Excel® 2007 Power Programming with VBA

Excel® 2007 Power Programming with VBA

by John Walkenbach

Wiley Publishing, Inc.

Wiley Publishing, Inc.

Excel® 2007 Power Programming with VBA

Published by
Wiley Publishing, Inc.
111 River Street
Hoboken, NJ 07030-5774
www.wiley.com

Copyright © 2007 by Wiley Publishing, Inc., Indianapolis, Indiana

Published by Wiley Publishing, Inc., Indianapolis, Indiana

Published simultaneously in Canada

Library of Congress Control Number: 2006939606

ISBN: 978-0-470-04401-8

Manufactured in the United States of America

10 9 8 7 6 5 4 3 2

WILEY

About the Author

John Walkenbach is author of about 50 spreadsheet books and lives in southern Arizona. Visit his Web site: `http://j-walk.com`.

wAcquisitions, Editorial, and Media Development

Senior Project Editor: Christopher Morris

(Previous Edition: Linda Morris)

Senior Acquisitions Editor: Bob Woerner

Copy Editor: Andy Hollandbeck

Technical Editor: Niek Otten

Editorial Manager: Kevin Kirschner

Media Development Specialists:
Angela Denny, Kate Jenkins,
Steven Kudirka, Kit Malone

Media Development Coordinator:
Laura Atkinson

Media Project Supervisor: Laura Moss

Media Development Manager:
Laura VanWinkle

Editorial Assistant: Amanda Foxworth

Sr. Editorial Assistant: Cherie Case

Composition Services

Project Coordinator: Kristie Rees

Layout and Graphics: Denny Hager,
Joyce Haughey, Jennifer Mayberry,
Heather Ryan

Proofreader: John Greenough

Indexer: Johnna VanHoose

Anniversary Logo Design: Richard Pacifico

Publishing and Editorial for Technology Dummies

Richard Swadley, Vice President and Executive Group Publisher

Andy Cummings, Vice President and Publisher

Mary Bednarek, Executive Acquisitions Director

Mary C. Corder, Editorial Director

Publishing for Consumer Dummies

Diane Graves Steele, Vice President and Publisher

Joyce Pepple, Acquisitions Director

Composition Services

Gerry Fahey, Vice President of Production Services

Debbie Stailey, Director of Composition Services

Preface

Welcome to *Excel 2007 Power Programming with VBA*. If your job involves developing spreadsheets that others will use — or if you simply want to get the most out of Excel — you've come to the right place.

Topics Covered

This book focuses on Visual Basic for Applications (VBA), the programming language built into Excel (and other applications that make up Microsoft Office). More specifically, it will show you how to write programs that automate various tasks in Excel. This book covers everything from recording simple macros through creating sophisticated user-oriented applications and utilities.

This book does *not* cover Microsoft Visual Studio Tools for Office (VSTO). VSTO is a relatively new technology that uses Visual Basic .NET and Microsoft Visual C#. VSTO can also be used to control Excel and other Microsoft Office applications.

What You Need to Know

This is not a book for beginning Excel users. If you have no experience with Excel, a better choice might be my *Excel 2007 Bible,* which provides comprehensive coverage of all the features of Excel. That book is meant for users of all levels.

To get the most out of this book, you should be a relatively experienced Excel user. I didn't spend much time writing basic how-to information. In fact, I assume that you know the following:

- How to create workbooks, insert sheets, save files, and so on

- How to navigate through a workbook

- How to use the Excel 2007 Ribbon

- How to enter formulas

- How to use Excel's worksheet functions

- How to name cells and ranges

- How to use basic Windows features, such as file management techniques and the Clipboard

If you don't know how to perform the preceding tasks, you could find some of this material over your head, so consider yourself warned. If you're an experienced spreadsheet user who hasn't used Excel 2007, Chapter 2 presents a brief overview of what this product offers.

What You Need to Have

To make the best use of this book, you need a copy of Excel 2007. Although most of the material also applies to Excel 2000 and later versions, I assume that you are using Excel 2007. Although Excel 2007 is radically different from its predecessors, the VBA environment has not changed at all. If you plan to develop applications that will be used in earlier versions of Excel, I strongly suggest that you *don't* use Excel 2007 for your development work.

Most of the material in this book also applies to Excel for Macintosh. However, I did no compatibility testing with the Mac version, so you're on your own.

Any computer system that can run Windows will suffice, but you'll be much better off with a fast machine with plenty of memory. Excel is a large program, and using it on a slower system or a system with minimal memory can be extremely frustrating.

I recommend using a high-resolution video driver (1024×768 is adequate, and 1600×1200 is even better). For optimal results, try a dual-monitor system and place Excel on one screen and the Visual Basic Editor on the other. You'll soon become spoiled.

To use the examples on the companion CD, you also need a CD-ROM drive.

Conventions in This Book

Take a minute to skim this section and learn some of the typographic conventions used throughout this book.

Excel commands

Excel 2007 features a brand new "menu-less" user interface. In place of a menu system, Excel uses a context-sensitive Ribbon system. The words along the top (such as Insert, View, and so on) are known as *tabs*. Click a tab, and the Ribbon of icons displays the commands that are most suited to the task at hand. Each icon has a name that is (usually) displayed next to or below the icon. The icons are arranged in groups, and the group name appears below the icons.

The convention I use in this book is to indicate the tab name, followed by the group name, followed by the icon name. So, for example, the command used to toggle word wrap within a cell is indicated as:

Home⇨Alignment⇨Wrap Text

The large round icon in the upper left corner of Excel 2007's window is knows as the Office Button. When I refer to commands that use the Office Button, I abbreviate it as Office. For example, the following command displays the Excel Options dialog box:

```
Office ⇨ Excel Options
```

VBA editor commands

The VBA editor is the window in which you work with your VBA code. The VBA editor uses the traditional menu-and-toolbar interface. A command like the following means to click the Tools menu and select the References menu item:

Tools⇨References

Keyboard conventions

You need to use the keyboard to enter data. In addition, you can work with menus and dialog boxes directly from the keyboard — a method that you might find easier if your hands are already positioned over the keys.

INPUT

Input that you type from the keyboard appears in boldface — for example, enter **=SUM(B2: B50)** into cell B51.

More lengthy input usually appears on a separate line in a monospace font. For example, I might instruct you to enter the following formula:

```
=VLOOKUP(StockNumber,PriceList,2)
```

VBA CODE

This book contains many snippets of VBA code as well as complete procedure listings. Each listing appears in a monospace font; each line of code occupies a separate line. (I copied these listings directly from the VBA module and pasted them into my word processor.) To make the code easier to read, I often use one or more tabs to create indentations. Indentation is optional, but it does help to delineate statements that go together.

If a line of code doesn't fit on a single line in this book, I use the standard VBA line continuation sequence: At the end of a line, a space followed by an underscore character indicates that the line of code extends to the next line. For example, the following two lines are a single code statement:

```
If Right(ActiveCell, 1) = "!" Then ActiveCell _
  = Left(ActiveCell, Len(ActiveCell) - 1)
```

You can enter this code either on two lines, exactly as shown, or on a single line without the underscore character.

FUNCTIONS, FILENAMES, AND NAMED RANGES

Excel's worksheet functions appear in uppercase font, like so: "Enter a SUM formula in cell C20." VBA procedure names, properties, methods, and objects appear in monospace font: "Execute the `GetTotals` procedure." I often use mixed upper- and lowercase to make these names easier to read.

I also use the monospace font for filenames and named ranges in a worksheet — for example: Open `myfile.xlsm` and select the range named `data`.

Mouse conventions

If you're reading this book, you're well versed in mouse usage. The mouse terminology I use is all standard fare: pointing, clicking, right-clicking, dragging, and so on.

What the Icons Mean

Throughout the book, I use icons to call your attention to points that are particularly important:

NEW

I use this icon to indicate that the material discussed is new to Excel 2007.

NOTE

I use Note icons to tell you that something is important — perhaps a concept that could help you master the task at hand or something fundamental for understanding subsequent material.

TIP

Tip icons indicate a more efficient way of doing something or a technique that might not be obvious.

CD-ROM

These icons indicate that an example file is on the companion CD-ROM. (See "About the Companion CD-ROM," later in this Preface.) This CD holds many of the examples that I show in the book.

CAUTION

I use Caution icons when the operation that I'm describing can cause problems if you're not careful.

CROSS-REFERENCE

I use the Cross Reference icon to refer you to other chapters that have more to say on a subject.

How This Book Is Organized

The chapters of this book are grouped into eight main parts.

Part I: Some Essential Background

In this part, I set the stage for the rest of the book. Chapter 1 presents a brief history of spreadsheets so that you can see how Excel fits into the big picture. In Chapter 2, I offer a conceptual overview of Excel 2007 — quite useful for experienced spreadsheet users who are switching to Excel. In Chapter 3, I cover the essentials of formulas, including some clever techniques that might be new to you. Chapter 4 covers the ins and outs of the various files used and generated by Excel.

Part II: Excel Application Development

This part consists of just two chapters. In Chapter 5, I broadly discuss the concept of a spreadsheet application. Chapter 6 goes into more detail and covers the steps typically involved in a spreadsheet application development project.

Part III: Understanding Visual Basic for Applications

Chapters 7 through 11 make up Part III, and these chapters include everything that you need to know to learn VBA. In this part, I introduce you to VBA, provide programming fundamentals, and detail how to develop VBA subroutines and functions. Chapter 11 contains many useful VBA examples.

Part IV: Working with UserForms

The four chapters in this part cover custom dialog boxes (also known as *UserForms*). Chapter 12 presents some built-in alternatives to creating custom UserForms. Chapter 13 provides an introduction to UserForms and the various controls that you can use. Chapters 14 and 15 present many examples of custom dialog boxes, ranging from basic to advanced.

Part V: Advanced Programming Techniques

Part V covers additional techniques that are often considered advanced. The first three chapters discuss how to develop utilities and how to use VBA to work with pivot tables and charts. Chapter 19 covers *event handling,* which enables you to execute procedures automatically when certain events occur. Chapter 20 discusses various techniques that you can use to interact with other applications (such as Word). Chapter 21 concludes Part V with an in-depth discussion of creating add-ins.

Part VI: Developing Applications

The chapters in Part VI deal with important elements of creating user-oriented applications. Chapter 22 discusses how to modify the new Ribbon interface. Chapter 23 describes how to modify Excel's shortcut menus. Chapter 24 presents several different ways to provide online help for your applications. In Chapter 25, I present some basic information about developing user-oriented applications, and I describe such an application in detail.

Part VII: Other Topics

The six chapters in Part VII cover additional topics. Chapter 26 presents information regarding compatibility. In Chapter 27, I discuss various ways to use VBA to work with files. In Chapter 28, I explain how to use VBA to manipulate Visual Basic components such as UserForms and modules. Chapter 29 covers the topic of class modules. Chapter 30 explains how to work with color in Excel. I finish the part with a useful chapter that answers many common questions about Excel programming.

Part VIII: Appendixes

Four appendixes round out the book. Appendix A contains useful information about Excel resources online. Appendix B is a reference guide to all VBA's keywords (statements and functions). I explain VBA error codes in Appendix C, and Appendix D describes the files available on the companion CD-ROM.

About the Companion CD-ROM

The inside back cover of this book contains a CD-ROM that holds many useful examples that I discuss in the text. When I write about computer-related material, I emphasize learning by example. I know that I learn more from a well-thought-out example than from reading a dozen pages in a book. I assume that this is true for many other people. Consequently, I spent more time developing the examples on the CD-ROM than I did writing chapters.

The files on the companion CD-ROM are not compressed, so you can access them directly from the CD.

CROSS-REFERENCE

Refer to Appendix D for a description of each file on the CD-ROM.

About the Power Utility Pak Offer

Toward the back of the book, you'll find a coupon that you can redeem for a discounted copy of my popular Power Utility Pak software. PUP is an award-winning collection of useful Excel utilities and many new worksheet functions. I developed this package exclusively with VBA.

I think you'll find this product useful in your day-to-day work with Excel. You can also purchase the complete VBA source code for a nominal fee. Studying the code is an excellent way to pick up some useful programming techniques.

You can take Power Utility Pak for a test drive by installing the 30-day trial version available at my Web site:

http://j-walk.com/ss

How to Use This Book

You can use this book any way that you please. If you choose to read it from cover to cover, be my guest. But because I'm dealing with intermediate-to-advanced subject matter, the chapter order is often immaterial. I suspect that most readers will skip around, picking up useful tidbits here and there. If you're faced with a challenging task, you might try the index first to see whether the book specifically addresses your problem.

Reach Out

The publisher and I want your feedback. After you've had a chance to use this book, please take a moment to visit the Wiley Publishing Web site to give us your comments. (Go to www.wiley.com and then click the Contact Us link.) Please be honest in your evaluation. If you thought a particular chapter didn't tell you enough, let us know. Of course, I would prefer to receive comments like, "This is the best book I've ever read," or "Thanks to this book, I was promoted and now make $112,000 a year."

I get at least a half dozen questions every day, via e-mail, from people who have read my books. I appreciate the feedback. Unfortunately, I simply don't have the time to reply to questions. Appendix A provides a good list of sources that *can* answer your questions.

I also invite you to visit my Web site, which contains lots of Excel-related material. Despite the massive attempts to make this book completely accurate, a few errors have probably crept into its pages. My Web site includes a list of any such errors. The URL is

http://j-walk.com/ss/w

Contents at a Glance

Table of Contents

Part II: Excel Application Development

Part IV: Working with UserForms

Part V: Advanced Programming Techniques

Part VII: Other Topics

Part VIII: Appendixes

Part I

Some Essential Background

Chapter 1
Excel 2007: Where It Came From

Chapter 2
Excel in a Nutshell

Chapter 3
Formula Tricks and Techniques

Chapter 4
Understanding Excel's Files

Chapter 1

Excel 2007: Where It Came From

In This Chapter

To fully appreciate the application development features available in Excel 2007, it's important to understand where this product came from and how it fits into the overall scheme of things.

◆ A history of spreadsheets — where they came from, who makes them, and what differentiates them

◆ A discussion of Excel's evolution

◆ An analysis of why Excel is a good tool for developers

If you've worked with personal computers and spreadsheets over the past decade, this information may be old hat. If you're a trivia buff, this chapter is a gold mine. Study this information, and you'll be a hit at the next computer geek party that you attend.

A Brief History of Spreadsheets

Most of us tend to take spreadsheet software for granted. In fact, it may be hard to fathom, but there really was a time when electronic spreadsheets were not available. Back then, people relied instead on clumsy mainframes or calculators and spent hours doing what now takes minutes.

It all started with VisiCalc

The world's first electronic spreadsheet, *VisiCalc*, was conjured up by Dan Bricklin and Bob Frankston back in 1978, when personal computers were pretty much unheard of in the office environment. VisiCalc was written for the Apple II computer, which was an interesting little machine that is something of a toy by today's standards. (But in its day, the Apple II kept me mesmerized for days at a time.) VisiCalc essentially laid the foundation for future spreadsheets, and its row-and-column–based layout and formula syntax are still found in modern spreadsheet products. VisiCalc caught on quickly, and many forward-looking companies purchased the Apple II for the sole purpose of developing their budgets with VisiCalc. Consequently, VisiCalc is often credited for much of the Apple II's initial success.

In the meantime, another class of personal computers was evolving; these PCs ran the CP/M operating system. A company called Sorcim developed SuperCalc, which was a spreadsheet that also attracted a legion of followers.

When the IBM PC arrived on the scene in 1981, legitimizing personal computers, VisiCorp wasted no time porting VisiCalc to this new hardware environment, and Sorcim soon followed with a PC version of SuperCalc.

By current standards, both VisiCalc and SuperCalc were extremely crude. For example, text entered into a cell could not extend beyond the cell — a lengthy title had to be entered into multiple cells. Nevertheless, the ability to automate the budgeting tedium was enough to lure thousands of accountants from paper ledger sheets to floppy disks.

TIP

You can download a copy of the original VisiCalc from Dan Bricklin's Web site. And yes, nearly 30 years later, this 27K program still runs on today's PCs (see Figure 1-1). You can find it at www.bricklin.com.

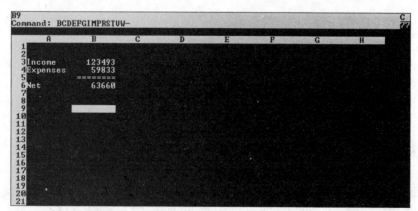

Figure 1-1: VisiCalc, running in a DOS window on a PC running Windows XP.

Lotus 1-2-3

Envious of VisiCalc's success, a small group of computer freaks at a start-up company in Cambridge, Massachusetts, refined the spreadsheet concept. Headed by Mitch Kapor and Jonathan Sachs, the company designed a new product and launched the software industry's first full-fledged marketing blitz. I remember seeing a large display ad for 1-2-3 in *The Wall Street Journal.* It was the first time that I'd ever seen software advertised in a general interest publication.

Released in January 1983, Lotus Development Corporation's 1-2-3 was an instant success. Despite its $495 price tag (yes, people really paid that much for software), it quickly outsold VisiCalc, rocketing to the top of the sales charts, where it remained for many years.

Lotus 1-2-3 improved on all the basics embodied in VisiCalc and SuperCalc and was also the first program to take advantage of the new and unique features found in the powerful 16-bit IBM PC AT. For example, 1-2-3 bypassed the slower DOS calls and wrote text directly to display memory, giving it a snappy and responsive feel that was unusual for the time. The online help system was a breakthrough, and the ingenious "moving bar" menu style set the standard for many years.

One feature that really set 1-2-3 apart, though, was its macro capability — a powerful tool that enabled spreadsheet users to record their keystrokes to automate many procedures. When such a macro was "played back," the original keystrokes were sent to the application. Although this was a far cry from today's macro capability, 1-2-3 macros were definitely a step in the right direction.

1-2-3 was not the first integrated package, but it was the first successful one. It combined (1) a powerful electronic spreadsheet with (2) elementary graphics and (3) some limited but handy database features. Easy as 1, 2, 3 — get it?

Lotus followed up the original 1-2-3 Release 1 with Release 1A in April 1983. This product enjoyed tremendous success and put Lotus in the enviable position of virtually owning the spreadsheet market. In September 1985, Release 1A was replaced by Release 2, which was a major upgrade that was superseded by the bug-fixed Release 2.01 the following July. Release 2 introduced *add-ins,* which are special-purpose programs that can be attached to give an application new features and extend the application's useful life. Release 2 also had improved memory management, more functions, 8,192 rows (four times as many as its predecessor), and added support for a math coprocessor. Release 2 also included some significant enhancements to the macro language.

Not surprisingly, the success of 1-2-3 spawned many *clones* — work-alike products that usually offered a few additional features and sold at a much lower price. Among the more notable were Paperback Software's VP Planner series and Mosaic Software's Twin. Lotus eventually took legal action against Paperback Software for copyright infringement (for copying the "look and feel" of 1-2-3); the successful suit essentially put Paperback out of business.

In the summer of 1989, Lotus shipped DOS and OS/2 versions of the long-delayed 1-2-3 Release 3. This product literally added a dimension to the familiar row-and-column–based spreadsheet: It extended the paradigm by adding multiple spreadsheet pages. The idea wasn't really new, however; a relatively obscure product called Boeing Calc originated the 3-D spreadsheet concept, and SuperCalc 5 and CubeCalc also incorporated it.

1-2-3 Release 3 offered features that users wanted — features that ultimately became standard fare: multilayered worksheets, the capability to work with multiple files simultaneously, file linking, improved graphics, and direct access to external database files. But it still lacked an important feature that users were begging for: a way to produce high-quality printed output.

Release 3 began life with a reduced market potential because it required an 80286-based PC and a minimum of 1MB of RAM — fairly hefty requirements in 1989. But Lotus had an ace up its corporate sleeve. Concurrent with the shipping of Release 3, the company surprised nearly everyone by announcing an upgrade of Release 2.01. (The product materialized a few months later as 1-2-3 Release 2.2.) Release 3 was *not* a replacement for Release 2, as most analysts had expected. Rather, Lotus made the brilliant move of splitting the spreadsheet market into two segments: those with high-end hardware and those with more mundane equipment.

1-2-3 Release 2.2 wasn't a panacea for spreadsheet buffs, but it was a significant improvement. The most important Release 2.2 feature was *Allways,* an add-in that gave users the ability to churn out attractive reports, complete with multiple typefaces, borders, and shading. In addition, users could view the results onscreen in a WYSIWYG (What You See Is What You Get) manner. Allways didn't, however, let users issue any worksheet commands while they viewed and formatted their work in WYSIWYG mode. Despite this rather severe limitation, most 1-2-3 users were overjoyed with this new capability because they could finally produce near-typeset-quality output.

In May 1990, Microsoft released Windows 3.0. As you probably know, Windows changed the way that people used personal computers. Apparently, the decision makers at Lotus weren't convinced that Windows was a significant product, and the company was slow getting out of the gate with its first Windows spreadsheet, 1-2-3 for Windows, which wasn't introduced until late 1991. Worse, this product was, in short, a dud. It didn't really capitalize on the Windows environment and disappointed many users. It also disappointed at least one book author. My very first book was titled *PC World 1-2-3 For Windows Complete Handbook*. I think it sold fewer than 1,000 copies.

Serious competition from Lotus never materialized. Consequently, Excel, which had already established itself as the premier Windows spreadsheet, became the overwhelming Windows spreadsheet market leader and has never left that position. Lotus came back with 1-2-3 Release 4 for Windows in June 1993, which was a vast improvement over the original. Release 5 for Windows appeared in mid-1994.

Also in mid-1994, Lotus unveiled 1-2-3 Release 4.0 for DOS. Many analysts (including myself) expected a product more compatible with the Windows product. But we were wrong; DOS Release 4.0 was simply an upgraded version of Release 3.4. Because of the widespread acceptance of Windows, that was the last DOS version of 1-2-3 to see the light of day.

Over the years, spreadsheets became less important to Lotus (its flagship product turns out to be Notes). In mid-1995, IBM purchased Lotus Development Corporation. Two more versions of 1-2-3 became available, but it seems to be a case of too little, too late. Excel clearly dominates the spreadsheet market, and 1-2-3 users are an increasingly rare breed.

Quattro Pro

The other significant player in the spreadsheet world is (or, I should say, *was*) Borland International. In 1994, Novell purchased WordPerfect International and Borland's entire spreadsheet business. In 1996, WordPerfect and Quattro Pro were both purchased by Corel Corporation.

Borland started in spreadsheets in 1987 with a product called *Quattro*. Word has it that the internal code name was *Buddha* because the program was intended to "assume the Lotus position" in the market (that is, #1). Essentially a clone of 1-2-3, Quattro offered a few additional features and an arguably better menu system at a much lower price. Importantly, users could opt for a 1-2-3-like menu system that let them use familiar commands and also ensured compatibility with 1-2-3 macros.

In the fall of 1989, Borland began shipping Quattro Pro, which was a more powerful product that built upon the original Quattro and trumped 1-2-3 in just about every area. For example, the first Quattro Pro let you work with multiple worksheets in movable and resizable windows — although it did *not* have a graphical user interface (GUI). More trivia: Quattro Pro was based on an obscure product called Surpass, which Borland acquired.

Released in late 1990, Quattro Pro Version 2.0 added 3-D graphs and a link to Borland's Paradox database. A mere six months later — much to the chagrin of Quattro Pro book authors — Version 3.0 appeared, featuring an optional graphical user interface and a slide show feature. In the spring of 1992, Version 4 appeared with customizable SpeedBars and an innovative analytical graphics feature. Version 5, which came out in 1994, had only one significant new feature: worksheet notebooks (that is, 3-D worksheets).

Like Lotus, Borland was slow to jump on the Windows bandwagon. When Quattro Pro for Windows finally shipped in the fall of 1992, however, it provided some tough competition for the other two Windows spreadsheets, Excel 4.0 and 1-2-3 Release 1.1 for Windows. Importantly, Quattro Pro for Windows had an innovative feature, known as the *UI Builder*, that let developers and advanced users easily create custom user interfaces.

Also worth noting was a lawsuit between Lotus and Borland. Lotus won the suit, forcing Borland to remove the 1-2-3 macro compatibility and 1-2-3 menu option from Quattro Pro. This ruling was eventually overturned in late 1994, however, and Quattro Pro can now include 1-2-3 compatibility features (as if anyone really cares). Both sides spent millions of dollars on this lengthy legal fight, and when the dust cleared, no real winner emerged.

Borland followed up the original Quattro Pro for Windows with Version 5, which was upgraded to Version 6 after Novell took over Borland's spreadsheet business. As I write, the current version of Quattro Pro is Version 13, which is part of WordPerfect Office X3.

There was a time when Quattro Pro seemed the ultimate solution for spreadsheet developers. But then Excel 5 arrived.

Microsoft Excel

And now on to the good stuff.

Most people don't realize that Microsoft's experience with spreadsheets extends back to the early '80s. Over the years, Microsoft's spreadsheet offerings have come a long way, from the barely adequate MultiPlan to the powerful Excel 2007.

In 1982, Microsoft released its first spreadsheet, *MultiPlan*. Designed for computers running the CP/M operating system, the product was subsequently ported to several other platforms, including Apple II, Apple III, XENIX, and MS-DOS.

MultiPlan essentially ignored existing software user-interface standards. Difficult to learn and use, it never earned much of a following in the United States. Not surprisingly, Lotus 1-2-3 pretty much left MultiPlan in the dust.

Excel sort of evolved from MultiPlan, first surfacing in 1985 on the Macintosh. Like all Mac applications, Excel was a graphics-based program (unlike the character-based MultiPlan). In November 1987, Microsoft released the first version of Excel for Windows (labeled Excel 2.0 to correspond with the Macintosh version). Because Windows was not in widespread use at the time, this version included a runtime version of Windows — a special version that had just enough features to run Excel and nothing else. Less than a year later, Microsoft released Excel Version 2.1. In July 1990, Microsoft released a minor upgrade (2.1d) that was compatible with Windows 3.0. Although these 2.x versions were quite rudimentary by current standards (see Figure 1-2) and didn't have the attractive, sculpted look of later versions, they attracted a small but loyal group of supporters and provided an excellent foundation for future development.

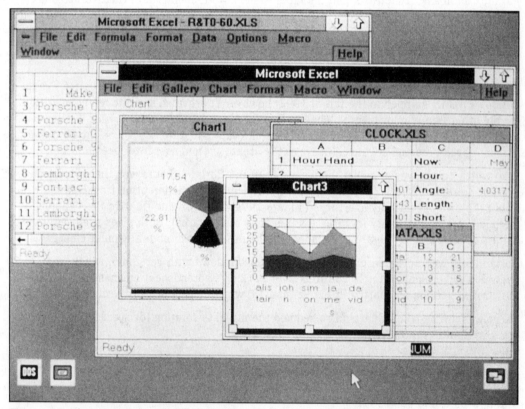

Figure 1-2: The original Excel 2.1 for Windows. This product has come a long way.

(Photo courtesy of Microsoft)

Excel's first macro language also appeared in Version 2. The XLM macro language consisted of functions that were evaluated in sequence. It was quite powerful, but very difficult to learn and use. As you'll see, the XLM macro language was replaced by Visual Basic for Applications (VBA), which is the topic of this book.

Meanwhile, Microsoft developed a version of Excel (numbered 2.20) for OS/2 Presentation Manager, released in September 1989 and upgraded to Version 2.21 about 10 months later. OS/2 never quite caught on, despite continued efforts by IBM.

In December 1990, Microsoft released Excel 3 for Windows, which boasted a significant improvement in both appearance and features (see Figure 1-3). The upgrade included a toolbar, drawing capabilities, a powerful optimization feature (Solver), add-in support, Object Linking and Embedding (OLE) support, 3-D charts, macro buttons, simplified file consolidation, workgroup editing, and the ability to wrap text in a cell. Excel 3 also had the capability to work with external databases (via the Q+E program). The OS/2 version upgrade appeared five months later.

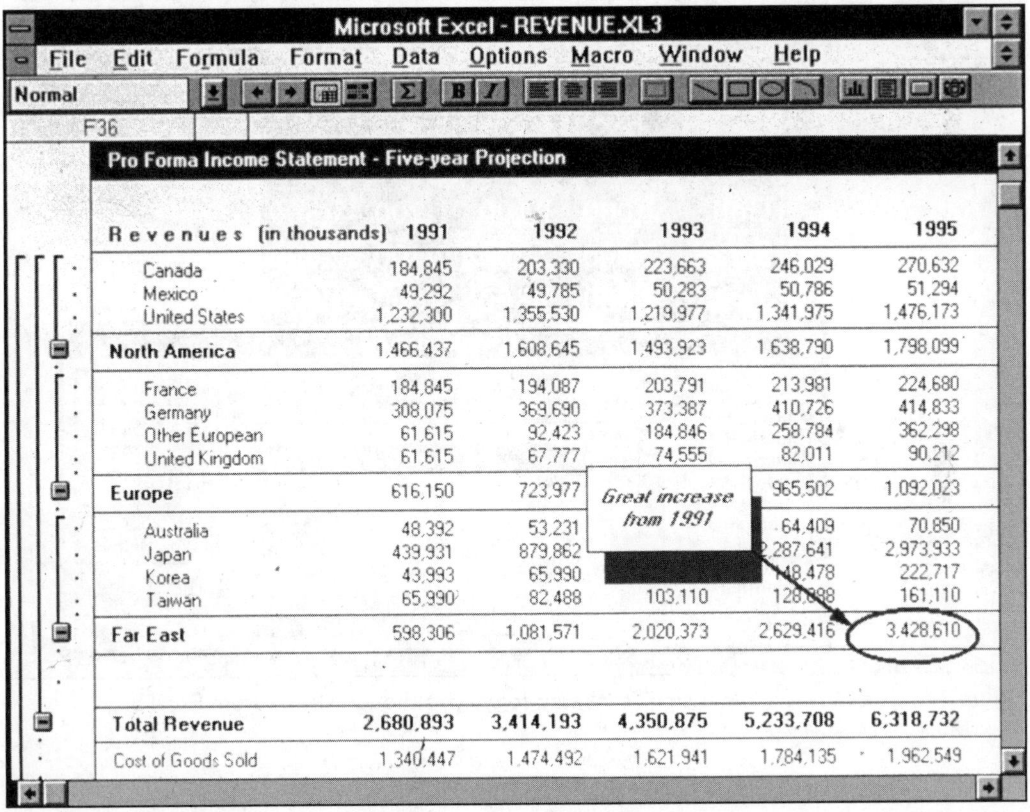

Figure 1-3: Excel 3 was a vast improvement over the original release.

(Photo courtesy of Microsoft)

Version 4, released in the spring of 1992, not only was easier to use but also had more power and sophistication for advanced users (see Figure 1-4). Excel 4 took top honors in virtually every spreadsheet product comparison published in the trade magazines. In the meantime, the relationship between Microsoft and IBM became increasingly strained; Excel 4 was never released for OS/2, and Microsoft has stopped making versions of Excel for OS/2.

Excel 5 hit the streets in early 1994 and immediately earned rave reviews. Like its predecessor, it finished at the top of every spreadsheet comparison published in the leading trade magazines. Despite stiff competition from 1-2-3 Release 5 for Windows and Quattro Pro for Windows 5 — both were fine products that could handle just about any spreadsheet task thrown their way — Excel 5 continued to rule the roost. This version, by the way, was the first to feature VBA.

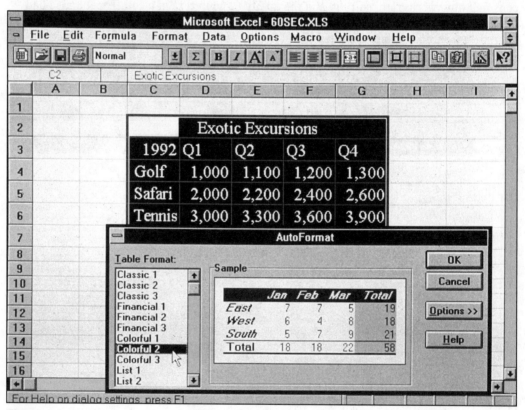

Figure 1-4: Excel 4 was another significant step forward, although still far from Excel 5.

(Photo courtesy of Microsoft)

Excel 95 (also known as Excel 7) was released concurrently with Microsoft Windows 95. (Microsoft skipped over Version 6 to make the version numbers consistent across its Office products.) On the surface, Excel 95 didn't appear to be much different from Excel 5. Much of the core code was rewritten, however, and speed improvements were apparent in many areas. Importantly, Excel 95 used the same file format as Excel 5, which is the first time that an Excel upgrade didn't use a new file format. This compatibility wasn't perfect, however, because Excel 95 included a few enhancements in the VBA language. Consequently, it was possible to develop an application using Excel 95 that would load but not run properly in Excel 5.

In early 1997, Microsoft released Office 97, which included Excel 97. Excel 97 is also known as Excel 8. This version included dozens of general enhancements plus a completely new interface for developing VBA-based applications. In addition, the product offered a new way of developing custom dialog boxes (called UserForms rather than dialog sheets). Microsoft tried to make Excel 97 compatible with previous versions, but the compatibility was far from perfect. Many applications that were developed using Excel 5 or Excel 95 required some tweaking before they would work with Excel 97 or later versions.

CROSS-REFERENCE

I discuss compatibility issues in Chapter 26.

Excel 2000 was released in early 1999 and was also sold as part of Office 2000. The enhancements in Excel 2000 dealt primarily with Internet capabilities, although a few significant changes were apparent in the area of programming.

Excel 2002 (sometimes known as Excel XP) hit the market in mid-2001. Like its predecessor, it didn't offer a raft of significant new features. Rather, it had a number of minor new features and several refinements of existing features. Perhaps the most compelling new feature was the ability to repair damaged files and save your work when Excel crashed.

Excel 2003 (released in Fall 2003) was perhaps the most disappointing upgrade ever. This version had very few new features. Microsoft touted the ability to import and export eXtensible Markup Language (XML) files and map the data to specific cells in a worksheet — but very few users actually need such a feature. In addition, Microsoft introduced some "rights management" features that let you place restrictions on various parts of a workbook (for example, allow only certain users to view a particular worksheet). In addition, Excel 2003 had a new Help system (which now puts the Help contents in the task pane) and a new "research" feature that lets you look up a variety of information in the task pane. (Some of these require a fee-based account.)

NOTE

For some reason, Microsoft chose to offer two sub-versions of Excel 2003. The XML and rights management features are available only in the standalone version of Excel and in the version of Excel that's included with the Professional version of Office 2003. Because of this, Excel developers may now need to deal with compatibility issues within a particular version!

Excel 2007, the focus of this book, is part of the Microsoft 2007 Office System. This upgrade is clearly the most significant ever. The user interface has been completely revamped. Menus and toolbars have been replaced by a new Ribbon UI (see Figure 1-5). Excel 2007's grid size is 1,000 times larger than in previous versions, and the product uses a new open XML file format. Other improvements include improved tables, conditional formatting enhancements, major cosmetic enhancements for charts, and document themes. It remains to be seen how the market will react to such an extreme upgrade. Clearly, Excel 2007 is easier for beginners, but long-time users will spend a lot of time wondering where to find their old commands.

So there you have it: 28 years of spreadsheet history condensed into a few pages. It has been an interesting ride, and I've been fortunate enough to have been involved with spreadsheets the entire time. Things have changed. Microsoft not only dominates the spreadsheet market, it virtually owns it. What little competition exists is primarily in the form of "open source" products such as OpenOffice and StarOffice. You'll also hear about up-and-coming Web spreadsheets such as Google Spreadsheets. In reality, these are not even considered minor threats to Microsoft. In fact, Microsoft's biggest competitor is itself. Users tend to settle on a particular version of Excel and have very little motivation to upgrade. Convincing users to upgrade to the radically different Excel 2007 may be one of Microsoft's biggest challenges yet.

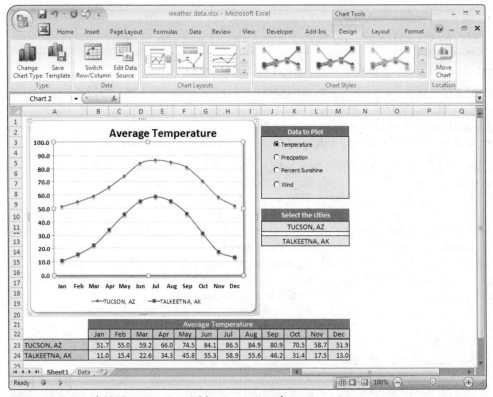

Figure 1-5: Excel 2007 uses a new Ribbon user interface.

Why Excel Is Great for Developers

Excel is a highly programmable product, and it's easily the best choice for developing spreadsheet-based applications.

For developers, Excel's key features include the following:

- *File structure:* The multisheet orientation makes it easy to organize an application's elements and store them in a single file. For example, a single workbook file can hold any number of worksheets and chart sheets. UserForms and VBA modules are stored with a workbook but are invisible to the end user.

- *Visual Basic for Applications:* This macro language lets you create structured programs directly in Excel. This book focuses on using VBA, which, as you'll discover, is extremely powerful and relatively easy to learn.

- *Easy access to controls:* Excel makes it very easy to add controls such as buttons, list boxes, and option buttons to a worksheet. Implementing these controls often requires little or no macro programming.

- *Custom dialog boxes:* You can easily create professional-looking dialog boxes by creating UserForms.

- *Custom worksheet functions:* With VBA, you can create custom worksheet functions to simplify formulas and calculations.

- *Customizable user interface:* Developers have lots of control over the user interface. In previous versions, this involved creating custom menus and toolbars. In Excel 2007, it involves modifying the Ribbon. Changing the Excel 2007 interface is not as easy as it was in previous versions, but it's still possible.

- *Customizable shortcut menus:* Using VBA, you can customize the right-click, context-sensitive shortcut menus.

- *Powerful data analysis options:* Excel's PivotTable feature makes it easy to summarize large amounts of data with very little effort.

- *Microsoft Query:* You can access important data directly from the spreadsheet environment. Data sources include standard database file formats, text files, and Web pages.

- *Data Access Objects (DAO) and ActiveX Data Objects (ADO):* These features make it easy to work with external databases by using VBA.

- *Extensive protection options:* Your applications can be kept confidential and protected from changes by casual users.

- *Ability to create "compiled" add-ins:* With a single command, you can create XLA add-in files that add new features to Excel.

- *Support for automation:* With VBA, you can control other applications that support automation. For example, your VBA macro can generate a report in Microsoft Word.

- *Ability to create Web pages:* It's easy to create a HyperText Markup Language (HTML) document from an Excel workbook. The HTML is very bloated, but it's readable by Web browsers.

Excel's Role in Microsoft's Strategy

Currently, most copies of Excel are sold as part of Microsoft Office — a suite of products that includes a variety of other programs. (The exact programs that you get depend on which version of Office you buy.) Obviously, it helps if the programs can communicate well with each other. Microsoft is at the forefront of this trend. All the Office products have extremely similar user interfaces, and all support VBA.

Therefore, after you hone your VBA skills in Excel, you'll be able to put them to good use in other applications — you just need to learn the object model for the other applications.

Chapter 2

Excel in a Nutshell

In This Chapter
In this chapter, I provide a broad overview of the major components of Excel 2007.

◆ An introduction to Excel's object orientation

◆ A conceptual overview of Excel 2007, including a description of its major features

◆ A list of the new features in Excel 2007

◆ Some tips and techniques that even advanced users may find helpful

This chapter will prove especially useful for casual Excel users who may not have discovered all of the features available. However, even experienced Excel users still may discover a thing or two by skimming through this chapter. For more details on a particular feature, consult the Help system or do a Web search.

Thinking in Terms of Objects

When you are developing applications with Excel (especially when you are dabbling with Visual Basic for Applications — VBA), it's helpful to think in terms of *objects*, or Excel elements that you can manipulate manually or via a macro. Here are some examples of Excel objects:

• The Excel application

• An Excel workbook

- A worksheet in a workbook

- A range or a table in a worksheet

- A ListBox control on a UserForm (a custom dialog box)

- A chart embedded in a worksheet

- A chart series on a chart

- A particular data point in a chart

You may notice that an *object hierarchy* exists here: The Excel object contains workbook objects, which contain worksheet objects, which contain range objects. This hierarchy comprises Excel's *object model*. Excel has more than 200 classes of objects that you can control directly or by using VBA. Other Microsoft Office 2007 products have their own object models.

 NOTE
Controlling objects is fundamental to developing applications. Throughout this book, you find out how to automate tasks by controlling Excel's objects, and you do so by using VBA. This concept becomes clearer in subsequent chapters.

Workbooks

One of the most common Excel objects is a *workbook*. Everything that you do in Excel takes place in a workbook, which is stored in a file that, by default, has an XLSX extension. An Excel workbook can hold any number of sheets (limited only by memory). There are four types of sheets:

- Worksheets

- Chart sheets

- XLM macro sheets (obsolete, but still supported)

- Dialog sheets (obsolete, but still supported)

You can open or create as many workbooks as you like (each in its own window), but at any given time, only one workbook is the *active workbook*. Similarly, only one sheet in a workbook is the *active sheet*. To activate a sheet, click its sheet tab at the bottom of the screen. To change a sheet's name, double-click the tab and enter the new text. Right-clicking a tab brings up a shortcut menu with additional options for the sheet, including changing its tab color, hiding the sheet, and so on.

You can also hide the window that contains a workbook by using the View ⇨ Window ⇨ Hide command. A hidden workbook window remains open, but it is not visible to the user.

Worksheets

The most common type of sheet is a worksheet, which is what people normally think of when they think of a spreadsheet. Worksheets contain cells, and the cells store data and formulas.

Every Excel 2007 worksheet has 16,384 columns and 1,048,576 rows. You can hide unneeded rows and columns to keep them out of view, but you cannot increase the number of rows or columns.

NOTE

Versions prior to Excel 2007 used the XLS binary format, and worksheets had only 65,536 rows and 256 columns. If you open such a file, Excel 2007 enters "compatibility mode" in order to work with the smaller worksheet grid. To convert such a file to the new format, save it as an XLSX or XLSM file. Then close the workbook and re-open it.

The real value of using multiple worksheets in a workbook is not access to more cells. Rather, multiple worksheets enable you to organize your work better. Back in the old days, when a file comprised a single worksheet, developers wasted a lot of time trying to organize the worksheet to hold their information efficiently. Now you can store information on any number of worksheets and still access it instantly by clicking a sheet tab.

As you know, a worksheet cell can hold a constant value or the result of a formula. The value may be a number, a date, a Boolean value (True or False), or text. Every worksheet also has an invisible drawing layer, which lets you insert graphic objects, such as charts, shapes, SmartArt, UserForm controls, pictures, and other embedded objects.

How Big Is a Worksheet?

It's interesting to stop and think about the actual size of a worksheet. Do the arithmetic (16,384 × 1,048,576), and you'll see that a worksheet has 17,179,869,184 cells. Remember that this is in just one worksheet. A single workbook can hold more than one worksheet.

If you're using a 1024 x 768 video mode with the default row heights and column widths, you can see 15 columns and 25 rows (or 375 cells) at a time — which is about .000002 percent of the entire worksheet. In other words, more than 45 million screens of information reside within a single worksheet.

If you were to enter a single digit into each cell at the relatively rapid clip of one cell per second, it would take you about 545 years, nonstop, to fill up a worksheet. To print the results of your efforts would require more than 40 million sheets of paper — a stack more than a mile high.

As you might suspect, filling an entire workbook with values is not possible. It's not even close to being possible. You would soon run out of memory, and Excel would probably crash.

You have complete control over the column widths and row heights — in fact, you can even hide rows and columns (as well as entire worksheets). You can specify any font size, and you have complete control over colors. Text in a cell can be displayed vertically (or at an angle) and can even be wrapped around to occupy multiple lines.

NEW

In the past, Excel was limited to a palette of 56 colors. With Excel 2007, the number of colors is virtually unlimited. In addition, Excel 2007 supports *document themes*. A single click lets you apply a new theme to a workbook, which can give it an entirely different look.

Chart sheets

A chart sheet normally holds a single chart. Many users ignore chart sheets, preferring to store charts on the worksheet's drawing layer. Using chart sheets is optional, but they make it a bit easier to print a chart on a page by itself, and they are especially useful for presentations. Figure 2-1 shows a pie chart on a chart sheet.

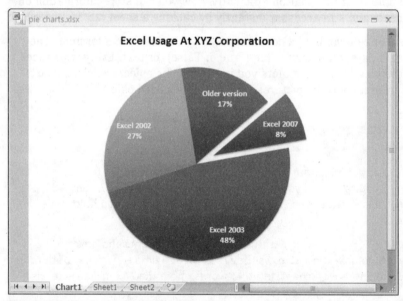

Figure 2-1: A pie chart on a chart sheet.

XLM macro sheets

An XLM macro sheet (also known as an *MS Excel 4 macro sheet*) is essentially a worksheet, but it has some different defaults. More specifically, an XLM macro sheet displays formulas rather than the results of formulas. In addition, the default column width is larger than in a normal worksheet.

What's New in Excel 2007?

Here's a quick-and-dirty overview of the new features in Excel 2007:

- A new tab-and-ribbon user interface
- New XML file formats
- Worksheet tables
- Significantly larger worksheet grid (1,048,576 rows x 16,384 columns)
- Ability to use more memory
- Unlimited conditional formats per cell
- 100 levels of undo
- Maximum formula length increased to 8,000 characters
- Supports 64 levels of nesting in a formula
- Formula AutoComplete
- Better-looking charts
- Workbook themes
- Skins
- Page Layout view
- New conditional formatting options
- Less confusing Excel Options dialog box
- New collaboration features (requires SharePoint)
- SmartArt and improved WordArt
- Compatibility checker
- Easier pivot tables
- Twelve new worksheet functions, plus integration of the Analysis ToolPak functions
- PDF output
- Resizable formula bar
- Many new templates
- More control over the status bar

As the name suggests, an XLM macro sheet is designed to hold XLM macros. As you may know, the XLM macro system is a holdover from previous versions of Excel (version 4.0 and earlier). Excel 2007 continues to support XLM macros for compatibility reasons — although it no longer provides the option of recording an XLM macro. This book does not cover the XLM macro system; instead, it focuses on the more powerful VBA macro system.

Excel 5/95 dialog sheets

In Excel 5 and Excel 95, you created a custom dialog box by inserting a special dialog sheet. Excel 97 and later versions still support these dialog sheets, but a much better alternative is available: UserForms. You work with UserForms in the Visual Basic Editor (VBE).

If you open a workbook that contains an Excel 5/95 dialog sheet, you can access the dialog sheet by clicking its tab.

I don't discuss Excel 5/95 dialog sheets in this book.

Excel's User Interface

The *user interface* (UI) is the means by which an end user communicates with a computer program. Generally speaking, a UI includes elements such as menus, toolbars, dialog boxes, keystroke combinations, and so on.

This section discusses the main components of Excel 2007's UI:

- The Ribbon
- Shortcut menus
- Dialog boxes
- Keyboard shortcuts
- Smart Tags
- Task pane

Introducing the Ribbon

If you've used Excel 2007 for more than a minute, you know that it has an entirely new UI. Menus and toolbars are gone, replaced with a brand new "tab and Ribbon" UI. Click a tab along the top (that is, a word such as Home, Insert, Page Layout), and the Ribbon displays the commands for that tab. Office 2007 is the first software in history to use this new interface, so the jury is still out regarding how it will be accepted.

The appearance of the commands on the Ribbon varies, depending on the width of the Excel window. When the window is too narrow to display everything, the commands adapt, and may seem to be missing. But the commands are still available. Figure 2-2 shows the Home tab of the Ribbon with all controls fully visible. Figure 2-3 shows the Ribbon when

Excel's window is narrower. Notice that some of the descriptive text is gone, but the icons remain. Figure 2-4 shows the extreme case, in which the window is very narrow. Some of the groups display a single icon. However, if you click the icon, all of the group commands are available to you.

Figure 2-2: The Home tab of the Ribbon.

Figure 2-3: The Home tab when Excel's window is narrower.

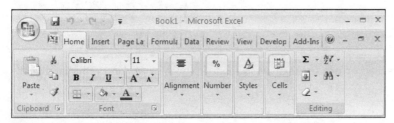

Figure 2-4: The Home tab when Excel's window is very narrow.

 TIP

If you would like to hide the Ribbon to increase your worksheet view, just double-click any of the tabs. The Ribbon goes away, and you'll be able to see about five additional rows of your worksheet. When you need to use the Ribbon again, just click any tab, and it comes back. You can also press Ctrl+F1 to toggle the Ribbon display on and off.

CONTEXTUAL TABS

In addition to the standard tabs, Excel 2007 includes "contextual tabs." Whenever an object (such as a chart, a table, a picture, or SmartArt) is selected, tools for working with that specific object are made available in the Ribbon.

Figure 2-5 shows the contextual tabs that appear when a pivot table is selected. In this case, Excel displays two contextual tabs: Options and Design. Notice that the contextual tabs contain a description (PivotTable Tools) in Excel's title bar. When contextual tabs are displayed, you can, of course, continue to use all of the other tabs.

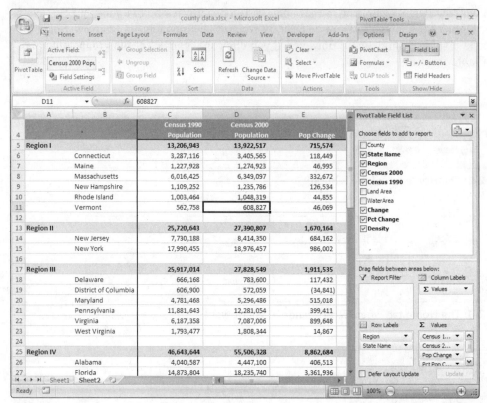

Figure 2-5: When you select an object, contextual tabs contain tools for working with that object.

TYPES OF COMMANDS ON THE RIBBON

For the most part, the commands in the Ribbon work just as you would expect them to. You'll encounter several different styles of commands on the Ribbon, as described next:

- *Simple buttons:* Click the button, and it does its thing. An example of a simple button is the Increase Font Size button in the Font group of the Home tab. Some buttons perform the action immediately; others display a dialog box so you can enter additional information. Button controls may or may not be accompanied by text.

- *Toggle buttons:* A toggle button is clickable and also conveys some type of information by displaying two different colors. An example is the Bold button in the Font group of the Home tab. If the active cell is not bold, the Bold button displays in its normal color. But if the active cell is already bold, the Bold button displays a different background color. If you click this button, it toggles the Bold attribute for the selection.

- *Simple drop-downs:* If the Ribbon command has a small downward-pointing arrow, then the command is a drop-down. Click it, and additional commands appear below it. An example of a simple drop-down is the Merge and Center command in the Alignment group of the Home Tab. When you click this control, you see four options related to merging and centering information.

- *Split buttons:* A split button control combines a one-click button (on the top) with a drop-down (on the bottom). If you click the button part, the command is executed. If you click the drop-down part, you choose from a list of related commands. You can identify a split button because it displays in two colors when you hover the mouse over it. An example of a split button is the Paste command in the Clipboard group of the Home tab. Clicking the top part of this control pastes the information from the Clipboard. If you click the bottom part of the control, you get a list of paste-related commands. See Figure 2-6.

- *Check boxes:* A check box control turns something on or off. An example is the Gridlines control in the Show/Hide group of the View tab. When the Gridlines check box is checked, the sheet displays gridlines. When the control is not checked, the sheet gridlines are not displayed.

- *Spinners:* An example of a spinner control is in the Scale to Fit group of the Page Layout tab. Click the top part of the spinner to increase the value; click the bottom part of the spinner to decrease the value.

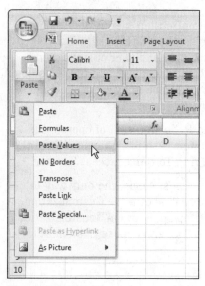

Figure 2-6: The Paste command is a split button control.

 CROSS-REFERENCE

Refer to Chapter 22 for information about customizing Excel's Ribbon.

Some of the Ribbon groups contain a small icon on the right side, known as a dialog launcher. For example, if you examine the Home ⇨ Alignment group, you'll see this icon (refer to Figure 2-7). Click it, and it displays the Format Cells dialog box, with the Number tab preselected. This dialog box provides options that aren't available in the Ribbon.

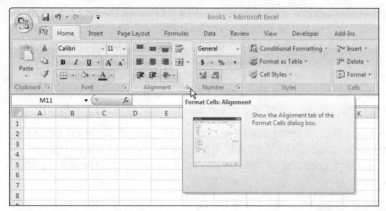

Figure 2-7: This small dialog launcher icon displays a dialog box that has additional options.

THE QUICK ACCESS TOOLBAR

In previous versions of Excel, end users were free to customize their menus and toolbars. Things have changed in Excel 2007. Although the Ribbon can be customized, it's a task best left for a knowledgeable developer. In Excel 2007, the only end-user customization option is the Quick Access Toolbar (QAT). Normally, the QAT is displayed on the left side of the title bar. Alternatively, you can display the QAT below the Ribbon by right-clicking the QAT and selecting Place Quick Access Toolbar Below Ribbon.

By default, the QAT contains these tools: Save, Undo, and Redo. You can, of course, customize the QAT by adding other commands that you use often. To add a command from the Ribbon to your QAT, right-click the command and choose Add To Quick Access Toolbar.

Excel has commands that aren't available in the Ribbon. In most cases, the only way to access these commands is to add them to your QAT. Figure 2-8 shows the Customization section of the Excel Options dialog box. This is your one-stop shop for QAT customization. A quick way to display this dialog box is to right-click the QAT and choose Customize Quick Access Toolbar.

ACCESSING THE RIBBON BY USING YOUR KEYBOARD

At first glance, you may think that the Ribbon is completely mouse-centric. After all, none of the commands has the traditional underlined letter to indicate the Alt+keystrokes. But, in fact, the Ribbon is *very* keyboard friendly. The trick is to press the Alt key to display the pop-up "keytips." Each Ribbon control has a letter (or series of letters) that you type to issue the command.

TIP

It's not necessary to hold down the Alt key as you type the keytip letters.

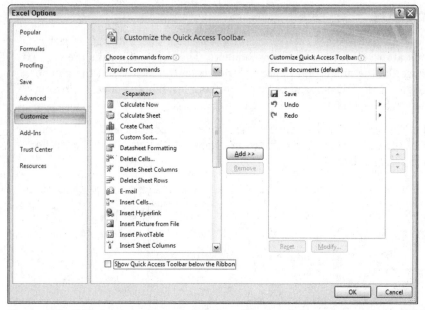

Figure 2-8: Add new icons to your QAT by using the Customization section of the Excel Options dialog box.

Figure 2-9 shows how the Home tab looks after I press the Alt key to display the keytips. If you press one of the keytips, the screen then displays more keytips. For example, to use the keyboard to align the cell contents to the left, press Alt, followed by H (for Home) and then AL (for Align Left). If you're a keyboard fan (like me), it will just take a few times before you memorize the keystrokes required for common commands.

Figure 2-9: Pressing Alt displays the keytips.

After you press Alt, you can also use the left and right arrow keys to scroll through the tabs. When you reach the proper tab, press the down-arrow key to enter the Ribbon. Then use the left- and right-arrow keys to scroll through the Ribbon commands. When you reach the command you need, press Enter to execute it. This method isn't as efficient as using the keytips, but it is a quick way to take a quick look at the choices on the Ribbon.

Shortcut menus

The only menus that remain in Excel 2007 are shortcut menus. These menus appear when you right-click after selecting one or more objects. The shortcut menus are context-sensitive. In other words, the menu that appears depends on the location of the mouse pointer when you right-click. You can right-click just about anything — a cell, a row or column border, a workbook title bar, a toolbar, and so on.

Right-clicking some objects displays a mini-toolbar above the shortcut menu. This toolbar provides quick access to commonly used formatting commands. Figure 2-10 shows the mini-toolbar when a cell is selected.

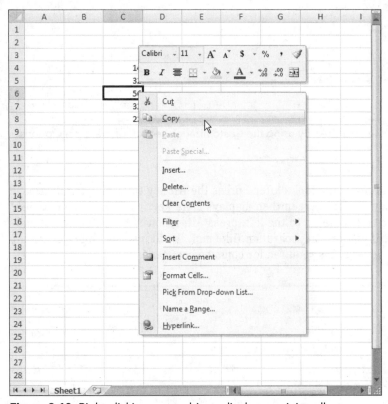

Figure 2-10: Right-clicking some objects displays a mini-toolbar.

Although you cannot customize the Ribbon by using VBA, you can use VBA to customize any of the shortcut menus.

CROSS-REFERENCE
Refer to Chapter 23 for more information about customizing shortcut menus.

Dialog boxes

Some of the Ribbon commands display a dialog box. In many cases, these dialog boxes contain additional controls that aren't available in the Ribbon.

You'll find two general classes of dialog boxes in Excel:

- *Modal dialog boxes:* When a modal dialog box is displayed, it must be closed in order to execute the commands. An example is the Format Cells dialog box. None of the options you specify are executed until you click OK. Use the Cancel button to close the dialog box without making any changes.

- *Modeless dialog boxes:* These are "stay on top" dialog boxes. For example, if you're working with a chart using the Format dialog box, changes that you make are reflected immediately in the chart. Modeless dialog boxes usually have a Close button rather than an OK button and a Cancel button.

Many of Excel's dialog boxes use a notebook tab metaphor, which makes a single dialog box function as several different dialog boxes. In older dialog boxes, the tabs are usually along the top. But in newer dialog boxes (such as the one shown in Figure 2-11), the tabs are along the left side.

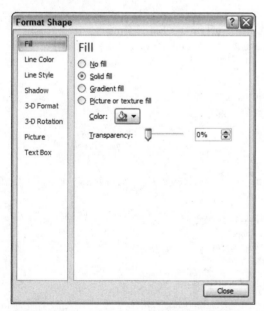

Figure 2-11: Tabbed dialog boxes make many options accessible without overwhelming the user.

Developers can create custom dialog boxes by using the UserForm feature. As you'll see, it's possible to create a wide variety of dialog boxes, including tabbed dialog boxes.

CROSS-REFERENCE

Refer to Part IV for information about creating and working with UserForms.

Keyboard shortcuts

Excel has *many* useful keyboard shortcuts. For example, you can press Ctrl+D to copy a cell to selected cells below it. If you're a newcomer to Excel — or you just want to improve your efficiency — I urge you to check out the Help system (access the Accessibility main topic, and go from there). Learning these shortcuts is key to becoming proficient in Excel. The Help file has tables that summarize useful keyboard commands and shortcuts.

And, as I noted previously, you can access the Ribbon commands by using the keyboard.

Smart Tags

A *Smart Tag* is a small icon that appears automatically in your worksheet after you perform certain actions. Clicking a Smart Tag reveals several options. For example, if you copy and paste a range of cells, Excel generates a Smart Tag that appears below the pasted range (see Figure 2-12) and provides you with several options regarding the formatting of the pasted data.

If you don't like these Smart Tags, you can turn them off in the Excel Options dialog box. Choose Office ➪ Excel Options and click the Advanced tab. Use the controls in the section labeled Cut, Copy And Paste.

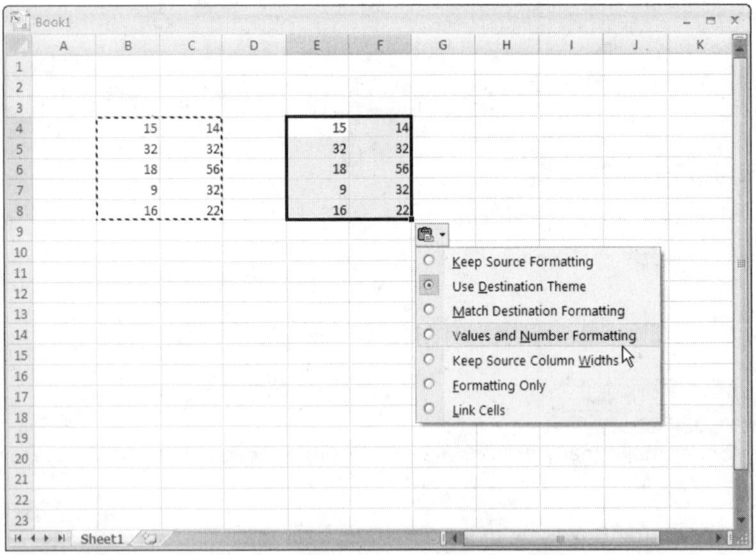

Figure 2-12: This Smart Tag appears when you paste a copied range.

Task pane

Excel 2002 introduced a new UI element known as the task pane. This is a multipurpose user interface element that is normally docked on the right side of Excel's window (but you can drag it anywhere). The task pane is used for a variety of purposes, including displaying the Office Clipboard, displaying a pivot table field list, inserting clip art, providing research assistance, and mapping eXtensible Markup Language (XML) data. Figure 2-13 shows the Clip Art task pane.

Figure 2-13: Locating clip art is one of several uses for the task pane.

What's New in the Visual Basic Editor?

Nothing.

Most of Excel 2007's updated object model is accessible in your VBA code, but the VB Editor is exactly the same as it was in Excel 2003.

Customizing the Display

Excel offers a great deal of flexibility regarding what is displayed onscreen (status bar, formula bar, toolbars, and so on). These commands are located in the View tab.

In fact, Excel makes it possible to develop an application that doesn't even look like a spreadsheet. For example, by choosing View ⇨ Workbook Views ⇨ Full Screen, you can get rid of everything except the title bar, thereby maximizing the amount of information visible. To exit full-screen mode, right-click any cell and choose Close Full Screen from the shortcut menu.

 NEW

Excel 2007 places a zoom control in the right side of the status bar, making it easier than ever to zoom in or out. In addition, you can right-click the status bar and specify the type of information you'd like to see.

Data Entry

Data entry in Excel is quite straightforward. Excel interprets each cell entry as one of the following:

- A numeric value (including date and time values)
- Text
- A Boolean value (True or False)
- A formula

Formulas always begin with an equal sign (=). Excel accommodates habitual 1-2-3 users, however, and accepts an each-at symbol (@), a plus sign (+), or a minus sign (–) as the first character in a formula. Excel automatically adjusts the entry after you press Enter.

Formulas, Functions, and Names

Formulas are what make a spreadsheet a spreadsheet. Excel has some advanced formula-related features that are worth knowing. They enable you to write array formulas, use an intersection operator, include links, and create *megaformulas* (my term for a lengthy and incomprehensible — but very efficient — formula).

CROSS-REFERENCE

Chapter 3 covers formulas and presents lots of tricks and tips.

Excel also has some useful auditing capabilities that help you identify errors or track the logic in an unfamiliar spreadsheet. To access these features, use the commands in the Formulas ➪ Formula Auditing group.

You may find the Formulas ➪ Formula Auditing ➪ Error Checking command useful. It will scan your worksheet and identify possibly erroneous formulas. In Figure 2-14, Excel identifies a possibly inconsistent formula and provides some options.

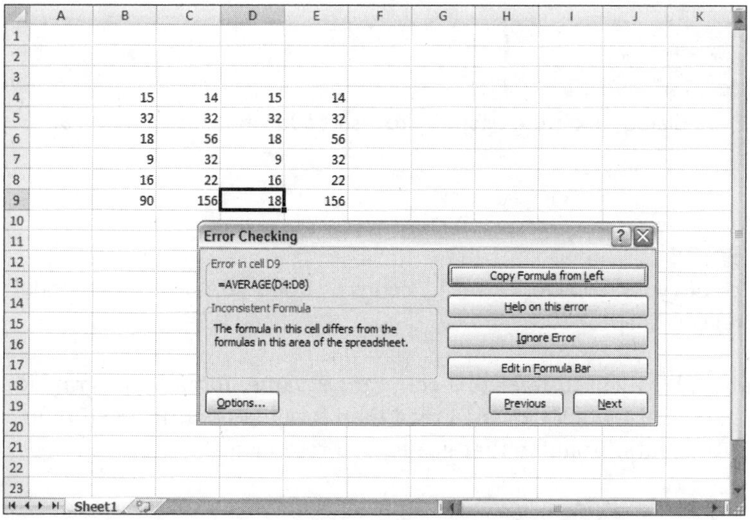

Figure 2-14: Excel can monitor your formulas for possible errors.

Worksheet functions enable you to perform calculations or operations that would otherwise be impossible. Excel provides a huge number of built-in functions.

The easiest way to locate the function that you need is to use the Insert Function dialog box, as shown in Figure 2-15. Access this dialog box by clicking the Insert Function button on the formula bar (or by pressing Shift+F3). After you select a function, Excel displays its Function Arguments dialog box, which assists with specifying the function's arguments.

NEW

In Excel 2007, the Analysis ToolPak functions are now built-in. In other words, you can use these function even if the Analysis ToolPak add-in is not installed.

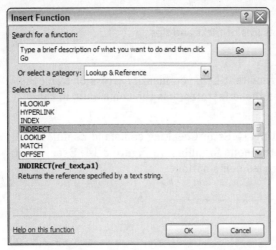

Figure 2-15: The Insert Function dialog box is the best way to insert a function into a formula.

 CROSS-REFERENCE

Excel also lets you create your own worksheet functions by using VBA. For details about this powerful feature, see Chapter 10.

A *name* is an identifier that enables you to refer to a cell, range, value, formula, or graphic object. Formulas that use names are much easier to read than formulas that use cell references, and it's much easier to create formulas that use named references.

 CROSS-REFERENCE

I discuss names in Chapter 3. As you can see there, Excel handles names in some unique ways.

Selecting Objects

Selecting objects in Excel conforms to standard Windows practices. You can select a range of cells by clicking and dragging (it's more efficient to learn the keyboard shortcuts, however). Clicking an object that has been placed on the drawing layer selects the object. To select multiple objects or noncontiguous cells, press Ctrl while you select the objects or cells.

NOTE

Clicking a chart selects a specific object within the chart. To select the chart object itself, press Ctrl while you click the chart.

If an object has a macro assigned to it, you'll find that clicking the object executes the macro. To actually select such an object, right-click it and press Esc to hide the shortcut menu. Or press Ctrl while you click the object.

Formatting

Excel provides two types of formatting: numeric formatting and stylistic formatting.

Numeric formatting

Numeric formatting refers to how a number appears in the cell. In addition to choosing from an extensive list of predefined formats, you can create your own formats (see Figure 2-16). The procedure is thoroughly explained in the Help system.

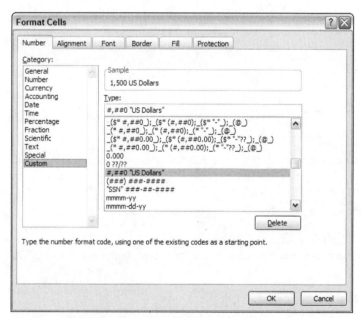

Figure 2-16: Excel's numeric formatting options are very flexible.

Excel applies some numeric formatting automatically, based on the entry. For example, if you precede a number with a currency symbol (a dollar sign in the U.S.), Excel applies Currency number formatting. A new feature in Excel 2007 enables you to apply number formatting conditionally, using the conditional formatting feature.

Stylistic formatting

Stylistic formatting refers to the formatting that you apply to make your work look good. Many Ribbon buttons offer direct access to common formatting options, but you'll want to access the object's Format dialog box for the full range of formatting options.

The easiest way to get to the correct dialog box and format an object is to select the object and press Ctrl+1. You could also right-click the object and choose Format *xxx* (where *xxx* is the selected object) from the shortcut menu. Either of these actions brings up a tabbed dialog box that holds all the formatting options for the selected object.

Excel's conditional formatting feature is particularly useful. This feature, accessed by choosing Home ➪ Styles ➪ Conditional Formatting, allows you to specify formatting that will be applied only if certain conditions are met. For example, you can make cells that exceed a specified value appear in a different color.

NEW

Excel 2007 has several new conditional formatting options, including data bars, color scales, and icon sets. Figure 2-17 shows the new data bars conditional formatting option that displays a histogram directly in the cells.

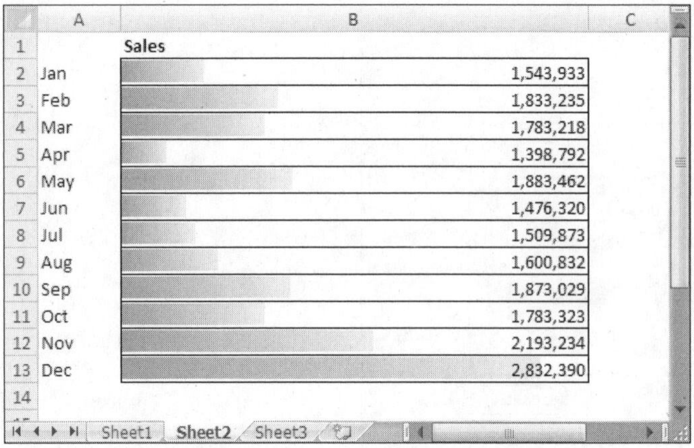

	A	B	C
1	Sales		
2	Jan		1,543,933
3	Feb		1,833,235
4	Mar		1,783,218
5	Apr		1,398,792
6	May		1,883,462
7	Jun		1,476,320
8	Jul		1,509,873
9	Aug		1,600,832
10	Sep		1,873,029
11	Oct		1,783,323
12	Nov		2,193,234
13	Dec		2,832,390
14			

Sheet1 Sheet2 Sheet3

Figure 2-17: The data bars option is one of the new conditional formatting features in Excel 2007.

Protection Options

Excel offers a number of different protection options. For example, you can protect formulas from being overwritten or modified, protect a workbook's structure, password-protect a workbook, and protect your VBA code.

Protecting formulas from being overwritten

In many cases, you might want to protect your formulas from being overwritten or modified. To do so, perform the following steps:

1. Select the cells that *may* be overwritten.

2. Right-click and choose Format Cells from the shortcut menu.

3. In the Format Cells dialog box, click the Protection tab.

4. In the Protection tab, clear the Locked check box.

5. Click OK to close the Format Cells dialog box.

6. Select Review ➪ Changes ➪ Protect Sheet to display the Protect Sheet dialog box, as shown in Figure 2-18.

Figure 2-18: The Protect Sheet dialog box.

7. In the Protect Sheet dialog box, select the options that correspond to the actions to allow, specify a password if desired, and then click OK.

 NOTE
By default, all cells are locked. The locked status of a cell has no effect, however, unless you have a protected worksheet.

You can also hide your formulas so they won't appear in Excel's formula bar when the cell is activated. To do so, select the formula cells and make sure that the Hidden check box is marked in the Protection tab of the Format Cells dialog box.

Protecting a workbook's structure

When you protect a workbook's structure, you can't add or delete sheets. Choose the Review ⇨ Changes ⇨ Protect Workbook command to display the Protect Workbook dialog box, as shown in Figure 2-19. Make sure that you enable the Structure check box. If you also mark the Windows check box, the window can't be moved or resized.

Figure 2-19: The Protect Workbook dialog box.

Applying password protection to a workbook

In some cases, you might want to limit access to a workbook to only those who know the password.

To save a workbook file with a password, choose Office ⇨ Prepare ⇨ Encrypt Document.. Then, in the Encrypt Document dialog box (see Figure 2-20), specify a password and click OK. Then save your workbook.

Figure 2-20: Use the Encrypt Document dialog box to save a workbook with a password.

Protecting VBA code with a password

If your workbook contains VBA code, you may wish to use a password to prevent others from viewing or modifying your macros. To apply a password to the VBA code in a workbook, activate the VBE (Alt+F11) and select your project in the Projects window. Then choose Tools ⇨ *xxxx* Properties (where *xxxx* corresponds to your Project name). This displays the Project Properties dialog box.

In the Project Properties dialog box, click the Protection tab (see Figure 2-21). Enable the Lock Project for Viewing check box and enter a password (twice). Click OK and then save your file. When the file is closed and then reopened, a password will be required to view or modify the code.

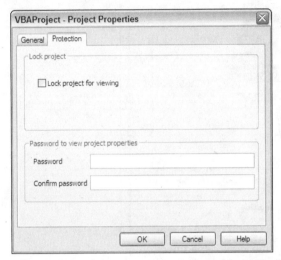

Figure 2-21: Protecting a VBA project with the Project Properties dialog box.

 CAUTION

It's important to keep in mind that Excel is not really a secure application. The protection features, even when used with a password, are intended to prevent casual users from accessing various components of your workbook. Anyone who really wants to defeat your protection can probably do so by using readily available password-cracking utilities (or by knowing a few "secrets").

Charts

Excel is perhaps the most commonly used application in the world for creating charts. As I mention earlier in this chapter, you can store charts on a chart sheet or float them on a worksheet.

 NEW

Excel 2007 still hasn't introduced any new chart types, but charts are easier to create, and they most definitely look much better. Figure 2-22 shows an Excel 2007 chart that uses some of the new formatting options.

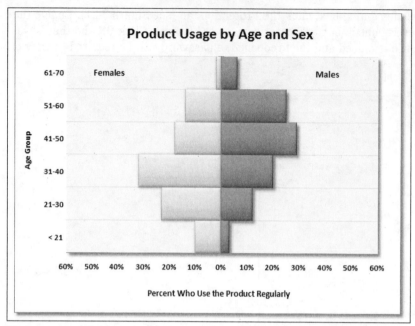

Figure 2-22: Excel 2007 charts have improved in the looks department.

You can also create pivot charts. A *pivot chart* is linked to a pivot table, and you can view various graphical summaries of your data by using the same techniques used in a pivot table.

Excel offers extensive chart customization options, and over the years, quite a few chart-making tricks have made the rounds. These tricks enable you to create charts that you might think are impossible.

Shapes and SmartArt

As I mention earlier in this chapter, each worksheet has an invisible drawing layer that holds charts, pictures, controls (such as buttons and list boxes), and shapes.

Excel enables you to easily draw a wide variety of geometric shapes directly on your worksheet. To access the Shape gallery, choose Insert ➪ Illustrations ➪ Shapes. The shapes are highly customizable, and you can even add text. You can also group objects into a single object, which is easier to size or position.

NEW

A new feature in Office 2007 is SmartArt, which you use to create a wide variety of customizable diagrams. Figure 2-23 shows an example of a SmartArt diagram.

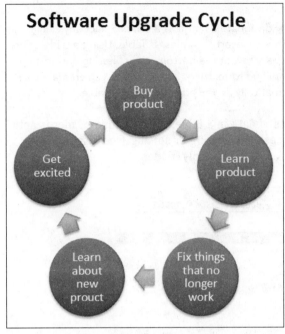

Figure 2-23: A SmartArt diagram.

Database Access

Over the years, most spreadsheets have enabled users to work with simple flat database tables. Excel has some slick tools.

Databases fall into two categories:

- *Worksheet databases:* The entire database is stored in a worksheet, limiting the size of the database.

- *External databases:* The data is stored in one or more files and is accessed as needed.

Worksheet databases

Generally, a rectangular range of data that contains column headers can be considered a worksheet database.

NEW

Excel 2007 enables you to specifically designate a range as a table. Select any cell in your rectangular range of data and choose Insert ⇨ Tables ⇨ Table. Using a table offers many advantages: an automatic summary row at the bottom, easy filtering and sorting, auto-fill formulas in columns, and simplified formatting. In addition, if you create a chart from a table, the chart expands automatically as you add rows to the table.

Particularly useful is working with columns of data in a table. Each column header is actually a drop-down list that contains easy access for filtering or sorting (see Figure 2-24). Table rows that don't meet the filter criteria are temporarily hidden.

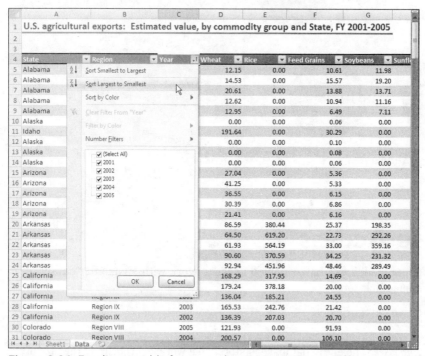

Figure 2-24: Excel's new table feature makes it easy to sort and filter rows.

External databases

To work with external database tables, use the commands in the Data ⇨ Get External Data group. Excel 2007 can work with a wide variety of external databases.

Internet Features

Excel includes a number of features that relate to the Internet. For example, you can save a worksheet or an entire workbook in HyperText Markup Language (HTML) format, accessible in a Web browser. In addition, you can insert clickable hyperlinks (including e-mail addresses) directly in cells.

 CAUTION

In previous versions, HTML was a "round-trip" file format. In other words, you could save a workbook in HTML format and then reopen it in Excel, and nothing would be lost. That's no longer the case with Excel 2007. HTML is now considered an export-only format.

You can also create Web queries to bring in data stored in a corporate intranet or on the Internet. Figure 2-25 shows an example of a Web query.

New Web Query

Address: http://moneycentral.msn.com/investor/market/ra   Go   Options...

Click ➡ next to the tables you want to select, then click Import.

Currency	In US Dollar	Per US Dollar
Argentine Peso	0.32383	3.08800
Australian Dollar	0.75637	1.32210
Brazilian Real	0.46468	2.15200
British Pound	1.88857	0.52950
Canadian Dollar	0.90196	1.10870
Chinese Yuan	0.12538	7.97600
Euro	1.27649	0.78340
Hong Kong Dollar	0.12855	7.77930
Indian Rupee	0.02154	46.42300
Japanese Yen	0.00853	117.29000

Cross-Currency Table
Currency Converter
New Stocks
IPO Center
News by Topic
Companies
Stock Market
Economy
Industry
Related Links
E-mail & Alerts

Import   Cancel

Figure 2-25: Create a Web Query to import data into a worksheet.

Analysis Tools

Excel is certainly no slouch when it comes to analysis. After all, that's what most people use a spreadsheet for. Most analysis tasks can be handled with formulas, but Excel offers many other options.

Outlines

A worksheet outline is often an excellent way to work with hierarchical data such as budgets. Excel can create an outline (horizontal, vertical, or both) automatically, or you can do so manually. After the outline is created, you can collapse or expand it to display various levels of detail.

Analysis ToolPak

In previous versions of Excel, the Analysis ToolPak add-in provided additional special-purpose analysis tools and worksheet functions, primarily statistical in nature. In Excel 2007, these features are built in. These tools make Excel suitable for casual statistical analysis.

Pivot tables

Pivot tables are among Excel's most powerful tools. A pivot table is capable of summarizing data in a handy table, and this table can be arranged in many ways. In addition, a pivot table can be manipulated entirely by VBA. Data for a pivot table comes from a worksheet database or an external database and is stored in a special cache, which enables Excel to recalculate rapidly after a pivot table is altered. Figure 2-26 shows a pivot table.

CROSS-REFERENCE

See Chapter 17 for information about manipulating pivot tables with VBA.

Solver

For specialized linear and nonlinear problems, Excel's Solver add-in calculates solutions to what-if scenarios based on adjustable cells, constraint cells, and, optionally, cells that must be maximized or minimized.

XML features

One of the few new features introduced in Excel 2003 dealt with XML files. (XML is an accepted standard that enables exchange of data between different applications.) You can import data from an XML file and then map the data to specific worksheet cells.

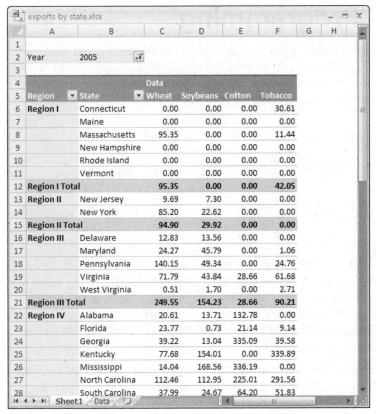

Figure 2-26: Excel's pivot table feature has many applications.

Add-Ins

An *add-in* is a program that's attached to an application to give it additional functionality. To attach an Excel add-in, use the Add-Ins tab in the Excel Options dialog box.

In addition to the add-ins that ship with Excel, you can download additional add-ins from Microsoft's Web site (http://office.microsoft.com), and you can purchase or download many third-party add-ins from online services. You can use the coupon in the back of the book to acquire a discounted copy of the Power Utility Pak add-in. And, as I detail in Chapter 21, it's *very* easy to create your own add-ins.

Macros and Programming

Excel has two built-in macro programming languages: XLM and VBA. The original XLM macro language is obsolete, and it has been replaced by VBA. Excel 2003 can still execute most XLM macros, and you can even create new ones. However, you cannot record XLM macros. You'll want to use VBA to develop new macros.

 CROSS-REFERENCE

Part III of this book is devoted to the VBA language.

File Format

A key consideration is file compatibility. Excel 97 through Excel 2003 all use the same file format, so file compatibility is not a problem for these four versions. Excel 2007, however, uses a new file format. Fortunately, Microsoft has made a "compatibility pack" available for earlier versions of Excel. This compatibility pack enables older versions of Excel to read and write the new XLSX file format.

It's important to understand the difference between file compatibility and feature compatibility. For example, even though the compatibility pack enables Excel 2003 to open files created by Excel 2007, it cannot handle features that were introduced in later versions.

 CROSS-REFERENCE

Refer to Chapter 4 for more information about Excel's file format, and read Chapter 26 for more information about compatibility issues for developers.

Excel's Help System

One of Excel's most important features is its Help system. When you get stuck, simply click the question mark below the title bar (or press F1). Excel's Help window appears, and you can search or use the Table of Contents.

 TIP

The Search button in the Help window is actually a drop-down control. Use the options to help narrow your search or to specify the source to search (see Figure 2-27).

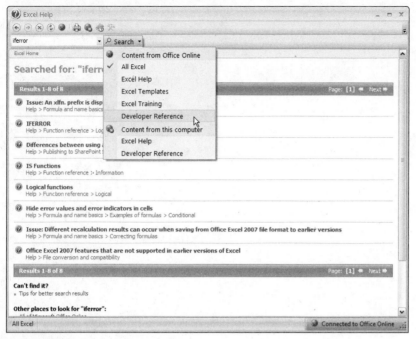

Figure 2-27: Excel's Help window.

Chapter 3

Formula Tricks and Techniques

In This Chapter

This chapter provides an overview of Excel's formula-related features and describes some techniques that might be new to you.

- ◆ An overview of Excel formulas
- ◆ Differentiating between absolute and relative references in formulas
- ◆ Understanding and using names
- ◆ Introducing array formulas
- ◆ Counting and summing cells
- ◆ Working with dates and times
- ◆ Creating megaformulas

Virtually every successful spreadsheet application uses formulas. In fact, constructing formulas can certainly be construed as a type of programming.

 NOTE

For a much more comprehensive treatment of Excel formulas and functions, refer to my book, *Excel 2007 Formulas* (Wiley).

About Formulas

Formulas, of course, are what make a spreadsheet a spreadsheet. If it weren't for formulas, your worksheet would just be a static document — something that could be produced by a word processor that has great support for tables.

Excel has a huge assortment of built-in functions, has excellent support for names, and even supports *array formulas* (a special type of formula that can perform otherwise impossible calculations).

A formula entered into a cell can consist of any of the following elements:

- Operators such as + (for addition) and * (for multiplication)
- Cell references (including named cells and ranges)
- Numbers or text strings
- Worksheet functions (such as SUM or AVERAGE)

A formula in Excel 2007 can consist of up to 8,000 characters. After you enter a formula into a cell, the cell displays the result of the formula. The formula itself appears in the formula bar when the cell is activated.

Calculating Formulas

You've probably noticed that the formulas in your worksheet get calculated immediately. If you change a cell that a formula uses, the formula displays a new result with no effort on your part. This is what happens when the Excel Calculation mode is set to Automatic. In this mode (which is the default mode), Excel uses the following rules when calculating your worksheet:

- When you make a change — enter or edit data or formulas, for example — Excel immediately calculates those formulas that depend on the new or edited data.
- If it's in the middle of a lengthy calculation, Excel temporarily suspends calculation when you need to perform other worksheet tasks; it resumes when you're finished.
- Formulas are evaluated in a natural sequence. In other words, if a formula in cell D12 depends on the result of a formula in cell D11, cell D11 is calculated before D12.

Sometimes, however, you might want to control when Excel calculates formulas. For example, if you create a worksheet with thousands of complex formulas, operations can slow to a snail's pace while Excel does its thing. In such a case, you should set Excel's calculation mode to Manual. Use the Calculation Options control in the Formulas ➪ Calculation group.

When you're working in Manual Calculation mode, Excel displays *Calculate* in the status bar when you have any uncalculated formulas. You can press the following shortcut keys to recalculate the formulas:

- *F9* calculates the formulas in all open workbooks.

- *Shift+F9* calculates the formulas in the active worksheet only. Other worksheets in the same workbook won't be calculated.

- *Ctrl+Alt+F9* forces a recalculation of everything in all workbooks. Use it if Excel (for some reason) doesn't seem to be calculating correctly, or if you want to force a recalculation of formulas that use custom functions created with Visual Basic for Applications (VBA).

- *Ctrl+Alt+Shift+F9* rechecks all dependent formulas, and calculates all cells in all workbooks (including cells not marked as needing to be calculated).

NOTE

Excel's Calculation mode isn't specific to a particular worksheet. When you change Excel's Calculation mode, it affects all open workbooks, not just the active workbook.

Cell and Range References

Most formulas reference one or more cells. This reference can be made by using the cell's or range's address or name (if it has one). Cell references come in four styles:

- *Relative:* The reference is fully relative. When the formula is copied, the cell reference adjusts to its new location. Example: A1.

- *Absolute:* The reference is fully absolute. When the formula is copied, the cell reference does not change. Example: $A$1.

- *Row Absolute:* The reference is partially absolute. When the formula is copied, the column part adjusts, but the row part does not change. Example: A$1.

- *Column Absolute:* The reference is partially absolute. When the formula is copied, the row part adjusts, but the column part does not change. Example: $A1.

By default, all cell and range references are relative. To change a reference, you must manually add the dollar signs. Or, when editing a cell in the formula bar, move the cursor to a cell address and press F4 repeatedly to cycle through all four types of cell referencing.

Why use references that aren't relative?

If you think about it, you'll realize that the only reason why you would ever need to change a reference is if you plan to copy the formula. Figure 3-1 demonstrates why this is so. The formula in cell C3 is

```
=$B3*C$2
```

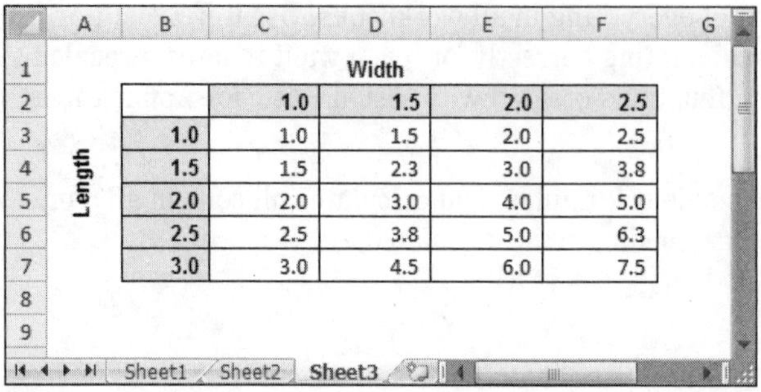

		Width			
		1.0	1.5	2.0	2.5
Length	1.0	1.0	1.5	2.0	2.5
	1.5	1.5	2.3	3.0	3.8
	2.0	2.0	3.0	4.0	5.0
	2.5	2.5	3.8	5.0	6.3
	3.0	3.0	4.5	6.0	7.5

Figure 3-1: An example of using nonrelative references in a formula.

This formula calculates the area for various lengths (listed in column B) and widths (listed in row 3). After the formula is entered, it can then be copied down to C7 and across to F7. Because the formula uses absolute references to row 2 and column B and relative references for other rows and columns, each copied formula produces the correct result. If the formula used only relative references, copying the formula would cause all the references to adjust and thus produce incorrect results.

About R1C1 notation

Normally, Excel uses what's known as *A1 notation:* Each cell address consists of a column letter and a row number. However, Excel also supports *R1C1 notation.* In this system, cell A1 is referred to as cell R1C1, cell A2 as R2C1, and so on.

To change to R1C1 notation, access the Formulas tab of the Excel Options dialog box. Place a check mark next to R1C1 Reference Style. After you do so, you'll notice that the column letters all change to numbers. All the cell and range references in your formulas are also adjusted.

Table 3-1 presents some examples of formulas that use standard notation and R1C1 notation. The formula is assumed to be in cell B1 (also known as R1C2).

TABLE 3-1   COMPARING SIMPLE FORMULAS IN TWO NOTATIONS

Standard	R1C1
=A1+1	=RC[–1]+1
=$A$1+1	=R1C1+1
=$A1+1	=RC1+1
=A$1+1	=R1C[–1]+1
=SUM(A1:A10)	=SUM(RC[–1]:R[9]C[–1])
=SUM($A$1:$A$10)	=SUM(R1C1:R10C1)

If you find R1C1 notation confusing, you're not alone. R1C1 notation isn't too bad when you're dealing with absolute references. But when relative references are involved, the brackets can be very confusing.

The numbers in brackets refer to the relative position of the references. For example, R[–5]C[–3] specifies the cell that's five rows above and three columns to the left. On the other hand, R[5]C[3] references the cell that's five rows below and three columns to the right. If the brackets are omitted, the notation specifies the same row or column. For example, R[5]C refers to the cell five rows below in the same column.

Although you probably won't use R1C1 notation as your standard system, it *does* have at least one good use. Using R1C1 notation makes it very easy to spot an erroneous formula. When you copy a formula, every copied formula is exactly the same in R1C1 notation. This is true regardless of the types of cell references that you use (relative, absolute, or mixed). Therefore, you can switch to R1C1 notation and check your copied formulas. If one looks different from its surrounding formulas, there's a good chance that it might be incorrect.

In addition, if you write VBA code to create worksheet formulas, you might find it easier to create the formulas by using R1C1 notation.

Referencing other sheets or workbooks

When a formula refers to other cells, the references need not be on the same sheet as the formula. To refer to a cell in a different worksheet, precede the cell reference with the sheet name followed by an exclamation point. Here's an example of a formula that uses a cell reference in a different worksheet (Sheet2):

```
=Sheet2!A1+1
```

You can also create link formulas that refer to a cell in a different workbook. To do so, precede the cell reference with the workbook name (in square brackets), the worksheet name, and an exclamation point. Here's an example:

```
=[Budget.xlsx]Sheet1!A1
```

If the workbook name in the reference includes one or more spaces, you must enclose it (and the sheet name) in single quotation marks. For example:

```
='[Budget For 2008.xlsx]Sheet1'!A1
```

Referencing Data in a Table

Excel 2007 supports a special type of range that has been designated as a table (using the Insert ⇨ Tables ⇨ Table command). Tables add a few new twists to formulas.

When you enter a formula into a cell in a table, Excel automatically copies the formula to all of the other cells in the column — but only if the column was empty. This is known as a calculated column. If you add a new row to the table, the calculated column formula is entered automatically for the new row. Most of the time, this is exactly what you want. If you don't like the idea of Excel entering formulas for you, use the SmartTag to turn this feature off. The SmartTag appears after Excel enters the calculated column formula.

Excel 2007 also supports "structured referencing" for referring to cells within a table. The table in the accompanying figure is named Table1.

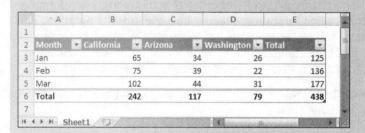

You can create formulas that refer to cells within the table by using the column headers. In some cases, this may make your formulas easier to understand. But the real advantage is that your formulas will continue to be valid if rows are added or removed from the table. For example, these are all valid formulas:

```
=SUM(Table1[Washington])
=Table1[[#Totals],[California]]
=Table1[[#Headers],[California]]
=SUM(Table1[[#This Row],[California]:[Washington]])
```

The last formula, which uses [#This Row], is valid only if it's in a cell in one of the rows occupied by the table.

If the linked workbook is closed, you must add the complete path to the workbook reference. Here's an example:

```
='C:\Budgeting\Excel Files\[Budget For 2008.xlsx]Sheet1'!A1
```

Although you can enter link formulas directly, you can also create the reference by using normal pointing methods. To do so, the source file must be open. When you do so, Excel creates absolute cell references. If you plan to copy the formula to other cells, make the references relative.

Working with links can be tricky. For example, if you choose the Office ➪ Save As command to make a backup copy of the source workbook, you automatically change the link formulas to refer to the new file (not usually what you want to do). Another way to mess up your links is to rename the source workbook when the dependent workbook is not open.

Using Names

One of the most useful features in Excel is its ability to provide meaningful names for various items. For example, you can name cells, ranges, rows, columns, charts, and other objects. You can even name values or formulas that don't appear in cells in your worksheet (see the "Naming constants" section, later in this chapter).

Naming cells and ranges

Excel provides several ways to name a cell or range:

- Choose Formulas ➪ Named Cells ➪ Name a Range to display the New Name dialog box.

- Use the Name Manager dialog box (Formulas ➪ Defined Names ➪ Name Manager or press Ctrl+F3). This is not the most efficient method because it requires clicking the New button in the Name Manger dialog box, which displays the New Name dialog box.

- Select the cell or range and then type a name in the Name box and press Enter. The Name box is the drop-down control displayed to the left of the formula bar.

- If your worksheet contains text that you would like to use for names of adjacent cells or ranges, select the text and the cells to be named and choose Formulas ➪ Defined Names ➪ Create from Selection. In Figure 3-2, for example, B3:E3 is named *North,* B4:E4 is named *South,* and so on. Vertically, B3:B6 is named *Qtr1,* C3:C6 is named *Qtr2,* and so on.

Using names is especially important if you write VBA code that uses cell or range references. The reason? VBA does not automatically update its references if you move a cell or range that's referred to in a VBA statement. For example, if your VBA code writes a value to `Range("C4")`, the data will be written to the wrong cell if the user inserts a new row above or a new column to the left of cell C4. Using a reference to a named cell, such as `Range("InterestRate")`, avoids these potential problems.

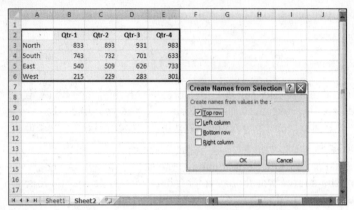

Figure 3-2: Excel makes it easy to create names that use descriptive text in your worksheet.

Applying names to existing references

When you create a name for a cell or a range, Excel doesn't automatically use the name in place of existing references in your formulas. For example, assume that you have the following formula in cell F10:

```
=A1–A2
```

If you define the names *Income* for A1 and *Expenses* for A2, Excel will not automatically change your formula to

```
=Income-Expenses
```

However, it's fairly easy to replace cell or range references with their corresponding names. Start by selecting the range that contains the formulas that you want to modify. Then choose the Formulas ➪ Defined Names ➪ Name a Range ➪ Apply Names. In the Apply Names dialog box, select the names that you want to apply and then click OK. Excel replaces the range references with the names in the selected cells.

 NOTE

Unfortunately, there is no way to automatically unapply names. In other words, if a formula uses a name, you can't convert the name to an actual cell or range reference. Even worse, if you delete a name that is used in a formula, the formula does not revert to the cell or range address — it simply returns a #NAME? error.

My Power Utility Pak add-in (available at a discount by using the coupon in the back of the book) includes a utility that scans all formulas in a selection and automatically replaces names with their cell addresses.

Hidden Names

Some Excel macros and add-ins create hidden names. These are names that exist in a workbook but don't appear in the Name Manager dialog box. For example, the Solver add-in creates a number of hidden names. Normally, you can just ignore these hidden names. However, sometimes these hidden names create a problem. If you copy a sheet to another workbook, the hidden names are also copied, and they might create a link that is very difficult to track down.

You can use the following VBA procedure to delete all hidden names in the workbook:

```
Sub DeleteHiddenNames()
    Dim n As Name
    Dim Count As Integer
    For Each n In ActiveWorkbook.Names
        If Not n.Visible Then
            n.Delete
            Count = Count + 1
        End If
    Next n
    MsgBox Count & " hidden names were deleted."
End Sub
```

Intersecting names

Excel has a special operator called the *intersection operator* that comes into play when you're dealing with ranges. This operator is a space character. Using names with the intersection operator makes it very easy to create meaningful formulas. For this example, refer to Figure 3-2. If you enter the following formula into a cell

```
=Qtr_2 South
```

the result is 732 — the intersection of the Qtr2 range and the South range.

Naming columns and rows

Excel lets you name complete rows and columns. In the preceding example, the name *Qtr1* is assigned to the range B3:B6. Alternatively, *Qtr1* could be assigned to all of column B, *Qtr2* to column C, and so on. You also can do the same horizontally so that *North* refers to row 3, *South* to row 4, and so on.

The intersection operator works exactly as before, but now you can add more regions or quarters without having to change the existing names.

When naming columns and rows, make sure that you don't store any extraneous information in named rows or columns. For example, remember that if you insert a value in cell C7, it is included in the *Qtr1* range.

Scoping names

A named cell or range normally has a workbook-level *scope*. In other words, you can use the name in any worksheet in the workbook.

Another option is to create names that have a worksheet-level scope. To create a worksheet-level name, define the name by preceding it with the worksheet name followed by an exclamation point: for example, *Sheet1!Sales*. If the name is used on the sheet in which it is designed, you can omit the sheet qualifier when you reference the name. You can, however, reference a worksheet-level name on a different sheet if you precede the name with the sheet qualifier.

The Name Manager dialog box (Formulas ➪ Defined Names ➪ Name Manager) makes it easy to identify names by their scope (see Figure 3-3). Note that you can sort the names within this dialog box. For example, click the Scope column header, and the names are sorted by scope.

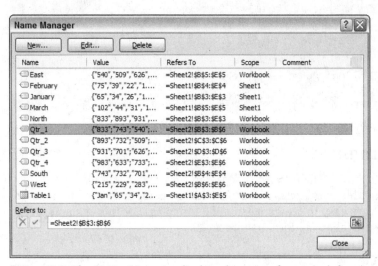

Figure 3-3: The Name Manager displays the scope for each defined name.

Naming constants

Virtually every experienced Excel user knows how to create cell and range names (although not all Excel users actually do so). But most Excel users do not know that you can use names to refer to values that don't appear in your worksheet — that is, *constants*.

Suppose that many formulas in your worksheet need to use a particular interest rate value. One approach is to type the interest rate into a cell and give that cell a name, such as *InterestRate*. After doing so, you can use that name in your formulas, like this:

```
=InterestRate*A3
```

An alternative is to call up the New Name dialog box (Formulas ➪ Defined Names ➪ Define Name) and enter the interest rate directly into the Refers To box (see Figure 3-4). Then you can use the name in your formulas just as if the value were stored in a cell. If the interest rate changes, just change the definition for *InterestRate,* and Excel updates all the cells that contain this name.

Figure 3-4: Excel lets you name constants that don't appear in worksheet cells.

TIP

This technique also works for text. For example, you can define the name IWC to stand for *International Widget Corporation.* Then you can enter **=IWC** into a cell, and the cell displays the full name.

Naming formulas

In addition to naming cells, ranges, and constants, you can also create named formulas. To do so, enter a formula directly into the Refers To field in the New Name dialog box.

NOTE

This is a very important point: The formula that you enter uses cell references relative to the active cell at the time that you create the named formula.

Figure 3-5 shows a formula (=A1^B1) entered directly in the Refers To box in the New Name dialog box. In this case, the active cell is C1, so the formula refers to the two cells to its left. (Notice that the cell references are relative.) After this name is defined, entering **=Power** into a cell raises the value two cells to the left to the power represented by the cell directly to the left. For example, if B10 contains 3 and C10 contains 4, entering the following formula into cell D10 returns a value of 81 (3 to the 4th power):

```
=Power
```

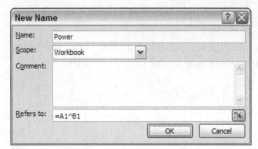

Figure 3-5: You can name a formula that doesn't appear in any worksheet cell.

When you display the New Name dialog box after creating the named formula, the Refers To box displays a formula that is relative to the current active cell. For example, if cell D32 is the active cell, the Refers To box displays

```
=Sheet1!B32^Sheet1!C32
```

Notice that Excel appends the worksheet name to the cell references used in your formula. This, of course, will cause the named formula to produce incorrect results if you use it on a worksheet other than the one in which it was defined. If you would like to use this named formula on a sheet other than Sheet1, you need to remove the sheet references from the formula (but keep the exclamation points). For example:

```
=!A1^!B1
```

After you understand the concept, you might discover some new uses for named formulas. One distinct advantage is apparent if you need to modify the formula. You can just change the formula one time rather than edit each occurrence of the formula.

 CD-ROM

The companion CD-ROM contains a workbook with several examples of named formulas. The workbook is called `named formulas.xlsx`.

 TIP

When you're working in the New Name dialog box, the Refers To field is normally in "point mode," which makes it easy to enter a range reference by clicking in the worksheet. Press F2 to toggle between point mode and normal editing mode, which allows you to use the arrow keys to edit the formula.

The Secret to Understanding Cell and Range Names

Excel users often refer to *named ranges* and *named cells*. In fact, I use these terms frequently throughout this chapter. Actually, this terminology is not quite accurate.

Here's the secret to understanding names:

When you create a name for a cell or a range in Excel, you're actually creating a named formula — a formula that doesn't exist in a cell. Rather, these named formulas exist in Excel's memory.

When you work with the New Name dialog box, the Refers To field contains the formula, and the Name field contains the formula's name. You'll find that the contents of the Refers To field always begin with an equal sign — which makes it a formula.

This is not exactly an earthshaking revelation, but keeping this "secret" in mind could help you understand what's going on behind the scenes when you create and use names in your workbooks.

Naming objects

In addition to providing names for cells and ranges, you can give more meaningful names to objects such as pivot tables and shapes. This can make it easier to refer to such objects, especially when you refer to them in your VBA code.

To change the name of a nonrange object, use the Name box, which is located to the left of the formula bar. Just select the object, type the new name in the Name box, and then press Enter.

 NOTE

If you simply click elsewhere in your workbook after typing the name in the Name box, the name won't stick. You must press Enter.

For some reason, Excel 2007 does not allow you to use the Name box to rename a chart. You must use Chart Tools ➪ Layout ➪ Properties ➪ Chart Name.

Formula Errors

It's not uncommon to enter a formula and receive an error in return. One possibility is that the formula you entered is the cause of the error. Another possibility is that the formula refers to a cell that has an error value. The latter scenario is known as the *ripple effect* — a single error value can make its way to lots of other cells that contain formulas that depend on the cell. The tools in the Formulas ➪ Formula Auditing group can help you trace the source of formula errors.

Table 3-2 lists the types of error values that may appear in a cell that has a formula.

TABLE 3-2   EXCEL ERROR VALUES

Error Value	Explanation
#DIV/0!	The formula is trying to divide by 0 (zero) (an operation that's not allowed on this planet). This error also occurs when the formula attempts to divide by a cell that is empty.
#N/A	The formula is referring (directly or indirectly) to a cell that uses the NA worksheet function to signal the fact that data is not available. A LOOKUP function that can't locate a value also returns #N/A.
#NAME?	The formula uses a name that Excel doesn't recognize. This can happen if you delete a name that's used in the formula or if you have unmatched quotes when using text. A formula will also display this error if it uses a function defined in an add-in and that add-in is not installed.
#NULL!	The formula uses an intersection of two ranges that don't intersect. (This concept is described earlier in the chapter.)
#NUM!	There is a problem with a function argument; for example, the SQRT function is attempting to calculate the square root of a negative number. This error also appears if a calculated value is too large or small. Excel does not support non-zero values less than 1E–307 or greater than 1E+308 in absolute value.
#REF!	The formula refers to a cell that isn't valid. This can happen if that cell has been deleted from the worksheet.
#VALUE!	The formula includes an argument or operand of the wrong type. An *operand* is a value or cell reference that a formula uses to calculate a result. This error also occurs if your formula uses a custom VBA worksheet function that contains an error.
#####	A cell displays a series of hash marks under two conditions: the column is not wide enough to display the result, or the formula returns a negative date or time value.

Array Formulas

In Excel terminology, an *array* is a collection of cells or values that is operated on as a group. An *array formula* is a special type of formula that works with arrays. An array formula can produce a single result, or it can produce multiple results — with each result displayed in a separate cell.

For example, when you multiply a 1 x 5 array by another 1 x 5 array, the result is a third 1 x 5 array. In other words, the result of this kind of operation occupies five cells; each element in the first array is multiplied by each corresponding element in the second array to create five new values, each getting its own cell. The array formula that follows multiplies the values in A1:A5 by the corresponding values in B1:B5. This array formula is entered into five cells simultaneously:

```
{=A1:A5*B1:B5}
```

NOTE

You enter an array formula by pressing Ctrl+Shift+Enter. To remind you that a formula is an array formula, Excel surrounds it with curly braces in the formula bar. When I present an array formula in this book, I enclose it in curly braces to distinguish it from a normal formula. Don't enter the braces yourself.

An array formula example

Excel's array formulas enable you to perform individual operations on each cell in a range in much the same way that a programming language's looping feature enables you to work with elements of an array. If you've never used array formulas before, this section will get your feet wet with a hands-on example.

Figure 3-6 shows a worksheet with text in A1:A5. The goal of this exercise is to create a *single formula* that returns the sum of the total number of characters in the range. Without the *single formula* requirement, you would write a formula with the LEN function, copy it down the column, and then use the SUM function to add the results of the intermediate formulas.

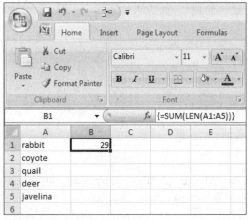

Figure 3-6: Cell B1 contains an array formula that returns the total number of characters contained in range A1:A5. Notice the brackets in the formula bar.

To demonstrate how an array formula can occupy more than one cell, create the worksheet shown in the figure and then try this:

1. Select the range B1:B5.

2. Type the following formula:

   ```
   =LEN(A1:A5)
   ```

3. Press Ctrl+Shift+Enter.

The preceding steps enter a single array formula into five cells. Enter a SUM formula that adds the values in B1:B5, and you'll see that the total number of characters in A1:A5 is 29.

Here's the key point: It's not necessary to actually *display* those five array elements. Rather, Excel can store the array in memory. Knowing this, you can type the following single array formula in any blank cell (*Remember:* Don't type the curly brackets, and make sure that you enter it by pressing Ctrl+Shift+Enter):

```
{=SUM(LEN(A1:A5))}
```

This formula essentially creates a five-element array (in memory) that consists of the length of each string in A1:A5. The SUM function uses this array as its argument, and the formula returns 29.

An array formula calendar

Figure 3-7 shows a worksheet set up to display a calendar for any month (change the month, and the calendar updates). Believe it or not, the calendar is created with a single array formula that occupies 42 cells.

The array formula, entered in the range B5:H10, is:

```
{=IF(MONTH(DATE(YEAR(B3),MONTH(B3),1))<>MONTH(DATE(YEAR(B3),
MONTH(B3),1)-(WEEKDAY(DATE(YEAR(B3),MONTH(B3),1))-1)
+{0;1;2;3;4;5}*7+{1,2,3,4,5,6,7}-1),"",
DATE(YEAR(B3),MONTH(B3),1)-(WEEKDAY(DATE(YEAR(B3),
MONTH(B3),1))-1)+{0;1;2;3;4;5}*7+{1,2,3,4,5,6,7}-1)}
```

 CD-ROM

The companion CD-ROM contains a workbook with the calendar example, as well as several additional array formula examples. The file is named `array formula examples.xlsx`.

Figure 3-7: A single multicell array formula is all it takes to make a calendar for any month in any year.

Array formula pros and cons

The advantages of using array formulas rather than single-cell formulas include the following:

- They can sometimes use less memory.
- They can make your work much more efficient.
- They can eliminate the need for intermediate formulas.
- They can enable you to do things that would be difficult or impossible otherwise.

A few disadvantages of using array formulas are the following:

- Using many complex array formulas can sometimes slow your spreadsheet recalculation time to a crawl.
- They can make your worksheet more difficult for others to understand.
- You must remember to enter an array formula with a special key sequence (by pressing Ctrl+Shift+Enter).

Counting and Summing Techniques

I spend quite a bit of time reading the Excel newsgroups on the Internet, and it seems that many of the questions deal with conditional counting or summing. In an attempt to answer most of these questions, I present a number of formula examples that deal with counting various things on a worksheet, based on single or multiple criteria. You can adapt these formulas to your own needs.

NEW

Excel 2007 includes two new counting and summing functions that aren't available in previous versions (COUNTIFS and SUMIFS). Therefore, I present two versions of some formulas: an Excel 2007–only version and an array formula that works with all recent versions of Excel.

Figure 3-8 shows a simple worksheet to demonstrate the formulas that follow. The following range names are defined:

- *Month:* A2:A10
- *Region:* B2:B10
- *Sales:* C2:C10

	A	B	C	D	E	F	G	H
1	Month	Region	Sales			XL 2007	All versions	Description
2	Jan	North	100				3	Count of Region
3	Jan	South	200				2	Count of Sales where Sales=300
4	Jan	West	300				2	Count of Sales where Sales>300
5	Feb	North	150				8	Count of Sales where Sales <> 100
6	Feb	South	250				6	Count of Regions with five letters
7	Feb	West	350				6	Count of Regions that contain the letter "h"
8	Mar	North	200			1	1	Count of Sales where Month ="Jan" and Sales >200
9	Mar	South	300			1	1	Count of Sales where Month="Jan" AND Region="North"
10	Mar	West	400			2	2	Count of Sales where Month = "Jan" AND Region="North" or "South"
11						4	4	Count of Sales between 300 and 400
12								
13								
14						XL 2007	All versions	Description
15							1,600	Sum of Sales greater than 200
16							600	Sum of Sales where Month = "Jan"
17							1,350	Sum of Sales where Month = "Jan" or "Feb"
18						100	100	Sum of Sales where Month="Jan" AND Region="North"
19						500	500	Sum of Sales where Month="Jan" AND Region<>"North"
20						300	500	Sum of Sales where Month="Jan" and Sales>= 200
21						1,350	1,350	Sum of Sales between 300 and 400
22								

Figure 3-8: This simple worksheet demonstrates some useful formulas for counting and summing.

CD-ROM

This workbook (including the formula examples) is available on the companion CD-ROM. The file is named `counting and summing examples.xlsx`.

Counting formula examples

Table 3-3 contains formulas that demonstrate a variety of counting techniques.

TABLE 3-3   COUNTING FORMULA EXAMPLES

Formula	Description
=COUNTIF(Region,"North")	Counts the number of rows in which Region = "North"
=COUNTIF(Sales,300)	Counts the number of rows in which Sales = 300
=COUNTIF(Sales,">300")	Counts the number of rows in which Sales > 300
=COUNTIF(Sales,"<>100")	Counts the number of rows in which Sales <> 100
=COUNTIF(Region,"?????")	Counts the number of rows in which Region contains five letters
=COUNTIF(Region,"*h*")	Counts the number of rows in which Region contains the letter H (not case-sensitive)
=COUNTIFS(Month,"Jan",Sales,">200")	Counts the number of rows in which Month = "Jan" and Sales > 200 (Excel 2007 only)
{=SUM((Month="Jan")*(Sales>200))}	An array formula that counts the number of rows in which Month = "Jan" and Sales > 200
=COUNTIFS(Month,"Jan",Region,"North")	Counts the number of rows in which Month = "Jan" and Region = "North" (Excel 2007 only)
{=SUM((Month="Jan")*(Region="North"))}	An array formula that counts the number of rows in which Month = "Jan" and Region = "North"
=COUNTIFS(Month,"Jan",Region,"North")+ COUNTIFS(Month,"Jan",Region,"South")	Counts the number of rows in which Month = "Jan" and Region = "North" or "South" (Excel 2007 only)
{=SUM((Month="Jan")*((Region="North")+ (Region="South")))}	An array formula that counts the number of rows in which Month = "Jan" and Region = "North" or "South"
=COUNTIFS(Sales,">=300",Sales,"<=400")	Counts the number of rows in which Sales is between 300 and 400 (Excel 2007 only)
{=SUM((Sales>=300)*(Sales<=400))}	An array formula that counts the number of rows in which Sales is between 300 and 400

Summing formula examples

Table 3-4 shows a number of formula examples that demonstrate a variety of summing techniques.

TABLE 3-4 SUMMING FORMULA EXAMPLES

Formula	Description
=SUMIF(Sales,">200")	Sum of all Sales over 200
=SUMIF(Month,"Jan",Sales)	Sum of Sales in which Month = "Jan"
=SUMIF(Month,"Jan",Sales)+ SUMIF(Month,"Feb",Sales)	Sum of Sales in which Month ="Jan" or "Feb"
=SUMIFS(Sales,Month,"Jan",Region,"North")	Sum of Sales in which Month="Jan" and Region="North"
=SUMIFS(Sales,Month,"Jan",Region,"North")	Sum of Sales in which Month="Jan" and Region="North" (Excel 2007 only)
{=SUM((Month="Jan")*(Region="North")*Sales)}	An array formula that returns the sum of Sales in which Month="Jan" and Region="North"
=SUMIFS(Sales,Month,"Jan",Region,"<>North")	Sum of Sales in which Month="Jan" and Region <> "North" (Excel 2007 only)
{=SUM((Month="Jan")*(Region<>"North")*Sales)}	An array formula that returns the sum of Sales in which Month="Jan" and Region <> "North"
=SUMIFS(Sales,Month,"Jan",Sales,">=200")	Sum of Sales in which Month="Jan" and Sales>=200 (Excel 2007 only)
{=SUM((Month="Jan")*(Sales>=200)*(Sales))}	An array formula that returns the sum of Sales in which Month="Jan" and Sales>=200
=SUMIFS(Sales,Sales,">=300",Sales,"<=400")	Sum of Sales between 300 and 400 (Excel 2007 only)
{=SUM((Sales>=300)*(Sales<=400)*(Sales))}	An array formula that returns the sum of Sales between 300 and 400

Other counting tools

Other ways to count or sum cells that meet certain criteria are:

- Filtering (using a table)
- Advanced filtering
- The DCOUNT and DSUM functions
- Pivot tables

For more information, consult the Help system.

Working with Dates and Times

Excel uses a serial number system to store dates. The earliest date that Excel can understand is January 1, 1900. This date has a serial number of 1. January 2, 1900, has a serial number of 2, and so on.

Most of the time, you don't have to be concerned with Excel's serial number date system. You simply enter a date in a familiar date format, and Excel takes care of the details behind the scenes. For example, if you need to enter August 15, 2007, you can simply enter the date by typing **August 15, 2007** (or use any of a number of different date formats). Excel interprets your entry and stores the value 39309, which is the serial number for that date.

 NOTE

In this chapter, I assume the U.S. date system. If your computer uses a different date system, you'll need to adjust accordingly. For example, you might need to enter **15 August 2007**.

Entering dates and times

When working with times, you simply enter the time into a cell in a recognized format. Excel's system for representing dates as individual values is extended to include decimals that represent portions or fractions of days. In other words, Excel perceives all time with the same system whether that time is a particular day, a certain hour, or a specific second. For example, the date serial number for August 15, 2007, is 39309. Noon (halfway through the day) is represented internally as 39309.5. Again, you normally don't have to be concerned with these fractional serial numbers.

Because dates and times are stored as serial numbers, it stands to reason that you can add and subtract dates and times. For example, you can enter a formula to calculate the number of days between two dates. If cells A1 and A2 both contain dates, the following formula returns the number of intervening days:

```
=A2-A1
```

TIP

When performing calculations with time, things get a bit trickier. When you enter a time without an associated date, the date is assumed to be January 0, 1900 (date serial number 0). This is not a problem — unless your calculation produces a negative time value. When this happens, Excel displays an error (displayed as #########). The solution? Switch to the 1904 date system. Display the Excel Options dialog box, click the Advanced tab, and then enable the Use 1904 Date System check box. Be aware that switching to the 1904 date system can cause problems with dates already entered in your file or dates in workbooks that are linked to your file.

TIP

In some cases, you may need to use time values to represent duration, rather than a point in time. For example, you may need to sum the number of hours worked in a week. When you add time values, you can't display more than 24 hours. For each 24-hour period, Excel simply adds another day to the total. The solution is to change the number formatting to use square brackets around the hour part of the format. The following number format, for example, displays more than 24 hours:

```
[hh]:mm
```

Using pre-1900 dates

The world, of course, didn't begin on January 1, 1900. People who work with historical information when using Excel often need to work with dates before January 1, 1900. Unfortunately, the only way to work with pre-1900 dates is to enter the date into a cell as text. For example, you can enter the following into a cell, and Excel won't complain:

```
July 4, 1776
```

You can't, however, perform any manipulation on dates that are actually text. For example, you can't change its formatting, you can't determine which day of the week this date occurred on, and you can't calculate the date that occurs seven days later. (See Figure 3-9.)

	A	B	C	D	E	F	G	H
4	**Examples: President Birthdays**							
5								
6	**President**	**Year**	**Month**	**Day**	**XDATE**	**XDATEDIF**	**XDATEYEARDIF**	**XDATEDOW**
7	George Washington	1732	2	22	February 22, 1732	100,376	274	Friday
8	John Adams	1735	10	30	October 30, 1735	99,030	271	Sunday
9	Thomas Jefferson	1743	4	13	April 13, 1743	96,308	263	Saturday
10	James Madison	1751	3	16	March 16, 1751	93,414	255	Tuesday
11	James Monroe	1758	4	28	April 28, 1758	90,814	248	Friday
12	John Quincy Adams	1767	7	11	July 11, 1767	87,453	239	Saturday
13	Andrew Jackson	1767	3	15	March 15, 1767	87,571	239	Sunday
14	Martin Van Buren	1782	12	5	December 5, 1782	81,827	224	Thursday
15	William Henry Harrison	1773	2	9	February 9, 1773	85,413	233	Tuesday
16	John Tyler	1790	3	29	March 29, 1790	79,156	216	Monday
17	James K. Polk	1795	11	2	November 2, 1795	77,112	211	Monday
18	Zachary Taylor	1784	11	24	November 24, 1784	81,107	222	Wednesday
19	Millard Fillmore	1800	1	7	January 7, 1800	75,585	206	Tuesday

Sheet1 Sheet2

Figure 3-9: The Extended Date Functions add-in lets you work with pre-1900 dates.

Creating Megaformulas

Often, spreadsheets require intermediate formulas to produce a desired result. In other words, a formula may depend on other formulas, which in turn depend on other formulas. After you get all these formulas working correctly, it's often possible to eliminate the intermediate formulas and use what I refer to as a single *megaformula* instead. The advantages? You use fewer cells (less clutter), the file size is smaller, and recalculation may even be a bit faster. The main disadvantage is that the formula may be impossible to decipher or modify.

Here's an example: Imagine a worksheet that has a column with thousands of people's names. And suppose that you've been asked to remove all the middle names and middle initials from the names — but not all the names have a middle name or initial. Editing the cells manually would take hours, and even Excel's Data ➪ Data Tools ➪ Convert Text to Table command isn't much help. So you opt for a formula-based solution. Although this is not a difficult task, it normally involves several intermediate formulas.

Figure 3-10 shows the results of the more conventional solution, which requires six intermediate formulas shown in Table 3-5. The names are in column A; the end result goes in column H. Columns B through G hold the intermediate formulas.

	A	B	C	D	E	F	G	H
1	Name	Formula-1	Formula-2	Formula-3	Formula-4	Formula-5	Formula-6	Result
2	Bob Smith	Bob Smith	4	#VALUE!	4	Bob	Smith	Bob Smith
3	Mike A. Jones	Mike A. Jones	5	8	8	Mike	Jones	Mike Jones
4	Jim Ray Johnson	Jim Ray Johnson	4	8	8	Jim	Johnson	Jim Johnson
5	Tom Alvin Jacobs	Tom Alvin Jacobs	4	10	10	Tom	Jacobs	Tom Jacobs
6	John Q. Public	John Q. Public	5	8	8	John	Public	John Public
7	R.J Smith	R.J Smith	4	#VALUE!	4	R.J	Smith	R.J Smith
8	R. Jay Smith	R. Jay Smith	3	7	7	R.	Smith	R. Smith
9	Tim Jones	Tim Jones	4	#VALUE!	4	Tim	Jones	Tim Jones
10								

Sheet1

Figure 3-10: Removing the middle names and initials requires six intermediate formulas.

TABLE 3-5   INTERMEDIATE FORMULAS WRITTEN IN ROW 2 IN FIGURE 3-9

Column	Intermediate Formula	What It Does
B	=TRIM(A2)	Removes excess spaces.
C	=FIND(" ",B2,1)	Locates the first space.
D	=FIND(" ",B2,C2+1)	Locates the second space. Returns #VALUE! if there is no second space.
E	=IF(ISERROR(D2),C2,D2)	Uses the first space if no second space exists.
F	=LEFT(B2,C2)	Extracts the first name.
G	=RIGHT(B2,LEN(B2)-E2)	Extracts the last name.
H	=F2&G2	Concatenates the two names.

You can eliminate the six intermediate formulas by creating a megaformula. You do so by creating all the intermediate formulas and then going back into the final result formula and replacing each cell reference with a copy of the formula in the cell referred to (without the equal sign). Fortunately, you can use the Clipboard to copy and paste. Keep repeating this process until cell H2 contains nothing but references to cell A2. You end up with the following megaformula in one cell:

```
=LEFT(TRIM(A2),FIND
(" ",TRIM(A2),1))&RIGHT(TRIM(A2),LEN(TRIM(A2))-
IF(ISERROR(FIND(" ",TRIM(A2),FIND(" ",TRIM(A2),1)+1)),
FIND(" ",TRIM(A2),1),FIND(" ",TRIM(A2),FIND
(" ",TRIM(A2),1)+1)))
```

When you're satisfied that the megaformula is working, you can delete the columns that hold the intermediate formulas because they are no longer used.

The megaformula performs exactly the same tasks as all the intermediate formulas — although it's virtually impossible for anyone to figure out, even the author. If you decide to use megaformulas, make sure that the intermediate formulas are performing correctly before you start building a megaformula. Even better, keep a single copy of the intermediate formulas somewhere in case you discover an error or need to make a change.

Another way to approach this problem is to create a custom worksheet function in VBA. Then you could replace the megaformula with a simple formula, such as

```
=NOMIDDLE(A1)
```

In fact, I wrote such a function to compare it with intermediate formulas and megaformulas. The listing follows.

```
Function NOMIDDLE(n) As String
    Dim FirstName As String, LastName As String
    n = Application.WorksheetFunction.Trim(n)
    FirstName = Left(n, InStr(1, n, " "))
    LastName = Right(n, Len(n) - InStrRev(n, " "))
    NOMIDDLE = FirstName & LastName
End Function
```

 CD-ROM

A workbook that contains the intermediate formulas, the megaformula, and the NOMIDDLE VBA function is available on the companion CD-ROM. The workbook is named `megaformula.xlsm`.

Because a megaformula is so complex, you may think that using one would slow down recalculation. Actually, that's not the case. As a test, I created a worksheet that used a megaformula to process 150,000 names. Then I created another worksheet that used six intermediate formulas. The megaformula version calculated a bit faster, and produced a much smaller file.

The actual results will vary significantly, depending on system speed, amount of memory installed, and the actual formula.

The VBA function was much slower — I abandoned the timed test after 10 minutes. This is fairly typical of VBA functions; they are always slower than built-in Excel functions.

Chapter 4

Understanding Excel's Files

In This Chapter
These topics are covered in this chapter.

◆ A description of the various ways to start Excel

◆ A discussion of the files that Excel can open and save

◆ An introduction to the new XML file format in Excel 2007

◆ Details about how Excel uses the Windows Registry

If you plan to do any advanced work with Excel, it's critical that you become familiar with some of the internal workings of Excel and understand what happens when the application is launched. It's also important to have an understanding of the various files used and generated by Excel.

Starting Excel

Excel can be started in various ways, depending on how it's installed. These include clicking an icon on the Desktop, using the Windows Start button, and double-clicking a file associated with the Excel application. All methods ultimately launch the `excel.exe` executable file.

When Excel starts, it performs the following actions:

- It reads its settings stored in the Windows Registry.
- It opens the `*.xlb` menu/toolbar customization file.
- It opens all add-ins that are installed (that is, those that are checked in the Add-Ins dialog box).
- It opens any workbooks that are in the XLStart directory.
- It opens any workbooks that are in the alternate startup directory (specified in the Advanced tab of the Excel Options dialog box).
- It displays an empty workbook — unless the user specified a workbook to open or one or more files were found in the XLStart or alternate startup directory.

 TIP

If you want to change the default formats (or content) of blank workbooks that you create, create a default workbook and save it as a template with the name `Book.xltx` in your XLStart folder. For details on creating and using template files, refer to Excel's Help.

Excel can be installed in any location. But in most cases, the Excel executable file is located in the default installation directory:

```
C:\Program Files\Microsoft Office\Office12\EXCEL.EXE
```

You can create one or more shortcuts to this executable file, and the shortcuts can be customized with various parameters, or command line switches. These command line switches are listed in Table 4-1.

TABLE 4-1   EXCEL COMMAND LINE SWITCHES

Switch	What It Does
filename	Opens the specified file. The filename is a parameter and does not require a switch.
/r filename	Opens the specified file in read-only mode.
/t filename	Opens the specified file as a template.
/n filename	Opens the specified file as a template (same as /t).
/e	Starts Excel without creating a new workbook and without displaying its splash screen.
/p directory	Sets the active path to a directory other than the default directory.

Switch	What It Does
/s	Starts Excel in Safe mode and does not load any add-ins or files in the XLStart or alternate startup file directories.
/embedded	Starts an invisible instance of Excel (not recommended).
/m	Forces Excel to create a new workbook that contains a single Microsoft Excel 4.0 macro sheet (obsolete).

You can experiment with these command line switches by using the Windows Start ⇨ Run command. Put the path to Excel in quotes, followed by a space, and then the command line switch. Figure 4-1 shows an example.

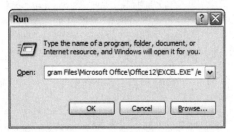

Figure 4-1: Starting Excel from the Windows Run dialog box.

One way to specify any of these switches is to edit the properties of the shortcut that starts Excel. For example, if there are times when you'd like Excel to start and use a folder named c:\xlfiles as its default folder, you can customize a Windows shortcut. In this case, you need to use the /p switch and specify the folder.

NOTE

The instructions that follow are for Windows XP.

Start with an icon that launches Excel. Right-click the icon and choose Properties. In the Shortcut Properties dialog box, click the Shortcut tab and enter the following in the Target field (see Figure 4-2):

```
"C:\Program Files\Microsoft Office\Office12\EXCEL.EXE" /p c:\xlfiles
```

Keep in mind that the path to excel.exe can vary for different installations and for different versions.

You can also assign a shortcut key to launch Excel, which can be useful. If Excel is already running, pressing the shortcut key activates Excel.

Figure 4-2: Customizing a shortcut to launch Excel.

NOTE

You can run multiple instances of Excel on a single system. Each instance is treated as a separate task. Most people have pretty good success running multiple *versions* of Excel on a single system. For best results, install the versions in the order of their release dates.

File Types

Although the Excel 2007 default file format is an XLSX workbook file, the program can also open and save a wide variety of other files. This section provides an overview of the file types that Excel 2007 can handle.

NOTE

Excel 2007 no longer supports Lotus or Quattro spreadsheet file formats.

Excel file formats

Excel 2007 uses a new default file format. However, it can still read and write older Excel file formats.

TIP

To change the default file save setting, choose Office ⇨ Excel Options and click the Save tab in the Excel Options dialog box. You'll find a drop-down list that lets you select the default file format.

Table 4-2 lists the Excel file types that Excel 2007 supports. Keep in mind that an Excel workbook or add-in file can have any extension that you like. In other words, these files don't need to be stored with the standard extensions shown in the table.

TABLE 4-2   EXCEL FILE TYPES

File Type	Extension	Read/Write	Notes
Excel Workbook	xlsx	Yes/Yes	The default Excel 2007 file format. It cannot store VBA or XLM macro code.
Excel Macro-Enabled Workbook	xlsm	Yes/Yes	The Excel 2007 file format for workbooks that contain macros.
Excel Binary Workbook	xlsb	Yes/Yes	The Excel 2007 binary file format (BIFF12). This is an updated version of the previous XLS (BIFF8) format.
Template	xltx	Yes/Yes	The Excel 2007 file format for a template. It cannot store VBA or XLM macro code.
Macro-Enabled Template	xltxm	Yes/Yes	The Excel 2007 file format for a template that contains macros.
Excel Add-In	xlam	Yes/Yes	The Excel 2007 file format for add-ins. It can store VBA and XLM macros.
Excel 97–Excel 2003 Workbook	xls	Yes/Yes	The Excel binary format (BIFF8) that's compatible with Excel 97 through Excel 2003.
Excel 97–Excel 2003 Template	xlt	Yes/Yes	The Excel binary template format (BIFF8) that's compatible with Excel 97 through Excel 2003.
Excel 97–Excel 2003 Add-In	xla	Yes/Yes	The Excel binary format (BIFF8) for add-ins that's compatible with Excel 97 through Excel 2003.

continued

TABLE 4-2   EXCEL FILE TYPES *(continued)*

File Type	Extension	Read/Write	Notes
Microsoft Excel 5.0/95 Workbook	xls	Yes/Yes	The Excel binary format (BIFF5) that's compatible with Excel 5.0 and Excel 95.
XML Spreadsheet 2003	xml	Yes/Yes	Microsoft's XML Spreadsheet 2003 file format (XMLSS).
XML Data	xml	Yes/Yes	A general XML file that contains data.

 NOTE
Microsoft Office XP and Office 2003 users can install the Microsoft Office Compatibility Pack, which allows them to open and save documents in the Office 2007 file formats. The Compatibility Pack is available at `http://office.microsoft.com`.

Text file formats

When you attempt to load a text file into Excel, the Text Import Wizard might kick in to help you specify how you want the file retrieved.

 TIP
To bypass the Text Import Wizard, press Shift when you click OK in the Open dialog box.

Table 4-3 lists the text file types supported by Excel 2007. All text file formats are limited to a single worksheet.

TABLE 4-3   TEXT FILE TYPES

File Type	Extension	Read/Write	Notes
CSV (comma separated variable)	csv	Yes/Yes	Columns are delimited with a comma, and rows are delimited with a carriage return. Excel supports subtypes for Macintosh and MS-DOS.
Formatted Text	prn	Yes/Yes	Columns are delimited with a space character, and rows are delimited with a carriage return.

File Type	Extension	Read/Write	Notes
Text	txt	Yes/Yes	Columns are delimited with a tab, and rows are delimited with a carriage return. Excel supports subtypes for Macintosh, MS-DOS, and Unicode.
Data Interchange Format (DIF)	dif	Yes/Yes	The file format originally used by VisiCalc.
Symbolic Link (SYLK)	slk	Yes/Yes	The file format originally used by Multiplan.

Database file formats

Table 4-4 lists the database file types supported by Excel 2007. All database file formats are limited to a single worksheet.

TABLE 4-4   DATABASE FILE TYPES

File Type	Extension	Read/Write	Notes
Access	mdb, mde, accdb, accde	Yes/No	You can open one table from the database.
dBASE	dbf	Yes/No	The file format originally created by Ashton-Tate
Others	Various	Yes/No	By using the commands in the Data ⇨ Get External Data group, you can import data from various data sources that have connections or queries defined on your system.

Other file formats

Table 4-5 lists the other file types supported by Excel 2007.

Workspace Files

A *workspace file* is a special file that contains information about an Excel workspace. For example, if you have a project that uses two workbooks and you like to have the workbook windows arranged in a particular way, you can save an XLW file to save this window configuration. Then, whenever you open the XLW file, Excel restores the desired workspace.

To save a workspace, choose View ➪ Window ➪ Save Workspace, and provide a name when prompted.

To open a workspace file, use Office ➪ Open and select Workspaces (*.xlw) from the Files of Type drop-down list.

It's important to understand that a workspace file does *not* include the workbooks — only the configuration information that makes those workbooks visible in your Excel workspace. So if you need to distribute a workspace to someone else, make sure that you include the workbook files as well as the XLW file.

TABLE 4-5   OTHER FILE TYPES

File Type	Extension	Read/Write	Notes
Hypertext Markup Language (HTML)	htm, html	Yes/Yes	Excel 2007 no longer supports "round-tripping" for HTML files.
Single File Web Page	mht, mhtml	Yes/Yes	Also known as Archived Web Page. The only browser that can display these files is Microsoft Internet Explorer.
Portable Document Format (PDF)	pdf	No/Yes	The file format originated by Adobe. Requires a free add-in from Microsoft.
XML Paper Specification	xps	No/Yes	Microsoft's alternative to Adobe's PDF. Requires a free add-in from Microsoft.

Working with Template Files

A *template* is essentially a model that serves as the basis for something else. An Excel template is a workbook that's used to create other workbooks. You can save any workbook as a template file (XLTX extension). Doing so is useful if you tend to create similar files on a

Part I

regular basis. For example, you might need to generate a monthly sales report. You can save some time by creating a template that holds the necessary formulas and charts for your report. When you start new files based on the template, you need only plug in the values.

Viewing templates

Excel 2007 gives you access to many templates. To explore the Excel templates, choose Office ⇨ New to display the New Workbook dialog box. The template categories appear as tabs in the New Workbook dialog box. In addition, the right side of the dialog box displays a list of templates that you've used recently.

The Microsoft Office Online section contains a number of categories. Click a category, and you'll see the available templates. To use a template, select it and click Download. Figure 4-3 shows some of templates available in the Invoices category.

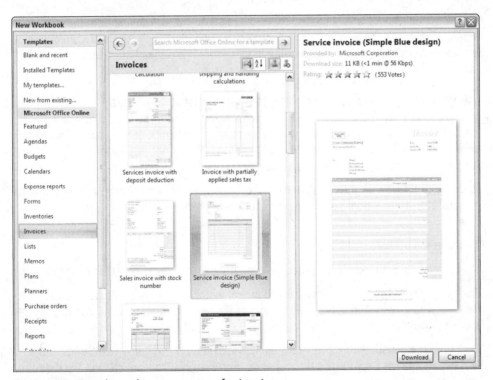

Figure 4-3: Templates that you can use for invoices.

Microsoft Office Online has a wide variety of templates, and some are better than others. If you download a few duds, don't give up. Even though a template may not be perfect, you can often modify a template to meet your needs. Modifying an existing template is often easier than creating a workbook from scratch.

NOTE

The location of the Templates folder varies, depending on the version of Excel. To find the location of your Templates folder, execute the following VBA statement:

```
MsgBox Application.TemplatesPath
```

Creating templates

Excel supports three types of templates:

- *The default workbook template:* Used as the basis for new workbooks. This file is named `book.xltx`.

- *The default worksheet template:* Used as the basis for new worksheets that are inserted into a workbook. This file is named `sheet.xltx`.

- *Custom workbook templates:* Usually, these are ready-to-run workbooks that include formulas, but they can be as simple or as complex as you like. Typically, these templates are set up so that a user can simply plug in values and get immediate results.

USING THE WORKBOOK TEMPLATE TO CHANGE WORKBOOK DEFAULTS

Every new workbook that you create starts out with some default settings. For example, the workbook has three worksheets, the worksheets have gridlines, text appears in Calibri 11-point font, columns are 8.43 units wide, and so on. If you're not happy with any of the default workbook settings, you can change them.

Making changes to Excel's default workbook is fairly easy to do, and it can save you lots of time in the long run. Here's how you change Excel's workbook defaults:

1. Open a new workbook.

2. Add or delete sheets to give the workbook the number of worksheets that you want.

3. Make any other changes that you want to make, which can include column widths, named styles, page setup options, and many of the settings that are available in the Options dialog box.

    To change the default formatting for cells, choose Home ➪ Styles ➪ Cell Styles and then modify the settings for the Normal style. For example, you can change the default font, size, or number format.

4. When your workbook is set up to your liking, choose Office ➪ Save As.

5. In the Save As dialog box, select Template (*.xltx) from the box labeled Save As Type.

6. Enter **book.xltx** for the filename.

7. Save the file in your \XLStart folder (*not* in your Templates folder).

8. Close the file.

TIP

The \XLStart folder may be located in either of these directories:

```
C:\Documents and Settings\<username>\Application
Data\Microsoft\Excel\XLStart
C:\Program Files\Microsoft Office\Office12\XLStart
```

To determine the location of \XLStart, execute this VBA statement:

```
MsgBox Application.StartupPath
```

After you perform the preceding steps, the new default workbook that appears when Excel is started is based on the `book.xltx` workbook template. You can also press Ctrl+N to create a workbook based on this template. If you ever want to revert back to the standard default workbook, just delete the `book.xltx` file.

NOTE

If you choose File ⇨ New, and select Blank Workbook from the New Workbook dialog box, the workbook will not be based on the `book.xltx` template. I don't know if this is a bug, or if it's by design.

USING THE WORKSHEET TEMPLATE TO CHANGE WORKSHEET DEFAULTS

When you insert a new worksheet into a workbook, Excel uses its built-in worksheet defaults for the worksheet. This includes items such as column width, row height, and so on. If you don't like the default settings for a new worksheet, you can change them by following these steps:

1. Start with a new workbook and delete all the sheets except one.

2. Make any changes that you want to make, which can include column widths, named styles, page setup options, and many of the settings that are available in the Excel Options dialog box.

3. When your workbook is set up to your liking, select Office ⇨ Save As.

4. In the Save As dialog box, select Template (*.xltx) from the Save As Type box.

5. Enter **sheet.xltx** for the filename.

6. Save the file in your \XLStart folder (*not* in your Templates folder).

7. Close the file.

8. Close and restart Excel.

After performing this procedure, all new sheets that you insert by clicking the Insert Worksheet button (which is next to the last sheet tab) will be formatted like your `sheet.xltx` template. You can also press Shift+F11 to insert a new worksheet.

Creating workbook templates

The `book.xltx` and `sheet.xltx` templates discussed in the preceding section are two special types of templates that determine default settings for new workbooks and new worksheets. This section discusses other types of templates, referred to as *workbook templates*, which are simply workbooks that you set up as the basis for new workbooks or worksheets.

Why use a workbook template? The simple answer is that it saves you from repeating work. Assume that you create a monthly sales report that consists of your company's sales by region, plus several summary calculations and charts. You can create a template file that consists of everything except the input values. Then, when it's time to create your report, you can open a workbook based on the template, fill in the blanks, and be finished.

NOTE

You could, of course, just use the previous month's workbook and save it with a different name. This is prone to errors, however, because you easily can forget to use the Save As command and accidentally overwrite the previous month's file. Another option is to use the New From Existing icon in the New Workbook dialog box. This creates a new workbook from an existing one, but gives a different name to ensure that the old file is not overwritten.

When you create a workbook that is based on a template, the default workbook name is the template name with a number appended. For example, if you create a new workbook based on a template named `Sales Report.xltx`, the workbook's default name is `Sales Report1.xlsx`. The first time that you save a workbook that is created from a template, Excel displays its Save As dialog box so that you can give the template a new name if you want to.

A *custom template* is essentially a normal workbook, and it can use any Excel feature, such as charts, formulas, and macros. Usually, a template is set up so that the user can enter values and get immediate results. In other words, most templates include everything but the data, which is entered by the user.

NOTE

If your template contains macros, it must be saved as an Excel Macro-Enabled Template, with an XLTM extension.

Inside an Excel File

As I've noted, Excel 2007 uses a new XML format for its workbooks, templates, and add-ins. These files are actually ZIP compressed files. As such, they can be "unzipped" and examined.

Previous versions of Excel used a binary file format. Although the binary file format specifications are known, working with binary files is not easy. The Excel 2007 XML file format, on the other hand, is an "open format." As such, these files can be created and manipulated using other software.

Dissecting a file

In this section, I describe the various parts within a typical Excel XLSM (macro-enabled) workbook file. The workbook, named `sample.xlsm`, is shown in Figure 4-4. It has one worksheet, one chart sheet, and a simple VBA macro. The worksheet contains a table, a button (from the Forms controls), a SmartArt diagram, and a photo of a flower.

CD

The `sample.xlsm` workbook is available on the companion CD-ROM.

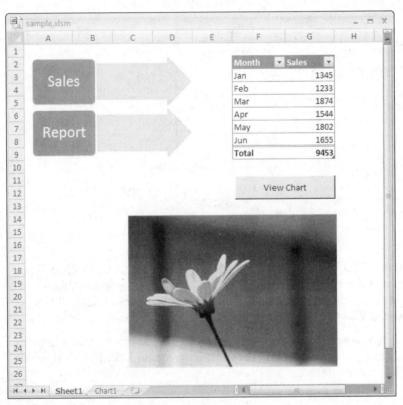

Figure 4-4: A simple workbook.

To view the innards of an Excel 2007 file, you need to open an Explorer window and add a ZIP extension to the filename. So the `sample.xlsm` file is renamed to `sample.xlsm.zip`. You can then open the file by using any unzipping program. I use the zip feature built into Windows XP.

TIP

You may prefer to extract the zipped files into an uncompressed directory. Doing so makes it easier to view the files. In Windows, right-click the filename and choose Extract All.

The first thing that you notice is that the file contains a directory structure. The left panel of Figure 4-5 shows the fully expanded directory structure for the workbook file. The actual directories will vary with the workbook.

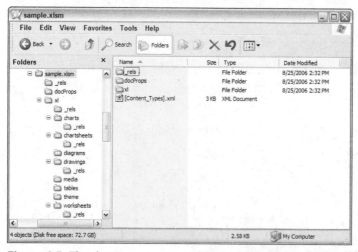

Figure 4-5: The directory structure of the workbook file.

With a few exceptions, all of the files are text files. More specifically, they are XML files. You can view them in a text file editor, an XML editor, a Web browser, or even in Excel. Figure 4-6 shows one of these files viewed in the Firefox browser. The non-XML files include graphic images and VBA projects (these are stored in binary format).

This XML file has three root-level folders, and some of these have subfolders. You'll notice that many of the folders contain a _rels folder. These folders contain XML files that define the relationships to other parts within the package.

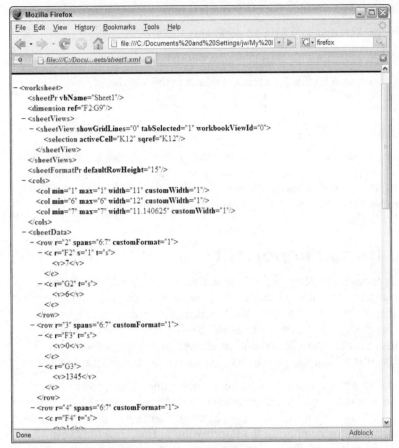

Figure 4-6: Viewing an XML file in a Web browser.

Following is a list of the folders in the `sample.xlsm` workbook:

- *_rels:* Contains information about the package relationships.

- *docProps:* Contains XML files that describe the file properties and application settings.

- *xl:* This folder holds the meat of the file. The name varies with the Office document type (xl, ppt, word, and so on). You'll find several XML files that contain settings for the workbook. And if your workbook contains VBA code, it will be in a binary file with a BIN extension. The xl folder has several subfolders (some workbooks may have more or fewer subfolders, depending on the content):

    - *charts:* Contains an XML file for each chart. This file contains the chart settings.

    - *chartsheets:* Contains an XML file with data for each chart sheet in the workbook.

    - *diagrams:* Contains XML files that describe the diagrams (SmartArt) in the workbook.

    - *drawings*: Contains an XML file with data for each "drawing." Drawings include items such as buttons, charts, and images.

- *media:* Contains embedded media, such GIF and JPG files.
- *tables:* Contains an XML file with data for each table.
- *theme:* Contains an XML file with data about the workbook's theme.
- *worksheets:* Contains an XML file for each worksheet in the workbook.

TIP

If you add a ZIP extension to an Excel file, you can still open it in Excel. Excel doesn't care what the file's extension is. Also, you can save a workbook with a ZIP extension. In the Save As dialog box, add a ZIP extension and then place double quotation marks around the entire file name. For example: **"Myworkbook.xlsx.zip"**.

Why is the file format important?

The new "open" XML file formats for Microsoft Office represent a significant step for the computing community. For the first time, it's relatively easy to read and write Excel workbooks using software other than Excel. For example, it's possible to write a program to modify thousands of Excel workbook files without even opening Excel. Such a program could insert a new worksheet into every file. The programmer, of course, would need to have excellent knowledge of the XML file structures, but such a task is definitely doable.

Importantly, the new file formats are much less prone to corruption (compared to the old binary formats). I saved a workbook file and then deleted one of the worksheet XML files. When I tried to reopen it in Excel, I got the message shown in Figure 4-7. Excel was able to tell that the file was damaged by comparing the information in the .res files with what's actually in the file. In this case, Excel was able to repair the file and open it. The deleted worksheet was re-inserted, but it was empty.

Figure 4-7: Excel can often repair a damaged workbook file.

In addition, the zipped XML files are usually smaller than comparable binary files. And, finally, the structured nature of the files makes it possible to extract individual elements (for example, all graphic images).

The typical Excel user won't need to examine or modify the XML components of a workbook file. But, as a developer, you may want to write code that changes Excel's Ribbon user interface. If that's the case, you *will* need to be at least somewhat familiar with the structure of a workbook XML file.

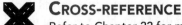

CROSS-REFERENCE
Refer to Chapter 22 for more information about modifying Excel's Ribbon.

The QAT File

The only user interface element in Excel 2007 that's customizable by the end user is the Quick Access Toolbar. The information for the QAT is stored in a file named Excel.qat, and this file is located here:

```
C:\Documents and Settings\<username>\Local Settings\Application Data\
Microsoft\OFFICE
```

This file is updated whenever a change is made to the QAT. It's updated immediately, not when Excel is closed.

`Excel.qat` is an XML file, and you can view it using an XML editor, a Web browser, or Excel. To view this file in Excel, follow these steps:

1. Make a copy of the `Excel.qat` file.

2. Add an XML extension to the copy of the file so that the name is `Excel.qat.xml`.

3. Choose Office ⇨ Open to open the file or just drag it into Excel's window.

4. You'll see a dialog box with some options; choose As an XML Table.

Figure 4-8 shows an imported `Excel.qat` file (the file is displayed as a table). This QAT has three commands in addition to the eleven default commands. Of the default commands, only three are visible.

	A	B	C
1	**idQ**	**visible**	
2	mso:FileNewDefault	FALSE	
3	mso:FileOpen	FALSE	
4	mso:FileSave	TRUE	
5	mso:FileSendAsAttachment	FALSE	
6	mso:FilePrintQuick	FALSE	
7	mso:FilePrintPreview	FALSE	
8	mso:Spelling	FALSE	
9	mso:Undo	TRUE	
10	mso:Redo	TRUE	
11	mso:SortAscendingExcel	FALSE	
12	mso:SortDescendingExcel	FALSE	
13	mso:SheetRowsInsert	TRUE	
14	mso:WindowSaveWorkspace	TRUE	
15	mso:OleObjectctInsert	TRUE	
16			

◄ ◄ ► ►◄   Sheet1

Figure 4-8: Viewing a QAT data file in Excel.

It's possible to share a QAT with other users. For example, you may have customized your QAT with two dozen useful tools. If a colleague is impressed, just give him a copy of your `Excel.qat` file and tell him where to put it.

Don't attempt to modify the `Excel.qat` file unless you know what you're doing.

The XLB File

Excel stores customized toolbar and menu bar configurations in an XLB file. Even though Excel 2007 doesn't officially support custom toolbars and menus in the way that it did in previous versions, it still uses an XLB file.

When you exit Excel, the current toolbar configuration is saved in a file named `Excel12.xlb`. This file is (most likely) located here:

```
C:\Documents and Settings\<username>\Application Data\Microsoft\Excel
```

This binary file contains information regarding the position and visibility of all custom toolbars and custom menu bars, plus modifications that you've made to built-in toolbars or menu bars.

Add-In Files

An *add-in* is essentially an Excel workbook file with a few important differences:

- The workbook's `IsAddin` property is `True` — which means that it can be loaded and unloaded by using the Add-Ins dialog box. Access this dialog box by choosing Office ➪ Excel Options. Click the Add-Ins tab, select Excel Add-Ins from the Manage list, and click Go.

- The workbook is hidden and cannot be unhidden by the user. Consequently, an add-in is never the active workbook.

- When using VBA, the workbook is not part of the `Workbooks` collection.

Many add-ins provide new features or functions to Excel. You can access these new features as if they were built into the product.

You can create your own add-ins from workbook files. In fact, creating add-ins is the preferred method of distributing some types of Excel applications. Excel 2007 add-ins have an XLAM extension by default.

NOTE

Besides XLAM add-ins, Excel supports XLL add-ins and COM add-ins. These types of add-ins are created using software other than Excel. This book discusses only XLAM add-ins.

CROSS-REFERENCE

Chapter 21 covers the topic of add-ins in detail.

Excel Settings in the Registry

The Excel Options dialog box has dozens of user-specified options. Excel uses the Windows Registry to store these settings and retrieve them when Excel is started. In this section, I provide some background information about the Windows Registry and discuss how Excel uses the Registry to store its settings.

About the Registry

The *Windows Registry* is essentially a central hierarchical database that is used by the operating system and by application software. The Registry first appeared in Windows 95 and replaces the old INI files that stored Windows and application settings.

CROSS-REFERENCE

Your VBA macros can also read and write information to the Registry. Refer to Chapter 11 for details.

You can use the Registry Editor program to browse the Registry — and even edit its contents if you know what you're doing. The Registry Editor is named `regedit.exe`. Before beginning your explorations, take a minute to read the upcoming sidebar (titled "Before You Edit the Registry . . ."). Figure 4-9 shows what the Registry Editor looks like.

The Registry consists of keys and values, arranged in a hierarchy. The top-level keys are:

- HKEY_CLASSES_ROOT
- HKEY_CURRENT_USER
- HKEY_LOCAL_MACHINE
- HKEY_USERS
- HKEY_CURRENT_CONFIG
- HKEY_DYN_DATA

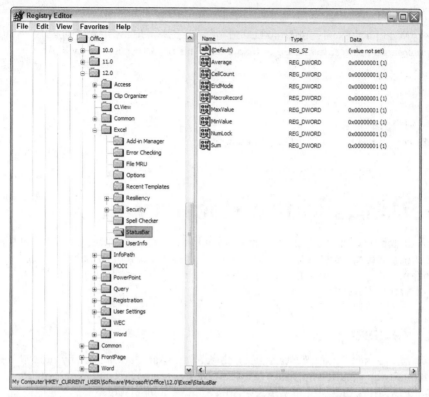

Figure 4-9: The Registry Editor lets you browse and make changes to the Registry.

Excel's settings

Information used by Excel 2007 is stored in this Registry section:

```
HKEY_CURRENT_USER\Software\Microsoft\Office\12.0\Excel
```

Before You Edit the Registry . . .

You can use the `regedit.exe` program to change anything in the Registry, including information that is critical to your system's operation. In other words, if you change the wrong piece of information, Windows may no longer work properly.

Get into the habit of choosing the File ⇨ Export command in Regedit. This command enables you to save an ASCII version of the entire Registry or just a specific branch of the Registry. If you find that you messed up something, you can always import the ASCII file to restore the Registry to its previous condition (choose the Registry ⇨ Import Registry File command). Refer to the Help file for Regedit for details.

In this section of the Registry, you'll find a number of keys that contain specific values that determine how Excel operates.

The Registry settings are updated automatically by Excel when Excel closes.

 NOTE

It's important to understand that Excel reads the Windows Registry only once — when it starts up. In addition, Excel updates the Registry settings only when Excel closes normally. If Excel crashes (unfortunately, not an uncommon occurrence), the Registry information is not updated. For example, if you change one of Excel's settings, such as the visibility of the Formula bar, this setting is not written to the Registry until Excel closes by normal means.

Table 4-6 lists the Registry sections that are relevant to Excel 2007. You might not find all these sections in your Registry database.

TABLE 4-6   EXCEL CONFIGURATION INFORMATION IN THE REGISTRY

Section	Description
Add-in Manager	Lists add-ins that appear in the Add-Ins dialog box. Add-ins that are included with Excel do not appear in this list. If you have an add-in entry in this list box that you no longer use, you can remove it by using the Registry Editor.
Converters	Lists additional (external) file converters that are not built into Excel.
Error Checking	Holds the settings for formula error checking.
File MRU	Holds information about the most recently used files (which appears in the Recent Documents list when you click the Office button).
Options	A catch-all section; holds a wide variety of settings.
Recent Templates	Stores the names of templates you've used recently.
Resiliency	Information used for recovering documents.
Security	Specifies the security options for opening files that contain macros.
Spell Checker	Stores information about your spelling checker options.
StatusBar	Stores the user choices for what appears in the status bar.
UserInfo	Stores information about the user.

Although you can change most of the settings via the Excel Options dialog box, a few settings cannot be changed directly from Excel (but you can use the Registry Editor to make changes). For example, when you select a range of cells, you may prefer that the selected cells appear in high contrast white-on-black. There is no way to specify this in Excel, but you can add a new Registry key like this:

1. Open the Registry Editor and locate this section:

   `HKEY_CURRENT_USER\Software\Microsoft\Office\12.0\Excel\Options`

2. Right-click and select New ⇨ DWORD Value.

3. Name this value **Options6**.

4. Right-click the Options6 key and select Modify.

5. In the Edit DWORD Value dialog box, click the Decimal option and enter **16** (see Figure 4-10).

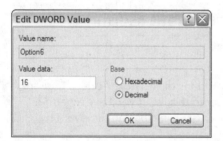

Figure 4-10: Setting a value for a Registry setting.

When you restart Excel, range selections will appear with a black background rather than gray. If you don't like this look, just delete the Options6 Registry entry.

TIP

If you have trouble starting Excel, it's possible that the Registry keys have become corrupt. You can try using the Registry Editor to delete the entire Excel section:

HKEY_CURRENT_USER\Software\Microsoft\Office\12.0\Excel

The next time Excel is started, it will rebuild the Registry keys. You will, however, lose all of the customization information that was stored there.

Part II

Excel Application Development

Chapter 5

What Is a Spreadsheet Application?

In This Chapter

In this chapter, I attempt to describe how people use spreadsheets in the real world. This is a topic that's germane to this entire book because it can help you determine how much effort you should devote to a particular development project. By the time you finish this chapter, you should have a pretty good idea of what I mean by a *spreadsheet application.* And after you've made it through the rest of the book, you'll be well on your way to developing your own spreadsheet applications with Excel. But, first, it's time to get down to the basics:

◆ A working definition of a spreadsheet application

◆ The difference between a spreadsheet user and a spreadsheet developer

◆ A system for classifying spreadsheet users to help you conceptualize the audience for your applications

◆ A discussion of why people use spreadsheets

◆ A taxonomy of the basic types of spreadsheets

You've probably been working with spreadsheets for several years, but chances are good that your primary focus has been on simply generating spreadsheets to get the job done. You probably never gave much thought to more global issues like those discussed in this chapter: the different types of spreadsheet users, how to classify various types of spreadsheets, and even basic questions such as why people use spreadsheets. If the title of this book attracted your attention, it's important for you to understand these issues so that you can become an effective power programmer. I first discuss the concept of a spreadsheet application. This is, after all, the desired result of your power-programming efforts.

Spreadsheet Applications

For the purposes of this book, a *spreadsheet application* is *a spreadsheet file* (or group of related files) that is designed so that someone other than the developer can perform useful work without extensive training. According to this definition, most of the spreadsheet files that you've developed probably don't qualify as spreadsheet applications. You may have dozens or hundreds of spreadsheet files on your hard drive, but it's a safe bet that most of them aren't really designed for others to use.

A good spreadsheet application has the following characteristics:

- It enables the end user to perform a task that he or she probably would not be able to do otherwise.

- It provides the appropriate solution to the problem. (A spreadsheet environment isn't always the optimal approach.)

- It accomplishes what it is supposed to do. This may be an obvious prerequisite, but it's not at all uncommon for applications to fail this test.

- It produces accurate results and is free of bugs.

- It uses appropriate and efficient methods and algorithms to accomplish its job.

- It traps errors before the user is forced to deal with them.

 NOTE

Note that errors and bugs are not the same. Attempting to divide by zero is an *error,* whereas failure to identify that error before it occurs is a bug.

- It does not allow the user to delete or modify important components accidentally (or intentionally).

- Its user interface is clear and consistent so that the user always knows how to proceed.

- Its formulas, macros, and user interface elements are well documented, allowing for subsequent changes, if necessary.

- It is designed so that it can be modified in simple ways without making major changes. A basic fact of life is that a user's needs change over time.

- It has an easily accessible help system that provides useful information on at least the major procedures.

- It is designed to be portable and to run on any system that has the proper software (in this case, a copy of the appropriate version of Excel).

It should come as no surprise that it is possible to create spreadsheet applications for many different usage levels, ranging from simple fill-in-the-blank templates to extremely complex applications that use a custom interface and that may not even look like spreadsheets.

The Developer and the End User

I've already used the terms *developer* and *end user,* and you will see them frequently throughout this book. Because you've gotten this far, I think I can safely assume that you're either a spreadsheet application developer or a potential developer.

My definitions regarding developers and end users are simple. The person who creates the spreadsheet application is the *developer.* For joint projects, there are multiple developers: a development *team.* The person who uses the results of the developer's spreadsheet programming efforts is the *end user* (which I often shorten to simply *user*). In many cases, there will be multiple end users, and often the developer is one of the users.

Who are developers? What do they do?

I've spent about 20 years trading methodologies and hanging out (usually in a "virtual" manner online) with the motley crew of folks who call themselves spreadsheet developers. I divide them into two primary groups:

- *Insiders* are developers who are intimately involved with the users and thoroughly understand their needs. In many cases, these developers are also users of the application. Often, they develop an application in response to a particular problem.

- *Outsiders* are developers who are hired to produce a solution to a problem. In most cases, developers in this category are familiar with the business in general but not with the specifics of the application they are developing. In other cases, these developers are already employed by the company that requests the application (but they normally work in a different department).

Some developers devote full time to development efforts. These developers may be either insiders or outsiders. A fair number of consultants (outsiders) make a decent living developing spreadsheet applications on a freelance basis.

Other spreadsheet developers don't work full time at the task and may not even realize they are developing spreadsheet applications. These developers are often office computer gurus who seem to know everything about computers and software. These folks often create spreadsheet applications as a way to make their lives easier — the time spent developing a well-designed application for others can often save hours of training time and can greatly reduce the time spent answering others' questions.

Spreadsheet developers are typically involved in the following activities, often performing most or all of each task on their own:

- Determining the needs of the user
- Planning an application that meets these needs
- Determining the most appropriate user interface
- Creating the spreadsheet, formulas, macros, and user interface
- Testing the application under all reasonable sets of conditions
- Making the application relatively user-friendly (often based on results from the testing)
- Making the application aesthetically appealing and intuitive
- Documenting the development effort
- Distributing the application to users
- Updating the application if and when it's necessary

CROSS-REFERENCE
I discuss these developer activities in more detail in Chapter 6.

Developers must have a thorough understanding of their development environment (in this case, Excel). And there's certainly a lot to know when it comes to Excel. Developing non-trivial spreadsheet applications with Excel requires an in-depth knowledge of formulas, functions, macros, custom dialog boxes, user interface elements, and add-ins. Most Excel users, of course, don't meet these qualifications and have no intention of ever learning these details — which brings me to the next topic: classifying spreadsheet users.

Classifying spreadsheet users

Over the years, I've found that it's often useful to classify people who use spreadsheets (including both developers and end users) along two dimensions: their *degree of experience* with spreadsheets and their *interest in learning* about spreadsheets.

To keep things simple, each of these two dimensions has three levels. These levels can be combined in nine combinations, which are shown in Table 5-1. In reality, only seven segments are worth thinking about because both moderately experienced and very experienced spreadsheet users generally have at least *some* interest in spreadsheets. (After all, that's what motivated them to get their experience.) Users who have a lot of spreadsheet experience and a low level of interest would make very bad developers.

TABLE 5-1 CLASSIFICATION OF SPREADSHEET USERS BY EXPERIENCE AND INTEREST

	No Interest	Moderately Interested	Very Interested
Little Experience	User	User	User/Potential Developer
Moderately Experienced	N/A	User	Developer
Very Experienced	N/A	User	Developer

It should be clear that spreadsheet developers must have a great deal of experience with spreadsheets as well as a high interest in spreadsheets. Those with little spreadsheet experience but a great deal of interest are potential developers. All they need is more experience. If you're reading this book, you probably fall into one of the boxes in the last column of the table.

The audience for spreadsheet applications

The remaining segments in the preceding table comprise spreadsheet end users, whom you can think of as the consumers of spreadsheet applications. When you develop a spreadsheet application for others to use, you need to know which of these groups of people will actually be using your application.

Users with little experience and no interest in learning more about spreadsheets make up a large percentage of all spreadsheet users, probably the largest group of all. These are the people who need to use a spreadsheet for their jobs but who view the spreadsheet simply as a means to an end. Typically, they know very little about computers and software, and they usually have no interest in learning anything more than what's required to get their work done. They might even feel a bit intimidated by computers. Often, these users don't even know which version of Excel they use, and they are largely unfamiliar with what it can do. Obviously, applications developed for this group must be user-friendly. By that I mean straightforward, unintimidating, easy to use, and as foolproof as possible.

From the developer's point of view, a more interesting group is comprised of users who have little or moderate spreadsheet experience but who are interested in learning more. These users understand the concept of formulas, use worksheet functions, and generally have a good idea of what the product is capable of doing. These users generally appreciate the work that you put into an application and are often impressed by your efforts. Even better, they'll often make excellent suggestions for improving your applications. Applications developed for this group should also be user-friendly, but they can also be more complex and customizable than applications designed for the less experienced and less interested groups.

Solving Problems with Excel

In the previous sections, I cover the basic concept of a spreadsheet application, discuss the end users and developers of such applications, and even attempt to figure out why people use spreadsheets at all. Now, it's time to take a look at the types of tasks that are appropriate for spreadsheet applications.

You might already have a good idea of the types of tasks for which you can use a spreadsheet. Traditionally, spreadsheet software has been used for numerical applications that are largely interactive. Corporate budgets are an excellent example of this. After the model has been set up (that is, after formulas have been developed), working with a budget is simply a matter of plugging in amounts and observing the bottom-line totals. Often, budgeters simply need to allocate fixed resources among various activities and present the results in a reasonably attractive (or at least legible) format. Excel, of course, is ideal for this.

Budget-type problems, however, probably account for only a small percentage of your spreadsheet-development time. If you're like me, you've learned that uses for Excel can often extend well beyond the types of tasks for which spreadsheets were originally designed.

Here are just a few examples of nontraditional ways that Excel can be used:

- *As a presentation device:* For example, with minimal effort, you can create an attractive, interactive, on-screen slideshow with only Excel. PowerPoint is a better choice, but Excel will do in a pinch.

- *As a data-entry tool:* For repetitive data-entry tasks, a spreadsheet is often the most efficient route to take. The data can then be exported to a variety of formats for use in other programs.

- *As a database manager:* If you're dealing with a fairly small amount of data, you may find it much easier to manage it using Excel rather than a program like Access.

- *As a forms generator:* For creating attractive printed forms, many find it easier to use Excel's formatting capabilities than to learn a desktop publishing package.

- *As a text processor:* Excel's text functions and macro capability enable you to manipulate text in ways that are impossible using a word processor.

- *As a platform for simple games:* Clearly, Excel was not designed with this in mind. However, I've downloaded (and written) some interesting strategy games by using the tools found in Excel and other spreadsheets.

You can probably think of many more examples for this list.

Ironically, the versatility of spreadsheets is a double-edged sword. On one hand, it's tempting to try to use a spreadsheet for every problem that crops up. On the other hand, you'll often be spinning your wheels by trying to use a spreadsheet for a problem that's better suited for a different solution.

Basic Spreadsheet Types

In this section, I classify spreadsheets into several basic types to provide a better perspective on how spreadsheet applications fit into the overall scheme of things. This is all quite arbitrary, of course, and is based solely on my own experience. Moreover, there is quite a bit of overlap between the categories, but they cover most of the spreadsheets that I've seen and developed.

My names for these categories are as follows:

- Quick-and-dirty
- For-your-eyes-only
- Single-user applications
- Spaghetti applications
- Utility applications
- Add-ins that contain worksheet functions
- Single-block budgets
- What-if models
- Data storage and access
- Database front ends
- Turnkey applications

I discuss each of these categories in the following sections.

Quick-and-dirty spreadsheets

This is probably the most common type of spreadsheet. Most of the spreadsheets in this category are fairly small and are developed to quickly solve a problem or answer a question. Here's an example: You're about to buy a new car, and you want to figure out your monthly payment for various loan amounts. Or perhaps you need to generate a chart that shows your company's sales by month, so you quickly enter 12 values and whip out a chart, which you paste into your word processor.

In both of the preceding cases, you can probably input the entire model in a few minutes, and you certainly won't take the time to document your work. You probably won't even think of developing any macros or custom dialog boxes. In fact, you might not even deem these simple spreadsheets worthy of saving to disk. Obviously, spreadsheets in this category are not applications.

For-your-eyes-only spreadsheets

As the name implies, no one except you — the creator — will ever see or use the spreadsheets that fall into this category. An example of this type might be a file in which you keep information relevant to your income taxes. You open the file whenever a check comes in the mail, you incur an expense that can be justified as business, you buy tax-deductible Girl Scout cookies, and so on. Another example is a spreadsheet that you use to keep track of your employees' time records (sick leave, vacation, and so on).

Spreadsheets in this category differ from quick-and-dirty spreadsheets in that you use them more than once, so you save these spreadsheets to files. But, again, they're not worth spending a great deal of time on. You might apply some simple formatting, but that's about it. This type of spreadsheet also lacks any type of error detection because you understand how the formulas are set up; you know enough to avoid inputting data that will produce erroneous results. If an error does crop up, you immediately know what caused it.

Spreadsheets in this category don't qualify as applications, although they sometimes increase in sophistication over time.

Single-user applications

This is a spreadsheet application that only the developer uses, but its complexity extends beyond the spreadsheets in the for-your-eyes-only category. For example, I developed a workbook to keep track of registered users for my shareware applications. It started out as a simple worksheet database (for my eyes only), but then I realized that I could also use it to generate mailing labels and invoices. One day I spent an hour or so writing macros and then realized that I had converted this workbook from a for-your-eyes-only spreadsheet to a single-user application.

Creating single-user applications for yourself is an excellent way to get practice with Excel's developer's tools. For example, you can learn to create custom dialog boxes, modify the user interface, write Visual Basic for Applications (VBA) macros, and so on.

 TIP
Working on a meaningful project (even if it's meaningful only to you) is the best way to learn advanced features in Excel — or any other software, for that matter.

Spaghetti applications

An all-too-common type of spreadsheet is what I call a *spaghetti application*. The term stems from the fact that the parts of the application are difficult to follow, much like a plate of spaghetti. Most of these spreadsheets begin life as a reasonably focused, single-user application. But over time, they are passed along to others who make their own modifications. As requirements change and employees come and go, new parts are added and others are ignored. Before too long, the original purpose of the workbook may have been forgotten. The result is a file that is used frequently, but no one really understands exactly how it all works.

Everyone who's involved with it knows that the spaghetti application should be completely reworked. But because nobody really understands it, the situation tends to worsen over time. Spreadsheet consultants make a lot of money untangling such applications. I've found that, in many cases, the most efficient solution is to redefine the users' needs and build a new application from scratch.

Utility applications

Good as it is, I still find quite a bit lacking in Excel. This brings me to the next category of spreadsheets: *utility applications*. Utilities are special tools designed to perform a single recurring task. For example, if you often import text into Excel, you may want some additional text-handling commands, such as the ability to convert selected text to uppercase (without using formulas). The solution? Develop a text-handling utility that does exactly what you want.

 NOTE

The Power Utility Pak is a collection of utility applications for Excel. I developed these utilities to extend Excel's functionality. These utilities work just like normal Excel commands. You can download a trial version of the Power Utility Pak from my Web site (www.j-walk.com/ss), and you can get a discounted copy of the full version by using the coupon located at the back of the book. And if you're interested, the complete VBA source code is also available for a small fee.

The best utility applications are very general in nature. Most macros are designed to perform a specific operation on a specific type of data found in a specific type of workbook. A good utility essentially works like a command normally found in Excel. In other words, the utility needs to recognize the context in which a command is executed and take appropriate action. This usually requires quite a bit of error-handling code so that the utility can handle any situation that comes up.

Utility applications always use macros and may or may not use custom dialog boxes. Fortunately, Excel makes it relatively easy to create such utilities, and they can be converted to add-ins and attached to Excel's user interface so that they appear to be part of Excel.

 CROSS-REFERENCE

The topic of creating utilities is so important that I devote an entire chapter to it. Chapter 16 discusses how to create custom Excel utilities with VBA.

Add-ins that contain worksheet functions

As you know, Excel has many worksheet functions that you can use in formulas. Chances are that you've needed a particular function, only to find that it doesn't exist. The solution? Create your own by using VBA. Custom worksheet functions can often simplify your formulas and make your spreadsheet easier to maintain.

CROSS-REFERENCE

In Chapter 10, you'll find everything you need to know about creating custom worksheet functions, including lots of examples.

Single-block budgets

By a *single-block budget*, I mean a spreadsheet (not necessarily a budget model) that essentially consists of one block of cells. The top row might contain names that correspond to time (months, quarters, or years), and the left column usually contains categories of some type. Typically, the bottom row and right column contain formulas that add the numbers together. There may or may not be formulas that compute subtotals within the block.

This is a very common type of spreadsheet. In most cases, simple single-block budget models are not good candidates for applications because they are simple to begin with, but there *are* exceptions. For example, you might consider converting such a spreadsheet into an application if the model is an unwieldy 3-D spreadsheet, needs to include consolidations from other files, or will be used by departmental managers who might not understand spreadsheets.

What-if models

Many consider the what-if model category to be the epitome of spreadsheets at their best. The ability to instantly recalculate thousands of formulas makes spreadsheet software the ideal tool for financial modeling and other models that depend on the values of several variables. If you think about it, just about any spreadsheet that contains formulas is a what-if model (which are often distributed as templates). Changing the value of a cell used in a formula is akin to asking "what if . . .?" My view of this category, however, is a bit more sophisticated. It includes spreadsheets designed exclusively for systematically analyzing the effects of various inputs.

What-if models often benefit from additional work to make them more user-friendly, especially if the model will be used for a lengthy period of time. Creating a good user interface on an application can make it very easy for anyone to use, including computer-illiterates. As an example, you might create an interface that lets users provide names for various sets of assumptions and then lets them instantly view the results of a selected scenario and create a perfectly formatted summary chart with the click of a button.

Data storage and access spreadsheets

A large percentage of Excel workbooks consist of one or more database tables (sometimes known as *lists*). These are used to track just about anything you can think of. Most people find that it's much easier to view and manipulate data in a spreadsheet than it is using normal database software. If the tables are set up properly, they can be summarized with a pivot table.

NEW

Microsoft is aware of the large number of users who use Excel for tables, and Excel 2007 has improved support for tables.

Spreadsheets in this category are often candidates for applications, especially if end users need to perform things like data validation and pivot table summaries.

For more sophisticated database applications, such as those that use multiple tables with relationships between them, you'll be better off using a real database program such as Access.

Database front ends

Increasingly, spreadsheet products are used to access external databases. Spreadsheet users can access data stored in external files, even if they come in a variety of formats, by using tools that Excel provides. When you create an application that does this, it's sometimes referred to as an *executive information system*, or *EIS*. This sort of system combines data from several sources and summarizes it for users.

Accessing external databases from a spreadsheet often strikes fear in the hearts of beginning users. Creating an executive information system is therefore an ideal sort of Excel application because its chief goal is usually ease of use.

Turnkey applications

The final category of spreadsheet types is the most complex. By *turnkey,* I mean ready to go, with little or no preparation by the end user. For example, the user loads the file and is presented with a user interface that makes user choices perfectly clear. Turnkey applications may not even look as if they are being powered by a spreadsheet, and, often, the user interacts completely with dialog boxes rather than cells. I've heard these types of applications referred to as "dictator applications" because the user can perform only the operations that the developer has allowed.

Actually, many of the categories just described can be converted into turnkey applications. The critical common elements, as I discuss throughout the remainder of the book, are good planning, error handling, and user interface design.

Part II

Chapter 6

Essentials of Spreadsheet Application Development

In This Chapter

My goal in this chapter is to provide you with some general guidelines that you may find useful while you learn to create effective applications with Excel.

- ◆ A discussion of the basic steps involved in spreadsheet application development

- ◆ Determining end user needs and planning applications to meet those needs

- ◆ Guidelines for developing and testing your applications

- ◆ Documenting your development efforts and writing user documentation

There is no simple, sure-fire recipe for developing an effective spreadsheet application. Everyone has his or her own style for creating such applications, and I haven't discovered one best way that works for everyone. In addition, every project is different and, therefore, requires its own approach. Finally, the demands and technical expertise of the people you work with (or for) also play a role in how the development process proceeds.

As I mention in the preceding chapter, spreadsheet developers typically perform the following activities:

- Determine the needs of the user(s)
- Plan an application that meets these needs
- Determine the most appropriate user interface
- Create the spreadsheet, formulas, macros, and user interface
- Test and debug the application
- Attempt to make the application bulletproof
- Make the application aesthetically appealing and intuitive
- Document the development effort
- Develop user documentation and help systems
- Distribute the application to the user
- Update the application when necessary

Not all these steps are required for each application, and the order in which these activities are performed varies from project to project. Each of these activities is described in the pages that follow, and in most cases, the technical details are covered in subsequent chapters.

Determining User Needs

When you undertake a new Excel project, one of your first steps is to identify exactly what the end users require. Failure to thoroughly assess the end users' needs early on often results in additional work later when you have to adjust the application so that it does what it was supposed to do in the first place.

In some cases, you'll be intimately familiar with the end users — you might even be an end user yourself. In other cases (for example, a consultant developing a project for a new client), you may know little or nothing about the users or their situations.

How do you determine the needs of the user? If you've been asked to develop a spreadsheet application, it's a good idea to meet with the end users and ask very specific questions. Better yet, get everything in writing, create flow diagrams, pay attention to minor details, and do anything else to ensure that the product you deliver is the product that is needed.

Here are some guidelines that may help to make this phase easier:

- Don't presume that you know what the user needs. Second-guessing at this stage almost always causes problems later on.
- If possible, talk directly to the end users of the application, not just their supervisor or manager.

- Learn what, if anything, is currently being done to meet the users' needs. You might be able to save some work by simply adapting an existing application. At the very least, looking at current solutions will familiarize you with the operation.

- Identify the resources available at the user's site. For example, try to determine whether there are any hardware or software limitations that you must work around.

- If possible, determine the specific hardware systems that will be used. If your application will be used on slower systems, you need to take that into account. See the later section "System speed."

- Identify which version(s) of Excel is (are) in use. Although Microsoft does everything in its power to urge users to upgrade to the latest version of the software, the majority of Excel users have not upgraded to the most recent version.

- Understand the skill levels of the end users. This information will help you design the application appropriately.

- Determine how long the application will be used and whether any changes are anticipated during the lifetime of the project. Knowing this may influence the amount of effort that you put into the project and help you plan for changes.

One final note: Don't be surprised if the project specifications change before you complete the application. This is quite common, and you are in a better position if you expect changes rather than being surprised by them. Just make sure that your contract (if you have one) addresses the issue of changing specifications.

Planning an Application That Meets User Needs

After you determine the end users' needs, it's very tempting to jump right in and start fiddling around in Excel. Take it from someone who suffers from this problem: Try to restrain yourself. Builders don't construct a house without a set of blueprints, and you shouldn't build a spreadsheet application without some type of plan. The formality of your plan depends on the scope of the project and your general style of working, but you should spend at least *some* time thinking about what you're going to do and coming up with a plan of action.

Before rolling up your sleeves and settling down at your keyboard, you'll benefit by taking some time to consider the various ways you can approach the problem. Here is where a thorough knowledge of Excel pays off. Avoiding blind alleys before you stumble into them is always a good idea.

If you ask a dozen Excel experts to design an application based on very precise specifications, chances are that you'll get a dozen different implementations of the project that meet those specifications. Of those solutions, some will definitely be better than the others because Excel often provides several different options to accomplish a task. If you know

Excel inside and out, you'll have a good idea of the potential methods at your disposal, and you can choose the one most appropriate for the project at hand. Often, a bit of creative thinking yields an unusual approach that's vastly superior to other methods.

So at the beginning stage of this planning period, consider some general options, such as these:

- *File structure:* Think about whether you want to use one workbook with multiple sheets, several single-sheet workbooks, or a template file.

- *Data structure:* You should always consider how your data will be structured. This includes using external database files versus storing everything in worksheets.

- *Formulas versus VBA:* Should you use formulas or write Visual Basic for Applications (VBA) procedures to perform calculations? Both methods have advantages and disadvantages.

- *Add-in or workbook file:* In some cases, an add-in might be the best choice for your final product. Or, perhaps you might use an add-in in conjunction with a standard workbook.

- *Version of Excel:* Will your Excel application be used with Excel 2007 only? With Excel 2000 or Excel 2002? What about Excel 97, Excel 95, and Excel 5? Will it also be run on a Macintosh? These are very important considerations because each new version of Excel adds features that aren't available in previous versions. The new user interface in Excel 2007 makes it more challenging than ever to create an application that works with older versions.

- *Error handling:* Error handling is a major issue with applications. You need to determine how your application will detect and deal with errors. For example, if your application applies formatting to the active worksheet, you need to be able to handle a case in which a chart sheet is active.

- *Use of special features:* If your application needs to summarize a lot of data, you might want to consider using Excel's pivot table feature. Or, you might want to use Excel's data validation feature as a check for valid data entry.

- *Performance issues:* The time to start thinking about increasing the speed and efficiency of your application is at the development stage, not when the application is completed and users are complaining.

- *Level of security:* As you may know, Excel provides several protection options to restrict access to particular elements of a workbook. For example, you can lock cells so that formulas cannot be changed, and you can assign a password to prevent unauthorized users from viewing or accessing specific files. Determining up front exactly what you need to protect — and what level of protection is necessary — will make your job easier.

NOTE

Be aware that Excel's protection features are not 100-percent effective — far from it. If you desire complete and absolute security for your application, Excel probably isn't the best platform.

Learning While You Develop

Now a few words about reality: Excel is a moving target. Excel's upgrade cycle is approximately 18–24 months, which means that you have fewer than two years to get up to speed with its current innovations before you have even more innovations to contend with.

Excel 5, which introduced VBA, represented a major paradigm shift for Excel developers. Thousands of people up until that point earned their living developing Excel applications (in Excel 2, 3, and 4) that were largely based on the XLM macro language. Beginning with Excel 5, dozens of new tools became available, and developers, for the most part, eagerly embraced them.

When Excel 97 became available, developers faced yet another shift. This new version introduced a new file format, the Visual Basic Editor (VBE), and UserForms as a replacement for dialog sheets. Excel 2000, 2002, and 2003 introduced additional features, but these changes were not as radical as those in previous upgrades.

Excel 2007 is perhaps the most significant upgrade ever. The key challenge is dealing with the new Ribbon user interface. In the past, creating custom menus and toolbars was relatively easy and could be done entirely using VBA. But, as you'll see, modifying the Ribbon requires quite a bit of additional work, and you'll need to go beyond VBA to make it happen. In addition, the new file formats will require some additional considerations. You may find it more efficient to create two versions of your applications: One for Excel 2007, and one for Excel 2003 and earlier versions.

VBA is not difficult to learn, but it definitely takes time to become comfortable with it — and even more time to master it. Consequently, it's not uncommon to be in the process of learning VBA while you're developing applications with it. In fact, I think it's impossible to learn VBA without developing applications. If you're like me, you'll find it much easier to learn VBA if you have a project that requires it. Learning VBA just for the sake of learning VBA usually doesn't work.

You'll probably have to deal with many other project-specific considerations in this phase. The important thing is that you consider all options and don't settle on the first solution that comes to mind.

Another design consideration is remembering to plan for change. You'll do yourself a favor if you make your application as generic as possible. For example, don't write a procedure that works with only a specific range of cells. Rather, write a procedure that accepts any range as an argument. When the inevitable changes are requested, such a design makes it easier for you to carry out the revisions. Also, you might find that the work that you do for one project is similar to the work that you do for another. Keeping reusability in mind when you are planning a project is always a good idea.

One thing that I've learned from experience is to avoid letting the end user completely guide your approach to a problem. For example, suppose you meet with a manager who tells you that the department needs application to write text files that will be imported into another application. Don't confuse the user's need with the solution. The user's real need is to share data. Using an intermediate text file to do it is just one possible solution to the need. There might be other ways to approach the problem that are superior. In other words, don't let the users define their problem by stating it in terms of a solution approach. Determining the best approach is *your* job.

Determining the Most Appropriate User Interface

When you develop spreadsheets that others will use, you need to pay special attention to the user interface. By *user interface,* I mean the method by which the user interacts with the application and executes your VBA macros.

Excel 2007 makes some of these decisions irrelevant. Custom menus and toolbars are, for all intents and purposes, obsolete. This means that developers must learn how to work with the Ribbon.

Excel provides several features that are relevant to user interface design:

- Ribbon customizations
- Shortcut menu customization
- Shortcut keys
- Custom dialog boxes (UserForms)
- Controls (such as a ListBox or a CommandButton) placed directly on a worksheet

I discuss these features briefly in the following sections and cover them more thoroughly in later chapters.

Customizing the Ribbon

The new Ribbon UI in Excel 2007 is a dramatic shift in user interface design. Fortunately, the developer has a fair amount of control over the Ribbon. Unfortunately, modifying the Ribbon isn't a simple task.

CROSS-REFERENCE

See Chapter 22 for information about working with the Ribbon.

Menu and Toolbar Compatibility

Excel 2007 still supports custom menus and toolbars, but the way these UI elements are handled may not be to your liking.

The following figure shows a custom menu and toolbar displayed in Excel 2003. The menu and toolbar were created using my Power Utility Pak add-in. Each menu item and toolbar button executes a macro.

As shown in the following figure, when the Power Utility Pak add-in is installed in Excel 2007, the custom menu appears in a group labeled Add-Ins ➪ Menu Commands, and the custom toolbar is in a group labeled Add-Ins ➪ Custom Toolbars (the toolbars cannot be moved or resized). These Ribbon groups display the menu additions and toolbars for all the applications or add-ins that are loaded. The menu items and toolbar buttons still function, but the designer's original UI conception has been compromised.

continued

Part II

continued

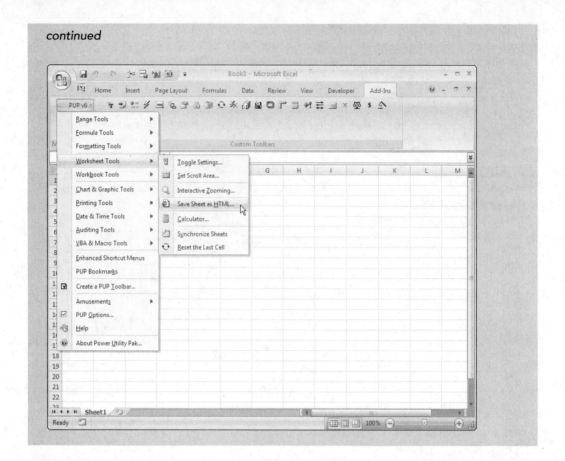

Customizing shortcut menus

Excel 2007 still allows the VBA developer to customize the right-click shortcut menus. Figure 6-1 shows a customized shortcut menu that appears when you right-click a row number. Notice that this shortcut menu has six menu items (at the bottom) that aren't normally available.

CROSS-REFERENCE

Chapter 23 describes how to work with shortcut menus using VBA.

Creating shortcut keys

Another user interface option at your disposal is to create custom shortcut keys. Excel lets you assign a Ctrl key (or Shift+Ctrl key) combination (shortcut) to a macro. When the user presses the key combination, the macro executes.

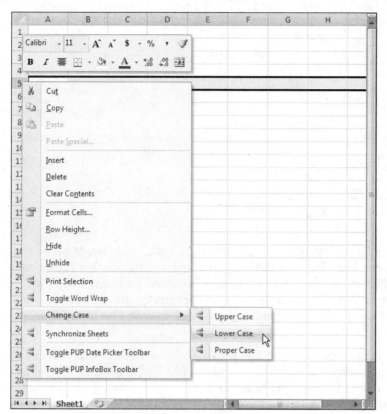

Figure 6-1: An example of a customized shortcut menu.

Be aware, however, of these two caveats: First, you must make it clear to the user which keys are active and what they do; second, you need to be careful not to assign a key combination that's already used for something else. A key combination that you assign to a macro takes precedence over the built-in shortcut keys. For example, Ctrl+S is a built-in Excel shortcut key used to save the current file. If you assign this key combination to a macro, you lose the capability to save the file with Ctrl+S. Remember that shortcut keys are case-sensitive, so you can use a combination such as Ctrl+Shift+S.

Creating custom dialog boxes

Anyone who has used a personal computer for any length of time is undoubtedly familiar with dialog boxes. Consequently, custom Excel dialog boxes can play a major role in the user interfaces that you design for your applications. Figure 6-2 shows an example of a custom dialog box.

Figure 6-2: A dialog box created with Excel's UserForm feature.

A custom dialog box is known as a *UserForm*. A UserForm can solicit user input, get a user's options or preferences, and direct the flow of your entire application. You create and edit UserForms in the VBE. The elements that make up a UserForm (buttons, drop-down lists, check boxes, and so on) are called *controls* — more specifically, *ActiveX controls.* Excel provides a standard assortment of ActiveX controls, and you can also incorporate third-party controls.

After adding a control to a dialog box, you can link it to a worksheet cell so that it doesn't require any macros (except a simple macro to display the dialog box). Linking a control to a cell is easy, but it's not always the best way to get user input from a dialog box. Most of the time, you want to develop VBA macros that work with your custom dialog boxes.

CROSS-REFERENCE
I cover UserForms in detail in Part IV.

Using ActiveX controls on a worksheet

Excel also lets you add the UserForm ActiveX controls to a worksheet's *drawing layer* (an invisible layer on top of a sheet that holds pictures, charts, and other objects). Figure 6-3 shows a simple worksheet model with several UserForm controls inserted directly on the worksheet. This sheet contains the following ActiveX controls: a Checkbox, a ScrollBar, and two sets of OptionButtons. This workbook uses no macros. Rather, the controls are linked to worksheet cells.

CD-ROM
This workbook is available on the companion CD-ROM. The file is named worksheet controls.xlsx.

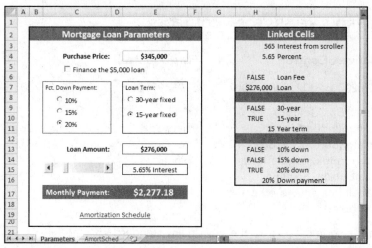

Figure 6-3: You can add dialog box controls to worksheets and link them to cells.

Perhaps the most common control is a CommandButton. By itself, a CommandButton doesn't do anything, so you need to attach a macro to each CommandButton.

Using dialog box controls directly in a worksheet often eliminates the need for custom dialog boxes. You can often greatly simplify the operation of a spreadsheet by adding a few ActiveX controls (or Form controls) to a worksheet. This lets the user make choices by operating familiar controls rather than making entries into cells.

Access these controls by using the Developer ⇨ Controls ⇨ Insert command (see Figure 6-4).

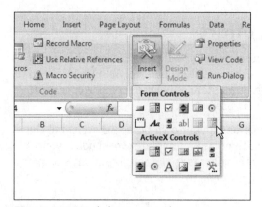

Figure 6-4: Worksheet controls.

The controls come in two types: Form Controls and ActiveX Controls. Both sets of controls have their advantages and disadvantages. Generally, the Form controls are easier to use, but the ActiveX controls are a bit more flexible. Table 6-1 summarizes these two classes of controls.

TABLE 6-1   ACTIVEX CONTROLS VERSUS FORM CONTROLS

	ActiveX Controls	Form Controls
Excel versions	97, 2000, 2002, 2003, 2007	5, 95, 97, 2000, 2002, 2003, 2007
Controls available	CheckBox, TextBox, CommandButton, OptionButton, ListBox, ComboBox, ToggleButton, SpinButton, ScrollBar, Label, Image (and others can be added)	Label, GroupBox, Button, CheckBox, OptionButton, ListBox, DropDown (ComboBox), ScrollBar, Spinner
Macro code storage	In the code module for the Sheet	In any standard VBA module
Macro name	Corresponds to the control name (for example, CommandButton1_Click)	Any name you specify
Correspond to . . .	UserForm controls	Pre–Excel 97 Dialog Sheet controls
Customization	Extensive, using the Properties box	Minimal
Respond to events	Yes	Click or Change events only

Executing the development effort

After you identify user needs, determine the approach that you'll take to meet those needs, and decide on the components that you'll use for the user interface, it's time to get down to the nitty-gritty and start creating the application. This step, of course, comprises a great deal of the total time that you spend on a particular project.

How you go about developing the application depends on your own personal style and the nature of the application. Except for simple fill-in-the-blanks template workbooks, your application will probably use macros. Developing the macros is the tough part. It's easy to create macros in Excel, but it's difficult to create *good* macros.

Concerning Yourself with the End User

In this section, I discuss the important development issues that surface as your application becomes more and more workable and as the time to package and distribute your work grows nearer.

Testing the application

How many times have you used a commercial software application, only to have it bomb out on you at a crucial moment? Most likely, the problem was caused by insufficient testing that didn't catch all the bugs. All nontrivial software has bugs, but in the best software, the bugs are simply more obscure. As you'll see, you sometimes must work around the bugs in Excel to get your application to perform properly.

After you create your application, you need to test it. This is one of the most crucial steps; it's not uncommon to spend as much time testing and debugging an application as you did creating the application in the first place. Actually, you should be doing a great deal of testing during the development phase. After all, whether you're writing a VBA routine or creating formulas in a worksheet, you want to make sure that the application is working the way it's supposed to work.

Like standard compiled applications, spreadsheet applications that you develop are prone to bugs. A *bug* can be defined as (1) something that does happen but shouldn't happen while a program (or application) is running, or (2) something that doesn't happen when it should happen. Both species of bugs are equally nasty, and you should plan on devoting a good portion of your development time to testing the application under all reasonable conditions and fixing any problems that you find. In some cases, unfortunately, the problems aren't entirely your fault. Excel, too, has its problems (see the "Bugs? In Excel?" sidebar).

Part II

Bugs? In Excel?

You might think that a product like Excel, which is used by millions of people throughout the world, would be relatively free of bugs. Think again. Excel is such a complex piece of software that it is only natural to expect some problems with it. And Excel *does* have some problems.

Getting a product like Excel out the door is not easy, even for a company like Microsoft with seemingly unlimited resources. Releasing a software product involves compromises and trade-offs. It's commonly known that most major software vendors release their products with full knowledge that they contain bugs. Most of the bugs are considered insignificant enough to ignore. Software companies could postpone their releases by a few months and fix many of them, but software, like everything else, is ruled by economics. The benefits of delaying a product's release often do not exceed the costs involved. Although Excel definitely has its share of bugs, my guess is that the majority of Excel users never encounter one.

In this book, I point out the problems with Excel that I know about. You'll surely discover some more on your own. Some problems occur only with a particular version of Excel — and under a specific configuration involving hardware and/or software. These are the worst bugs of all because they aren't easily reproducible.

So what's a developer to do? It's called a *workaround*. If something that you try to do doesn't work — and all indications say that it *should* work — it's time to move on to Plan B. Frustrating? Sure. A waste of your time? Absolutely. It's all part of being a developer.

What about Beta Testing?

Software manufacturers typically have a rigorous testing cycle for new products. After extensive internal testing, the pre-release product is usually sent to a group of interested users for *beta testing*. This phase often uncovers additional problems that are usually corrected before the product's final release.

If you're developing an Excel application that more than a few people will use, you might want to consider a beta test. This enables your application to be used in its intended setting on different hardware (usually) and by the intended users.

The beta period should begin after you've completed all your own testing and you feel that the application is ready to distribute. You'll need to identify a group of users to help you. The process works best if you distribute everything that will ultimately be included in your application: user documentation, the installation program, help, and so on. You can evaluate the beta test in a number of ways, including face-to-face discussions, questionnaires, and phone calls.

You almost always become aware of problems that you need to correct or improvements that you need to make before you undertake a widespread distribution of the application. Of course, a beta testing phase takes additional time, and not all projects can afford that luxury.

I probably don't need to tell you to thoroughly test any spreadsheet application that you develop for others. And depending on its eventual audience, you might want to make your application bulletproof. In other words, try to anticipate all the errors and screw-ups that could possibly occur, making concerted efforts to avoid them — or, at least, to handle them gracefully. This not only helps the end user but also makes it easier on you and protects your reputation. Also consider using beta testing; your end users are likely candidates because they are the ones who will be using your product. See the upcoming sidebar "What about Beta Testing?"

Although you cannot conceivably test for all possibilities, your macros should be able to handle common types of errors. For example, what if the user enters a text string instead of a numeric value? What if the user tries to run your macro when a workbook isn't open? What if he or she cancels a dialog box without making any selections? What happens if the user presses Ctrl+F6 and jumps to the next window? When you gain experience, issues like these become very familiar, and you account for them without even thinking.

Making the application bulletproof

If you think about it, it's fairly easy to destroy a spreadsheet. Erasing one critical formula or value can cause errors throughout the entire worksheet — and perhaps even other dependent worksheets. Even worse, if the damaged workbook is saved, it replaces the good copy on disk. Unless a backup procedure is in place, the user of your application could be in trouble, and *you'll* probably be blamed for it.

Obviously, it's easy to see why you need to add some protection when users — especially novices — will be using your worksheets. Excel provides several techniques for protecting worksheets and parts of worksheets:

- *Lock specific cells:* You can lock specific cells (by using the Protection tab in the Format Cells dialog box) so that they cannot be changed. This takes effect only when the document is protected with the Review ➪ Changes ➪ Protect Sheet command. The Protect Sheet dialog box has options that allow you to specify which actions can be performed on a protected sheet. See Figure 6-5.

Figure 6-5: Using the Protect Sheet dialog box to specify what users can and cannot do.

- *Hide the formulas in specific cells:* You can hide the formulas in specific cells (by using the Protection tab in the Format Cells dialog box) so that others can't see them. Again, this takes effect only when the document is protected by choosing the Review ➪ Changes ➪ Protect Sheet command.

- *Protect an entire workbook:* You can protect an entire workbook — the structure of the workbook, the window position and size, or both. Use the Review ➪ Changes ➪ Protect Workbook command for this purpose.

- *Lock objects on the worksheet:* Use the Properties tab in the Size and Properties dialog box to lock objects (such as shapes) and prevent them from being moved or changed. To access the Size and Properties dialog box, select the object and then click the dialog box launcher in the Drawing Tools ➪ Format ➪ Size group. Locking objects takes effect only when the document is protected via the Review ➪ Changes ➪ Protect Sheet command. By default, all objects are locked.

- *Hide rows, columns, sheets, and documents:* You can hide rows, columns, sheets, and entire workbooks. This helps prevent the worksheet from looking cluttered and also provides some protection against prying eyes.

Part II

How Secure Are Excel's Passwords?

As far as I know, Microsoft has never advertised Excel as a secure program. And for good reason: It's actually quite easy to circumvent Excel's password system. Several commercial programs are available that can break passwords. Excel 2002 and later versions seem to have stronger security than previous versions, but they can still be cracked by a determined user. Bottom line? Don't think of password protection as foolproof. Sure, it will be effective for the casual user. But if someone *really* wants to break your password, he can probably do so.

- *Designate an Excel workbook as read-only recommended:* You can designate an Excel workbook as read-only recommended (and use a password) to ensure that the file cannot be overwritten with any changes. You do this in the General Options dialog box. Display this dialog box by choosing File ➪ Save As. In the Save As dialog box, click the Tools button and choose General Options.

- *Assign a password:* You can assign a password to prevent unauthorized users from opening your file. You do this in the General Options dialog box. Display this dialog box by choosing File ➪ Save As. In the Save As dialog box, click the Tools button and choose General Options.

- *Use a password-protected add-in:* You can use a password-protected add-in, which doesn't allow the user to change *anything* on its worksheets.

Making the application aesthetically appealing and intuitive

If you've used many different software packages, you've undoubtedly seen examples of poorly designed user interfaces, difficult-to-use programs, and just plain ugly screens. If you're developing spreadsheets for other people, you should pay particular attention to how the application looks.

How a computer program looks can make all the difference in the world to users, and the same is true with the applications that you develop with Excel. Beauty, however, is in the eye of the beholder. If your skills lean more in the analytical direction, consider enlisting the assistance of someone with a more aesthetic sensibility to provide help with design.

The good news is that Excel 2007 makes it relatively easy to create better-looking spreadsheets. If you stick with the pre-designed cell styles, your work stands a good chance of looking good. And, with the click of a mouse, you can apply a new theme that completely transforms the look of the workbook — and still looks good. Unfortunately, Excel 2007 adds nothing new in the area of UserForm design, so you're on your own in that area.

End users appreciate a good-looking user interface, and your applications will have a much more polished and professional look if you devote some additional time to design and aesthetic considerations. An application that looks good demonstrates that its developer cared enough about the product to invest some extra time and effort. Take the following suggestions into account:

- *Strive for consistency:* When designing dialog boxes, for example, try to emulate Excel's dialog box look and feel whenever possible. Be consistent with formatting, fonts, text size, and colors.

- *Keep it simple:* A common mistake that developers make is trying to cram too much information into a single screen or dialog box. A good rule is to present only one or two chunks of information at a time.

- *Break down input screens:* If you use an input screen to solicit information from the user, consider breaking it up into several, less crowded screens. If you use a complex dialog box, you might want to break it up by using a MultiPage control, which lets you create a familiar tabbed dialog box.

- *Don't overdo color:* Use color sparingly. It's very easy to overdo it and make the screen look gaudy.

- *Monitor typography and graphics:* Pay attention to numeric formats and use consistent typefaces, font sizes, and borders.

Evaluating aesthetic qualities is very subjective. When in doubt, strive for simplicity and clarity.

NOTE

Previous versions of Excel used a pallet of 56 colors. That restriction has been removed, and Excel 2007 supports more than 16 million colors.

Creating a user Help system

With regard to user documentation, you basically have two options: paper-based documentation or electronic documentation. Providing electronic help is standard fare in Windows applications. Fortunately, your Excel applications can also provide help — even context-sensitive help. Developing help text takes quite a bit of additional effort, but for a large project, it may be worth it. Figure 6-6 shows an example of a custom Help system in compiled HTML format.

Another point to consider is support for your application. In other words, who gets the phone call if the user encounters a problem? If you aren't prepared to handle routine questions, you need to identify someone who is. In some cases, you want to arrange it so that only highly technical or bug-related issues escalate to the developer.

CROSS-REFERENCE

In Chapter 24, I discuss several alternatives for providing help for your applications.

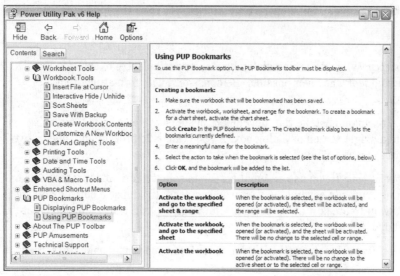

Figure 6-6: An example of custom help file for an Excel add-in.

Documenting the development effort

Putting a spreadsheet application together is one thing. Making it understandable for other people is another. As with traditional programming, it's important that you thoroughly document your work. Such documentation helps you if you need to go back to it (and you will), and it helps anyone else whom you might pass it on to.

TIP

You might want to consider a couple of things when you document your project. For example, if you were hired to develop an Excel application, you might not want to share all your hard-earned secrets by thoroughly documenting *everything*. If this is the case, you should maintain two versions: one thoroughly documented (for your own reference) and the other partially documented (for other users).

How do you document a workbook application? You can either store the information in a worksheet or use another file. You can even use a paper document if you prefer. Perhaps the easiest way is to use a separate worksheet to store your comments and key information for the project. For VBA code, use comments liberally. (VBA text preceded with an apostrophe is ignored because that text is designated a comment.) Although an elegant piece of VBA code can seem perfectly obvious to you today, when you come back to it in a few months, your reasoning might be completely obscured unless you use the VBA comment feature.

Why Is There No Runtime Version of Excel?

When you distribute your application, you need to be sure that each end user has a licensed copy of the appropriate version of Excel. It's illegal to distribute a copy of Excel along with your application. Why, you might ask, doesn't Microsoft provide a runtime version of Excel? A *runtime version* is an executable program that can load files but not create them. With a runtime version, the end user wouldn't need a copy of Excel to run your application. (This is common with database programs.)

I've never seen a clear or convincing reason why Microsoft does not have a runtime version of Excel, and no other spreadsheet manufacturer offers a runtime version of its product, either. The most likely reason is that spreadsheet vendors fear that doing so would reduce sales of the software. Or, it could be that developing a runtime version would require a tremendous amount of programming that would just never pay off.

On a related note . . . Microsoft does offer an Excel file *viewer*. This product lets you view Excel files if you don't own a copy of Excel. Macros, however, will not execute. You can get a copy of this free file viewer from the Microsoft Web site (`http://office.microsoft.com/downloads`).

Distributing the application to the user

You've completed your project, and you're ready to release it to the end users. How do you go about doing this? You can choose from many ways to distribute your application, and the method that you choose depends on many factors.

You could just hand over a CD-ROM, scribble a few instructions, and be on your way. Or, you may want to install the application yourself — but this is not always feasible. Another option is to develop an official setup program that performs the task automatically. You can write such a program in a traditional programming language, purchase a generic setup program, or write your own in VBA.

Excel 2000 and later incorporates technology to enable developers to digitally sign their applications. This process is designed to help end users identify the author of an application, to ensure that the project has not been altered, and to help prevent the spread of macro viruses or other potentially destructive code. To digitally sign a project, you first apply for a digital certificate from a formal certificate authority (or, you can self-sign your project by creating your own digital certificate). Refer to the Help system or the Microsoft Web site for additional information.

Updating the application when necessary

After you distribute your application, you're finished with it, right? You can sit back, enjoy yourself, and try to forget about the problems that you encountered (and solved) during the course of developing your application. In rare cases, yes, you may be finished. More often, however, the users of your application will not be completely satisfied. Sure, your application adheres to all the *original* specifications, but things change. Seeing an application working frequently causes the user to think of other things that the application could be doing. I'm talking *updates*.

When you need to update or revise your application, you'll appreciate that you designed it well in the first place and that you fully documented your efforts. If not, well . . . we learn from our experiences.

Other Development Issues

You need to keep several other issues in mind when developing an application — especially if you don't know exactly who will be using the application. If you're developing an application that will have widespread use (a shareware application, for example), you have no way of knowing how the application will be used, what type of system it will run on, or what other software will be running concurrently.

The user's installed version of Excel

With every new release of Excel, the issue of compatibility rears its head. As I write this, Excel 2007 has just been released — yet many large corporations are still using Excel 2000 and some use even earlier versions.

Unfortunately, there is no guarantee that an application developed for, say, Excel 2000 will work perfectly with later versions of Excel. If you need your application to work with a variety of Excel versions, the best approach is to work with the lowest version — and then test it thoroughly with all other versions.

Things get even more complicated when you consider Excel's sub-versions. Microsoft distributes service releases (SRs) to correct problems. For example, users might have the original Excel 2000, Excel 2000 with SR-1, or Excel 2000 with SR-2. And it gets even more complicated with Excel 2003. Excel 2007 has a quite a few known problems, and it's likely that at least some of them will be corrected in a future service release.

CROSS-REFERENCE
I discuss compatibility issues in Chapter 26.

Language issues

Consider yourself very fortunate if all your end users have the English language version of Excel. Non-English versions of Excel aren't always 100-percent compatible, so that means additional testing on your part. In addition, keep in mind that two users can both be using the English language version of Excel yet use different Windows regional settings. In some cases, you may need to be aware of potential problems.

CROSS-REFERENCE

I briefly discuss language issues in Chapter 26.

System speed

You're probably a fairly advanced computer user and tend to keep your hardware reasonably up to date. In other words, you have a fairly powerful system that is probably better than the average user's system. In some cases, you'll know exactly what hardware the end users of your applications are using. If so, it's vitally important that you test your application on that system. A procedure that executes almost instantaneously on your system may take several seconds on another system. In the world of computers, several seconds may be unacceptable.

TIP

When you gain more experience with VBA, you'll discover that there are ways to get the job done, and there are ways to get the job done fast. It's a good idea to get into the habit of coding for speed. Other chapters in this book will certainly help you out in this area.

Video modes

As you probably know, users' video displays vary widely. A video resolution of 1024 x 768 is most common, but many systems are set up with an 800 x 600 display. Higher resolution displays and even dual displays are becoming increasingly common. Just because you have a super-high-resolution monitor, you can't assume that everyone else does.

Video resolution can be a problem if your application relies on specific information being displayed on a single screen. For example, if you develop an input screen that uses 1280 x 1024 mode, users with a 1024 x 768 display will not be able to see the whole input screen without scrolling or zooming. Also, it's important to realize that a *restored* (that is, not maximized or minimized) workbook is displayed at its previous window size and position. In the extreme case, it's possible that a window saved by using a high-resolution display may be completely off the screen when opened on a system running in a lower resolution.

Unfortunately, there's no way to automatically scale things so that they look the same regardless of the display resolution. In some cases, you can zoom the worksheet (using the Zoom control in the status bar), but doing so reliably may be difficult. Unless you're certain of the video resolution that the users of your application will use, you should probably design your application so it works with the lowest common denominator — 800 x 600 mode.

As you will learn later in the book (see Chapter 10), it's possible to determine the user's video resolution by using Windows API calls from VBA. In some cases, you may want to programmatically adjust things depending on the user's video resolution.

Part

Understanding Visual Basic for Applications

Chapter 7

Introducing Visual Basic for Applications

In This Chapter

This chapter introduces you to Visual Basic for Applications (VBA) and the objects that make up Excel.

- ◆ An introduction to VBA — the programming language built into Excel

- ◆ How VBA differs from traditional spreadsheet macro languages and how it differs from the Visual Basic language

- ◆ How to use the Visual Basic Editor (VBE)

- ◆ How to work in the Code windows in the VBE and customize the VBE environment

- ◆ How to use Excel's macro recorder

- ◆ An overview of objects, collections, properties, and methods

- ◆ A case study of the Comment object

- ◆ Specific information and examples of working with Range objects

- ◆ How to access a lot of information about Excel objects, properties, and methods

Programming Excel essentially boils down to manipulating objects, which you do by writing instructions in a language that Excel can understand: VBA.

Some BASIC Background

Many hard-core programmers scoff at the idea of programming in BASIC. The name itself (an acronym for Beginner's All-purpose Symbolic Instruction Code) suggests that it's not a professional language. In fact, BASIC was first developed in the early 1960s as a way to teach programming techniques to college students. BASIC caught on quickly and is available in hundreds of dialects for many types of computers.

BASIC has evolved and improved over the years. For example, in many early implementations, BASIC was an *interpreted* language. Each line was interpreted before it was executed, causing slow performance. Most modern dialects of BASIC allow the code to be compiled — converted to machine code — which results in faster and more efficient execution

BASIC gained quite a bit of respectability in 1991 when Microsoft released Visual Basic for Windows. This product made it easy for the masses to develop standalone applications for Windows. Visual Basic has very little in common with early versions of BASIC, but Visual Basic is the foundation on which VBA was built.

About VBA

Excel 5 was the first application on the market to feature Visual Basic for Applications (VBA). VBA is best thought of as Microsoft's common application scripting language, and it's included with most Office 2007 applications and even in applications from other vendors. Therefore, if you master VBA by using Excel, you'll be able to jump right in and write macros for other Microsoft (and some non-Microsoft) products. Even better, you'll be able to create complete solutions that use features across various applications.

Object models

The secret to using VBA with other applications lies in understanding the *object model* for each application. VBA, after all, simply manipulates objects, and each product (Excel, Word, Access, PowerPoint, and so forth) has its own unique object model. You can program an application by using the objects that the application exposes.

Excel's object model, for example, exposes several very powerful data analysis objects, such as worksheets, charts, pivot tables, and numerous mathematical, financial, engineering, and general business functions. With VBA, you can work with these objects and develop automated procedures. While you work with VBA in Excel, you gradually build an understanding of the object model. **Warning:** It will be very confusing at first. Eventually, however, the pieces come together — and all of a sudden, you realize that you've mastered it!

Is VBA Becoming Obsolete?

For the past few years, I've heard rumors that Microsoft is going to remove VBA from the Office applications and replace it with .NET. My understanding is that these rumors are completely unfounded. Sure, Microsoft has developed another way to automate Office applications, but VBA will be around for quite a while — at least in Excel for Windows. As I write this, Microsoft announced that VBA would no longer be part of Excel for Macintosh.

Why will VBA survive? Because literally millions of VBA-based solutions are in use and VBA is much easier to learn and use than the alternative.

VBA versus XLM

Before version 5, Excel used a powerful (but very cryptic) macro language called *XLM*. Later versions of Excel (including Excel 2007) still execute XLM macros, but the capability to record macros in XLM was removed beginning with Excel 97. As a developer, you should be aware of XLM (in case you ever encounter macros written in that system), but you should use VBA for your development work.

 NOTE

Don't confuse the XLM macro language with eXtensible Markup Language (XML). Although these terms share the same letters, they have nothing in common. *XML* is a storage format for structured data. The Office 2007 applications use XML as their default file format.

The Basics of VBA

Before I get into the meat of things, I suggest that you read through the material in this section to get a broad overview of where I'm heading. These are the topics that I cover in the remainder of this chapter.

Following is a quick-and-dirty summary of what VBA is all about:

- *Code:* You perform actions in VBA by executing VBA code.

  You write (or record) VBA code, which is stored in a VBA module.

- *Module:* VBA modules are stored in an Excel workbook, but you view or edit a module by using the Visual Basic Editor (VBE).

  A VBA module consists of procedures.

- *Procedures:* A procedure is basically a unit of computer code that performs some action. VBA supports two types of procedures: `Sub` procedures and `Function` procedures.

  - `Sub`: A `Sub` procedure consists of a series of statements and can be executed in a number of ways.

    Here's an example of a simple `Sub` procedure called `Test`: This procedure calculates a simple sum and then displays the result in a message box.

    ```
    Sub Test()
        Sum = 1 + 1
        MsgBox "The answer is " & Sum
    End Sub
    ```

  - `Function`: A VBA module can also have `Function` procedures. A `Function` procedure returns a single value (or possibly an array). A `Function` can be called from another VBA procedure or used in a worksheet formula.

    Here's an example of a `Function` named `AddTwo`:

    ```
    Function AddTwo(arg1, arg2)
        AddTwo = arg1 + arg2
    End Function
    ```

- *Objects:* VBA manipulates objects contained in its host application. (In this case, Excel is the host application.)

  Excel provides you with more than 100 classes of objects to manipulate. Examples of objects include a workbook, a worksheet, a range on a worksheet, a chart, and a drawn rectangle. Many more objects are at your disposal, and you can manipulate them by using VBA code.

  Object classes are arranged in a hierarchy.

  Objects can act as containers for other objects. For example, Excel is an object called `Application`, and it contains other objects, such as `Workbook` and `CommandBar` objects. The `Workbook` object contains other objects, such as `Worksheet` objects and `Chart` objects. A `Worksheet` object contains objects such as `Range` objects, `PivotTable` objects, and so on. The arrangement of these objects is referred to as Excel's *object model.*

- *Collections:* Like objects form a *collection.*

  For example, the `Worksheets` collection consists of all the worksheets in a particular workbook. The `CommandBars` collection consists of all `CommandBar` objects. Collections are objects in themselves.

- *Object hierarchy:* When you refer to a contained or member object, you specify its position in the object hierarchy by using a period (also known as a *dot*) as a separator between the container and the member.

  For example, you can refer to a workbook named `Book1.xlsx` as

  ```
  Application.Workbooks("Book1.xlsx")
  ```

This refers to the `Book1.xlsx` workbook in the `Workbooks` collection. The `Workbooks` collection is contained in the Excel `Application` object. Extending this to another level, you can refer to `Sheet1` in `Book1` as

```
Application.Workbooks("Book1.xlsx").Worksheets("Sheet1")
```

You can take it to still another level and refer to a specific cell as follows:

```
Application.Workbooks("Book1.xlsx").Worksheets("Sheet1").Range("A1")
```

- *Active objects:* If you omit a specific reference to an object, Excel uses the active objects.

  If `Book1` is the active workbook, the preceding reference can be simplified as

```
Worksheets("Sheet1").Range("A1")
```

  If you know that `Sheet1` is the active sheet, you can simplify the reference even more:

```
Range("A1")
```

- *Objects properties:* Objects have *properties.* A property can be thought of as a *setting* for an object. For example, a range object has properties such as `Value` and `Name`. A chart object has properties such as `HasTitle` and `Type`. You can use VBA to determine object properties and also to change them.

  You refer to properties by combining the object with the property, separated by a period. For example, you can refer to the value in cell A1 on `Sheet1` as

```
Worksheets("Sheet1").Range("A1").Value
```

- *VBA variables:* You can assign values to VBA variables. Think of a variable as a name that you can use to store a particular value.

  To assign the value in cell A1 on `Sheet1` to a variable called `Interest`, use the following VBA statement:

```
Interest = Worksheets("Sheet1").Range("A1").Value
```

- *Object methods:* Objects have methods. A *method* is an action that is performed with the object. For example, one of the methods for a `Range` object is `ClearContents`. This method clears the contents of the range.

  You specify methods by combining the object with the method, separated by a period. For example, to clear the contents of cell A1 on the active worksheet, use this:

```
Range("A1").ClearContents
```

- *Standard programming constructs:* VBA also includes all the constructs of modern programming languages, including arrays, looping, and so on.

- *Events:* Some objects recognize specific events, and you can write VBA code that is executed when the event occurs. For example, opening a workbook triggers a `Workbook_Open` event. Changing a cell in a worksheet triggers a `Worksheet_Change` event.

Believe it or not, the preceding section pretty much describes VBA. Now it's just a matter of learning the details.

An Analogy

If you like analogies, here's one for you. It might help you understand the relationships between objects, properties, and methods in VBA. In this analogy, I compare Excel with a fast-food restaurant chain.

The basic unit of Excel is a `Workbook` object. In a fast-food chain, the basic unit is an individual restaurant. With Excel, you can add workbooks and close workbooks, and the set of all the open workbooks is known as `Workbooks` (a collection of `Workbook` objects). Similarly, the management of a fast-food chain can add restaurants and close restaurants — and all the restaurants in the chain can be viewed as the `Restaurants` collection — a collection of `Restaurant` objects.

An Excel workbook is an object, but it also contains other objects, such as worksheets, charts, VBA modules, and so on. Furthermore, each object in a workbook can contain its own objects. For example, a `Worksheet` object can contain `Range` objects, `PivotTable` objects, `Shape` objects, and so on.

Continuing with the analogy, a fast-food restaurant (like a workbook) contains objects such as the `Kitchen`, `DiningArea`, and `Tables` (a collection). Furthermore, management can add or remove objects from the `Restaurant` object. For example, management can add more tables to the `Tables` collection. Each of these objects can contain other objects. For example, the `Kitchen` object has a `Stove` object, `VentilationFan` object, `Chef` object, `Sink` object, and so on.

So far, so good. This analogy seems to work. Let's see whether I can take it further.

Excel objects have properties. For example, a `Range` object has properties such as `Value` and `Name`, and a `Shape` object has properties such as `Width`, and `Height`. Not surprisingly, objects in a fast-food restaurant also have properties. The `Stove` object, for example, has properties such as `Temperature` and `NumberofBurners`. The `VentilationFan` has its own set of properties (`TurnedOn`, `RPM`, and so forth).

Besides properties, Excel's objects also have methods, which perform operations on objects. For example, the `ClearContents` method erases the contents of a `Range` object. An object in a fast-food restaurant also has methods. You can easily envision a `ChangeThermostat` method for a `Stove` object, or a `SwitchOn` method for a `VentilationFan` object.

With Excel, methods sometimes change an object's properties. The `ClearContents` method for a `Range` changes the `Range` `Value` property. Similarly, the `ChangeThermostat` method on a `Stove` object affects its `Temperature` property.

With VBA, you can write procedures to manipulate Excel's objects. In a fast-food restaurant, the management can give orders to manipulate the objects in the restaurants. ("Turn on the stove and switch the ventilation fan to high.") Now is it clear?

Introducing the Visual Basic Editor

All your VBA work is done in the Visual Basic Editor (VBE). The VBE is a separate application that works seamlessly with Excel. By *seamlessly*, I mean that Excel takes care of the details of opening the VBE when you need it. You can't run VBE separately; Excel must be running in order for the VBE to run.

NOTE

VBA modules are stored in workbook files. However, the VBA modules aren't visible unless you activate the VBE.

Displaying Excel's Developer tab

The Excel 2007 Ribbon does not display the Developer tab by default. If you're going to be working with VBA, it's essential that you turn on the Developer tab:

1. Choose Office ➪ Excel Options.

2. In the Excel Options dialog box, click the Popular tab.

3. Place a checkmark next to Show Developer Tab in the Ribbon.

After you perform these steps, Excel displays a new tab, as shown in Figure 7-1.

Figure 7-1: By default, the Developer tab is not displayed.

Activating the VBE

When you're working in Excel, you can switch to the VBE by using either of the following techniques:

- Press Alt+F11.

- Choose Developer ➪ Code ➪ Visual Basic.

In addition, you can access two special modules as follows. (These special VBA modules are used for event handler procedures, which I describe in Chapter 19.)

Part III

What's New in the VBE?

Excel 2007 has dozens of significant new features, including a brand-spanking-new user interface. If you're expecting new things in the VBE, you're out of luck. The Excel 2007 VBE is exactly like the Excel 2003 VBE.

- Right-click a sheet tab and choose View Code (this takes you to the code module for the sheet).

- Right-click a workbook's title bar and choose View Code (this takes you to the code module for the workbook). If the workbook window is maximized in Excel, the title bar is not visible.

Figure 7-2 shows the VBE. Chances are that your VBE window won't look exactly like the window shown in the figure. This window is highly customizable — you can hide windows, change their sizes, dock them, rearrange them, and so on.

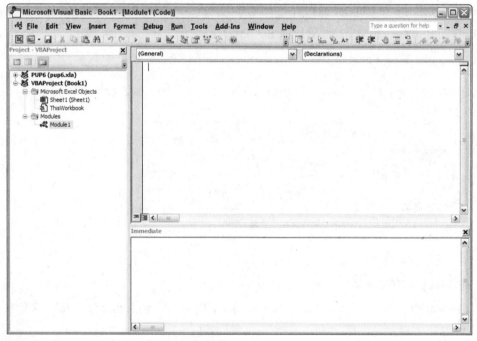

Figure 7-2: The Visual Basic Editor window.

The VBE windows

The VBE has a number of parts. I briefly describe some of the key components in the sections that follow.

VBE MENU BAR

The VBE menu bar works like every other menu bar that you've encountered. It contains commands that you use to work with the various components in the VBE. Also, you'll find that many of the menu commands have shortcut keys associated with them. For example, the View ⇨ Immediate Window command has a shortcut key of Ctrl+G.

TIP

The VBE also features shortcut menus. As you'll discover, you can right-click virtually anything in a VBE window to get a shortcut menu of common commands.

VBE TOOLBARS

The Standard toolbar, which is directly under the menu bar by default, is one of six VBE toolbars available (the menu bar is also considered a toolbar). You can customize toolbars, move them around, display other toolbars, and so forth. Choose View ⇨ Toolbars ⇨ Customize to work with VBE toolbars.

PROJECT EXPLORER WINDOW

The Project Explorer window displays a tree diagram that consists of every workbook that is currently open in Excel (including add-ins and hidden workbooks). Each workbook is known as a *project*. I discuss the Project Explorer window in more detail in the next section ("Working with the Project Explorer").

If the Project Explorer window is not visible, press Ctrl+R. To hide the Project Explorer window, click the Close button in its title bar or right-click anywhere in the Project Explorer window and select Hide from the shortcut menu.

CODE WINDOW

A Code window (sometimes known as a Module window) contains VBA code. Every item in a project's tree has an associated code window. To view a code window for an object, double-click the object in the Project Explorer window. For example, to view the code window for the Sheet1 object, double-click Sheet1 in the Project Explorer window. Unless you've added some VBA code, the Code window is empty.

Another way to view the Code window for an object is to select the object in the Project Explorer window and then click the View Code button in the toolbar at the top of the Project Explorer window.

I discuss Code windows later on in this chapter (see "Working with Code Windows").

IMMEDIATE WINDOW

The Immediate window is most useful for executing VBA statements directly, testing statements, and debugging your code. This window might or might not be visible. If the Immediate window isn't visible, press Ctrl+G. To close the Immediate window, click the Close button in its title bar (or right-click anywhere in the Immediate window and select Hide from the shortcut menu).

Working with the Project Explorer

When you're working in the VBE, each Excel workbook and add-in that's currently open is considered a *project*. You can think of a project as a collection of objects arranged as an expandable tree. You can expand a project by clicking the plus sign (+) at the left of the project's name in the Project Explorer window. You contract a project by clicking the minus sign (–) to the left of a project's name. If you try to expand a project that's protected with a password, you are prompted to enter the password.

 NOTE

The top of the Project Explorer window contains three icons. The third icon, named *Toggle Folder,* controls whether the objects in a project are displayed in a hierarchy or are shown in a single non-hierarchical list.

Figure 7-3 shows a Project Explorer window with three projects listed (one add-in and two workbooks).

Figure 7-3: A Project Explorer window with three projects listed.

 CAUTION

When you activate the VBE, you cannot assume that the code module that's displayed corresponds to the highlighted object in the Project Explorer window. To make sure that you're working in the correct code module, always double-click the object in the Project Explorer window.

If you have many workbooks and add-ins loaded, the Project Explorer window can be a bit overwhelming. Unfortunately, you can't hide projects in the Project Explorer window. However, you probably want to keep the project outlines contracted if you're not working on them.

When viewing the Project Explorer in folder view, every project expands to show at least one node called Microsoft Excel Objects. This node expands to show an item for each worksheet and chart sheet in the workbook (each sheet is considered an object) and another object called `ThisWorkbook` (which represents the `Workbook` object). If the project has any VBA modules, the project listing also shows a Modules node, and the modules are listed there. A project can also contain a node called Forms that contains `UserForm` objects (also known as custom dialog boxes). If your project has any class modules, it displays another node called Class Modules. Similarly, if your project has any references, you see another node called References. The References node is a bit misleading because references can't contain any VBA code.

Adding a new VBA module

To add a new VBA module to a project, select the project's name in the Project Explorer window and choose Insert ⇨ Module. Or you can just right-click the project's name and choose Insert ⇨ Module from the shortcut menu.

When you record a macro, Excel automatically inserts a VBA module to hold the recorded code.

Removing a VBA module

If you need to remove a VBA module or a class module from a project, select the module's name in the Project Explorer window and choose File ⇨ Remove *xxx* (where *xxx* is the name of the module). Or you can right-click the module's name and choose Remove *xxx* from the shortcut menu. You are asked whether you want to export the module before removing it. See the next section for details. You cannot remove code modules associated with the workbook (the `ThisWorkbook` code module) or with a sheet (for example, the `Sheet1` code module).

Exporting and importing objects

Except for those listed under the `References` node, every object in a project can be saved to a separate file. Saving an individual object in a project is called *exporting*. And it stands to reason that you can also *import* objects into a project. Exporting and importing objects might be useful if you want to use a particular object (such as a VBA module or a UserForm) in a different project.

To export an object, select it in the Project Explorer window and choose File ⇨ Export File (or press Ctrl+E). You get a dialog box that asks for a filename. Note that the object remains in the project (only a copy of it is exported). If you export a `UserForm` object, any code associated with the UserForm is also exported.

To import a file into a project, select the project's name in the Project Explorer window and choose File ⇨ Import File. You get a dialog box that asks for a file. You can import only a file that has been exported by choosing the File ⇨ Export File command.

TIP

If you would like to copy a module or UserForm object to another project, it's not really necessary to export and then import the object. Make sure that both projects are open; then simply activate the Project Explorer and drag the object from one project to the other.

Working with Code Windows

When you become proficient with VBA, you'll be spending *lots* of time working in code windows. Each object in a project has an associated code window. To summarize, these objects can be

- The workbook itself (ThisWorkbook in the Project Explorer window)

- A worksheet or chart sheet in a workbook (for example, Sheet1 or Chart1 in the Project Explorer window)

- A VBA module

- A *class module* (a special type of module that lets you create new object classes)

- A UserForm

Minimizing and maximizing windows

Depending on how many workbooks and add-ins are open, the VBE can have lots of code windows, and things can get a bit confusing. Code windows are much like worksheet windows in Excel. You can minimize them, maximize them, hide them, rearrange them, and so on. Most people find it most efficient to maximize the Code window that they're working in. Doing so enables you to see more code and keeps you from getting distracted. To maximize a Code window, click the maximize button in its title bar or just double-click its title bar. To restore a Code window (make it nonmaximized), click the Restore button in its title bar.

Sometimes, you might want to have two or more Code windows visible. For example, you might want to compare the code in two modules or perhaps copy code from one module to another. To view two or more Code windows at once, make sure the active code window isn't maximized. Then drag and resize the windows that you want to view.

Minimizing a code window gets it out of the way. You can also click the Close button in a Code window's title bar to close the window completely. To open it again, just double-click the appropriate object in the Project Explorer window.

The VBE doesn't let you close a workbook. You must reactivate Excel and close it from there. You can, however, use the Immediate window to close a workbook or an add-in. Just activate the Immediate window, type a VBA statement like the one that follows, and press Enter:

```
Workbooks("myaddin.xlam").Close
```

As you'll see, this statement executes the `Close` method of the `Workbook` object, which closes a workbook. In this case, the workbook happens to be an add-in.

Storing VBA code

In general, a code window can hold four types of code:

- `Sub` procedures: A *procedure* is a set of instructions that performs some action.

- `Function` procedures: A *function* is a set of instructions that returns a single value or an array (similar in concept to a worksheet function, such as SUM).

- `Property` procedures: These are special procedures used in class modules.

- Declarations: A *declaration* is information about a variable that you provide to VBA. For example, you can declare the data type for variables you plan to use.

A single VBA module can store any number of `Sub` procedures, `Function` procedures, and declarations. How you organize a VBA module is completely up to you. Some people prefer to keep all their VBA code for an application in a single VBA module; others like to split up the code into several different modules.

NOTE

Although you have lots of flexibility regarding where to store your VBA code, there are some restrictions. Event handler procedures must be located in the Code window for the object that responds to the event. For example, if you write a procedure that executes when the workbook is opened, that procedure must be located in the Code window for the `ThisWorkbook` object, and the procedure must have a special name. This concept will become clearer when I discuss events (Chapter 19) and UserForms (Part IV).

Entering VBA code

Before you can do anything meaningful, you must have some VBA code in a Code window. This VBA code must be within a procedure. A procedure consists of VBA statements. For now, I focus on one type of Code window: a VBA module.

You can add code to a VBA module in three ways:

- *Enter the code manually:* Use your keyboard to type your code.

- *Use the macro-recorder feature:* Use Excel's macro-recorder feature to record your actions and convert them into VBA code.

- *Copy and paste:* Copy the code from another module and paste it into the module that you're working in.

Pause for a Terminology Break

Throughout this book, I use the terms *routine*, *procedure*, and *macro*. Programming people typically use the word *procedure* to describe an automated task. In Excel, a procedure is also known as a *macro*. Technically, a procedure can be a Sub procedure or a Function procedure, both of which are sometimes called *routines*. I use all these terms pretty much interchangeably. There is, however, an important difference between Sub procedures and Function procedures. This distinction becomes apparent in Chapters 9 and 10.

ENTERING CODE MANUALLY

Sometimes, the most direct route is the best one. Entering code directly involves . . . well, entering the code directly. In other words, you type the code by using your keyboard. You can use the Tab key to indent the lines that logically belong together — for example, the conditional statements between an If and an End If statement. This isn't necessary, but it makes the code easier to read, so it's a good habit to acquire.

Entering and editing text in a VBA module works just as you would expect. You can select text, copy it or cut it, and then paste it to another location.

A single instruction in VBA can be as long as you need it to be. For readability's sake, however, you might want to break a lengthy instruction into two or more lines. To do so, end the line with a space followed by an underscore character; then press Enter and continue the instruction on the following line. The following code, for example, is a single VBA statement split over four lines.

```
MsgBox "Can't find " & UCase(SHORTCUTMENUFILE) _
    & vbCrLf & vbCrLf & "The file should be located in " _
    & ThisWorkbook.Path & vbCrLf & vbCrLf _
    & "You may need to reinstall BudgetMan", vbCritical, APPNAME
```

Notice that I indented the last three lines of this statement. Doing so is optional, but it helps clarify the fact that these four lines are, in fact, a single statement.

 TIP

Like Excel, the VBE has multiple levels of Undo and Redo. Therefore, if you find that you deleted an instruction that you shouldn't have, you can click the Undo button (or press Ctrl+Z) repeatedly until the instruction comes back. After undoing, you can click the Redo button (or press Ctrl+Y) to redo changes that were previously undone. This feature can be a lifesaver, so I recommend that you play around with it until you understand how it works.

Try this: Insert a VBA module into a project and then enter the following procedure into the Code window of the module:

```
Sub SayHello()
    Msg = "Is your name " & Application.UserName & "?"
    Ans = MsgBox(Msg, vbYesNo)
    If Ans = vbNo Then
        MsgBox "Oh, never mind."
    Else
        MsgBox "I must be clairvoyant!"
    End If
End Sub
```

Figure 7-4 shows how this looks in a VBA module.

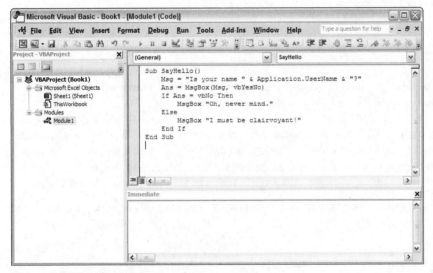

Figure 7-4: Your first VBA procedure.

 NOTE

While you enter the code, notice that the VBE makes some adjustments to the text that you enter. For example, if you omit the space before or after an equal sign (=), VBE inserts the space for you. Also, the color of some of the text is changed. This is all perfectly normal, and you'll appreciate it later.

To execute the `SayHello` procedure, make sure that the cursor is located anywhere within the text that you typed. Then do any of the following:

- Press F5.

- Choose Run ⇨ Run Sub/UserForm.

- Click the Run Sub/UserForm button on the Standard toolbar.

If you entered the code correctly, the procedure executes, and you can respond to a simple dialog box (see Figure 7-5) that displays the username, as listed in Excel's Options dialog box. Notice that Excel is activated when the macro executes. At this point, it's not important that you understand how the code works; that becomes clear later in this chapter and in subsequent chapters.

Figure 7-5: The result of running the procedure in Figure 7-4.

 NOTE

Most of the time, you'll be executing your macros from Excel. However, it's often more efficient to test your macro by running it directly from the VBE.

What you did was write a VBA Sub procedure (also known as a *macro*). When you issued the command to execute the macro, the VBE quickly compiled the code and executed it. In other words, each instruction was evaluated, and Excel simply did what it was told to do. You can execute this macro any number of times, although it tends to lose its appeal after a while.

For the record, this simple procedure uses the following concepts (all of which I cover later in the book):

- Declaring a procedure (the first line)
- Assigning a value to variables (Msg and Ans)
- Concatenating strings (using the & operator)
- Using a built-in VBA function (MsgBox)
- Using built-in VBA constants (vbYesNo and vbNo)
- Using an If-Then-Else construct
- Ending a procedure (the last line)

Not bad for a first effort, eh?

USING THE MACRO RECORDER

Another way to get code into a VBA module is to record your actions by using the Excel macro recorder.

No matter how hard you try, there is absolutely no way to record the SayHello procedure shown previously. As you'll see, recording macros is very useful, but it has some limitations.

In fact, when you record a macro, you almost always need to make some adjustments or enter some code manually.

This next example shows how to record a macro that simply changes the page setup to landscape orientation. If you want to try this, start with a blank workbook and follow these steps:

1. Activate a worksheet in the workbook (any worksheet will do).

2. Choose Developer ➪ Code ➪ Record Macro.

   Excel displays its Record Macro dialog box.

3. Click OK to accept the default setting for the macro.

   Excel automatically inserts a new VBA module into the workbook's VBA project. From this point on, Excel converts your actions into VBA code. Notice that Excel's status bar displays a blue square. You can click that control to stop recording.

4. Choose Page Layout ➪ Page Setup ➪ Orientation ➪ Landscape.

5. Select Developer ➪ Code ➪ Stop Recording or click the blue square in the status bar.

   Excel stops recording your actions.

To take a look at the macro, activate the VBE (pressing Alt+F11 is the easiest way) and locate the project in the Project Explorer window. Double-click the `Modules` node to expand it. Then double-click the `Module1` item to display the code window. (If the project already had a `Module1`, the new macro will be in `Module2`.) The code generated by this single command follows. Remember that code lines preceded by an apostrophe are comments and are not executed.

```
Sub Macro1()
'
' Macro1 Macro
'
'
    With ActiveSheet.PageSetup
        .PrintTitleRows = ""
        .PrintTitleColumns = ""
    End With
    ActiveSheet.PageSetup.PrintArea = ""
    With ActiveSheet.PageSetup
        .LeftHeader = ""
        .CenterHeader = ""
        .RightHeader = ""
        .LeftFooter = ""
        .CenterFooter = ""
        .RightFooter = ""
        .LeftMargin = Application.InchesToPoints(0.7)
        .RightMargin = Application.InchesToPoints(0.7)
        .TopMargin = Application.InchesToPoints(0.75)
```

```
            .BottomMargin = Application.InchesToPoints(0.75)
            .HeaderMargin = Application.InchesToPoints(0.3)
            .FooterMargin = Application.InchesToPoints(0.3)
            .PrintHeadings = False
            .PrintGridlines = False
            .PrintComments = xlPrintNoComments
            .PrintQuality = 600
            .CenterHorizontally = False
            .CenterVertically = False
            .Orientation = xlLandscape
            .Draft = False
            .PaperSize = xlPaperLetter
            .FirstPageNumber = xlAutomatic
            .Order = xlDownThenOver
            .BlackAndWhite = False
            .Zoom = 100
            .PrintErrors = xlPrintErrorsDisplayed
            .OddAndEvenPagesHeaderFooter = False
            .DifferentFirstPageHeaderFooter = False
            .ScaleWithDocHeaderFooter = True
            .AlignMarginsHeaderFooter = True
            .EvenPage.LeftHeader.Text = ""
            .EvenPage.CenterHeader.Text = ""
            .EvenPage.RightHeader.Text = ""
            .EvenPage.LeftFooter.Text = ""
            .EvenPage.CenterFooter.Text = ""
            .EvenPage.RightFooter.Text = ""
            .FirstPage.LeftHeader.Text = ""
            .FirstPage.CenterHeader.Text = ""
            .FirstPage.RightHeader.Text = ""
            .FirstPage.LeftFooter.Text = ""
            .FirstPage.CenterFooter.Text = ""
            .FirstPage.RightFooter.Text = ""
        End With
    End Sub
```

You might be surprised by the amount of code generated by this single command. (I know I was the first time I tried something like this.) Although you changed only one simple setting in the Page Setup tab, Excel generates code that affects dozens of print settings.

This brings up an important concept. The Excel macro recorder is not the most efficient way to generate VBA code. More often than not, the code produced when you record a macro is overkill. Consider the recorded macro that switches to landscape mode. Practically every statement in that macro is extraneous. You can simplify this macro considerably by deleting the extraneous code. This makes the macro easier to read, and the macro also runs faster because it doesn't do things that are unnecessary. In fact, this macro can be simplified to the following:

```
Sub Macro1()
    With ActiveSheet.PageSetup
        .Orientation = xlLandscape
    End With
End Sub
```

I deleted all the code except for the line that sets the Orientation property. Actually, this macro can be simplified even more because the With-End With construct isn't necessary when you're changing only one property:

```
Sub Macro1()
    ActiveSheet.PageSetup.Orientation = xlLandscape
End Sub
```

In this example, the macro changes the Orientation property of the PageSetup object on the active sheet. By the way, xlLandscape is a built-in constant that's provided to make things easier for you. The variable xlLandscape has a value of 2, and xlPortrait has a value of 1. The following macro works the same as the preceding Macro1.

```
Sub Macro1a()
    ActiveSheet.PageSetup.Orientation = 2
End Sub
```

Most would agree that it's easier to remember the name of the constant than the arbitrary numbers. You can use the Help system to learn the relevant constants for a particular command.

You could have entered this procedure directly into a VBA module. To do so, you would have to know which objects, properties, and methods to use. Obviously, it's much faster to record the macro, and this example has a built-in bonus: You also learned that the PageSetup object has an Orientation property.

NOTE

A point that I make clear throughout this book is that recording your actions is perhaps the best way to learn VBA. When in doubt, try recording. Although the result might not be exactly what you want, chances are that it will steer you in the right direction. You can use the Help system to check out the objects, properties, and methods that appear in the recorded code.

CROSS-REFERENCE

I discuss the macro recorder in more detail later in this chapter. See the section, "The Macro Recorder."

Unfortunately, some Excel actions simply can't be recorded. For example, turn on the macro recorder and record your actions while you insert a Shape and apply formatting to it.

You'll find that the recorded macro is completely empty. Why? Because Microsoft didn't deem enabling this type of action important enough to delay the release of Office 2007.

COPYING VBA CODE

So far, I've covered typing code directly into a module and recording your actions to generate VBA code. The final method of getting code into a VBA module is to copy it from another module. For example, you may have written a procedure for one project that would also be useful in your current project. Rather than re-enter the code, you can simply open the workbook, activate the module, and use the normal Clipboard copy-and-paste procedures to copy it into your current VBA module. After you've finished pasting, you can modify the code as necessary.

TIP

As I note previously in this chapter, you can also import to a file an entire module that has been exported.

Customizing the VBE Environment

If you're serious about becoming an Excel programmer, you'll be spending a lot of time with the VBE window. To help make things as comfortable as possible, the VBE provides quite a few customization options.

When the VBE is active, choose Tools ➪ Options. You see a dialog box with four tabs: Editor, Editor Format, General, and Docking. I discuss some of the most useful options on these tabs in the sections that follow. By the way, don't confuse this with the Excel Options dialog box, which you bring up by choosing Office ➪ Excel Options in Excel.

Using the Editor tab

Figure 7-6 shows the options that you access by clicking the Editor tab of the Options dialog box.

AUTO SYNTAX CHECK OPTION

The Auto Syntax Check setting determines whether the VBE pops up a dialog box if it discovers a syntax error while you're entering your VBA code. The dialog box tells you roughly what the problem is. If you don't choose this setting, VBE flags syntax errors by displaying them in a different color from the rest of the code, and you don't have to deal with any dialog boxes popping up on your screen.

I keep this setting turned off because I find the dialog boxes annoying, and I can usually figure out what's wrong with an instruction. But if you're new to VBA, you might find this assistance helpful.

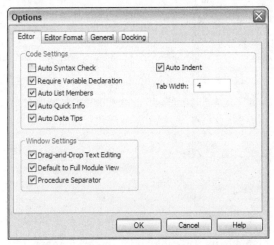

Figure 7-6: The Editor tab of the Options dialog box.

REQUIRE VARIABLE DECLARATION OPTION

If the Require Variable Declaration option is set, VBE inserts the following statement at the beginning of each new VBA module that you insert:

```
Option Explicit
```

If this statement appears in your module, you must explicitly define each variable that you use. This is an excellent habit to get into, although it does require some additional effort on your part. If you don't declare your variables, they will all be of the Variant data type, which is flexible but not efficient in terms of storage or speed. I discuss variable declaration in more depth in Chapter 8.

NOTE

Changing the Require Variable Declaration option affects only new modules, not existing modules.

AUTO LIST MEMBERS OPTION

If the Auto List Members option is set, VBE provides some help when you're entering your VBA code by displaying a list of member items for an object. These items include methods and properties for the object that you typed.

This option is very helpful, and I always keep it turned on. Figure 7-7 shows an example of Auto List Members (which will make a lot more sense when you actually start writing VBA code). In this example, VBE is displaying a list of members for the Application object. You can just select an item from the list and press Tab, thus avoiding typing it (or, double-click an item). Using the Auto List Members list also ensures that the item is spelled correctly.

Part III

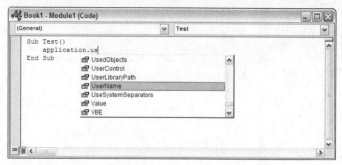

Figure 7-7: An example of Auto List Members.

Auto Quick Info option

If the Auto Quick Info option is set, the VBE displays information about the arguments available for functions, properties, and methods while you type. This can be very helpful, and I always leave this setting on. Figure 7-8 shows this feature in action. It's displaying the syntax for the Cells property.

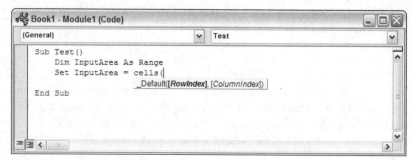

Figure 7-8: An example of Auto Quick Info offering help about the Cells property.

Auto Data Tips option

If the Auto Data Tips option is set, you can hover your mouse pointer over a variable, and VBE displays the value of the variable. This technique works only when the procedure is paused while debugging. When you enter the wonderful world of debugging, you'll definitely appreciate this option. I always keep this option turned on.

Auto Indent option

The Auto Indent setting determines whether VBE automatically indents each new line of code by the same amount as the previous line. I'm a big fan of using indentations in my code, so I keep this option on. You can also specify the number of characters to indent; the default is four.

TIP

Use the Tab key, not the space bar, to indent your code. Using the Tab key results in more consistent spacing. In addition, you can use Shift+Tab to unindent a line of code. These keys also work if you select more than one statement.

DRAG-AND-DROP TEXT EDITING OPTION

The Drag-and-Drop Text Editing option, when enabled, lets you copy and move text by dragging and dropping. I keep this option turned on, but I never use drag-and-drop editing. I prefer to use keyboard shortcuts for copying and pasting.

DEFAULT TO FULL MODULE VIEW OPTION

The Default to Full Module View option specifies how procedures are viewed. If this option is set, procedures in the code window appear as a single scrollable window. If this option is turned off, you can see only one procedure at a time. I keep this setting turned on.

PROCEDURE SEPARATOR OPTION

When the Procedure Separator option is turned on, the VBE displays separator bars between procedures in a code window (assuming that the Default to Full Module View option is also selected). I like the visual cues that show where my procedures end, so I keep this option turned on.

Using the Editor Format tab

Figure 7-9 shows the Editor Format tab of the Options dialog box. The options on this tab control the appearance of the VBE itself.

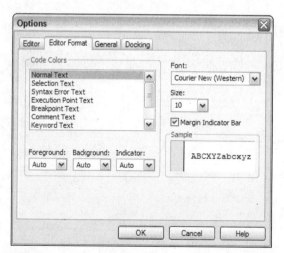

Figure 7-9: The Editor Format tab of the Options dialog box.

CODE COLORS OPTION

The Code Colors option lets you set the text color (foreground and background) and the indicator color displayed for various elements of VBA code. This is largely a matter of individual preference. Personally, I find the default colors to be just fine. But for a change of scenery, I occasionally play around with these settings.

FONT OPTION

The Font option lets you select the font that's used in your VBA modules. For best results, stick with a fixed-width font (monofont) such as Courier New. In a *fixed-width font*, all characters are exactly the same width. This makes your code much more readable because the characters are nicely aligned vertically and you can easily distinguish multiple spaces.

SIZE SETTING

The Size setting specifies the size of the font in the VBA modules. This setting is a matter of personal preference determined by your video display resolution and your eyesight. The default size of 10 (points) works for me.

MARGIN INDICATOR BAR OPTION

The Margin Indicator Bar option controls the display of the vertical margin indicator bar in your modules. You should keep this turned on; otherwise, you won't be able to see the helpful graphical indicators when you're debugging your code.

Using the General tab

Figure 7-10 shows the options available under the General tab in the Options dialog box. In almost every case, the default settings are just fine.

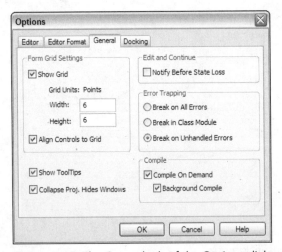

Figure 7-10: The General tab of the Options dialog box.

CROSS-REFERENCE

The Error Trapping setting determines what happens when an error is encountered. If you write any error-handling code, make sure that the Break on Unhandled Errors option is set. If the Break on All Errors option is set, error-handling code is ignored (which is hardly ever what you want). I discuss error-handling techniques in Chapter 9.

Using the Docking tab

Figure 7-11 shows the Docking tab of the Options dialog box. These options determine how the various windows in the VBE behave. When a window is docked, it is fixed in place along one of the edges of the VBE window. This makes it much easier to identify and locate a particular window. If you turn off all docking, you have a big mess of windows that are very confusing. Generally, you'll find that the default settings work fine.

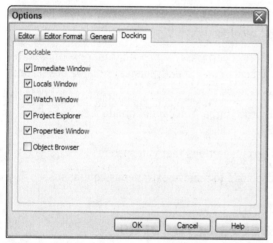

Figure 7-11: The Docking tab of the Options dialog box.

To dock a window, just drag it to the desired location. For example, you might want to dock the Project Explorer window to the left side of the screen. Just drag its title bar to the left, and you see an outline that shows it docked. Release the mouse and it is docked.

NOTE

Docking windows in the VBE has always been a bit problematic. Often, you find that some windows simply refuse to be docked. I've found that if you persist long enough, the procedure will eventually work. Unfortunately, I don't have any secret window-docking techniques.

The Macro Recorder

Earlier in this chapter, I discuss the *macro recorder,* which is a tool that converts your Excel actions into VBA code. This section covers the macro recorder in more detail.

NOTE

This is another reminder to make sure that Excel displays the Developer tab in the Ribbon. If you don't see this tab, refer to " Displaying Excel's Developer tab" earlier in this chapter.

The macro recorder is an *extremely* useful tool, but remember the following points:

- The macro recorder is appropriate only for simple macros or for recording a small part of a more complex macro.

- Not all the actions you make in Excel get recorded.

- The macro recorder cannot generate code that performs *looping* (that is, repeating statements), assigns variables, executes statements conditionally, displays dialog boxes, and so on.

- The macro recorder always creates Sub procedures. You cannot create a Function procedure by using the macro recorder.

- The code that is generated depends on certain settings that you specify.

- You'll often want to clean up the recorded code to remove extraneous commands.

What the macro recorder actually records

The Excel macro recorder translates your mouse and keyboard actions into VBA code. I could probably write several pages describing how this is done, but the best way to show you is by example. Follow these steps:

1. Start with a blank workbook.

2. Make sure that the Excel window is not maximized. You don't want it to fill the entire screen.

3. Press Alt+F11 to activate the VBE window.

   Note: Make sure that this window is not maximized. Otherwise, you won't be able to see the VBE window and Excel's window at the same time.

4. Resize and arrange Excel's window and the VBE window so both are visible. (For best results, minimize any other applications that are running.)

5. Activate Excel, choose Developer ➪ Code ➪ Record Macro and then click OK to start the macro recorder.

6. Activate the VBE window.

7. In the Project Explorer window, double-click `Module1` to display that module in the code window.

8. Close the Project Explorer window in the VBE to maximize the view of the code window.

Your screen layout should look something like the example in Figure 7-12. The size of the windows depends on your video resolution.

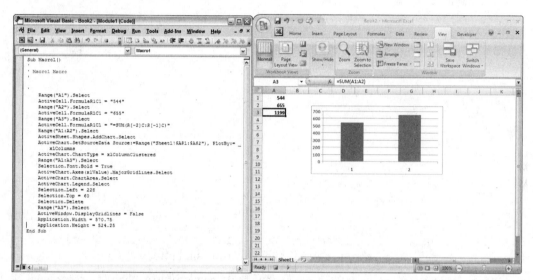

Figure 7-12: A convenient window arrangement for watching the macro recorder do its thing.

Now move around in the worksheet and select various Excel commands. Watch while the code is generated in the window that displays the VBA module. Select cells, enter data, format cells, use the Ribbon commands, create a chart, manipulate graphic objects, and so on. I guarantee that you'll be enlightened while you watch the code being spit out before your very eyes.

Relative or absolute?

When recording your actions, Excel normally records *absolute references* to cells. In other words, when you select a cell, it will remember that exact cell (not the cell relative to the current active cell). To demonstrate how this works, perform these steps and examine the code:

1. Activate a worksheet and start the macro recorder.

2. Activate cell B1.

3. Enter **Jan** into cell B1.

4. Move to cell C1 and enter **Feb.**

5. Continue this process until you've entered the first six months of the year in B1:G1.

6. Click cell B1 to activate it again.

7. Stop the macro recorder and examine the new code in the VBE.

Excel generates the following code:

```
Sub Macro1()
    Range("B1").Select
    ActiveCell.FormulaR1C1 = "Jan"
    Range("C1").Select
    ActiveCell.FormulaR1C1 = "Feb"
    Range("D1").Select
    ActiveCell.FormulaR1C1 = "Mar"
    Range("E1").Select
    ActiveCell.FormulaR1C1 = "Apr"
    Range("F1").Select
    ActiveCell.FormulaR1C1 = "May"
    Range("G1").Select
    ActiveCell.FormulaR1C1 = "Jun"
    Range("B1").Select
End Sub
```

To execute this macro, choose Developer ➪ Code ➪ Macros (or press Alt+F8) and select `Macro1` (or whatever the macro is named) and click the Run button.

The macro, when executed, re-creates the actions that you performed when you recorded it. These same actions occur regardless of which cell is active when you execute the macro. Recording a macro using absolute references always produces the exact same results.

In some cases, however, you want your recorded macro to work with cell locations in a *relative* manner. For example, you'd probably want such a macro to start entering the month names in the active cell. In such a case, you want to use relative recording to record the macro.

You control how references are recorded by using the Developer ➪ Code ➪ Use Relative References button. This button is a toggle. When the button appears in a different color, the macro recorder records relative references. When the button appears in the standard color, the macro recorder records absolute references. You can change the recording method at any time, even in the middle of recording.

To see how this works, erase the cells in B1:D1 and then perform the following steps:

1. Activate cell B1.

2. Choose Developer ➪ Code ➪ Record Macro.

3. Click OK to begin recording.

4. Click the Use Relative Reference button to change the recording mode to relative.

After you click this button, it appears in a different color.

5. Enter the first six months' names in B1:G1, as in the previous example.

6. Select cell B1.

7. Stop the macro recorder.

With the recording mode set to relative, the code that Excel generates is quite different:

```
Sub Macro2()
    ActiveCell.FormulaR1C1 = "Jan"
    ActiveCell.Offset(0, 1).Range("A1").Select
    ActiveCell.FormulaR1C1 = "Feb"
    ActiveCell.Offset(0, 1).Range("A1").Select
    ActiveCell.FormulaR1C1 = "Mar"
    ActiveCell.Offset(0, 1).Range("A1").Select
    ActiveCell.FormulaR1C1 = "Apr"
    ActiveCell.Offset(0, 1).Range("A1").Select
    ActiveCell.FormulaR1C1 = "May"
    ActiveCell.Offset(0, 1).Range("A1").Select
    ActiveCell.FormulaR1C1 = "Jun"
    ActiveCell.Offset(0, -5).Range("A1").Select
End Sub
```

You can execute this macro by activating a worksheet and then choosing the Developer ⇨ Code ⇨ Macros command. Select the macro name and then click the Run button.

You'll also notice that I varied the procedure slightly in this example: I activated the beginning cell *before* I started recording. This is an important step when you record macros that use the active cell as a base.

Although it looks rather complicated, this macro is actually quite simple. The first statement simply enters Jan into the active cell. (It uses the active cell because it's not preceded by a statement that selects a cell.) The next statement uses the Select method (along with the Offset property) to move the selection one cell to the right. The next statement inserts more text, and so on. Finally, the original cell is selected by calculating a relative offset rather than an absolute cell. Unlike the preceding macro, this one always starts entering text in the active cell.

 NOTE

You'll notice that this macro generates code that appears to reference cell A1 — which might seem strange because cell A1 was not even involved in the macro. This is simply a by-product of how the macro recorder works. (I discuss the Offset property later in this chapter.) At this point, all you need to know is that the macro works as it should.

The point here is that the recorder has two distinct modes, and you need to be aware of which mode you're recording in. Otherwise, the result will not be what you expected.

By the way, the code generated by Excel is more complex than it need be, and it's not even the most efficient way to code the operation. The macro that follows, which I entered manually, is a simpler and faster way to perform this same operation. This example demonstrates that VBA doesn't have to select a cell before it puts information into it — an important concept that can speed things up considerably.

```
Sub Macro3()
    ActiveCell.Offset(0, 0) = "Jan"
    ActiveCell.Offset(0, 1) = "Feb"
    ActiveCell.Offset(0, 2) = "Mar"
    ActiveCell.Offset(0, 3) = "Apr"
    ActiveCell.Offset(0, 4) = "May"
    ActiveCell.Offset(0, 5) = "Jun"
End Sub
```

In fact, this macro can be made even more efficient by using the With-End With construct:

```
Sub Macro4()
    With ActiveCell
        .Offset(0, 0) = "Jan"
        .Offset(0, 1) = "Feb"
        .Offset(0, 2) = "Mar"
        .Offset(0, 3) = "Apr"
        .Offset(0, 4) = "May"
        .Offset(0, 5) = "Jun"
    End With
End Sub
```

Or, if you're a VBA guru, you can impress your colleagues by using a single statement:

```
Sub Macro5()
    ActiveCell.Resize(,6)=Array("Jan","Feb","Mar","Apr","May","Jun")
End Sub
```

Recording options

When you record your actions to create VBA code, you have several options in the Record Macro dialog box. The following paragraphs describe your options.

MACRO NAME

You can enter a name for the procedure that you are recording. By default, Excel uses the names Macro1, Macro2, and so on for each macro that you record. I usually just accept the default name and change the name of the procedure later. You, however, might prefer to name the macro before you record it. The choice is yours.

The Personal Macro Workbook

When you record a macro, one of your options is to record it to your Personal Macro Workbook. If you create some VBA macros that you find particularly useful, you might want to store these routines on your Personal Macro Workbook. This is a workbook named `Personal.xlsb` that is stored in your XLStart directory. Whenever you start Excel, this workbook is loaded, and you have access to the macros stored in the workbook. `Personal.xlsb` a hidden workbook, so it's out of your way when you're working in Excel.

The `Personal.xlsb` file doesn't exist until you record a macro to it.

SHORTCUT KEY

The Shortcut key option lets you execute the macro by pressing a shortcut key combination. For example, if you enter **w** (lowercase), you can execute the macro by pressing Ctrl+W. If you enter **W** (uppercase), the macro comes alive when you press Ctrl+Shift+W. Keep in mind that a shortcut key assigned to a macro overrides a built-in shortkey key (if one exists). For example, if you assign Ctrl+B to a macro, you won't be able to use the key combination to toggle the bold attribute in cells.

You can always add or change a shortcut key at any time, so you don't need to set this option while recording a macro.

STORE MACRO IN

The Store Macro In option tells Excel where to store the macro that it records. By default, Excel puts the recorded macro in a module in the active workbook. If you prefer, you can record it in a new workbook (Excel opens a blank workbook) or in your Personal Macro Workbook. (Read more about this in the sidebar, "The Personal Macro Workbook.")

NOTE

Excel remembers your choice, so the next time you record a macro, it defaults to the same location you used previously.

Cleaning up recorded macros

Earlier in this chapter, you see how recording your actions while you issue a single command (the Page Layout ⇨ Page Setup ⇨ Orientation command) produces an enormous amount of VBA code. This is an example of how, in many cases, the recorded code includes extraneous commands that you can delete.

About the Code Examples

Throughout this book, I present many small snippets of VBA code to make a point or to provide an example. Often, this code might consist of just a single statement. In some cases, the example consists of only an *expression*, which isn't a valid instruction by itself.

For example, the following is an expression:

```
Range("A1").Value
```

To test an expression, you must evaluate it. The MsgBox function is a handy tool for this:

```
MsgBox Range("A1").Value
```

To try out these examples, put the statement within a procedure in a VBA module, like this:

```
Sub Test()
' statement goes here
End Sub
```

Then put the cursor anywhere within the procedure and press F5 to execute it. Also, make sure that the code is being executed within the proper context. For example, if a statement refers to Sheet1, make sure that the active workbook actually has a sheet named Sheet1.

If the code is just a single statement, you can use the VBE Immediate window. The Immediate window is very useful for executing a statement "immediately" — without having to create a procedure. If the Immediate window is not displayed, press Ctrl+G in the VBE.

Just type the VBA statement in the Immediate window and press Enter. To evaluate an expression in the Immediate window, precede the expression with a question mark (?). The question mark is a shortcut for Print. For example, you can type the following into the Immediate window:

```
? Range("A1").Value
```

The result of this expression is displayed in the next line of the Immediate window.

It's also important to understand that the macro recorder doesn't always generate the most efficient code. If you examine the generated code, you see that Excel generally records what is selected (that is, an object) and then uses the Selection object in subsequent statements. For example, here's what is recorded if you select a range of cells and then use some buttons on the Home tab to change the numeric formatting and apply bold and italic:

```
Range("A1:C5").Select
Selection.Style = "Comma"
Selection.Font.Bold = True
Selection.Font.Italic = True
```

The recorded VBA code works, but it's just one way to perform these actions. You can also use the more efficient `With-End With` construct, as follows:

```
Range("A1:C5").Select
With Selection
    .Style = "#,##0.00"
    .Font.Bold = True
    .Font.Italic = True
End With
```

Or you can avoid the `Select` method altogether and write the code even more efficiently, like this:

```
With Range("A1:C5")
    .Style = "#,##0.00"
    .Font.Bold = True
    .Font.Italic = True
End With
```

If speed is essential in your application, you always want to examine any recorded VBA code closely to make sure that it's as efficient as possible.

You, of course, need to understand VBA thoroughly before you start cleaning up your recorded macros. But for now, just be aware that recorded VBA code isn't always the best, most efficient code.

About Objects and Collections

If you've worked through the first part of this chapter, you have an overview of VBA and you know the basics of working with VBA modules in the VBE. You've also seen some VBA code and were exposed to concepts like objects and properties. This section gives you some additional details about objects and collections of objects.

When you work with VBA, you must understand the concept of objects and Excel's object model. It helps to think of objects in terms of a *hierarchy*. At the top of this model is the `Application` object — in this case, Excel itself. But if you're programming in VBA with Microsoft Word, the `Application` object is Word.

The object hierarchy

The `Application` object (that is, Excel) contains other objects. Here are a few examples of objects contained in the `Application` object:

- `Workbooks` (a collection of all `Workbook` objects)
- `Windows` (a collection of all `Window` objects)
- `AddIns` (a collection of all `AddIn` objects)

Some objects can contain other objects. For example, the `Workbooks` collection consists of all open `Workbook` objects, and a `Workbook` object contains other objects, a few of which are as follows:

- `Worksheets` (a collection of `Worksheet` objects)
- `Charts` (a collection of `Chart` objects)
- `Names` (a collection of `Name` objects)

Each of these objects, in turn, can contain other objects. The `Worksheets` collection consists of all `Worksheet` objects in a `Workbook`. A `Worksheet` object contains many other objects, which include the following:

- `ChartObjects` (a collection of `ChartObject` objects)
- `Range`
- `PageSetup`
- `PivotTables` (a collection of `PivotTable` objects)

If this seems confusing, trust me, it *will* make sense, and you'll eventually realize that this object hierarchy setup is quite logical and well structured. By the way, the complete Excel object model is covered in the Help system.

About collections

Another key concept in VBA programming is collections. A *collection* is a group of objects of the same class, and a collection is itself an object. As I note earlier, `Workbooks` is a collection of all `Workbook` objects currently open. `Worksheets` is a collection of all `Worksheet` objects contained in a particular `Workbook` object. You can work with an entire collection of objects or with an individual object in a collection. To reference a single object from a collection, you put the object's name or index number in parentheses after the name of the collection, like this:

```
Worksheets("Sheet1")
```

If `Sheet1` is the first worksheet in the collection, you could also use the following reference:

```
Worksheets(1)
```

You refer to the second worksheet in a `Workbook` as `Worksheets(2)`, and so on.

There is also a collection called `Sheets`, which is made up of all sheets in a workbook, whether they're worksheets or chart sheets. If `Sheet1` is the first sheet in the workbook, you can reference it as follows:

```
Sheets(1)
```

Referring to objects

When you refer to an object using VBA, you often must qualify the object by connecting object names with a period (also known as a *dot operator*). What if you had two workbooks open and they both had a worksheet named Sheet1? The solution is to qualify the reference by adding the object's container, like this:

```
Workbooks("Book1").Worksheets("Sheet1")
```

Without the workbook qualifier, VBA would look for Sheet1 in the active workbook.

To refer to a specific range (such as cell A1) on a worksheet named Sheet1 in a workbook named Book1, you can use the following expression:

```
Workbooks("Book1").Worksheets("Sheet1").Range("A1")
```

The fully qualified reference for the preceding example also includes the Application object, as follows:

```
Application.Workbooks("Book1").Worksheets("Sheet1").Range("A1")
```

Most of the time, however, you can omit the Application object in your references; it is assumed. If the Book1 object is the active workbook, you can even omit that object reference and use this:

```
Worksheets("Sheet1").Range("A1")
```

And — I think you know where I'm going with this — if Sheet1 is the active worksheet, you can use an even simpler expression:

```
Range("A1")
```

 NOTE

Contrary to what you might expect, Excel does not have an object that refers to an individual cell that is called Cell. A single cell is simply a Range object that happens to consist of just one element.

Simply referring to objects (as in these examples) doesn't do anything. To perform anything meaningful, you must read or modify an object's properties or else specify a method to be used with an object.

Properties and Methods

It's easy to be overwhelmed with properties and methods; there are literally thousands available. In this section, I describe how to access properties and methods of objects.

Object properties

Every object has properties. For example, a `Range` object has a property called `Value`. You can write VBA code to display the `Value` property or write VBA code to set the `Value` property to a specific value. Here's a procedure that uses the VBA `MsgBox` function to pop up a box that displays the value in cell A1 on `Sheet1` of the active workbook:

```
Sub ShowValue()
    Msgbox Worksheets("Sheet1").Range("A1").Value
End Sub
```

 NOTE

The VBA `MsgBox` function provides an easy way to display results while your VBA code is executing. I use it extensively throughout this book.

The code in the preceding example displays the current setting of the `Value` property of a specific cell: cell A1 on a worksheet named `Sheet1` in the active workbook. Note that if the active workbook does not have a sheet named `Sheet1`, the macro generates an error.

What if you want to change the `Value` property? The following procedure changes the value displayed in cell A1 by changing the cell's `Value` property:

```
Sub ChangeValue()
    Worksheets("Sheet1").Range("A1").Value = 123.45
End Sub
```

After executing this routine, cell A1 on `Sheet1` has the value 123.45.

You might want to enter these procedures into a module and experiment with them.

 NOTE

Most objects have a default property. For a `Range` object, the default property is the `Value` property. Therefore, you can omit the `.Value` part from the preceding code, and it has the same effect. However, it's usually considered good programming practice to include the property in your code, even if it is the default property.

The statement that follows accesses the `HasFormula` and the `Formula` properties of a `Range` object.

```
If Range("A1").HasFormula Then MsgBox Range("A1").Formula
```

I use an `If-Then` construct to display a message box conditionally: If the cell has a formula, then display the formula by accessing the `Formula` property. If cell A1 does not have a formula, nothing happens.

The `Formula` property is a read-write property, so you can also specify a formula by using VBA:

```
Range("D12").Formula = "=RAND()*100"
```

Object methods

In addition to properties, objects also have methods. A *method* is an action that you perform with an object. Here's a simple example that uses the `Clear` method on a `Range` object. After you execute this procedure, A1:C3 on `Sheet1` is empty and all cell formatting is removed.

```
Sub ZapRange()
    Worksheets("Sheet1").Range("A1:C3").Clear
End Sub
```

Specifying Arguments for Methods and Properties

An issue that often leads to confusion among new VBA programmers concerns arguments for methods and properties. Some methods use arguments to further clarify the action to be taken, and some properties use arguments to further specify the property value. In some cases, one or more of the arguments are optional.

If a method uses arguments, place the arguments after the name of the method, separated by commas. If the method uses optional arguments, you can insert blank placeholders for the optional arguments. Read on to discover how to insert these placeholders.

Consider the `Protect` method for a workbook object. Check the Help system, and you'll find that the `Protect` method takes three arguments: password, structure, and windows. These arguments correspond to the options in the Protect Workbook dialog box.

If you want to protect a workbook named `MyBook.xlsx`, for example, you might use a statement like this:

```
Workbooks("MyBook.xlsx").Protect "xyzzy", True, False
```

In this case, the workbook is protected with a password (argument 1). Its structure is protected (argument 2) but not its windows (argument 3).

If you don't want to assign a password, you can use a statement like this:

```
Workbooks("MyBook.xlsx").Protect , True, False
```

continued

continued

Notice that the first argument is omitted and that I specified the placeholder by using a comma.

Another approach, which makes your code more readable, is to use named arguments. Here's an example of how you use named arguments for the preceding example:

```
Workbooks("MyBook.xlsx").Protect Structure:=True, Windows:=False
```

Using named arguments is a good idea, especially for methods that have many optional arguments and also when you need to use only a few of them. When you use named arguments, there is no need to use a placeholder for missing arguments.

For properties (and methods) that return a value, you must use parentheses around the arguments. For example, the Address property of a Range object takes five arguments, all of which are optional. Because the Address property returns a value, the following statement is not valid because the parentheses are omitted:

```
MsgBox Range("A1").Address False    ' invalid
```

The proper syntax for such a statement requires parentheses, as follows:

```
MsgBox Range("A1").Address(False)
```

The statement could also be written by using a named argument:

```
MsgBox Range("A1").Address(rowAbsolute:=False)
```

These nuances will become clearer as you gain more experience with VBA.

If you'd like to delete the values in a range but keep the formatting, use the ClearContents method of the Range object.

Most methods also take arguments to define the action further. Here's an example that copies cell A1 to cell B1 by using the Copy method of the Range object. In this example, the Copy method has one argument (the destination of the copy). Notice that I use the line continuation character sequence (a space followed by an underscore) in this example. You can omit the line continuation sequence and type the statement on a single line.

```
Sub CopyOne()
    Worksheets("Sheet1").Range("A1").Copy _
        Worksheets("Sheet1").Range("B1")
End Sub
```

The Comment Object: A Case Study

To help you better understand the properties and methods available for an object, I focus on a particular object: the Comment object. In Excel, you create a Comment object when you choose the Review ⇨ Comments ⇨ New Comment command to enter a cell comment. In the sections that follow, you get a feel for working with objects.

Viewing Help for the Comment object

One way to learn about a particular object is to look it up in the Help system. Figure 7-13 shows some Help topics for the Comment object. I found this Help screen by typing **comment** in the VBE Type a Question for Help box (to the right of the menu bar). Notice that the Help Table of Contents displays the properties and methods for this object.

Properties of a Comment object

The Comment object has five properties. Table 7-1 contains a list of these properties, along with a brief description of each. If a property is *read-only*, your VBA code can read the property but cannot change it.

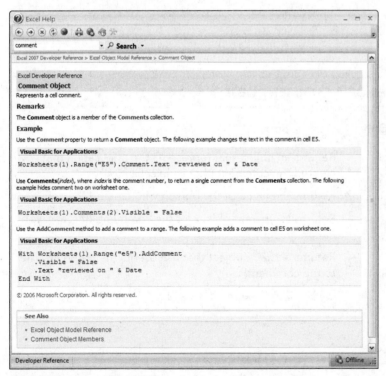

Figure 7-13: The main help screen for the Comment object.

Using the Help System

The easiest way to get specific help about a particular object, property, or method is to type the word in a code window and press F1. If there is any ambiguity about the word that you typed, you get a dialog box like the one shown in the following figure.

Unfortunately, the items listed in the dialog box are not always clear, so it may require some trial and error to locate the correct help topic. The dialog box in the figure appears when you type Comment and then press F1. In this case, although `Comment` is an object, it may behave like a property. Clicking the first item displays the help topic for the `Comment` object; clicking the second item displays the help topic for the `Comment` property.

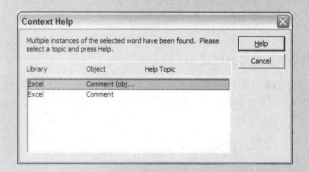

TABLE 7-1   PROPERTIES OF A COMMENT OBJECT

Property	Read-Only	Description
`Application`	Yes	Returns an object that represents the application that created the comment (that is, Excel).
`Author`	Yes	Returns the name of the person who created the comment.
`Parent`	Yes	Returns the parent object for the comment. (It is always a `Range` object.)
`Shape`	Yes	Returns a `Shape` object that represents the shape attached to the comment.
`Visible`	No	Is `True` if the comment is visible.

Methods of a Comment object

Table 7-2 shows the methods that you can use with a `Comment` object. Again, these methods perform common operations that you may have performed manually with a comment at some point . . . but you probably never thought of these operations as methods.

TABLE 7-2   METHODS OF A COMMENT OBJECT

Method	Description
Delete	Deletes a comment.
Next	Returns a `Comment` object that represents the next comment in the worksheet.
Previous	Returns a `Comment` object that represents the previous comment in the worksheet.
Text	Returns or sets the text in a comment (takes three arguments).

NOTE
You might be surprised to see that `Text` is a method rather than a property. This leads to an important point: The distinction between properties and methods isn't always clear-cut, and the object model isn't perfectly consistent. In fact, it's not really important that you distinguish between properties and methods. As long as you get the syntax correct, it doesn't matter whether a word in your code is a property or a method.

The Comments collection

Recall that a collection is a group of like objects. Every worksheet has a `Comments` collection, which consists of all `Comment` objects on the worksheet. If the worksheet has no comments, this collection is empty. Comments appear in the collection based on their position in the worksheet: Left-to-right and then top-to-bottom.

For example, the following code refers to the first comment on `Sheet1` of the active workbook:

```
Worksheets("Sheet1").Comments(1)
```

The following statement displays the text contained in the first comment on `Sheet1`:

```
MsgBox Worksheets("Sheet1").Comments(1).Text
```

Unlike most objects, a `Comment` object does not have a `Name` property. Therefore, to refer to a specific comment, you must either use an index number or (more frequently) use the `Comment` property of a `Range` object to return a specific comment.

The `Comments` collection is also an object and has its own set of properties and methods. For example, the `Comments` collection has a `Count` property that stores the number of items in the collection — which is the number of `Comment` objects in the active worksheet. The following statement displays the total number of comments on the active worksheet.

```
MsgBox ActiveSheet.Comments.Count
```

The next example shows the address of the cell that has the first comment:

```
MsgBox ActiveSheet.Comments(1).Parent.Address
```

Here, `Comments(1)` returns the first `Comment` object in the `Comments` collection. The `Parent` property of the `Comment` object returns its container, which is a `Range` object. The message box displays the `Address` property of the Range. The net effect is that the statement displays the address of the cell that contains the first comment.

You can also loop through all the comments on a sheet by using the `For Each–Next` construct. (Looping is explained in Chapter 8.) Here's an example that displays a separate message box for each comment on the active worksheet:

```
For Each cmt in ActiveSheet.Comments
    MsgBox cmt.Text
Next cmt
```

If you'd rather not deal with a series of message boxes, use this procedure to print the comments to the Immediate window in the VBE:

```
For Each cmt in ActiveSheet.Comments
    Debug.Print cmt.Text
Next cmt
```

About the Comment property

In this section, I've been discussing the `Comment` object. If you dig through the Help system, you'll find that a `Range` object has a property named `Comment`. If the cell contains a comment, the `Comment` *property* returns a `Comment` *object*. For example, the following statement refers to the `Comment` object in cell A1:

```
Range("A1").Comment
```

If this were the first comment on the sheet, you could refer to the same `Comment` object as follows:

```
ActiveSheet.Comments(1)
```

To display the comment in cell A1 in a message box, use a statement like this:

```
MsgBox Range("A1").Comment.Text
```

If cell A1 does not contain a comment, this statement generates an error.

NOTE
The fact that a property can return an object is a very important concept — a difficult one to grasp, perhaps, but critical to mastering VBA.

Objects within a Comment object

Working with properties is confusing at first because some properties actually return objects. Suppose that you want to determine the background color of a particular comment on Sheet1. If you look through the list of properties for a Comment object, you won't find anything that relates to color. Rather, you must do this:

1. Use the Comment object's Shape property to return the Shape object that's contained in the comment.

2. Use the Shape object's Fill property to return a FillFormat object.

3. Use the FillFormat object's ForeColor property to return a ColorFormat object.

4. Use the ColorFormat object's RGB property to get the color value.

Put another way, getting at the interior color for a Comment object involves accessing other objects contained in the Comment object. Here's a look at the object hierarchy that's involved:

```
Application (Excel)
  Workbook object
   Worksheet object
    Comment object
     Shape object
      FillFormat object
       ColorFormat object
```

I'll be the first to admit it: This can get very confusing! But, as an example of the elegance of VBA, the code to change the color of a comment can be written with a single statement:

```
Worksheets("Sheet1").Comments(1).Shape.Fill.ForeColor _
    .RGB = RGB(0, 255, 0)
```

Or, if you use the SchemeColor property (which ranges from 0 to 80), the code is:

```
Worksheets("Sheet1").Comments(1).Shape.Fill.ForeColor _
    .SchemeColor = 12
```

Part III

This type of referencing is certainly not intuitive at first, but it will eventually make sense. Fortunately, recording your actions in Excel almost always yields some insights regarding the hierarchy of the objects involved.

By the way, to change the color of the text in a comment, you need to access the `Comment` object's `TextFrame` object, which contains the `Characters` object, which contains the `Font` object. Then you have access to the `Font` object's `Color` or `ColorIndex` properties. Here's an example that sets `ColorIndex` property to 5:

```
Worksheets("Sheet1").Comments(1) _
  .Shape.TextFrame.Characters.Font.ColorIndex = 5
```

CROSS-REFERENCE
Refer to Chapter 30 for more information on colors.

Determining whether a cell has a comment

The following statement displays the comment in cell A1 of the active sheet:

```
MsgBox Range("A1").Comment.Text
```

If cell A1 does not have a comment, executing this statement generates a cryptic error message: `Object variable or With block variable not set`.

To determine whether a particular cell has a comment, you can write code to check whether the `Comment` object is `Nothing`. (Yes, `Nothing` is a valid keyword.) The following statement displays `True` if cell A1 does not have a comment:

```
MsgBox Range("A1").Comment Is Nothing
```

Note that I use the `Is` keyword and not an equal sign.

You can take this one step further and write a statement that displays the cell comment only if the cell actually has a comment (and does not generate an error if the cell lacks a comment). The statement that follows accomplishes this task:

```
If Not Range("A1").Comment Is Nothing Then _
  MsgBox Range("A1").Comment.Text
```

Notice that I used the `Not` keyword, which negates the `True` value that's returned if the cell has no comment. The statement, in essence, uses a double-negative to test a condition: If the comment is not nothing, then display it. If this is confusing, think about it for a while and it will make sense.

Adding a new Comment object

You may have noticed that the list of methods for the Comment object doesn't include a method to add a new comment. This is because the AddComment method belongs to the Range object. The following statement adds a comment (an empty comment) to cell A1 on the active worksheet:

```
Range("A1").AddComment
```

If you consult the Help system, you discover that the AddComment method takes an argument that represents the text for the comment. Therefore, you can add a comment and then add text to the comment with a single statement, like this:

```
Range("A1").AddComment "Formula developed by JW."
```

NOTE

The AddComment method generates an error if the cell already contains a comment. To avoid the error, your code can check whether the cell has a comment before adding one.

CD-ROM

If you'd like to see these Comment object properties and methods in action, check out the example workbook on the companion CD-ROM. This workbook, named comment object.xlsm, contains several examples that manipulate Comment objects with VBA code. You probably won't understand all the code, but you will get a feel for how you can use VBA to manipulate an object.

Some Useful Application Properties

When you're working with Excel, only one workbook at a time can be active. And if the sheet is a worksheet, one cell is the active cell (even if a multicell range is selected). VBA knows about active workbooks, worksheets, and cells, and lets you refer to these active objects in a simplified manner. This is often useful because you won't always know the exact workbook, worksheet, or range that you want to operate on. VBA handles this by providing properties of the Application object. For example, the Application object has an ActiveCell property that returns a reference to the active cell. The following instruction assigns the value 1 to the active cell:

```
ActiveCell.Value = 1
```

Notice that I omitted the reference to the Application object in the preceding example because it is assumed. It's important to understand that this instruction will fail if the active sheet is not a worksheet. For example, if VBA executes this statement when a chart sheet is active, the procedure halts and you get an error message.

If a range is selected in a worksheet, the active cell is a cell within the selected range. In other words, the active cell is always a single cell (never a multicell range).

The `Application` object also has a `Selection` property that returns a reference to whatever is selected, which could be a single cell (the active cell), a range of cells, or an object such as `ChartObject`, `TextBox`, or `Shape`.

Table 7-3 lists the other `Application` properties that are useful when working with cells and ranges.

TABLE 7-3   SOME USEFUL PROPERTIES OF THE APPLICATION OBJECT

Property	Object Returned
ActiveCell	The active cell.
ActiveChart	The active chart sheet or chart contained in a `ChartObject` on a worksheet. This property is `Nothing` if a chart is not active.
ActiveSheet	The active sheet (worksheet or chart).
ActiveWindow	The active window.
ActiveWorkbook	The active workbook.
Selection	The object selected. (It could be a `Range` object, `Shape`, `ChartObject`, and so on.)
ThisWorkbook	The workbook that contains the VBA procedure being executed.

The advantage of using these properties to return an object is that you don't need to know which cell, worksheet, or workbook is active; nor do you need to provide a specific reference to it. This allows you to write VBA code that is not specific to a particular workbook, sheet, or range. For example, the following instruction clears the contents of the active cell, even though the address of the active cell is not known:

```
ActiveCell.ClearContents
```

The example that follows displays a message that tells you the name of the active sheet:

```
MsgBox ActiveSheet.Name
```

If you want to know the name and directory path of the active workbook, use a statement like this:

```
MsgBox ActiveWorkbook.FullName
```

If a range on a worksheet is selected, you can fill the entire range with a value by executing a single statement. In the following example, the `Selection` property of the `Application` object returns a `Range` object that corresponds to the selected cells. The instruction simply modifies the `Value` property of this `Range` object, and the result is a range filled with a single value:

```
Selection.Value = 12
```

Note that if something other than a range is selected (such as a `ChartObject` or a `Shape`), the preceding statement generates an error because `ChartObject` and `Shape` objects don't have a `Value` property.

The following statement, however, enters a value of 12 into the `Range` object that was selected before a non-`Range` object was selected. If you look up the `RangeSelection` property in the Help system, you find that this property applies only to a `Window` object.

```
ActiveWindow.RangeSelection.Value = 12
```

To find out how many cells are selected in the active window, access the `Count` property. Here's an example:

```
MsgBox ActiveWindow.RangeSelection.Count
```

Working with Range Objects

Much of the work that you will do in VBA involves cells and ranges in worksheets. The earlier discussion on relative versus absolute macro recording (see "Relative or absolute?") exposes you to working with cells in VBA, but you need to know a lot more.

A `Range` object is contained in a `Worksheet` object and consists of a single cell or range of cells on a single worksheet. In the sections that follow, I discuss three ways of referring to `Range` objects in your VBA code:

- The `Range` property of a `Worksheet` or `Range` class object
- The `Cells` property of a `Worksheet` object
- The `Offset` property of a `Range` object

The Range property

The `Range` property returns a `Range` object. If you consult the Help system for the `Range` property, you learn that this property has two syntaxes:

```
object.Range(cell1)
object.Range(cell1, cell2)
```

Working with Merged Cells

Working with merged cells can be tricky. If a range contains merged cells, you may need to take some special action with the macros. For example, if cells A1:D1 are merged, the statement that follows selects columns A through D (not just column B, as you might expect):

```
Columns("B:B").Select
```

I don't know if this unexpected behavior is intentional or if it's a bug. However, it can cause your macro to behave in a manner that you didn't expect. Merged cells also cause problems with sorting.

To determine if a particular range contains any merged cells, you can use the following VBA function. The function returns True if any cell in the argument range is a merged cell (refer to Chapter 10 for more information about Function procedures).

```
Function ContainsMergedCells(rng As Range)
    Dim cell As Range
    ContainsMergedCells = False
    For Each cell In rng
        If cell.MergeCells Then
            ContainsMergedCells = True
            Exit Function
        End If
    Next cell
End Function
```

To refer to merged cells, you can reference the entire merged range or just the upper-left cell within the merged range. For example, if a worksheet contains four cells merged into one (A1, B1, A2, and B1), reference the merged cells using either of the following expressions:

```
Range("A1:B2")
Range("A1")
```

If you attempt to assign a value to a cell in a merged range that's not the upper-left cell, VBA ignores the instruction and does not generate an error. For example, the following statement has no effect if A1:B2 is merged:

```
Range("B2").Value = 43
```

Some operations cause Excel to display a confirmation message. For example, if A1:B2 is merged, the following statement generates a message: `This operation will cause some merged cells to unmerge. Do you wish to continue?`

```
Range("B2").Delete
```

Bottom line? Be careful with merged cells. Clearly, this feature was not very well thought out before it was implemented.

The `Range` property applies to two types of objects: a `Worksheet` object or a `Range` object. Here, `cell1` and `cell2` refer to placeholders for terms that Excel recognizes as identifying the range (in the first instance) and delineating the range (in the second instance). Following are a few examples of using the `Range` property.

You've already seen examples like the following one earlier in the chapter. The instruction that follows simply enters a value into the specified cell. In this case, it puts the value `12.3` into cell A1 on `Sheet1` of the active workbook:

```
Worksheets("Sheet1").Range("A1").Value = 12.3
```

The `Range` property also recognizes defined names in workbooks. Therefore, if a cell is named `Input`, you can use the following statement to enter a value into that named cell:

```
Worksheets("Sheet1").Range("Input").Value = 100
```

The example that follows enters the same value into a range of 20 cells on the active sheet. If the active sheet is not a worksheet, this causes an error message:

```
ActiveSheet.Range("A1:B10").Value = 2
```

The next example produces exactly the same result as the preceding example:

```
Range("A1", "B10") = 2
```

The sheet reference is omitted, however, so the active sheet is assumed. Also, the value property is omitted, so the default property (which is `Value` for a `Range` object) is assumed. This example also uses the second syntax of the `Range` property. With this syntax, the first argument is the cell at the top left of the range, and the second argument is the cell at the lower right of the range.

The following example uses the Excel range intersection operator (a space) to return the intersection of two ranges. In this case, the intersection is a single cell, C6. Therefore, this statement enters 3 into cell C6:

```
Range("C1:C10 A6:E6") = 3
```

And finally, this next example enters the value 4 into five cells: that is, a noncontiguous range. The comma serves as the union operator:

```
Range("A1,A3,A5,A7,A9") = 4
```

So far, all the examples have used the `Range` property on a `Worksheet` object. As I mentioned, you can also use the `Range` property on a `Range` object. This can be rather confusing, but bear with me.

Following is an example of using the `Range` property on a `Range` object. (In this case, the `Range` object is the active cell.) This example treats the `Range` object as if it were the upper-left cell in the worksheet, and then it enters a value of 5 into the cell that *would be*

B2. In other words, the reference returned is relative to the upper-left corner of the Range object. Therefore, the statement that follows enters a value of 5 into the cell directly to the right and one row below the active cell:

```
ActiveCell.Range("B2") = 5
```

I *said* this is confusing. Fortunately, there is a much clearer way to access a cell relative to a range: the Offset property. I discuss this property after the next section.

The Cells property

Another way to reference a range is to use the Cells property. You can use the Cells property, like the Range property, on Worksheet objects and Range objects. Check the Help system, and you see that the Cells property has three syntaxes:

```
object.Cells(rowIndex, columnIndex)
object.Cells(rowIndex)
object.Cells
```

I'll give you some examples that demonstrate how to use the Cells property. The first example enters the value 9 into cell A1 on Sheet1. In this case, I'm using the first syntax, which accepts the index number of the row (from 1 to 1048576) and the index number of the column (from 1 to 16384):

```
Worksheets("Sheet1").Cells(1, 1) = 9
```

Here's an example that enters the value 7 into cell D3 (that is, row 3, column 4) in the active worksheet:

```
ActiveSheet.Cells(3, 4) = 7
```

You can also use the Cells property on a Range object. When you do so, the Range object returned by the Cells property is relative to the upper-left cell of the referenced Range. Confusing? Probably. An example might help clear this up. The following instruction enters the value 5 into the active cell. Remember, in this case, the active cell is treated as if it were cell A1 in the worksheet:

```
ActiveCell.Cells(1, 1) = 5
```

 NOTE

The real advantage of this type of cell referencing will be apparent when I discuss variables and looping (see Chapter 8). In most cases, you don't use actual values for the arguments; rather, you use variables.

To enter a value of 5 into the cell directly below the active cell, you can use the following instruction:

```
ActiveCell.Cells(2, 1) = 5
```

Think of the preceding example as though it said this: "Start with the active cell and consider this cell as cell A1. Place 5 in the cell in the second row and the first column."

The second syntax of the `Cells` method uses a single argument that can range from 1 to 17,179,869,184. This number is equal to the number of cells in an Excel 2007 worksheet. The cells are numbered starting from A1 and continuing right and then down to the next row. The 16,384th cell is XFD1; the 16,385th is A2.

The next example enters the value 2 into cell SZ1 (which is the 520th cell in the worksheet) of the active worksheet:

```
ActiveSheet.Cells(520) = 2
```

To display the value in the last cell in a worksheet (XFD1048576), use this statement:

```
MsgBox ActiveSheet.Cells(17179869184)
```

This syntax can also be used with a `Range` object. In this case, the cell returned is relative to the `Range` object referenced. For example, if the `Range` object is A1:D10 (40 cells), the `Cells` property can have an argument from 1 to 40 and can return one of the cells in the `Range` object. In the following example, a value of 2000 is entered into cell A2 because A2 is the fifth cell (counting from the top, to the right, and then down) in the referenced range:

```
Range("A1:D10").Cells(5) = 2000
```

 NOTE

In the preceding example, the argument for the `Cells` property is not limited to values between 1 and 40. If the argument exceeds the number of cells in the range, the counting continues as if the range were taller than it actually is. Therefore, a statement like the preceding one could change the value in a cell that's outside of the range A1:D10. The statement that follows, for example, changes the value in cell A11:

```
Range("A1:D10").Cells(41)=2000
```

The third syntax for the `Cells` property simply returns all cells on the referenced worksheet. Unlike the other two syntaxes, in this one, the return data is not a single cell. This example uses the `ClearContents` method on the range returned by using the `Cells` property on the active worksheet. The result is that the content of every cell on the worksheet is cleared:

```
ActiveSheet.Cells.ClearContents
```

The Offset property

The Offset property, like the Range and Cells properties, also returns a Range object. But unlike the other two methods that I discussed, the Offset property applies only to a Range object and no other class. Its syntax is as follows:

```
object.Offset(rowOffset, columnOffset)
```

The Offset property takes two arguments that correspond to the relative position from the upper-left cell of the specified Range object. The arguments can be positive (down or to the right), negative (up or to the left), or zero. The example that follows enters a value of 12 into the cell directly below the active cell:

```
ActiveCell.Offset(1,0).Value = 12
```

The next example enters a value of 15 into the cell directly above the active cell:

```
ActiveCell.Offset(-1,0).Value = 15
```

If the active cell is in row 1, the Offset property in the preceding example generates an error because it cannot return a Range object that doesn't exist.

The Offset property is quite useful, especially when you use variables within looping procedures. I discuss these topics in the next chapter.

When you record a macro using the relative reference mode, Excel uses the Offset property to reference cells relative to the starting position (that is, the active cell when macro recording begins). For example, I used the macro recorder to generate the following code. I started with the cell pointer in cell B1, entered values into B1:B3, and then returned to B1.

```
Sub Macro1()
    ActiveCell.FormulaR1C1 = "1"
    ActiveCell.Offset(1, 0).Range("A1").Select
    ActiveCell.FormulaR1C1 = "2"
    ActiveCell.Offset(1, 0).Range("A1").Select
    ActiveCell.FormulaR1C1 = "3"
    ActiveCell.Offset(-2, 0).Range("A1").Select
End Sub
```

Notice that the macro recorder uses the FormulaR1C1 property. Normally, you want to use the Value property to enter a value into a cell. However, using FormulaR1C1 or even Formula produces the same result.

Also notice that the generated code references cell A1 — a cell that was even involved in the macro. This notation is a quirk in the macro recording procedure that makes the code more complex than necessary. You can delete all references to Range("A1"), and the macro still works perfectly:

```
Sub Modified Macro1()
    ActiveCell.FormulaR1C1 = "1"
    ActiveCell.Offset(1, 0).Select
    ActiveCell.FormulaR1C1 = "2"
    ActiveCell.Offset(1, 0).Select
    ActiveCell.FormulaR1C1 = "3"
    ActiveCell.Offset(-2, 0).Select
End Sub
```

In fact, here's a much more efficient version of the macro (which I wrote myself) that doesn't do any selecting:

```
Sub Macro1()
    ActiveCell = 1
    ActiveCell.Offset(1, 0) = 2
    ActiveCell.Offset(2, 0) = 3
End Sub
```

Things to Know about Objects

The preceding sections introduced you to objects (including collections), properties, and methods. But I've barely scratched the surface.

Essential concepts to remember

In this section, I note some additional concepts that are essential for would-be VBA gurus. These concepts become clearer when you work with VBA and read subsequent chapters:

- *Objects have unique properties and methods.*

  Each object has its own set of properties and methods. Some objects, however, share some properties (for example, `Name`) and some methods (such as `Delete`).

- *You can manipulate objects without selecting them.*

  This might be contrary to how you normally think about manipulating objects in Excel. The fact is that it's usually more efficient to perform actions on objects without selecting them first. When you record a macro, Excel generally selects the object first. This is not necessary and may actually make your macro run more slowly.

- *It's important that you understand the concept of collections.*

  Most of the time, you refer to an object indirectly by referring to the collection that it's in. For example, to access a `Workbook` object named `Myfile`, reference the `Workbooks` collection as follows:

  ```
  Workbooks("Myfile.xlsx")
  ```

This reference returns an object, which is the workbook with which you are concerned.

- *Properties can return a reference to another object.*

  For example, in the following statement, the Font property returns a Font object contained in a Range object. Bold is a property of the Font object, not the Range object.

  ```
  Range("A1").Font.Bold = True
  ```

- *There can be many different ways to refer to the same object.*

  Assume that you have a workbook named Sales, and it's the only workbook open. Then assume that this workbook has one worksheet, named Summary. You can refer to the sheet in any of the following ways:

  ```
  Workbooks("Sales.xlsx").Worksheets("Summary")
  Workbooks(1).Worksheets(1)
  Workbooks(1).Sheets(1)
  Application.ActiveWorkbook.ActiveSheet
  ActiveWorkbook.ActiveSheet
  ActiveSheet
  ```

  The method that you use is usually determined by how much you know about the workspace. For example, if more than one workbook is open, the second and third methods are not reliable. If you want to work with the active sheet (whatever it may be), any of the last three methods would work. To be absolutely sure that you're referring to a specific sheet on a specific workbook, the first method is your best choice.

Learning more about objects and properties

If this is your first exposure to VBA, you're probably a bit overwhelmed by objects, properties, and methods. I don't blame you. If you try to access a property that an object doesn't have, you get a runtime error, and your VBA code grinds to a screeching halt until you correct the problem.

Fortunately, there are several good ways to learn about objects, properties, and methods.

READ THE REST OF THE BOOK

Don't forget, the name of this chapter is "Introducing Visual Basic for Applications." The remainder of this book covers many additional details and provides many useful and informative examples.

RECORD YOUR ACTIONS

The absolute best way to become familiar with VBA, without question, is to simply turn on the macro recorder and record some actions that you perform in Excel. This is a quick way to learn the relevant objects, properties, and methods for a task. It's even better if the VBA module in which the code is being recorded is visible while you're recording.

USE THE HELP SYSTEM

The main source of detailed information about Excel's objects, methods, and procedures is the Help system. Many people forget about this resource.

USE THE OBJECT BROWSER

The *Object Browser* is a handy tool that lists every property and method for every object available. When the VBE is active, you can bring up the Object Browser in any of the following three ways:

- Press F2.

- Choose the View ⇨ Object Browser command from the menu.

- Click the Object Browser tool on the Standard toolbar.

The Object Browser is shown in Figure 7-14.

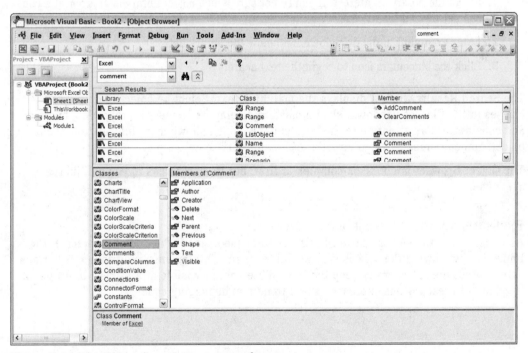

Figure 7-14: The Object Browser is a great reference source.

The drop-down list in the upper-left corner of the Object Browser includes a list of all object libraries that you have access to:

- Excel itself

- MSForms (used to create custom dialog boxes)

- Office (objects common to all Microsoft Office applications)

- Stdole (OLE automation objects)

- VBA

- The current project (the project that's selected in the Project Explorer) and any work-books referenced by that project

Your selection in this upper-left drop-down list determines what is displayed in the Classes window, and your selection in the Classes window determines what is visible in the Members Of window.

After you select a library, you can search for a particular text string to get a list of properties and methods that contain the text. You do so by entering the text in the second drop-down list and then clicking the binoculars (Search) icon. For example, assume that you're working on a project that manipulates cell comments:

1. Select the library of interest. If you're not sure which object library is appropriate, you can select <All Libraries>.

2. Enter **Comment** in the drop-down list below the library list.

3. Click the binoculars icon to begin the text search.

The Search Results window displays the matching text. Select an object to display its classes in the Classes window. Select a class to display its members (properties, methods, and constants). Pay attention to the bottom pane, which shows more information about the object. You can press F1 to go directly to the appropriate help topic.

The Object Browser might seem complex at first, but its usefulness to you will increase over time.

EXPERIMENT WITH THE IMMEDIATE WINDOW

As I describe in the sidebar earlier in this chapter (see "About the Code Examples"), the Immediate window of the VBE is very useful for testing statements and trying out various VBA expressions. I generally keep the Immediate window visible at all times, and I use it frequently to test various expressions and to help in debugging code.

Chapter 8

VBA Programming Fundamentals

In This Chapter

In the preceding chapter, I introduce you to Visual Basic for Applications (VBA); now it's time to get better acquainted. This chapter discusses some of the key language elements and programming concepts in VBA.

- ◆ Understanding VBA language elements, including variables, data types, constants, and arrays

- ◆ Using VBA built-in functions

- ◆ Manipulating objects and collections

- ◆ Controlling the execution of your procedures

If you've used other programming languages, much of this information may sound familiar. VBA has a few unique wrinkles, however; so even experienced programmers may find some new information.

VBA Language Elements: An Overview

In Chapter 7, I present an overview of objects, properties, and methods, but I don't tell you much about how to manipulate objects so that they do meaningful things. This chapter gently nudges you in that direction by exploring the VBA *language elements,* which are the keywords and control structures that you use to write VBA routines.

To get the ball rolling, I start by presenting a simple VBA Sub procedure. The following code, which is stored in a VBA module, calculates the sum of the first 100 positive integers. When the code finishes executing, the procedure displays a message with the result.

```
Sub VBA_Demo()
'    This is a simple VBA Example
    Dim Total As Integer, i As Integer
    Total = 0
    For i = 1 To 100
        Total = Total + i
    Next i
    MsgBox Total
End Sub
```

This procedure uses some common VBA language elements, including:

- A comment (the line that begins with an apostrophe)
- A variable declaration statement (the line that begins with Dim)
- Two variables (Total and i)
- Two assignment statements (Total = 0 and Total = Total + i)
- A looping structure (For-Next)
- A VBA function (MsgBox)

All these language elements are discussed in subsequent sections of this chapter.

 NOTE

VBA procedures need not manipulate any objects. The preceding procedure, for example, doesn't do anything with objects. It simply works with numbers.

Entering VBA Code

VBA code, which resides in a VBA module, consists of instructions. The accepted practice is to use one instruction per line. This standard is not a requirement, however; you can use a colon to separate multiple instructions on a single line. The following example combines four instructions on one line:

```
Sub OneLine()
    x= 1: y= 2: z= 3: MsgBox x + y + z
End Sub
```

Most programmers agree that code is easier to read if you use one instruction per line:

```
Sub OneLine()
    x = 1
    y = 2
    z = 3
    MsgBox x + y + z
End Sub
```

Each line can be as long as you like; the VBA module window scrolls to the left when you reach the right side. For lengthy lines, you may want to use VBA's line continuation sequence: a space followed by an underscore (_).For example:

```
Sub LongLine()
    SummedValue = _
        Worksheets("Sheet1").Range("A1").Value + _
        Worksheets("Sheet2").Range("A1").Value
End Sub
```

When you record macros, Excel often uses underscores to break long statements into multiple lines.

After you enter an instruction, VBA performs the following actions to improve readability:

- *It inserts spaces between operators.* If you enter `Ans=1+2` (without spaces), for example, VBA converts it to

  ```
  Ans = 1 + 2
  ```

- *It adjusts the case of the letters for keywords, properties, and methods.* If you enter the following text: `Result=activesheet.range("a1").value=12`

  VBA converts it to

  ```
  Result = ActiveSheet.Range("a1").Value = 12
  ```

  Notice that text within quotation marks (in this case, `"a1"`) is not changed.

- *Because VBA variable names are not case-sensitive, the interpreter by default adjusts the names of all variables with the same letters so that their case matches the case of letters that you most recently typed.* For example, if you first specify a variable as `myvalue` (all lowercase) and then enter the variable as `MyValue` (mixed case), VBA changes all other occurrences of the variable to `MyValue`. An exception occurs if you declare the variable with `Dim` or a similar statement; in this case, the variable name always appears as it was declared.

- *VBA scans the instruction for syntax errors.* If VBA finds an error, it changes the color of the line and might display a message describing the problem. Choose the Visual Basic Editor Tools ➪ Options command to display the Options dialog box, where you control the error color (use the Editor Format tab) and whether the error message is displayed (use the Auto Syntax Check option in the Editor tab).

Part III

Comments

A *comment* is descriptive text embedded within your code and ignored by VBA. It's a good idea to use comments liberally to describe what you're doing because an instruction's purpose is not always obvious.

You can use a complete line for your comment, or you can insert a comment *after* an instruction on the same line. A comment is indicated by an apostrophe. VBA ignores any text that follows an apostrophe — except when the apostrophe is contained within quotation marks — up until the end of the line. For example, the following statement does not contain a comment, even though it has an apostrophe:

```
Msg = "Can't continue"
```

The following example shows a VBA procedure with three comments:

```
Sub Comments()
'    This procedure does nothing of value
    x = 0    'x represents nothingness
'    Display the result
    MsgBox x
End Sub
```

Although the apostrophe is the preferred comment indicator, you can also use the Rem keyword to mark a line as a comment. For example:

```
Rem -- The next statement prompts the user for a filename
```

The Rem keyword is essentially a holdover from old versions of BASIC and is included in VBA for the sake of compatibility. Unlike the apostrophe, Rem can be written only at the beginning of a line, not on the same line as another instruction.

 TIP

Using comments is definitely a good idea, but not all comments are equally beneficial. To be useful, comments should convey information that's not immediately obvious from reading the code. Otherwise, you're just chewing up valuable bytes.

Following are a few general tips on making the best use of comments:

- Use comments to describe briefly the purpose of each procedure that you write.
- Use comments to describe changes that you make to a procedure.
- Use comments to indicate that you're using functions or constructs in an unusual or nonstandard manner.

- Use comments to describe the purpose of variables so that you and other people can decipher otherwise cryptic names.

- Use comments to describe workarounds that you develop to overcome Excel bugs or limitations.

- Write comments *while* you code rather than after.

TIP

In some cases, you might want to test a procedure without including a particular instruction or group of instructions. Instead of deleting the instruction, simply turn it into a comment by inserting an apostrophe at the beginning. VBA then ignores the instruction(s) when the routine is executed. To convert the comment back to an instruction, just delete the apostrophe.

The Visual Basic Editor (VBE) Edit toolbar contains two very useful buttons. Select a group of instructions and then click the Comment Block button to convert the instructions to comments. The Uncomment Block button converts a group of comments back to instructions. These buttons are very useful, so you might want to copy them to your Standard toolbar.

Part III

Variables, Data Types, and Constants

VBA's main purpose in life is to manipulate data. Some data resides in objects, such as worksheet ranges. Other data is stored in variables that you create.

A *variable* is simply a named storage location in your computer's memory. Variables can accommodate a wide variety of *data types* — from simple Boolean values (`True` or `False`) to large, double-precision values (see the following section). You assign a value to a variable by using the equal sign operator (more about this in the upcoming section, "Assignment Statements").

You make your life easier if you get into the habit of making your variable names as descriptive as possible. VBA does, however, have a few rules regarding variable names:

- You can use alphabetic characters, numbers, and some punctuation characters, but the first character must be alphabetic.

- VBA does not distinguish between case. To make variable names more readable, programmers often use mixed case (for example, `InterestRate` rather than `interestrate`).

- You cannot use spaces or periods. To make variable names more readable, programmers often use the underscore character (`Interest_Rate`).

- Special type declaration characters (#, $, %, &, or !) cannot be embedded in a variable name.

- Variable names can be as long as 254 characters — but using such long variable names is not recommended.

The following list contains some examples of assignment expressions that use various types of variables. The variable names are to the left of the equal sign. Each statement assigns the value to the right of the equal sign to the variable on the left.

```
x = 1
InterestRate = 0.075
LoanPayoffAmount = 243089.87
DataEntered = False
x = x + 1
MyNum = YourNum * 1.25
UserName = "Bob Johnson"
DateStarted = #12/14/2006#
```

VBA has many *reserved words,* which are words that you cannot use for variable or procedure names. If you attempt to use one of these words, you get an error message. For example, although the reserved word Next might make a very descriptive variable name, the following instruction generates a syntax error:

```
Next = 132
```

Unfortunately, syntax error messages aren't always very descriptive. The preceding instruction generates this error message: Compile error: Syntax error. It would be nice if the error message were something like Reserved word used as a variable. So if an instruction produces a strange error message, check the VBA Help system to ensure that your variable name doesn't have a special use in VBA.

Defining data types

VBA makes life easy for programmers because it can automatically handle all the details involved in dealing with data. Not all programming languages make it so easy. For example, some languages are *strictly typed,* which means that the programmer must explicitly define the data type for every variable used.

Data type refers to how data is stored in memory — as integers, real numbers, strings, and so on. Although VBA can take care of data typing automatically, it does so at a cost: slower execution and less efficient use of memory. As a result, letting VBA handle data typing may present problems when you're running large or complex applications. Another advantage of explicitly declaring your variables as a particular data type is that VBA can perform some additional error checking at the compile stage. These errors might otherwise be difficult to locate.

Table 8-1 lists VBA's assortment of built-in data types. (Note that you can also define custom data types, which I describe later in this chapter in "User-Defined Data Types.")

TABLE 8-1   VBA BUILT-IN DATA TYPES

Data Type	Bytes Used	Range of Values
Byte	1 byte	0 to 255
Boolean	2 bytes	True or False
Integer	2 bytes	-32,768 to 32,767
Long	4 bytes	-2,147,483,648 to 2,147,483,647
Single	4 bytes	-3.402823E38 to -1.401298E-45 (for negative values); 1.401298E-45 to 3.402823E38 (for positive values)
Double	8 bytes	-1.79769313486232E308 to -4.94065645841247E-324 (negative values); 4.94065645841247E-324 to 1.79769313486232E308 (for positive values)
Currency	8 bytes	-922,337,203,685,477.5808 to 922,337,203,685,477.5807
Decimal	12 bytes	+/-79,228,162,514,264,337,593,543,950,335 with no decimal point; +/-7.9228162514264337593543950335 with 28 places to the right of the decimal
Date	8 bytes	January 1, 0100 to December 31, 9999
Object	4 bytes	Any object reference
String (variable length)	10 bytes + string length	0 to approximately 2 billion characters
String (fixed length)	Length of string	1 to approximately 65,400 characters
Variant (with numbers)	16 bytes	Any numeric value up to the range of a double data type. It can also hold special values such as Empty, Error, Nothing, and Null.
Variant (with characters)	22 bytes + string length	0 to approximately 2 billion
User-defined	Varies	Varies by element

Part III

Benchmarking Variant Data Types

To test whether data typing is important, I developed the following routine, which performs some meaningless calculations in a loop and then displays the procedure's total execution time:

```vba
Sub TimeTest()
    Dim x As Long, y As Long
    Dim A As Double, B As Double, C As Double
    Dim i As Long, j As Long
    Dim StartTime As Date, EndTime As Date
'   Store the starting time
    StartTime = Timer
'   Perform some calculations
    x = 0
    y = 0
    For i = 1 To 5000
        x = x + 1
        y = x + 1
        For j = 1 To 5000
            A = x + y + i
            B = y - x - i
            C = x / y * i
        Next j
    Next i
'   Get ending time
    EndTime = Timer
'   Display total time in seconds
    MsgBox Format(EndTime - StartTime, "0.0")
End Sub
```

On my system, this routine took 5.1 seconds to run (the time will vary, depending on your system's processor speed). I then commented out the Dim statements, which declare the data types. That is, I turned the Dim statements into comments by adding an apostrophe at the beginning of the lines. As a result, VBA used the default data type, Variant. I ran the procedure again. It took 14.7 seconds, almost three times as long as before.

The moral is simple: If you want your VBA applications to run as fast as possible, declare your variables!

A workbook that contains this code is available on the companion CD-ROM in a file named timing text.xlsm.

NOTE

The Decimal data type is rather unusual because you cannot actually declare it. In fact, it is a subtype of a variant. You need to use the VBA CDec function to convert a variant to the Decimal data type.

Generally, it's best to use the data type that uses the smallest number of bytes yet still can handle all the data that will be assigned to it. When VBA works with data, execution speed is a function of the number of bytes that VBA has at its disposal. In other words, the fewer bytes used by data, the faster VBA can access and manipulate the data.

For worksheet calculation, Excel uses the Double data type, so that's a good choice for processing numbers in VBA when you don't want to lose any precision. For integer calculations, you can use the Integer type (which is limited to values less than or equal to 32,767). Otherwise, use the Long data type. In fact, using the Long data type even for values less than 32,767 is recommended, because this data type may be a bit faster than using the Integer type. When dealing with Excel worksheet row numbers, you want to use the Long data type because the number of rows in a worksheet exceeds the maximum value for the Integer data type.

Declaring variables

If you don't declare the data type for a variable that you use in a VBA routine, VBA uses the default data type, Variant. Data stored as a Variant acts like a chameleon: It changes type, depending on what you do with it.

The following procedure demonstrates how a variable can assume different data types:

```
Sub VariantDemo()
    MyVar = "123"
    MyVar = MyVar / 2
    MyVar = "Answer: " & MyVar
    MsgBox MyVar
End Sub
```

In the VariantDemo procedure, MyVar starts out as a three-character string. Then this string is divided by two and becomes a numeric data type. Next, MyVar is appended to a string, converting MyVar back to a string. The MsgBox statement displays the final string: Answer: 61.5.

To further demonstrate the potential problems in dealing with Variant data types, try executing this procedure:

```
Sub VariantDemo2()
    MyVar = "123"
    MyVar = MyVar + MyVar
    MyVar = "Answer: " & MyVar
    MsgBox MyVar
End Sub
```

The message box displays Answer: 123123. This is probably *not* what you wanted. When dealing with variants that contain text strings, the + operator performs string concatenation.

DETERMINING A DATA TYPE

You can use the VBA TypeName function to determine the data type of a variable. Here's a modified version of the previous procedure. This version displays the data type of MyVar at each step. You see that it starts out as a string, is then converted to a double, and finally ends up as a string again.

```
Sub VariantDemo2()
    MyVar = "123"
    MsgBox TypeName(MyVar)
    MyVar = MyVar / 2
    MsgBox TypeName(MyVar)
    MyVar = "Answer: " & MyVar
    MsgBox TypeName(MyVar)
    MsgBox MyVar
End Sub
```

Thanks to VBA, the data type conversion of undeclared variables is automatic. This process might seem like an easy way out, but remember that you sacrifice speed and memory — and you run the risk of errors that you may not even know about.

Declaring each variable in a procedure before you use it is an excellent habit. Declaring a variable tells VBA its name and data type. Declaring variables provides two main benefits:

- *Your programs run faster and use memory more efficiently.* The default data type, Variant, causes VBA to repeatedly perform time-consuming checks and reserve more memory than necessary. If VBA knows the data type, it doesn't have to investigate, and it can reserve just enough memory to store the data.

- *You avoid problems involving misspelled variable names.* This assumes that you use Option Explicit to force yourself to declare all variables (see the next section). Say that you use an undeclared variable named CurrentRate. At some point in your routine, however, you insert the statement CurentRate = .075. This misspelled variable name, which is very difficult to spot, will likely cause your routine to give incorrect results.

FORCING YOURSELF TO DECLARE ALL VARIABLES

To force yourself to declare all the variables that you use, include the following as the first instruction in your VBA module:

```
Option Explicit
```

When this statement is present, VBA will not even execute a procedure if it contains an undeclared variable name. VBA issues the error message shown in Figure 8-1, and you must declare the variable before you can proceed.

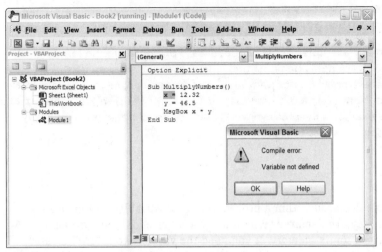

Figure 8-1: VBA's way of telling you that your procedure contains an undeclared variable.

TIP

To ensure that the `Option Explicit` statement is inserted automatically whenever you insert a new VBA module, enable the Require Variable Declaration option in the Editor tab of the VBE Options dialog box (choose Tools ➪ Options). I highly recommend doing so. Be aware, however, that this option does not affect existing modules.

Scoping variables

A variable's *scope* determines in which modules and procedures the variable can be used. Table 8-2 lists the three ways in which a variable can be scoped.

TABLE 8-2   VARIABLE SCOPE

Scope	How a Variable with This Scope Is Declared
Single procedure	Include a `Dim` or `Static` statement within the procedure.
Single module	Include a `Dim` or `Private` statement before the first procedure in a module.
All modules	Include a `Public` statement before the first procedure in a module.

I discuss each scope further in the following sections.

A Note about the Examples in This Chapter

This chapter contains many examples of VBA code, usually presented in the form of simple procedures. These examples demonstrate various concepts as simply as possible. Most of these examples do not perform any particularly useful task; in fact, the task can often be performed in a different (perhaps more efficient) way. In other words, don't use these examples in your own work. Subsequent chapters provide many more code examples that *are* useful.

LOCAL VARIABLES

A *local variable* is a variable declared within a procedure. Local variables can be used only in the procedure in which they are declared. When the procedure ends, the variable no longer exists, and Excel frees up its memory. If you need the variable to retain its value when the procedure ends, declare it as a `Static` variable. (See "Static variables," later in this section.)

The most common way to declare a local variable is to place a `Dim` statement between a `Sub` statement and an `End Sub` statement. `Dim` statements usually are placed right after the `Sub` statement, before the procedure's code.

 NOTE

If you're curious about this word, `Dim` is a shortened form of *Dimension*. In old versions of BASIC, this statement was used exclusively to declare the dimensions for an array. In VBA, the `Dim` keyword is used to declare any variable, not just arrays.

The following procedure uses six local variables declared by using `Dim` statements:

```
Sub MySub()
    Dim x As Integer
    Dim First As Long
    Dim InterestRate As Single
    Dim TodaysDate As Date
    Dim UserName As String
    Dim MyValue
'   - [The procedure's code goes here] -
End Sub
```

Notice that the last `Dim` statement in the preceding example doesn't declare a data type; it simply names the variable. As a result, that variable becomes a variant.

You also can declare several variables with a single `Dim` statement. For example:

```
Dim x As Integer, y As Integer, z As Integer
Dim First As Long, Last As Double
```

CAUTION

Unlike some languages, VBA does not let you declare a group of variables to be a particular data type by separating the variables with commas. For example, the following statement, although valid, does *not* declare all the variables as integers:

```
Dim i, j, k As Integer
```

In VBA, only k is declared to be an integer; the other variables are declared variants. To declare i, j, and k as integers, use this statement:

```
Dim i As Integer, j As Integer, k As Integer
```

If a variable is declared with a local scope, other procedures in the same module can use the same variable name, but each instance of the variable is unique to its own procedure.

In general, local variables are the most efficient because VBA frees up the memory that they use when the procedure ends.

Another Way of Data-Typing Variables

Like most other dialects of BASIC, VBA lets you append a character to a variable's name to indicate the data type. For example, you can declare the MyVar variable as an integer by tacking % onto the name:

```
Dim MyVar%
```

Type-declaration characters exist for most VBA data types. Data types not listed in the following table don't have type-declaration characters.

Data Type	Type-Declaration Character
Integer	%
Long	&
Single	!
Double	#
Currency	@
String	$

This method of data typing is essentially a holdover from BASIC; it's better to declare your variables by using the other techniques described in this chapter. I list these type declaration characters here just in case you encounter them in an older program.

Part III

MODULE-WIDE VARIABLES

Sometimes, you want a variable to be available to all procedures in a module. If so, just declare the variable *before* the module's first procedure (outside of any procedures or functions).

In the following example, the Dim statement is the first instruction in the module. Both Procedure1 and Procedure2 have access to the CurrentValue variable.

```
Dim CurrentValue as Integer

Sub Procedure1()
'    - [Code goes here] -
End Sub

Sub Procedure2()
'    - [Code goes here] -
End Sub
```

Normally, the value of a module-wide variable does not change when a procedure ends normally (that is, when it reaches the End Sub or End Function statement). An exception is if the procedure is halted with an End statement. When VBA encounters an End statement, all module-wide variables lose their values.

PUBLIC VARIABLES

To make a variable available to all the procedures in all the VBA modules in a project, declare the variable at the module level (before the first procedure declaration) by using the Public keyword rather than Dim. Here's an example:

```
Public CurrentRate as Long
```

The Public keyword makes the CurrentRate variable available to any procedure in the VBA project, even those in other modules within the project. You must insert this statement before the first procedure in a module (any module). This type of declaration must appear in a standard VBA module, not in a code module for a sheet or a UserForm.

STATIC VARIABLES

Static variables are a special case. They are declared at the procedure level, and they retain their value when the procedure ends normally. However, if the procedure is halted by an End statement, static variables *do* lose their values.

You declare static variables by using the Static keyword:

```
Sub MySub()
    Static Counter as Integer
    - [Code goes here] -
End Sub
```

Variable Naming Conventions

Some programmers name variables so that users can identify their data types by just looking at their names. Personally, I don't use this technique very often because I think it makes the code more difficult to read, but you might find it helpful.

The naming convention involves using a standard lowercase prefix for the variable's name. For example, if you have a Boolean variable that tracks whether a workbook has been saved, you might name the variable bWasSaved. That way, it is clear that the variable is a Boolean variable. The following table lists some standard prefixes for data types:

Data Type	Prefix
Boolean	b
Integer	i
Long	l
Single	s
Double	d
Currency	c
Date/Time	dt
String	str
Object	obj
Variant	v
User-defined	u

Part III

Working with constants

A variable's value may change while a procedure is executing (that's why it's called a *variable*). Sometimes, you need to refer to a named value or string that never changes: a *constant*.

Using constants throughout your code in place of hard-coded values or strings is an excellent programming practice. For example, if your procedure needs to refer to a specific value (such as an interest rate) several times, it's better to declare the value as a constant and use the constant's name rather than its value in your expressions. This technique not only makes your code more readable, it also makes it easier to change should the need arise — you have to change only one instruction rather than several.

DECLARING CONSTANTS

You declare constants with the `Const` statement. Here are some examples:

```
Const NumQuarters as Integer = 4
Const Rate = .0725, Period = 12
Const ModName as String = "Budget Macros"
Public Const AppName as String = "Budget Application"
```

The second example doesn't declare a data type. Consequently, VBA determines the data type from the value. The `Rate` variable is a `Double`, and the `Period` variable is an `Integer`. Because a constant never changes its value, you normally want to declare your constants as a specific data type.

Like variables, constants also have a scope. If you want a constant to be available within a single procedure only, declare it after the `Sub` or `Function` statement to make it a local constant. To make a constant available to all procedures in a module, declare it before the first procedure in the module. To make a constant available to all modules in the work-book, use the `Public` keyword and declare the constant before the first procedure in a module. For example:

```
Public Const InterestRate As Double = 0.0725
```

 NOTE

If your VBA code attempts to change the value of a constant, you get an error (`Assignment to constant not permitted`). This is what you would expect. A constant is a constant, not a variable.

USING PREDEFINED CONSTANTS

Excel and VBA make available many predefined constants, which you can use without declaring. In fact, you don't even need to know the value of these constants to use them. The macro recorder generally uses constants rather than actual values. The following procedure uses a built-in constant (`xlLandscape`) to set the page orientation to landscape for the active sheet:

```
Sub SetToLandscape()
    ActiveSheet.PageSetup.Orientation = xlLandscape
End Sub
```

I discovered the `xlLandscape` constant by recording a macro. I also could have found this information in the Help system. And, if you have the `AutoList Members` option turned on, you can often get some assistance while you enter your code (see Figure 8-2). In many cases, VBA lists all the constants that can be assigned to a property.

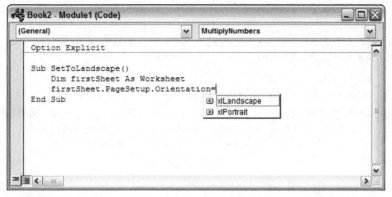

Figure 8-2: VBA displays a list of constants that can be assigned to a property.

The actual value for `xlLandscape` is 2 (which you can discover by using the Immediate window). The other built-in constant for changing paper orientation is `xlPortrait`, which has a value of 1. Obviously, if you use the built-in constants, you don't really need to know their values.

NOTE

The Object Browser, which I discuss briefly in Chapter 7, can display a list of all Excel and VBA constants. In the VBE, press F2 to bring up the Object Browser.

Working with strings

Like Excel, VBA can manipulate both numbers and text (strings). There are two types of strings in VBA:

- *Fixed-length strings* are declared with a specified number of characters. The maximum length is 65,535 characters.

- *Variable-length strings* theoretically can hold up to 2 billion characters.

Each character in a string requires 1 byte of storage, plus a small amount of storage for the header of each string. When you declare a variable with a `Dim` statement as data type `String`, you can specify the length if you know it (that is, a fixed-length string), or you can let VBA handle it dynamically (a variable-length string).

In the following example, the `MyString` variable is declared to be a string with a maximum length of 50 characters. `YourString` is also declared as a string; but it's a variable-length string, so its length is unfixed.

```
Dim MyString As String * 50
Dim YourString As String
```

Working with dates

You can use a string variable to store a date, but if you do, it's not a real date (meaning you can't perform date calculations with it). Using the Date data type is a better way to work with dates.

A variable defined as a date uses 8 bytes of storage and can hold dates ranging from January 1, 0100 to December 31, 9999. That's a span of nearly 10,000 years — more than enough for even the most aggressive financial forecast! The Date data type is also useful for storing time-related data. In VBA, you specify dates and times by enclosing them between two hash marks (#).

NOTE

The range of dates that VBA can handle is much larger than Excel's own date range, which begins with January 1, 1900. Therefore, be careful that you don't attempt to use a date in a worksheet that is outside of Excel's acceptable date range.

Here are some examples of declaring variables and constants as Date data types:

```
Dim Today As Date
Dim StartTime As Date
Const FirstDay As Date = #1/1/2007#
Const Noon = #12:00:00#
```

CAUTION

Dates are always defined using month/day/year format, even if your system is set up to display dates in a different format (for example, day/month/year).

About Excel's Date Bug

It is commonly known that Excel has a date bug: It incorrectly assumes that the year 1900 is a leap year. Even though there was no February 29, 1900, Excel accepts the following formula and displays the result as the 29th day of February, 1900:

```
=Date(1900,2,29)
```

VBA does not have this date bug. The VBA equivalent of Excel's DATE function is DateSerial. The following expression (correctly) returns March 1, 1900:

```
DateSerial(1900,2,29)
```

Therefore, Excel's date serial number system does not correspond exactly to the VBA date serial number system. These two systems return different values for dates between January 1, 1900 and February 28, 1900.

If you use a message box to display a date, it is displayed according to your system's short date format. Similarly, a time is displayed according to your system's time format (either 12- or 24-hour). You can modify these system settings by using the Regional Settings option in the Windows Control Panel.

CD-ROM

The companion CD-ROM includes a workbook that contains several VBA worksheet functions that enable you to work with dates prior to January 1, 1900. The file is named `extended date functions.xlsm`. You'll also find a Word document (`extended date functions help.docx`) that describes the functions..

Assignment Statements

An *assignment statement* is a VBA instruction that makes a mathematical evaluation and assigns the result to a variable or an object. Excel's Help system defines *expression* as "a combination of keywords, operators, variables, and constants that yields a string, number, or object. An expression can perform a calculation, manipulate characters, or test data."

I couldn't have said it better myself. Much of the work done in VBA involves developing (and debugging) expressions. If you know how to create formulas in Excel, you'll have no trouble creating expressions in VBA. With a worksheet formula, Excel displays the result in a cell. The result of a VBA expression, on the other hand, can be assigned to a variable or used as a property value.

VBA uses the equal sign (=) as its assignment operator. The following are examples of assignment statements (the expressions are to the right of the equal sign):

```
x = 1
x = x + 1
x = (y * 2) / (z  * 2)
FileOpen = True
FileOpen = Not FileOpen
Range("TheYear").Value = 2007
```

TIP

Expressions can be very complex. You might want to use the line continuation sequence (space followed by an underscore) to make lengthy expressions easier to read.

Often, expressions use functions. These functions can be built-in VBA functions, Excel's worksheet functions, or custom functions that you develop in VBA. I discuss built-in VBA functions later in this chapter (see "Built-in Functions").

Operators play a major role in VBA. Familiar operators describe mathematical operations, including addition (+), multiplication (*), division (/), subtraction (–), exponentiation (^), and string concatenation (&). Less-familiar operators are the backslash (\) (used in integer division) and the Mod operator (used in modulo arithmetic). The Mod operator returns the remainder of one number divided by another. For example, the following expression returns 2:

```
17 Mod 3
```

VBA also supports the same comparison operators used in Excel formulas: equal to (=), greater than (>), less than (<), greater than or equal to (>=), less than or equal to (<=), and not equal to (<>).

The order of precedence for operators in VBA is exactly the same as in Excel (see Table 8-3). And, of course, you can use parentheses to change the natural order of precedence.

TABLE 8-3   OPERATOR PRECEDENCE

Operator	Operation	Order of Precedence
^	Exponentiation	1
* and /	Multiplication and division	2
+ and –	Addition and subtraction	3
&	Concatenation	4
=, <, >, <=, >=, <>	Comparison	5

In the statement that follows, x is assigned the value 10 because the multiplication operator has a higher precedence than the addition operator.

```
x = 4 + 3 * 2
```

To avoid ambiguity, you might prefer to write the statement as follows:

```
x = 4 + (3 * 2)
```

In addition, VBA provides a full set of logical operators, shown in Table 8-4. For complete details on these operators (including examples), use the VBA Help system.

TABLE 8-4 VBA LOGICAL OPERATORS

Operator	What It Does
Not	Performs a logical negation on an expression
And	Performs a logical conjunction on two expressions
Or	Performs a logical disjunction on two expressions
Xor	Performs a logical exclusion on two expressions
Eqv	Performs a logical equivalence on two expressions
Imp	Performs a logical implication on two expressions

The following instruction uses the Not operator to toggle the grid-line display in the active window. The DisplayGridlines property takes a value of either True or False. Therefore, using the Not operator changes False to True and True to False.

```
ActiveWindow.DisplayGridlines = _
   Not ActiveWindow.DisplayGridlines
```

The following expression performs a logical And operation. The MsgBox statement displays True only when Sheet1 is the active sheet *and* the active cell is in Row 1. If either or both of these conditions are not true, the MsgBox statement displays False.

```
MsgBox ActiveSheet.Name = "Sheet1" And ActiveCell.Row = 1
```

The following expression performs a logical Or operation. The MsgBox statement displays True when either Sheet1 *or* Sheet2 is the active sheet.

```
MsgBox ActiveSheet.Name = "Sheet1" _
   Or ActiveSheet.Name = "Sheet2"
```

Arrays

An *array* is a group of elements of the same type that have a common name. You refer to a specific element in the array by using the array name and an index number. For example, you can define an array of 12 string variables so that each variable corresponds to the name of a month. If you name the array MonthNames, you can refer to the first element of the array as MonthNames(0), the second element as MonthNames(1), and so on, up to MonthNames(11).

Declaring arrays

You declare an array with a `Dim` or `Public` statement, just as you declare a regular variable. You can also specify the number of elements in the array. You do so by specifying the first index number, the keyword `To`, and the last index number — all inside parentheses. For example, here's how to declare an array comprising exactly 100 integers:

```
Dim MyArray(1 To 100) As Integer
```

TIP

When you declare an array, you need specify only the upper index, in which case VBA assumes that 0 is the lower index. Therefore, the two statements that follow have the same effect:

```
Dim MyArray(0 to 100) As Integer
Dim MyArray(100) As Integer
```

In both cases, the array consists of 101 elements.

By default, VBA assumes zero-based arrays. If you would like VBA to assume that 1 is the lower index for all arrays that declare only the upper index, include the following statement before any procedures in your module:

```
Option Base 1
```

Declaring multidimensional arrays

The array examples in the preceding section are one-dimensional arrays. VBA arrays can have up to 60 dimensions, although it's rare to need more than three dimensions (a 3-D array). The following statement declares a 100-integer array with two dimensions (2-D):

```
Dim MyArray(1 To 10, 1 To 10) As Integer
```

You can think of the preceding array as occupying a 10 x 10 matrix. To refer to a specific element in a 2-D array, you need to specify two index numbers. For example, here's how you can assign a value to an element in the preceding array:

```
MyArray(3, 4) = 125
```

Following is a declaration for a 3-D array that contains 1,000 elements (visualize this array as a cube).

```
Dim MyArray(1 To 10, 1 To 10, 1 To 10) As Integer
```

Reference an item within the array by supplying three index numbers:

```
MyArray(4, 8, 2) = 0
```

Declaring dynamic arrays

A *dynamic array* doesn't have a preset number of elements. You declare a dynamic array with a blank set of parentheses:

```
Dim MyArray() As Integer
```

Before you can use a dynamic array in your code, however, you must use the ReDim statement to tell VBA how many elements are in the array. This is often done by using a variable, the value of which isn't known until the procedure is executing. For example, if the variable x contains a number, you can define the array's size by using this statement:

```
ReDim MyArray (1 to x)
```

You can use the ReDim statement any number of times, changing the array's size as often as you need to. When you change an array's dimensions the existing values are destroyed. If you would like to preserve the existing values, use ReDim Preserve. For example:

```
ReDim Preserve MyArray (1 to y)
```

Arrays crop up later in this chapter when I discuss looping ("Looping blocks of instructions").

Object Variables

An *object variable* is a variable that represents an entire object, such as a range or a worksheet. Object variables are important for two reasons:

- They can simplify your code significantly.
- They can make your code execute more quickly.

Object variables, like normal variables, are declared with the Dim or Public statement. For example, the following statement declares InputArea as a Range object variable:

```
Dim InputArea As Range
```

Use the Set keyword to assign an object to the variable. For example:

```
Set InputArea = Range("C16:E16")
```

To see how object variables simplify your code, examine the following procedure, which does not use an object variable:

```
Sub NoObjVar()
    Worksheets("Sheet1").Range("A1").Value = 124
    Worksheets("Sheet1").Range("A1").Font.Bold = True
    Worksheets("Sheet1").Range("A1").Font.Italic = True
End Sub
```

This routine enters a value into cell A1 of Sheet1 on the active workbook and then bold-faces and italicizes the cell's contents. That's a lot of typing. To reduce wear and tear on your fingers (and make your code more efficient), you can condense the routine with an object variable:

```
Sub ObjVar()
    Dim MyCell As Range
    Set MyCell = Worksheets("Sheet1").Range("A1")
    MyCell.Value = 124
    MyCell.Font.Bold = True
    MyCell.Font.Italic = True
End Sub
```

After the variable MyCell is declared as a Range object, the Set statement assigns an object to it. Subsequent statements can then use the simpler MyCell reference in place of the lengthy Worksheets("Sheet1").Range("A1") reference.

TIP

After an object is assigned to a variable, VBA can access it more quickly than it can a normal, lengthy reference that has to be resolved. So when speed is critical, use object variables. One way to think about this is in terms of *dot processing*. Every time VBA encounters a dot, as in Sheets(1).Range("A1"), it takes time to resolve the reference. Using an object variable reduces the number of dots to be processed. The fewer the dots, the faster the processing time. Another way to improve the speed of your code is by using the With-End With construct, which also reduces the number of dots to be processed. I discuss this construct later in this chapter.

The true value of object variables becomes apparent when I discuss looping later in this chapter.

User-Defined Data Types

VBA lets you create custom, or *user-defined*, data types (a concept much like Pascal records or C structures). A user-defined data type can ease your work with some types of data. For example, if your application deals with customer information, you might want to create a user-defined data type named CustomerInfo, as follows:

```
Type CustomerInfo
    Company As String
    Contact As String
    RegionCode As Long
    Sales As Double
End Type
```

 NOTE
You define custom data types at the top of your module before any procedures.

After you create a user-defined data type, you use a `Dim` statement to declare a variable as that type. Usually, you define an array. For example:

```
Dim Customers(1 To 100) As CustomerInfo
```

Each of the 100 elements in this array consists of four components (as specified by the user-defined data type, `CustomerInfo`). You can refer to a particular component of the record as follows:

```
Customers(1).Company = "Acme Tools"
Customers(1).Contact = "Tim Robertson"
Customers(1).RegionCode = 3
Customers(1).Sales = 150674.98
```

You can also work with an element in the array as a whole. For example, to copy the information from `Customers(1)` to `Customers(2)`, use this instruction:

```
Customers(2) = Customers(1)
```

The preceding example is equivalent to the following instruction block:

```
Customers(2).Company = Customers(1).Company
Customers(2).Contact = Customers(1).Contact
Customers(2).RegionCode = Customers(1).RegionCode
Customers(2).Sales = Customers(1).Sales
```

Built-in Functions

Like most programming languages, VBA has a variety of built-in functions that simplify calculations and operations. Many VBA functions are similar (or identical) to Excel worksheet functions. For example, the VBA function **UCase, which converts a string argument to uppercase, is equivalent to the Excel** worksheet function UPPER.

Part III

CROSS-REFERENCE

Appendix B contains a complete list of VBA functions, with a brief description of each. All are thoroughly described in the VBA Help system.

TIP

To get a list of VBA functions while you're writing your code, type **VBA** followed by a period (.). The VBE displays a list of all its members, including functions (see Figure 8-3). The functions are preceded by a green icon.

If this technique doesn't work for you, make sure that the Auto List Members option is selected. Choose Tools ➪ Options and then click the Editor tab.

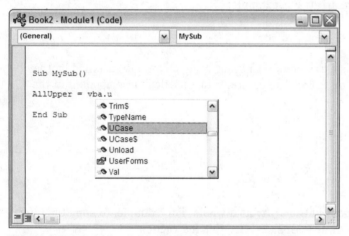

Figure 8-3: Displaying a list of VBA functions in the VBE.

You use functions in VBA expressions in much the same way that you use functions in worksheet formulas. Here's a simple procedure that calculates the square root of a variable (using the VBA Sqr function), stores the result in another variable, and then displays the result:

```
Sub ShowRoot()
    Dim MyValue As Double
    Dim SquareRoot As Double
    MyValue = 25
    SquareRoot = Sqr(MyValue)
    MsgBox SquareRoot
End Sub
```

The VBA Sqr function is equivalent to the Excel SQRT worksheet function.

You can use many (but not all) of Excel's worksheet functions in your VBA code. The `WorksheetFunction` object, which is contained in the `Application` object, holds all the worksheet functions that you can call from your VBA procedures.

To use a worksheet function in a VBA statement, just precede the function name with

```
Application.WorksheetFunction
```

The MsgBox Function

The `MsgBox` function is one of the most useful VBA functions. Many of the examples in this chapter use this function to display the value of a variable.

This function often is a good substitute for a simple custom dialog box. It's also an excellent debugging tool because you can insert `MsgBox` functions at any time to pause your code and display the result of a calculation or assignment.

Most functions return a single value, which you assign to a variable. The `MsgBox` function not only returns a value, but also displays a dialog box that the user can respond to. The value returned by the `MsgBox` function represents the user's response to the dialog. You can use the `MsgBox` function even when you have no interest in the user's response but want to take advantage of the message display.

The official syntax of the `MsgBox` function has five arguments (those in square brackets are optional):

```
MsgBox(prompt[, buttons][, title][, helpfile, context])
```

- `prompt`: (Required) The message displayed in the pop-up display.

- `buttons`: (Optional) A value that specifies which buttons and which icons, if any, appear in the message box. Use built-in constants — for example, `vbYesNo`.

- `title`: (Optional) The text that appears in the message box's title bar. The default is `Microsoft Excel`.

- `helpfile`: (Optional) The name of the help file associated with the message box.

- `context`: (Optional) The context ID of the help topic. This represents a specific help topic to display. If you use the `context` argument, you must also use the `helpfile` argument.

You can assign the value returned to a variable, or you can use the function by itself without an assignment statement. This example assigns the result to the variable `Ans`.

```
Ans = MsgBox("Continue?", vbYesNo + vbQuestion, "Tell me")
If Ans = vbNo Then Exit Sub
```

continued

continued

Notice that I used the sum of two built-in constants (vbYesNo + vbQuestion) for the buttons argument. Using vbYesNo displays two buttons in the message box: one labeled Yes and one labeled No. (See the results in the accompanying figure.) Adding vbQuestion to the argument also displays a question mark icon (see the accompanying figure). When the first statement is executed, Ans contains one of two values, represented by the constant vbYes or vbNo. In this example, if the user clicks the No button, the procedure ends.

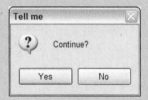

See Chapter 12 for more information about the MsgBox function.

The following example demonstrates how to use an Excel worksheet function in a VBA procedure. Excel's infrequently used ROMAN function converts a decimal number into a Roman numeral.

```
Sub ShowRoman()
    Dim DecValue As Long
    Dim RomanValue As String
    DecValue = 2007
    RomanValue = Application.WorksheetFunction.Roman(DecValue)
    MsgBox RomanValue
End Sub
```

When you execute this procedure, the MsgBox function displays the string MMVII. Fans of old movies are often dismayed when they learn that Excel doesn't have a function to convert a Roman numeral to its decimal equivalent.

Keep in mind that you cannot use worksheet functions that have an equivalent VBA function. For example, VBA cannot access the Excel SQRT worksheet function because VBA has its own version of that function: Sqr. Therefore, the following statement generates an error:

```
MsgBox Application.WorksheetFunction.Sqrt(123)    'error
```

 CROSS-REFERENCE

As I describe in Chapter 10, you can use VBA to create custom worksheet functions that work just like Excel's built-in worksheet functions.

Manipulating Objects and Collections

As an Excel programmer, you'll spend a lot of time working with objects and collections. Therefore, you want to know the most efficient ways to write your code to manipulate these objects and collections. VBA offers two important constructs that can simplify working with objects and collections:

- With-End With constructs
- For Each-Next constructs

With-End With constructs

The With-End With instruction construct enables you to perform multiple operations on a single object. To start understanding how the With-End With construct works, examine the following procedure, which modifies five properties of a selection's formatting (the selection is assumed to be a Range object):

```
Sub ChangeFont1()
    Selection.Font.Name = "Cambria"
    Selection.Font.Bold = True
    Selection.Font.Italic = True
    Selection.Font.Size = 12
    Selection.Font.Underline = xlUnderlineStyleSingle
    Selection.Font.ThemeColor = xlThemeColorAccent1
End Sub
```

This procedure can be rewritten using the With-End With construct. The following procedure performs exactly like the preceding one:

```
Sub ChangeFont2()
    With Selection.Font
        .Name = "Cambria"
        .Bold = True
        .Italic = True
        .Size = 12
        .Underline = xlUnderlineStyleSingle
        .ThemeColor = xlThemeColorAccent1
    End With
End Sub
```

Some people think that the second incarnation of the procedure is actually more difficult to read. Remember, though, that the objective is increased speed. Although the first version may be more straightforward and easier to understand, a procedure that uses the With-End With construct to change several properties of an object can be faster than the equivalent procedure that explicitly references the object in each statement.

Part III

NOTE

When you record a VBA macro, Excel uses the `With-End With` construct every chance it gets. To see a good example of this construct, try recording your actions while you change the page orientation using the Page Layout ➪ Page Setup ➪ Orientation command.

For Each-Next constructs

Recall from the preceding chapter that a *collection* is a group of related objects. For example, the `Workbooks` collection is a collection of all open `Workbook` objects, and there are many other collections that you can work with.

Suppose that you want to perform some action on all objects in a collection. Or suppose that you want to evaluate all objects in a collection and take action under certain conditions. These are perfect occasions for the `For Each-Next` construct because you don't have to know how many elements are in a collection to use the `For Each-Next` construct.

The syntax of the `For Each-Next` construct is

```
For Each element In collection
    [instructions]
    [Exit For]
    [instructions]
Next [element]
```

The following procedure uses the `For Each-Next` construct with the `Worksheets` collection in the active workbook. When you execute the procedure, the `MsgBox` function displays each worksheet's `Name` property. (If there are five worksheets in the active workbook, the `MsgBox` function is called five times.)

```
Sub CountSheets()
    Dim Item as Worksheet
    For Each Item In ActiveWorkbook.Worksheets
        MsgBox Item.Name
    Next Item
End Sub
```

NOTE

In the preceding example, `Item` is an object variable (more specifically, a `Worksheet` object). There's nothing special about the name `Item`; you can use any valid variable name in its place.

The next example uses `For Each-Next` to cycle through all objects in the `Windows` collection and count the number of windows that are hidden.

```
Sub HiddenWindows()
    Dim Cnt As Integer
```

```
    Dim Win As Window
    Cnt = 0
    For Each Win In Windows
        If Not Win.Visible Then Cnt = Cnt + 1
    Next Win
    MsgBox Cnt & " hidden windows."
End Sub
```

For each window, if the window is hidden, the Cnt variable is incremented. When the loop ends, the message box displays the value of Cnt.

Here's an example that closes all workbooks except the active workbook. This procedure uses the If-Then construct to evaluate each workbook in the Workbooks collection.

```
Sub CloseInactive()
    Dim Book as Workbook
    For Each Book In Workbooks
        If Book.Name <> ActiveWorkbook.Name Then Book.Close
    Next Book
End Sub
```

A common use for the For Each-Next construct is to loop through all cells in a range. The next example of For Each-Next is designed to be executed after the user selects a range of cells. Here, the Selection object acts as a collection that consists of Range objects because each cell in the selection is a Range object. The procedure evaluates each cell and uses the VBA UCase function to convert its contents to uppercase. (Numeric cells are not affected.)

```
Sub MakeUpperCase()
    Dim Cell as Range
    For Each Cell In Selection
        Cell.Value = UCase(Cell.Value)
    Next Cell
End Sub
```

VBA provides a way to exit a For-Next loop before all the elements in the collection are evaluated. Do this with an Exit For statement. The example that follows selects the first negative value in Row 1 of the active sheet.

```
Sub SelectNegative()
    Dim Cell As Range
    For Each Cell In Range("1:1")
        If Cell.Value < 0 Then
            Cell.Select
            Exit For
        End If
    Next Cell
End Sub
```

This example uses an If-Then construct to check the value of each cell. If a cell is negative, it is selected, and then the loop ends when the Exit For statement is executed.

Controlling Code Execution

Some VBA procedures start at the top and progress line by line to the bottom. Macros that you record, for example, always work in this fashion. Often, however, you need to control the flow of your routines by skipping over some statements, executing some statements multiple times, and testing conditions to determine what the routine does next.

The preceding section describes the For Each-Next construct, which is a type of loop. This section discusses the additional ways of controlling the execution of your VBA procedures:

- GoTo statements
- If-Then constructs
- Select Case constructs
- For-Next loops
- Do While loops
- Do Until loops

GoTo statements

The most straightforward way to change the flow of a program is to use a GoTo statement. This statement simply transfers program execution to a new instruction, which must be preceded by a label (a text string followed by a colon, or a number with no colon). VBA procedures can contain any number of labels, but a GoTo statement cannot branch outside of a procedure.

The following procedure uses the VBA InputBox function to get the user's name. If the name is not *Howard,* the procedure branches to the WrongName label and ends. Otherwise, the procedure executes some additional code. The Exit Sub statement causes the procedure to end.

```
Sub GoToDemo()
    UserName = InputBox("Enter Your Name:")
    If UserName <> "Howard" Then GoTo WrongName
    MsgBox ("Welcome Howard...")
'   -[More code here] -
    Exit Sub
WrongName:
    MsgBox "Sorry. Only Howard can run this."
End Sub
```

This simple procedure works, but it's not an example of good programming. In general, you should use the GoTo statement only when there is no other way to perform an action. In fact, the only time you *really* need to use a GoTo statement in VBA is for error handling (refer to Chapter 9).

Finally, it goes without saying that the preceding example is *not* intended to demonstrate an effective security technique!

If-Then constructs

Perhaps the most commonly used instruction grouping in VBA is the If-Then construct. This common instruction is one way to endow your applications with decision-making capability. Good decision making is the key to writing successful programs.

The basic syntax of the If-Then construct is

```
If condition Then true_instructions [Else false_instructions]
```

The If-Then construct is used to execute one or more statements conditionally. The Else clause is optional. If included, the Else clause lets you execute one or more instructions when the condition that you're testing is not True.

The following procedure demonstrates an If-Then structure without an Else clause. The example deals with time, and VBA uses a date-and-time serial number system similar to Excel's. The time of day is expressed as a fractional value — for example, noon is represented as .5. The VBA Time function returns a value that represents the time of day, as reported by the system clock. In the following example, a message is displayed if the time is before noon. If the current system time is greater than or equal to .5, the procedure ends, and nothing happens.

```
Sub GreetMe1()
    If Time < 0.5 Then MsgBox "Good Morning"
End Sub
```

Another way to code this routine is to use multiple statements, as follows:

```
Sub GreetMe1a()
    If Time < 0.5 Then
        MsgBox "Good Morning"
    End If
End Sub
```

Notice that the If statement has a corresponding End If statement. In this example, only one statement is executed if the condition is True. You can, however, place any number of statements between the If and End If statements.

If you want to display a different greeting when the time of day is after noon, add another If-Then statement, like so:

```
Sub GreetMe2()
    If Time < 0.5 Then MsgBox "Good Morning"
    If Time >= 0.5 Then MsgBox "Good Afternoon"
End Sub
```

Notice that I used >= (greater than or equal to) for the second If-Then statement. This covers the remote chance that the time is precisely 12:00 noon.

Another approach is to use the Else clause of the If-Then construct. For example,

```
Sub GreetMe3()
    If Time < 0.5 Then MsgBox "Good Morning" Else _
        MsgBox "Good Afternoon"
End Sub
```

Notice that I used the line continuation sequence; If-Then-Else is actually a single statement.

If you need to execute multiple statements based on the condition, use this form:

```
Sub GreetMe3a()
    If Time < 0.5 Then
        MsgBox "Good Morning"
        ' Other statements go here
    Else
        MsgBox "Good Afternoon"
        ' Other statements go here
    End If
End Sub
```

If you need to expand a routine to handle three conditions (for example, morning, afternoon, and evening), you can use either three If-Then statements or a form that uses ElseIf. The first approach is the simpler:

```
Sub GreetMe4()
    If Time < 0.5 Then MsgBox "Good Morning"
    If Time >= 0.5 And Time < 0.75 Then MsgBox "Good Afternoon"
    If Time >= 0.75 Then MsgBox "Good Evening"
End Sub
```

The value 0.75 represents 6:00 p.m. — three-quarters of the way through the day and a good point at which to call it an evening.

In the preceding examples, every instruction in the procedure gets executed, even if the first condition is satisfied (that is, it's morning). A more efficient procedure would include a structure that ends the routine when a condition is found to be True. For example, it might display the Good Morning message in the morning and then exit without evaluating the other, superfluous conditions. True, the difference in speed is inconsequential when you design a procedure as small as this routine. But for more complex applications, you need another syntax:

```
If condition Then
    [true_instructions]
[ElseIf condition-n Then
    [alternate_instructions]]
[Else
    [default_instructions]]
End If
```

Here's how you can use this syntax to rewrite the GreetMe procedure:

```
Sub GreetMe5()
    If Time < 0.5 Then
        MsgBox "Good Morning"
    ElseIf Time >= 0.5 And Time < 0.75 Then
        MsgBox "Good Afternoon"
    Else
        MsgBox "Good Evening"
    End If
End Sub
```

With this syntax, when a condition is True, the conditional statements are executed and the If-Then construct ends. In other words, the extraneous conditions are not evaluated. Although this syntax makes for greater efficiency, some find the code to be more difficult to understand.

The following procedure demonstrates yet another way to code this example. It uses nested If-Then-Else constructs (without using ElseIf). This procedure is efficient and also easy to understand. Note that each If statement has a corresponding End If statement.

```
Sub GreetMe6()
    If Time < 0.5 Then
        MsgBox "Good Morning"
    Else
        If Time >= 0.5 And Time < 0.75 Then
            MsgBox "Good Afternoon"
        Else
            If Time >= 0.75 Then
                MsgBox "Good Evening"
            End If
        End If
    End If
End Sub
```

The following is another example that uses the simple form of the If-Then construct. This procedure prompts the user for a value for Quantity and then displays the appropriate discount based on that value. Note that Quantity is declared as a Variant data type. This is because Quantity contains an empty string (not a numeric value) if the InputBox is cancelled. To keep it simple, this procedure does not perform any other error checking. For example, it does not ensure that the quantity entered is a non-negative numeric value.

```vba
Sub Discount1()
    Dim Quantity As Variant
    Dim Discount As Double
    Quantity = InputBox("Enter Quantity: ")
    If Quantity = "" Then Exit Sub
    If Quantity >= 0 Then Discount = 0.1
    If Quantity >= 25 Then Discount = 0.15
    If Quantity >= 50 Then Discount = 0.2
    If Quantity >= 75 Then Discount = 0.25
    MsgBox "Discount: " & Discount
End Sub
```

Notice that each If-Then statement in this procedure is always executed, and the value for Discount can change. The final value, however, is the desired value.

The following procedure is the previous one rewritten to use the alternate syntax. In this case, the procedure ends after executing the True instruction block.

```vba
Sub Discount2()
    Dim Quantity As Variant
    Dim Discount As Double
    Quantity = InputBox("Enter Quantity: ")
    If Quantity = "" Then Exit Sub
    If Quantity >= 0 And Quantity < 25 Then
        Discount = 0.1
    ElseIf Quantity < 50 Then
        Discount = 0.15
    ElseIf Quantity < 75 Then
        Discount = 0.2
    Else
        Discount = 0.25
    End If
    MsgBox "Discount: " & Discount
End Sub
```

I find nested If-Then structures rather cumbersome. As a result, I usually use the If-Then structure only for simple binary decisions. When you need to choose among three or more alternatives, the Select Case structure (discussed next) is often a better construct to use.

VBA's IIf Function

VBA offers an alternative to the `If-Then` construct: the `IIf` function. This function takes three arguments and works much like Excel's IF worksheet function. The syntax is

```
IIf(expr, truepart, falsepart)
```

- **expr**: (Required) Expression you want to evaluate.
- **truepart**: (Required) Value or expression returned if `expr` is `True`.
- **falsepart**: (Required) Value or expression returned if `expr` is `False`.

The following instruction demonstrates the use of the `IIf` function. The message box displays `Zero` if cell A1 contains a zero or is empty and displays `Nonzero` if cell A1 contains anything else.

```
MsgBox IIf(Range("A1") = 0, "Zero", "Nonzero")
```

It's important to understand that the third argument (`falsepart`) is always evaluated, even if the first argument (`expr`) is `True`. Therefore, the following statement generates an error if the value of n is 0 (zero):

```
MsgBox IIf(n = 0, 0, 1 / n)
```

Select Case constructs

The `Select Case` construct is useful for choosing among three or more options. This construct also works with two options and is a good alternative to `If-Then-Else`. The syntax for `Select Case` is as follows:

```
Select Case testexpression
    [Case expressionlist-n
        [instructions-n]]
    [Case Else
        [default_instructions]]
End Select
```

The following example of a `Select Case` construct shows another way to code the `GreetMe` examples that I presented in the preceding section:

```
Sub GreetMe()
    Dim Msg As String
    Select Case Time
        Case Is < 0.5
            Msg = "Good Morning"
        Case 0.5 To 0.75
            Msg = "Good Afternoon"
        Case Else
```

```
          Msg = "Good Evening"
     End Select
     MsgBox Msg
End Sub
```

And here's a rewritten version of the Discount example using a Select Case construct. This procedure assumes that Quantity is always an integer value. For simplicity, the procedure performs no error checking.

```
Sub Discount3()
     Dim Quantity As Variant
     Dim Discount As Double
     Quantity = InputBox("Enter Quantity: ")
     Select Case Quantity
          Case ""
               Exit Sub
          Case 0 To 24
               Discount = 0.1
          Case 25 To 49
               Discount = 0.15
          Case 50 To 74
               Discount = 0.2
          Case Is >= 75
               Discount = 0.25
     End Select
     MsgBox "Discount: " & Discount
End Sub
```

The Case statement also can use a comma to separate multiple values for a single case. The following procedure uses the VBA WeekDay function to determine whether the current day is a weekend (that is, the Weekday function returns 1 or 7). The procedure then displays an appropriate message.

```
Sub GreetUser1()
     Select Case Weekday(Now)
          Case 1, 7
               MsgBox "This is the weekend"
          Case Else
               MsgBox "This is not the weekend"
     End Select
End Sub
```

The following example shows another way to code the previous procedure:

```
Sub GreetUser2()
     Select Case Weekday(Now)
          Case 2, 3, 4, 5, 6
               MsgBox "This is not the weekend"
```

```
        Case Else
            MsgBox "This is the weekend"
    End Select
End Sub
```

Any number of instructions can be written below each `Case` statement, and they all are executed if that case evaluates to `True`. If you use only one instruction per case, as in the preceding example, you might want to put the instruction on the same line as the `Case` keyword (but don't forget the VBA statement-separator character, the colon). This technique makes the code more compact. For example:

```
Sub Discount3()
    Dim Quantity As Variant
    Dim Discount As Double
    Quantity = InputBox("Enter Quantity: ")
    Select Case Quantity
        Case "": Exit Sub
        Case  0 To 24: Discount = 0.1
        Case 25 To 49: Discount = 0.15
        Case 50 To 74: Discount = 0.2
        Case Is >= 75: Discount = 0.25
    End Select
    MsgBox "Discount: " & Discount
End Sub
```

TIP

VBA exits a `Select Case` construct as soon as a `True` case is found. Therefore, for maximum efficiency, you should check the most likely case first.

`Select Case` structures can also be nested. The following procedure, for example, uses the VBA `TypeName` function to determine what is selected (a range, nothing, or anything else). If a range is selected, the procedure executes a nested `Select Case` and tests for the number of cells in the range. If one cell is selected, it displays `One cell is selected`. Otherwise, it displays a message with the number of selected rows.

```
Sub SelectionType()
    Select Case TypeName(Selection)
        Case "Range"
            Select Case Selection.Count
                Case 1
                    MsgBox "One cell is selected"
                Case Else
                    MsgBox Selection.Rows.Count & " rows"
            End Select
        Case "Nothing"
            MsgBox "Nothing is selected"
```

```
        Case Else
            MsgBox "Something other than a range"
    End Select
End Sub
```

This procedure also demonstrates the use of `Case Else`, a catch-all case. You can nest `Select Case` constructs as deeply as you need, but make sure that each `Select Case` statement has a corresponding `End Select` statement.

This procedure demonstrates the value of using indentation in your code to clarify the structure. For example, take a look at the same procedure without the indentations:

```
Sub SelectionType()
Select Case TypeName(Selection)
Case "Range"
Select Case Selection.Count
Case 1
MsgBox "One cell is selected"
Case Else
MsgBox Selection.Rows.Count & " rows"
End Select
Case "Nothing"
MsgBox "Nothing is selected"
Case Else
MsgBox "Something other than a range"
End Select
End Sub
```

Fairly incomprehensible, eh?

Looping blocks of instructions

Looping is the process of repeating a block of instructions. You might know the number of times to loop, or the number could be determined by the values of variables in your program.

The following code, which enters consecutive numbers into a range, demonstrates what I call a *bad loop*. The procedure uses two variables to store a starting value (`StartVal`) and the total number of cells to fill (`NumToFill`). This loop uses the `GoTo` statement to control the flow. If the `Cnt` variable, which keeps track of how many cells are filled, is less than the value of `NumToFill`, program control loops back to `DoAnother`.

```
Sub BadLoop()
    Dim StartVal As Integer
    Dim NumToFill As Integer
    Dim Cnt As Integer
    StartVal = 1
    NumToFill = 100
    ActiveCell.Value = StartVal
```

```
    Cnt = 1
DoAnother:
    ActiveCell.Offset(Cnt, 0).Value = StartVal + Cnt
    Cnt = Cnt + 1
    If Cnt < NumToFill Then GoTo DoAnother Else Exit Sub
End Sub
```

This procedure works as intended, so why is it an example of bad looping? Programmers generally frown on using a GoTo statement when not absolutely necessary. Using GoTo statements to loop is contrary to the concept of structured coding (see the "What Is Structured Programming?" sidebar). In fact, a GoTo statement makes the code much more difficult to read because it's almost impossible to represent a loop using line indentations. In addition, this type of unstructured loop makes the procedure more susceptible to error. Furthermore, using lots of labels results in *spaghetti code* — code that appears to have little or no structure and flows haphazardly.

Because VBA has several structured looping commands, you almost never have to rely on GoTo statements for your decision making.

FOR-NEXT LOOPS

The simplest type of a good loop is a For-Next loop. Its syntax is

```
For counter = start To end [Step stepval]
    [instructions]
    [Exit For]
    [instructions]
Next [counter]
```

Following is an example of a For-Next loop that doesn't use the optional Step value or the optional Exit For statement. This routine executes the Sum = Sum + Sqr(Count) statement 100 times and displays the result — that is, the sum of the square roots of the first 100 integers.

```
Sub SumSquareRoots()
    Dim Sum As Double
    Dim Count As Integer
    Sum = 0
    For Count = 1 To 100
        Sum = Sum + Sqr(Count)
    Next Count
    MsgBox Sum
End Sub
```

In this example, Count (the loop counter variable) starts out as 1 and increases by 1 each time the loop repeats. The Sum variable simply accumulates the square roots of each value of Count.

What Is Structured Programming?

Hang around with programmers, and sooner or later you'll hear the term *structured programming*. You'll also discover that structured programs are considered superior to unstructured programs.

So what is structured programming? And can you do it with VBA?

The basic premise of structured programming is that a routine or code segment should have only one entry point and one exit point. In other words, a body of code should be a standalone unit, and program control should not jump into or exit from the middle of this unit. As a result, structured programming rules out the GoTo statement. When you write structured code, your program progresses in an orderly manner and is easy to follow — as opposed to spaghetti code, in which a program jumps around.

A structured program is easier to read and understand than an unstructured one. More important, it's also easier to modify.

VBA is a structured language. It offers standard structured constructs, such as If-Then-Else and Select Case and the For-Next, Do Until, and Do While loops. Furthermore, VBA fully supports modular code construction.

If you're new to programming, it's a good idea to form good structured-programming habits early.

CAUTION

When you use For-Next loops, it's important to understand that the loop counter is a normal variable — nothing special. As a result, it's possible to change the value of the loop counter within the block of code executed between the For and Next statements. This is, however, a bad practice and can cause unpredictable results. In fact, you should take precautions to ensure that your code does not change the loop counter.

You can also use a Step value to skip some values in the loop. Here's the same procedure rewritten to sum the square roots of the odd numbers between 1 and 100:

```
Sub SumOddSquareRoots()
    Dim Sum As Double
    Dim Count As Integer
    Sum = 0
    For Count = 1 To 100 Step 2
        Sum = Sum + Sqr(Count)
    Next Count
    MsgBox Sum
End Sub
```

In this procedure, Count starts out as 1 and then takes on values of 3, 5, 7, and so on. The final value of Count used within the loop is 99. When the loop ends, the value of Count is 101.

A `Step` value in a `For-Next` loop can also be negative. The procedure that follows deletes Rows 2, 4, 6, 8, and 10 of the active worksheet:

```
Sub DeleteRows()
    Dim RowNum As Long
    For RowNum = 10 To 2 Step -2
        Rows(RowNum).Delete
    Next RowNum
End Sub
```

You may wonder why I used a negative `Step` value in the `DeleteRows` procedure. If you use a positive `Step` value, as shown in the following procedure, incorrect rows are deleted. That's because the row numbers below a deleted row get a new row number. For example, when Row 2 is deleted, Row 3 becomes the new Row 2. Using a negative `Step` value ensures that the correct rows are deleted.

```
Sub DeleteRows2()
    Dim RowNum As Long
    For RowNum = 2 To 10 Step 2
        Rows(RowNum).Delete
    Next RowNum
End Sub
```

The following procedure performs the same task as the `BadLoop` example found at the beginning of the "Looping blocks of instructions" section. I eliminate the `GoTo` statement, however, converting a bad loop into a good loop that uses the `For-Next` structure.

```
Sub GoodLoop()
    Dim StartVal As Integer
    Dim NumToFill As Integer
    Dim Cnt As Integer
    StartVal = 1
    NumToFill = 100
    For Cnt = 0 To NumToFill - 1
        ActiveCell.Offset(Cnt, 0).Value = StartVal + Cnt
    Next Cnt
End Sub
```

`For-Next` loops can also include one or more `Exit For` statements within the loop. When this statement is encountered, the loop terminates immediately and control passes to the statement following the `Next` statement of the current `For-Next` loop. The following example demonstrates use of the `Exit For` statement. This procedure determines which cell has the largest value in Column A of the active worksheet:

```
Sub ExitForDemo()
    Dim MaxVal As Double
    Dim Row As Long
    MaxVal = Application.WorksheetFunction.Max(Range("A:A"))
```

```
    For Row = 1 To 1048576
        If Cells(Row, 1).Value = MaxVal Then
            Exit For
        End If
    Next Row
    MsgBox "Max value is in Row " & Row
    Cells(Row, 1).Activate
End Sub
```

The maximum value in the column is calculated by using the Excel MAX function, and the value is assigned to the MaxVal variable. The For-Next loop checks each cell in the column. If the cell being checked is equal to MaxVal, the Exit For statement terminates the loop and the statements following the Next statement are executed. These statements display the row of the maximum value and activate the cell.

NOTE

The ExitForDemo procedure is presented to demonstrate how to exit from a For-Next loop. However, it is not the most efficient way to activate the largest value in a range. In fact, a single statement does the job:

```
    Range("A:A").Find(Application.WorksheetFunction.Max _
        (Range("A:A"))).Activate
```

The previous examples use relatively simple loops. But you can have any number of statements in the loop, and you can even nest For-Next loops inside other For-Next loops. Here's an example that uses nested For-Next loops to initialize a 10 x 10 x 10 array with the value −1. When the procedure is finished, each of the 1,000 elements in MyArray contains −1.

```
Sub NestedLoops()
    Dim MyArray(1 to 10, 1 to 10, 1 to 10)
    Dim i As Integer, j As Integer, k As Integer
    For i = 1 To 10
        For j = 1 To 10
            For k = 1 To 10
                MyArray(i, j, k) = -1
            Next k
        Next j
    Next i
End Sub
```

DO WHILE LOOPS

This section describes another type of looping structure available in VBA. Unlike a For-Next loop, a Do While loop executes as long as a specified condition is met.

A `Do While` loop can have either of two syntaxes:

```
Do [While condition]
    [instructions]
    [Exit Do]
    [instructions]
Loop
```

or

```
Do
    [instructions]
    [Exit Do]
    [instructions]
Loop [While condition]
```

As you can see, VBA lets you put the `While` condition at the beginning or the end of the loop. The difference between these two syntaxes involves the point in time when the condition is evaluated. In the first syntax, the contents of the loop may never be executed. In the second syntax, the statements inside the loop are always executed at least one time.

The following examples insert a series of dates into the active worksheet. The dates correspond to the days in the current month, and the dates are entered in a column beginning at the active cell.

 NOTE

These examples use some VBA date-related functions:

- `Date` returns the current date.
- `Month` returns the month number for a date supplied as its argument.
- `DateSerial` returns a date for the year, month, and day supplied as arguments.

The first example demonstrates a `Do While` loop that tests the condition at the beginning of the loop: The EnterDates1 procedure writes the dates of the current month to a worksheet column, beginning with the active cell.

```
Sub EnterDates1()
'   Do While, with test at the beginning
    Dim TheDate As Date
    TheDate = DateSerial(Year(Date), Month(Date), 1)
    Do While Month(TheDate) = Month(Date)
        ActiveCell = TheDate
        TheDate = TheDate + 1
        ActiveCell.Offset(1, 0).Activate
    Loop
End Sub
```

This procedure uses a variable, TheDate, which contains the dates that are written to the worksheet. This variable is initialized with the first day of the current month. Inside of the loop, the value of TheDate is entered into the active cell, TheDate is incremented, and the next cell is activated. The loop continues while the month of TheDate is the same as the month of the current date.

The following procedure has the same result as the EnterDates1 procedure, but it uses the second Do While loop syntax, which checks the condition at the end of the loop.

```
Sub EnterDates2()
'    Do While, with test at the end
    Dim TheDate As Date
    TheDate = DateSerial(Year(Date), Month(Date), 1)
    Do
        ActiveCell = TheDate
        TheDate = TheDate + 1
        ActiveCell.Offset(1, 0).Activate
    Loop While Month(TheDate) = Month(Date)
End Sub
```

The following is another Do While loop example. This procedure opens a text file, reads each line, converts the text to uppercase, and then stores it in the active sheet, beginning with cell A1 and continuing down the column. The procedure uses the VBA EOF function, which returns True when the end of the file has been reached. The final statement closes the text file.

```
Sub DoWhileDemo1()
    Dim LineCt As Long
    Dim LineOfText As String
    Open "c:\data\textfile.txt" For Input As #1
    LineCt = 0
    Do While Not EOF(1)
        Line Input #1, LineOfText
        Range("A1").Offset(LineCt, 0) = UCase(LineOfText)
        LineCt = LineCt + 1
    Loop
    Close #1
End Sub
```

 ## CROSS-REFERENCE

For additional information about reading and writing text files using VBA, see Chapter 27.

Do While loops can also contain one or more Exit Do statements. When an Exit Do statement is encountered, the loop ends immediately and control passes to the statement following the Loop statement.

Do Until loops

The Do Until loop structure is very similar to the Do While structure. The difference is evident only when the condition is tested. In a Do While loop, the loop executes *while* the condition is True; in a Do Until loop, the loop executes *until* the condition is True.

Do Until also has two syntaxes:

```
Do [Until condition]
    [instructions]
    [Exit Do]
    [instructions]
Loop
```

or

```
Do
    [instructions]
    [Exit Do]
    [instructions]
Loop [Until condition]
```

The two examples that follow perform the same action as the Do While date entry examples in the previous section. The difference in these two procedures is where the condition is evaluated (at the beginning or at the end of the loop).

```
Sub EnterDates3()
'   Do Until, with test at beginning
    Dim TheDate As Date
    TheDate = DateSerial(Year(Date), Month(Date), 1)
    Do Until Month(TheDate) <> Month(Date)
        ActiveCell = TheDate
        TheDate = TheDate + 1
        ActiveCell.Offset(1, 0).Activate
    Loop
End Sub
```

```
Sub EnterDates4()
'   Do Until, with test at end
    Dim TheDate As Date
    TheDate = DateSerial(Year(Date), Month(Date), 1)
    Do
        ActiveCell = TheDate
        TheDate = TheDate + 1
        ActiveCell.Offset(1, 0).Activate
    Loop Until Month(TheDate) <> Month(Date)
End Sub
```

Part III

The following example was originally presented for the Do While loop but has been rewritten to use a Do Until loop. The only difference is the line with the Do statement. This example makes the code a bit clearer because it avoids the negative required in the Do While example.

```
Sub DoUntilDemo1()
    Dim LineCt As Long
    Dim LineOfText As String
    Open "c:\data\textfile.txt" For Input As #1
    LineCt = 0
    Do Until EOF(1)
        Line Input #1, LineOfText
        Range("A1").Offset(LineCt, 0) = UCase(LineOfText)
        LineCt = LineCt + 1
    Loop
    Close #1
End Sub
```

NOTE

VBA supports yet another type of loop, While Wend. This looping structure is included primarily for compatibility purposes. I mention it here in case you ever encounter such a loop. Here's how the date entry procedure looks when it's coded to use a While Wend loop:

```
Sub EnterDates5()
    Dim TheDate As Date
    TheDate = DateSerial(Year(Date), Month(Date), 1)
    While Month(TheDate) = Month(Date)
        ActiveCell = TheDate
        TheDate = TheDate + 1
        ActiveCell.Offset(1, 0).Activate
    Wend
End Sub
```

Chapter 9

Working with VBA Sub Procedures

In This Chapter

A *procedure* holds a group of Visual Basic for Applications (VBA) statements that accomplishes a desired task. Most VBA code is contained in procedures. This chapter focuses on `Sub` procedures.

◆ Declaring and creating VBA `Sub` procedures

◆ Executing procedures

◆ Passing arguments to a procedure

◆ Using error-handling techniques

◆ An example of developing a useful procedure

 CROSS-REFERENCE

VBA also supports `Function` procedures, which I discuss in Chapter 10. Chapter 11 has many additional examples of procedures, both `Sub` and `Function`, that you can incorporate into your work.

About Procedures

A *procedure* is a series of VBA statements that resides in a VBA module, which you access in the Visual Basic Editor (VBE). A module can hold any number of procedures.

237

You have a number of ways to *call*, or execute, procedures. A procedure is executed from beginning to end, but it can also be ended prematurely.

TIP

A procedure can be any length, but many people prefer to avoid creating extremely long procedures that perform many different operations. You may find it easier to write several smaller procedures, each with a single purpose. Then, design a main procedure that calls those other procedures. This approach can make your code easier to maintain.

Some procedures are written to receive arguments. An *argument* is simply information that is used by the procedure and that is passed to the procedure when it is executed. Procedure arguments work much like the arguments that you use in Excel worksheet functions. Instructions within the procedure generally perform logical operations on these arguments, and the results of the procedure are usually based on those arguments.

Declaring a Sub procedure

A procedure declared with the `Sub` keyword must adhere to the following syntax:

```
[Private | Public][Static] Sub name ([arglist])
    [instructions]
    [Exit Sub]
    [instructions]
End Sub
```

- `Private`: (Optional) Indicates that the procedure is accessible only to other procedures in the same module.

- `Public`: (Optional) Indicates that the procedure is accessible to all other procedures in all other modules in the workbook. If used in a module that contains an `Option Private Module` statement, the procedure is not available outside the project.

- `Static`: (Optional) Indicates that the procedure's variables are preserved when the procedure ends.

- `Sub`: (Required) The keyword that indicates the beginning of a procedure.

- `name`: (Required) Any valid procedure name.

- `arglist`: (Optional) Represents a list of variables, enclosed in parentheses, that receive arguments passed to the procedure. Use a comma to separate arguments. If the procedure uses no arguments, a set of empty parentheses is required.

- `instructions`: (Optional) Represents valid VBA instructions.

- `Exit Sub`: (Optional) A statement that forces an immediate exit from the procedure prior to its formal completion.

- `End Sub`: (Required) Indicates the end of the procedure.

Naming Procedures

Every procedure must have a name. The rules governing procedure names are generally the same as for variable names. Ideally, a procedure's name should describe what its contained processes do. A good rule is to use a name that includes a verb and a noun (for example, `ProcessDate`, `PrintReport`, `Sort_Array`, or `CheckFilename`). Avoid meaningless names such as `DoIt`, `Update`, and `Fix`.

Some programmers use sentence-like names that describe the procedure (for example, `WriteReportToTextFile` and `Get_Print_Options_ and_Print_Report`).

NOTE

With a few exceptions, all VBA instructions in a module must be contained within procedures. Exceptions include module-level variable declarations, user-defined data type definitions, and a few other instructions that specify module-level options (for example, `Option Explicit`).

Scoping a procedure

In the preceding chapter, I note that a variable's *scope* determines the modules and procedures in which the variable can be used. Similarly, a procedure's scope determines which other procedures can call it.

PUBLIC PROCEDURES

By default, procedures are *public* — that is, they can be called by other procedures in any module in the workbook. It's not necessary to use the `Public` keyword, but programmers often include it for clarity. The following two procedures are both public:

```
Sub First()
'    ... [code goes here] ...
End Sub

Public Sub Second()
'    ... [code goes here] ...
End Sub
```

PRIVATE PROCEDURES

Private procedures can be called by other procedures in the same module but not by procedures in other modules.

NOTE

When a user displays the Macro dialog box, Excel shows only the public procedures. Therefore, if you have procedures that are designed to be called only by other procedures in the same module, you should make sure that those procedures are declared as `Private`. Doing so prevents the user from running these procedures from the Macro dialog box.

The following example declares a private procedure named `MySub`:

```
Private Sub MySub()
'    ... [code goes here] ...
End Sub
```

TIP

You can force all procedures in a module to be private — even those declared with the `Public` keyword — by including the following statement before your first `Sub` statement:

```
Option Private Module
```

If you write this statement in a module, you can omit the `Private` keyword from your `Sub` declarations.

Excel's macro recorder normally creates new `Sub` procedures called `Macro1`, `Macro2`, and so on. These procedures are all public procedures, and they will never use any arguments.

Executing Sub Procedures

In this section, I describe the various ways to *execute,* or call, a VBA `Sub` procedure:

- With the Run Sub/UserForm command (in the VBE). Or you can press the F5 shortcut key or use the Run Sub/UserForm button on the Standard toolbar.

- From Excel's Macro dialog box.

- By using the Ctrl key shortcut assigned to the procedure (assuming that you assigned one).

- By clicking a button or a shape on a worksheet. The button or shape must have the procedure assigned to it.

- From another procedure that you write. `Sub` and `Function` procedures can execute other procedures.

- From a custom control in the Ribbon. In addition, built-in Ribbon controls can be "repurposed" to execute a macro.

- From a customized shortcut menu.

- When an event occurs. These events include opening the workbook, saving the workbook, closing the workbook, changing a cell's value, activating a sheet, and many other things.

- From the Immediate window in the VBE. Just type the name of the procedure, including any arguments that may apply, and press Enter.

I discuss these methods of executing procedures in the following sections.

NOTE

In many cases, a procedure will not work properly unless it is executed in the appropriate context. For example, if a procedure is designed to work with the active worksheet, it will fail if a chart sheet is active. A good procedure incorporates code that checks for the appropriate context and exits gracefully if it can't proceed.

Executing a procedure with the Run Sub/UserForm command

The VBE Run Sub/UserForm menu command is used primarily to test a procedure while you are developing it. You would never require a user to activate the VBE to execute a procedure. Choose Run ➪ Run Sub/UserForm in the VBE to execute the current procedure (in other words, the procedure that contains the cursor). Or, press F5, or use the Run Sub/UserForm button on the Standard toolbar.

If the cursor is not located within a procedure when you issue the Run Sub/UserForm command, VBE displays its Macro dialog box so that you can select a procedure to execute.

Executing a procedure from the Macro dialog box

Choosing Excel's Developer ➪ Code ➪ Macros command displays the Macro dialog box, as shown in Figure 9-1. (You can also press Alt+F8 to access this dialog box.) Use the Macros In drop-down box to limit the scope of the macros displayed (for example, show only the macros in the active workbook).

The Macro dialog box does *not* display

- `Function` procedures

- `Sub` procedures declared with the `Private` keyword

- `Sub` procedures that require one or more arguments

- `Sub` procedures contained in add-ins

Figure 9-1: The Macro dialog box.

TIP

Even though procedures stored in an add-in are not listed in the Macro dialog box, you still can execute such a procedure if you know the name. Simply type the procedure name in the Macro Name field in the Macro dialog box and then click Run.

Executing a procedure with a Ctrl+shortcut key combination

You can assign a Ctrl+shortcut key combination to any procedure that doesn't use any arguments. If you assign the Ctrl+U key combo to a procedure named `UpdateCustomerList`, for example, pressing Ctrl+U executes the that procedure.

When you begin recording a macro, the Record Macro dialog box gives you the opportunity to assign a shortcut key. However, you can assign a shortcut key at any time. To assign a Ctrl shortcut key to a procedure (or to change a procedure's shortcut key), follow these steps:

1. Activate Excel and choose Developer ➪ Code ➪ Macros.

2. Select the appropriate procedure from the list box in the Macro dialog box.

3. Click the Options button to display the Macro Options dialog box (see Figure 9-2).

4. Enter a character into the Ctrl+ text box.

   Note: The character that you enter into the Ctrl+ text box is case-sensitive. If you enter a lowercase *s*, the shortcut key combo is Ctrl+S. If you enter an uppercase *S*, the short-cut key combo is Ctrl+Shift+S.

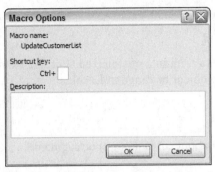

Figure 9-2: The Macro Options dialog box lets you assign a Ctrl key shortcut and an optional description to a procedure.

5. Enter a description (optional). If you enter a description for a macro, it is displayed at the bottom of the Macro dialog box when the procedure is selected in the list box.

6. Click OK to close the Macro Options dialog box, and then click Close to close the Macro dialog box.

CAUTION

If you assign one of Excel's predefined shortcut key combinations to a procedure, your key assignment takes precedence over the predefined key assignment. For example, Ctrl+S is the Excel predefined shortcut key for saving the active workbook. But if you assign Ctrl+S to a procedure, pressing Ctrl+S no longer saves the active workbook.

TIP

The following keyboard keys are *not* used by Excel 2007 for Ctrl+key combinations: E, J, M, and Q. Excel doesn't use too many Ctrl+Shift+key combinations. In fact, you can use any of them *except* F, L, N, O, P, and W.

Executing a procedure from the Ribbon

If you're willing to go through a bit of effort, you can write XML code to add a new button (or other control) to the Ribbon and assign your macro to that control. Note that modifying the Ribbon is done outside of Excel, and it cannot be done using VBA.

CROSS-REFERENCE

Refer to Chapter 22 for more information about customizing the Ribbon.

Executing a procedure from a customized shortcut menu

A macro can also be executed by clicking a menu item in a customized shortcut menu. A shortcut menu appears when you right-click an object or range in Excel.

CROSS-REFERENCE

Refer to Chapter 23 for more information about customizing shortcut menus.

Executing a procedure from another procedure

One of the most common ways to execute a procedure is from another VBA procedure. You have three ways to do this:

- Enter the procedure's name, followed by its arguments (if any) separated by commas.

- Use the `Call` keyword followed by the procedure's name and then its arguments (if any) enclosed in parentheses and separated by commas.

- Use the `Run` method of the `Application` object. The `Run` method is useful when you need to run a procedure whose name is assigned to a variable. You can then pass the variable as an argument to the `Run` method.

The following example demonstrates the first method. In this case, the `MySub` procedure processes some statements (not shown), executes the `UpdateSheet` procedure, and then executes the rest of the statements.

```
Sub MySub()
'    ... [code goes here] ...
    UpdateSheet
'    ... [code goes here] ...
End Sub

Sub UpdateSheet()
'    ... [code goes here] ...
End Sub
```

The following example demonstrates the second method. The `Call` keyword executes the `Update` procedure, which requires one argument; the calling procedure passes the argument to the called procedure. I discuss procedure arguments later in this chapter (see "Passing Arguments to Procedures").

```
Sub MySub()
    MonthNum = InputBox("Enter the month number: ")
    Call UpdateSheet(MonthNum)
```

```
'   ... [code goes here] ...
End Sub

Sub UpdateSheet(MonthSeq)
'   ... [code goes here] ...
End Sub
```

TIP

Even though it's optional, some programmers always use the `Call` keyword just to make it perfectly clear that another procedure is being called.

The next example uses the `Run` method to execute the `UpdateSheet` procedure and then to pass `MonthNum` as the argument:

```
Sub MySub()
    MonthNum = InputBox("Enter the month number: ")
    Application.Run "UpdateSheet", MonthNum
'   ... [code goes here] ...
End Sub

Sub UpdateSheet(MonthSeq)
'   ... [code goes here] ...
End Sub
```

Perhaps the best reason to use the `Run` method is when the procedure name is assigned to a variable. In fact, it's the only way to execute a procedure in such a way. The following example demonstrates this. The `Main` procedure uses the VBA `WeekDay` function to determine the day of the week (an integer between 1 and 7, beginning with Sunday). The `SubToCall` variable is assigned a string that represents a procedure name. The `Run` method then calls the appropriate procedure (either `WeekEnd` or `Daily`).

```
Sub Main()
    Dim SubToCall As String
    Select Case WeekDay(Now)
        Case 1, 7: SubToCall = "WeekEnd"
        Case Else: SubToCall = "Daily"
    End Select
        Application.Run SubToCall
End Sub

Sub WeekEnd()
    MsgBox "Today is a weekend"
'   Code to execute on the weekend
'   goes here
```

Part III

```
End Sub

Sub Daily()
    MsgBox "Today is not a weekend"
'   Code to execute on the weekdays
'   goes here
End Sub
```

CALLING A PROCEDURE IN A DIFFERENT MODULE

If VBA can't locate a called procedure in the current module, it looks for public procedures in other modules in the same project.

If you need to call a private procedure from another procedure, both procedures must reside in the same module.

You can't have two procedures with the same name in the same module, but you can have identically named procedures in different modules within the project. You can force VBA to execute an *ambiguously named* procedure — that is, another procedure in a different module that has the same name. To do so, precede the procedure name with the module name and a dot. For example, say that you define procedures named MySub in Module1 and Module2. If you want a procedure in Module2 to call the MySub in Module1, you can use either of the following statements:

```
Module1.MySub
Call Module1.MySub
```

If you do not differentiate between procedures that have the same name, you get an Ambiguous name detected error message.

CALLING A PROCEDURE IN A DIFFERENT WORKBOOK

In some cases, you may need your procedure to execute another procedure defined in a different workbook. To do so, you have two options: Either establish a reference to the other workbook or use the Run method and specify the workbook name explicitly.

To add a reference to another workbook, choose the VBE's Tools ➪ References command. Excel displays the References dialog box (see Figure 9-3), which lists all available references, including all open workbooks. Simply check the box that corresponds to the workbook that you want to add as a reference and then click OK. After you establish a reference, you can call procedures in the workbook as if they were in the same workbook as the calling procedure.

A referenced workbook does not have to be open; it is treated like a separate object library. Use the Browse button in the References dialog box to establish a reference to a workbook that isn't open.

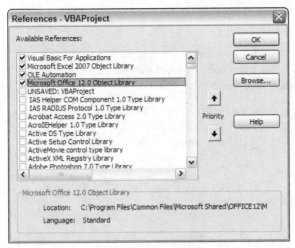

Figure 9-3: The References dialog box lets you establish a reference to another workbook.

The workbook names that appear in the list of references are listed by their VBE project names. By default, every project is initially named *VBAProject*. Therefore, the list may contain several identically named items. To distinguish a project, change its name in the Project Properties dialog box. Click the project name in the Project window and then choose Tools ⇨ xxxx Properties (where xxxx is the current project name). In the Project Properties dialog box, click the General tab and change the name displayed in the Project Name field.

The list of references displayed in the References dialog box also includes object libraries and ActiveX controls that are registered on your system. Your Excel 2007 workbooks always include references to the following object libraries:

- Visual Basic for Applications

- Microsoft Excel 12.0 Object Library

- OLE Automation

- Microsoft Office 12.0 Object Library

- Microsoft Forms 2.0 Object Library (optional, included only if your project includes a UserForm)

NOTE

Any additional references to other workbooks that you add are also listed in your project outline in the Project Explorer window in the VBE. These references are listed under a node called References.

Why Call Other Procedures?

If you're new to programming, you may wonder why anyone would ever want to call a procedure from another procedure. You may ask, "Why not just put the code from the called procedure into the calling procedure and keep things simple?"

One reason is to clarify your code. The simpler your code, the easier it is to maintain and modify. Smaller routines are easier to decipher and then debug. Examine the accompanying procedure, which does nothing but call other procedures. This procedure is very easy to follow.

```
Sub Main()
    Call GetUserOptions
    Call ProcessData
    Call CleanUp
    Call CloseItDown
End Sub
```

Calling other procedures also eliminates redundancy. Suppose that you need to perform an operation at ten different places in your routine. Rather than enter the code ten times, you can write a procedure to perform the operation and then simply call the procedure ten times.

Also, you may have a series of general-purpose procedures that you use frequently. If you store these in a separate module, you can import the module to your current project and then call these procedures as needed — which is much easier than copying and pasting the code into your new procedures.

Creating several small procedures rather than a single large one is often considered good programming practice. A modular approach not only makes your job easier but also makes life easier for the people who wind up working with your code.

If you've established a reference to a workbook that contains the procedure YourSub, for example, you can use either of the following statements to call YourSub:

```
YourSub
Call YourSub
```

To precisely identify a procedure in a different workbook, specify the project name, module name, and procedure name by using the following syntax:

```
MyProject.MyModule.MySub
```

Alternatively, you can use the Call keyword:

```
Call MyProject.MyModule.MySub
```

Another way to call a procedure in a different workbook is to use the Run method of the Application object. This technique does not require that you establish a reference, but the workbook that contains the procedure must be open. The following statement executes the Consolidate procedure located in a workbook named budget macros.xlsm:

```
Application.Run "'budget macros.xlsm'!Consolidate"
```

Executing a procedure by clicking an object

Excel provides a variety of objects that you can place on a worksheet or chart sheet, and you can attach a macro to any of these objects. These objects fall into several classes:

- ActiveX controls

- Forms controls

- Inserted objects (Shapes, SmartArt, WordArt, charts, and pictures)

 NOTE

The Developer ➪ Controls ➪ Insert drop-down list contains two types of controls that you can insert on a worksheet: Form controls and ActiveX controls. The ActiveX controls are similar to the controls that you use in a UserForm. The Forms controls were designed for Excel 5 and Excel 95, but they can still be used in later versions (and may be preferable in some cases).

Unlike the Form controls, the ActiveX controls cannot be used to execute an arbitrary macro. An ActiveX control executes a specially-named macro. For example, if you insert an ActiveX button control named CommandButton1, clicking the button executes a macro named CommandButton1_Click, which must be located in the code module for the sheet on which the control was inserted.

Refer to Chapter 13 for information about using controls on worksheets.

To assign a procedure to a Button object from the Form controls, follow these steps:

1. Select Developer ➪ Controls ➪ Insert and click the button in the Form Controls group.

2. Click the worksheet to create the button. Or, you can drag your mouse on the worksheet to change the default size of the button.

   Excel jumps right in and displays the Assign Macro dialog box (see Figure 9-4). It proposes a macro that's based on the button's name.

3. Select or enter the macro that you want to assign to the button and then click OK.

You can always change the macro assignment by right-clicking the button and choosing Assign Macro.

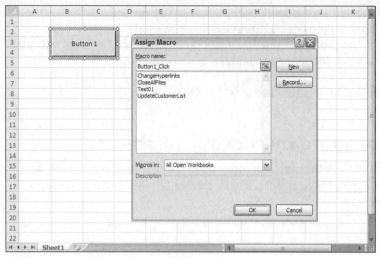

Figure 9-4: Assigning a macro to a button.

To assign a macro to a Shape, SmartArt, WordArt, chart, or picture, right-click the object and choose Assign Macro from the shortcut menu.

Executing a procedure when an event occurs

You might want a procedure to execute when a particular event occurs. Examples of events include opening a workbook, entering data into a worksheet, saving a workbook, clicking a CommandButton ActiveX control, and many others. A procedure that is executed when an event occurs is an *event handler* procedure. Event handler procedures are characterized by the following:

- They have special names that are made up of an object, an underscore, and the event name. For example, the procedure that is executed when a workbook is opened is Workbook_Open.

- They are stored in the Code module for the particular object.

CROSS-REFERENCE

Chapter 19 is devoted to event handler procedures.

Executing a procedure from the Immediate window

You also can execute a procedure by entering its name in the Immediate window of the VBE. If the Immediate window is not visible, press Ctrl+G. The Immediate window executes VBA statements while you enter them. To execute a procedure, simply enter the name of the procedure in the Immediate window and press Enter.

This method can be quite useful when you're developing a procedure because you can insert commands to display results in the Immediate window. The following procedure demonstrates this technique:

```
Sub ChangeCase()
    Dim MyString As String
    MyString = "This is a test"
    MyString = UCase(MyString)
    Debug.Print MyString
End Sub
```

Figure 9-5 shows what happens when you enter **ChangeCase** in the Immediate window: The Debug.Print statement displays the result immediately.

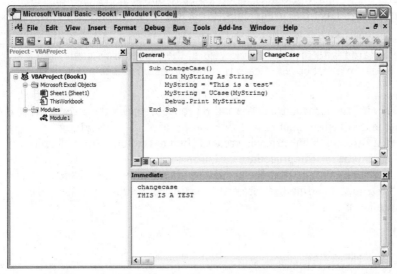

Figure 9-5: Executing a procedure by entering its name in the Immediate window.

Passing Arguments to Procedures

A procedure's *arguments* provide it with data that it uses in its instructions. The data that's passed by an argument can be any of the following:

- A variable
- A constant
- An array
- An object

The use of arguments by procedures is very similar to worksheet functions in the following respects:

- A procedure may not require any arguments.

- A procedure may require a fixed number of arguments.

- A procedure may accept an indefinite number of arguments.

- A procedure may require some arguments, leaving others optional.

- A procedure may have all optional arguments.

For example, a few of Excel's worksheet functions, such as RAND and NOW, use no arguments. Others, such as COUNTIF, require two arguments. Others still, such as SUM, can use up to 255 arguments. Still other worksheet functions have optional arguments. The PMT function, for example, can have five arguments (three are required; two are optional).

Most of the procedures that you've seen so far in this book have been declared without arguments. They were declared with just the Sub keyword, the procedure's name, and a set of empty parentheses. Empty parentheses indicate that the procedure does not accept arguments.

The following example shows two procedures. The Main procedure calls the ProcessFile procedure three times (the Call statement is in a For-Next loop). Before calling ProcessFile, however, a three-element array is created. Inside the loop, each element of the array becomes the argument for the procedure call. The ProcessFile procedure takes one argument (named TheFile). Notice that the argument goes inside parentheses in the Sub statement. When ProcessFile finishes, program control continues with the statement after the Call statement.

```
Sub Main()
    Dim File(1 To 3) As String
    Dim i as Integer
    File(1) = "dept1.xlsx"
    File(2) = "dept2.xlsx"
    File(3) = "dept3.xlsx"
    For i = 1 To 3
        Call ProcessFile(File(i))
    Next i
End Sub


Sub ProcessFile(TheFile)
    Workbooks.Open FileName:=TheFile
'    ...[more code here]...
End Sub
```

You can also, of course, pass *literals* (that is, not variables) to a procedure. For example:

```
Sub Main()
    Call ProcessFile("budget.xlsx")
End Sub
```

You can pass an argument to a procedure in two ways:

- **By reference:** Passing an argument by reference (the default method) simply passes the memory address of the variable. Changes to the argument within the procedure are made to the original variable.

- **By value:** Passing an argument by value passes a *copy* of the original variable. Consequently, changes to the argument within the procedure are not reflected in the original variable.

The following example demonstrates this concept. The argument for the Process procedure is passed by reference (the default method). After the Main procedure assigns a value of 10 to MyValue, it calls the Process procedure and passes MyValue as the argument. The Process procedure multiplies the value of its argument (named YourValue) by 10. When Process ends and program control passes back to Main, the MsgBox function displays MyValue: 100.

```
Sub Main()
    Dim MyValue As Integer
    MyValue = 10
    Call Process(MyValue)
    MsgBox MyValue
End Sub

Sub Process(YourValue)
    YourValue = YourValue * 10
End Sub
```

If you don't want the called procedure to modify any variables passed as arguments, you can modify the called procedure's argument list so that arguments are passed to it by *value* rather than by *reference*. To do so, precede the argument with the ByVal keyword. This technique causes the called routine to work with a copy of the passed variable's data — not the data itself. In the following procedure, for example, the changes made to YourValue in the Process procedure do not affect the MyValue variable in Main. As a result, the MsgBox function displays 10 and not 100.

```
Sub Process(ByVal YourValue)
    YourValue = YourValue * 10
End Sub
```

Using Public Variables versus Passing Arguments to a Procedure

In Chapter 8, I point out how a variable declared as `Public` (at the top of the module) is available to all procedures in the module. In some cases, you might want to access a `Public` variable rather than pass the variable as an argument when calling another procedure.

For example, the procedure that follows passes the value of `MonthVal` to the `ProcessMonth` procedure:

```
Sub MySub()
    Dim MonthVal as Integer
'   ... [code goes here]
    MonthVal = 4
    Call ProcessMonth(MonthVal)
'   ... [code goes here]
End Sub
```

An alternative approach, which doesn't use an argument, is

```
Public MonthVal as Integer

Sub MySub()
'   ... [code goes here]
    MonthVal = 4
    Call ProcessMonth2
'   ... [code goes here]
End Sub
```

In the revised code, because `MonthVal` is a public variable, the `ProcessMonth2` procedure can access it, thus eliminating the need for an argument for the `ProcessMonth2` procedure.

In most cases, you'll be content to use the default reference method of passing arguments. However, if your procedure needs to use data passed to it in an argument — and you must keep the original data intact — you'll want to pass the data by value.

A procedure's arguments can mix and match by value and by reference. Arguments preceded with `ByVal` are passed by value; all others are passed by reference.

 NOTE

If you pass a variable defined as a user-defined data type to a procedure, it must be passed by reference. Attempting to pass it by value generates an error.

Because I didn't declare a data type for any of the arguments in the preceding examples, all the arguments have been of the `Variant` data type. But a procedure that uses arguments can define the data types directly in the argument list. The following is a `Sub` statement for a procedure with two arguments of different data types. The first is declared as an integer, and the second is declared as a string.

```
Sub Process(Iterations As Integer, TheFile As String)
```

When you pass arguments to a procedure, the data that is passed as the argument must match the argument's data type. For example, if you call `Process` in the preceding example and pass a string variable for the first argument, you get an error: `ByRef argument type mismatch`.

NOTE

Arguments are relevant to both `Sub` procedures and `Function` procedures. In fact, arguments are more often used in `Function` procedures. In Chapter 10, where I focus on `Function` procedures, I provide additional examples of using arguments with your routines, including how to handle optional arguments.

Error-Handling Techniques

When a VBA procedure is running, errors can occur, as you undoubtedly know. These include either *syntax errors* (which you must correct before you can execute a procedure) or *runtime errors* (which occur while the procedure is running). This section deals with runtime errors.

CAUTION

For error-handling procedures to work, the Break on All Errors setting *must* be turned off. In the VBE, choose Tools ⇨ Options and click the General tab in the Options dialog box. If Break on All Errors is selected, VBA ignores your error-handling code. You'll usually want to use the Break on Unhandled Errors option.

Normally, a runtime error causes VBA to stop, and the user sees a dialog box that displays the error number and a description of the error. A good application doesn't make the user deal with these messages. Rather, it incorporates error-handling code to trap errors and take appropriate actions. At the very least, your error-handling code can display a more meaningful error message than the one VBA pops up.

CROSS-REFERENCE

Appendix C lists all the VBA error codes and descriptions.

Trapping errors

You can use the On Error statement to specify what happens when an error occurs. Basically, you have two choices:

- *Ignore the error and let VBA continue.* Your code can later examine the Err object to determine what the error was and then take action if necessary.

- *Jump to a special error-handling section of your code to take action.* This section is placed at the end of the procedure and is also marked by a label.

To cause your VBA code to continue when an error occurs, insert the following statement in your code:

```
On Error Resume Next
```

Some errors are inconsequential and can be ignored without causing a problem. But you may want to determine what the error was. When an error occurs, you can use the Err object to determine the error number. The VBA Error function can be used to display the text that corresponds to the Err.Number value. For example, the following statement displays the same information as the normal Visual Basic error dialog box (the error number and the error description):

```
MsgBox "Error " & Err & ": " & Error(Err.Number)
```

Figure 9-6 shows a VBA error message, and Figure 9-7 shows the same error displayed in a message box. You can, of course, make the error message a bit more meaningful to your end users by using more descriptive text.

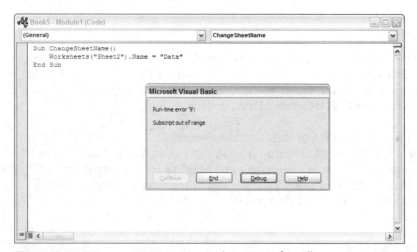

Figure 9-6: VBA error messages aren't always user friendly.

Figure 9-7: You can create a message box to display the error code and description.

NOTE

Referencing Err is equivalent to accessing the Number property of the Err object. Therefore, the following two statements have the same effect:

```
MsgBox Err
MsgBox Err.Number
```

You also use the On Error statement to specify a location in your procedure to jump to when an error occurs. You use a label to mark the location. For example:

```
On Error GoTo ErrorHandler
```

Error-handling examples

The first example demonstrates an error that can safely be ignored. The SpecialCells method selects cells that meet a certain criterion.

NOTE

The SpecialCells method is equivalent to choosing the Home ⇨ Editing ⇨ Find & Select ⇨ Go To Special command. The Go To Special dialog box provides you with a number of choices. For example, you can select cells that contain a numeric constant (non-formula).

In the example that follows, the SpecialCells method selects all the cells in the current range selection that contain a formula that returns a number. If no cells in the selection qualify, VBA displays the error message shown in Figure 9-8. Using the On Error Resume Next statement simply prevents the error message from appearing.

```
Sub SelectFormulas()
    On Error Resume Next
    Selection.SpecialCells(xlFormulas, xlNumbers).Select
    On Error GoTo 0
'    ...[more code goes here]
End Sub
```

The On Error GoTo 0 statement restores normal error handling for the remaining statements in the procedure.

Microsoft Visual Basic

Run-time error '1004':

No cells were found.

| Continue | End | Debug | Help |

Figure 9-8: The SpecialCells method generates this error if no cells are found.

The following procedure uses an additional statement to determine whether an error did occur:

```
Sub SelectFormulas2()
    On Error Resume Next
    Selection.SpecialCells(xlFormulas, xlNumbers).Select
    If Err.Number = 1004 Then MsgBox "No formula cells were found."
    On Error GoTo 0
'    ...[more code goes here]
End Sub
```

If the `Number` property of `Err` is equal to anything except 0, then an error occurred. The `If` statement checks to see if `Err.Number` is equal to 1004 and displays a message box if it is. In this example, the code is checking for a specific error number. To check for any error, use a statement like this:

```
If Err.Number <> 0 Then MsgBox "An error occurred."
```

The next example demonstrates error handling by jumping to a label.

```
Sub ErrorDemo()
    On Error GoTo Handler
    Selection.Value = 123
    Exit Sub
Handler:
    MsgBox "Cannot assign a value to the selection."
End Sub
```

The procedure attempts to assign a value to the current selection. If an error occurs (for example, a range is not selected or the sheet is protected), the assignment statement results in an error. The `On Error` statement specifies a jump to the `Handler` label if an error occurs. Notice the use of the `Exit Sub` statement before the label. This prevents the error-handling code from being executed if no error occurs. If this statement is omitted, the error message is displayed even if an error does not occur.

Sometimes, you can take advantage of an error to get information. The example that follows simply checks whether a particular workbook is open. It does not use any error handling.

```
Sub CheckForFile1()
    Dim FileName As String
    Dim FileExists As Boolean
    Dim book As Workbook
    FileName = "BUDGET.XLSX"
    FileExists = False

'   Cycle through all workbooks
    For Each book In Workbooks
        If UCase(book.Name) = FileName Then FileExists = True
    Next book

'   Display appropriate message
    If FileExists Then
        MsgBox FileName & " is open."
    Else
        MsgBox FileName & " is not open."
    End If
End Sub
```

Here, a `For Each-Next` loop cycles through all objects in the `Workbooks` collection. If the workbook is open, the `FileExists` variable is set to `True`. Finally, a message is displayed that tells the user whether the workbook is open.

The preceding routine can be rewritten to use error handling to determine whether the file is open. In the example that follows, the `On Error Resume Next` statement causes VBA to ignore any errors. The next instruction attempts to reference the workbook by assigning the workbook to an object variable (by using the `Set` keyword). If the workbook is not open, an error occurs. The `If-Then-Else` structure checks the value property of `Err` and displays the appropriate message.

```
Sub CheckForFile()
    Dim FileName As String
    Dim x As Workbook
    FileName = "BUDGET.XLSX"
    On Error Resume Next
    Set x = Workbooks(FileName)
    If Err = 0 Then
        MsgBox FileName & " is open."
    Else
        MsgBox FileName & " is not open."
    End If
    On Error GoTo 0
End Sub
```

CROSS-REFERENCE

Chapter 11 presents several additional examples that use error handling.

A Realistic Example That Uses Sub Procedures

In this chapter, I describe the basics of creating Sub procedures. Most of the previous examples, I will admit, have been rather wimpy. The remainder of this chapter is a real-life exercise that demonstrates many of the concepts covered in this and the preceding two chapters.

This section describes the development of a useful utility that qualifies as an application as defined in Chapter 5. More important, I demonstrate the *process* of analyzing a problem and then solving it with VBA. I wrote this section with VBA newcomers in mind. As a result, I don't simply present the code, but I also show how to find out what you need to know to develop the code.

CD-ROM

The completed application can be found on the companion CD-ROM.

The goal

The goal of this exercise is to develop a utility that rearranges a workbook by alphabetizing its sheets (something that Excel cannot do on its own). If you tend to create workbooks that consist of many sheets, you know that it can be difficult to locate a particular sheet. If the sheets are ordered alphabetically, however, it's easier to find a desired sheet.

Project requirements

Where to begin? One way to get started is to list the requirements for your application. When you develop your application, you can check your list to ensure that you're covering all the bases.

Here's the list of requirements that I compiled for this example application:

1. It should sort the sheets (that is, worksheets and chart sheets) in the active workbook in ascending order of their names.

2. It should be easy to execute.

3. It should always be available. In other words, the user shouldn't have to open a workbook to use this utility.

4. It should work properly for any workbook that's open.

5. It should not display any VBA error messages.

What you know

Often, the most difficult part of a project is figuring out where to start. In this case, I started by listing things that I know about Excel that may be relevant to the project requirements:

- Excel doesn't have a command that sorts sheets. Therefore, recording a macro to alphabetize the sheets is not an option.

- I can move a sheet easily by dragging its sheet tab.

  Mental note: Turn on the macro recorder and drag a sheet to a new location to find out what kind of code this action generates.

- Excel also has a Move or Copy dialog box, which is displayed when I right-click a sheet tab and choose Move or Copy. Would recording a macro of this command generate different code than moving a sheet manually?

- I'll need to know how many sheets are in the active workbook. I can get this information with VBA.

- I'll need to know the names of all the sheets. Again, I can get this information with VBA.

- Excel has a command that sorts data in worksheet cells.

  Mental note: Maybe I can transfer the sheet names to a range and use this feature. Or, maybe VBA has a sorting method that I can take advantage of.

- Thanks to the Macro Options dialog box, it's easy to assign a shortcut key to a macro.

- If a macro is stored in the Personal Macro Workbook, it will always be available.

- I need a way to test the application while I develop it. For certain, I don't want to be testing it using the same workbook in which I'm developing the code.

  Mental note: Create a dummy workbook for testing purposes.

- If I develop the code properly, VBA won't display any errors.

  Mental note: Wishful thinking . . .

The approach

Although I still didn't know exactly how to proceed, I could devise a preliminary, skeleton plan that describes the general tasks required:

1. Identify the active workbook.

2. Get a list of all the sheet names in the workbook.

3. Count the sheets.

4. Sort the sheet names (somehow).

5. Rearrange the sheets so they correspond to the sorted sheet names.

What you need to know

I saw a few holes in the plan. I knew that I had to determine the following:

- How to identify the active workbook

- How to count the sheets in the active workbook

- How to get a list of the sheet names

- How to sort the list

- How to rearrange the sheets according to the sorted list

TIP

When you lack critical information about specific methods or properties, you can consult this book or the VBA Help system. You may eventually discover what you need to know. Your best bet, however, is to turn on the macro recorder and examine the code that it generates when you perform some relevant actions. You will almost always get some clues as to how to proceed.

Some preliminary recording

Here's an example of using the macro recorder to learn about VBA. I started with a workbook that contained three worksheets. Then I turned on the macro recorder and specified my Personal Macro Workbook as the destination for the macro. With the macro recorder running, I dragged the third worksheet to the first sheet position. Here's the code that was generated by the macro recorder:

```
Sub Macro1()
    Sheets("Sheet3").Select
    Sheets("Sheet3").Move Before:=Sheets(1)
End Sub
```

I searched the VBA Help for *Move* and discovered that it's a method that moves a sheet to a new location in the workbook. It also takes an argument that specifies the location for the sheet. This information is very relevant to the task at hand. Curious, I then turned on the macro recorder to see whether using the Move or Copy dialog box would generate different code. It didn't.

Next, I needed to find out how many sheets were in the active workbook. I searched Help for the word *Count* and found out that it's a property of a collection. I activated the Immediate window in the VBE and typed the following statement:

```
? ActiveWorkbook.Count
```

Error! After a little more thought, I realized that I needed to get a count of the sheets within a workbook. So I tried this:

```
? ActiveWorkbook.Sheets.Count
```

Success. Figure 9-9 shows the result. More useful information.

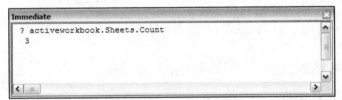

Figure 9-9: Use the VBE Immediate window to test a statement.

What about the sheet names? Time for another test. I entered the following statement in the Immediate window:

```
? ActiveWorkbook.Sheets(1).Name
```

This told me that the name of the first sheet is Sheet3, which is correct (because I'd moved it). More good information to keep in mind.

Then I remembered something about the For Each-Next construct: It is useful for cycling through each member of a collection. After consulting the Help system, I created a short procedure to test it:

```
Sub Test()
    For Each Sht In ActiveWorkbook.Sheets
        MsgBox Sht.Name
    Next Sht
End Sub
```

Another success. This macro displayed three message boxes, each showing a different sheet name.

Finally, it was time to think about sorting options. From the Help system, I learned that the Sort method applies to a Range object. So one option was to transfer the sheet names to a range and then sort the range, but that seemed like overkill for this application. I thought that a better option was to dump the sheet names into an array of strings and then sort the array by using VBA code.

Initial setup

Now I knew enough to get started writing some serious code. Before doing so, however, I needed to do some initial setup work. To re-create my steps, follow these instructions:

1. Create an empty workbook with five worksheets, named Sheet1, Sheet2, Sheet3, Sheet4, and Sheet5.

2. Move the sheets around randomly so that they aren't in any particular order.

3. Save the workbook as Test.xlsx.

4. Activate the VBE and select the Personal.xlsb project in the Project Window.

   If Personal.xlsb doesn't appear in the Project window in the VBE, it means that you've never used the Personal Macro Workbook. To have Excel create this workbook for you, simply record a macro (any macro) and specify the Personal Macro Workbook as the destination for the macro.

5. Insert a new VBA module in Personal.xlsb (choose Insert ➪ Module).

6. Create an empty Sub procedure called SortSheets (see Figure 9-10).

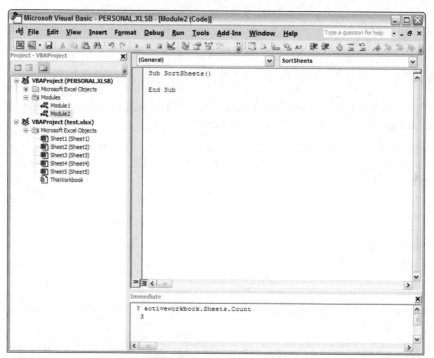

Figure 9-10: An empty procedure in a module located in the Personal Macro Workbook.

Actually, you can store this macro in any module in the Personal Macro Workbook. However, it's a good idea to keep each macro (or group of related macros) in a separate module. That way, you can easily export the module and import it into a different project later on.

7. Activate Excel. Choose Developer ➪ Code ➪ Macros to display the Macro dialog box.

8. In the Macro dialog box, select the SortSheets procedure and click the Options button to assign a shortcut key to this macro. The Ctrl+Shift+S key combination is a good choice.

Code writing

Now it's time to write some code. I knew that I needed to put the sheet names into an array of strings. Because I don't know yet how many sheets are in the active workbook, I used a Dim statement with empty parentheses to declare the array. I knew that I could use ReDim afterward to redimension the array for the actual number of elements.

I entered the following code, which inserts the sheet names into the SheetNames array. I also added a MsgBox function within the loop just to assure me that the sheets' names were indeed being entered into the array.

```
Sub SortSheets()
'   Sorts the sheets of the active workbook
    Dim SheetNames() as String
    Dim i as Long
    Dim SheetCount as Long
    SheetCount = ActiveWorkbook.Sheets.Count
    ReDim SheetNames(1 To SheetCount)
    For i = 1 To SheetCount
        SheetNames(i) = ActiveWorkbook.Sheets(i).Name
        MsgBox SheetNames(i)
    Next i
End Sub
```

To test the preceding code, I activated the Test.xlsx workbook and pressed Ctrl+Shift+S. Five message boxes appeared, each displaying the name of a sheet in the active workbook. So far, so good.

By the way, I'm a major proponent of testing your work as you go. When you're convinced that your code is working correctly, remove the MsgBox statement. (These message boxes become annoying after a while.)

TIP

Rather than use the MsgBox function to test your work, you can use the Print method of the Debug object to display information in the Immediate window. For this example, use the following statement in place of the MsgBox statement:

```
Debug.Print SheetNames(i)
```

This technique is much less intrusive than using MsgBox statements. Just make sure that you remember to remove the statement when you're finished.

At this point, the `SortSheets` procedure simply creates an array of sheet names corresponding to the sheets in the active workbook. Two steps remain: Sort the elements in the `SheetNames` array and then rearrange the sheets to correspond to the sorted array.

Writing the Sort procedure

It was time to sort the `SheetNames` array. One option was to insert the sorting code in the `SortSheets` procedure, but I thought a better approach was to write a general-purpose sorting procedure that I could reuse with other projects (sorting arrays is a common operation).

You might be a bit daunted by the thought of writing a sorting procedure. The good news is that it's relatively easy to find commonly used routines that you can use or adapt. The Internet, of course, is a great source for such information.

You can sort an array in many ways. I chose the *bubble sort* method; although it's not a particularly fast technique, it's easy to code. Blazing speed is not really a requirement in this particular application.

The bubble sort method uses a nested `For-Next` loop to evaluate each array element. If the array element is greater than the next element, the two elements swap positions. This evaluation is repeated for every pair of items (that is, *n* − 1 times).

 CROSS-REFERENCE

In Chapter 11, I present some other sorting routines and compare them in terms of speed.

Here's the sorting procedure I developed (after consulting a few programming Web sites to get some ideas):

```
Sub BubbleSort(List() As String)
    Dim First As Long, Last As Long
    Dim i As Long, j As Long
    Dim Temp As String
    First = LBound(List)
    Last = UBound(List)
    For i = First To Last - 1
        For j = i + 1 To Last
            If List(i) > List(j) Then
                Temp = List(j)
                List(j) = List(i)
                List(i) = Temp
            End If
        Next j
    Next i
End Sub
```

This procedure accepts one argument: a one-dimensional array named List. An array passed to a procedure can be of any length. I used the LBound and UBound functions to define the lower bound and upper bound of the array to the variables First and Last, respectively.

Here's a little temporary procedure that I used to test the BubbleSort procedure:

```
Sub SortTester()
    Dim x(1 To 5) As String
    Dim i As Long
    x(1) = "dog"
    x(2) = "cat"
    x(3) = "elephant"
    x(4) = "aardvark"
    x(5) = "bird"
    Call BubbleSort(x)
    For i = 1 To 5
        Debug.Print i, x(i)
    Next i
End Sub
```

The SortTester routine creates an array of five strings, passes the array to BubbleSort, and then displays the sorted array in the Immediate window. I eventually deleted this code because it served its purpose.

After I was satisfied that this procedure worked reliably, I modified SortSheets by adding a call to the BubbleSort procedure, passing the SheetNames array as an argument. At this point, my module looked like this:

```
Sub SortSheets()
    Dim SheetNames() As String
    Dim SheetCount as Long
    Dim i as Long
    SheetCount = ActiveWorkbook.Sheets.Count
    ReDim SheetNames(1 To SheetCount)
    For i = 1 To SheetCount
        SheetNames(i) = ActiveWorkbook.Sheets(i).Name
    Next i
    Call BubbleSort(SheetNames)
End Sub

Sub BubbleSort(List() As String)
'   Sorts the List array in ascending order
    Dim First As Long, Last As Long
    Dim i As Long, j As Long
    Dim Temp As String
    First = LBound(List)
    Last = UBound(List)
```

```
    For i = First To Last - 1
        For j = i + 1 To Last
            If List(i) > List(j) Then
                Temp = List(j)
                List(j) = List(i)
                List(i) = Temp
            End If
        Next j
    Next i
End Sub
```

When the SheetSort procedure ends, it contains an array that consists of the sorted sheet names in the active workbook. To verify this, you can display the array contents in the VBE Immediate window by adding the following code at the end of the SortSheets procedure (if the Immediate window is not visible, press Ctrl+G):

```
For i = 1 To SheetCount
    Debug.Print SheetNames(i)
Next i
```

So far, so good. Next step: Write some code to rearrange the sheets to correspond to the sorted items in the SheetNames array.

The code that I recorded earlier proved useful. Remember the instruction that was recorded when I moved a sheet to the first position in the workbook?

```
Sheets("Sheet3").Move Before:=Sheets(1)
```

After a little thought, I was able to write a For-Next loop that would go through each sheet and move it to its corresponding sheet location, specified in the SheetNames array:

```
For i = 1 To SheetCount
    Sheets(SheetNames(i)).Move Before:=Sheets(i)
Next i
```

For example, the first time through the loop, the loop counter i is 1. The first element in the SheetNames array is (in this example) Sheet1. Therefore, the expression for the Move method within the loop evaluates to

```
Sheets("Sheet1").Move Before:= Sheets(1)
```

The second time through the loop, the expression evaluates to

```
Sheets("Sheet2").Move Before:= Sheets(2)
```

I then added the new code to the SortSheets procedure:

```
Sub SortSheets()
    Dim SheetNames() As String
    Dim SheetCount as Long
    Dim i as Long
    SheetCount = ActiveWorkbook.Sheets.Count
    ReDim SheetNames(1 To SheetCount)
    For i = 1 To SheetCount
        SheetNames(i) = ActiveWorkbook.Sheets(i).Name
    Next i
    Call BubbleSort(SheetNames)
    For i = 1 To SheetCount
        ActiveWorkbook.Sheets(SheetNames(i)).Move _
            Before:=ActiveWorkbook.Sheets(i)
    Next i
End Sub
```

I did some testing, and it seemed to work just fine for the Test.xlsx workbook.

Time to clean things up. I made sure that all the variables used in the procedures were declared, and then I added a few comments and blank lines to make the code easier to read. The SortSheets procedure looked like the following:

```
Sub SortSheets()
'    This routine sorts the sheets of the
'    active workbook in ascending order.
'    Use Ctrl+Shift+S to execute

    Dim SheetNames() As String
    Dim SheetCount As Long
    Dim i As Long

'    Determine the number of sheets & ReDim array
    SheetCount = ActiveWorkbook.Sheets.Count
    ReDim SheetNames(1 To SheetCount)

'    Fill array with sheet names
    For i = 1 To SheetCount
        SheetNames(i) = ActiveWorkbook.Sheets(i).Name
    Next i

'    Sort the array in ascending order
    Call BubbleSort(SheetNames)

'    Move the sheets
```

```
      For i = 1 To SheetCount
          ActiveWorkbook.Sheets(SheetNames(i)).Move _
              Before:= ActiveWorkbook.Sheets(i)
      Next i
End Sub
```

Everything seemed to be working. To test the code further, I added a few more sheets to
Test.xlsx and changed some of the sheet names. It worked like a charm.

More testing

I was tempted to call it a day. However, just because the procedure worked with the
Test.xlsx workbook didn't mean that it would work with all workbooks. To test it further,
I loaded a few other workbooks and retried the routine. I soon discovered that the applica-
tion was not perfect. In fact, it was far from perfect. I identified the following problems:

- Workbooks with many sheets took a long time to sort because the screen was continually updated during the move operations.

- The sorting didn't always work. For example, in one of my tests, a sheet named
  SUMMARY (all uppercase) appeared before a sheet named Sheet1. This problem was
  caused by the BubbleSort procedure — an uppercase *U* is "greater than" a lowercase *h*.

- If Excel had no visible workbook windows, pressing the Ctrl+Shift+S shortcut key
  combo caused the macro to fail.

- If the workbook's structure was protected, the Move method failed.

- After sorting, the last sheet in the workbook became the active sheet. Changing the
  user's active sheet is not a good practice; it's better to keep the user's original sheet
  active.

- If I interrupted the macro by pressing Ctrl+Break, VBA displayed an error message.

- The macro cannot be reversed (that is, the Undo command is disabled). If the user accidentally presses Ctrl+Shift+S, the workbook sheets are sorted and the only way to get
  them back to their original order is by doing it manually.

Fixing the problems

Fixing the screen-updating problem was a breeze. I inserted the following instruction to
turn off screen updating while the sheets are being moved:

```
Application.ScreenUpdating = False
```

This statement causes Excel's windows to freeze while the macro is running. A beneficial
side effect is that it also speeds up the macro considerably. After the macro completes it
operation, screen updating is turned back on automatically.

It was also easy to fix the problem with the `BubbleSort` procedure: I used VBA's `UCase` function to convert the sheet names to uppercase for the comparison. This caused all the comparisons were made by using uppercase versions of the sheet names. The corrected line read as follows:

```
If UCase(List(i)) > UCase(List(j)) Then
```

TIP

Another way to solve the "case" problem is to add the following statement to the top of your module:

```
Option Compare Text
```

This statement causes VBA to perform string comparisons based on a case-insensitive text sort order. In other words, *A* is considered the same as *a*.

To prevent the error message that appears when no workbooks are visible, I added some error checking. I used `On Error Resume Next` to ignore the error and then checked the value of `Err`. If `Err` is not equal to 0, it means that an error occurred. Therefore, the procedure ends. The error-checking code is

```
On Error Resume Next
SheetCount = ActiveWorkbook.Sheets.Count
If Err <> 0 Then Exit Sub ' No active workbook
```

It occurred to me that I could avoid using `On Error Resume Next`. The following statement is a more direct approach to determining whether a workbook is not visible and doesn't require any error handling. This statement can go at the top of the `SortSheets` procedure:

```
If ActiveWorkbook Is Nothing Then Exit Sub
```

There's usually a good reason that a workbook's structure is protected. I decided that the best approach was to not attempt to unprotect the workbook. Rather, the code should display a message box warning and let the user unprotect the workbook and re-execute the macro. Testing for a protected workbook structure was easy — the `ProtectStructure` property of a `Workbook` object returns `True` if a workbook is protected. I added the following block of code:

```
'   Check for protected workbook structure
    If ActiveWorkbook.ProtectStructure Then
        MsgBox ActiveWorkbook.Name & " is protected.", _
            vbCritical, "Cannot Sort Sheets."
        Exit Sub
    End If
```

Part III

If the workbook's structure is protected, the user sees the message box shown in Figure 9-11.

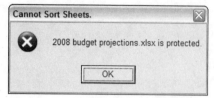

Figure 9-11: This message box tells the user that the sheets cannot be sorted.

To reactivate the original active sheet after the sorting was performed, I wrote code that assigned the original sheet to an object variable (OldActiveSheet) and then activated that sheet when the routine was finished. Here's the statement that assigns the variable:

```
Set OldActive = ActiveSheet
```

This statement activates the original active worksheet:

```
OldActive.Activate
```

Pressing Ctrl+Break normally halts a macro, and VBA usually displays an error message. But because one of my goals was to avoid VBA error messages, I inserted a command to prevent this situation. From the online help, I discovered that the Application object has an EnableCancelKey property that can disable Ctrl+Break. So I added the following statement at the top of the routine:

```
Application.EnableCancelKey = xlDisabled
```

 CAUTION

Be very careful when you disable the Cancel key. If your code gets caught in an infinite loop, there is no way to break out of it. For best results, insert this statement only after you're sure that everything is working properly.

To prevent the problem of accidentally sorting the sheets, I added the following statement to the procedure, before the Ctrl+Break key is disabled:

```
    If MsgBox("Sort the sheets in the active workbook?", _
        vbQuestion + vbYesNo) <> vbYes Then Exit Sub
```

When the user executes the SortSheets procedure, he sees the message box in Figure 9-12.

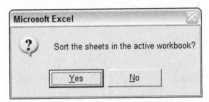

Figure 9-12: This message box appears before the sheets are sorted.

After I made all these corrections, the `SortSheets` procedure looked like this:

```vba
Option Explicit
Sub SortSheets()
'   This routine sorts the sheets of the
'   active workbook in ascending order.
'   Use Ctrl+Shift+S to execute

    Dim SheetNames() As String
    Dim i As Long
    Dim SheetCount As Long
    Dim OldActiveSheet As Object

    If ActiveWorkbook Is Nothing Then Exit Sub ' No active workbook
    SheetCount = ActiveWorkbook.Sheets.Count

'   Check for protected workbook structure
    If ActiveWorkbook.ProtectStructure Then
        MsgBox ActiveWorkbook.Name & " is protected.", _
            vbCritical, "Cannot Sort Sheets."
        Exit Sub
    End If

'   Make user verify
    If MsgBox("Sort the sheets in the active workbook?", _
      vbQuestion + vbYesNo) <> vbYes Then Exit Sub

'   Disable Ctrl+Break
    Application.EnableCancelKey = xlDisabled

'   Get the number of sheets
    SheetCount = ActiveWorkbook.Sheets.Count

'   Redimension the array
    ReDim SheetNames(1 To SheetCount)

'   Store a reference to the active sheet
```

```
    Set OldActiveSheet = ActiveSheet

'   Fill array with sheet names
    For i = 1 To SheetCount
        SheetNames(i) = ActiveWorkbook.Sheets(i).Name
    Next i

'   Sort the array in ascending order
    Call BubbleSort(SheetNames)

'   Turn off screen updating
    Application.ScreenUpdating = False

'   Move the sheets
    For i = 1 To SheetCount
        ActiveWorkbook.Sheets(SheetNames(i)).Move _
            Before:=ActiveWorkbook.Sheets(i)
    Next i

'   Reactivate the original active sheet
    OldActiveSheet.Activate
End Sub
```

Utility availability

Because the SortSheets macro is stored in the Personal Macro Workbook, it is available whenever Excel is running. At this point, the macro can be executed by selecting the macro's name from the Macro dialog box (Alt+F8 displays this dialog box) or by pressing Ctrl+Shift+S.

Evaluating the project

So there you have it. The utility meets all the original project requirements: It sorts all sheets in the active workbook, it can be executed easily, it's always available, it seems to work for any workbook, and I have yet to see it display a VBA error message.

 NOTE

The procedure still has one slight problem: The sorting is strict and may not always be "logical." For example, after sorting, Sheet10 is placed before Sheet2. Most would want Sheet2 to be listed before Sheet10.

Chapter 10

Creating Function Procedures

In This Chapter

A *function* is a VBA procedure that performs some calculations and returns a value. You can use these functions in your Visual Basic for Applications (VBA) code or in formulas.

◆ The difference between Sub procedures and Function procedures

◆ How to create custom functions

◆ About Function procedures and function arguments

◆ How to create a function that emulates Excel's SUM function

◆ How to debug functions, deal with the Insert Function dialog box, and use add-ins to store custom functions

◆ How to call the Windows Application Programming Interface (API) to perform otherwise impossible feats

VBA enables you to create Sub procedures and Function procedures. I cover Sub procedures in the preceding chapter, and in this chapter I discuss Function procedures.

 CROSS-REFERENCE

Chapter 11 has many useful and practical examples of Function procedures. You can incorporate many of these techniques into your work.

Sub Procedures versus Function Procedures

You can think of a Sub procedure as a command that can be executed either by the user or by another procedure. Function procedures, on the other hand, usually return a single value (or an array), just like Excel worksheet functions and VBA built-in functions. As with built-in functions, your Function procedures can use arguments.

Function procedures are quite versatile and can be used in two situations:

- As part of an expression in a VBA procedure
- In formulas that you create in a worksheet

In fact, you can use a Function procedure anywhere that you can use an Excel worksheet function or a VBA built-in function. As far as I know, the only exception is that you can't use a VBA function in a data validation formula.

Why Create Custom Functions?

You are undoubtedly familiar with Excel worksheet functions; even novices know how to use the most common worksheet functions, such as SUM, AVERAGE, and IF. By my count, Excel contains 340 predefined worksheet functions. If that's not enough, however, you can create custom functions by using VBA.

 NEW
Excel 2007 incorporates all the functions that are included in the Analysis ToolPak add-in.

With all the functions available in Excel and VBA, you might wonder why you would ever need to create new functions. The answer: to simplify your work. With a bit of planning, custom functions are very useful in worksheet formulas and VBA procedures.

Often, for example, you can create a custom function that can significantly shorten your formulas. And shorter formulas are more readable and easier to work with. I should also point out, however, that custom functions used in your formulas are usually much slower than built-in functions. And, of course, the user must enable macros in order to use these functions.

When you create applications, you may notice that some procedures repeat certain calculations. In such cases, consider creating a custom function that performs the calculation. Then you can simply call the function from your procedure. A custom function can eliminate the need for duplicated code, thus reducing errors.

Also, co-workers often can benefit from your specialized functions. And some may be willing to pay you to create custom functions that save them time and work.

Although many cringe at the thought of creating custom worksheet functions, the process is not difficult. In fact, I *enjoy* creating custom functions. I especially like how my custom functions appear in the Insert Function dialog box along with Excel built-in functions, as if I'm re-engineering the software in some way.

In this chapter, I tell you what you need to know to start creating custom functions, and I provide lots of examples.

An Introductory Function Example

Without further ado, this section presents an example of a VBA `Function` procedure.

A custom function

The following is a custom function defined in a VBA module. This function, named `RemoveVowels`, uses a single argument. The function returns the argument, but with all the vowels removed.

```
Function RemoveVowels(Txt) As String
' Removes all vowels from the Txt argument
    Dim i As Long
    RemoveVowels = ""
    For i = 1 To Len(Txt)
        If Not UCase(Mid(Txt, i, 1)) Like "[AEIOU]" Then
            RemoveVowels = RemoveVowels & Mid(Txt, i, 1)
        End If
    Next i
End Function
```

This certainly isn't the most useful function I've written, but it demonstrates some key concepts related to functions. I explain how this function works later, in the "Analyzing the custom function" section.

CAUTION

When you create custom functions that will be used in a worksheet formula, make sure that the code resides in a normal VBA module. If you place your custom functions in a code module for a `UserForm`, a `Sheet`, or `ThisWorkbook`, they will not work in your formulas.

Part III

Using the function in a worksheet

When you enter a formula that uses the `RemoveVowels` function, Excel executes the code to get the value. Here's an example of how you would use the function in a formula:

```
=RemoveVowels(A1)
```

See Figure 10-1 for examples of this function in action. The formulas are in column B, and they use the text in column A as their arguments. As you can see, the function returns the single argument, but with the vowels removed.

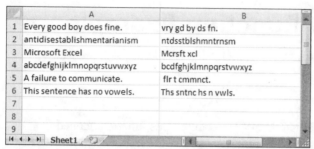

	A	B
1	Every good boy does fine.	vry gd by ds fn.
2	antidisestablishmentarianism	ntdsstblshmntrnsm
3	Microsoft Excel	Mcrsft xcl
4	abcdefghijklmnopqrstuvwxyz	bcdfghjklmnpqrstvwxyz
5	A failure to communicate.	flr t cmmnct.
6	This sentence has no vowels.	Ths sntnc hs n vwls.
7		
8		
9		

Figure 10-1: Using a custom function in a worksheet formula.

Actually, the function works pretty much like any built-in worksheet function. You can insert it in a formula by choosing Formulas ➪ Function Library ➪ Insert Function or by clicking the Insert Function Wizard icon to the left of the formula bar. Either of these actions displays the Insert Function dialog box. In the Insert Function dialog box, your custom functions are located, by default, in the User Defined category.

You can also nest custom functions and combine them with other elements in your formulas. For example, the following formula nests the `RemoveVowels` function inside Excel's UPPER function. The result is the original string (sans vowels), converted to uppercase.

```
=UPPER(RemoveVowels(A1))
```

Using the function in a VBA procedure

In addition to using custom functions in worksheet formulas, you can also use them in other VBA procedures. The following VBA procedure, which is defined in the same module as the custom `RemoveVowels` function, first displays an input box to solicit some text from the user. Then the procedure uses the VBA built-in `MsgBox` function to display the user input after it's processed by the `RemoveVowels` function (see Figure 10-2). The original input appears as the caption in the message box.

```
Sub ZapTheVowels()
    Dim UserInput as String
    UserInput = InputBox("Enter some text:")
    MsgBox RemoveVowels(UserInput), , UserInput
End Sub
```

In the example shown in Figure 10-2, the string entered in response to the InputBox function was Excel Power Programming With VBA. The MsgBox function displays the text without vowels.

Figure 10-2: Using a custom function in a VBA procedure.

Analyzing the custom function

Function procedures can be as complex as you need them to be. Most of the time, they are more complex and much more useful than this sample procedure. Nonetheless, an analysis of this example may help you understand what is happening.

Here's the code, again:

```
Function RemoveVowels(Txt) As String
' Removes all vowels from the Txt argument
    Dim i As Long
    RemoveVowels = ""
    For i = 1 To Len(Txt)
        If Not UCase(Mid(Txt, i, 1)) Like "[AEIOU]" Then
            RemoveVowels = RemoveVowels & Mid(Txt, i, 1)
        End If
    Next i
End Function
```

Notice that the procedure starts with the keyword Function, rather than Sub, followed by the name of the function (RemoveVowels). This custom function uses only one argument (Txt), enclosed in parentheses. As String defines the data type of the function's return value. Excel uses the Variant data type if no data type is specified.

The second line is simply an optional comment that describes what the function does. This is followed by a Dim statement, which declares the variable (i) used in the procedure as type Long.

What Custom Worksheet Functions Can't Do

When you develop custom functions, it's important to understand a key distinction between functions that you call from other VBA procedures and functions that you use in worksheet formulas. `Function` procedures used in worksheet formulas must be passive. For example, code within a `Function` procedure cannot manipulate ranges or change things on the worksheet. An example can help make this clear.

You might be tempted to write a custom worksheet function that changes a cell's formatting. For example, it could be useful to have a formula that uses a custom function to change the color of text in a cell based on the cell's value. Try as you might, however, such a function is impossible to write. No matter what you do, the function won't change the worksheet. Remember, a function simply returns a value. It cannot perform actions with objects.

That said, I should point out one notable exception. It is possible to change the text in a cell *comment* by using a custom VBA function. Here's the function:

```
Function ModifyComment(Cell As Range, Cmt As String)
    Cell.Comment.Text Cmt
End Function
```

Here's an example of using this function in a formula. The formula replaces the comment in cell A1 with new text. The function will not work if cell A1 doesn't have a comment.

```
=ModifyComment(A1,"Hey, I changed your comment")
```

NOTE

Notice that I use the function name as a variable here. When a function ends, it always returns the current value of the variable that corresponds to the function's name.

The next five instructions make up a `For-Next` loop. The procedure loops through each character in the input and builds the string. The first instruction within the loop uses VBA's `Mid` function to return a single character from the input string and converts this character to uppercase. That character is then compared to a list of characters by using Excel's `Like` operator. In other words, the `If` clause is true if the character is not A, E, I, O, or U. In such a case, the character is appended to the `RemoveVowels` variable.

When the loop is finished, `RemoveVowels` consists of the input string with all the vowels removed. This string is the value that the function returns.

The procedure ends with an `End Function` statement.

Keep in mind that the coding for this function can be done in a number of different ways. Here's a function that accomplishes the same result but is coded differently:

```
Function RemoveVowels(txt) As String
' Removes all vowels from the Txt argument
    Dim i As Long
    Dim TempString As String
    TempString = ""
    For i = 1 To Len(txt)
        Select Case ucase(Mid(txt, i, 1))
            Case "A", "E", "I", "O", "U"
                'Do nothing
            Case Else
                TempString = TempString & Mid(txt, i, 1)
        End Select
    Next i
    RemoveVowels = TempString
End Function
```

In this version, I used a string variable (TempString) to store the vowel-less string as it is being constructed. Then, before the procedure ends, I assigned the contents of TempString to the function's name. This version also uses a Select Case construct rather than an If-Then construct.

 CD-ROM

Both versions of this function are available on the companion CD-ROM. The file is named remove vowels.xlsm.

Function Procedures

A custom Function procedure has much in common with a Sub procedure. (For more information on Sub procedures, see Chapter 9.)

Declaring a function

The syntax for declaring a function is as follows:

```
[Public | Private][Static] Function name ([arglist])[As type]
    [instructions]
    [name = expression]
    [Exit Function]
    [instructions]
    [name = expression]
End Function
```

The `Function` procedure contains the following elements:

- `Public`: (Optional) Indicates that the `Function` procedure is accessible to all other procedures in all other modules in all active Excel VBA projects.

- `Private`: (Optional) Indicates that the `Function` procedure is accessible only to other procedures in the same module.

- `Static`: (Optional) Indicates that the values of variables declared in the `Function` procedure are preserved between calls.

- `Function`: (Required) Indicates the beginning of a procedure that returns a value or other data.

- *name*: (Required) Represents any valid `Function` procedure name, which must follow the same rules as a variable name.

- *arglist*: (Optional) Represents a list of one or more variables that represent arguments passed to the `Function` procedure. The arguments are enclosed in parentheses. Use a comma to separate pairs of arguments.

- *type*: (Optional) Is the data type returned by the `Function` procedure.

- *instructions*: (Optional) Are any number of valid VBA instructions.

- `Exit Function`: (Optional) Is a statement that forces an immediate exit from the `Function` procedure prior to its completion.

- `End Function`: (Required) Is a keyword that indicates the end of the `Function` procedure.

The main thing to remember about a custom function written in VBA is that a value is always assigned to its name a minimum of one time, generally when it has completed execution.

To create a custom function, start by inserting a VBA module. (Or you can use an existing module.) Enter the keyword `Function`, followed by the function name and a list of its arguments (if any) in parentheses. You can also declare the data type of the return value by using the `As` keyword (this is optional, but recommended). Insert the VBA code that performs the work, making sure that the appropriate value is assigned to the term corresponding to the function name at least once within the body of the `Function` procedure. End the function with an `End Function` statement.

Function names must adhere to the same rules as variable names. If you plan to use your custom function in a worksheet formula, be careful if the function name is also a cell address. For example, if you use something like `J21` as a function name, it must be entered with apostrophes:

```
='J21'(A1)
```

The best advice is to avoid using function names that are also cell references, including named ranges. And, avoid using function names that correspond to Excel's built-in function names. If there is a function name conflict, Excel always uses its built-in function.

A function's scope

In Chapter 9, I discuss the concept of a procedure's scope (public or private). The same discussion applies to functions: A function's scope determines whether it can be called by procedures in other modules or in worksheets.

Here are a few things to keep in mind about a function's scope:

- If you don't declare a function's scope, its default is `Public`.

- Functions declared `As Private` do not appear in Excel's Paste Function dialog box. Therefore, when you create a function that should be used only in a VBA procedure, you should declare it `Private` so that users don't try to use it in a formula.

- If your VBA code needs to call a function that's defined in another workbook, set up a reference to the other workbook by choosing the Visual Basic Editor (VBE) Tools ⇨ References command.

Executing function procedures

Although you can execute a `Sub` procedure in many ways, you can execute a `Function` procedure in only three ways:

- Call it from another procedure
- Use it in a worksheet formula
- Call it from the VBE Immediate window

FROM A PROCEDURE

You can call custom functions from a procedure the same way that you call built-in functions. For example, after you define a function called `SumArray`, you can enter a statement like the following:

```
Total = SumArray(MyArray)
```

This statement executes the `SumArray` function with `MyArray` as its argument, returns the function's result, and assigns it to the `Total` variable.

You also can use the `Run` method of the `Application` object. Here's an example:

```
Total = Application.Run ("SumArray", "MyArray")
```

The first argument for the Run method is the function name. Subsequent arguments represent the argument(s) for the function. The arguments for the Run method can be literal strings (as shown above), numbers, or variables.

IN A WORKSHEET FORMULA

Using custom functions in a worksheet formula is like using built-in functions except that you must ensure that Excel can locate the Function procedure. If the Function procedure is in the same workbook, you don't have to do anything special. If it's in a different workbook, you may have to tell Excel where to find it.

You can do so in three ways:

- *Precede the function name with a file reference.* For example, if you want to use a function called CountNames that's defined in an open workbook named Myfuncs.xlsm, you can use the following reference:

  =Myfuncs.xlsm!CountNames(A1:A1000)

  If you insert the function with the Insert Function dialog box, the workbook reference is inserted automatically.

- *Set up a reference to the workbook.* You do so by choosing the VBE Tools ⇨ References command. If the function is defined in a referenced workbook, you don't need to use the worksheet name. Even when the dependent workbook is assigned as a reference, the Paste Function dialog box continues to insert the workbook reference (although it's not necessary).

- *Create an add-in.* When you create an add-in from a workbook that has Function procedures, you don't need to use the file reference when you use one of the functions in a formula. The add-in must be installed, however. I discuss add-ins in Chapter 21.

You'll notice that unlike Sub procedures, your Function procedures do not appear in the Macro dialog box when you issue the Tools ⇨ Macro ⇨ Macros command. In addition, you can't choose a function when you issue the VBE Run ⇨ Sub/UserForm command (or press F5) if the cursor is located in a Function procedure. (You get the Macro dialog box that lets you choose a macro to run.) As a result, you need to do a bit of extra up-front work to test your functions while you're developing them. One approach is to set up a simple procedure that calls the function. If the function is designed to be used in worksheet formulas, you'll want to enter a simple formula to test it.

FROM THE VBE IMMEDIATE WINDOW

The final way to call Function procedure is from the VBE Immediate window. This method is generally used only for testing purposes. Figure 10-3 shows an example.

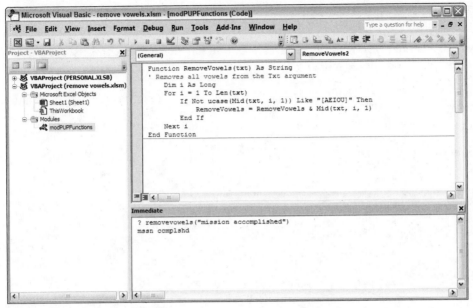

Figure 10-3: Calling a Function procedure from the Immediate Window.

Function Arguments

Keep in mind the following points about Function procedure arguments:

- Arguments can be variables (including arrays), constants, literals, or expressions.
- Some functions do not have arguments.
- Some functions have a fixed number of required arguments (from 1 to 60).
- Some functions have a combination of required and optional arguments.

NOTE

If your formula uses a custom worksheet function and it returns #VALUE!, there is an error in your function. The error could be caused by logical errors in your code or by passing incorrect arguments to the function. See "Debugging Functions" later in this chapter.

Part III

Reinventing the Wheel

Just for fun, I wrote my own version of Excel's UPPER function (which converts a string to all uppercase) and named it `UpCase`:

```
Function UpCase(InString As String) As String
'    Converts its argument to all uppercase.
    Dim StringLength As Integer
    Dim i As Integer
    Dim ASCIIVal As Integer
    Dim CharVal As Integer

    StringLength = Len(InString)
    UpCase = InString
    For i = 1 To StringLength
        ASCIIVal = Asc(Mid(InString, i, 1))
        CharVal = 0
        If ASCIIVal >= 97 And ASCIIVal <= 122 Then
            CharVal = -32
            Mid(UpCase, i, 1) = Chr(ASCIIVal + CharVal)
        End If
    Next i
End Function
```

Note: A workbook that contains this function is on the companion CD-ROM in a file named `upper case.xlsm`.

Notice that I resisted the urge to take the easy route — using the VBA `UCase` function.

I was curious to see how the custom function differed from the built-in function, so I created a worksheet that called the function 20,000 times, using random names. The worksheet took about 40 seconds to calculate. I then substituted Excel's UPPER function and ran the test again. The recalculation time was virtually instantaneous. I don't claim that my `UpCase` function is the optimal algorithm for this task, but it's safe to say that a custom function will never match the speed of Excel's built-in functions.

Function Examples

In this section, I present a series of examples that demonstrate how to use arguments effectively with functions. By the way, this discussion also applies to `Sub` procedures.

Functions with no argument

Like `Sub` procedures, `Function` procedures need not have arguments. Excel, for example, has a few built-in functions that don't use arguments, including RAND, TODAY, and NOW. You can create similar functions.

This section contains examples of functions that don't use an argument.

CD-ROM

A workbook that contains these functions is available on the companion CD-ROM. The file is named no argument.xlsm.

Here's a simple example of a function that doesn't use an argument. The following function returns the UserName property of the Application object. This name appears in the Options dialog box (General tab) and is stored in the Windows Registry.

```
Function User()
'    Returns the name of the current user
     User = Application.UserName
End Function
```

When you enter the following formula, the cell returns the name of the current user (assuming that it's listed properly in the Registry):

```
=User()
```

NOTE

When you use a function with no arguments in a worksheet formula, you must include a set of empty parentheses. This requirement is not necessary if you call the function in a VBA procedure, although including the empty parentheses does make it clear that you're calling a function.

To use this function in another procedure, you can assign it to a variable, use it in an expression, or use it as an argument for another function.

The following example calls the User function and uses the return value as an argument for the MsgBox statement. The concatenation operator (&) joins the literal string with the result of the User function.

```
Sub ShowUser()
    MsgBox "Your name is " & User()
End Sub
```

This example demonstrates how you can create a *wrapper* function that simply returns a property or the result of a VBA function. Following are three additional wrapper functions that take no argument.

```
Function ExcelDir() As String
'    Returns the directory in which Excel is installed
     ExcelDir = Application.Path
```

```
End Function

Function SheetCount()
'    Returns the number of sheets in the workbook
     SheetCount = Application.Caller.Parent.Parent.Sheets.Count
End Function

Function SheetName()
'    Returns the name of the worksheet
     SheetName = Application.Caller.Parent.Name
End Function
```

Controlling Function Recalculation

When you use a custom function in a worksheet formula, when is it recalculated?

Custom functions behave like Excel's built-in worksheet functions. Normally, a custom function is recalculated only when it needs to be — which is only when any of the function's arguments are modified. You can, however, force functions to recalculate more frequently. Adding the following statement to a `Function` procedure makes the function recalculate whenever the sheet is recalculated. If you're using automatic calculation mode, a calculation occurs whenever any cell is changed.

```
Application.Volatile True
```

The `Volatile` method of the `Application` object has one argument (either `True` or `False`). Marking a `Function` procedure as volatile forces the function to be calculated whenever recalculation occurs for any cell in the worksheet.

For example, the custom `StaticRand` function can be changed to emulate Excel's RAND function using the `Volatile` method, as follows:

```
Function NonStaticRand()
'    Returns a random number that
'    changes with each calculation
     Application.Volatile True
     NonStaticRand = Rnd()
End Function
```

Using the `False` argument of the `Volatile` method causes the function to be recalculated only when one or more of its arguments change as a result of a recalculation. (If a function has no arguments, this method has no effect.)

To force an entire recalculation, including nonvolatile custom functions, press Ctrl+Alt+F9. This key combination will, for example, generate new random numbers for the `StaticRand` function presented in this chapter.

Here's another example of a function that doesn't take an argument. I used to use Excel's RAND function to quickly fill a range of cells with values. But I didn't like the fact that the random numbers change whenever the worksheet is recalculated. So I remedied this by converting the formulas to values.

Then I realized that I could create a custom function that returned random numbers that didn't change. I used the VBA built-in Rnd function, which returns a random number between 0 and 1. The custom function is as follows:

```
Function StaticRand()
'    Returns a random number that doesn't
'    change when recalculated
     StaticRand = Rnd()
End Function
```

If you want to generate a series of random integers between 0 and 1,000, you can use a formula such as this:

```
=INT(StaticRand()*1000)
```

The values produced by this formula never change when the worksheet is calculated normally. However, you can force the formula to recalculate by pressing Ctrl+Alt+F9

A function with one argument

This section describes a function for sales managers who need to calculate the commissions earned by their sales forces. The calculations in this example are based on the following table:

Monthly Sales	Commission Rate
0–$9,999	8.0%
$10,000–$19,999	10.5%
$20,000–$39,999	12.0%
$40,000+	14.0%

Note that the commission rate is nonlinear and also depends on the month's total sales. Employees who sell more earn a higher commission rate.

There are several ways to calculate commissions for various sales amounts entered into a worksheet. If you're not thinking too clearly, you might waste lots of time and come up with a lengthy formula such as this:

```
=IF(AND(A1>=0,A1<=9999.99),A1*0.08,
 IF(AND(A1>=10000,A1<=19999.99),A1*0.105,
 IF(AND(A1>=20000,A1<=39999.99),A1*0.12,
 IF(A1>=40000,A1*0.14,0))))
```

This is a bad approach for a couple of reasons. First, the formula is overly complex, making it difficult to understand. Second, the values are hard-coded into the formula, making the formula difficult to modify.

A better (non-VBA) approach is to use a lookup table function to compute the commissions. For example, the following formula uses VLOOKUP to retrieve the commission value from a range named Table and multiplies that value by the value in cell A1.

```
=VLOOKUP(A1,Table,2)*A1
```

Yet another approach (which eliminates the need to use a lookup table) is to create a custom function such as the following:

```
Function Commission(Sales)
    Const Tier1 = 0.08
    Const Tier2 = 0.105
    Const Tier3 = 0.12
    Const Tier4 = 0.14
'   Calculates sales commissions
    Select Case Sales
        Case 0 To 9999.99: Commission = Sales * Tier1
        Case 1000 To 19999.99: Commission = Sales * Tier2
        Case 20000 To 39999.99: Commission = Sales * Tier3
        Case Is >= 40000: Commission = Sales * Tier4
    End Select
End Function
```

After you enter this function in a VBA module, you can use it in a worksheet formula or call the function from other VBA procedures.

Entering the following formula into a cell produces a result of 3,000; the amount — 25,000 — qualifies for a commission rate of 12 percent:

```
=Commission(25000)
```

Even if you don't need custom functions in a worksheet, creating Function procedures can make your VBA coding much simpler. For example, if your VBA procedure calculates sales commissions, you can use the exact same function and call it from a VBA procedure.

Here's a tiny procedure that asks the user for a sales amount and then uses the
`Commission` function to calculate the commission due:

```
Sub CalcComm()
    Dim Sales as Long
    Sales = InputBox("Enter Sales:")
    MsgBox "The commission is " & Commission(Sales)
End Sub
```

The `CalcComm` procedure starts by displaying an input box that asks for the sales amount.
Then it displays a message box with the calculated sales commission for that amount.

This `Sub` procedure works, but it is rather crude. Following is an enhanced version that
displays formatted values and keeps looping until the user clicks No (see Figure 10-4).

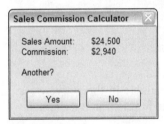

Figure 10-4: Using a function to display the result of a calculation.

```
Sub CalcComm()
    Dim Sales As Long
    Dim Msg As String, Ans As String

'   Prompt for sales amount
    Sales = Val(InputBox("Enter Sales:", _
     "Sales Commission Calculator"))

'   Build the Message
    Msg = "Sales Amount:" & vbTab & Format(Sales, "$#,##0.00")
    Msg = Msg & vbCrLf & "Commission:" & vbTab
    Msg = Msg & Format(Commission(Sales), "$#,##0.00")
    Msg = Msg & vbCrLf & vbCrLf & "Another?"

'   Display the result and prompt for another
    Ans = MsgBox(Msg, vbYesNo, "Sales Commission Calculator")
    If Ans = vbYes Then CalcComm
End Sub
```

This function uses two VBA built-in constants: `vbTab` represents a tab (to space the output), and `vbCrLf` specifies a carriage return and line feed (to skip to the next line). VBA's
`Format` function displays a value in a specified format (in this case, with a dollar sign,
comma, and two decimal places).

Use Arguments, Not Cell References

All ranges that are used in a custom function should be passed as arguments. Consider the following function, which returns the value in A1, multiplied by 2:

```
Function DoubleCell()
    DoubleCell = Range("A1") * 2
End Function
```

Although this function works, there are times when it may return an incorrect result. Excel's calculation engine cannot account for ranges in your code that are not passed as arguments. Therefore, in some cases, all precedents may not be calculated before the function's value is returned. The `DoubleCell` function should be written as follows, with A1 passed as the argument:

```
Function DoubleCell(cell)
    DoubleCell = cell * 2
End Function
```

In both of these examples, the `Commission` function must be available in the active workbook; otherwise, Excel displays an error message saying that the function is not defined.

A function with two arguments

Imagine that the aforementioned hypothetical sales managers implement a new policy to help reduce turnover: The total commission paid is increased by 1 percent for every year that the salesperson has been with the company.

I modified the custom `Commission` function (defined in the preceding section) so that it takes two arguments. The new argument represents the number of years. Call this new function `Commission2`:

```
Function Commission2(Sales, Years)
'    Calculates sales commissions based on
'    years in service
    Const Tier1 = 0.08
    Const Tier2 = 0.105
    Const Tier3 = 0.12
    Const Tier4 = 0.14
    Select Case Sales
        Case 0 To 9999.99: Commission2 = Sales * Tier1
        Case 1000 To 19999.99: Commission2 = Sales * Tier2
        Case 20000 To 39999.99: Commission2 = Sales * Tier3
        Case Is >= 40000: Commission2 = Sales * Tier4
    End Select
    Commission2 = Commission2 + (Commission2 * Years / 100)
End Function
```

Pretty simple, eh? I just added the second argument (Years) to the Function statement and included an additional computation that adjusts the commission.

Here's an example of how you can write a formula using this function (it assumes that the sales amount is in cell A1 and the number of years the salesperson has worked is in cell B1):

```
=Commission2(A1,B1)
```

CD-ROM
All of these commission-related procedures are available on the companion CD-ROM in a file named commission functions.xlsm.

A function with an array argument

A Function procedure also can accept one or more arrays as arguments, process the array(s), and return a single value. The array can also consist of a range of cells.

The following function accepts an array as its argument and returns the sum of its elements:

```
Function SumArray(List) As Double
    Dim Item As Variant
    SumArray = 0
    For Each Item In List
        If WorksheetFunction.IsNumber(Item) Then _
            SumArray = SumArray + Item
    Next Item
End Function
```

Excel's ISNUMBER function checks to see whether each element is a number before adding it to the total. Adding this simple error-checking statement eliminates the type-mismatch error that occurs when you try to perform arithmetic with something other than a number.

The following procedure demonstrates how to call this function from a Sub procedure. The MakeList procedure creates a 100-element array and assigns a random number to each element. Then the MsgBox function displays the sum of the values in the array by calling the SumArray function.

```
Sub MakeList()
    Dim Nums(1 To 100) As Double
    Dim i as Integer
    For i = 1 To 100
        Nums(i) = Rnd * 1000
    Next i
    MsgBox SumArray(Nums)
End Sub
```

Notice that the SumArray function doesn't declare the data type of its argument (it's a variant). Because it's not declared as a specific numeric type, the function also works in your worksheet formulas in which the argument is a Range object. For example, the following formula returns the sum of the values in A1:C10:

```
=SumArray(A1:C10)
```

You might notice that, when used in a worksheet formula, the SumArray function works very much like Excel's SUM function. One difference, however, is that SumArray does not accept multiple arguments. Understand that this example is for educational purposes only. Using the SumArray function in a formula offers absolutely no advantages over the Excel SUM function.

 CD

This example, named array argument.xlsm, is available on the companion CD-ROM.

A function with optional arguments

Many of Excel's built-in worksheet functions use optional arguments. An example is the LEFT function, which returns characters from the left side of a string. Its syntax is

```
LEFT(text,num_chars)
```

The first argument is required, but the second is optional. If the optional argument is omitted, Excel assumes a value of 1. Therefore, the following two formulas return the same result:

```
=LEFT(A1,1)
=LEFT(A1)
```

The custom functions that you develop in VBA also can have optional arguments. You specify an optional argument by preceding the argument's name with the keyword Optional. In the argument list, optional arguments must appear after any required arguments.

Following is a simple function example that returns the user's name. The function's argument is optional.

```
Function User(Optional UpperCase As Variant)
    If IsMissing(UpperCase) Then UpperCase = False
    User = Application.UserName
    If UpperCase Then User = UCase(User)
End Function
```

If the argument is False or omitted, the user's name is returned without any changes. If the argument is True, the user's name is converted to uppercase (using the VBA UCase function) before it is returned. Notice that the first statement in the procedure uses the VBA `IsMissing` function to determine whether the argument was supplied. If the argument is missing, the statement sets the `UpperCase` variable to `False` (the default value).

All the following formulas are valid, and the first two produce the same result:

```
=User()
=User(False)
=User(True)
```

NOTE

If you need to determine whether an optional argument was passed to a function, you must declare the optional argument as a `Variant` data type. Then you can use the `IsMissing` function within the procedure, as demonstrated in this example.

The following is another example of a custom function that uses an optional argument. This function randomly chooses one cell from an input range and returns that cell's contents. If the second argument is `True`, the selected value changes whenever the worksheet is recalculated (that is, the function is made volatile). If the second argument is `False` (or omitted), the function is not recalculated unless one of the cells in the input range is modified.

```
Function DrawOne(Rng As Variant, Optional Recalc As Variant = False)
'       Chooses one cell at random from a range

'       Make function volatile if Recalc is True
        Application.Volatile Recalc

'       Determine a random cell
        DrawOne = Rng(Int((Rng.Count) * Rnd + 1))
End Function
```

Notice that the second argument for `DrawOne` includes the `Optional` keyword, along with a default value.

All the following formulas are valid, and the first two have the same effect:

```
=DrawOne(A1:A100)
=DrawOne(A1:A100,False)
=DrawOne(A1:A100,True)
```

This function might be useful for choosing lottery numbers, picking a winner from a list of names, and so on.

CD-ROM

This function is available on the companion CD-ROM. The filename is `draw.xlsm`.

A function that returns a VBA array

VBA includes a useful function called `Array`. The `Array` function returns a variant that contains an array (that is, multiple values). If you're familiar with array formulas in Excel, you have a head start on understanding VBA's `Array` function. You enter an array formula into a cell by pressing Ctrl+Shift+Enter. Excel inserts curly braces around the formula to indicate that it's an array formula.

CROSS-REFERENCE

See Chapter 3 for more details on array formulas.

NOTE

It's important to understand that the array returned by the `Array` function is not the same as a normal array that's made up of elements of the `Variant` data type. In other words, a variant array is not the same as an array of variants.

The `MonthNames` function, which follows, is a simple example that uses VBA's `Array` function in a custom function:

```
Function MonthNames()
    MonthNames = Array("Jan", "Feb", "Mar", "Apr","May", "Jun", _
        "Jul", "Aug", "Sep", "Oct", "Nov", "Dec")
End Function
```

The `MonthNames` function returns a horizontal array of month names. You can create a multicell array formula that uses the `MonthNames` function. Here's how to use it: Make sure that the function code is present in a VBA module. Then in a worksheet, select multiple cells in a row (start by selecting 12 cells). Then enter the formula that follows (without the braces) and press Ctrl+Shift+Enter:

```
{=MonthNames()}
```

What if you'd like to generate a vertical list of month names? No problem; just select a vertical range, enter the following formula (without the braces), and then press Ctrl+Shift+Enter:

```
{=TRANSPOSE(MonthNames())}
```

This formula uses the Excel TRANSPOSE function to convert the horizontal array to a vertical array.

The following example is a variation on the MonthNames function:

```
Function MonthNames(Optional MIndex)
    Dim AllNames As Variant
    Dim MonthVal As Long
    AllNames = Array("Jan", "Feb", "Mar", "Apr", _
        "May", "Jun", "Jul", "Aug", "Sep", "Oct", _
        "Nov", "Dec")
    If IsMissing(MIndex) Then
        MonthNames = AllNames
    Else
        Select Case MIndex
            Case Is >= 1
                Determine month value (for example, 13=1)
                MonthVal = ((MIndex - 1) Mod 12)
                MonthNames = AllNames(MonthVal)
            Case Is <= 0 ' Vertical array
                MonthNames = Application.Transpose(AllNames)
        End Select
    End If
End Function
```

Notice that I use the VBA IsMissing function to test for a missing argument. In this situation, it is not possible to specify the default value for the missing argument in the argument list of the function because the default value is defined within the function. You can use the IsMissing function only if the optional argument is a variant.

This enhanced function uses an optional argument that works as follows:

- *If the argument is missing*, the function returns a horizontal array of month names.

- *If the argument is less than or equal to 0*, the function returns a vertical array of month names. It uses Excel's TRANSPOSE function to convert the array.

- *If the argument is greater than or equal to 1*, it returns the month name that corresponds to the argument value.

NOTE

This procedure uses the Mod operator to determine the month value. The Mod operator returns the remainder after dividing the first operand by the second. Keep in mind that the AllNames array is zero-based and that indices range from 0 to 11. In the statement that uses the Mod operator, 1 is subtracted from the function's argument. Therefore, an argument of 13 returns 0 (corresponding to Jan), and an argument of 24 returns 11 (corresponding to Dec).

You can use this function in a number of ways, as illustrated in Figure 10-5.

	A	B	C	D	E	F	G	H	I	J	K	L
1	Jan	Feb	Mar	Apr	May	Jun	Jul	Aug	Sep	Oct	Nov	Dec
2												
3	1	Jan		Jan		Mar						
4	2	Feb		Feb								
5	3	Mar		Mar								
6	4	Apr		Apr								
7	5	May		May								
8	6	Jun		Jun								
9	7	Jul		Jul								
10	8	Aug		Aug								
11	9	Sep		Sep								
12	10	Oct		Oct								
13	11	Nov		Nov								
14	12	Dec		Dec								
15												

Sheet1

Figure 10-5: Different ways of passing an array or a single value to a worksheet.

Range A1:L1 contains the following formula entered as an array. Start by selecting A1:L1, enter the formula (without the braces), and then press Ctrl+Shift+Enter.

```
{=MonthNames()}
```

Range A3:A14 contains integers from 1 to 12. Cell B3 contains the following (nonarray) formula, which was copied to the 11 cells below it:

```
=MonthNames(A3)
```

Range D3:D14 contains the following formula entered as an array:

```
{=MonthNames(-1)}
```

Range F3 contains this (nonarray) formula:

```
=MonthNames(3)
```

Remember: To enter an array formula, you must press Ctrl+Shift+Enter.

 NOTE

The lower bound of an array, created using the `Array` function, is determined by the lower bound specified with the `Option Base` statement at the top of the module. If there is no `Option Base` statement, the default lower bound is 0.

CD-ROM

A workbook that demonstrates the `MonthNames` function is available on the companion CD-ROM. The file is named `month names.xslm`.

A function that returns an error value

In some cases, you might want your custom function to return a particular error value. Consider the RemoveVowels function, which I presented earlier in this chapter:

```
Function RemoveVowels(Txt) As String
' Removes all vowels from the Txt argument
    Dim i As Long
    RemoveVowels = ""
    For i = 1 To Len(Txt)
        If Not UCase(Mid(Txt, i, 1)) Like "[AEIOU]" Then
            RemoveVowels = RemoveVowels & Mid(Txt, i, 1)
        End If
    Next i
End Function
```

When used in a worksheet formula, this function removes the vowels from its single-cell argument. If the argument is a numeric value, this function returns the value as a string. You may prefer that the function returns an error value (#N/A), rather than the numeric value converted to a string.

You might be tempted simply to assign a string that looks like an Excel formula error value. For example:

```
RemoveVowels = "#N/A"
```

Although the string *looks* like an error value, it is not treated as such by other formulas that may reference it. To return a *real* error value from a function, use the VBA CVErr function, which converts an error number to a real error.

Fortunately, VBA has built-in constants for the errors that you want to return from a custom function. These errors are Excel formula error values and not VBA runtime error values. These constants are as follows:

- xlErrDiv0 (for #DIV/0!)

- xlErrNA (for #N/A)

- xlErrName (for #NAME?)

- xlErrNull (for #NULL!)

- xlErrNum (for #NUM!)

- xlErrRef (for #REF!)

- xlErrValue (for #VALUE!)

Part III

To return a #N/A error from a custom function, you can use a statement like this:

```
RemoveVowels = CVErr(xlErrNA)
```

The revised `RemoveVowels` function follows. This function uses an If-Then construct to take a different action if the argument is not text. It uses Excel's ISTEXT function to determine whether the argument is text. If the argument is text, the function proceeds normally. If the cell doesn't contain text (or is empty), the function returns the #N/A error.

```
Function RemoveVowels(Txt) As Variant
' Removes all vowels from the Txt argument
' Returns #VALUE if Txt is not a string
    Dim i As Long
    RemoveVowels = ""
    If Application.WorksheetFunction.IsText(Txt) Then
        For i = 1 To Len(Txt)
            If Not UCase(Mid(Txt, i, 1)) Like "[AEIOU]" Then
                RemoveVowels = RemoveVowels & Mid(Txt, i, 1)
            End If
        Next i
    Else
        RemoveVowels = CVErr(xlErrNA)
    End If
End Function
```

 NOTE

Notice that I also changed the data type for the function's return value. Because the function can now return something other than a string, I changed the data type to `Variant`.

A function with an indefinite number of arguments

Some Excel worksheet functions take an indefinite number of arguments. A familiar example is the SUM function, which has the following syntax:

```
SUM(number1,number2...)
```

The first argument is required, but you can have as many as 254 additional arguments in Excel 2007. Here's an example of a SUM function with four range arguments:

```
=SUM(A1:A5,C1:C5,E1:E5,G1:G5)
```

You can even mix and match the argument types. For example, the following example uses three arguments: the first is a range, the second is a value, and the third is an expression.

```
=SUM(A1:A5,12,24*3)
```

You can create Function procedures that have an indefinite number of arguments. The trick is to use an array as the last (or only) argument, preceded by the keyword ParamArray.

NOTE

ParamArray can apply only to the last argument in the procedure's argument list. It is always a Variant data type, and it is always an optional argument (although you don't use the Optional keyword).

Following is a function that can have any number of single-value arguments. (It doesn't work with multicell range arguments.) It simply returns the sum of the arguments.

```
Function SimpleSum(ParamArray arglist() As Variant) As Double
    For Each arg In arglist
        SimpleSum = SimpleSum + arg
    Next arg
End Function
```

To modify this function so it works with multicell range arguments, you need to add another loop, which processes each cell in each of the arguments:

```
Function SimpleSum(ParamArray arglist() As Variant) As Double
    Dim cell As Range
    For Each arg In arglist
        For Each cell In arg
            SimpleSum = SimpleSum + cell
        Next cell
    Next arg
End Function
```

The SimpleSum function is similar to Excel's SUM function, but it's not nearly as flexible. Try it out by using various types of arguments, and you'll see that it fails if any of the cells contains a non-value.

Emulating Excel's SUM Function

In this section, I present a custom function called MySum. Unlike the SimpleSum function listed in the previous section, the MySum function emulates Excel's SUM function (almost) perfectly.

Before you look at the code for MySum, take a minute to think about the Excel SUM function. It is, in fact, very versatile. It can have as many as 255 arguments (even "missing" arguments), and the arguments can be numerical values, cells, ranges, text representations of numbers, logical values, and even embedded functions. For example, consider the following formula:

```
=SUM(B1,5,"6",,TRUE,SQRT(4),A1:A5,D:D,C2*C3)
```

This perfectly valid formula contains all the following types of arguments, listed here in the order of their presentation:

- A single cell reference
- A literal value
- A string that looks like a value
- A missing argument
- A logical TRUE value
- An expression that uses another function
- A simple range reference
- A range reference that includes an entire column
- An expression that calculates the product of two cells

The MySum function (see Listing 10-1) handles all these argument types.

 CD-ROM

A workbook containing the MySum function is available on the companion CD-ROM. The file is named mysum function.xlsm.

Listing 10-1: MySum Function

```
Function MySum(ParamArray args() As Variant) As Variant
' Emulates Excel's SUM function

' Variable declarations
    Dim i As Variant
    Dim TempRange As Range, cell As Range
    Dim ECode As String
    Dim m, n
    MySum = 0
```

```
' Process each argument
  For i = 0 To UBound(args)
'    Skip missing arguments
    If Not IsMissing(args(i)) Then
'      What type of argument is it?
      Select Case TypeName(args(i))
        Case "Range"
'          Create temp range to handle full row or column ranges
          Set TempRange = Intersect(args(i).Parent.UsedRange, _
            args(i))
          For Each cell In TempRange
            If IsError(cell) Then
              MySum = cell ' return the error
              Exit Function
            End If
            If cell = True Or cell = False Then
              MySum = MySum + 0
            Else
              If IsNumeric(cell) Or IsDate(cell) Then _
                MySum = MySum + cell
              End If
          Next cell
        Case "Variant()"
            n = args(i)
            For m = LBound(n) To UBound(n)
              MySum = MySum(MySum, n(m)) 'recursive call
            Next m
        Case "Null"  'ignore it
        Case "Error" 'return the error
          MySum = args(i)
          Exit Function
        Case "Boolean"
'          Check for literal TRUE and compensate
          If args(i) = "True" Then MySum = MySum + 1
        Case "Date"
          MySum = MySum + args(i)
        Case Else
          MySum = MySum + args(i)
      End Select
    End If
  Next i
End Function
```

Figure 10-6 shows a workbook with various formulas that use SUM and MySum. As you can see, the functions return identical results.

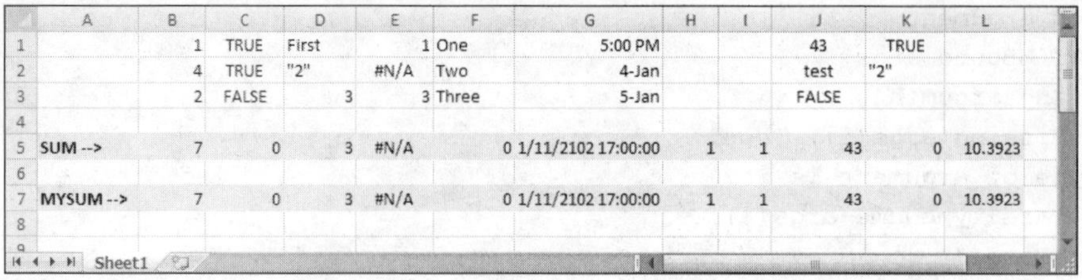

	A	B	C	D	E	F	G	H	I	J	K	L
1		1	TRUE	First	1	One	5:00 PM			43	TRUE	
2		4	TRUE	"2"	#N/A	Two	4-Jan			test	"2"	
3		2	FALSE		3	3 Three	5-Jan			FALSE		
4												
5	SUM -->	7	0		3	#N/A	0 1/11/2102 17:00:00	1	1	43	0	10.3923
6												
7	MYSUM -->	7	0		3	#N/A	0 1/11/2102 17:00:00	1	1	43	0	10.3923
8												
9												

Sheet1

Figure 10-6: Comparing SUM with MySum.

If you're interested in learning how this function works, create a formula that uses the function. Then, set a breakpoint in the code and step through the statements line by line. (See "Debugging Functions," later in this chapter.) Try this for several different argument types, and you'll soon have a good feel for how this function works. As you study the code for MySum, keep the following points in mind:

- Missing arguments (determined by the IsMissing function) are simply ignored.

- The procedure uses VBA's TypeName function to determine the type of argument (Range, Error, and so on). Each argument type is handled differently.

- For a range argument, the function loops through each cell in the range, determines the type of data in the cell, and (if appropriate) adds its value to a running total.

- The data type for the function is Variant because the function needs to return an error if any of its arguments is an error value.

- If an argument contains an error (for example, #DIV/0!), the MySum function simply returns the error — just as Excel's SUM function does.

- Excel's SUM function considers a text string to have a value of 0 unless it appears as a literal argument (that is, as an actual value, not a variable). Therefore, MySum adds the cell's value only if it can be evaluated as a number. (VBA's IsNumeric function is used for this.)

- For range arguments, the function uses the Intersect method to create a temporary range that consists of the intersection of the range and the sheet's used range. This handles cases in which a range argument consists of a complete row or column, which would take forever to evaluate.

You might be curious about the relative speeds of SUM and MySum. MySum, of course, is much slower, but just how much slower depends on the speed of your system and the formulas themselves. On my system, a worksheet with 1,000 SUM formulas recalculates instantly. After I replace the SUM functions with MySum functions, it takes about eight seconds. MySum may be improved a bit, but it can never come close to SUM's speed.

By the way, I hope you understand that the point of this example is *not* to create a new SUM function. Rather, it demonstrates how to create custom worksheet functions that look and work like those built into Excel.

Debugging Functions

When you're using a formula in a worksheet to test a Function procedure, VBA runtime errors do not appear in the all-too-familiar, pop-up error box. If an error occurs, the formula simply returns an error value (#VALUE!). Luckily, this does not present a problem for debugging functions because you have several possible workarounds:

- *Place MsgBox functions at strategic locations to monitor the value of specific variables.* Message boxes in Function procedures *do* pop up when the procedure is executed. But make sure that you have only one formula in the worksheet that uses your function, or message boxes will appear for each formula that is evaluated, which is a repetition that will quickly become annoying.

- *Test the procedure by calling it from a Sub procedure, not from a worksheet formula.* Runtime errors are displayed in the usual manner, and you can either fix the problem (if you know it) or jump right into the Debugger.

- *Set a breakpoint in the function and then step through the function.* You then can access all the standard VBA debugging tools. To set a breakpoint, move the cursor to the statement at which you want to pause execution and then choose Debug ➪ Toggle Breakpoint (or press F9). When the function is executing, press F8 to step through the procedure line-by-line.

- *Use one or more temporary Debug.Print statements in your code to write values to the VBE Immediate window.* For example, if you want to monitor a value inside of a loop, use something like the following routine:

```
Function VowelCount(r) As Long
    Dim Count As Long
    Dim i As Long
    Dim Ch As String * 1
    Count = 0
    For i = 1 To Len(r)
        Ch = UCase(Mid(r, i, 1))
        If Ch Like "[AEIOU]" Then
            Count = Count + 1
            Debug.Print Ch, i
        End If
    Next i
    VowelCount = Count
End Function
```

In this case, the values of two variables, Ch and i, are printed to the Immediate window whenever the Debug.Print statement is encountered. Figure 10-7 shows the result when the function has an argument of Tucson Arizona.

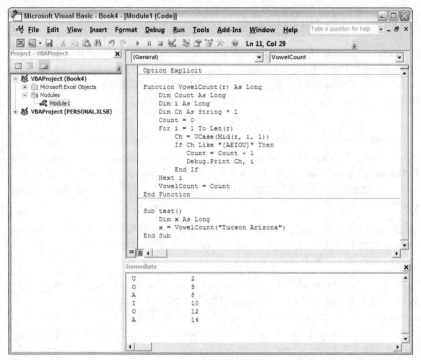

Figure 10-7: Use the Immediate window to display results while a function is running.

Dealing with the Insert Function Dialog Box

Excel's Insert Function dialog box is a handy tool. When you are creating a worksheet formula, this tool lets you select a particular worksheet function from a list of functions (see Figure 10-8). These functions are grouped into various categories to make it easier to locate a particular function. The Insert Function dialog box also displays your custom worksheet functions, and the Function Arguments dialog box prompts you for a function's arguments.

NOTE

Custom `Function` procedures defined with the `Private` keyword do not appear in the Insert Function dialog box. If you develop a function that's intended to be used only in your other VBA procedures, you should declare it by using the `Private` keyword. However, declaring the function as `Private` does not prevent it from being used in a worksheet formula. It just prevents the function from displaying in the Insert Function dialog box.

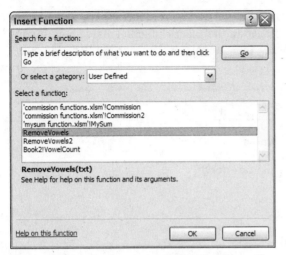

Figure 10-8: Inserting a custom function into a formula.

By default, custom functions are listed under the User Defined category, but you can have them appear under a different category if you like. You also can add some text to describe the function. (I highly recommend this step.)

In the Insert Function dialog box, notice that the workbook name is also displayed for functions that are defined in a workbook other than the active workbook.

NOTE

The Insert Function dialog box enables you to search for a function by keyword. Unfortunately, this search feature cannot be used to locate custom functions created in VBA.

Specifying a function category

Oddly, Excel does not provide a direct way to assign a custom function to a category. If you would like your custom function to appear in a function category other than User Defined, you must write and execute some VBA code.

The following statement assigns the function named `Commission` to the Financial category (category number 1):

```
Application.MacroOptions Macro:="Commission", Category:=1
```

NOTE

You need to execute this statement only one time (not each time the workbook is opened). From then on, every time the workbook is opened, the function will appear in the category that you specified.

Table 10-1 lists the category numbers that you can use. Notice that a few of these categories (10 through 13) are normally not displayed in the Insert Function dialog box. If you assign your function to one of these categories, the category will appear in the dialog box.

TABLE 10-1   FUNCTION CATEGORIES

Category Number	Category Name
0	All (no specific category)
1	Financial
2	Date & Time
3	Math & Trig
4	Statistical
5	Lookup & Reference
6	Database
7	Text
8	Logical
9	Information
10	Commands
11	Customizing
12	Macro Control
13	DDE/External
14	User Defined
15	Engineering
16	Cube*

*The Cube category is new to Excel 2007

Adding a function description

When you select a function in the Insert Function dialog box, a brief description of the function appears. You can specify a description for your custom function in two ways: Either use the Macro dialog box or write VBA code.

NOTE

If you don't provide a description for your custom function, the Insert Function dialog box displays the following text: No help available.

DESCRIBING YOUR FUNCTION IN THE MACRO DIALOG BOX

Follow these steps to provide a description for a custom function:

1. Create your function in the VBE.

2. Activate Excel, making sure that the workbook that contains the function is the active workbook.

3. Choose Developer ⇨ Code ⇨ Macros (or press Alt+F8).

   The Macro dialog box lists available procedures, but your functions will not be in the list.

4. Type the name of your function in the Macro Name box.

5. Click the Options button to display the Macro Options dialog box.

6. Enter the function description in the Description box (see Figure 10-9). The Shortcut Key field is irrelevant for functions.

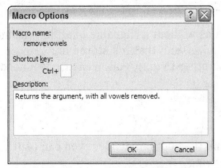

Figure 10-9: Provide a function description in the Macro Options dialog box.

7. Click OK and then click Cancel.

After you perform the preceding steps, the Insert Function dialog box displays the description that you entered in Step 6 when the function is selected.

CROSS-REFERENCE

For information on creating a custom help topic accessible from the Insert Function dialog box, refer to Chapter 24.

When you use the Insert Function dialog box to enter a function, the Function Arguments dialog box is displayed after you click OK. For built-in functions, the Function Arguments dialog box displays a description for each of the function's arguments. Unfortunately, you cannot provide such descriptions for custom function arguments.

DESCRIBING YOUR FUNCTION WITH VBA CODE

Another way to provide a description for a custom function is to write VBA code. The following statement assigns a description for the function named Commission:

```
Application.MacroOptions _
    Macro:= "Commission", _
    Description:= "Calculates sales commissions"
```

You need to execute this statement only one time (not each time the workbook is opened).

Using Add-ins to Store Custom Functions

You might prefer to store frequently used custom functions in an add-in file. A primary advantage of doing this is that you can use the functions in any workbook.

In addition, the functions can be used in formulas without a filename qualifier. Assume that you have a custom function named ZapSpaces, and that it's stored in Myfuncs.xlsm. To use this function in a formula in a workbook other than Myfuncs.xlsm, you need to enter the following formula:

```
=Myfuncs.xlsm!ZapSpaces(A1:C12)
```

If you create an add-in from Myfuncs.xlsm and the add-in is loaded, you can omit the file reference and enter a formula such as the following:

```
=ZapSpaces(A1:C12)
```

CROSS-REFERENCE
I discuss add-ins in Chapter 21.

CAUTION
A potential problem with using add-ins to store custom functions is that your workbook is dependent on the add-in file. If you need to share your workbook with a colleague, you also need to share a copy of the add-in that contains the functions.

Using the Windows API

VBA can borrow methods from other files that have nothing to do with Excel or VBA — for example, the Dynamic Link Library (DLL) files that Windows and other software use. As a result, you can do things with VBA that would otherwise be outside the language's scope.

The Windows *Application Programming Interface* (API) is a set of functions available to Windows programmers. When you call a Windows function from VBA, you're accessing the Windows API. Many of the Windows resources used by Windows programmers are available in *DLLs*, which store programs and functions and are linked at runtime rather than at compile time.

Excel itself uses several DLLs, for example. The code in many of these DLLs could have been compiled right into the `excel.exe` executable file, but the designers chose to store it in DLLs, which are loaded only when needed. This technique makes Excel's main executable file smaller. In addition, it is a more efficient use of memory because the library is loaded only when it's needed.

DLLs are also used to share code. For example, most Windows programs use dialog boxes to open and save files. Windows comes with a DLL that has the code to generate several standard dialog boxes. Programmers thus can call this DLL rather than write their own routines.

If you're a C programmer, you can produce your own DLLs and use them from VBA. In addition, Microsoft's Visual Basic language (but not VBA) also has the capability to create DLL files that can be called from Excel.

Windows API examples

Before you can use a Windows API function, you must declare the function at the top of your code module. If the code module is for a `UserForm`, `Sheet`, or `ThisWorkbook`, you must declare the API function as `Private`.

An API function must be declared precisely. The declaration statement tells VBA:

- Which API function you're using
- In which library the API function is located
- The API function's arguments

After you declare an API function, you can use it in your VBA code.

Determining the Windows directory

Following is an example of an API function declaration:

```
Declare Function GetWindowsDirectoryA Lib "kernel32" _
  (ByVal lpBuffer As String, ByVal nSize As Long) As Long
```

This function, which has two arguments, returns the name of the directory in which Windows is installed (something that is not normally possible using VBA). After calling the function, the Windows directory is contained in `lpBuffer`, and the length of the directory string is contained in `nSize`.

After inserting the `Declare` statement at the top of your module, you can access the function by calling the `GetWindowsDirectoryA` function. The following is an example of calling the function and displaying the result in a message box:

```
Sub ShowWindowsDir()
    Dim WinPath As String * 255
    Dim WinDir As String
    WinPath = Space(255)
    WinDir = Left(WinPath, GetWindowsDirectoryA _
      (WinPath, Len(WinPath)))
    MsgBox WinDir, vbInformation, "Windows Directory"
End Sub
```

Executing the `ShowWindowsDir` procedure displays a message box with the Windows directory.

Often, you'll want to create a *wrapper* for API functions. In other words, you create your own function that uses the API function. This greatly simplifies using the API function. Here's an example of a wrapper VBA function:

```
Function WindowsDir() As String
'   Returns the Windows directory
    Dim WinPath As String * 255
    WinPath = Space(255)
    WindowsDir = Left(WinPath, GetWindowsDirectoryA _
        (WinPath, Len(WinPath)))
End Function
```

After declaring this function, you can call it from another procedure:

```
MsgBox WindowsDir()
```

You can even use the function in a worksheet formula:

```
=WindowsDir()
```

CD-ROM

This example is available on the companion CD-ROM. The filename is `windows directory.xlsm`.

The reason for using API calls is to perform actions that would otherwise be impossible (or at least very difficult). If your application needs to find the path of the Windows directory, you could search all day and not find a function in Excel or VBA to do the trick. But knowing how to access the Windows API may solve your problem.

 CAUTION

When you work with API calls, system crashes during testing are not uncommon, so save your work often.

Detecting the Shift key

Here's another example: Suppose you've written a VBA macro that will be executed from button on a worksheet. Furthermore, suppose you want the macro to perform differently if the user presses the Shift key when the button is clicked. Normally, there is no way to detect whether the Shift key is pressed. But you can use the GetKeyState API function to find out. The GetKeyState function tells you whether a particular key is pressed. It takes a single argument, nVirtKey, which represents the code for the key that you are interested in.

 CROSS-REFERENCE

Chapter 11 has several additional examples of using Windows API functions.

The following code demonstrates how to detect whether the Shift key is pressed when the Button_Click event handler procedure is executed. Notice that I define a constant for the Shift key (using a hexadecimal value) and then use this constant as the argument for GetKeyState. If GetKeyState returns a value less than zero, it means that the Shift key was pressed; otherwise, the Shift key was not pressed.

```
Declare Function GetKeyState Lib "user32" _
   (ByVal nVirtKey As Long) As Integer

Sub Button_Click()
    Const VK_SHIFT As Integer = &H10
    If GetKeyState(VK_SHIFT) < 0 Then
        MsgBox "Shift is pressed"
    Else
        MsgBox "Shift is not pressed"
    End If
End Sub
```

 CD-ROM

A workbook named key press.xlsm on the companion CD-ROM demonstrates how to detect the following keys (as well as any combinations): Ctrl, Shift, and Alt.

Part III

Learning more about API functions

Working with the Windows API functions can be tricky. Many programming reference books list the declarations for common API calls and often provide examples. Usually, you can simply copy the declarations and use the functions without really understanding the details. In reality (at least the reality that I've seen), most Excel programmers take a cookbook approach to API functions. The Internet has hundreds of examples that can be copied and pasted and that work quite reliably.

CD-ROM

The companion CD-ROM includes a file named win32api.txt, which is a text file that contains Windows API declarations and constants. You can open this file with a text editor and copy the appropriate declarations to a VBA module.

Chapter 11

VBA Programming Examples and Techniques

In This Chapter

I believe that learning programming concepts is accelerated by a heavy emphasis on examples. And based on the feedback that I've received from readers of previous editions of this book, I have plenty of company. VBA programmers especially benefit from a hands-on approach. A well-thought-out example usually communicates a concept much better than a description of the underlying theory. I decided, therefore, not to write a reference book that painstakingly describes every nuance of VBA. Rather, I prepared numerous examples to demonstrate useful Excel programming techniques.

- ◆ Examples of using VBA to work with ranges

- ◆ Examples of using VBA to work with workbooks and sheets

- ◆ Custom functions for use in your VBA procedures and in worksheet formulas

- ◆ Examples of miscellaneous VBA tricks and techniques

- ◆ Examples of using Windows Application Programming Interface (API) functions

The previous chapters in this part provide enough information to get you started. The Help system provides all the details that I left out. In this chapter, I pick up the pace and present examples that solve practical problems while furthering your knowledge of VBA.

I've categorized this chapter's examples into six groups:

- Working with ranges
- Working with workbooks and sheets
- VBA techniques
- Functions that are useful in your VBA procedures
- Functions that you can use in worksheet formulas
- Windows API calls

 CROSS-REFERENCE

Subsequent chapters in this book present additional feature-specific examples: charts, pivot tables, events, UserForms, and so on.

Working with Ranges

The examples in this section demonstrate how to manipulate worksheet ranges with VBA.

Copying a range

Excel's macro recorder is useful not so much for generating usable code, but for discovering the names of relevant objects, methods, and properties. The code that's generated by the macro recorder isn't always the most efficient, but it can usually provide you with several clues.

For example, recording a simple copy-and-paste operation generates five lines of VBA code:

```
Sub Macro1()
    Range("A1").Select
    Selection.Copy
```

```
    Range("B1").Select
    ActiveSheet.Paste
    Application.CutCopyMode = False
End Sub
```

Notice that the generated code selects cell A1, copies it, and then selects cell B1 and performs the paste operation. But in VBA, it's not necessary to select an object to work with it. You would never learn this important point by mimicking the preceding recorded macro code, where two statements incorporate the Select method. This procedure can be replaced with the following much simpler routine, which doesn't select any cells. It also takes advantage of the fact that the Copy method can use an argument that represents the destination for the copied range:

```
Sub CopyRange()
    Range("A1").Copy Range("B1")
End Sub
```

Both of these macros assume that a worksheet is active and that the operation takes place on the active worksheet. To copy a range to a different worksheet or workbook, simply qualify the range reference for the destination. The following example copies a range from Sheet1 in File1.xlsx to Sheet2 in File2.xlsx. Because the references are fully qualified, this example works regardless of which workbook is active.

```
Sub CopyRange2()
    Workbooks("File1.xlsx").Sheets("Sheet1").Range("A1").Copy _
        Workbooks("File2.xlsx").Sheets("Sheet2").Range("A1")
End Sub
```

Another way to approach this task is to use object variables to represent the ranges, as shown in the code that follows:

```
Sub CopyRange3()
    Dim Rng1 As Range, Rng2 As Range
    Set Rng1 = Workbooks("File1.xlsx").Sheets("Sheet1").Range("A1")
    Set Rng2 = Workbooks("File2.xlsx").Sheets("Sheet2").Range("A1")
    Rng1.Copy Rng2
End Sub
```

As you might expect, copying is not limited to one single cell at a time. The following procedure, for example, copies a large range. Notice that the destination consists of only a single cell (which represents the upper-left cell for the destination).

```
Sub CopyRange4()
    Range("A1:C800").Copy Range("D1")
End Sub
```

Part III

Moving a range

The VBA instructions for moving a range are very similar to those for copying a range, as the following example demonstrates. The difference is that you use the Cut method instead of the Copy method. Note that you need to specify only the upper-left cell for the destination range.

The following example moves 18 cells (in A1:C6) to a new location, beginning at cell H1:

```
Sub MoveRange1()
    Range("A1:C6").Cut Range("H1")
End Sub
```

Copying a variably sized range

In many cases, you need to copy a range of cells, but you don't know the exact row and column dimensions of the range. For example, you might have a workbook that tracks weekly sales, and the number of rows changes weekly when you add new data.

Figure 11-1 shows a common type of worksheet. This range consists of several rows, and the number of rows changes each week. Because you don't know the exact range address at any given time, writing a macro to copy the range requires some additional coding.

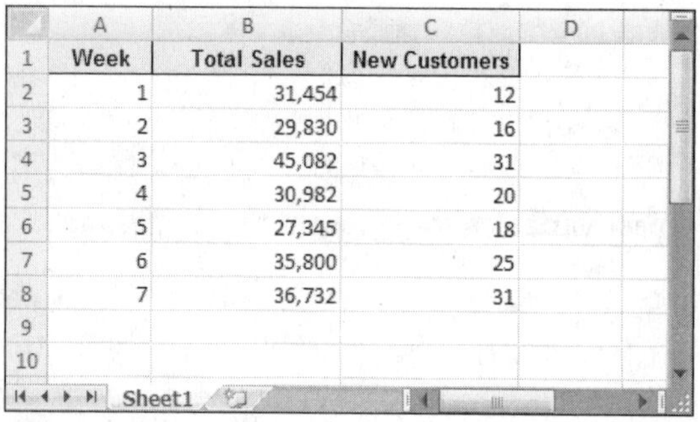

	A	B	C	D
1	Week	Total Sales	New Customers	
2	1	31,454	12	
3	2	29,830	16	
4	3	45,082	31	
5	4	30,982	20	
6	5	27,345	18	
7	6	35,800	25	
8	7	36,732	31	
9				
10				

Sheet1

Figure 11-1: The number of rows in the data range changes every week.

The following macro demonstrates how to copy this range from Sheet1 to Sheet2 (beginning at cell A1). It uses the CurrentRegion property, which returns a Range object that corresponds to the block of cells around a particular cell (in this case, A1).

```
Sub CopyCurrentRegion2()
    Range("A1").CurrentRegion.Copy Sheets("Sheet2").Range("A1")
End Sub
```

Tips for Working with Ranges

When you work with ranges, keep the following points in mind:

- Your code doesn't need to select a range in order to work with it.

- If your code does select a range, its worksheet must be active. You can use the `Activate` method of the `Worksheets` collection to activate a particular sheet.

- The macro recorder doesn't always generate the most efficient code. Often, you can create your macro by using the recorder and then edit the code to make it more efficient.

- It's a good idea to use named ranges in your VBA code. For example, referring to `Range("Total")` is better than `Range("D45")`. In the latter case, if you add a row above row 45, the cell address will change. You would then need to modify the macro so that it uses the correct range address (D46).

- If you rely on the macro recorder when selecting ranges, make sure that you record the macro using relative references. Use the Developer ⇨ Code ⇨ Use Relative References control.

- When running a macro that works on each cell in the current range selection, the user might select entire columns or rows. In most cases, you don't want to loop through every cell in the selection. Your macro should create a subset of the selection consisting of only the nonblank cells. See "Looping through a selected range efficiently," later in this chapter.

- Excel allows multiple selections. For example, you can select a range, press Ctrl, and select another range. You can test for this in your macro and take appropriate action. See "Determining the type of selected range," later in this chapter.

NOTE

Using the `CurrentRegion` property is equivalent to choosing the Home ⇨ Editing ⇨ Find & Select ⇨ Go To Special command and selecting the Current Region option (or by using the Ctrl+Shift+* shortcut). To see how this works, record your actions while you issue that command. Generally, the `CurrentRegion` property setting consists of a rectangular block of cells surrounded by one or more blank rows or columns.

Selecting or otherwise identifying various types of ranges

Much of the work that you will do in VBA will involve working with ranges — either selecting a range or identifying a range so that you can do something with the cells.

In addition to the `CurrentRegion` property (which I discussed earlier), you should also be aware of the `End` method of the `Range` object. The `End` method takes one argument, which determines the direction in which the selection is extended. The following statement selects a range from the active cell to the last non-empty cell:

```
Range(ActiveCell, ActiveCell.End(xlDown)).Select
```

As you might expect, three other constants simulate key combinations in the other directions: `xlUp`, `xlToLeft`, and `xlToRight`.

CAUTION

Be careful when using the `End` method. If the active cell is at the perimeter of a range or if the range contains one or more empty cells, the `End` method may not produce the desired results.

CD-ROM

The companion CD-ROM includes a workbook that demonstrates several common types of range selections. When you open this workbook, named `range selections.xlsm`, the code adds a new menu item to the shortcut menu that appears when you right-click a cell: `Selection Demo`. This menu contains commands that enable the user to make various types of selections, as shown in Figure 11-2.

The following macro is in the example workbook. The `SelectCurrentRegion` macro simulates pressing Ctrl+Shift+*.

```
Sub SelectCurrentRegion()
    ActiveCell.CurrentRegion.Select
End Sub
```

Often, you won't want to actually select the cells. Rather, you'll want to work with them in some way (for example, format them). The cell-selecting procedures can easily be adapted. The following procedure was adapted from `SelectCurrentRegion`. This procedure doesn't select cells; it applies formatting to the range that's defined as the current region around the active cell. The other procedures in the example workbook can also be adapted in this manner.

```
Sub FormatCurrentRegion()
    ActiveCell.CurrentRegion.Font.Bold = True
End Sub
```

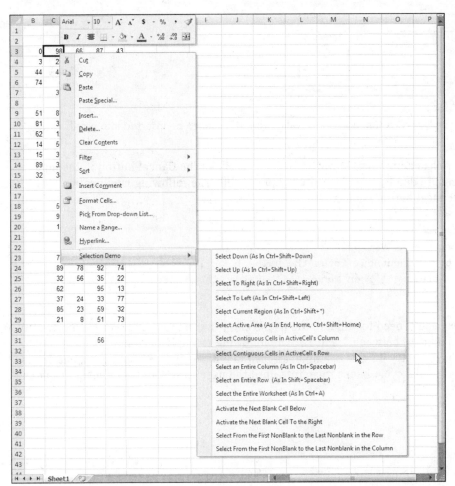

Figure 11-2: This workbook uses a custom shortcut menu to demonstrate how to select variably sized ranges by using VBA.

Prompting for a cell value

The following procedure demonstrates how to ask the user for a value and then insert it into cell A1 of the active worksheet:

```
Sub GetValue1()
    Range("A1").Value = InputBox("Enter the value")
End Sub
```

Figure 11-3 shows how the input box looks.

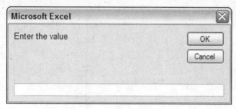

Figure 11-3: The InputBox function gets a value from the user to be inserted into a cell.

This procedure has a problem, however. If the user clicks the Cancel button in the input box, the procedure deletes any data already in the cell. The following modification takes no action if the Cancel button is clicked:

```
Sub GetValue2()
    Dim UserEntry As Variant
     UserEntry = InputBox("Enter the value")
    If UserEntry <> "" Then Range("A1").Value = UserEntry
End Sub
```

In many cases, you'll need to validate the user's entry in the input box. For example, you may require a number between 1 and 12. The following example demonstrates one way to validate the user's entry. In this example, an invalid entry is ignored, and the input box is displayed again. This cycle keeps repeating until the user enters a valid number or clicks Cancel.

```
Sub GetValue3()
    Dim UserEntry As Variant
    Dim Msg As String
    Const MinVal As Integer = 1
    Const MaxVal As Integer = 12
    Msg = "Enter a value between " & MinVal & " and " & MaxVal
    Do
        UserEntry = InputBox(Msg)
        If UserEntry = "" Then Exit Sub
        If IsNumeric(UserEntry) Then
            If UserEntry >= MinVal And UserEntry <= MaxVal Then Exit Do
        End If
        Msg = "Your previous entry was INVALID."
        Msg = Msg & vbNewLine
        Msg = Msg & "Enter a value between " & MinVal & " and " & MaxVal
    Loop
    ActiveSheet.Range("A1").Value = UserEntry
End Sub
```

As you can see in Figure 11-4, the code also changes the message displayed if the user makes an invalid entry.

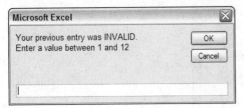

Figure 11-4: Validate a user's entry with the VBA `InputBox` function.

CD-ROM

The three `GetValue` procedures are available on the companion CD-ROM. The filename is `inputbox demo.xlsm`.

Entering a value in the next empty cell

A common requirement is to enter a value into the next empty cell in a column or row. The following example prompts the user for a name and a value and then enters the data into the next empty row (see Figure 11-5).

```
Sub GetData()
    Dim NextRow As Long
    Dim Entry1 As String, Entry2 As String
  Do
    'Determine next empty row
    NextRow = Cells(Rows.Count, 1).End(xlUp).Row + 1

'   Prompt for the data
    Entry1 = InputBox("Enter the name")
    If Entry1 = "" Then Exit Sub
    Entry2 = InputBox("Enter the amount")
    If Entry2 = "" Then Exit Sub

'   Write the data
    Cells(NextRow, 1) = Entry1
    Cells(NextRow, 2) = Entry2
  Loop
End Sub
```

To keep things simple, this procedure doesn't perform any validation. Notice that the loop continues indefinitely. I use `Exit Sub` statements to get out of the loop when the user clicks Cancel in the input box.

Part III

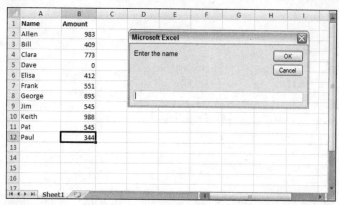

Figure 11-5: A macro for inserting data into the next empty row in a worksheet.

 CD-ROM

The GetData procedure is available on the companion CD-ROM. The filename is next empty cell.xlsm.

Notice the statement that determines the value of the NextRow variable. If you don't understand how this works, try the manual equivalent: Activate the last cell in column A, press End, and then press the up-arrow key. At this point, the last nonblank cell in column A will be selected. The Row property returns this row number, and it is incremented by 1 in order to get the row of the cell below it (the next empty row). Rather than hard-code the last cell in column A, I used Rows.Count so this procedure will work with previous versions of Excel (which have fewer rows).

Note that this technique of selecting the next empty cell has a slight glitch. If the column is completely empty, it will calculate row 2 as the next empty row. It would be fairly easy to write additional code to account for this possibility.

Pausing a macro to get a user-selected range

In some situations, you may need an interactive macro. For example, you can create a macro that pauses while the user specifies a range of cells. The procedure in this section describes how to do this with Excel's InputBox method.

 NOTE

Do not confuse Excel's InputBox method with VBA's InputBox function. Although these two items have the same name, they are not the same.

The Sub procedure that follows demonstrates how to pause a macro and let the user select a range. The code then inserts a formula into each cell of the specified range.

```vba
Sub GetUserRange()
    Dim UserRange As Range

    Prompt = "Select a range for the random numbers."
    Title = "Select a range"

'   Display the Input Box
    On Error Resume Next
    Set UserRange = Application.InputBox( _
        Prompt:=Prompt, _
        Title:=Title, _
        Default:=ActiveCell.Address, _
        Type:=8) 'Range selection
    On Error GoTo 0

'   Was the Input Box canceled?
    If UserRange Is Nothing Then
        MsgBox "Canceled."
    Else
        UserRange.Formula = "=RAND()"
    End If
End Sub
```

The input box is shown in Figure 11-6.

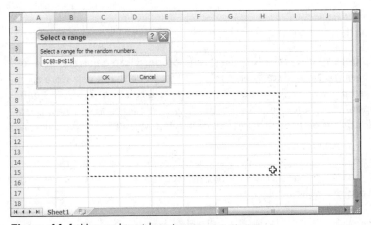

Figure 11-6: Use an input box to pause a macro.

 CD-ROM

This example, named `prompt for a range.xlsm`, is available on the companion CD-ROM.

Specifying a `Type` argument of 8 for the InputBox method is the key to this procedure. Also, note the use of `On Error Resume Next`. This statement ignores the error that occurs if the user clicks the Cancel button. If so, the `UserRange` object variable is not defined. This example displays a message box with the text `Canceled`. If the user clicks OK, the macro continues. Using `On Error GoTo 0` resumes normal error handling.

By the way, it's not necessary to check for a valid range selection. Excel takes care of this for you.

CAUTION

Make sure that screen updating is not turned off when you use the InputBox method to select a range. Otherwise, you won't be able to make a worksheet selection. Use the `ScreenUpdating` property of the `Application` object to control screen updating while a macro is running.

Counting selected cells

You can create a macro that works with the selected range of cells. Use the `Count` property of the `Range` object to determine how many cells are contained in a range selection (or any range, for that matter). For example, the following statement displays a message box that contains the number of cells in the current selection:

```
MsgBox Selection.Count
```

CAUTION

With the larger worksheet size in Excel 2007, the `Count` property can generate an error. The `Count` property uses the `Long` data type, so the largest value that it can store is 2,147,483,647. For example, if the user selects 2,048 complete columns (2,147,483,648 cells), the `Count` property generates an error. Fortunately, Microsoft added a new property: `CountLarge`. `CountLarge` uses the `Double` data type, which can handle values up to 1.79+E^308.

Bottom line? In the vast majority of situations, the `Count` property will work fine. If there's a chance that you may need to count more cells (such as all cells in a worksheet), use `CountLarge` instead of `Count`.

If the active sheet contains a range named `data`, the following statement assigns the number of cells in the `data` range to a variable named `CellCount`:

```
CellCount = Range("data").Count
```

You can also determine how many rows or columns are contained in a range. The following expression calculates the number of columns in the currently selected range:

```
Selection.Columns.Count
```

And, of course, you can also use the Rows property to determine the number of rows in a range. The following statement counts the number of rows in a range named data and assigns the number to a variable named RowCount:

```
RowCount = Range("data").Rows.Count
```

Determining the type of selected range

Excel supports several types of range selections:

- A single cell
- A contiguous range of cells
- One or more entire columns
- One or more entire rows
- The entire worksheet
- Any combination of the above (that is, a multiple selection)

As a result, when your VBA procedure processes a user-selected range, you can't make any presumptions about what that range might be.

In the case of a multiple range selection, the Range object comprises separate areas. To determine whether a selection is a multiple selection, use the Areas method, which returns an Areas collection. This collection represents all the ranges within a multiple range selection.

You can use an expression like the following to determine whether a selected range has multiple areas:

```
NumAreas = Selection.Areas.Count
```

If the NumAreas variable contains a value greater than 1, the selection is a multiple selection.

Following is a function named AreaType, which returns a text string that describes the type of range selection.

```
Function AreaType(RangeArea As Range) As String
'    Returns the type of a range in an area
    Select Case True
        Case RangeArea.Cells.CountLarge = 1
            AreaType = "Cell"
        Case RangeArea.CountLarge = Cells.CountLarge
            AreaType = "Worksheet"
        Case RangeArea.Rows.Count = Cells.Rows.Count
            AreaType = "Column"
```

```
        Case RangeArea.Columns.Count = Cells.Columns.Count
            AreaType = "Row"
        Case Else
            AreaType = "Block"
    End Select
End Function
```

This function accepts a `Range` object as its argument and returns one of five strings that describe the area: `Cell`, `Worksheet`, `Column`, `Row`, or `Block`. The function uses a `Select Case` construct to determine which of five comparison expressions is `True`. For example, if the range consists of a single cell, the function returns `Cell`. If the number of cells in the range is equal to the number of cells in the worksheet, it returns `Worksheet`. If the number of rows in the range equals the number of rows in the worksheet, it returns `Column`. If the number of columns in the range equals the number of columns in the worksheet, the function returns `Row`. If none of the `Case` expressions is `True`, the function returns `Block`.

Notice that I used the `CountLarge` property when counting cells. As I noted previously in this chapter, the number of selected cells in Excel 2007 could potentially exceed the limit of the `Count` property.

 CD-ROM

This example is available on the companion CD-ROM in a file named about range selection.xlsm. The workbook contains a procedure (named `RangeDescription`) that uses the `AreaType` function to display a message box that describes the current range selection. Figure 11-7 shows an example. Understanding how this routine works will give you a good foundation for working with `Range` objects.

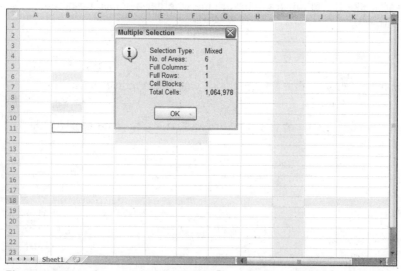

Figure 11-7: A VBA procedure analyzes the currently selected range.

NOTE

You might be surprised to discover that Excel allows multiple selections to be identical. For example, if you hold down Ctrl and click five times in cell A1, the selection will have five identical areas. The `RangeDescription` procedure takes this into account and does not count the same cell multiple times.

Looping through a selected range efficiently

A common task is to create a macro that evaluates each cell in a range and performs an operation if the cell meets a certain criterion. The procedure that follows is an example of such a macro. The `ColorNegative` procedure sets the cell's background color to red for cells that contain a negative value. For non-negative value cells, it sets the background color to none.

NOTE

This example is for educational purposes only. Using Excel's conditional formatting is a much better approach.

```
Sub ColorNegative()
'    Makes negative cells red
    Dim cell As Range
    If TypeName(Selection) <> "Range" Then Exit Sub
    Application.ScreenUpdating = False
    For Each cell In Selection
        If cell.Value < 0 Then
            cell.Interior.Color = RGB(255, 0, 0)
        Else
            cell.Interior.Color = xlNone
        End If
    Next cell
End Sub
```

The `ColorNegative` procedure certainly works, but it has a serious flaw. For example, what if the used area on the worksheet were small, but the user selects an entire column? Or ten columns? Or the entire worksheet? There's no need to process all of those empty cells, and the user would probably give up before all the cells were evaluated.

A better solution (`ColorNegative2`) follows. In this revised procedure, I create a `Range` object variable, `WorkRange`, which consists of the intersection of the selected range and the worksheet's used range. Figure 11-8 shows an example; the entire column D is selected (1,048,576 cells). The worksheet's used range, however, consists of the range B2:I18. Therefore, the intersection of these ranges is D2:D18, which is a much smaller range than the original selection. The time difference between processing 16 cells versus processing 1,048,576 cells is significant.

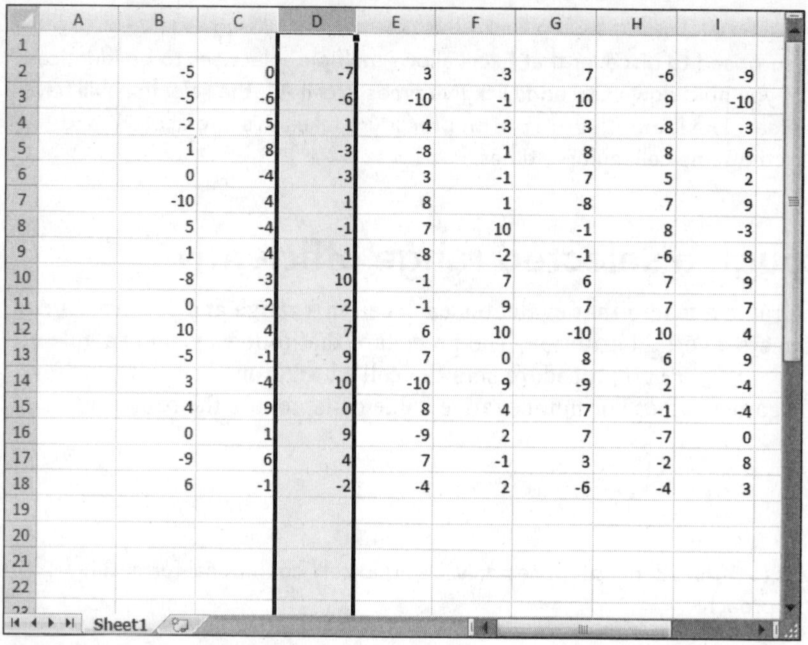

	A	B	C	D	E	F	G	H	I
1									
2		-5	0	-7	3	-3	7	-6	-9
3		-5	-6	-6	-10	-1	10	9	-10
4		-2	5	1	4	-3	3	-8	-3
5		1	8	-3	-8	1	8	8	6
6		0	-4	-3	3	-1	7	5	2
7		-10	4	1	8	1	-8	7	9
8		5	-4	-1	7	10	-1	8	-3
9		1	4	1	-8	-2	-1	-6	8
10		-8	-3	10	-1	7	6	7	9
11		0	-2	-2	-1	9	7	7	7
12		10	4	7	6	10	-10	10	4
13		-5	-1	9	7	0	8	6	9
14		3	-4	10	-10	9	-9	2	-4
15		4	9	0	8	4	7	-1	-4
16		0	1	9	-9	2	7	-7	0
17		-9	6	4	7	-1	3	-2	8
18		6	-1	-2	-4	2	-6	-4	3
19									
20									
21									
22									

Figure 11-8: Using the intersection of the used range and the selected ranged results in fewer cells to process.

```
Sub ColorNegative2()
'   Makes negative cells red
    Dim WorkRange As Range
    Dim cell As Range
    If TypeName(Selection) <> "Range" Then Exit Sub
    Application.ScreenUpdating = False
    Set WorkRange = Application.Intersect(Selection, _
      ActiveSheet.UsedRange)
    For Each cell In WorkRange
        If cell.Value < 0 Then
            cell.Interior.Color = RGB(255, 0, 0)
        Else
            cell.Interior.Color = xlNone
        End If
    Next cell
End Sub
```

The ColorNegative2 procedure is an improvement, but it's still not as efficient as it could be because it processes empty cells. A third revision, ColorNegative3, is quite a bit longer, but it's much more efficient. I use the SpecialCells method to generate two subsets of the selection: One subset (ConstantCells) includes only the cells with numeric constants; the other subset (FormulaCells) includes only the cells with numeric formulas. The code processes the cells in these subsets by using two For Each–Next constructs. The net effect: Only non-blank, non-text cells are evaluated, thus speeding up the macro considerably.

```vba
Sub ColorNegative3()
'   Makes negative cells red
    Dim FormulaCells As Range, ConstantCells As Range
    Dim cell As Range
    If TypeName(Selection) <> "Range" Then Exit Sub
    Application.ScreenUpdating = False

'   Create subsets of original selection
    On Error Resume Next
    Set FormulaCells = Selection.SpecialCells(xlFormulas, xlNumbers)
    Set ConstantCells = Selection.SpecialCells(xlConstants, xlNumbers)
    On Error GoTo 0

'   Process the formula cells
    If Not FormulaCells Is Nothing Then
        For Each cell In FormulaCells
            If cell.Value < 0 Then
                cell.Interior.Color = RGB(255, 0, 0)
            Else
                cell.Interior.Color = xlNone
            End If
        Next cell
    End If

'   Process the constant cells
    If Not ConstantCells Is Nothing Then
        For Each cell In ConstantCells
            If cell.Value < 0 Then
                cell.Interior.Color = RGB(255, 0, 0)
            Else
                cell.Interior.Color = xlNone
            End If
        Next cell
    End If
End Sub
```

NOTE

The On Error statement is necessary because the SpecialCells method generates an error if no cells qualify.

CD-ROM

A workbook that contains the three `ColorNegative` procedures is available on the companion CD-ROM. The file is named `efficient looping.xlsm`.

Deleting all empty rows

The following procedure deletes all empty rows in the active worksheet. This routine is fast and efficient because it doesn't check all rows. It checks only the rows in the used range, which is determined by using the `UsedRange` property of the `Worksheet` object.

```
Sub DeleteEmptyRows()
    Dim LastRow As Long
    Dim r As Long
    Dim Counter As Long
    Application.ScreenUpdating = False
    LastRow = ActiveSheet.UsedRange.Rows.Count + _
      ActiveSheet.UsedRange.Rows(1).Row - 1
    For r = LastRow To 1 Step -1
        If Application.WorksheetFunction.CountA(Rows(r)) = 0 Then
            Rows(r).Delete
            Counter = Counter + 1
        End If
    Next r
    Application.ScreenUpdating = True
    MsgBox Counter & " empty rows were deleted."
End Sub
```

The first step is to determine the last used row and then assign this row number to the `LastRow` variable. This is not as simple as you might think because the used range may or may not begin in row 1. Therefore, `LastRow` is calculated by determining the number of rows in the used range, adding the first row number in the used range, and subtracting 1.

The procedure uses Excel's COUNTA worksheet function to determine whether a row is empty. If this function returns 0 for a particular row, the row is empty. Notice that the procedure works on the rows from bottom to top and also uses a negative step value in the `For-Next` loop. This is necessary because deleting rows causes all subsequent rows to move up in the worksheet. If the looping occurred from top to bottom, the counter within the loop would not be accurate after a row is deleted.

The macro uses another variable, `Counter`, to keep track of how many rows were deleted. This number is displayed in a message box when the procedure ends.

CD-ROM

A workbook that contains this example is available on the companion CD-ROM in a file named `delete empty rows.xlsm`.

Duplicating rows a variable number of times

The example in this section demonstrates how to use VBA to create duplicates of a row. Figure 11-9 shows a worksheet for an office raffle. Column A contains the name, and column B contains the number of tickets purchased by each person. Column C contains a random number (generated by the RAND function). The winner will be determined by sorting the data based on column 3 (the highest random number wins).

	A	B	C	D	E
1	Name	No. Tickets	Random		
2	Alan	1	0.75245004		
3	Barbara	2	0.72935607		
4	Charlie	1	0.41277549		
5	Dave	5	0.06281273		
6	Frank	3	0.34540676		
7	Gilda	1	0.8052792		
8	Hubert	1	0.97467075		
9	Inez	2	0.62376896		
10	Mark	1	0.64050016		
11	Norah	10	0.70054717		
12	Penelope	2	0.67441042		
13	Rance	1	0.3963156		
14	Wendy	2	0.25597381		
15					

H ◄ ► H Sheet1

Figure 11-9: The goal is to duplicate rows based on the value in column B.

The goal is to duplicate the rows so each person will have a row for each ticket purchased. For example, Barbara purchased two tickets, so she should have two rows. The procedure to insert the new rows is shown here:

```
Sub DupeRows()
  Dim cell As Range
' 1st cell with number of tickets
  Set cell = Range("B2")
  Do While Not IsEmpty(cell)
    If cell > 1 Then
      Range(cell.Offset(1, 0), cell.Offset(cell.Value - 1, _
        0)).EntireRow.Insert
      Range(cell, cell.Offset(cell.Value - 1, 1)).EntireRow.FillDown
    End If
    Set cell = cell.Offset(cell.Value, 0)
  Loop
End Sub
```

The cell object variable is initialized to cell B2, the first cell that has a number. The loop inserts new rows and then copies the row using the FillDown method. The cell variable is incremented to the next person, and the loop continues until an empty cell is encountered. Figure 11-10 shows the worksheet after running this procedure.

	A	B	C	D
1	Name	No. Tickets	Random	
2	Alan	1	0.20078745	
3	Barbara	2	0.8125618	
4	Barbara	2	0.98978267	
5	Charlie	1	0.90960581	
6	Dave	5	0.2255792	
7	Dave	5	0.49645822	
8	Dave	5	0.46617908	
9	Dave	5	0.47803568	
10	Dave	5	0.86463447	
11	Frank	3	0.52724143	
12	Frank	3	0.12248409	
13	Frank	3	0.1170304	
14	Gilda	1	0.8736246	
15	Hubert	1	0.7854768	
16	Inez	2	0.06544751	
17	Inez	2	0.48685292	
18	Mark	1	0.42300247	
19	Norah	10	0.2847447	
20	Norah	10	0.98165866	
21	Norah	10	0.64097199	

Sheet1

Figure 11-10: New rows were added, according to the value in column B.

CD-ROM

A workbook that contains this example is available on the companion CD-ROM. The file is named `duplicate rows.xlsm`.

Determining whether a range is contained in another range

The following `InRange` function accepts two arguments, both `Range` objects. The function returns `True` if the first range is contained in the second range.

```
Function InRange(rng1, rng2) As Boolean
'    Returns True if rng1 is a subset of rng2
    InRange = False
    If rng1.Parent.Parent.Name = rng2.Parent.Parent.Name Then
        If rng1.Parent.Name = rng2.Parent.Name Then
            If Union(rng1, rng2).Address = rng2.Address Then
                InRange = True
            End If
        End If
    End If
End Function
```

The `InRange` function may appear a bit more complex than it needs to be because the code needs to ensure that the two ranges are in the same worksheet and workbook. Notice that the procedure uses the `Parent` property, which returns an object's container object. For example, the following expression returns the name of the worksheet for the `rng1` object reference:

```
rng1.Parent.Name
```

The following expression returns the name of the workbook for `rng1`:

```
rng1.Parent.Parent.Name
```

VBA's `Union` function returns a `Range` object that represents the union of two `Range` objects. The union consists of all the cells from both ranges. If the address of the union of the two ranges is the same as the address of the second range, the first range is contained within the second range.

CD-ROM

A workbook that contains this function is available on the companion CD-ROM in a file named `inrange function.xlsm`.

Determining a cell's data type

Excel provides a number of built-in functions that can help determine the type of data contained in a cell. These include ISTEXT, ISLOGICAL, and ISERROR. In addition, VBA includes functions such as `IsEmpty`, `IsDate`, and `IsNumeric`.

The following function, named `CellType`, accepts a range argument and returns a string (`Blank`, `Text`, `Logical`, `Error`, `Date`, `Time`, or `Number`) that describes the data type of the upper-left cell in the range. You can use this function in a worksheet formula or from another VBA procedure.

```
Function CellType(Rng)
'    Returns the cell type of the upper left
'    cell in a range
    Dim TheCell As Range
    Set TheCell = Rng.Range("A1")
    Select Case True
        Case IsEmpty(TheCell)
            CellType = "Blank"
        Case Application.IsText(TheCell)
            CellType = "Text"
        Case Application.IsLogical(TheCell)
            CellType = "Logical"
        Case Application.IsErr(TheCell)
            CellType = "Error"
        Case IsDate(TheCell)
            CellType = "Date"
```

```
        Case InStr(1, TheCell.Text, ":") <> 0
            CellType = "Time"
        Case IsNumeric(TheCell)
            CellType = "Number"
    End Select
End Function
```

Notice the use of the `Set TheCell` statement.. The `CellType` function accepts a range argument of any size, but this statement causes it to operate on only the upper-left cell in the range (which is represented by the `TheCell` variable).

CD-ROM

A workbook that contains this function is available on the companion CD-ROM. The file is named `celltype function.xlsm`.

Reading and writing ranges

Many VBA tasks involve transferring values either from an array to a range or from a range to an array. For some reason, Excel reads from ranges much faster than it writes to ranges. The `WriteReadRange` procedure that follows demonstrates the relative speeds of writing and reading a range.

This procedure creates an array and then uses `For-Next` loops to write the array to a range and then read the range back into the array. It calculates the time required for each operation by using the Excel `Timer` function.

```
Sub WriteReadRange()
    Dim MyArray()
    Dim Time1 As Double
    Dim NumElements As Long, i As Long
    Dim WriteTime As String, ReadTime As String
    Dim Msg As String

    NumElements = 60000
    ReDim MyArray(1 To NumElements)

'   Fill the array
    For i = 1 To NumElements
        MyArray(i) = i
    Next i

'   Write the array to a range
    Time1 = Timer
    For i = 1 To NumElements
        Cells(i, 1) = MyArray(i)
    Next i
```

```
    WriteTime = Format(Timer - Time1, "00:00")

'   Read the range into the array
    Time1 = Timer
    For i = 1 To NumElements
        MyArray(i) = Cells(i, 1)
    Next i
    ReadTime = Format(Timer - Time1, "00:00")

'   Show results
    Msg = "Write: " & WriteTime
    Msg = Msg & vbCrLf
    Msg = Msg & "Read: " & ReadTime
    MsgBox Msg, vbOKOnly, NumElements & " Elements"
End Sub
```

On my system, it took 12 seconds to write a 60,000-element array to a range but only 1 second to read the range into an array.

A better way to write to a range

The example in the preceding section uses a For-Next loop to transfer the contents of an array to a worksheet range. In this section, I demonstrate a more efficient way to accomplish this.

Start with the example that follows, which illustrates the most obvious (but not the most efficient) way to fill a range. This example uses a For-Next loop to insert its values in a range.

```
Sub LoopFillRange()
'   Fill a range by looping through cells

    Dim CellsDown As Long, CellsAcross As Integer
    Dim CurrRow As Long, CurrCol As Integer
    Dim StartTime As Double
    Dim CurrVal As Long

'   Get the dimensions
    CellsDown = InputBox("How many cells down?")
    If CellsDown = 0 Then Exit Sub
    CellsAcross = InputBox("How many cells across?")
    If CellsAcross = 0 Then Exit Sub

'   Record starting time
    StartTime = Timer

'   Loop through cells and insert values
    CurrVal = 1
```

```
        Application.ScreenUpdating = False
        For CurrRow = 1 To CellsDown
            For CurrCol = 1 To CellsAcross
                ActiveCell.Offset(CurrRow - 1, _
                CurrCol - 1).Value = CurrVal
                CurrVal = CurrVal + 1
            Next CurrCol
        Next CurrRow

    '   Display elapsed time
        Application.ScreenUpdating = True
        MsgBox Format(Timer - StartTime, "00.00") & " seconds"
    End Sub
```

The example that follows demonstrates a much faster way to produce the same result. This code inserts the values into an array and then uses a single statement to transfer the contents of an array to the range.

```
Sub ArrayFillRange()
'   Fill a range by transferring an array

    Dim CellsDown As Long, CellsAcross As Integer
    Dim i As Long, j As Integer
    Dim StartTime As Double
    Dim TempArray() As Long
    Dim TheRange As Range
    Dim CurrVal As Long

'   Get the dimensions
    CellsDown = InputBox("How many cells down?")
    If CellsDown = 0 Then Exit Sub
    CellsAcross = InputBox("How many cells across?")
    If CellsAcross = 0 Then Exit Sub

'   Record starting time
    StartTime = Timer

'   Redimension temporary array
    ReDim TempArray(1 To CellsDown, 1 To CellsAcross)

'   Set worksheet range
    Set TheRange = ActiveCell.Range(Cells(1, 1), _
        Cells(CellsDown, CellsAcross))

'   Fill the temporary array
    CurrVal = 0
```

```
    Application.ScreenUpdating = False
    For i = 1 To CellsDown
        For j = 1 To CellsAcross
            TempArray(i, j) = CurrVal + 1
            CurrVal = CurrVal + 1
        Next j
    Next i

'   Transfer temporary array to worksheet
    TheRange.Value = TempArray

'   Display elapsed time
    Application.ScreenUpdating = True
    MsgBox Format(Timer - StartTime, "00.00") & " seconds"
End Sub
```

On my system, using the loop method to fill a 500 x 256–cell range (128,000 cells) took 12.81 seconds. The array transfer method took only 0.20 seconds to generate the same results — more than 60 times faster! The moral of this story? If you need to transfer large amounts of data to a worksheet, avoid looping whenever possible.

CD-ROM

A workbook that contains the `WriteReadRange`, `LoopFillRange`, and `ArrayFillRange` procedures is available on the companion CD-ROM. The file is named `loop vs array fill range.xlsm`.

Transferring one-dimensional arrays

The example in the preceding section involves a two-dimensional array, which works out nicely for row-and-column-based worksheets.

When transferring a one-dimensional array to a range, the range must be horizontal — that is, one row with multiple *columns*. If you need the data in a vertical range instead, you must first transpose the array to make it vertical. You can use Excel's TRANSPOSE function to do this. The following example transfers a 100-element array to a vertical worksheet range (A1:A100):

```
Range("A1:A100").Value = Application.WorksheetFunction.Transpose(MyArray)
```

Transferring a range to a variant array

This section discusses yet another way to work with worksheet data in VBA. The following example transfers a range of cells to a two-dimensional variant array. Then message boxes display the upper bounds for each dimension of the variant array.

```
Sub RangeToVariant()
    Dim x As Variant
    x = Range("A1:L600").Value
    MsgBox UBound(x, 1)
    MsgBox UBound(x, 2)
End Sub
```

In this example, the first message box displays 600 (the number of rows in the original range), and the second message box displays 12 (the number of columns). You'll find that transferring the range data to a variant array is virtually instantaneous.

The following example reads a range (named `data`) into a variant array, performs a simple multiplication operation on each element in the array, and then transfers the variant array back to the range.

```
Sub RangeToVariant2()
    Dim x As Variant
    Dim r As Long, c As Integer

'    Read the data into the variant
    x = Range("data").Value

'    Loop through the variant array
    For r = 1 To UBound(x, 1)
        For c = 1 To UBound(x, 2)
'            Multiply by 2
            x(r, c) = x(r, c) * 2
        Next c
    Next r

'    Transfer the variant back to the sheet
    Range("data") = x
End Sub
```

You'll find that this procedure runs amazingly fast.

 CD-ROM

A workbook that contains this example is available on the companion CD-ROM. The file is named `variant transfer.xlsm`.

Selecting cells by value

The example in this section demonstrates how to select cells based on their value. Oddly enough, Excel does not provide a direct way to perform this operation. My `SelectByValue` procedure follows. In this example, the code selects cells that contain a negative value, but this can be changed easily.

```vba
Sub SelectByValue()
    Dim Cell As Object
    Dim FoundCells As Range
    Dim WorkRange As Range

    If TypeName(Selection) <> "Range" Then Exit Sub

'   Check all or selection?
    If Selection.CountLarge = 1 Then
        Set WorkRange = ActiveSheet.UsedRange
    Else
        Set WorkRange = Application.Intersect(Selection, ActiveSheet.UsedRange)
    End If

'   Reduce the search to numeric cells only
    On Error Resume Next
    Set WorkRange = WorkRange.SpecialCells(xlConstants, xlNumbers)
    If WorkRange Is Nothing Then Exit Sub
    On Error GoTo 0

'   Loop through each cell, add to the FoundCells range if it qualifies
    For Each Cell In WorkRange
        If Cell.Value < 0 Then
            If FoundCells Is Nothing Then
                Set FoundCells = Cell
            Else
                Set FoundCells = Union(FoundCells, Cell)
            End If
        End If
    Next Cell

'   Show message, or select the cells
    If FoundCells Is Nothing Then
        MsgBox "No cells qualify."
    Else
        FoundCells.Select
    End If
End Sub
```

The procedure starts by checking the selection. If it's a single cell, then the entire worksheet is searched. If the selection is at least two cells, then only the selected range is searched. The range to be searched is further refined by using the SpecialCells method to create a Range object that consists only of the numeric constants.

The code within the For-Next loop examines the cell's value. If it meets the criterion (less than 0), then the cell is added to the FoundCells Range object by using the Union method. Note that you can't use the Union method for the first cell. If the FoundCells range contains no cells, attempting to use the `Union` method will generate an error. Therefore, the code checks whether `FoundCells` is `Nothing`.

When the loop ends, the `FoundCells` object will consist of the cells that meet the criterion (or will be `Nothing` if no cells were found). If no cells are found, a message box appears. Otherwise, the cells are selected.

CD-ROM

This example is available on the companion CD-ROM. The file is named `select by value.xlsm`.

Copying a noncontiguous range

If you've ever attempted to copy a noncontiguous range selection, you discovered that Excel doesn't support such an operation. Attempting to do so brings up an error message: *That command cannot be used on multiple selections.*

When you encounter a limitation in Excel, you can often circumvent it by creating a macro. The example is this section is a VBA procedure that allows you to copy a multiple selection to another location.

```
Sub CopyMultipleSelection()
    Dim SelAreas() As Range
    Dim PasteRange As Range
    Dim UpperLeft As Range
    Dim NumAreas As Long, i As Long
    Dim TopRow As Long, LeftCol As Long
    Dim RowOffset As Long, ColOffset As Long

    If TypeName(Selection) <> "Range" Then Exit Sub

'   Store the areas as separate Range objects
    NumAreas = Selection.Areas.Count
    ReDim SelAreas(1 To NumAreas)
    For i = 1 To NumAreas
        Set SelAreas(i) = Selection.Areas(i)
    Next

'   Determine the upper-left cell in the multiple selection
    TopRow = ActiveSheet.Rows.Count
    LeftCol = ActiveSheet.Columns.Count
    For i = 1 To NumAreas
        If SelAreas(i).Row < TopRow Then TopRow = SelAreas(i).Row
        If SelAreas(i).Column < LeftCol Then LeftCol = SelAreas(i).Column
```

```
    Next
    Set UpperLeft = Cells(TopRow, LeftCol)


'   Get the paste address
    On Error Resume Next
    Set PasteRange = Application.InputBox _
      (Prompt:="Specify the upper-left cell for the paste range:", _
      Title:="Copy Multiple Selection", _
      Type:=8)
    On Error GoTo 0
'   Exit if canceled
    If TypeName(PasteRange) <> "Range" Then Exit Sub


'   Make sure only the upper-left cell is used
    Set PasteRange = PasteRange.Range("A1")


'   Copy and paste each area
    For i = 1 To NumAreas
        RowOffset = SelAreas(i).Row - TopRow
        ColOffset = SelAreas(i).Column - LeftCol
        SelAreas(i).Copy PasteRange.Offset(RowOffset, ColOffset)
    Next i
End Sub
```

Figure 11-11 shows the prompt to select the destination location.

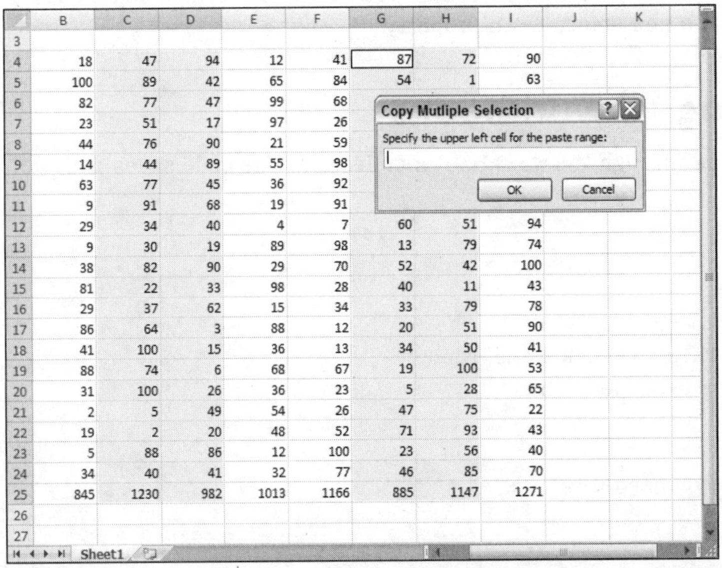

Figure 11-11: Using Excel's InputBox method to prompt for a cell location.

CD-ROM

The companion CD-ROM contains a workbook with this example, plus another version that warns the user if data will be overwritten. The file is named `copy multiple selection.xlsm`.

Working with Workbooks and Sheets

The examples in this section demonstrate various ways to use VBA to work with workbooks and worksheets.

Saving all workbooks

The following procedure loops through all workbooks in the `Workbooks` collection and saves each file that has been saved previously:

```
Public Sub SaveAllWorkbooks()
    Dim Book As Workbook
    For Each Book In Workbooks
        If Book.Path <> "" Then Book.Save
    Next Book
End Sub
```

Notice the use of the `Path` property. If a workbook's `Path` property is empty, the file has never been saved (it's a new workbook). This procedure ignores such workbooks and saves only the workbooks that have a non-empty `Path` property.

Saving and closing all workbooks

The following procedure loops through the `Workbooks` collection. The code saves and closes all workbooks.

```
Sub CloseAllWorkbooks()
    Dim Book As Workbook
    For Each Book In Workbooks
        If Book.Name <> ThisWorkbook.Name Then
            Book.Close savechanges:=True
        End If
    Next Book
    ThisWorkbook.Close savechanges:=True
End Sub
```

The procedure uses an `If` statement within the `For-Next` loop to determine whether the workbook is the workbook that contains the code. This is necessary because closing the workbook that contains the procedure would end the code, and subsequent workbooks would not be affected.

Hiding all but the selection

The example in this section hides all rows and columns except those in the current range selection. Figure 11-12 shows an example.

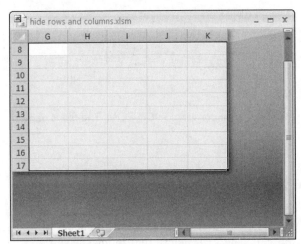

Figure 11-12: All rows and columns are hidden, except for a range (G8:K17).

```
Sub HideRowsAndColumns()
    Dim row1 As Long, row2 As Long
    Dim col1 As Long, col2 As Long

    If TypeName(Selection) <> "Range" Then Exit Sub

'   If last row or last column is hidden, unhide all and quit
    If Rows(Rows.Count).EntireRow.Hidden Or _
       Columns(Columns.Count).EntireColumn.Hidden Then
        Cells.EntireColumn.Hidden = False
        Cells.EntireRow.Hidden = False
        Exit Sub
    End If

    row1 = Selection.Rows(1).Row
    row2 = row1 + Selection.Rows.Count - 1
    col1 = Selection.Columns(1).Column
```

```
      col2 = col1 + Selection.Columns.Count - 1

      Application.ScreenUpdating = False
      On Error Resume Next
'     Hide rows
      Range(Cells(1, 1), Cells(row1 - 1, 1)).EntireRow.Hidden = True
      Range(Cells(row2 + 1, 1), Cells(Rows.Count, 1)).EntireRow.Hidden = True
'     Hide columns
      Range(Cells(1, 1), Cells(1, col1 - 1)).EntireColumn.Hidden = True
      Range(Cells(1, col2 + 1), Cells(1, Columns.Count)).EntireColumn.Hidden = True
End Sub
```

If the range selection consists of a noncontiguous range, the first Area is used as the basis for hiding rows and columns.

 CD-ROM

A workbook with this example is available on the companion CD-ROM. The file is named hide rows and columns.xlsm.

Synchronizing worksheets

If you use multisheet workbooks, you probably know that Excel cannot synchronize the sheets in a workbook. In other words, there is no automatic way to force all sheets to have the same selected range and upper-left cell. The VBA macro that follows uses the active worksheet as a base and then performs the following on all other worksheets in the workbook:

- Selects the same range as the active sheet.
- Makes the upper-left cell the same as the active sheet.

Following is the listing for the subroutine:

```
Sub SynchSheets()
'    Duplicates the active sheet's active cell and upper left cell
'    Across all worksheets
     If TypeName(ActiveSheet) <> "Worksheet" Then Exit Sub
     Dim UserSheet As Worksheet, sht As Worksheet
     Dim TopRow As Long, LeftCol As Integer
     Dim UserSel As String

     Application.ScreenUpdating = False

'    Remember the current sheet
```

```
    Set UserSheet = ActiveSheet

'   Store info from the active sheet
    TopRow = ActiveWindow.ScrollRow
    LeftCol = ActiveWindow.ScrollColumn
    UserSel = ActiveWindow.RangeSelection.Address

'   Loop through the worksheets
    For Each sht In ActiveWorkbook.Worksheets
        If sht.Visible Then 'skip hidden sheets
            sht.Activate
            Range(UserSel).Select
            ActiveWindow.ScrollRow = TopRow
            ActiveWindow.ScrollColumn = LeftCol
        End If
    Next sht

'   Restore the original position
    UserSheet.Activate
    Application.ScreenUpdating = True
End Sub
```

CD-ROM

A workbook with this example is available on the companion CD-ROM in a file named
synchronize sheets.xlsm.

VBA Techniques

The examples in this section illustrate common VBA techniques that you might be able to
adapt to your own projects.

Toggling a Boolean property

A *Boolean property* is one that is either True or False. The easiest way to toggle a
Boolean property is to use the Not operator, as shown in the following example, which toggles the WrapText property of a selection.

```
Sub ToggleWrapText()
'   Toggles text wrap alignment for selected cells
    If TypeName(Selection) = "Range" Then
        Selection.WrapText = Not ActiveCell.WrapText
    End If
End Sub
```

Note that the active cell is used as the basis for toggling. When a range is selected and the property values in the cells are inconsistent (for example, some cells are bold, and others are not), it is considered *mixed,* and Excel uses the active cell to determine how to toggle. If the active cell is bold, for example, all cells in the selection are made not bold when you click the Bold button. This simple procedure mimics the way Excel works, which is usually the best practice.

Note also that this procedure uses the TypeName function to check whether the selection is a range. If the selection isn't a range, nothing happens.

You can use the Not operator to toggle many other properties. For example, to toggle the display of row and column borders in a worksheet, use the following code:

```
ActiveWindow.DisplayHeadings = Not _
    ActiveWindow.DisplayHeadings
```

To toggle the display of grid lines in the active worksheet, use the following code:

```
ActiveWindow.DisplayGridlines = Not _
    ActiveWindow.DisplayGridlines
```

Determining the number of printed pages

If you need to determine the number of printed pages for a worksheet printout, you can use Excel's Print Preview feature and view the page count displayed at the bottom of the screen. The VBA procedure that follows calculates the number of printed pages for the active sheet by counting the number of horizontal and vertical page breaks:

```
Sub PageCount()
    MsgBox (ActiveSheet.HPageBreaks.Count + 1) * _
        (ActiveSheet.VPageBreaks.Count + 1) & " pages"
End Sub
```

The following VBA procedure loops through all worksheets in the active workbook and displays the total number of printed pages, as shown in Figure 11-13:

```
Sub ShowPageCount()
    Dim PageCount As Integer
    Dim sht As Worksheet
    PageCount = 0
    For Each sht In Worksheets
        PageCount = PageCount + (sht.HPageBreaks.Count + 1) * _
            (sht.VPageBreaks.Count + 1)
    Next sht
    MsgBox "Total printed pages = " & PageCount
End Sub
```

Figure 11-13: Using VBA to count the number of printed pages in a workbook.

 CD-ROM

A workbook that contains this example is on the companion CD-ROM in a file named page count.xlsm.

Displaying the date and time

If you understand the serial number system that Excel uses to store dates and times, you won't have any problems using dates and times in your VBA procedures.

The `DateAndTime` procedure displays a message box with the current date and time, as depicted in Figure 11-14. This example also displays a personalized message in the message box title bar.

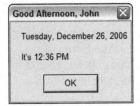

Figure 11-14: A message box displaying the date and time.

The procedure uses the `Date` function as an argument for the `Format` function. The result is a string with a nicely formatted date. I used the same technique to get a nicely formatted time.

```
Sub DateAndTime()
    Dim TheDate As String, TheTime As String
    Dim Greeting As String
    Dim FullName As String, FirstName As String
    Dim SpaceInName As Long

    TheDate = Format(Date, "Long Date")
    TheTime = Format(Time, "Medium Time")

'   Determine greeting based on time
    Select Case Time
        Case Is < TimeValue("12:00"): Greeting = "Good Morning, "
```

```
        Case Is >= TimeValue("17:00"): Greeting = "Good Evening, "
        Case Else: Greeting = "Good Afternoon, "
    End Select

'   Append user's first name to greeting
    FullName = Application.UserName
    SpaceInName = InStr(1, FullName, " ", 1)

'   Handle situation when name has no space
    If SpaceInName = 0 Then SpaceInName = Len(FullName)
    FirstName = Left(FullName, SpaceInName)
    Greeting = Greeting & FirstName

'   Show the message
    MsgBox TheDate & vbCrLf & vbCrLf & "It's " & TheTime, vbOKOnly, Greeting
End Sub
```

In the preceding example, I used named formats (`Long Date` and `Medium Time`) to ensure that the macro will work properly regardless of the user's international settings. You can, however, use other formats. For example, to display the date in mm/dd/yy format, you can use a statement like the following:

```
TheDate = Format(Date, "mm/dd/yy")
```

I used a `Select Case` construct to base the greeting displayed in the message box's title bar on the time of day. VBA time values work just as they do in Excel. If the time is less than .5 (noon), it's morning. If it's greater than .7083 (5 p.m.), it's evening. Otherwise, it's afternoon. I took the easy way out and used VBA's `TimeValue` function, which returns a time value from a string.

The next series of statements determines the user's first name, as recorded in the General tab in Excel's Options dialog box. I used VBA's `InStr` function to locate the first space in the user's name. When I first wrote this procedure, I didn't consider a username that has no space. So when I ran this procedure on a machine with a username of *Nobody,* the code failed — which goes to show you that I can't think of everything, and even the simplest procedures can run aground. (By the way, if the user's name is left blank, Excel always substitutes the name *User.*) The solution to this problem was to use the length of the full name for the `SpaceInName` variable so that the `Left` function extracts the full name.

The `MsgBox` function concatenates the date and time but uses the built-in `vbCrLf` constant to insert a line break between them. `vbOKOnly` is a predefined constant that returns 0, causing the message box to appear with only an OK button. The final argument is the `Greeting`, constructed earlier in the procedure.

CD-ROM

The `DateAndTime` procedure is available on the companion CD-ROM in a file named `date and time.xlsm`.

Getting a list of fonts

If you need to get a list of all installed fonts, you'll find that Excel does not provide a direct way to retrieve that information. In previous editions of this book, I presented a technique that read the font names from the Font control on the Formatting toolbar. Excel 2007 no longer has a Formatting toolbar, and it's impossible to access the controls on the Ribbon using VBA. For compatibility purposes, however, Excel 2007 still supports the old CommandBar properties and methods — it's just that they don't work as you would expect.

In any case, I was able to modify my old procedure so it works reliably in Excel 2007. The ShowInstalledFonts macro displays a list of the installed fonts in column A of the active worksheet. It creates a temporary toolbar (a CommandBar object), adds the Font control, and reads the fonts from that control. The temporary toolbar is then deleted.

```
Sub ShowInstalledFonts()
    Dim FontList As CommandBarControl
    Dim TempBar As CommandBar
    Dim i As Long

'   Create temporary CommandBar
    Set TempBar = Application.CommandBars.Add
    Set FontList = TempBar.Controls.Add(ID:=1728)

'   Put the fonts into column A
    Range("A:A").ClearContents
    For i = 0 To FontList.ListCount - 1
        Cells(i + 1, 1) = FontList.List(i + 1)
    Next i

'   Delete temporary CommandBar
    TempBar.Delete
End Sub
```

TIP

As an option, you can display each font name in the actual font (as shown in Figure 11-15). To do so, add this statement inside of the For-Next loop:

```
Cells(i+1,1).Font.Name = FontList.List(i+1)
```

Be aware, however, that using many fonts in a workbook can eat up lots of system resources, and it could even crash your system.

CD-ROM

This procedure is available on the companion CD-ROM. The file is named list fonts.xlsm.

Part III

Figure 11-15: Listing font names in the actual fonts.

Sorting an array

Although Excel has a built-in command to sort worksheet ranges, VBA doesn't offer a method to sort arrays. One viable (but cumbersome) workaround is to transfer your array to a worksheet range, sort it by using Excel's commands, and then return the result to your array. But if speed is essential, it's better to write a sorting routine in VBA.

In this section, I cover four different sorting techniques:

- *Worksheet sort* transfers an array to a worksheet range, sorts it, and transfers it back to the array. This procedure accepts an array as its only argument.

- *Bubble sort* is a simple sorting technique (also used in the Chapter 9 sheet-sorting example). Although easy to program, the bubble-sorting algorithm tends to be rather slow, especially when the number of elements is large.

- *Quick sort* is a much faster sorting routine than bubble sort, but it is also more difficult to understand. This technique works only with `Integer` and `Long` data types.

- *Counting sort* is lightning fast, but also difficult to understand. Like the quick sort, this technique works only with `Integer` and `Long` data types.

CD-ROM

The companion CD-ROM includes a workbook application (named `sorting demo.xlsm`) that demonstrates these sorting methods. This workbook is useful for comparing the techniques with arrays of varying sizes.

Figure 11-16 shows the dialog box for this project. I tested the sorting procedures with seven different array sizes, ranging from 100 to 100,000 elements. The arrays contained random numbers (of type `Long`).

Figure 11-16: Comparing the time required to perform sorts of various array sizes.

Table 11-1 shows the results of my tests. A 0.00 entry means that the sort was virtually instantaneous (less than .01 second).

TABLE 11-1   SORTING TIMES (IN SECONDS) FOR FOUR SORT ALGORITHMS USING RANDOMLY FILLED ARRAYS

Array Elements	Excel Worksheet Sort	VBA Bubble Sort	VBA Quick Sort	VBA Counting Sort
100	0.05	0.00	0.00	0.02
500	0.05	0.02	0.00	0.02
1,000	0.06	0.08	0.01	0.02
5,000	0.14	1.92	0.02	0.03
10,000	0.22	8.23	0.03	0.03
50,000	0.97	186.56	0.27	0.08
100,000	1.97	713.03	0.50	0.14

Part III

The worksheet sort algorithm is amazingly fast, especially when you consider that the array is transferred to the sheet, sorted, and then transferred back to the array.

The bubble sort algorithm is reasonably fast with small arrays, but for larger arrays (more than 5,000 elements), forget it. The quick sort and counting sort algorithm are both very fast, but they are limited to `Integer` and `Long` data types.

Processing a series of files

One common use for macros, of course, is to repeat an operation a number of times. The example in this section demonstrates how to execute a macro on several different files stored on disk. This example — which may help you set up your own routine for this type of task — prompts the user for a file specification and then processes all matching files. In this case, processing consists of importing the file and entering a series of summary formulas that describe the data in the file.

 NOTE

In previous editions of this book, I used the `FileSearch` object. Excel 2007 no longer supports the `FileSearch` object, so I resorted to the more cumbersome `Dir` function.

```
Sub BatchProcess()
    Dim FileSpec As String
    Dim i As Integer
    Dim FileName As String
    Dim FileList() As String
    Dim FoundFiles As Integer

'   Specify path and file spec
    FileSpec = ThisWorkbook.Path & "\" & "text??.txt"
    FileName = Dir(FileSpec)

'   Was a file found?
    If FileName <> "" Then
        FoundFiles = 1
        ReDim Preserve FileList(1 To FoundFiles)
        FileList(FoundFiles) = FileName
    Else
        MsgBox "No files were found that match " & FileSpec
        Exit Sub
    End If

'   Get other filenames
    Do
        FileName = Dir
```

```
        If FileName = "" Then Exit Do
        FoundFiles = FoundFiles + 1
        ReDim Preserve FileList(1 To FoundFiles)
        FileList(FoundFiles) = FileName & "*"
    Loop

'   Loop through the files and process them
    For i = 1 To FoundFiles
        Call ProcessFiles(FileList(i))
    Next i
End Sub
```

CD-ROM

This example, named `batch processing.xlsm`, is on the companion CD-ROM. It uses three additional files (also on the CD): `text01.txt`, `text02.txt`, and `text03.txt`. You'll need to modify the routine to import other text files.

The matching filenames are stored in an array named `FoundFiles`, and the procedure uses a `For-Next` loop to process the files. Within the loop, the processing is done by calling the `ProcessFiles` procedure, which follows. This simple procedure uses the `OpenText` method to import the file and then inserts five formulas. You may, of course, substitute your own routine in place of this one:

```
Sub ProcessFiles(FileName As String)
'   Import the file
    Workbooks.OpenText FileName:=FileName, _
        Origin:=xlWindows, _
        StartRow:=1, _
        DataType:=xlFixedWidth, _
        FieldInfo:= _
        Array(Array(0, 1), Array(3, 1), Array(12, 1))
'   Enter summary formulas
    Range("D1").Value = "A"
    Range("D2").Value = "B"
    Range("D3").Value = "C"
    Range("E1:E3").Formula = "=COUNTIF(B:B,D1)"
    Range("F1:F3").Formula = "=SUMIF(B:B,D1,C:C)"
End Sub
```

CROSS-REFERENCE

For more information about working with files using VBA, refer to Chapter 27.

Some Useful Functions for Use in Your Code

In this section, I present some custom utility functions that you may find useful in your own applications and that may provide inspiration for creating similar functions. These functions are most useful when called from another VBA procedure. Therefore, they are declared by using the `Private` keyword and thus will not appear in Excel's Insert Function dialog box.

CD-ROM

The examples in this section are available on the companion CD-ROM. The file is named `VBA utility functions.xlsm`.

The FileExists function

This function takes one argument (a path with filename) and returns `True` if the file exists:

```
Private Function FileExists(fname) As Boolean
'    Returns TRUE if the file exists
    FileExists = (Dir(fname) <> "")
End Function
```

The FileNameOnly function

This function accepts one argument (a path with filename) and returns only the filename. In other words, it strips out the path.

```
Private Function FileNameOnly(pname) As String
'    Returns the filename from a path/filename string
    Dim i As Integer, length As Integer, temp As String
    Dim Cnt As Integer
'    Count the path separator characters
    Cnt = 0
    For i = 1 To Len(pname)
        If Mid(pname, i, 1) = Application.PathSeparator Then
            Cnt = Cnt + 1
        End If
    Next i
    FileNameOnly = Split(pname, Application.PathSeparator, Cnt)
End Function
```

If the argument is `c:\excel files\2007\backup\budget.xls`, the function returns the string `budget.xls`.

The `FileNameOnly` function works with any path and filename (even if the file *does not* exist). If the file exists, the following function is a simpler way to strip off the path and return only the filename.

```
Private Function FileNameOnly2(pname) As String
    FileNameOnly2 = Dir(pname)
End Function
```

The PathExists function

This function accepts one argument (a path) and returns `True` if the path exists:

```
Private Function PathExists(pname) As Boolean
'   Returns TRUE if the path exists
  If Dir(pname, vbDirectory) = "" Then
    PathExists = False
  Else
    PathExists = (GetAttr(pname) And vbDirectory) = vbDirectory
  End If
End Function
```

The RangeNameExists function

This function accepts a single argument (a range name) and returns `True` if the range name exists in the active workbook:

```
Private Function RangeNameExists(nname) As Boolean
'   Returns TRUE if the range name exists
    Dim n As Name
    RangeNameExists = False
    For Each n In ActiveWorkbook.Names
        If UCase(n.Name) = UCase(nname) Then
            RangeNameExists = True
            Exit Function
        End If
    Next n
End Function
```

Another way to write this function follows. This version attempts to create an object variable using the name. If doing so generates an error, then the name does not exist.

```
Private Function RangeNameExists2(nname) As Boolean
'   Returns TRUE if the range name exists
    Dim n As Range
    On Error Resume Next
    Set n = Range(nname)
```

```
    If Err.Number = 0 Then RangeNameExists2 = True _
        Else RangeNameExists2 = False
End Function
```

The SheetExists function

This function accepts one argument (a worksheet name) and returns `True` if the worksheet exists in the active workbook:

```
Private Function SheetExists(sname) As Boolean
'   Returns TRUE if sheet exists in the active workbook
    Dim x As Object
    On Error Resume Next
    Set x = ActiveWorkbook.Sheets(sname)
    If Err.Number = 0 Then SheetExists = True _
        Else SheetExists = False
End Function
```

The WorkbookIsOpen function

This function accepts one argument (a workbook name) and returns `True` if the workbook is open:

```
Private Function WorkbookIsOpen(wbname) As Boolean
'   Returns TRUE if the workbook is open
    Dim x As Workbook
    On Error Resume Next
    Set x = Workbooks(wbname)
    If Err.Number = 0 Then WorkbookIsOpen = True _
        Else WorkbookIsOpen = False
End Function
```

Retrieving a value from a closed workbook

VBA does not include a method to retrieve a value from a closed workbook file. You can, however, take advantage of Excel's ability to work with linked files. This section contains a custom VBA function (`GetValue`, which follows) that retrieves a value from a closed workbook. It does so by calling an *XLM macro*, which is an old-style macro used in versions prior to Excel 5. Fortunately, Excel still supports this old macro system.

```
Private Function GetValue(path, file, sheet, ref)
'   Retrieves a value from a closed workbook
    Dim arg As String

'   Make sure the file exists
```

```
    If Right(path, 1) <> "\" Then path = path & "\"
    If Dir(path & file) = "" Then
        GetValue = "File Not Found"
        Exit Function
    End If

'   Create the argument
    arg = "'" & path & "[" & file & "]" & sheet & "'!" & _
        Range(ref).Range("A1").Address(, , xlR1C1)

'   Execute an XLM macro
    GetValue = ExecuteExcel4Macro(arg)
End Function
```

Testing for Membership in a Collection

The following function procedure is a generic function that you can use to determine whether an object is a member of a collection:

```
Private Function IsInCollection(Coln As Object, _
    Item As String) As Boolean
    Dim Obj As Object
    On Error Resume Next
    Set Obj = Coln(Item)
    IsInCollection = Not Obj Is Nothing
End Function
```

This function accepts two arguments: the collection (an object) and the item (a string) that might or might not be a member of the collection. The function attempts to create an object variable that represents the item in the collection. If the attempt is successful, the function returns True; otherwise, it returns False.

You can use the IsInCollection function in place of three other functions listed in this chapter: RangeNameExists, SheetExists, and WorkbookIsOpen. To determine whether a range named Data exists in the active workbook, call the IsInCollection function with this statement:

```
MsgBox IsInCollection(ActiveWorkbook.Names, "Data")
```

To determine whether a workbook named Budget is open, use this statement:

```
MsgBox IsInCollection(Workbooks, "budget.xlsx")
```

To determine whether the active workbook contains a sheet named Sheet1, use this statement.

```
MsgBox IsInCollection(ActiveWorkbook.Worksheets, "Sheet1")
```

Part III

The GetValue function takes four arguments:

- path: The drive and path to the closed file (for example, "d:\files")
- file: The workbook name (for example, "budget.xlsx")
- sheet: The worksheet name (for example, "Sheet1")
- ref: The cell reference (for example, "C4")

The following Sub procedure demonstrates how to use the GetValue function. It simply displays the value in cell A1 in Sheet1 of a file named 2007budget.xlsx, located in the XLFiles\Budget directory on drive C.

```
Sub TestGetValue()
    Dim p As String, f As String
    Dim s As String, a As String

    p = "c:\XLFiles\Budget"
    f = "2007budget.xlsx"
    s = "Sheet1"
    a = "A1"
    MsgBox GetValue(p, f, s, a)
End Sub
```

Another example follows. This procedure reads 1,200 values (100 rows and 12 columns) from a closed file and then places the values into the active worksheet.

```
Sub TestGetValue2()
    Dim p As String, f As String
    Dim s As String, a As String
    Dim r As Long, c As Long

    p = "c:\XLFiles\Budget"
    f = "2007Budget.xlsx"
    s = "Sheet1"
    Application.ScreenUpdating = False
    For r = 1 To 100
        For c = 1 To 12
            a = Cells(r, c).Address
            Cells(r, c) = GetValue(p, f, s, a)
        Next c
    Next r
End Sub
```

NOTE

The `GetValue` function does not work if used in a worksheet formula. Actually, there is no need to use this function in a formula. You can simply create a link formula to retrieve a value from a closed file.

CD-ROM

This example is available on the companion CD-ROM. The file is named `value from a closed workbook.xlsm`. The example uses a file named `myworkbook.xlsx` for the closed file.

Some Useful Worksheet Functions

The examples in this section are custom functions that can be used in worksheet formulas. Remember, these `Function` procedures must be defined in a VBA module (not a code module associated with `ThisWorkbook`, a `Sheet`, or a `UserForm`).

CD-ROM

The examples in this section are available on the companion CD-ROM in a file named `worksheet functions.xlsm`.

Returning cell formatting information

This section contains a number of custom functions that return information about a cell's formatting. These functions are useful if you need to sort data based on formatting (for example, sort such that all bold cells are together). Keep in mind that these functions work only with explicitly-applied formatting; they do not work for formatting applied using conditional formatting.

CAUTION

You'll find that these functions aren't always updated automatically. This is because changing formatting, for example, doesn't trigger Excel's recalculation engine. To force a global recalculation (and update all the custom functions), press Ctrl+Alt+F9.

Alternatively, you can add the following statement to your function:

```
Application.Volatile
```

When this statement is present, then pressing F9 will recalculate the function.

The following function returns TRUE if its single-cell argument has bold formatting. If a range is passed as the argument, the function uses the upper-left cell of the range.

```
Function IsBold(cell) As Boolean
'    Returns TRUE if cell is bold
     IsBold = cell.Range("A1").Font.Bold
End Function
```

The following function returns TRUE if its single-cell argument has italic formatting:

```
Function IsItalic(cell) As Boolean
'    Returns TRUE if cell is italic
     IsItalic = cell.Range("A1").Font.Italic
End Function
```

Both of the preceding functions will return an error if the cell has mixed formatting — for example, if only *some* characters are bold. The following function returns TRUE only if all characters in the cell are bold:

```
Function AllBold(cell) As Boolean
'    Returns TRUE if all characters in cell are bold
     If IsNull(cell.Font.Bold) Then
         AllBold = False
     Else
         AllBold = cell.Font.Bold
     End If
End Function
```

The ALLBOLD function can be simplified as follows:

```
Function AllBold (cell) As Boolean
'    Returns TRUE if all characters in cell are bold
     AllBold = Not IsNull(cell.Font.Bold)
End Function
```

The `FillColor` function returns an integer that corresponds to the color index of the cell's interior. The actual color depends on the workbook theme that's applied. If the cell's interior is not filled, the function returns –4142.

```
Function FillColor(cell) As Integer
'    Returns an integer corresponding to
'    cell's interior color
     FillColor = cell.Range("A1").Interior.ColorIndex
End Function
```

A talking worksheet

The `SayIt` function uses Excel's text-to-speech generator to "speak" it's argument (which can be literal text or a cell reference).

```
Function SayIt(txt)
    Application.Speech.Speak (txt)
    SayIt = txt
End Function
```

This function has some amusement possibilities, but it can also be useful. For example, use the function in a formula like this:

```
=IF(SUM(A:A)>25000,SayIt("Goal Reached"))
```

If the sum of the values in column A exceeds 25,000, you'll hear the synthesized voice tell you that the goal has been reached. You can also use the `Speak` method at the end of a lengthy procedure. That way, you can do something else and you'll get an audible notice when the procedure ends.

Displaying the date when a file was saved or printed

An Excel workbook contains several built-in document properties, accessible from the `BuiltinDocumentProperties` property of the `Workbook` object. The following function returns the date and time that the workbook was last saved:

```
Function LastSaved()
    Application.Volatile
    LastSaved = ThisWorkbook. _
      BuiltinDocumentProperties("Last Save Time")
End Function
```

The following function is similar, but it returns the date and time when the workbook was last printed or previewed. If the workbook has never been printed or previewed, the function returns a #VALUE error.

```
Function LastPrinted()
    Application.Volatile
    LastPrinted = ThisWorkbook. _
      BuiltinDocumentProperties("Last Print Date")
End Function
```

If you use these functions in a formula, you might need to force a recalculation (by pressing F9) to get the current values of these properties.

NOTE

Quite a few additional built-in properties are available, but Excel does not use all of them. For example, attempting to access the Number of Bytes property will generate an error. For a list of all built-in properties, consult the Help.

The preceding `LastSaved` and `LastPrinted` functions are designed to be stored in the workbook in which they are used. In some cases, you might want to store the function in a different workbook (for example, `personal.xlsb`) or in an add-in. Because these functions reference `ThisWorkbook`, they will not work correctly. Following are more general-purpose versions of these functions. These functions use `Application.Caller`, which returns a `Range` object that represents the cell that calls the function. The use of `Parent.Parent` returns the workbook (that is, the parent of the parent of the `Range` object — a `Workbook` object). This topic is explained further in the next section.

```
Function LastSaved2()
    Application.Volatile
    LastSaved2 = Application.Caller.Parent.Parent. _
      BuiltinDocumentProperties("Last Save Time")
End Function
```

Understanding object parents

As you know, Excel's object model is a hierarchy: Objects are contained in other objects. At the top of the hierarchy is the `Application` object. Excel contains other objects, and these objects contain other objects, and so on. The following hierarchy depicts how a `Range` object fits into this scheme:

> `Application` object
>> `Workbook` object
>>> `Worksheet` object
>>>> `Range` object

In the lingo of object-oriented programming, a `Range` object's parent is the `Worksheet` object that contains it. A `Worksheet` object's parent is the `Workbook` object that contains the worksheet, and a `Workbook` object's parent is the `Application` object.

How can this information be put to use? Examine the `SheetName` VBA function that follows. This function accepts a single argument (a range) and returns the name of the worksheet that contains the range. It uses the `Parent` property of the `Range` object. The `Parent` property returns an object: the object that contains the `Range` object.

```
Function SheetName(ref) As String
    SheetName = ref.Parent.Name
End Function
```

The next function, WorkbookName, returns the name of the workbook for a particular cell. Notice that it uses the Parent property twice. The first Parent property returns a Worksheet object, and the second Parent property returns a Workbook object.

```
Function WorkbookName(ref) As String
    WorkbookName = ref.Parent.Parent.Name
End Function
```

The AppName function that follows carries this exercise to the next logical level, accessing the Parent property three times. This function returns the name of the Application object for a particular cell. It will, of course, always return Microsoft Excel.

```
Function AppName(ref) As String
    AppName = ref.Parent.Parent.Parent.Name
End Function
```

Counting cells between two values

The following function, named CountBetween, returns the number of values in a range (first argument) that fall between values represented by the second and third arguments:

```
Function CountBetween(InRange, num1, num2) As Long
'   Counts number of values between num1 and num2
    With Application.WorksheetFunction
        If num1 <= num2 Then
            CountBetween = .CountIf(InRange, ">=" & num1) - _
                .CountIf(InRange, ">" & num2)
        Else
            CountBetween = .CountIf(InRange, ">=" & num2) - _
                .CountIf(InRange, ">" & num1)
        End If
    End With
End Function
```

Note that this function uses Excel's COUNTIF function. In fact, the CountBetween function is essentially a wrapper that can simplify your formulas.

Following is an example formula that uses the CountBetween function. The formula returns the number of cells in A1:A100 that are greater than or equal to 10 and less than or equal to 20.

```
=CountBetween(A1:A100,10,20)
```

Using this VBA function is simpler than entering the following lengthy (and somewhat confusing) formula:

```
=COUNTIF(A1:A100,">=10")-COUNTIF(A1:A100,">20")
```

Counting visible cells in a range

The `CountVisible` function that follows accepts a range argument and returns the number of non-empty visible cells in the range. A cell is not visible if it's in a hidden row or a hidden column.

```
Function CountVisible(rng)
'    Counts visible cells
    Dim CellCount As Long
    Dim cell As Range
    Application.Volatile
    CellCount = 0
    Set rng = Intersect(rng.Parent.UsedRange, rng)
    For Each cell In rng
       If Not IsEmpty(cell) Then
          If Not cell.EntireRow.Hidden And _
              Not cell.EntireColumn.Hidden Then _
              CellCount = CellCount + 1
       End If
    Next cell
    CountVisible = CellCount
End Function
```

This function loops through each cell in the range, first checking whether the cell is empty. If it's not empty, it checks the hidden properties of the cell's row and column. If neither the row nor column is hidden, the `CellCount` variable is incremented.

The `CountVisible` function is useful when you're working with AutoFilters or outlines. Both of these features make use of hidden rows.

TIP

If you're using Excel 2003 or later, the `CountVisible` function is no longer required. You can use Excel's SUBTOTAL function instead. For example, to count the visible numeric cells in a range named data, use this formula:

```
=SUBTOTAL(103,data)
```

This formula works even if rows or columns are hidden manually. In previous versions, the SUBTOTAL function worked correctly only if the cells were hidden by using AutoFilters or outlines.

Determining the last non-empty cell in a column or row

In this section, I present two useful functions: `LastInColumn` returns the contents of the last non-empty cell in a column; `LastInRow` returns the contents of the last non-empty cell in a row. Each function accepts a range as its single argument. The range argument can be a complete column (for `LastInColumn`) or a complete row (for `LastInRow`). If the supplied argument is not a complete column or row, the function uses the column or row of the upper-left cell in the range. For example, the following formula returns the last value in column B:

```
=LastInColumn(B5)
```

The following formula returns the last value in row 7:

```
=LastInRow(C7:D9)
```

The `LastInColumn` function follows:

```
Function LastInColumn(rng As Range)
'   Returns the contents of the last non-empty cell in a column
    Dim LastCell As Range
    Application.Volatile
    With rng.Parent
        With .Cells(.Rows.Count, rng.Column)
            If Not IsEmpty(.Value) Then
                LastInColumn = .Value
            ElseIf IsEmpty(.End(xlUp)) Then
                LastInColumn = ""
            Else
                LastInColumn = .End(xlUp).Value
            End If
        End With
    End With
End Function
```

This function is rather complicated, so here are a few points that may help you understand it:

- `Application.Volatile` causes the function to be executed whenever the sheet is calculated.

- `Rows.Count` returns the number of rows in the worksheet. I used this, rather than hard-coding the value, because not all worksheets have the same number of rows.

- `rng.Column` returns the column number of the upper-left cell in the `rng` argument.

- Using `rng.Parent` causes the function to work properly even if the `rng` argument refers to a different sheet or workbook.

- The `End` method (with the `xlUp` argument) is equivalent to activating the last cell in a column, pressing End, and then pressing the up-arrow key.

- The `IsEmpty` function checks whether the cell is empty. If so, it returns an empty string. Without this statement, an empty cell would be returned as 0.

Part III

The LastInRow function follows. This is very similar to the LastInColumn function.

```
Function LastInRow(rng As Range)
'     Returns the contents of the last non-empty cell in a row
      Application.Volatile
      With rng.Parent
          With .Cells(rng.Row, .Columns.Count)
              If Not IsEmpty(.Value) Then
                  LastInRow = .Value
              ElseIf IsEmpty(.End(xlToLeft)) Then
                  LastInRow = ""
              Else
                  LastInRow = .End(xlToLeft).Value
              End If
          End With
      End With
End Function
```

Does a string match a pattern?

The IsLike function is very simple (but also very useful). This function returns TRUE if a text string matches a specified pattern.

This function, which follows, is remarkably simple. As you can see, the function is essentially a wrapper that lets you take advantage of VBA's powerful Like operator in your formulas.

```
Function IsLike(text As String, pattern As String) As Boolean
'     Returns true if the first argument is like the second
      IsLike = text Like pattern
End Function
```

This IsLike function takes two arguments:

- text: A text string or a reference to a cell that contains a text string
- pattern: A string that contains wildcard characters according to the following list:

Character(s) in pattern	Matches in text
?	Any single character
*	Zero or more characters
#	Any single digit (0–9)
[charlist]	Any single character in charlist
[!charlist]	Any single character not in charlist

The following formula returns TRUE because * matches any number of characters. It returns TRUE if the first argument is any text that begins with *g*.

```
=IsLike("guitar","g*")
```

The following formula returns TRUE because ? matches any single character. If the first argument were "Unit12", the function would return FALSE.

```
=IsLike("Unit1","Unit?")
```

The next formula returns TRUE because the first argument is a single character in the second argument.

```
=ISLIKE("a","[aeiou]")
```

The following formula returns TRUE if cell A1 contains *a, e, i, o, u, A, E, I, O,* or *U.* Using the UPPER function for the arguments makes the formula not case-sensitive.

```
=IsLike(UPPER(A1), UPPER("[aeiou]"))
```

The following formula returns TRUE if cell A1 contains a value that begins with 1 and has exactly three digits (that is, any integer between 100 and 199).

```
=IsLike(A1,"1##")
```

Extracting the nth element from a string

ExtractElement is a custom worksheet function (which can also be called from a VBA procedure) that extracts an element from a text string. For example, if a cell contains the following text, you can use the ExtractElement function to extract any of the substrings between the hyphens.

```
123-456-789-0133-8844
```

The following formula, for example, returns 0133, which is the fourth element in the string. The string uses a hyphen (-) as the separator.

```
=ExtractElement("123-456-789-0133-8844",4,"-")
```

The ExtractElement function uses three arguments:

- Txt: The text string from which you're extracting. This can be a literal string or a cell reference.
- n: An integer that represents the element to extract.
- Separator: A single character used as the separator.

NOTE

If you specify a space as the Separator character, multiple spaces are treated as a single space, which is almost always what you want. If n exceeds the number of elements in the string, the function returns an empty string.

The VBA code for the ExtractElement function follows:

```
Function ExtractElement(Txt, n, Separator) As String
'    Returns the nth element of a text string, where the
'    elements are separated by a specified separator character
    Dim AllElements As Variant
    AllElements = Split(Txt, Separator)
    ExtractElement = AllElements(n - 1)
End Function
```

This function uses VBA's Split function, which returns a variant array that contains each element of the text string. This array begins with 0 (not 1), so using n - 1 references the desired element.

The Split function was introduced in Excel 2000. For compatibility with older versions of Excel, you need to use the following function:

```
Function ExtractElement2(Txt, n, Separator) As String
'    Returns the nth element of a text string, where the
'    elements are separated by a specified separator character

    Dim Txt1 As String, TempElement As String
    Dim ElementCount As Integer, i As Integer

    Txt1 = Txt
'    If space separator, remove excess spaces
    If Separator = Chr(32) Then Txt1 = Application.Trim(Txt1)

'    Add a separator to the end of the string
    If Right(Txt1, Len(Txt1)) <> Separator Then _
        Txt1 = Txt1 & Separator

'    Initialize
    ElementCount = 0
    TempElement = ""

'    Extract each element
    For i = 1 To Len(Txt1)
        If Mid(Txt1, i, 1) = Separator Then
            ElementCount = ElementCount + 1
            If ElementCount = n Then
'                Found it, so exit
```

```
                ExtractElement2 = TempElement
                Exit Function
            Else
                TempElement = ""
            End If
        Else
            TempElement = TempElement & Mid(Txt1, i, 1)
        End If
    Next i
    ExtractElement2 = ""
End Function
```

A multifunctional function

This example describes a technique that may be helpful in some situations: making a single worksheet function act like multiple functions. For example, the following VBA listing is for a custom function called StatFunction. It takes two arguments: the range (rng) and the operation (op). Depending on the value of op, the function returns a value computed using any of the following worksheet functions: AVERAGE, COUNT, MAX, MEDIAN, MIN, MODE, STDEV, SUM, or VAR.

For example, you can use this function in your worksheet as follows:

```
=StatFunction(B1:B24,A24)
```

The result of the formula depends on the contents of cell A24, which should be a string such as Average, Count, Max, and so on. You can adapt this technique for other types of functions.

```
Function StatFunction(rng, op)
    Select Case UCase(op)
        Case "SUM"
            StatFunction = WorksheetFunction.Sum(rng)
        Case "AVERAGE"
            StatFunction = WorksheetFunction.Average(rng)
        Case "MEDIAN"
            StatFunction = WorksheetFunction.Median(rng)
        Case "MODE"
            StatFunction = WorksheetFunction.Mode(rng)
        Case "COUNT"
            StatFunction = WorksheetFunction.Count(rng)
        Case "MAX"
            StatFunction = WorksheetFunction.Max(rng)
        Case "MIN"
            StatFunction = WorksheetFunction.Min(rng)
        Case "VAR"
```

Part III

```
              StatFunction = WorksheetFunction.Var(rng)
       Case "STDEV"
              StatFunction = WorksheetFunction.StDev(rng)
       Case Else
              StatFunction = CVErr(xlErrNA)
     End Select
End Function
```

The SheetOffset function

You probably know that Excel's support for 3-D workbooks is limited. For example, if you need to refer to a different worksheet in a workbook, you must include the worksheet's name in your formula. This is not a big problem . . . until you attempt to copy the formula across other worksheets. The copied formulas continue to refer to the original worksheet name, and the sheet references are not adjusted as they would be in a true 3-D workbook.

The example discussed in this section is a VBA function (named SheetOffset) that enables you to address worksheets in a relative manner. For example, you can refer to cell A1 on the previous worksheet by using this formula:

```
=SheetOffset(-1,A1)
```

The first argument represents the relative sheet, and it can be positive, negative, or zero. The second argument must be a reference to a single cell. You can copy this formula to other sheets, and the relative referencing will be in effect in all the copied formulas.

The VBA code for the SheetOffset function follows:

```
Function SheetOffset(Offset As Long, Optional Cell As Variant)
'    Returns cell contents at Ref, in sheet offset
     Dim WksIndex As Long, WksNum As Long
     Dim wks As Worksheet
     Application.Volatile
     If IsMissing(Cell) Then Set Cell = Application.Caller
     WksNum = 1
     For Each wks In Application.Caller.Parent.Parent.Worksheets
         If Application.Caller.Parent.Name = wks.Name Then
             SheetOffset = Worksheets(WksNum + Offset).Range(Cell(1).Address)
             Exit Function
         Else
             WksNum = WksNum + 1
         End If
     Next wks
End Function
```

Returning the maximum value across all worksheets

If you need to determine the maximum value in cell B1 across a number of worksheets, you would use a formula such as this:

```
=MAX(Sheet1:Sheet4!B1)
```

This formula returns the maximum value in cell B1 for Sheet1, Sheet4, and all the sheets in between.

But what if you add a new sheet (Sheet5) after Sheet4? Your formula won't adjust automatically, so you need to edit it to include the new sheet reference:

```
=MAX(Sheet1:Sheet5!B1)
```

The MaxAllSheets function, which follows, accepts a single-cell argument and returns the maximum value in that cell across all worksheets in the workbook. The formula that follows, for example, returns the maximum value in cell B1 for all sheets in the workbook:

```
=MaxAllSheets(B1)
```

If you add a new sheet, there's no need to edit the formula:

```
Function MaxAllSheets(cell)
    Dim MaxVal As Double
    Dim Addr As String
    Dim Wksht As Object
    Application.Volatile
    Addr = cell.Range("A1").Address
    MaxVal = -9.9E+307
    For Each Wksht In cell.Parent.Parent.Worksheets
        If Wksht.Name = cell.Parent.Name And _
          Addr = Application.Caller.Address Then
        ' avoid circular reference
        Else
            If IsNumeric(Wksht.Range(Addr)) Then
                If Wksht.Range(Addr) > MaxVal Then _
                    MaxVal = Wksht.Range(Addr).Value
            End If
        End If
    Next Wksht
    If MaxVal = -9.9E+307 Then MaxVal = 0
    MaxAllSheets = MaxVal
End Function
```

The For Each statement uses the following expression to access the workbook:

```
cell.Parent.Parent.Worksheets
```

The parent of the cell is a worksheet, and the parent of the worksheet is the workbook. Therefore, the For Each-Next loop cycles among all worksheets in the workbook. The first If statement inside the loop performs a check to see whether the cell being checked is the cell that contains the function. If so, that cell is ignored to avoid a circular reference error.

NOTE

This function can be modified easily to perform other cross-worksheet calculations, such as minimum, average, sum, and so on.

Returning an array of nonduplicated random integers

The function in this section, RandomIntegers, returns an array of nonduplicated integers. The function is intended to be used in a multicell array formula.

```
{=RandomIntegers()}
```

Select a range and then enter the formula by pressing Ctrl+Shift+Enter. The formula returns an array of nonduplicated integers, arranged randomly. For example, if you enter the formula into a 50-cell range, the formulas will return nonduplicated integers from 1 to 50.

The code for RandomIntegers follows:

```
Function RandomIntegers()
    Dim FuncRange As Range
    Dim V() As Variant, ValArray() As Variant
    Dim CellCount As Double
    Dim i As Integer, j As Integer
    Dim r As Integer, c As Integer
    Dim Temp1 As Variant, Temp2 As Variant
    Dim RCount As Integer, CCount As Integer

'   Create Range object
    Set FuncRange = Application.Caller

'   Return an error if FuncRange is too large
    CellCount = FuncRange.Count
    If CellCount > 1000 Then
        RandomIntegers = CVErr(xlErrNA)
        Exit Function
    End If

'   Assign variables
    RCount = FuncRange.Rows.Count
    CCount = FuncRange.Columns.Count
```

```
    ReDim V(1 To RCount, 1 To CCount)
    ReDim ValArray(1 To 2, 1 To CellCount)

'   Fill array with random numbers
'   and consecutive integers
    For i = 1 To CellCount
        ValArray(1, i) = Rnd
        ValArray(2, i) = i
    Next i

'   Sort ValArray by the random number dimension
    For i = 1 To CellCount
        For j = i + 1 To CellCount
            If ValArray(1, i) > ValArray(1, j) Then
                Temp1 = ValArray(1, j)
                Temp2 = ValArray(2, j)
                ValArray(1, j) = ValArray(1, i)
                ValArray(2, j) = ValArray(2, i)
                ValArray(1, i) = Temp1
                ValArray(2, i) = Temp2
            End If
        Next j
    Next i

'   Put the randomized values into the V array
    i = 0
    For r = 1 To RCount
        For c = 1 To CCount
            i = i + 1
            V(r, c) = ValArray(2, i)
        Next c
    Next r
    RandomIntegers = V
End Function
```

Randomizing a range

The RangeRandomize function, which follows, accepts a range argument and returns an array that consists of the input range — in random order:

```
Function RangeRandomize(rng)
    Dim V() As Variant, ValArray() As Variant
    Dim CellCount As Double
    Dim i As Integer, j As Integer
    Dim r As Integer, c As Integer
    Dim Temp1 As Variant, Temp2 As Variant
```

```vba
    Dim RCount As Integer, CCount As Integer

'   Return an error if rng is too large
    CellCount = rng.Count
    If CellCount > 1000 Then
        RangeRandomize = CVErr(xlErrNA)
        Exit Function
    End If

'   Assign variables
    RCount = rng.Rows.Count
    CCount = rng.Columns.Count
    ReDim V(1 To RCount, 1 To CCount)
    ReDim ValArray(1 To 2, 1 To CellCount)

'   Fill ValArray with random numbers
'   and values from rng
    For i = 1 To CellCount
        ValArray(1, i) = Rnd
        ValArray(2, i) = rng(i)
    Next i

'   Sort ValArray by the random number dimension
    For i = 1 To CellCount
        For j = i + 1 To CellCount
            If ValArray(1, i) > ValArray(1, j) Then
                Temp1 = ValArray(1, j)
                Temp2 = ValArray(2, j)
                ValArray(1, j) = ValArray(1, i)
                ValArray(2, j) = ValArray(2, i)
                ValArray(1, i) = Temp1
                ValArray(2, i) = Temp2
            End If
        Next j
    Next i

'   Put the randomized values into the V array
    i = 0
    For r = 1 To RCount
        For c = 1 To CCount
            i = i + 1
            V(r, c) = ValArray(2, i)
        Next c
    Next r
    RangeRandomize = V
End Function
```

The code is very similar to that for the `RandomIntegers` function.

Figure 11-17 shows the function in use. The array formula in B2:B11 is:

```
{= RangeRandomize(A2:A11)}
```

This formula returns the contents of A2:A11, but in random order.

	A	B	C
1	**Original**	**Random**	
2	Aardvark	Giraffe	
3	Baboon	Cat	
4	Cat	Iguana	
5	Dog	Elephant	
6	Flephant	Aardvark	
7	Fox	Dog	
8	Giraffe	Hippo	
9	Hippo	Baboon	
10	Iguana	Javelina	
11	Javelina	Fox	
12			
13			

Sheet1 / Sheet2

Figure 11-17: The `RangeRandomize` function returns the contents of a range, in random order.

Windows API Calls

VBA has the capability to use functions that are stored in Dynamic Link Libraries (DLLs). The examples in this section use common Windows API calls to DLLs.

Determining file associations

In Windows, many file types are associated with a particular application. This association makes it possible to double-click the file to load it into its associated application.

The following function, named `GetExecutable`, uses a Windows API call to get the full path to the application associated with a particular file. For example, your system has many files with a `.txt` extension — one named `Readme.txt` is probably in your Windows directory right now. You can use the `GetExecutable` function to determine the full path of the application that opens when the file is double-clicked.

 NOTE

Windows API declarations must appear at the top of your VBA module.

```
Private Declare Function FindExecutableA Lib "shell32.dll" _
    (ByVal lpFile As String, ByVal lpDirectory As String, _
    ByVal lpResult As String) As Long

Function GetExecutable(strFile As String) As String
    Dim strPath As String
    Dim intLen As Integer
    strPath = Space(255)
    intLen = FindExecutableA(strFile, "\", strPath)
    GetExecutable = Trim(strPath)
End Function
```

Figure 11-18 shows the result of calling the GetExecutable function, with an argument of the filename for an MP3 audio file. The function returns the full path of the application that's associated with the file.

Figure 11-18: Determining the path and name of the application associated with a particular file.

CD-ROM

This example is available on the companion CD-ROM. The filename is file association.xlsm.

Determining disk drive information

VBA doesn't have a way to directly get information about disk drives. But with the assistance of three API functions, you can get just about all of the information you need.

Figure 11-19 shows the output from a VBA procedure that identifies all connected drives, determines the drive type, and calculates total space, used space, and free space. In the example shown, the system has six drives connected.

The code is rather lengthy, so I don't list it here, but the interested reader should be able to figure it out by examining the code on the CD-ROM.

CD-ROM

This example is available on the companion CD-ROM in a file named drive information.xlsm.

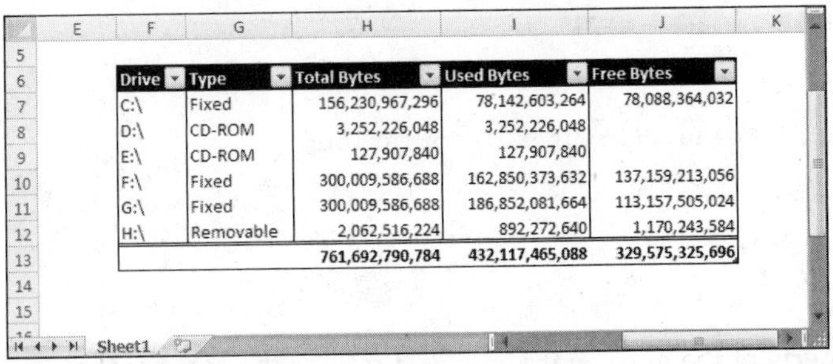

Drive	Type	Total Bytes	Used Bytes	Free Bytes
C:\	Fixed	156,230,967,296	78,142,603,264	78,088,364,032
D:\	CD-ROM	3,252,226,048	3,252,226,048	
E:\	CD-ROM	127,907,840	127,907,840	
F:\	Fixed	300,009,586,688	162,850,373,632	137,159,213,056
G:\	Fixed	300,009,586,688	186,852,081,664	113,157,505,024
H:\	Removable	2,062,516,224	892,272,640	1,170,243,584
		761,692,790,784	432,117,465,088	329,575,325,696

Figure 11-19: Using Windows API functions to get disk drive information.

Determining default printer information

The example in this section uses a Windows API function to return information about the active printer. The information is contained in a single text string. The example parses the string and displays the information in a more readable format.

```
Private Declare Function GetProfileStringA Lib "kernel32" _
  (ByVal lpAppName As String, ByVal lpKeyName As String, _
  ByVal lpDefault As String, ByVal lpReturnedString As _
  String, ByVal nSize As Long) As Long


Sub DefaultPrinterInfo()
    Dim strLPT As String * 255
    Dim Result As String
    Call GetProfileStringA _
      ("Windows", "Device", "", strLPT, 254)

    Result = Application.Trim(strLPT)
    ResultLength = Len(Result)

    Comma1 = InStr(1, Result, ",", 1)
    Comma2 = InStr(Comma1 + 1, Result, ",", 1)

'   Gets printer's name
    Printer = Left(Result, Comma1 - 1)

'   Gets driver
    Driver = Mid(Result, Comma1 + 1, Comma2 - Comma1 - 1)

'   Gets last part of device line
    Port = Right(Result, ResultLength - Comma2)

'   Build message
    Msg = "Printer:" & Chr(9) & Printer & Chr(13)
    Msg = Msg & "Driver:" & Chr(9) & Driver & Chr(13)
```

Part III

```
    Msg = Msg & "Port:" & Chr(9) & Port

'   Display message
    MsgBox Msg, vbInformation, "Default Printer Information"
End Sub
```

NOTE

The `ActivePrinter` property of the `Application` object returns the name of the active printer (and lets you change it), but there's no direct way to determine what printer driver or port is being used. That's why this function may be useful.

Figure 11-20 shows a sample message box returned by this procedure.

Figure 11-20: Getting information about the active printer by using a Windows API call.

CD-ROM

This example is available on the companion CD-ROM. The filename is `printer info.xlsm`.

Determining video display information

The example in this section uses Windows API calls to determine a system's current video mode for the primary display monitor. If your application needs to display a certain amount of information on one screen, knowing the display size helps you scale the text accordingly. In addition, the code determines the number of monitors. If more than one monitor is installed, the procedure reports the virtual screen size.

```
'32-bit API declaration
Declare Function GetSystemMetrics Lib "user32" _
   (ByVal nIndex As Long) As Long

Public Const SM_CMONITORS = 80
Public Const SM_CXSCREEN = 0
Public Const SM_CYSCREEN = 1
```

```
Public Const SM_CXVIRTUALSCREEN = 78
Public Const SM_CYVIRTUALSCREEN = 79


Sub DisplayVideoInfo()
    Dim numMonitors As Long
    Dim vidWidth As Long, vidHeight As Long
    Dim virtWidth As Long, virtHeight As Long
    Dim Msg As String

    numMonitors = GetSystemMetrics(SM_CMONITORS)
    vidWidth = GetSystemMetrics(SM_CXSCREEN)
    vidHeight = GetSystemMetrics(SM_CYSCREEN)
    virtWidth = GetSystemMetrics(SM_CXVIRTUALSCREEN)
    virtHeight = GetSystemMetrics(SM_CYVIRTUALSCREEN)

    If numMonitors > 1 Then
        Msg = numMonitors & " display monitors" & vbCrLf
        Msg = Msg & "Virtual screen: " & virtWidth & " X "
        Msg = Msg & virtHeight & vbCrLf & vbCrLf
        Msg = Msg & "The video mode on the primary display is: "
        Msg = Msg & vidWidth & " X " & vidHeight
    Else
        Msg = Msg & "The video display mode: "
        Msg = Msg & vidWidth & " X " & vidHeight
    End If
    MsgBox Msg
End Sub
```

Figure 11-21 shows the message box returned by this procedure when running on a dual-monitor system.

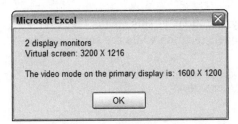

Figure 11-21: Using a Windows API call to determine the video display mode.

 CD-ROM

This example is available on the companion CD-ROM. The filename is `video mode.xlsm`.

Part III

Adding sound to your applications

The example in this section adds some sound capability to Excel. Specifically, it enables your application to play WAV or MIDI files. For example, you might like to play a short sound clip when a dialog box is displayed. Or maybe not. In any case, if you want Excel to play WAV or MIDI files, this section has what you need.

CD-ROM

The examples in this section are available on the companion CD-ROM in a file named sound.xlsm.

PLAYING A WAV FILE

The following example contains the API function declaration plus a simple procedure to play a sound file called sound.wav, which is presumed to be in the same directory as the workbook:

```
Private Declare Function PlaySound Lib "winmm.dll" _
  Alias "PlaySoundA" (ByVal lpszName As String, _
  ByVal hModule As Long, ByVal dwFlags As Long) As Long

Const SND_SYNC = &H0
Const SND_ASYNC = &H1
Const SND_FILENAME = &H20000

Sub PlayWAV()
    WAVFile = "sound.wav"
    WAVFile = ThisWorkbook.Path & "\" & WAVFile
    Call PlaySound(WAVFile, 0&, SND_ASYNC Or SND_FILENAME)
End Sub
```

In the preceding example, the WAV file is played asynchronously. This means that execution continues while the sound is playing. To stop code execution while the sound is playing, use this statement instead:

```
Call PlaySound(WAVFile, 0&, SND_SYNC Or SND_FILENAME)
```

PLAYING A MIDI FILE

If the sound file is a MIDI file, you'll need to use a different API call. The PlayMIDI procedure starts playing a MIDI file. Executing the StopMIDI procedure stops playing the MIDI file. This example uses a file named xfiles.mid.

```
Private Declare Function mciExecute Lib "winmm.dll" _
   (ByVal lpstrCommand As String) As Long

Sub PlayMIDI()
    MIDIFile = "xfiles.mid"
    MIDIFile = ThisWorkbook.Path & "\" & MIDIFile
    mciExecute ("play " & MIDIFile)
End Sub

Sub StopMIDI()
    MIDIFile = "xfiles.mid"
    MIDIFile = ThisWorkbook.Path & "\" & MIDIFile
    mciExecute ("stop " & MIDIFile)
End Sub
```

PLAYING SOUND FROM A WORKSHEET FUNCTION

The Alarm function, which follows, is designed to be used in a worksheet formula. It uses a Windows API function to play a sound file when a cell meets a certain condition.

```
Declare Function PlaySound Lib "winmm.dll" _
   Alias "PlaySoundA" (ByVal lpszName As String, _
   ByVal hModule As Long, ByVal dwFlags As Long) As Long

Function Alarm(Cell, Condition)
    Dim WAVFile As String
    Const SND_ASYNC = &H1
    Const SND_FILENAME = &H20000
    If Evaluate(Cell.Value & Condition) Then
        WAVFile = ThisWorkbook.Path & "\sound.wav"
        Call PlaySound(WAVFile, 0&, SND_ASYNC Or SND_FILENAME)
        Alarm = True
    Else
        Alarm = False
    End If
End Function
```

The Alarm function accepts two arguments: a cell reference and a condition (expressed as a string). The following formula, for example, uses the Alarm function to play a WAV file when the value in cell B13 is greater than or equal to 1000.

```
=ALARM(B13,">=1000")
```

The function uses VBA's Evaluate function to determine whether the cell's value matches the specified criterion. When the criterion is met (and the alarm has sounded), the function returns True; otherwise, it returns False.

CROSS-REFERENCE

The SayIt function, presented earlier in this chapter, is a much simpler way to use sound in a function.

Reading from and writing to the Registry

Most Windows applications use the Windows Registry database to store settings. (See Chapter 4 for some additional information about the Registry.) Your VBA procedures can read values from the Registry and write new values to the Registry. Doing so requires the following Windows API declarations:

```
Private Declare Function RegOpenKeyA Lib "ADVAPI32.DLL" _
    (ByVal hKey As Long, ByVal sSubKey As String, _
    ByRef hkeyResult As Long) As Long

Private Declare Function RegCloseKey Lib "ADVAPI32.DLL" _
    (ByVal hKey As Long) As Long

Private Declare Function RegSetValueExA Lib "ADVAPI32.DLL" _
    (ByVal hKey As Long, ByVal sValueName As String, _
    ByVal dwReserved As Long, ByVal dwType As Long, _
    ByVal sValue As String, ByVal dwSize As Long) As Long

Private Declare Function RegCreateKeyA Lib "ADVAPI32.DLL" _
    (ByVal hKey As Long, ByVal sSubKey As String, _
    ByRef hkeyResult As Long) As Long

Private Declare Function RegQueryValueExA Lib "ADVAPI32.DLL" _
    (ByVal hKey As Long, ByVal sValueName As String, _
    ByVal dwReserved As Long, ByRef lValueType As Long, _
    ByVal sValue As String, ByRef lResultLen As Long) As Long
```

CD-ROM

I developed two wrapper functions that simplify the task of working with the Registry: GetRegistry and WriteRegistry. These functions are available on the companion CD-ROM in a file named windows registry.xlsm. This workbook includes a procedure that demonstrates reading from the Registry and writing to the Registry.

READING FROM THE REGISTRY

The GetRegistry function returns a setting from the specified location in the Registry. It takes three arguments:

- `RootKey`: A string that represents the branch of the Registry to address. This string can be one of the following:

  - `HKEY_CLASSES_ROOT`

  - `HKEY_CURRENT_USER`

  - `HKEY_LOCAL_MACHINE`

  - `HKEY_USERS`

  - `HKEY_CURRENT_CONFIG`

  - `HKEY_DYN_DATA`

- `Path`: The full path of the Registry category being addressed.

- `RegEntry`: The name of the setting to retrieve.

Here's an example. If you'd like to find which graphic file, if any, is being used for the Desktop wallpaper, you can call `GetRegistry` as follows. (Notice that the arguments are not case-sensitive.)

```
RootKey = "hkey_current_user"
Path = "Control Panel\Desktop"
RegEntry = "Wallpaper"
MsgBox GetRegistry(RootKey, Path, RegEntry), _
    vbInformation, Path & "\RegEntry"
```

The message box will display the path and filename of the graphic file (or an empty string if wallpaper is not used).

WRITING TO THE REGISTRY

The `WriteRegistry` function writes a value to the Registry at a specified location. If the operation is successful, the function returns `True`; otherwise, it returns `False`. `WriteRegistry` takes the following arguments (all of which are strings):

- `RootKey`: A string that represents the branch of the Registry to address. This string may be one of the following:

  - `HKEY_CLASSES_ROOT`

  - `HKEY_CURRENT_USER`

  - `HKEY_LOCAL_MACHINE`

  - `HKEY_USERS`

  - `HKEY_CURRENT_CONFIG`

  - `HKEY_DYN_DATA`

- `Path`: The full path in the Registry. If the path doesn't exist, it is created.

- `RegEntry`: The name of the Registry category to which the value will be written. If it doesn't exist, it is added.

- `RegVal`: The value that you are writing.

Here's an example that writes a value representing the time and date Excel was started to the Registry. The information is written in the area that stores Excel's settings.

```
Sub Auto_Open()
    RootKey = "hkey_current_user"
    Path = "software\microsoft\office\12.0\excel\LastStarted"
    RegEntry = "DateTime"
    RegVal = Now()
    If WriteRegistry(RootKey, Path, RegEntry, RegVal) Then
        msg = RegVal & " has been stored in the registry."
            Else msg = "An error occurred"
    End If
    MsgBox msg
End Sub
```

If you store this routine in your personal macro workbook, the setting is automatically updated whenever you start Excel.

An Easier Way to Access the Registry

If you want to use the Windows Registry to store and retrieve settings for your Excel applications, you don't have to bother with the Windows API calls. Rather, you can use VBA's `GetSetting` and `SaveSetting` functions.

These two functions are described in the online Help, so I won't cover the details here. However, it's important to understand that these functions work only with the following key name:

`HKEY_CURRENT_USER\Software\VB and VBA Program Settings`

In other words, you can't use these functions to access *any* key in the Registry. Rather, these functions are most useful for storing information about your Excel application that you need to maintain between sessions.

Part

Working with UserForms

Chapter 12

Custom Dialog Box Alternatives

In This Chapter

Dialog boxes are, perhaps, the most important user interface element in Windows programs. Virtually every Windows program uses them, and most users have a good understanding of how they work. Excel developers implement custom dialog boxes by creating UserForms. However, VBA provides the means to display some built-in dialog boxes. This chapter covers the following topics:

- Using an input box to get user input
- Using a message box to display messages or get a simple response
- Selecting a file from a dialog box
- Selecting a directory
- Displaying Excel's built-in dialog boxes

Before I get into the nitty-gritty of creating UserForms, you might find it helpful to understand some of Excel's built-in tools that display dialog boxes. That's the focus of this chapter.

Before You Create That UserForm . . .

In some cases, you can save yourself the trouble of creating a custom dialog box by using one of several prebuilt dialog boxes. The sections that follow describe various dialog boxes that you can display without creating a UserForm.

Using an Input Box

An *input box* is a simple dialog box that allows the user to make a single entry. For example, you can use an input box to let the user enter text, a number, or even select a range. There are actually two ways to generate an InputBox: one by using a VBA function, and the other by using a method of the Application object.

The VBA InputBox function

The syntax for VBA's InputBox function is:

```
InputBox(prompt[,title][,default][,xpos][,ypos][,helpfile, context])
```

- prompt: Required. The text displayed in the InputBox.

- title: Optional. The caption of the InputBox window.

- default: Optional. The default value to be displayed in the dialog box.

- xpos, ypos: Optional. The screen coordinates of the upper-left corner of the window.

- helpfile, context: Optional. The help file and help topic.

The InputBox function prompts the user for a single piece of information. The function always returns a string, so it may be necessary to convert the results to a value.

The prompt may consist of about 1,024 characters (more or less, depending on the width of the characters used). In addition, you can provide a title for the dialog box and a default value and specify its position on the screen. And you can specify a custom help topic; if you do, the input box includes a Help button.

The following example, whose output is shown in Figure 12-1, uses the VBA InputBox function to ask the user for his or her full name. The code then extracts the first name and displays a greeting in a message box.

```
Sub GetName()
    Dim UserName As String
    Dim FirstSpace As Integer
    Do Until UserName <> ""
        UserName = InputBox("Enter your full name: ", _
```

```
                "Identify Yourself")
    Loop
    FirstSpace = InStr(UserName, " ")
    If FirstSpace <> 0 Then
        UserName = Left(UserName, FirstSpace - 1)
    End If
    MsgBox "Hello " & UserName
End Sub
```

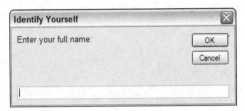

Figure 12-1: VBA's InputBox function at work.

Notice that this InputBox function is written in a Do Until loop to ensure that something is entered when the input box appears. If the user clicks Cancel or doesn't enter any text, UserName contains an empty string, and the input box reappears. The procedure then attempts to extract the first name by searching for the first space character (by using the InStr function) and then using the Left function to extract all characters before the first space. If a space character is not found, the entire name is used as entered.

As I mentioned, the InputBox function always returns a string. If the string returned by the InputBox function looks like a number, you can convert it to a value by using VBA's Val function. Or you can use Excel's InputBox method, which I describe in the next section.

Figure 12-2 shows another example of the VBA InputBox function. The user is asked to fill in the missing word. This example also illustrates the use of named arguments. The prompt text is retrieved from a worksheet cell.

```
Sub GetWord()
    Dim TheWord As String
    Dim p As String
    Dim t As String
    p = Range("A1")
    t = "What's the missing word?"
    TheWord = InputBox(prompt:=p, Title:=t)
    If UCase(TheWord) = "BATTLEFIELD" Then
        MsgBox "Correct."
    Else
        MsgBox "That is incorrect."
    End If
End Sub
```

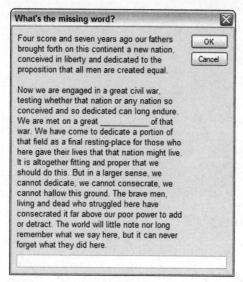

Figure 12-2: Using VBA's InputBox function with a long prompt.

 ## CD-ROM

The two examples in this section are available on the companion CD-ROM. The file is named VBA inputbox.xlsm.

The Excel InputBox method

Using Excel's InputBox method offers three advantages over VBA's InputBox function:

- You can specify the data type returned.
- The user can specify a worksheet range by dragging in the worksheet.
- Input validation is performed automatically.

The syntax for the Excel InputBox method is:

```
InputBox(Prompt [,Title][,Default][,Left][,Top][,HelpFile, HelpContextID]
[,Type])
```

- Prompt: Required. The text displayed in the input box.
- Title: Optional. The caption in the input box window.
- Default: Optional. The default value to be returned by the function if the user enters nothing.
- Left, Top: Optional. The screen coordinates of the upper-left corner of the window.

- `HelpFile, HelpContextID`: Optional. The help file and help topic.

- `Type`: Optional. A code for the data type returned, as listed in Table 12-1.

TABLE 12-1   CODES TO DETERMINE THE DATA TYPE RETURNED BY EXCEL'S INPUTBOX METHOD

Code	Meaning
0	A formula
1	A number
2	A string (text)
4	A logical value (`True` or `False`)
8	A cell reference, as a range object
16	An error value, such as #N/A
64	An array of values

Excel's InputBox method is quite versatile. To allow more than one data type to be returned, use the sum of the pertinent codes. For example, to display an input box that can accept text or numbers, set `type` equal to 3 (that is, 1 + 2, or *number* plus *text*). If you use 8 for the `type` argument, the user can enter a cell or range address manually or point to a range in the worksheet.

The `EraseRange` procedure, which follows, uses the InputBox method to allow the user to select a range to erase (see Figure 12-3). The user can either type the range address manually or use the mouse to select the range in the sheet.

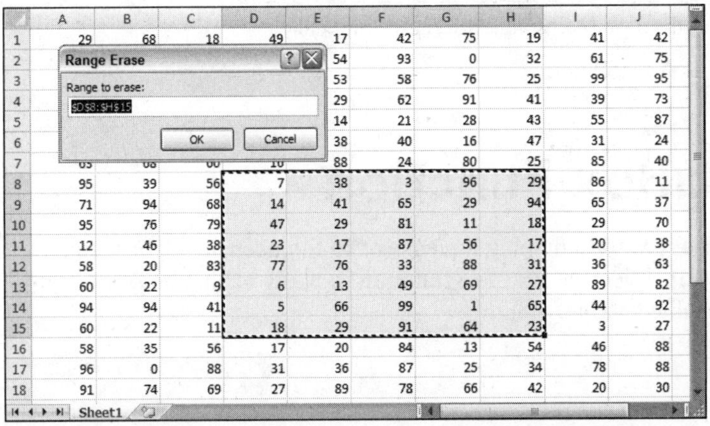

Figure 12-3: Using the InputBox method to specify a range.

The InputBox method with a `type` argument of 8 returns a `Range` object (note the `Set` keyword). This range is then erased (by using the `Clear` method). The default value displayed in the input box is the current selection's address. The `On Error` statement ends the procedure if the input box is canceled.

```
Sub EraseRange()
    Dim UserRange As Range
    On Error GoTo Canceled
    Set UserRange = Application.InputBox _
        (Prompt:="Range to erase:", _
        Title:="Range Erase", _
        Default:=Selection.Address, _
        Type:=8)
    UserRange.Clear
    UserRange.Select
Canceled:
End Sub
```

 CD-ROM

This example is available on the companion CD-ROM in a file named `inputbox method.xlsm`.

Yet another advantage of using Excel's InputBox method is that Excel performs input validation automatically. In the `GetRange` example, if you enter something other than a range address, Excel displays an informative message and lets the user try again (see Figure 12-4).

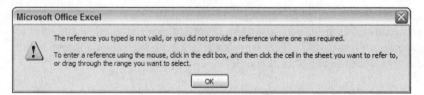

Figure 12-4: Excel's InputBox method performs validation automatically.

The VBA MsgBox Function

VBA's `MsgBox` function is an easy way to display a message to the user or to get a simple response (such as OK or Cancel). I use the `MsgBox` function in many of this book's examples as a way to display a variable's value.

The official syntax for `MsgBox` is as follows:

```
MsgBox(prompt[,buttons][,title][,helpfile, context])
```

- `prompt`: Required. The text displayed in the message box.
- `buttons`: Optional. A numeric expression that determines which buttons and icon are displayed in the message box. See Table 12-2.
- `title`: Optional. The caption in the message box window.
- `helpfile, context`: Optional. The helpfile and help topic.

You can easily customize your message boxes because of the flexibility of the `buttons` argument. (Table 12-2 lists the many constants that you can use for this argument.) You can specify which buttons to display, whether an icon appears, and which button is the default.

TABLE 12-2   CONSTANTS USED FOR BUTTONS IN THE MSGBOX FUNCTION

Constant	Value	Description
vbOKOnly	0	Display OK button only.
vbOKCancel	1	Display OK and Cancel buttons.
vbAbortRetryIgnore	2	Display Abort, Retry, and Ignore buttons.
vbYesNoCancel	3	Display Yes, No, and Cancel buttons.
vbYesNo	4	Display Yes and No buttons.
vbRetryCancel	5	Display Retry and Cancel buttons.
vbCritical	16	Display Critical Message icon.
vbQuestion	32	Display Warning Query icon.
vbExclamation	48	Display Warning Message icon.
vbInformation	64	Display Information Message icon.
vbDefaultButton1	0	First button is default.
vbDefaultButton2	256	Second button is default.
vbDefaultButton3	512	Third button is default.
vbDefaultButton4	768	Fourth button is default.

continued

Part IV

TABLE 12-2 CONSTANTS USED FOR BUTTONS IN THE MSGBOX FUNCTION
(continued)

Constant	Value	Description
vbSystemModal	4096	All applications are suspended until the user responds to the message box (might not work under all conditions).
vbMsgBoxHelpButton	16384	Display a Help button. However, there is no way to display any help if the button is clicked.

You can use the MsgBox function by itself (to simply display a message) or assign its result to a variable. When MsgBox does return a result, it represents the button clicked by the user. The following example displays a message and an OK button and does not return a result:

```
Sub MsgBoxDemo()
    MsgBox "Macro finished with no errors."
End Sub
```

To get a response from a message box, you can assign the results of the MsgBox function to a variable. In the following code, I use some built-in constants (described in Table 12-3) to make it easier to work with the values returned by MsgBox:

```
Sub GetAnswer()
    Dim Ans As Integer
    Ans = MsgBox("Continue?", vbYesNo)
    Select Case Ans
        Case vbYes
'       ...[code if Ans is Yes]...
        Case vbNo
'       ...[code if Ans is No]...
    End Select
End Sub
```

TABLE 12-3 CONSTANTS USED FOR MSGBOX RETURN VALUE

Constant	Value	Button Clicked
vbOK	1	OK
vbCancel	2	Cancel

Constant	Value	Button Clicked
vbAbort	3	Abort
vbRetry	4	Retry
vbIgnore	5	Ignore
vbYes	6	Yes
vbNo	7	No

The variable returned by the MsgBox function is an Integer data type. Actually, it's not even necessary to use a variable to utilize the result of a message box. The following procedure is another way of coding the GetAnswer procedure.

```
Sub GetAnswer2()
    If MsgBox("Continue?", vbYesNo) = vbYes Then
'        ...[code if Ans is Yes]...
    Else
'        ...[code if Ans is No]...
    End If
End Sub
```

The following function example uses a combination of constants to display a message box with a Yes button, a No button, and a question mark icon; the second button is designated as the default button (see Figure 12-5). For simplicity, I assigned these constants to the Config variable.

```
Private Function ContinueProcedure() As Boolean
    Dim Config As Integer
    Dim Ans As Integer
    Config = vbYesNo + vbQuestion + vbDefaultButton2
    Ans = MsgBox("An error occurred. Continue?", Config)
    If Ans = vbYes Then ContinueProcedure = True _
        Else ContinueProcedure = False
End Function
```

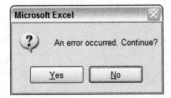

Figure 12-5: The buttons argument of the MsgBox function determines which buttons appear.

Part IV

The `ContinueProcedure` function can be called from another procedure. For example, the following statement calls the `ContinueProcedure` function (which displays the message box). If the function returns `False` (that is, the user selects No), the procedure ends. Otherwise, the next statement would be executed.

```
If Not ContinueProcedure() Then Exit Sub
```

The width of the message box depends on your video resolution. If you would like to force a line break in the message, use the `vbCrLf` (or `vbNewLine`) constant in the text. The following example displays the message in three lines. Figure 12-6 shows how it looks.

```
Sub MultiLine()
    Dim Msg As String
    Msg = "This is the first line." & vbCrLf & vbCrLf
    Msg = Msg & "This is the second line." & vbCrLf
    Msg = Msg & "And this is the last line."
    MsgBox Msg
End Sub
```

Figure 12-6: Splitting a message into multiple lines.

You can also insert a tab character by using the `vbTab` constant. The following procedure uses a message box to display the values in a 20 x 8 range of cells in A1:H20 (see Figure 12-7). It separates the columns by using a `vbTab` constant and inserts a new line by using the `vbCrLf` constant. The `MsgBox` function accepts a maximum string length of 1,023 characters, which will limit the number of cells that you can display.

```
Sub ShowRange()
    Dim Msg As String
    Dim r As Integer, c As Integer
    Msg = ""
    For r = 1 To 20
        For c = 1 To 8
            Msg = Msg & Cells(r, c) & vbTab
        Next c
        Msg = Msg & vbCrLf
    Next r
    MsgBox Msg
End Sub
```

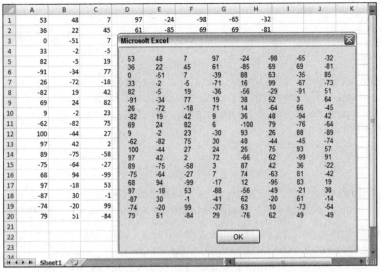

Figure 12-7: This message box displays text with tabs and line breaks.

CROSS-REFERENCE

Chapter 15 includes a UserForm example that emulates the MsgBox function.

The Excel GetOpenFilename Method

If your application needs to ask the user for a filename, you can use the InputBox function. But this approach is tedious and error-prone. A better approach is to use the GetOpenFilename method of the Application object, which ensures that your application gets a valid filename (as well as its complete path).

This method displays the normal Open dialog box, but it does *not* actually open the file specified. Rather, the method returns a string that contains the path and filename selected by the user. Then you can write code to do whatever you want with the filename.

The syntax for the GetOpenFilename method is as follows (all arguments are optional):

```
ApplicationGetOpenFilename(FileFilter, FilterIndex, Title, ButtonText,
MultiSelect)
```

- **FileFilter**: Optional. A string specifying file-filtering criteria.

- **FilterIndex**: Optional. The index number of the default file-filtering criteria.

- **Title**: Optional. The title of the dialog box. If omitted, the title is Open.

- `ButtonText`: For Macintosh only.

- `MultiSelect`: Optional. If `True`, multiple filenames can be selected. The default value is `False`.

The `FileFilter` argument determines what appears in the dialog box's Files of Type drop-down list. The argument consists of pairs of file filter strings followed by the wildcard file filter specification, with each part and each pair separated by commas. If omitted, this argument defaults to the following:

```
"All Files (*.*),*.*"
```

Notice that the first part of this string (`All Files (*.*)`) is the text displayed in the Files of Type drop-down list. The second part (`*.*`) actually determines which files are displayed.

The following instruction assigns a string to a variable named `Filt`. This string can then be used as a `FileFilter` argument for the GetOpenFilename method. In this case, the dialog box will allow the user to select from four different file types (plus an All Files option). Notice that I used VBA's line continuation sequence to set up the `Filt` variable; doing so makes it much easier to work with this rather complicated argument.

```
Filt = "Text Files (*.txt),*.txt," & _
       "Lotus Files (*.prn),*.prn," & _
       "Comma Separated Files (*.csv),*.csv," & _
       "ASCII Files (*.asc),*.asc," & _
       "All Files (*.*),*.*"
```

The `FilterIndex` argument specifies which `FileFilter` is the default, and the title argument is text that is displayed in the title bar. If the `MultiSelect` argument is `True`, the user can select multiple files, all of which are returned in an array.

The following example prompts the user for a filename. It defines five file filters.

```
Sub GetImportFileName()
    Dim Filt As String
    Dim FilterIndex As Integer
    Dim Title As String
    Dim FileName As Variant

'   Set up list of file filters
    Filt = "Text Files (*.txt),*.txt," & _
           "Lotus Files (*.prn),*.prn," & _
           "Comma Separated Files (*.csv),*.csv," & _
           "ASCII Files (*.asc),*.asc," & _
           "All Files (*.*),*.*"

'   Display *.* by default
```

```
      FilterIndex = 5

'     Set the dialog box caption
      Title = "Select a File to Import"

'     Get the file name
      FileName = Application.GetOpenFilename _
          (FileFilter:=Filt, _
           FilterIndex:=FilterIndex, _
           Title:=Title)

'     Exit if dialog box canceled
      If FileName = False Then
          MsgBox "No file was selected."
          Exit Sub
      End If

'     Display full path and name of the file
      MsgBox "You selected " & FileName
End Sub
```

Figure 12-8 shows the dialog box that appears when this procedure is executed and the user selects the Comma Separated Files filter.

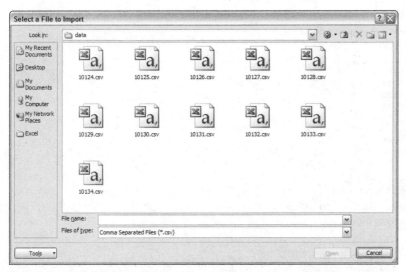

Figure 12-8: The GetOpenFilename method displays a dialog box used to specify a file.

The following example is similar to the previous example. The difference is that the user can press Ctrl or Shift and select multiple files when the dialog box is displayed. Notice that I check for the Cancel button click by determining whether `FileName` is an array. If the user doesn't click Cancel, the result is an array that consists of at least one element. In this example, a list of the selected files is displayed in a message box.

```
Sub GetImportFileName2()
    Dim Filt As String
    Dim FilterIndex As Integer
    Dim FileName As Variant
    Dim Title As String
    Dim i As Integer
    Dim Msg As String
'   Set up list of file filters
    Filt  = "Text Files (*.txt),*.txt," & _
            "Lotus Files (*.prn),*.prn," & _
            "Comma Separated Files (*.csv),*.csv," & _
            "ASCII Files (*.asc),*.asc," & _
            "All Files (*.*),*.*"
'   Display *.* by default
    FilterIndex = 5

'   Set the dialog box caption
    Title = "Select a File to Import"

'   Get the file name
    FileName = Application.GetOpenFilename _
        (FileFilter:=Filt, _
         FilterIndex:=FilterIndex, _
         Title:=Title, _
         MultiSelect:=True)

'   Exit if dialog box canceled
    If Not IsArray(FileName) Then
        MsgBox "No file was selected."
        Exit Sub
    End If

'   Display full path and name of the files
    For i = LBound(FileName) To UBound(FileName)
        Msg = Msg & FileName(i) & vbCrLf
    Next i
    MsgBox "You selected:" & vbCrLf & Msg
End Sub
```

The FileName variable is defined as a variant (not a string, as in the previous examples). This is done because FileName can potentially hold an array rather than a single filename.

The Excel GetSaveAsFilename Method

The GetSaveAsFilename method is very similar to the GetOpenFilename method. It displays a Save As dialog box and lets the user select (or specify) a file. It returns a filename and path but doesn't take any action. Like the GetOpenFilename method, all of the GetSaveAsFilename method's arguments are optional.

The syntax for this method is:

```
Application.GetSaveAsFilename(InitialFilename, FileFilter, FilterIndex, Title,
ButtonText)
```

The arguments are:

- `InitialFilename`: Optional. Specifies the suggested filename.
- `FileFilter`: Optional. A string specifying file-filtering criteria.
- `FilterIndex`: Optional. The index number of the default file-filtering criteria.
- `Title`: Optional. The title of the dialog box.
- `ButtonText`: For Macintosh only.

Prompting for a Directory

If you need to get a filename, the simplest solution is to use the GetOpenFileName method, as I describe earlier. But if you need to get a directory name only (no file), you have two choices.

- *A Windows API function.* This method is a bit more complicated but displays a commonly used (and familiar) dialog box. A limitation is that you can't specify a default or starting directory.
- *Excel's FileDialog object.* This method is much easier to implement, and the dialog box resembles the standard Open dialog box. The FileDialog object was introduced in Excel 2002, so it won't work with earlier versions of Excel.

Both of these techniques are described in the sections that follow.

 CD-ROM

The companion CD-ROM contains a workbook that demonstrates both of these methods. The file is named get directory.xlsm.

Using a Windows API function to select a directory

In this section, I present a function named GetDirectory that displays the dialog box shown in Figure 12-9 and returns a string that represents the selected directory. If the user clicks Cancel, the function returns an empty string.

Figure 12-9: Use an API function to display this dialog box.

The GetDirectory function takes one argument, which is optional. This argument is a string that will be displayed in the dialog box. If the argument is omitted, the dialog box displays Select a folder as the message.

Following are the API declarations required at the beginning of the workbook module. This function also uses a custom data type, called BROWSEINFO.

```
'32-bit API declarations
Declare Function SHGetPathFromIDList Lib "shell32.dll" _
   Alias "SHGetPathFromIDListA" (ByVal pidl As Long, ByVal _
   pszPath As String) As Long

Declare Function SHBrowseForFolder Lib "shell32.dll" _
   Alias "SHBrowseForFolderA" (lpBrowseInfo As BROWSEINFO) _
   As Long

Public Type BROWSEINFO
    hOwner As Long
    pidlRoot As Long
    pszDisplayName As String
    lpszTitle As String
    ulFlags As Long
```

```
        lpfn As Long
        lParam As Long
        iImage As Long
End Type
```

The `GetDirectory` function follows:

```
Function GetDirectory(Optional Msg) As String
    Dim bInfo As BROWSEINFO
    Dim path As String
    Dim r As Long, x As Long, pos As Integer

'   Root folder = Desktop
    bInfo.pidlRoot = 0&

'   Title in the dialog
    If IsMissing(Msg) Then
        bInfo.lpszTitle = "Select a folder."
    Else
        bInfo.lpszTitle = Msg
    End If

'   Type of directory to return
    bInfo.ulFlags = &H1

'   Display the dialog
    x = SHBrowseForFolder(bInfo)

'   Parse the result
    path = Space$(512)
    r = SHGetPathFromIDList(ByVal x, ByVal path)
    If r Then
        pos = InStr(path, Chr$(0))
        GetDirectory = Left(path, pos - 1)
    Else
        GetDirectory = ""
    End If
End Function
```

The simple procedure that follows demonstrates how to use the `GetDirectory` function in your code. Executing this procedure displays the dialog box. When the user clicks OK, the `MsgBox` function displays the full path of the selected directory. If the user clicks Cancel, the message box displays `Canceled`.

```
Sub GetAFolder1()
    Dim Msg As String
    Dim UserFile As String
```

```
    Msg = "Please select a location for the backup."
    UserFile = GetDirectory(Msg)
    If UserFile = "" Then
        MsgBox "Canceled"
    Else
        MsgBox UserFile
    End If
End Sub
```

NOTE

Unfortunately, there is no easy way to specify a default or starting directory.

Using the FileDialog object to select a directory

If users of your application all use Excel 2002 or later, you might prefer to use a much simpler technique that uses the FileDialog object.

The following procedure displays a dialog box (see Figure 12-10) that allows the user to select a directory. The selected directory name (or Canceled) is then displayed by using the MsgBox function.

```
Sub GetAFolder2()
'   For Excel 2002 and later
    With Application.FileDialog(msoFileDialogFolderPicker)
        .InitialFileName = Application.DefaultFilePath & "\"
        .Title = "Please select a location for the backup"
        .Show
        If .SelectedItems.Count = 0 Then
            MsgBox "Canceled"
        Else
            MsgBox .SelectedItems(1)
        End If
    End With
End Sub
```

The FileDialog object lets you specify the starting directory by specifying a value for the InitialFileName property. In this case, the code uses Excel's default file path as the starting directory.

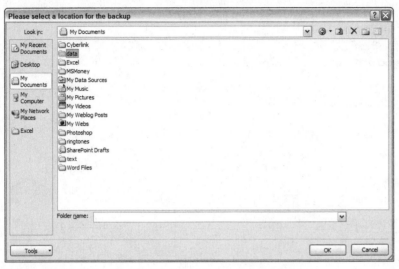

Figure 12-10: Using the FileDialog object to select a directory.

Displaying Excel's Built-In Dialog Boxes

Code that you write in VBA can execute many of Excel's Ribbon commands. And, if the command leads to a dialog box, your code can "make choices" in the dialog box (although the dialog box itself isn't displayed). For example, the following VBA statement is equivalent to choosing the Home ⇨ Editing ⇨ Find & Select ⇨ Go To command, specifying range A1:C3, and clicking OK. But the Go To dialog box never appears (which is what you want).

```
Application.Goto Reference:=Range("A1:C3")
```

In some cases, however, you may want to display one of Excel's built-in dialog boxes so that the end user can make the choices. You can do this by accessing the `Dialogs` collection of the `Application` object.

About the Dialogs collection

The `Dialogs` collection of the `Application` object consists of more than 200 members that represent most of Excel's built-in dialog boxes. Each has a predefined constant to make it easy to specify the dialog box that you need. For example, Excel's Go To dialog box is represented by the constant `xlDialogFormulaGoto`.

Part IV

Use the `Show` method to actually display the dialog box. Here's an example that displays the Go To dialog box (see Figure 12-11):

```
Application.Dialogs(xlDialogFormulaGoto).Show
```

Figure 12-11: This dialog box was displayed with a VBA statement.

When the Go To dialog box is shown, the user can specify a named range or enter a cell address to go to. This dialog box is the one that appears when you choose Home ⇨ Editing ⇨ Find & Select ⇨ Go To (or press F5).

You can also write code to determine how the user dismissed the dialog box. Do this by using a variable. In the following statement, the `Result` variable will be `True` if the user clicks OK and `False` if the user clicks Cancel or presses Esc.

```
Result = Application.Dialogs(xlDialogFormulaGoto).Show
```

 NOTE

Contrary to what you might expect, the `Result` variable does not hold the range that was specified in the Go To dialog box.

The statement below displays the Open dialog box (equivalent to selecting Office ⇨ Open):

```
Application.Dialogs(xlDialogOpen).Show
```

Unfortunately, the `Dialogs` collection is poorly documented, and the newer dialog boxes aren't even available. The next section describes a better way to display built-in dialog boxes — for Excel 2007 only.

Executing Ribbon commands

In previous versions of Excel, programmers created custom menus and toolbars by using the `CommandBar` object. In Excel 2007, the `CommandBar` object is still available, but it doesn't work like it has in the past.

CROSS-REFERENCE

Refer to Chapter 22 for more information about the `CommandBar` object.

The `CommandBar` object has also been enhanced in Excel 2007. You can use the `CommandBar` object to execute Ribbon commands using VBA. Many of the Ribbon commands display a dialog box. For example, the statement below displays the Go To dialog box:

```
Application.CommandBars.ExecuteMso("GoTo")
```

The `ExecuteMso` method accepts one argument, an `idMso` parameter that represents a Ribbon control. Unfortunately, these parameters are not listed in the Help system.

CD-ROM

The companion CD-ROM contains a file, `ribbon control names.xlsx`, that lists all of the Excel Ribbon command parameter names.

Following is another example. This statement, when executed, displays the Font tab of the Format Cells dialog box (see Figure 12-12):

```
Application.CommandBars.ExecuteMso("FormatCellsFontDialog")
```

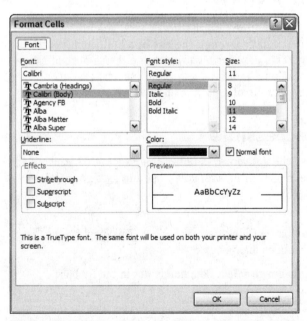

Figure 12-12: Using the ExecuteMso method to display a dialog box.

Executing an Old Menu Item Directly

Another technique to display a built-in dialog box requires knowledge of the pre-Excel 2007 toolbars (officially known as CommandBar objects). Although Excel 2007 no longer uses CommandBar objects, they are still supported for compatibility.

The following statement, for example, is equivalent to selecting the Go To menu item on the Edit menu:

```
Application.CommandBars("Worksheet Menu Bar"). _
    Controls("Edit").Controls("Go To...").Execute
```

This statement, when executed, displays the Go To dialog box. Notice that the menu item captions must match exactly (including the ellipsis after Go To).

Here's another example. This statement displays the Format Cells dialog box:

```
Application.CommandBars("Worksheet Menu Bar"). _
    Controls("Format").Controls("Cells...").Execute
```

It's probably not a good idea to rely on CommandBar objects because they may be removed from a future version of Excel.

Displaying a Data Form

Many people use Excel to manage lists in which the information is arranged in rows. Excel offers a simple way to work with this type of data through the use of a built-in data entry form that Excel can create automatically. This data form works with either a normal range of data or a range that has been designated as a table (by using the Insert ⇨ Tables ⇨ Table command). Figure 12-13 shows an example of a data form in use.

Making the data form accessible

For some reason, the command to access the data form is not in the Excel 2007 Ribbon. In order to access the data form from Excel's user interface, you must add it to your Quick Access Toolbar (QAT):

1. Right-click the QAT and select Customize Quick Access Toolbar. This displays the Customization panel of the Excel Options dialog box.

2. In the Choose Commands From drop-down, select Commands Not in the Ribbon.

3. In the list box on the left, select Form.

4. Click the Add button to add the selected command to your QAT.

5. Click OK to close the Excel Options dialog box.

   After performing these steps, a new icon will appear on your QAT.

	A	B	C	D	E	F	G	H	I	J	K
1	Agent	Date Listed	Area	List Price	Bedrooms	Baths	SqFt	Type	Pool	Sold	Per Sq Ft
2	Adams	10/9/2007	Central	$199,000	3	2.5	1,510	Condo	FALSE	FALSE	$132
3	Adams	8/19/2007	Central	$214,500	4	2.5	1,862	Single Family	TRUE	FALSE	$115
4	Adams	4/28/2007	Central	$265,000	4	3	1,905	Single Family	FALSE	FALSE	$139
5	Adams	7/19/2007	Central	$268,500	4	2.5	1,911	Single Family	FALSE	FALSE	$141
6	Adams	2/6/2007	Central	$275					UE	TRUE	$176
7	Adams	8/1/2007	Central	$309					UE	FALSE	$111
8	Adams	1/15/2007	Central	$325					LSE	TRUE	$186
9	Jenkins	1/29/2007	N. County	$1,200					UE	FALSE	$256
10	Romero	4/4/2007	N. County	$799					LSE	FALSE	$166
11	Hamilton	2/24/2007	N. County	$425					UE	FALSE	$176
12	Randolph	4/24/2007	N. County	$405					UE	TRUE	$166
13	Adams	4/21/2007	S. County	$208					UE	TRUE	$95
14	Shasta	3/24/2007	N. County	$398					LSE	FALSE	$152
15	Kelly	6/9/2007	N. County	$389					LSE	FALSE	$198
16	Shasta	8/17/2007	N. County	$389					LSE	FALSE	$125
17	Adams	6/6/2007	N. County	$379					LSE	FALSE	$154
18	Adams	2/8/2007	N. County	$379					LSE	TRUE	$161
19	Robinson	3/30/2007	N. County	$379					LSE	FALSE	$126
20	Barnes	6/26/2007	S. County	$208					LSE	FALSE	$116
21	Bennet	5/12/2007	Central	$229					LSE	TRUE	$112
22	Bennet	5/9/2007	Central	$545					UE	FALSE	$283
23	Shasta	7/15/2007	N. County	$374					LSE	FALSE	$95
24	Lang	5/3/2007	N. County	$369,900	3	2.5	2,030	Condo	TRUE	FALSE	$182
25	Romero	1/28/2007	N. County	$369,900	4	3	1,988	Condo	FALSE	TRUE	$186
26	Bennet	6/26/2007	S. County	$229,900	3	2.5	1,580	Single Family	TRUE	FALSE	$146

Data form dialog (Sheet1):
- 22 of 125
- Agent: Shasta
- Date Listed: 7/15/2007
- Area: N. County
- List Price: 374900
- Bedrooms: 4
- Baths: 3
- SqFt: 3927
- Type: Single Family
- Pool: FALSE
- Sold: FALSE
- Per Sq Ft: $95
- Buttons: New, Delete, Restore, Find Prev, Find Next, Criteria, Close

Sheet1

Figure 12-13: Some users prefer to use Excel's built-in data form for data-entry tasks.

To use a data entry form, you must arrange your data so that Excel can recognize it as a table. Start by entering headings for the columns in the first row of your data entry range. Select any cell in the table and click the Form button on your QAT. Excel then displays a dialog box customized to your data. You can use the Tab key to move between the text boxes and supply information. If a cell contains a formula, the formula result appears as text (not as an edit box). In other words, you cannot modify formulas from the data entry form.

When you complete the data form, click the New button. Excel enters the data into a row in the worksheet and clears the dialog box for the next row of data.

Displaying a data form by using VBA

Use the ShowDataForm method to display Excel's data form. The only requirement is that the active cell must be within a range. The following code activates cell A1 (which is in a table) and then displays the data form:

```
Sub DisplayDataForm()
    Range("A1").Select
    ActiveSheet.ShowDataForm
End Sub
```

CD-ROM

A workbook with this example is available on the companion CD-ROM. The file is named data form example.xlsm.

Part IV

Chapter 13

Introducing UserForms

In This Chapter
Excel makes it relatively easy to create custom dialog boxes for your applications. In fact, you can duplicate the look and feel of many of Excel's dialog boxes. This chapter provides an introduction to and overview of UserForms.

- ◆ Creating, showing, and unloading UserForms
- ◆ A discussion of the UserForm controls available to you
- ◆ Setting the properties of UserForm controls
- ◆ Controlling UserForms with VBA procedures
- ◆ A hands-on example of creating a UserForm
- ◆ An introduction to the types of events relevant to UserForms and controls
- ◆ Customizing your control Toolbox
- ◆ A handy checklist for creating UserForms

Excel developers have always had the ability to create custom dialog boxes for their applications. Beginning with Excel 97, things changed substantially — UserForms replaced the clunky old dialog sheets. You'll find that UserForms are *much* easier to work with, and they offer many additional capabilities. Even though UserForms have not been upgraded over the years, you'll find that this feature works well and is very flexible.

How Excel Handles Custom Dialog Boxes

A custom dialog box is created on a UserForm, and you access UserForms in the Visual Basic Editor (VBE).

Following is the typical sequence that you will follow when you create a UserForm:

1. Insert a new UserForm into your workbook's VB Project.

2. Write a procedure that will display the UserForm. This procedure will be located in a VBA module (not in the code module for the UserForm).

3. Add controls to the UserForm.

4. Adjust some of the properties of the controls that you added.

5. Write event handler procedures for the controls. These procedures, which are located in the code window for the UserForm, are executed when various events (such as a button click) occur.

Inserting a New UserForm

To insert a new UserForm, activate the VBE (press Alt+F11), select your workbook's project from the Project window, and then choose Insert ➪ UserForm. UserForms have default names like UserForm1, UserForm2, and so on.

TIP

You can change the name of a UserForm to make it easier to identify. Select the form and use the Properties window to change the Name property. (Press F4 if the Properties window is not displayed.) Figure 13-1 shows the Properties window when an empty UserForm is selected.

A workbook can have any number of UserForms, and each UserForm holds a single custom dialog box.

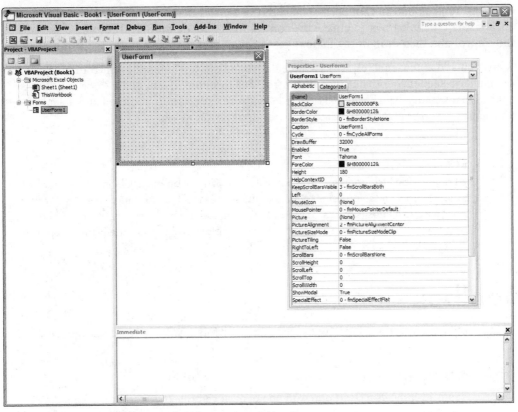

Figure 13-1: The Properties window for an empty UserForm.

Adding Controls to a UserForm

To add controls to a UserForm, use the Toolbox. (The VBE does not have menu commands that add controls.) If the Toolbox is not displayed, choose View ➪ Toolbox. Figure 13-2 shows the Toolbox.

Figure 13-2: Use the Toolbox to add controls to a UserForm.

Click the Toolbox button that corresponds to the control that you want to add and then click inside the dialog box to create the control (using its default size). Or you can click the control and then drag in the dialog box to specify the dimensions for the control.

When you add a new control, it is assigned a name that combines the control type with the numeric sequence for that type of control. For example, if you add a `CommandButton` control to an empty UserForm, it is named `CommandButton1`. If you then add a second `CommandButton` control, it is named `CommandButton2`.

TIP

It's a good idea to rename all the controls that you will be manipulating with your VBA code. Doing so lets you refer to meaningful names (such as `ProductListBox`) rather than generic names (such as `ListBox1`). To change the name of a control, use the Properties window in the VBE. Just select the object and change the Name property.

Toolbox Controls

In the sections that follow, I briefly describe the controls available to you in the Toolbox.

CD-ROM

Figure 13-3 shows a UserForm with one of each control. This workbook, named `all userform controls.xlsm`, is available on the companion CD-ROM.

TIP

Your UserForms can also use other ActiveX controls. See "Customizing the Toolbox," later in this chapter.

CheckBox

A `CheckBox` control is useful for getting a binary choice: yes or no, true or false, on or off, and so on. When a CheckBox is checked, it has a value of `True`; when it's not checked, the CheckBox value is `False`.

ComboBox

A `ComboBox` control presents a list of items in a drop-down box and displays only one item at a time. Unlike a `ListBox` control, a ComboBox can be set up to allow the user to enter a value that doesn't appear in the list of items.

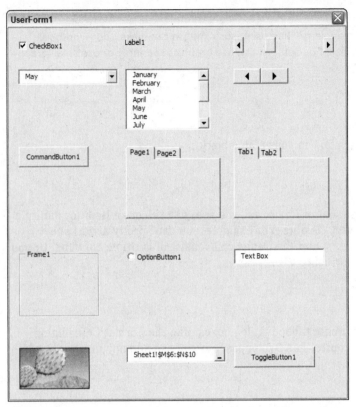

Figure 13-3: This UserForm has one of each of the 15 controls.

Part IV

CommandButton

Every dialog box that you create will probably have at least one CommandButton control. Usually, you'll want to have a CommandButton labeled OK and another labeled Cancel.

Frame

A Frame control is used to enclose other controls. You do this either for aesthetic purposes or to logically group a set of controls. A frame is particularly useful when the dialog box contains more than one set of OptionButton controls.

Image

An Image control is used to display a graphic image, which can come from a file or can be pasted from the Clipboard. You might want to use an Image control to display your company's logo in a dialog box. The graphics image is stored in the workbook. That way, if you distribute your workbook to someone else, you don't have to include a copy of the graphics file.

CAUTION
Some graphics files are very large, and using such images can make your workbook increase dramatically in size. For best results, use graphics sparingly or use small graphics files.

Label

A `Label` control simply displays text in your dialog box.

ListBox

The `ListBox` control presents a list of items, and the user can select an item (or multiple items). `ListBox` controls are very flexible. For example, you can specify a worksheet range that holds the ListBox items, and this range can consist of multiple columns. Or you can fill the ListBox with items by using VBA.

MultiPage

A `MultiPage` control lets you create tabbed dialog boxes, like the Format Cells dialog box. By default, a `MultiPage` control has two pages, but you can add any number of additional pages.

OptionButton

`OptionButton` controls are useful when the user needs to select one item from a small number of choices. OptionButtons are always used in groups of at least two. When one OptionButton is selected, the other OptionButtons in its group are deselected.

If your UserForm contains more than one set of OptionButtons, the OptionButtons in each set must share a unique `GroupName` property value. Otherwise, all OptionButtons become part of the same set. Alternatively, you can enclose the OptionButtons in a `Frame` control, which automatically groups the OptionButtons contained in the frame.

RefEdit

The `RefEdit` control is used when you need to let the user select a range in a worksheet.

ScrollBar

The `ScrollBar` control is similar to a `SpinButton` control. The difference is that the user can drag the ScrollBar button to change the control's value in larger increments. The `ScrollBar` control is most useful for selecting a value that extends across a wide range of possible values.

SpinButton

The SpinButton control lets the user select a value by clicking either of two arrows: one to increase the value and the other to decrease the value. A SpinButton is often used in conjunction with a TextBox control or Label control, which displays the current value of the SpinButton.

TabStrip

A TabStrip control is similar to a MultiPage control, but it's not as easy to use. A TabStrip control, unlike a MultiPage control, does not serve as a container for other objects. Generally, you'll find that the MultiPage control is much more versatile.

TextBox

A TextBox control lets the user input text.

ToggleButton

A ToggleButton control has two states: on and off. Clicking the button toggles between these two states, and the button changes its appearance. Its value is either True (pressed) or False (not pressed). I never use this control because I think a CheckBox is much clearer.

Using Controls on a Worksheet

Many of the UserForm controls can be embedded directly into a worksheet. These controls are accessible by using Excel's Developer ➪ Controls ➪ Insert command. Adding such controls to a worksheet requires much less effort than creating a UserForm. In addition, you may not have to create any macros because you can link a control to a worksheet cell. For example, if you insert a CheckBox control on a worksheet, you can link it to a particular cell by setting its LinkedCell property. When the CheckBox is checked, the linked cell displays TRUE. When the CheckBox is unchecked, the linked cell displays FALSE.

The accompanying figure shows a worksheet that contains some ActiveX controls. This workbook, named activex worksheet controls.xlsx, is available on the companion CD-ROM. The workbook uses linked cells and contains no macros.

continued

Part IV

continued

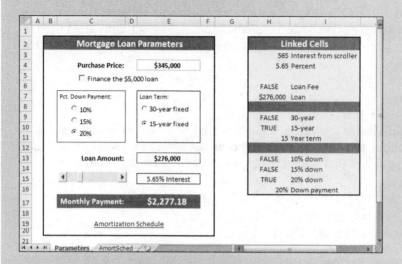

Adding controls to a worksheet can be a bit confusing because controls can come from two sources:

- *Form controls:* These controls are insertable objects.

- *ActiveX controls:* These controls are a subset of those that are available for use on UserForms.

You can use the controls from either of these sources, but it's important that you understand the distinctions between them. The Form controls work much differently than the ActiveX controls.

When you add an ActiveX control to a worksheet, Excel goes into *design mode*. In this mode, you can adjust the properties of any controls on your worksheet, add or edit event handler procedures for the control, or change its size or position. To display the Properties window for an ActiveX control, use the Developer ⇨ Controls ⇨ Properties command.

For simple buttons, I often use the `Button` control from the Form controls because it lets me attach any macro to it. If I use a `CommandButton` control from the ActiveX controls, clicking it will execute its event handler procedure (for example, `CommandButton1_Click`) in the code module for the `Sheet` object — you can't attach just any macro to it.

When Excel is in design mode, you can't try out the controls. To test the controls, you must exit design mode by clicking the Developer ⇨ Controls ⇨ Design mode button (which is a toggle).

Adjusting UserForm Controls

After a control is placed in a UserForm, you can move and resize the control by using standard mouse techniques.

TIP

You can select multiple controls by Shift-clicking or by clicking and dragging to lasso a group of controls.

A UserForm can contain vertical and horizontal grid lines (displayed as dots) that help you align the controls that you add. When you add or move a control, it *snaps* to the grid to help you line up the controls. If you don't like to see these grid lines, you can turn them off by choosing Tools ➪ Options in the VBE. In the Options dialog box, select the General tab and set your desired options in the Form Grid Settings section.

The Format menu in the VBE window provides several commands to help you precisely align and space the controls in a dialog box. Before you use these commands, select the controls that you want to work with. These commands work just as you would expect, so I don't explain them here. Figure 13-4 shows a dialog box with several `OptionButton` controls about to be aligned. Figure 13-5 shows the controls after being aligned and assigned equal vertical spacing.

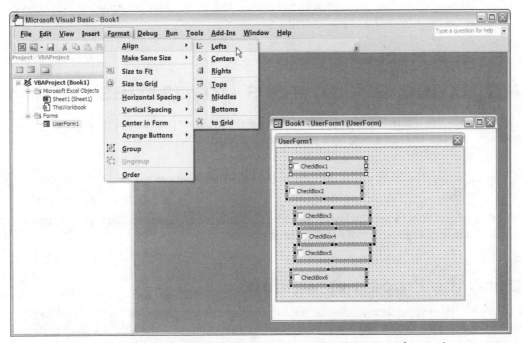

Figure 13-4: Use the Format ➪ Align command to change the alignment of controls.

Part IV

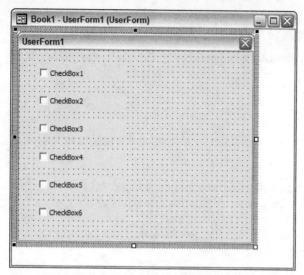

Figure 13-5: Six controls, aligned and evenly spaced.

TIP

When you select multiple controls, the last control that you select appears with white handles rather than the normal black handles. The control with the white handles is used as the basis for sizing or positioning.

Adjusting a Control's Properties

Every control has a number of properties that determine how the control looks and behaves. You can change a control's properties, as follows:

- *At design time* when you're developing the UserForm. You use the Properties window for this.

- *During runtime* when the UserForm is being displayed for the user. You use VBA instructions to change a control's properties at runtime.

Using the Properties window

In the VBE, the Properties window adjusts to display the properties of the selected item (which can be a control or the UserForm itself). In addition, you can select a control from the drop-down list at the top of the Properties window (see Figure 13-6).

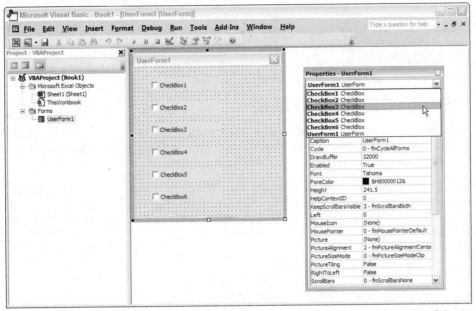

Figure 13-6: Selecting a control (CheckBox3) from the drop-down list at the top of the Properties window.

NOTE

The Properties window has two tabs. The Alphabetic tab displays the properties for the selected object in alphabetical order. The Categorized tab displays them grouped into logical categories. Both tabs contain the same properties but in a different order.

To change a property, just click it and specify the new property. Some properties can take on a finite number of values, selectable from a list. If so, the Properties window will display a button with a downward-pointing arrow. Click the button, and you'll be able to select the property's value from the list. For example, the `TextAlign` property can have any of the following values: `1 - fmTextAlignLeft`, `2 - fmTextAlignCenter`, or `3 - fmTextAlignRight`.

A few properties (for example, `Font` and `Picture`) display a small button with an ellipsis when selected. Click the button to display a dialog box associated with the property.

The `Image` control `Picture` property is worth mentioning because you can either select a graphic file that contains the image or paste an image from the Clipboard. When pasting an image, first copy it to the Clipboard; then select the `Picture` property for the `Image` control and press Ctrl+V to paste the Clipboard contents.

NOTE

If you select two or more controls at once, the Properties window displays only the properties that are common to the selected controls.

TIP

The UserForm itself has many properties that you can adjust. These properties are then used as defaults for controls that you add to the UserForm. For example, if you change the UserForm Font property, all controls added to the UserForm will use that font.

Common properties

Although each control has its own unique set of properties, many controls have some common properties. For example, every control has a Name property and properties that determine its size and position (Height, Width, Left, and Right).

If you're going to manipulate a control by using VBA, it's an excellent idea to provide a meaningful name for the control. For example, the first OptionButton that you add to a UserForm has a default name of OptionButton1. You refer to this object in your code with a statement such as the following:

```
OptionButton1.Value = True
```

But if you give the OptionButton a more meaningful name (such as obLandscape), you can use a statement such as this one:

```
obLandscape.Value = True
```

TIP

Many people find it helpful to use a name that also identifies the type of object. In the preceding example, I use ob as the prefix to identify the fact that this control is an OptionButton.

You can adjust the properties of several controls at once. For example, you might have several OptionButtons that you want left-aligned. You can simply select all the OptionButtons and then change the Left property in the Properties box. All the selected controls will then take on that new Left property value.

Learning more about properties

The best way to learn about the various properties for a control is to use the Help system. Simply click on a property in the Property window and press F1. Figure 13-7 shows an example of the type of help provided for a property.

Accommodating keyboard users

Many users prefer to navigate through a dialog box by using the keyboard: The Tab and Shift+Tab keystrokes cycle through the controls, and pressing a hot key (an underlined letter) operates the control. To make sure that your dialog box works properly for keyboard users, you must be mindful of two issues: tab order and accelerator keys.

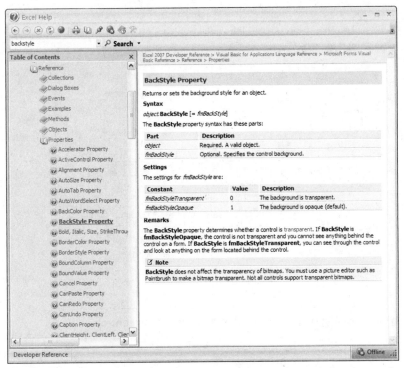

Figure 13-7: The Help system provides information about each property for every control.

CHANGING THE TAB ORDER OF CONTROLS

The *tab order* determines the sequence in which the controls are activated when the user presses Tab or Shift+Tab. It also determines which control has the initial *focus*. If a user is entering text into a `TextBox` control, for example, the TextBox has the focus. If the user clicks an OptionButton, the OptionButton has the focus. The control that's first in the tab order has the focus when a dialog box is first displayed.

To set the tab order of your controls, choose View ➪ Tab Order. You can also right-click the UserForm and choose Tab Order from the shortcut menu. In either case, Excel displays the Tab Order dialog box, as shown in Figure 13-8. The Tab Order dialog box lists all the controls, the sequence of which corresponds to the order in which controls pass the focus between each other in the UserForm. To move a control, select it and click the arrow keys up or down. You can choose more than one control (click while pressing Shift or Ctrl) and move them all at once.

Alternatively, you can set an individual control's position in the tab order via the Properties window. The first control in the tab order has a `TabIndex` property of 0. Changing the `TabIndex` property for a control may also affect the `TabIndex` property of other controls. These adjustments are made automatically to ensure that no control has a `TabIndex` greater than the number of controls. If you want to remove a control from the tab order, set its `TabStop` property to `False`.

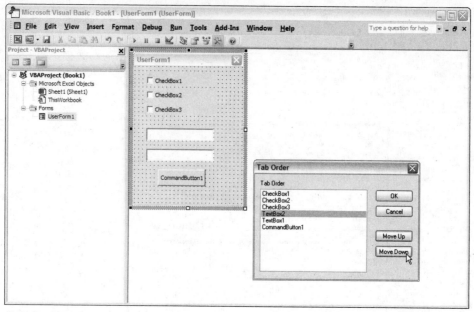

Figure 13-8: Use the Tab Order dialog box to specify the tab order of the controls.

NOTE

Some controls, such as `Frame` and `MultiPage`, act as containers for other controls. The controls inside a container have their own tab order. To set the tab order for a group of OptionButtons inside a `Frame` control, select the `Frame` control before you choose the View ⇨ Tab Order command.

SETTING HOT KEYS

You can assign an accelerator key, or hot key, to most dialog box controls. This allows the user to access the control by pressing Alt+ the hot key. Use the `Accelerator` property in the Properties window for this purpose.

TIP

Some controls, such as a `TextBox`, don't have an `Accelerator` property because they don't display a caption. You still can allow direct keyboard access to these controls by using a `Label` control. Assign an accelerator key to the Label and put it ahead of the TextBox in the tab order.

Testing a UserForm

You'll usually want to test your UserForm while you're developing it. There are three ways that you can test a UserForm without actually calling it from a VBA procedure:

- Choose the Run ⇨ Run Sub/UserForm command.
- Press F5.
- Click the Run Sub/UserForm button on the Standard toolbar.

These three techniques all trigger the UserForm's `Initialize` event. When a dialog box is displayed in this test mode, you can try out the tab order and the accelerator keys.

Displaying and Closing UserForms

In this section, I provide an overview of using VBA to work with UserForms.

Displaying a UserForm

To display a UserForm from VBA, you create a procedure that uses the `Show` method of the `UserForm` object. You cannot display a UserForm from Excel without using at least one line of VBA code. If your UserForm is named `UserForm1`, the following procedure displays the dialog box on that form:

```
Sub ShowForm()
    UserForm1.Show
End Sub
```

This procedure must be located in a standard VBA module and not in the code module for the UserForm.

When the UserForm is displayed, it remains visible onscreen until it is dismissed. Usually, you'll add a CommandButton to the UserForm that executes a procedure that dismisses the UserForm. The procedure can either unload the UserForm (with the `Unload` command) or hide the UserForm (with the `Hide` method of the `UserForm` object). This concept will become clearer as you work through various examples in this and subsequent chapters.

DISPLAYING A MODELESS USERFORM

By default, UserForms are displayed modally. This means that the UserForm must be dismissed before the user can do anything in the worksheet. You can also display a modeless UserForm. When a modeless UserForm is displayed, the user can continue working in Excel, and the UserForm remains visible. To display a modeless UserForm, use the following syntax:

```
UserForm1.Show vbModeless
```

Part IV

DISPLAYING A USERFORM BASED ON A VARIABLE

In some cases, you may have several UserForms, and your code makes a decision regarding which of them to display. If the name of the UserForm is stored as a string variable, you can use the Add method to add the UserForm to the UserForms collection and then use the Show method of the UserForms collection. Here's an example that assigns the name of a UserForm to the MyForm variable and then displays the UserForm.

```
MyForm = "UserForm1"
UserForms.Add(MyForm).Show
```

LOADING A USERFORM

VBA also has a Load statement. Loading a UserForm loads it into memory, but it is not visible until you use the Show method. To load a UserForm, use a statement like this:

```
Load UserForm1
```

If you have a complex UserForm, you might want to load it into memory before it is needed so that it will appear more quickly when you use the Show method. In the majority of situations, however, it's not necessary to use the Load statement.

Closing a UserForm

To close a UserForm, use the Unload command, as shown in this example:

```
Unload UserForm1
```

Or, if the code is located in the code module for the UserForm, you can use the following:

```
Unload Me
```

In this case, the keyword Me refers to the UserForm. Using Me rather than the UserForm's name eliminates the need to modify your code if you change the name of the UserForm.

Normally, your VBA code should include the Unload command after the UserForm has performed its actions. For example, your UserForm may have a CommandButton that serves as an OK button. Clicking this button executes a macro. One of the statements in the macro will unload the UserForm. The UserForm remains visible on the screen until the macro that contains the Unload statement finishes.

When a UserForm is unloaded, its controls are reset to their original values. In other words, your code will not be able to access the user's choices after the UserForm is unloaded. If the user's choice must be used later on (after the UserForm is unloaded), you need to store the value in a Public variable, declared in a standard VBA module. Or you could store the value in a worksheet cell.

NOTE

A UserForm is automatically unloaded when the user clicks the Close button (the X in the UserForm title bar). This action also triggers a UserForm `QueryClose` event, followed by a UserForm `Terminate` event.

UserForms also have a `Hide` method. When you invoke this method, the UserForm disappears, but it remains loaded in memory, so your code can still access the various properties of the controls. Here's an example of a statement that hides a UserForm:

```
UserForm1.Hide
```

Or, if the code is in the code module for the UserForm, you can use the following:

```
Me.Hide
```

If for some reason you would like your UserForm to disappear immediately while its macro is executing, use the `Hide` method at the top of the procedure. For example, in the following procedure, the UserForm disappears immediately when `CommandButton1` is clicked. The last statement in the procedure unloads the UserForm.

```
Private Sub CommandButton1_Click()
    Me.Hide
    For r = 1 To 10000
        Cells(r, 1) = r
    Next r
    Unload Me
End Sub
```

CROSS-REFERENCE

In Chapter 15, I describe how to display a progress indicator, which takes advantage of the fact that a UserForm remains visible while the macro executes.

About event handler procedures

After the UserForm is displayed, the user interacts with it — selecting an item from a ListBox, clicking a CommandButton, and so on. In official terminology, the user causes an *event* to occur. For example, clicking a CommandButton causes the `Click` event for the CommandButton. You need to write procedures that execute when these events occur. These procedures are sometimes known as *event handler* procedures.

NOTE

Event handler procedures must be located in the Code window for the UserForm. However, your event handler procedure can call another procedure that's located in a standard VBA module.

Part IV

Your VBA code can change the properties of the controls while the UserForm is displayed (that is, at runtime). For example, you could assign to a ListBox control a procedure that changes the text in a Label when an item is selected. This type of manipulation will become clearer later in this chapter.

Creating a UserForm: An Example

If you've never created a UserForm, you might want to walk through the example in this section. The example includes step-by-step instructions for creating a simple dialog box and developing a VBA procedure to support the dialog box.

This example uses a UserForm to obtain two pieces of information: a person's name and sex. The dialog box uses a TextBox control to get the name and three OptionButtons to get the sex (Male, Female, or Unknown). The information collected in the dialog box is then sent to the next blank row in a worksheet.

Creating the UserForm

Figure 13-9 shows the finished UserForm for this example. For best results, start with a new workbook with only one worksheet in it. Then follow these steps:

1. Press Alt+F11 to activate the VBE.

2. In the Project window, select the workbook's project and choose Insert ➪ UserForm to add an empty UserForm.

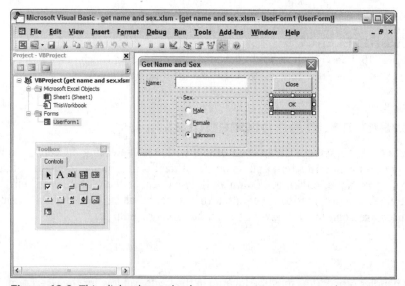

Figure 13-9: This dialog box asks the user to enter a name and a sex.

3. The UserForm's `Caption` property will have its default value: `UserForm1`. Use the Properties window to change the UserForm's `Caption` property to `Get Name and Sex`. (If the Properties window isn't visible, press F4.)

4. Add a `Label` control and adjust the properties as follows:

Property	Value
Accelerator	N
Caption	Name:
TabIndex	0

5. Add a `TextBox` control and adjust the properties as follows:

Property	Value
Name	TextName
TabIndex	1

6. Add a `Frame` control and adjust the properties as follows:

Property	Value
Caption	Sex
TabIndex	2

7. Add an `OptionButton` control inside the Frame and adjust the properties as follows:

Property	Value
Accelerator	M
Caption	Male
Name	OptionMale
TabIndex	0

Part IV

8. Add another `OptionButton` control inside the Frame and adjust the properties as follows:

Property	Value
Accelerator	F
Caption	Female
Name	OptionFemale
TabIndex	1

9. Add yet another `OptionButton` control inside the Frame and adjust the properties as follows:

Property	Value
Accelerator	U
Caption	Unknown
Name	OptionUnknown
TabIndex	2
Value	True

10. Add a `CommandButton` control *outside* the Frame and adjust the properties as follows:

Property	Value
Caption	OK
Default	True
Name	OKButton
TabIndex	3

11. Add another `CommandButton` control and adjust the properties as follow s:

Property	Value
Caption	Close
Cancel	True
Name	CloseButton
TabIndex	4

TIP

When you are creating several controls that are similar, you may find it easier to copy an existing control rather than create a new one. To copy a control, press Ctrl while you drag the control to make a new copy of it. Then adjust the properties on the copied control.

Writing code to display the dialog box

Next, you add an ActiveX CommandButton to the worksheet. This button will execute a procedure that displays the UserForm. Here's how:

1. Activate Excel. (Alt+F11 is the shortcut key combination.)

2. Choose Developer ⇨ Controls ⇨ Insert and click CommandButton from the ActiveX Controls section.

3. Drag in the worksheet to create the button.

If you like, you can change the caption for the worksheet CommandButton. To do so, right-click the button and choose CommandButton Object ⇨ Edit from the shortcut menu. You can then edit the text that appears on the CommandButton. To change other properties of the object, right-click and choose Properties. Then make the changes in the Properties box.

4. Double-click the CommandButton.

This activates the VBE. More specifically, the code module for the worksheet will be displayed, with an empty event handler procedure for the worksheet's CommandButton.

5. Enter a single statement in the `CommandButton1_Click` procedure (see Figure 13-10). This short procedure uses the `Show` method of an object (`UserForm1`) to display the UserForm.

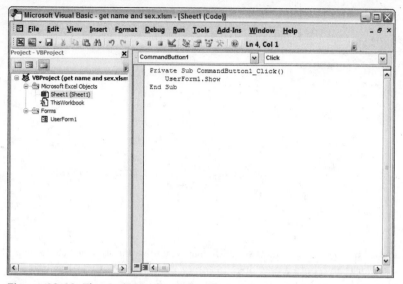

Figure 13-10: The CommandButton1_Click procedure is executed when the button on the worksheet is clicked.

Testing the dialog box

The next step is to try out the procedure that displays the dialog box.

NOTE

When you click the CommandButton on the worksheet, you'll find that nothing happens. Rather, the button is selected. That's because Excel is still in design mode — which happens automatically when you insert an ActiveX control. To exit design mode, click the Developer ⇨ Controls ⇨ Design Mode button. To make any changes to your CommandButton, you'll need to put Excel back into design mode.

When you exit design mode, clicking the button will display the UserForm (see Figure 13-11).

When the dialog box is displayed, enter some text into the text box and click OK. Nothing happens — which is understandable considering you haven't yet created any event handler procedures for the UserForm.

NOTE

Click the Close button in the UserForm title bar to get rid of the dialog box.

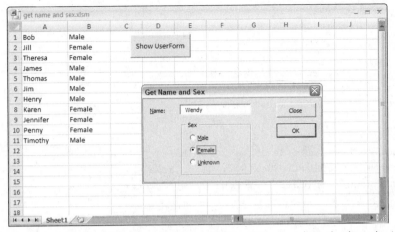

Figure 13-11: The CommandButton's Click event procedure displays the UserForm.

Adding event handler procedures

In this section, I explain how to write the procedures that will handle the events that occur when the UserForm is displayed. To continue the example, do the following:

1. Press Alt+F11 to activate the VBE.

2. Make sure the UserForm is displayed and double-click its Close button.

   This will activate the Code window for the UserForm and insert an empty procedure named `CloseButton_Click`. Notice that this procedure consists of the object's name, an underscore character, and the event that it handles.

3. Modify the procedure as follows. (This is the event handler for the `CloseButton`'s `Click` event.)

```
Private Sub CloseButton_Click()
    Unload UserForm1
End Sub
```

   This procedure, which is executed when the user clicks the Close button, simply unloads the UserForm.

4. Press Shift+F7 to redisplay `UserForm1` (or click the View Object icon at the top of the Project Explorer window).

5. Double-click the OK button and enter the following procedure. (This is the event handler for the `OKButton`'s `Click` event.)

```
Private Sub OKButton_Click()
    Dim NextRow As Long
'   Make sure Sheet1 is active
```

```
      Sheets("Sheet1").Activate

'     Determine the next empty row
      NextRow = _
        Application.WorksheetFunction.CountA(Range("A:A")) + 1
'     Transfer the name
      Cells(NextRow, 1) = TextName.Text

'     Transfer the sex
      If OptionMale Then Cells(NextRow, 2) = "Male"
      If OptionFemale Then Cells(NextRow, 2) = "Female"
      If OptionUnknown Then Cells(NextRow, 2) = "Unknown"

'     Clear the controls for the next entry
      TextName.Text = ""
      OptionUnknown = True
      TextName.SetFocus
  End Sub
```

6. Activate Excel and click the CommandButton again to display the UserForm. Run the procedure again.

You'll find that the UserForm controls now function correctly.

Here's how the OKButton_Click procedure works: First, the procedure makes sure that the proper worksheet (Sheet1) is active. It then uses Excel's COUNTA function to determine the next blank cell in column A. Next, it transfers the text from the TextBox control to column A. It then uses a series of If statements to determine which OptionButton was selected and writes the appropriate text (Male, Female, or Unknown) to column B. Finally, the dialog box is reset to make it ready for the next entry. Notice that clicking OK doesn't close the dialog box. To end data entry (and unload the UserForm), click the Close button.

Validating the data

Play around with this example some more, and you'll find that it has a small problem: It doesn't ensure that the user actually enters a name into the text box. To make sure the user enters a name, insert the following code in the OKButton_Click procedure, before the text is transferred to the worksheet. It ensures that the user enters a name (well, at least some text) in the TextBox. If the TextBox is empty, a message appears, and the focus is set to the TextBox so that the user can try again. The Exit Sub statement ends the procedure with no further action.

```
'   Make sure a name is entered
    If TextName.Text = "" Then
        MsgBox "You must enter a name."
        TextName.SetFocus
        Exit Sub
    End If
```

The finished dialog box

After making all these modifications, you'll find that the dialog box works flawlessly. (Don't forget to test the hot keys.) In real life, you'd probably need to collect more information than just name and sex. However, the same basic principles apply. You just need to deal with more UserForm controls.

CD-ROM

A workbook with this example is available on the companion CD-ROM in a file named get name and sex.xlsm.

Understanding UserForm Events

Each UserForm control (as well as the UserForm itself) is designed to respond to certain types of events, and these events can be triggered by a user or by Excel. For example, clicking a CommandButton generates a Click event for the CommandButton. You can write code that is executed when a particular event occurs.

Some actions generate multiple events. For example, clicking the upward arrow of a SpinButton control generates a SpinUp event and also a Change event. When a UserForm is displayed by using the Show method, Excel generates an Initialize event and an Activate event for the UserForm. (Actually, the Initialize event occurs when the UserForm is loaded into memory and before it is actually displayed.)

CROSS-REFERENCE

Excel also supports events associated with a Sheet object, Chart objects, and the ThisWorkbook object. I discuss these types of events in Chapter 18.

Learning about events

To find out which events are supported by a particular control, do the following:

1. Add a control to a UserForm.

2. Double-click the control to activate the code module for the UserForm. The VBE will insert an empty event handler procedure for the default event for the control.

3. Click the drop-down list in the upper-right corner of the module window, and you'll see a complete list of events for the control (see Figure 13-12).

4. Select an event from the list, and the VBE will create an empty event handler procedure for you.

Part IV

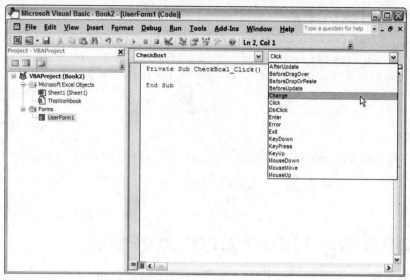

Figure 13-12: The event list for a CheckBox control.

NOTE

To find out specific details about an event, consult the Help system. The Help system also lists the events available for each control. When you locate an event for an object, make sure the Help system table of contents is displayed. Then you can see a list of all other events for the object.

CAUTION

Event handler procedures incorporate the name of the object in the procedure's name. Therefore, if you change the name of a control, you'll also need to make the appropriate changes to the control's event handler procedure(s). The name changes are not performed automatically! To make things easy on yourself, it's a good idea to provide names for your controls before you begin creating event handler procedures.

UserForm events

Several events are associated with showing and unloading a UserForm:

- `Initialize`: Occurs before a UserForm is loaded or shown but does not occur if the UserForm was previously hidden.

- `Activate`: Occurs when a UserForm is shown.

- `Deactivate`: Occurs when a UserForm is deactivated but does not occur if the form is hidden.

- QueryClose: Occurs before a UserForm is unloaded.

- Terminate: Occurs after the UserForm is unloaded.

NOTE

Often, it's critical that you choose the appropriate event for your event handler procedure and that you understand the order in which the events occur. Using the Show method invokes the Initialize and Activate events (in that order). Using the Load command invokes only the Initialize event. Using the Unload command triggers the QueryClose and Terminate events (in that order). Using the Hide method doesn't trigger either of these events.

CD-ROM

The companion CD-ROM contains a workbook (named userform events.xlsm) that monitors all these events and displays a message box when an event occurs. If you're confused about UserForm events, studying the code in this example should clear things up.

SpinButton events

To help clarify the concept of events, this section takes a close look at the events associated with a SpinButton control.

CD-ROM

The companion CD-ROM contains a workbook that demonstrates the sequence of events that occur for a SpinButton and the UserForm that contains it. The workbook, named spinbutton events.xlsm, contains a series of event-handler routines — one for each SpinButton and UserForm event. Each of these routines simply displays a message box that tells you the event that just fired.

Table 13-1 lists all the events for the SpinButton control.

TABLE 13-1 SPINBUTTON EVENTS

Event	Description
AfterUpdate	Occurs after the control is changed through the user interface.
BeforeDragOver	Occurs when a drag-and-drop operation is in progress.
BeforeDropOrPaste	Occurs when the user is about to drop or paste data onto the control.

continued

Part IV

TABLE 13-1   SPINBUTTON EVENTS *(continued)*

Event	Description
BeforeUpdate	Occurs before the control is changed.
Change	Occurs when the Value property changes.
Enter	Occurs before the control actually receives the focus from a control on the same UserForm.
Error	Occurs when the control detects an error and cannot return the error information to a calling program.
Exit	Occurs immediately before a control loses the focus to another control on the same form.
KeyDown	Occurs when the user presses a key and the object has the focus.
KeyPress	Occurs when the user presses any key that produces a typeable character.
KeyUp	Occurs when the user releases a key and the object has the focus.
SpinDown	Occurs when the user clicks the lower (or left) SpinButton arrow.
SpinUp	Occurs when the user clicks the upper (or right) SpinButton arrow.

A user can operate a SpinButton control by clicking it with the mouse or (if the control has the focus) by using the up-arrow and down-arrow keys.

MOUSE-INITIATED EVENTS

When the user clicks the upper SpinButton arrow, the following events occur in this precise order:

1. Enter (triggered only if the SpinButton did not already have the focus)
2. Change
3. SpinUp

KEYBOARD-INITIATED EVENTS

The user can also press Tab to set the focus to the SpinButton and then use the arrow keys to increment or decrement the control. If so, the following events occur (in this order):

1. Enter
2. KeyDown

3. Change

4. SpinUp (or SpinDown)

5. KeyUp

WHAT ABOUT CHANGES VIA CODE?

The SpinButton control can also be changed by VBA code — which also triggers the
appropriate event(s). For example, the following statement sets the SpinButton1 Value
property to 0 and also triggers the Change event for the SpinButton control — but only if
the SpinButton value was not already 0:

```
SpinButton1.Value = 0
```

You might think that you could disable events by setting the EnableEvents property of
the Application object to False. Unfortunately, this property applies only to events that
involve true Excel objects: Workbooks, Worksheets, and Charts.

Pairing a SpinButton with a TextBox

A SpinButton has a Value property, but this control doesn't have a caption in which to display its value. In many cases, however, you will want the user to see the SpinButton value.
And sometimes you'll want the user to be able to change the SpinButton value directly
instead of clicking the SpinButton repeatedly.

The solution is to pair a SpinButton with a TextBox, which enables the user to specify a
value either by typing it into the TextBox directly or by clicking the SpinButton to increment or decrement the value in the TextBox.

Figure 13-13 shows a simple example. The SpinButton's Min property is 1, and its Max
property is 100. Therefore, clicking the SpinButton's arrows will change its value to an
integer between 1 and 100.

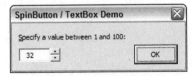

Figure 13-13: This SpinButton is paired with a TextBox.

CD-ROM

This workbook is available on the companion CD-ROM. The file is named spinbutton
and textbox.xlsm.

The code required to link a SpinButton with a TextBox is relatively simple. It's basically a matter of writing event handler procedures to ensure that the SpinButton's Value property is always in sync with the TextBox's Text property.

The following procedure is executed whenever the SpinButton's Change event is triggered. That is, the procedure is executed when the user clicks the SpinButton or changes its value by pressing the up arrow or down arrow.

```
Private Sub SpinButton1_Change()
    TextBox1.Text = SpinButton1.Value
End Sub
```

The procedure simply assigns the SpinButton's Value to the Text property of the TextBox control. Here, the controls have their default names (SpinButton1 and TextBox1). If the user enters a value directly into the TextBox, its Change event is triggered, and the following procedure is executed:

```
Private Sub TextBox1_Change()
    NewVal = Val(TextBox1.Text)
    If NewVal >= SpinButton1.Min And _
        NewVal <= SpinButton1.Max Then _
        SpinButton1.Value = NewVal
End Sub
```

This procedure starts by using VBA's Val function to convert the text in the TextBox to a value. (If the TextBox contains non-numeric text, the Val function returns 0.) The next statement determines whether the value is within the proper range for the SpinButton. If so, the SpinButton's Value property is set to the value entered in the TextBox.

The example is set up so that clicking the OK button (which is named OKButton) transfers the SpinButton's value to the active cell. The event handler for this CommandButton's Click event is as follows:

```
Private Sub OKButton_Click()
'   Enter the value into the active cell
    If CStr(SpinButton1.Value) = TextBox1.Text Then
        ActiveCell = SpinButton1.Value
        Unload Me
    Else
        MsgBox "Invalid entry.", vbCritical
        TextBox1.SetFocus
        TextBox1.SelStart = 0
        TextBox1.SelLength = Len(TextBox1.Text)
    End If
End Sub
```

About the Tag Property

Every UserForm and control has a `Tag` property. This property doesn't represent anything specific, and, by default, is empty. You can use the `Tag` property to store information for your own use.

For example, you might have a series of `TextBox` controls in a UserForm. The user may be required to enter text into some but not all of them. You can use the `Tag` property to identify (for your own use) which fields are required. In this case, you can set the `Tag` property to a string such as `Required`. Then when you write code to validate the user's entries, you can refer to the `Tag` property.

The following example is a function that examines all `TextBox` controls on `UserForm1` and returns the number of required `TextBox` controls that are empty:

```
Function EmptyCount()
  Dim ctl As Control
  EmptyCount= 0
  For Each ctl In UserForm1.Controls
    If TypeName(ctl) = "TextBox" Then
      If ctl.Tag = "Required" Then
        If ctl.Text = "" Then
          EmptyCount = EmptyCount + 1
        End If
      End If
    End If
  Next ctl
End Function
```

As you work with UserForms, you will probably think of other uses for the `Tag` property.

This procedure does one final check: It makes sure that the text entered in the TextBox matches the SpinButton's value. This is necessary in the case of an invalid entry. For example, if the user enters 3r into the TextBox, the SpinButton's value would not be changed, and the result placed in the active cell would not be what the user intended. Notice that the SpinButton's `Value` property is converted to a string by using the `CStr` function. This ensures that the comparison will not generate an error if a value is compared with text. If the SpinButton's value does not match the TextBox's contents, a message box is displayed. Notice that the focus is set to the `TextBox` object, and the contents are selected (by using the `SelStart` and `SelLength` properties). This makes it very easy for the user to correct the entry.

Referencing UserForm Controls

When working with controls on a UserForm, the VBA code is usually contained in the code window for the UserForm. You can also refer to UserForm controls from a general VBA module. To do so, you need to qualify the reference to the control by specifying the UserForm name. For example, consider the following procedure, which is located in a VBA module. It simply displays the UserForm named UserForm1.

```
Sub GetData()
    UserForm1.Show
End Sub
```

Assume that UserForm1 contains a text box (named TextBox1), and you want to provide a default value for the text box. You could modify the procedure as follows:

```
Sub GetData()
    UserForm1.TextBox1.Value = "John Doe"
    UserForm1.Show
End Sub
```

Understanding the Controls Collection

The controls on a UserForm make up a collection. For example, the following statement displays the number of controls on UserForm1:

```
MsgBox UserForm1.Controls.Count
```

VBA does *not* maintain a collection of each control type. For example, there is no collection of CommandButton controls. However, you can determine the type of control by using the TypeName function. The following procedure uses a For Each structure to loop through the Controls collection and then displays the number of CommandButton controls on UserForm1:

```
Sub CountButtons()
    Dim cbCount As Integer
    Dim ctl as Control
    cbCount = 0
    For Each ctl In UserForm1.Controls
        If TypeName(ctl) = "CommandButton" Then _
            cbCount = cbCount + 1
    Next ctl
    MsgBox cbCount
End Sub
```

Another way to set the default value is to take advantage of the UserForm's `Initialize` event. You can write code in the `UserForm_Initialize` procedure, which is located in the code module for the UserForm. Here's an example:

```
Private Sub UserForm_Initialize()
    TextBox1.Value = "John Doe"
End Sub
```

Notice that when the control is referenced in the code module for the UserForm, you don't need to qualify the references with the UserForm name. However, qualifying references to controls does have an advantage: You will then be able to take advantage of the Auto List Members feature, which lets you choose the control names from a drop-down list.

TIP

Rather than use the actual name of the UserForm, it is preferable to use `Me`. Then, if you change the name of the UserForm, you won't need to replace the references in your code.

Customizing the Toolbox

When a UserForm is active in the VBE, the Toolbox displays the controls that you can add to the UserForm. This section describes ways to customize the Toolbox.

Changing icons or tip text

If you would prefer a different icon or different tip text for a particular tool, right-click the toolbox control and select Customize *xxx* from the shortcut menu (where *xxx* is the control's name). This brings up a new dialog box that lets you change the ToolTip text, edit the icon, or load a new icon image from a file.

Adding new pages

The Toolbox initially contains a single tab. Right-click this tab and select New Page to add a new tab to the Toolbox. You can also change the text displayed on the tab by selecting Rename from the shortcut menu.

Customizing or combining controls

A very handy feature lets you customize a control and then save it for future use. You can, for instance, create a `CommandButton` control that's set up to serve as an OK button. For example, you can set the following properties: `Width`, `Height`, `Caption`, `Default`, and `Name`. Then drag the customized CommandButton to the Toolbox. This will create a new control. Right-click the new control to rename it or change its icon.

Part IV

You can also create a new Toolbox entry that consists of multiple controls. For example, you can create two CommandButtons that represent a UserForm's OK and Cancel buttons. Customize them as you want and then select them both and drag them to the Toolbox. In this case, you can use this new Toolbox control to add two customized buttons in one fell swoop.

This also works with controls that act as containers. For example, create a `Frame` control and add four customized OptionButtons, neatly spaced and aligned. Then drag the Frame to the Toolbox to create a customized `Frame` control.

TIP

You might want to place your customized controls on a separate page in the Toolbox. This lets you export the entire page so you can share it with other Excel users. To export a Toolbox page, right-click the tab and select Export Page.

CD-ROM

The companion CD-ROM contains a PAG file (named `newcontrols.pag`) that contains some customized controls. You can import this file as a new page in your Toolbox. Right-click a tab and select Import Page. Then locate the PAG file. Your Toolbox will resemble Figure 13-14. The new controls are: an exclamation point image, a "critical" red x image, a question mark image, an information image, an OK and Cancel button, a Frame with four OptionButton controls, a TextBox and a Spinner, and six CheckBox controls.

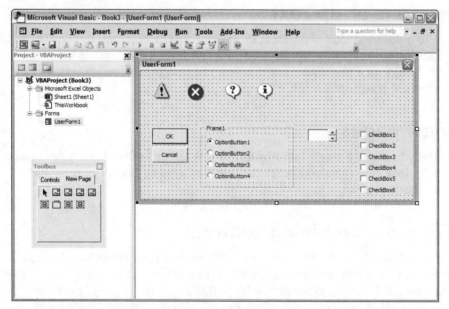

Figure 13-14: The Toolbox, with a new page of controls.

Adding new ActiveX controls

UserForms can use other ActiveX controls developed by Microsoft or other vendors. To add an additional ActiveX control to the Toolbox, right-click the Toolbox and select Additional Controls. This will display the dialog box shown in Figure 13-15.

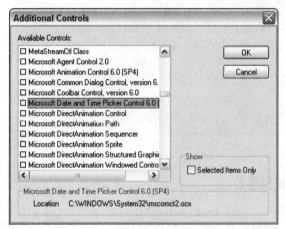

Figure 13-15: The Additional Controls dialog box lets you add other ActiveX controls.

The Additional Controls dialog box lists all ActiveX controls that are installed on your system. Select the control(s) that you want to add and then click OK to add an icon for each selected control.

CAUTION

Not all ActiveX controls that are installed on your system will work in Excel UserForms. In fact, most of them probably won't work. Also, some controls require a license in order to use them in an application. If you (or the users of your application) aren't licensed to use a particular control, an error will occur.

Creating UserForm Templates

You might find that when you design a new UserForm, you tend to add the same controls each time. For example, every UserForm might have two CommandButtons that serve as OK and Cancel buttons. In the previous section, I describe how to create a new control that combines these two (customized) buttons into a single control. Another option is to create your UserForm template and then export it so it can be imported into other projects. An advantage is that the event handler code for the controls is stored with the template.

Start by creating a UserForm that contains all the controls and customizations that you would need to reuse in other projects. Then make sure the UserForm is selected and choose File ⇨ Export File (or press Ctrl+E). You'll be prompted for a filename. Then, when you start your next project, choose File ⇨ Import File to load the saved UserForm.

Emulating Excel's Dialog Boxes

The look and feel of Windows dialog boxes differs from program to program. When developing applications for Excel, it's best to try to mimic Excel's dialog box style whenever possible.

In fact, a good way to learn how to create effective dialog boxes is to try to copy one of Excel's dialog boxes down to the smallest detail. For example, make sure that you get all the hot keys defined and be sure that the tab order is the same. To re-create one of Excel's dialog boxes, you need to test it under various circumstances and see how it behaves. I guarantee that your analysis of Excel's dialog boxes will improve your own dialog boxes.

You will find that it's impossible to duplicate some of Excel's dialog boxes.

A UserForm Checklist

Before you unleash a UserForm on end users, be sure that everything is working correctly. The following checklist should help you identify potential problems.

- Are similar controls the same size?
- Are the controls evenly spaced?
- Is the dialog box too overwhelming? If so, you may want to group the controls by using a MultiPage control.
- Can every control be accessed with a hot key?
- Are any of the hot keys duplicated?
- Is the tab order set correctly?
- Will your VBA code take appropriate action if the user presses Esc or clicks the Close button on the UserForm?
- Are there any misspellings in the text?
- Does the dialog box have an appropriate caption?
- Will the dialog box display properly at all video resolutions?
- Are the controls grouped logically (by function)?
- Do ScrollBar and SpinButton controls allow valid values only?
- Are ListBoxes set properly (Single, Multi, or Extended)? See Chapter 14 for details on ListBox controls.

Chapter 14

UserForm Examples

In This Chapter

This chapter presents many useful and informative examples that introduce you to some additional techniques that involve UserForms.

- ◆ Using a UserForm for a simple menu
- ◆ Selecting ranges from a UserForm
- ◆ Using a UserForm as a splash screen
- ◆ Changing the size of a UserForm while it's displayed
- ◆ Zooming and scrolling a sheet from a UserForm
- ◆ Understanding various techniques that involve a `ListBox` control
- ◆ Using an external control
- ◆ Using the `MultiPage` control
- ◆ Animating a `Label` control

You might be able to adapt these techniques to your own work. All the examples are available on the CD-ROM that accompanies this book.

 CROSS-REFERENCE

Chapter 15 contains additional examples of more advanced UserForm techniques.

Creating a UserForm "Menu"

Sometimes, you might want to use a UserForm as a type of menu. In other words, the UserForm presents some options, and the user makes a choice. This section presents two ways to do this: using CommandButtons or using a ListBox.

Using CommandButtons in a UserForm

Figure 14-1 shows an example of a UserForm that uses CommandButton controls as a simple menu. Setting up this sort of thing is very easy, and the code behind the UserForm is very straightforward. Each CommandButton has its own event handler procedure. For example, the following procedure is executed when CommandButton1 is clicked:

```
Private Sub CommandButton1_Click()
    Call Macro1
    Unload Me
End Sub
```

Figure 14-1: This dialog box uses CommandButtons as a menu.

This procedure simply calls Macro1 and closes the UserForm. The other buttons have similar event handler procedures.

Using a ListBox in a UserForm

Figure 14-2 shows another example that uses a ListBox as a menu. Before the UserForm is displayed, its Initialize event handler procedure is called. This procedure, which follows, uses the AddItem method to add six items to the ListBox:

```
Private Sub UserForm_Initialize()
    With ListBox1
        .AddItem "Macro1"
        .AddItem "Macro2"
        .AddItem "Macro3"
        .AddItem "Macro4"
        .AddItem "Macro5"
```

```
        .AddItem "Macro6"
    End With
End Sub
```

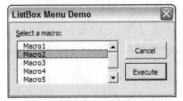

Figure 14-2: This dialog box uses a ListBox as a menu.

The Execute button also has a procedure to handle its `Click` event:

```
Private Sub ExecuteButton_Click()
    Select Case ListBox1.ListIndex
        Case -1
            MsgBox "Select a macro from the list."
            Exit Sub
        Case 0: Call Macro1
        Case 1: Call Macro2
        Case 2: Call Macro3
        Case 3: Call Macro4
        Case 4: Call Macro5
        Case 5: Call Macro6
    End Select
    Unload Me
End Sub
```

This procedure accesses the `ListIndex` property of the ListBox to determine which item is selected. The procedure uses a `Select Case` structure to execute the appropriate macro. If the `ListIndex` is –1, nothing is selected in the ListBox, and the user sees a message.

CD-ROM

The two examples in this section are available on the companion CD-ROM. The filename is `userform menus.xlsm`.

CROSS-REFERENCE

Chapter 15 shows a similar example in which you can use a UserForm to simulate a toolbar.

Part IV

Selecting Ranges from a UserForm

Many of Excel's built-in dialog boxes allow the user to specify a range. For example, the Goal Seek dialog box asks the user to select two single-cell ranges. The user can either type the range names directly or use the mouse to point and click in a sheet to make a range selection.

Your UserForms can also provide this type of functionality, thanks to the `RefEdit` control. The `RefEdit` control doesn't look exactly like the range selection control used in Excel's built-in dialog boxes, but it works in a similar manner. If the user clicks the small button on the right side of the control, the dialog box disappears temporarily, and a small range selector is displayed — which is exactly what happens with Excel's built-in dialog boxes.

NOTE

Unfortunately, the `RefEdit` control has a few quirks that still haven't been fixed. You'll find that this control does not allow the user to use shortcut range selection keys (for example, pressing End, followed by Shift+↓ will not select cells to the end of the column). In addition, after clicking the small button on the right side of the control (to temporarily hide the dialog box), you're limited to mouse selections only. The keyboard can't be used at all to make a selection.

Figure 14-3 shows a UserForm that contains a `RefEdit` control. This dialog box enables the user to perform a simple mathematical operation on all nonformula (and non-empty) cells in the selected range. The operation that's performed corresponds to the selected OptionButton.

CD-ROM

This example is available on the companion CD-ROM in a file named `range selection demo.xlsm`.

	A	B	C	D	E	F	G	H	I	J	K
1	-91	-43	92	-60	-73	76					
2	-26	49	53	29	-9	-53					
3	38	11	58	10	3	18					
4	45	12	-23	-14	-41	-22					
5	-85	-51	-94	-76	93	-25					
6	72	93	55	-90	63	34					
7	81	23	-76	-89	-97	72					
8	47	63	-74	42	87	47					
9	46	83	-17	77	-69	-62					
10	-84	-62	-10	55	-79	32					
11	16	15	-81	58	-6	-51	77				
12	-42	36	29	30	-55	-24	-21				
13	69	-54	89	-40	29	-77	-96				
14	-71	93	-12	-10	-75	-37	32				
15	18	-24	26	-34	52	-97	19				
16	-4	89	-94	-57	41	-64	66				
17											
18											

Range Selection Demo

Select the range to modify:
Sheet1!$B$3:$E$9

Operation
• Add   ○ Multiply
○ Subtract   ○ Divide

Operand:

Cancel
OK

H ◄ ► H   Sheet1   Sheet2

Figure 14-3: The RefEdit control shown here allows the user to select a range.

Following are a few things to keep in mind when using a RefEdit control:

- The RefEdit control returns a text string that represents a range address. You can convert this string to a Range object by using a statement such as

```
Set UserRange = Range(RefEdit1.Text)
```

- It's a good practice to initialize the RefEdit control to display the current range selection. You can do so in the UserForm_Initialize procedure by using a statement such as

```
RefEdit1.Text = ActiveWindow.RangeSelection.Address
```

- For best results, do not put a RefEdit control inside of a Frame or a MultiPage control. Doing so may cause Excel to crash.

- Don't assume that RefEdit will always return a valid range address. Pointing to a range isn't the only way to get text into this control. The user can type any text and can also edit or delete the displayed text. Therefore, you need to make sure that the range is valid. The following code is an example of a way to check for a valid range. If an invalid range is detected, the user is given a message, and focus is set to the RefEdit control so the user can try again.

```
On Error Resume Next
Set UserRange = Range(RefEdit1.Text)
If Err.Number <> 0 Then
    MsgBox "Invalid range selected"
    RefEdit1.SetFocus
    Exit Sub
End If
On Error GoTo 0
```

- The user can also click the worksheet tabs while selecting a range with the RefEdit control. Therefore, you can't assume that the selection is on the active sheet. However, if a different sheet is selected, the range address is preceded by a sheet name. For example:

```
Sheet2!$A$1:$C$4
```

- If you need to get a single cell selection from the user, you can pick out the upper-left cell of a selected range by using a statement such as

```
Set OneCell = Range(RefEdit1.Text).Range("A1")
```

CROSS-REFERENCE

As I discuss in Chapter 12, you can also use Excel's InputBox method to allow the user to select a range.

Creating a Splash Screen

Some developers like to display some introductory information when the application is opened. This is commonly known as a *splash screen*. You are undoubtedly familiar with Excel's splash screen, which appears for a few seconds when Excel is loading.

You can create a splash screen for your Excel application with a UserForm. This example is essentially a UserForm that displays automatically and then dismisses itself after five seconds.

CD-ROM

The companion CD-ROM contains a workbook that demonstrates this procedure. The file is named splash screen.xlsm.

Follow these instructions to create a splash screen for your project:

1. Create your workbook.

2. Activate the Visual Basic Editor (VBE) and insert a new UserForm into the project. The code in this example assumes that this form is named UserForm1.

3. Place any controls that you like on UserForm1. For example, you may want to insert an Image control that has your company's logo. Figure 14-4 shows an example.

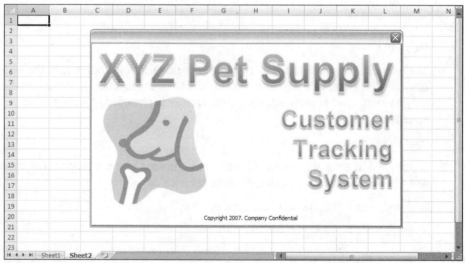

Figure 14-4: This splash screen is displayed briefly when the workbook is opened.

4. Insert the following procedure into the code module for the ThisWorkbook object:

```
Private Sub Workbook_Open()
    UserForm1.Show
End Sub
```

5. Insert the following procedure into the code module for `UserForm1`. For something other than a five-second delay, change the argument for the `TimeValue` function.

```
Private Sub UserForm_Activate()
    Application.OnTime Now + _
        TimeValue("00:00:05"), "KillTheForm"
End Sub
```

6. Insert the following procedure into a general VBA module:

```
Private Sub KillTheForm()
    Unload UserForm1
End Sub
```

When the workbook is opened, the `Workbook_Open` procedure is executed. The procedure in Step 4 displays the UserForm. At that time, the UserForm's `Activate` event occurs, which triggers the `UserForm_Activate` procedure (see Step 5). This procedure uses the `OnTime` method of the `Application` object to execute a procedure named `KillTheForm` at a particular time. In this case, the time is five seconds after the activation event. The `KillTheForm` procedure simply unloads the UserForm.

7. As an option, you can add a small CommandButton named `CancelButton`, set its `Cancel` property to `True`, and insert the following event handler procedure in the UserForm's code module:

```
Private Sub CancelButton_Click()
    KillTheForm
End Sub
```

Doing so lets the user cancel the splash screen before the time has expired by pressing Esc. You can even place this small button behind another object so it won't be visible.

CAUTION

Keep in mind that the splash screen is not displayed until the workbook is entirely loaded. In other words, if you would like to display the splash screen to give the user something to look at while the workbook is loading, this technique won't fill the bill.

TIP

If your application needs to run some VBA procedures at startup, you can display the UserForm modeless so that the code will continue running while the UserForm is displayed. To do so, change the `Workbook_Open` procedure as follows:

```
Private Sub Workbook_Open()
    UserForm1.Show vbModeless
    ' other code goes here
End Sub
```

Disabling a UserForm's Close Button

When a UserForm is displayed, clicking the Close button (the X in the upper-right corner) will unload the form. You might have a situation in which you don't want this to happen. For example, you might require that the UserForm be closed only by clicking a particular CommandButton.

Although you can't actually disable the Close button, you can prevent the user from closing a UserForm by clicking it. You can do so by monitoring the UserForm's QueryClose event.

The following procedure, which is located in the code module for the UserForm, is executed before the form is closed (that is, when the QueryClose event occurs):

```
Private Sub UserForm_QueryClose _
   (Cancel As Integer, CloseMode As Integer)
    If CloseMode = vbFormControlMenu Then
        MsgBox "Click the OK button to close the form."
        Cancel = True
    End If
End Sub
```

The UserForm_QueryClose procedure uses two arguments. The CloseMode argument contains a value that indicates the cause of the QueryClose event. If CloseMode is equal to vbFormControlMenu (a built-in constant), that means that the user clicked the Close button. If a message is displayed, the Cancel argument is set to True, and the form is not actually closed.

CD-ROM

The example in this section is available on the companion CD-ROM in a file named queryclose demo.xlsm.

NOTE

Keep in mind that a user can press Ctrl+Break to break out of the macro. In this example, pressing Ctrl+Break while the UserForm is displayed causes the UserForm to be dismissed. To prevent this from happening, execute the following statement prior to displaying the UserForm:

```
Application.EnableCancelKey = xlDisabled
```

Make sure that your application is debugged before you add this statement. Otherwise, you'll find that it's impossible to break out of an accidental endless loop.

Changing a UserForm's Size

Many applications use dialog boxes that change their own size. For example, Excel's Find and Replace dialog box (displayed when you choose Home ⇨ Editing ⇨ Find & Select ⇨ Replace) increases its height when the user clicks the Options button.

The example in this section demonstrates how to get a UserForm to change its size dynamically. Changing a dialog box's size is done by altering the Width or Height property of the UserForm object.

CROSS-REFERENCE

Refer to Chapter 15 for an example that allows the user to change the UserForm's size by dragging the lower-right corner.

Figure 14-5 shows the dialog box as it is first displayed, and Figure 14-6 shows it after the user clicks the Options button. Notice that the button's caption changes, depending on the size of the UserForm.

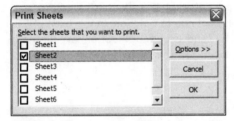

Figure 14-5: A sample dialog box in its standard mode.

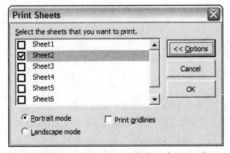

Figure 14-6: The same dialog box enlarged to show some options.

While you're creating the UserForm, set it to its largest size to enable you to work with the controls. Then use the UserForm_Initialize procedure to set it to its default (smaller) size.

Part IV

This example displays a list of worksheets in the active workbook and lets the user select which sheets to print. Following is the event handler that's executed when the CommandButton named OptionsButton is clicked:

```
Private Sub OptionsButton_Click()
    If OptionsButton.Caption = "Options >>" Then
        Me.Height = 164
        OptionsButton.Caption = "<< Options"
    Else
        Me.Height = 128
        OptionsButton.Caption = "Options >>"
    End If
End Sub
```

This procedure examines the Caption of the CommandButton and sets the UserForm's Height property accordingly.

 NOTE

When controls are not displayed because they are outside the visible portion of the UserForm, the accelerator keys for such controls continue to function. In this example, the user can press the Alt+L hot key (to select the Landscape mode option) even if that option is not visible. To block access to nondisplayed controls, you can write code to disable the controls when they are not displayed.

 CD-ROM

The example in this section is available on the companion CD-ROM. The file is named change userform size.xlsm.

Zooming and Scrolling a Sheet from a UserForm

The example in this section demonstrates how to use ScrollBar controls to allow sheet scrolling and zooming while a dialog box is displayed. Figure 14-7 shows how the example dialog box is set up. When the UserForm is displayed, the user can adjust the worksheet's zoom factor (from 10% to 400%) by using the ScrollBar at the top. The two ScrollBars in the bottom section of the dialog box allow the user to scroll the worksheet horizontally and vertically.

 CD-ROM

This example, named zoom and scroll sheet.xlsm, is available on the companion CD-ROM.

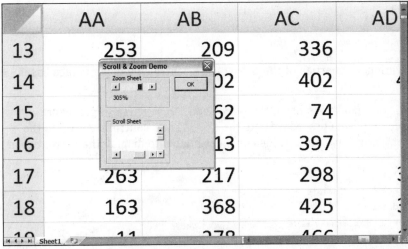

Figure 14-7: Here, ScrollBar controls allow zooming and scrolling of the worksheet.

If you look at the code for this example, you'll see that it's remarkably simple. The controls are initialized in the UserForm_Initialize procedure, which follows:

```
Private Sub UserForm_Initialize()
    LabelZoom.Caption = ActiveWindow.Zoom & "%"
'   Zoom
    With ScrollBarZoom
        .Min = 10
        .Max = 400
        .SmallChange = 1
        .LargeChange = 10
        .Value = ActiveWindow.Zoom
    End With

'   Horizontally scrolling
    With ScrollBarColumns
        .Min = 1
        .Max = ActiveSheet.UsedRange.Columns.Count
        .Value = ActiveWindow.ScrollColumn
        .LargeChange = 25
        .SmallChange = 1
    End With

'   Vertically scrolling
    With ScrollBarRows
        .Min = 1
        .Max = ActiveSheet.UsedRange.Rows.Count
        .Value = ActiveWindow.ScrollRow
        .LargeChange = 25
```

```
        .SmallChange = 1
    End With
End Sub
```

This procedure sets various properties of the ScrollBar controls by using values based on the active window.

When the ScrollBarZoom control is used, the ScrollBarZoom_Change procedure (which follows) is executed. This procedure sets the ScrollBar control's Value to the ActiveWindow's Zoom property value. It also changes a label to display the current zoom factor.

```
Private Sub ScrollBarZoom_Change()
    With ActiveWindow
        .Zoom = ScrollBarZoom.Value
        LabelZoom = .Zoom & "%"
    End With
End Sub
```

Worksheet scrolling is accomplished by the two procedures that follow. These procedures set the ScrollRow or ScrollColumns property of the ActiveWindow object equal to the appropriate ScrollBar control value.

```
Private Sub ScrollBarColumns_Change()
    ActiveWindow.ScrollColumn = ScrollBarColumns.Value
End Sub
```

```
Private Sub ScrollBarRows_Change()
    ActiveWindow.ScrollRow = ScrollBarRows.Value
End Sub
```

TIP

Rather than use the Change event in the preceding procedures, you can use the Scroll event. The difference is that the event is triggered when the ScrollBars are dragged — resulting in smooth zooming and scrolling. To use the Scroll event, just make the Change part of the procedure name Scroll.

ListBox Techniques

The ListBox control is extremely versatile, but it can be a bit tricky to work with. This section contains of a number of simple examples that demonstrate common techniques that involve the ListBox control.

NOTE

In most cases, the techniques described in this section also work with a `ComboBox` control.

About the ListBox control

Following are a few points to keep in mind when working with `ListBox` controls. Examples in the sections that follow demonstrate many of these points:

- The items in a ListBox can be retrieved from a range of cells (specified by the `RowSource` property), or they can be added by using VBA code (using the `AddItem` method).

- A ListBox can be set up to allow a single selection or a multiple selection. This is determined by the `MultiSelect` property.

- If a ListBox is not set up for a multiple selection, the value of the ListBox can be linked to a worksheet cell by using the `ControlSource` property.

- It's possible to display a ListBox with no items selected (the `ListIndex` property will be −1). However, after an item is selected, the user cannot deselect all items. The exception to this is if the `MultiSelect` property is `True`.

- A ListBox can contain multiple columns (controlled by the `ColumnCount` property) and even a descriptive header (controlled by the `ColumnHeads` property).

- The vertical height of a ListBox displayed in a UserForm window isn't always the same as the vertical height when the UserForm is actually displayed.

- The items in a ListBox can be displayed either as check boxes (if multiple selection is allowed) or as option buttons (if a single selection is allowed). This is controlled by the `ListStyle` property.

For complete details on the properties and methods for a `ListBox` control, consult the Help system.

Adding items to a ListBox control

Before displaying a UserForm that uses a `ListBox` control, you'll probably need to fill the ListBox with items. You can fill a ListBox at design time using items stored in a worksheet range or at runtime using VBA to add the items to the ListBox.

The two examples in this section presume that

- You have a UserForm named `UserForm1`.

- This UserForm contains a `ListBox` control named `ListBox1`.

- The workbook contains a sheet named `Sheet1`, and range A1:A12 contains the items to be displayed in the ListBox.

ADDING ITEMS TO A LISTBOX AT DESIGN TIME

To add items to a ListBox at design time, the ListBox items must be stored in a worksheet range. Use the RowSource property to specify the range that contains the ListBox items. Figure 14-8 shows the Properties window for a ListBox control. The RowSource property is set to Sheet1!A1:A12. When the UserForm is displayed, the ListBox will contain the 12 items in this range. The items appear in the ListBox at design time as soon as you specify the range for the RowSource property.

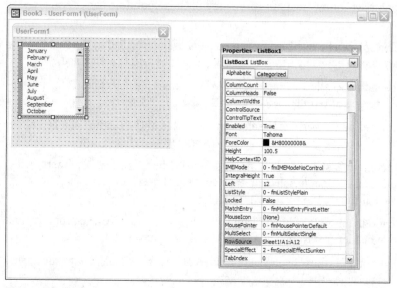

Figure 14-8: Setting the RowSource property at design time.

 CAUTION

In most cases, you'll want to include the worksheet name when you specify the RowSource property; otherwise, the ListBox will use the specified range on the active worksheet. In some cases, you might need to fully qualify the range by including the workbook name. For example:

```
[budget.xlsx]Sheet1!A1:A12
```

A better practice is to define a name for the range and use that name in your code. This will ensure that the proper range is used even if rows above the range are added or deleted.

ADDING ITEMS TO A LISTBOX AT RUNTIME

To add ListBox items at runtime, you have two choices:

- Set the RowSource property to a range address by using code.

- Write code that uses the AddItem method to add the ListBox items.

As you might expect, you can set the RowSource property via code rather than with the Properties window. For example, the following procedure sets the RowSource property for a ListBox before displaying the UserForm. In this case, the items consist of the cell entries in a range named Categories on the Budget worksheet.

```
UserForm1.ListBox1.RowSource = "Budget!Categories"
UserForm1.Show
```

If the ListBox items are not contained in a worksheet range, you can write VBA code to fill the ListBox before the dialog box appears. The following procedure fills the ListBox with the names of the months by using the AddItem method.

```
Sub ShowUserForm2()
'    Fill the list box
    With UserForm2.ListBox1
        .RowSource=""
        .AddItem "January"
        .AddItem "February"
        .AddItem "March"
        .AddItem "April"
        .AddItem "May"
        .AddItem "June"
        .AddItem "July"
        .AddItem "August"
        .AddItem "September"
        .AddItem "October"
        .AddItem "November"
        .AddItem "December"
    End With
    UserForm2.Show
End Sub
```

CAUTION

In the preceding code, notice that I set the RowSource property to an empty string. This is to avoid a potential error that occurs if the Properties window has a nonempty RowSource setting. If you try to add items to a ListBox that has a non-null RowSource setting, you'll get a "permission denied" error.

You can also use the AddItem method to retrieve ListBox items from a range. Here's an example that fills a ListBox with the contents of A1:A12 on Sheet1.

```
For Row = 1 To 12
  UserForm1.ListBox1.AddItem Sheets("Sheet1").Cells(Row, 1)
Next Row
```

Using the `List` property is even simpler. The statement that follows has the same effect as the preceding `For Next` loop.

```
UserForm1.ListBox1.List = Application.Transpose(Sheets("Sheet1").Range("A1:A12"))
```

Note that I used the `Transpose` function because the `List` property expects a horizontal array and the range is in a column rather than a row.

You can also use the `List` property if your data is stored in a one-dimensional array. For example, assume that you have an array named `MyList` that contains 50 elements. The following statement will create a 50-item list in `ListBox1`:

```
UserForm1.ListBox1.List = MyList
```

CD-ROM

The examples in this section are available on the companion CD-ROM. The file is named `fill listbox.xlsm`.

ADDING ONLY UNIQUE ITEMS TO A LISTBOX

In some cases, you might need to fill a ListBox with *unique* (nonduplicated) items from a list. For example, assume you have a worksheet that contains customer data. One of the columns might contain the state (see Figure 14-9). You would like to fill a ListBox with the state name of your customers, but you don't want to include duplicate state names.

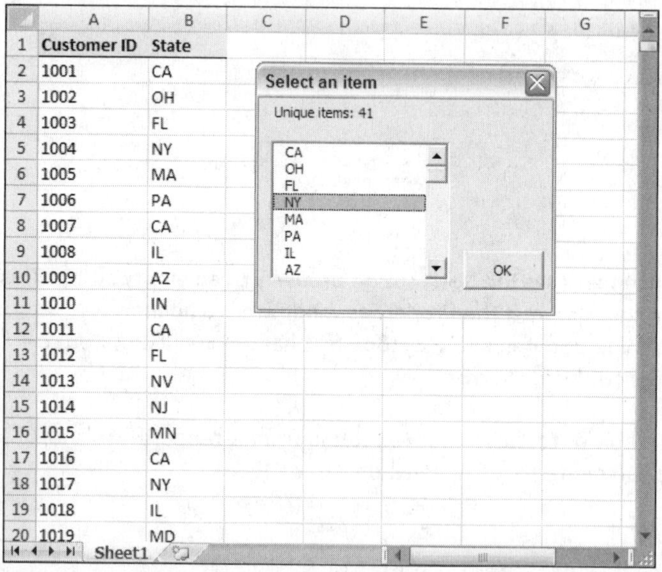

	A	B	C	D	E	F	G
1	Customer ID	State					
2	1001	CA					
3	1002	OH					
4	1003	FL					
5	1004	NY					
6	1005	MA					
7	1006	PA					
8	1007	CA					
9	1008	IL					
10	1009	AZ					
11	1010	IN					
12	1011	CA					
13	1012	FL					
14	1013	NV					
15	1014	NJ					
16	1015	MN					
17	1016	CA					
18	1017	NY					
19	1018	IL					
20	1019	MD					

Select an item

Unique items: 41

CA
OH
FL
NY
MA
PA
IL
AZ

OK

Sheet1

Figure 14-9: A Collection object is used to fill a ListBox with the unique items from column B.

One technique involves using a `Collection` object. You can add items to a `Collection` object with the following syntax:

```
object.Add item, key, before, after
```

The `key` argument, if used, must be a unique text string that specifies a separate key that can be used to access a member of the collection. The important word here is *unique.* If you attempt to add a non-unique key to a collection, an error occurs, and the item is not added. You can take advantage of this situation and use it to create a collection that consists only of unique items.

The following procedure starts by declaring a new `Collection` object named `NoDupes`. It assumes that a range named `Data` contains a list of items, some of which may be duplicated.

The code loops through the cells in the range and attempts to add the cell's value to the `NoDupes` collection. It also uses the cell's value (converted to a string) for the key argument. Using the `On Error Resume Next` statement causes VBA to ignore the error that occurs if the key is not unique. When an error occurs, the item is not added to the collection — which is just what you want. The procedure then transfers the items in the `NoDupes` collection to the ListBox. The UserForm also contains a label that displays the number of unique items.

```vba
Sub RemoveDuplicates1()
    Dim AllCells As Range, Cell As Range
    Dim NoDupes As New Collection

    On Error Resume Next
    For Each Cell In Range("State")
        NoDupes.Add Cell.Value, CStr(Cell.Value)
    Next Cell
    On Error GoTo 0

'   Add the non-duplicated items to a ListBox
    For Each Item In NoDupes
        UserForm1.ListBox1.AddItem Item
    Next Item

'   Display the count
    UserForm1.Label1.Caption = _
      "Unique items: " & NoDupes.Count

'   Show the UserForm
    UserForm1.Show
End Sub
```

CD-ROM

This example, named `listbox unique items1.xlsm`, is available on the companion CD-ROM. A workbook named `listbox unique items2.xlsm` has a slightly more sophisticated version of this technique and displays the items sorted.

Determining the selected item

The examples in preceding sections merely display a UserForm with a ListBox filled with various items. These procedures omit a key point: how to determine which item or items were selected by the user.

NOTE

This discussion assumes a single-selection `ListBox` object — one whose `MultiSelect` property is set to 0.

To determine which item was selected, access the ListBox's `Value` property. The statement that follows, for example, displays the text of the selected item in `ListBox1`.

```
MsgBox ListBox1.Value
```

If no item is selected, this statement will generate an error.

If you need to know the position of the selected item in the list (rather than the content of that item), you can access the ListBox's `ListIndex` property. The following example uses a message box to display the item number of the selected ListBox item:

```
MsgBox "You selected item #" & ListBox1.ListIndex
```

If no item is selected, the `ListIndex` property will return –1.

NOTE

The numbering of items in a ListBox begins with 0 — not 1. Therefore, the `ListIndex` of the first item is 0, and the `ListIndex` of the last item is equivalent to the value of the `ListCount` property less 1.

Determining multiple selections in a ListBox

A ListBox's `MultiSelect` property can be any of three values:

- 0 (`fmMultiSelectSingle`): Only one item can be selected. This is the default setting.
- 1 (`fmMultiSelectMulti`): Pressing the Space key or clicking selects or deselects an item in the list.

- 2 (`fmMultiSelectExtended`): Shift-clicking extends the selection from the previously selected item to the current item. You can also use Shift and one of the arrow keys to extend the selected items.

If the ListBox allows multiple selections (that is, if its `MultiSelect` property is either 1 or 2), trying to access the `ListIndex` or `Value` properties will result in an error. Instead, you need to use the `Selected` property, which returns an array whose first item has an index of 0. For example, the following statement displays `True` if the first item in the ListBox list is selected:

```
MsgBox ListBox1.Selected(0)
```

CD-ROM

The companion CD-ROM contains a workbook that demonstrates how to identify the selected item(s) in a ListBox. It works for single-selection and multiple-selection ListBoxes. The file is named `listbox selected items.xlsm`.

The following code, from the example workbook on the CD-ROM, loops through each item in the ListBox. If the item was selected, it appends the item's text to a variable called `Msg`. Finally, the names of all the selected items are displayed in a message box.

```
Private Sub OKButton_Click()
    Msg = ""
    For i = 0 To ListBox1.ListCount - 1
        If ListBox1.Selected(i) Then _
            Msg = Msg & ListBox1.List(i) & vbCrLf
    Next i
    MsgBox "You selected: " & vbCrLf & Msg
    Unload Me
End Sub
```

Figure 14-10 shows the result when multiple ListBox items are selected.

Multiple lists in a single ListBox

This example demonstrates how to create a ListBox in which the contents change depending on the user's selection from a group of OptionButtons.

Figure 14-11 shows the sample UserForm. The ListBox gets its items from a worksheet range. The procedures that handle the `Click` event for the `OptionButton` controls simply set the ListBox's `RowSource` property to a different range. One of these procedures follows:

```
Private Sub obMonths_Click()
    ListBox1.RowSource = "Sheet1!Months"
End Sub
```

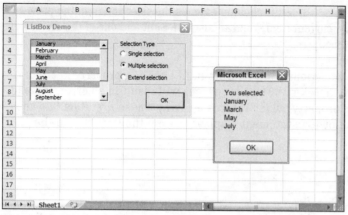

Figure 14-10: This message box displays a list of items selected in a ListBox.

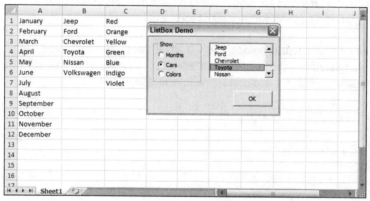

Figure 14-11: The contents of this ListBox depend on the OptionButton selected.

Clicking the OptionButton named obMonths changes the RowSource property of the ListBox to use a range named Months on Sheet1.

CD-ROM

This example, named listbox multiple lists.xlsm, is available on the companion CD-ROM.

ListBox item transfer

Some applications require a user to select several items from a list. It's often useful to create a new list of the selected items and display the new list in another ListBox. For an example of this situation, check out the Customization tab of the Excel Options dialog box.

Figure 14-12 shows a dialog box with two ListBoxes. The Add button adds the item selected in the left ListBox to the right ListBox. The Delete button removes the selected item from the list on the right. A check box determines the behavior when a duplicate item is added to the list: Namely, if the Allow Duplicates check box is not marked, a message box appears if the user attempts to add an item that's already on the list.

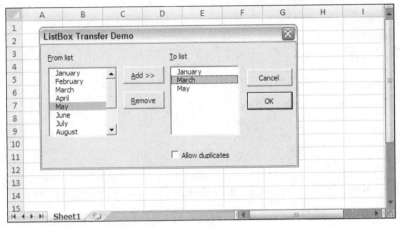

Figure 14-12: Building a list from another list.

The code for this example is relatively simple. Here's the procedure that is executed when the user clicks the Add button:

```
Private Sub AddButton_Click()
    If ListBox1.ListIndex = -1 Then Exit Sub
    If Not cbDuplicates Then
'       See if item already exists
        For i = 0 To ListBox2.ListCount - 1
            If ListBox1.Value = ListBox2.List(i) Then
                Beep
                Exit Sub
            End If
        Next i
    End If
    ListBox2.AddItem ListBox1.Value
End Sub
```

The code for the Remove button is even simpler:

```
Private Sub RemoveButton_Click()
    If ListBox2.ListIndex = -1 Then Exit Sub
    ListBox2.RemoveItem ListBox2.ListIndex
End Sub
```

Notice that both of these routines check to make sure that an item is actually selected. If the ListBox's `ListIndex` property is –1, no items are selected, and the procedure ends.

This example has two additional procedures that control whether the Remove button is enabled or disabled. These events are triggered when the `ListBox` is entered (either via a keystroke or a mouse click). The net effect is that the Remove button is enabled only when the user is working in `ListBox2`.

```
Private Sub ListBox1_Enter()
    RemoveButton.Enabled = False
End Sub

Private Sub ListBox2_Enter()
    RemoveButton.Enabled = True
End Sub
```

 CD-ROM

This example, named `listbox item transfer.xlsm`, is available on the companion CD-ROM.

Moving items in a ListBox

Often, the order of items in a list is important. The example in this section demonstrates how to allow the user to move items up or down in a ListBox. The VBE uses this type of technique to let you control the tab order of the items in a UserForm (right-click a UserForm and choose Tab Order from the shortcut menu).

Figure 14-13 shows a dialog box that contains a ListBox and two CommandButtons. Clicking the Move Up button moves the selected item up in the ListBox; clicking the Move Down button moves the selected item down.

Figure 14-13: The buttons allow the user to move items up or down in the ListBox.

 CD-ROM

This example, named `listbox move items.xlsm`, is available on the companion CD-ROM.

The event handler procedures for the two CommandButtons follow:

```
Private Sub MoveUpButton_Click()
    If ListBox1.ListIndex <= 0 Then Exit Sub
    NumItems = ListBox1.ListCount
    Dim TempList()
    ReDim TempList(0 To NumItems - 1)
'   Fill array with list box items
    For i = 0 To NumItems - 1
        TempList(i) = ListBox1.List(i)
    Next i
'   Selected item
    ItemNum = ListBox1.ListIndex
'   Exchange items
    TempItem = TempList(ItemNum)
    TempList(ItemNum) = TempList(ItemNum - 1)
    TempList(ItemNum - 1) = TempItem
    ListBox1.List = TempList
'   Change the list index
    ListBox1.ListIndex = ItemNum - 1
End Sub


Private Sub MoveDownButton_Click()
    If ListBox1.ListIndex = ListBox1.ListCount - 1 Then Exit Sub
    NumItems = ListBox1.ListCount
    Dim TempList()
    ReDim TempList(0 To NumItems - 1)
'   Fill array with list box items
    For i = 0 To NumItems - 1
        TempList(i) = ListBox1.List(i)
    Next i
'   Selected item
    ItemNum = ListBox1.ListIndex
'   Exchange items
    TempItem = TempList(ItemNum)
    TempList(ItemNum) = TempList(ItemNum + 1)
    TempList(ItemNum + 1) = TempItem
    ListBox1.List = TempList
'   Change the list index
    ListBox1.ListIndex = ItemNum + 1
End Sub
```

These procedures work fairly well, but you'll find that, for some reason, relatively rapid clicking doesn't always register. For example, you may click the Move Down button three times in quick succession, but the item only moves one or two positions. The solution is to add a new `DblClick` event handler for each CommandButton. These procedures, which simply call the `Click` procedures, are as follows:

```
Private Sub MoveUpButton_DblClick _
   (ByVal Cancel As MSForms.ReturnBoolean)
     Call MoveUpButton_Click
End Sub

Private Sub MoveDownButton_DblClick _
   (ByVal Cancel As MSForms.ReturnBoolean)
     Call MoveDownButton_Click
End Sub
```

Working with multicolumn ListBox controls

A normal ListBox has a single column for its contained items. You can, however, create a ListBox that displays multiple columns and (optionally) column headers. Figure 14-14 shows an example of a multicolumn ListBox that gets its data from a worksheet range.

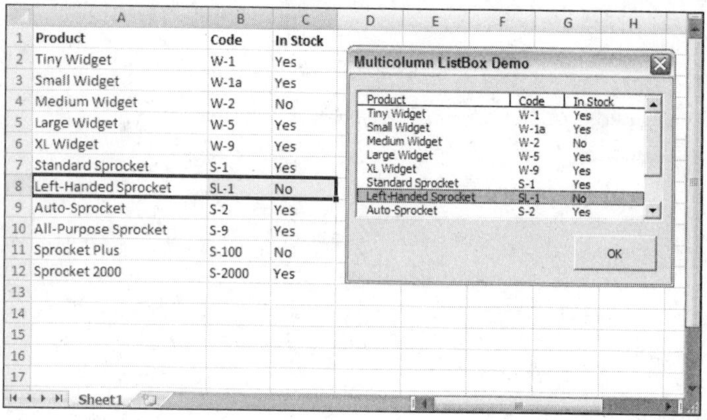

Figure 14-14: This ListBox displays a three-column list with column headers.

CD-ROM

This example, named `listbox multicolumn1.xlsm`, is available on the companion CD-ROM.

To set up a multicolumn ListBox that uses data stored in a worksheet range, follow these steps:

1. Make sure that the ListBox's `ColumnCount` property is set to the correct number of columns.

2. Specify the correct multicolumn range in the Excel worksheet as the ListBox's RowSource property.

3. If you want to display column headers, set the ColumnHeads property to True. Do not include the column headings on the worksheet in the range setting for the RowSource property. VBA will instead automatically use the row directly above the first row of the RowSource range.

4. Adjust the column widths by assigning a series of values, specified in *points* (1/72 of one inch) and separated by semicolons, to the ColumnWidths property. For example, for a three-column list box, the ColumnWidths property might be set to the following text string:

```
100;40;30
```

5. Specify the appropriate column as the BoundColumn property. The bound column specifies which column is referenced when an instruction polls the ListBox's Value property.

To fill a ListBox with multicolumn data without using a range, you first create a two-dimensional array and then assign the array to the ListBox's List property. The following statements demonstrate this using a 12-row x 2-column array named Data. The two-column ListBox shows the month names in column 1 and the number of the days in the month in column 2 (see Figure 14-15). Notice that the procedure sets the ColumnCount property to 2.

```
Private Sub UserForm_Initialize()
'   Fill the list box
    Dim Data(1 To 12, 1 To 2)
    For i = 1 To 12
        Data(i, 1) = Format(DateSerial(2007, i, 1), "mmmm")
    Next i
    For i = 1 To 12
        Data(i, 2) = Day(DateSerial(2007, i + 1, 1) - 1)
    Next i
    ListBox1.ColumnCount = 2
    ListBox1.List = Data
End Sub
```

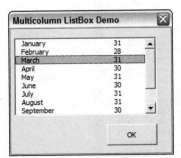

Figure 14-15: A two-column ListBox filled with data stored in an array.

Part IV

CD-ROM

This example is available on the companion CD-ROM. The file is named `listbox multicolumn2.xlsm`.

NOTE

There appears to be no way to specify column headers for the `ColumnHeads` property when the list source is a VBA array.

Using a ListBox to select worksheet rows

The example in this section displays a ListBox that consists of the entire used range of the active worksheet (see Figure 14-16). The user can select multiple items in the ListBox. Clicking the All button selects all items, and clicking the None button deselects all items. Clicking OK selects those corresponding rows in the worksheet. You can, of course, select multiple noncontiguous rows directly in the worksheet by pressing Ctrl while you click the row borders. However, you might find that selecting rows is easier when using this method.

CD-ROM

This example, named `listbox select rows.xlsm`, is available on the companion CD-ROM.

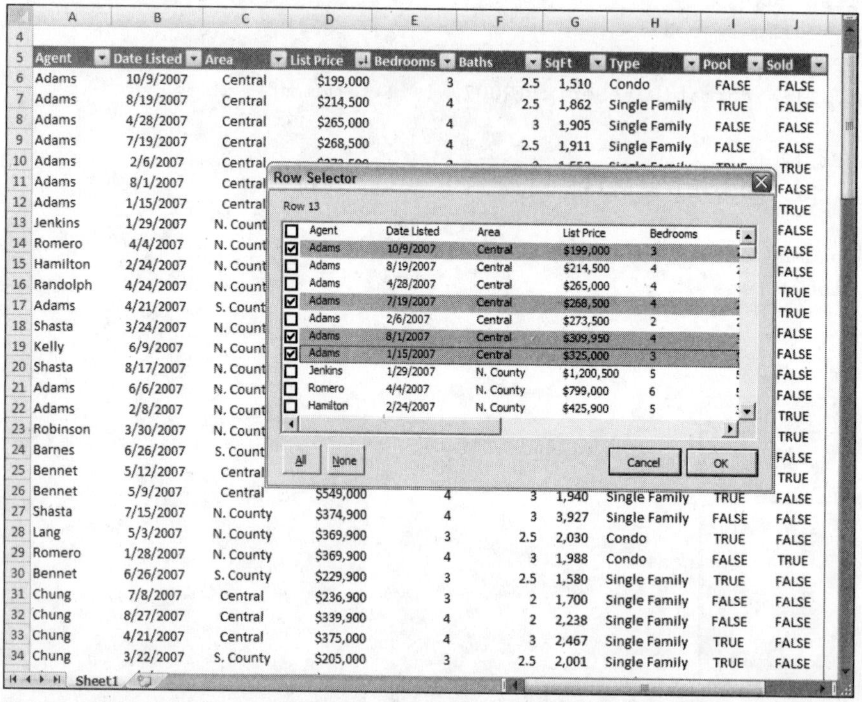

Figure 14-16: This ListBox makes it easy to select rows in a worksheet.

Selecting multiple items is possible because the ListBox's `MultiSelect` property is set to `1 - fmMultiSelectMulti`. The check boxes on each item are displayed because the ListBox's `ListStyle` property is set to `1 - fmListStyleOption`.

The UserForm's `Initialize` procedure follows. This procedure creates a `Range` object named `rng` that consists of the active sheet's used range. Additional code sets the ListBox's `ColumnCount` and `RowSource` properties and adjusts the `ColumnWidths` property so that the ListBox columns are proportional to the column widths in the worksheet.

```
Private Sub UserForm_Initialize()
    Dim ColCnt As Integer
    Dim rng As Range
    Dim cw As String
    Dim c As Integer
    ColCnt = ActiveSheet.UsedRange.Columns.Count
    Set rng = ActiveSheet.UsedRange
    With ListBox1
        .ColumnCount = ColCnt
        .RowSource = rng.Address
        cw = ""
        For c = 1 To .ColumnCount
            cw = cw & rng.Columns(c).Width & ";"
        Next c
        .ColumnWidths = cw
        .ListIndex = 0
    End With
End Sub
```

The All and None buttons (named `SelectAllButton` and `SelectNoneButton`, respectively) have simple event handler procedures as follows:

```
Private Sub SelectAllButton_Click()
    Dim r As Integer
    For r = 0 To ListBox1.ListCount - 1
        ListBox1.Selected(r) = True
    Next r
End Sub

Private Sub SelectNoneButton_Click()
    Dim r As Integer
    For r = 0 To ListBox1.ListCount - 1
        ListBox1.Selected(r) = False
    Next r
End Sub
```

The `OKButton_Click` procedure follows. This procedure creates a `Range` object named `RowRange` that consists of the rows that correspond to the selected items in the ListBox. To determine whether a row was selected, the code examines the `Selected` property of the `ListBox` control. Notice that it uses the `Union` function to add ranges to the `RowRange` object.

```
Private Sub OKButton_Click()
    Dim RowRange As Range
    RowCnt = 0
    For r = 0 To ListBox1.ListCount - 1
        If ListBox1.Selected(r) Then
            RowCnt = RowCnt + 1
            If RowCnt = 1 Then
                Set RowRange = ActiveSheet.UsedRange.Rows(r + 1)
            Else
                Set RowRange = _
                    Union(RowRange, ActiveSheet.UsedRange.Rows(r + 1))
            End If
        End If
    Next r
    If Not RowRange Is Nothing Then RowRange.Select
    Unload Me
End Sub
```

 CD-ROM

This example is available on the companion CD-ROM. The file is named `listbox select rows.xlsm`.

Using a ListBox to activate a sheet

The example in this section is just as useful as it is instructive. This example uses a multicolumn ListBox to display a list of sheets within the active workbook. The columns represent

- The sheet's name
- The type of sheet (worksheet, chart, or Excel 5/95 dialog sheet)
- The number of nonempty cells in the sheet
- Whether the sheet is visible

Figure 14-17 shows an example of the dialog box.

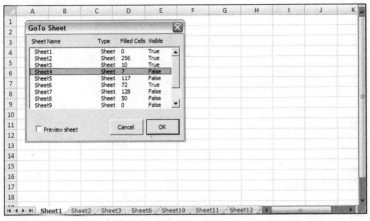

Figure 14-17: This dialog box lets the user activate a sheet.

The code in the `UserForm_Initialize` procedure (which follows) creates a two-dimensional array and collects the information by looping through the sheets in the active workbook. It then transfers this array to the ListBox.

```
Public OriginalSheet As Object

Private Sub UserForm_Initialize()
    Dim SheetData() As String
    Set OriginalSheet = ActiveSheet
    ShtCnt = ActiveWorkbook.Sheets.Count
    ReDim SheetData(1 To ShtCnt, 1 To 4)
    ShtNum = 1
    For Each Sht In ActiveWorkbook.Sheets
        If Sht.Name = ActiveSheet.Name Then _
          ListPos = ShtNum - 1
        SheetData(ShtNum, 1) = Sht.Name
        Select Case TypeName(Sht)
            Case "Worksheet"
                SheetData(ShtNum, 2) = "Sheet"
                SheetData(ShtNum, 3) = _
                  Application.CountA(Sht.Cells)
            Case "Chart"
                SheetData(ShtNum, 2) = "Chart"
                SheetData(ShtNum, 3) = "N/A"
            Case "DialogSheet"
                SheetData(ShtNum, 2) = "Dialog"
                SheetData(ShtNum, 3) = "N/A"
        End Select
        If Sht.Visible Then
            SheetData(ShtNum, 4) = "True"
        Else
```

```
            SheetData(ShtNum, 4) = "False"
        End If
        ShtNum = ShtNum + 1
    Next Sht
    With ListBox1
        .ColumnWidths = "100 pt;30 pt;40 pt;50 pt"
        .List = SheetData
        .ListIndex = ListPos
    End With
End Sub
```

The `ListBox1_Click` procedure follows:

```
Private Sub ListBox1_Click()
    If cbPreview Then _
        Sheets(ListBox1.Value).Activate
End Sub
```

The value of the `CheckBox` control (named `cbPreview`) determines whether the selected sheet is previewed when the user clicks an item in the ListBox.

Clicking the OK button (named `OKButton`) executes the `OKButton_Click` procedure, which follows:

```
Private Sub OKButton_Click()
    Dim UserSheet As Object
    Set UserSheet = Sheets(ListBox1.Value)
    If UserSheet.Visible Then
        UserSheet.Activate
    Else
        If MsgBox("Unhide sheet?", _
          vbQuestion + vbYesNoCancel) = vbYes Then
            UserSheet.Visible = True
            UserSheet.Activate
        Else
            OriginalSheet.Activate
        End If
    End If
    Unload Me
End Sub
```

The `OKButton_Click` procedure creates an object variable that represents the selected sheet. If the sheet is visible, it is activated. If it's not visible, the user is presented with a message box asking whether it should be unhidden. If the user responds in the affirmative, the sheet is unhidden and activated. Otherwise, the original sheet (stored in a public object variable named `OriginalSheet`) is activated.

Double-clicking an item in the ListBox has the same result as clicking the OK button. The `ListBox1_DblClick` procedure, which follows, simply calls the `OKButton_Click` procedure.

```
Private Sub ListBox1_DblClick(ByVal Cancel As MSForms.ReturnBoolean)
    Call OKButton_Click
End Sub
```

 CD-ROM

This example is available on the companion CD-ROM. The file is named `listbox activate sheet.xlsm`.

Using the MultiPage Control in a UserForm

The `MultiPage` control is very useful for UserForms that must display many controls. The `MultiPage` control lets you group the choices and place each group on a separate tab.

Figure 14-18 shows an example of a UserForm that contains a `MultiPage` control. In this case, the control has three pages, each with its own tab.

Part IV

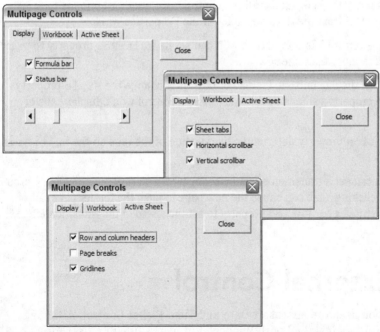

Figure 14-18: MultiPage groups your controls on pages, making them accessible from a tab.

CD-ROM

This example is available on the companion CD-ROM. The file is named `multipage control demo.xlsm`.

NOTE

The Toolbox also contains a control named `TabStrip`, which resembles a `MultiPage` control. However, unlike the `MultiPage` control, the `TabStrip` control is not a container for other objects. The `MultiPage` control is much more versatile, and I've never had a need to actually use the `TabStrip` control.

Using a `MultiPage` control can be a bit tricky. The following are some things to keep in mind when using this control:

- The tab (or page) that's displayed up front is determined by the control's `Value` function. A value of 0 displays the first tab, a value of 1 displays the second tab, and so on.

- By default, a `MultiPage` control has two pages. To add a new page in the VBE, right-click a tab and select New Page from the shortcut menu.

- When you're working with a `MultiPage` control, just click a tab to set the properties for that particular page. The Properties window will display the properties that you can adjust.

- You might find it difficult to select the actual `MultiPage` control because clicking the control selects a page within the control. To select the control itself, click its border. Or, you can use the Tab key to cycle among all the controls. Yet another option is to select the `MultiPage` control from the drop-down list in the Properties window.

- If your `MultiPage` control has lots of tabs, you can set its `MultiRow` property to `True` to display the tabs in more than one row.

- If you prefer, you can display buttons instead of tabs. Just change the `Style` property to 1. If the `Style` property value is 2, the `MultiPage` control won't display tabs or buttons.

- The `TabOrientation` property determines the location of the tabs on the `MultiPage` control.

- For each page, you can set a transition effect by changing the `TransitionEffect` property. For example, clicking a tab can cause the new page to push the former page out of the way. Use the `TransitionPeriod` property to set the speed of the transition effect.

Using an External Control

The example in this section uses the Microsoft Date and Time Picker Control. Although this is not an Excel control (it's installed with Windows), it works fine in a UserForm.

To make this control available, add a UserForm to a workbook and follow these steps:

1. Activate the VBE.

2. Right-click the Toolbox and choose Additional Controls.

   Select View ⇨ Toolbox if the Toolbox is not visible.

3. In the Additional Controls dialog box, scroll down and place a check mark next to Microsoft Date and Time Picker Control 6.0.

4. Click OK.

   Your Toolbox will display a new control.

Figure 14-19 shows the Date and Time Picker Control in a UserForm, along with the Property window. The Format property determines whether it works with dates or times.

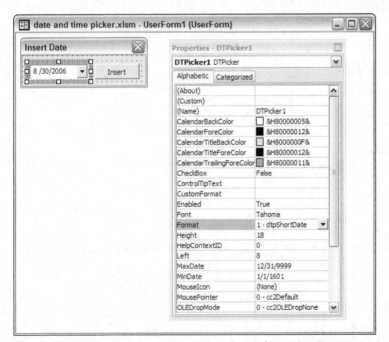

Figure 14-19: The Date and Time Picker Control in a UserForm.

Figure 14-20 shows this control being used. Clicking the drop-down button displays a calendar. When the user clicks a calendar date, that date is displayed in the control and is assigned to the Value property for the control. This dialog box is displayed modeless, so the user can select a new cell without closing the dialog box.

Part IV

When the UserForm is displayed, the Date and Time Picker displays the current date by setting its `Value` property in the `UserForm_Initialize` procedure:

```
Private Sub UserForm_Initialize()
    DTPicker1.Value = Date
End Sub
```

The code to handle the Insert button click is as follows:

```
Private Sub InsertButton_Click()
    ActiveCell = DTPicker1.Value
    ActiveCell.Columns.EntireColumn.AutoFit
End Sub
```

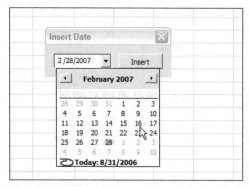

Figure 14-20: Inserting a date using the Date and Time Picker Control.

CD-ROM

This example, named `date and time picker.xlsm`, is available on the companion CD-ROM.

Animating a Label

The final example in this chapter demonstrates how to animate a `Label` control. The UserForm shown in Figure 14-21 is an interactive random number generator.

Two `TextBox` controls hold the lower and upper values for the random number. A `Label` control initially displays four question marks, but the text is animated to show random numbers when the user clicks the Start button. The Start button changes to a Stop button, and clicking it again stops the animation and displays the random number. Figure 14-22 shows the dialog box displaying a random number between 1 and 10,000.

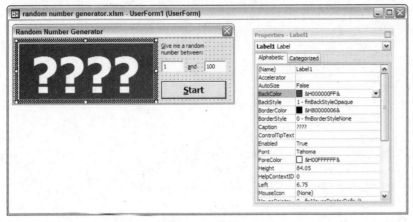

Figure 14-21: Generating a random number.

Figure 14-22: A random number has been chosen.

The code that's attached to the button is as follows:

```
Dim Stopped As Boolean

Private Sub StartStopButton_Click()
    Dim Low As Double, Hi As Double

    If StartStopButton.Caption = "Start" Then
'       validate low and hi values
        If Not IsNumeric(TextBox1.Text) Then
            MsgBox "Non-numeric starting value.", vbInformation
            With TextBox1
                .SelStart = 0
                .SelLength = Len(.Text)
                .SetFocus
            End With
            Exit Sub
        End If

        If Not IsNumeric(TextBox2.Text) Then
```

```
            MsgBox "Non-numeric ending value.", vbInformation
            With TextBox2
                .SelStart = 0
                .SelLength = Len(.Text)
                .SetFocus
            End With
            Exit Sub
        End If


'       Make sure they aren't in the wrong order
        Low = Application.Min(Val(TextBox1.Text), Val(TextBox2.Text))
        Hi = Application.Max(Val(TextBox1.Text), Val(TextBox2.Text))


'       Adjust font size, if necessary
        Select Case Application.Max(Len(TextBox1.Text), Len(TextBox2.Text))
            Case Is < 5: Label1.Font.Size = 72
            Case 5: Label1.Font.Size = 60
            Case 6: Label1.Font.Size = 48
            Case Else: Label1.Font.Size = 36
        End Select


        StartStopButton.Caption = "Stop"
        Stopped = False
        Randomize
        Do Until Stopped
            Label1.Caption = Int((Hi - Low + 1) * Rnd + Low)
            DoEvents ' Causes the animation
        Loop
    Else
        Stopped = True
        StartStopButton.Caption = "Start"
    End If
End Sub
```

Because the button serves two purposes (starting and stopping), the procedure uses a public variable, Stopped, to keep track of the state. The first part of the procedure consists of two If-Then structures to validate the contents of the TextBox controls. Two more statements ensure that the low value is in fact less than the high value. The next section adjusts the Label control's font size, based on the maximum value. The Do Until loop is responsible for generating and displaying the random numbers. Notice the DoEvents statement. This statement causes Excel to "yield" to the operating system. Without the statement, the Label control would not display each random number as it is generated. In other words, the DoEvents statement is what makes the animation possible.

The UserForm also contains a CommandButton that serves as a Cancel button. This control is positioned off the UserForm so it's not visible. This CommandButton has its Cancel property set to True, so pressing Esc is equivalent to clicking the button. It's click event handler procedure simply sets the Stopped variable to True and unloads the UserForm:

```
Private Sub CancelButton_Click()
    Stopped = True
    Unload Me
End Sub
```

CD-ROM

This example, named random number generator.xlsm, is available on the companion CD-ROM.

Chapter 15

Advanced UserForm Techniques

In This Chapter

This chapter picks up where Chapter 14 left off. Here, you'll find additional examples of UserForms.

- Using modeless UserForms
- Displaying a progress indicator
- Creating a *wizard* — an interactive series of dialog boxes
- Creating a function that emulates VBA's `MsgBox` function
- Allowing users to move UserForm controls
- Displaying a UserForm with no title bar
- Simulating a toolbar with a Userform
- Allowing users to resize a UserForm
- Handling multiple controls with a single event handler
- Using a dialog box to select a color
- Displaying a chart in a UserForm
- Using an enhanced data form
- Creating a moving tile puzzle

Most of these examples are advanced, and the majority focus on practical applications. But even the less-than-practical examples demonstrate some useful techniques.

 CROSS-REFERENCE

Chapter 28 contains still more UserForm examples. Specifically, you'll find information on how to create a UserForm on the fly.

A Modeless Dialog Box

Most dialog boxes that you encounter are *modal* dialog boxes, which must be dismissed from the screen before the user can do anything with the underlying application. Some dialogs, however, are *modeless*, which means the user can continue to work in the application while the dialog box is displayed.

To display a modeless UserForm, use a statement such as

```
UserForm1.Show vbModeless
```

The word `vbModeless` is a built-in constant that has a value of 0. Therefore, the following statement works identically:

```
UserForm1.Show 0
```

Figure 15-1 shows a modeless dialog box that displays information about the active cell. When the dialog box is displayed, the user is free to move the cell cursor, activate other sheets, and perform other Excel actions.

	A	B	C	D	E	F	G	H
1	9/3/2006							
2								
3	**Product**	**Sales**	**Units**	**Per Unit**	**Pct of Total**			
4	Widgets	$1,322.50	20	$66.13	89.7%			
5	Shapholytes	$902.44	6	$150.41	204.1%			
6	Hinkers	$322.40	8	$40.30	54.7%			
7	Ralimongers	$32.00	1	$32.00	43.4%			
8	Total:	$2,579.34	35	$73.70				
9								
10								

Cell: D5

Formula:	=B5/C5
Number Format:	$#,##0.00_);($#,##0.00)
Locked:	True

Close

Sheet1 / Sheet2 / Chart1

Figure 15-1: This modeless dialog box remains visible while the user continues working.

CD-ROM

This example, named `modeless userform1.xlsm`, is available on the companion CD-ROM.

The key is determining when to update the information in the dialog box. To do so, the example monitors two workbook events: `SheetSelectionChange` and `SheetActivate`. These event handler procedures are located in the code module for the `ThisWorkbook` object.

CROSS-REFERENCE

Refer to Chapter 19 for additional information about events.

The event handler procedures follow:

```
Private Sub Workbook_SheetSelectionChange _
   (ByVal Sh As Object, ByVal Target As Range)
    Call UpdateBox
End Sub


Private Sub Workbook_SheetActivate(ByVal Sh As Object)
    Call UpdateBox
End Sub
```

The two previous procedures call the `UpdateBox` procedure, which follows:

```
Sub UpdateBox()
    With UserForm1
'       Make sure a worksheet is active
        If TypeName(ActiveSheet) <> "Worksheet" Then
            .lblFormula.Caption = "N/A"
            .lblNumFormat.Caption = "N/A"
            .lblLocked.Caption = "N/A"
            Exit Sub
        End If

        .Caption = "Cell: " & ActiveCell.Address(False, False)
'       Formula
        If ActiveCell.HasFormula Then
            .lblFormula.Caption = ActiveCell.Formula
        Else
            .lblFormula.Caption = "(none)"
        End If
'       Number format
        .lblNumFormat.Caption = ActiveCell.NumberFormat
'       Locked
```

```
            .lblLocked.Caption = ActiveCell.Locked
    End With
End Sub
```

The `UpdateBox` procedure changes the UserForm's caption to show the active cell's address; then it updates the three `Label` controls (`lblFormula`, `lblNumFormat`, and `lblLocked`).

Following are a few points to help you understand how this example works:

- The UserForm is displayed modeless so that you can still access the worksheet while it's displayed.

- Code at the top of the procedure checks to make sure that the active sheet is a worksheet. If the sheet is not a worksheet, the `Label` controls are assigned the text N/A.

- The workbook monitors the active cell by using a `Selection_Change` event (which is located in the `ThisWorkbook` code module).

- The information is displayed in `Label` controls on the UserForm.

Figure 15-2 shows a more sophisticated version of this example. This version displays quite a bit of additional information about the selected cell. Long-time Excel users might notice the similarity to the Info window — a feature that was removed from Excel several years ago. The code is too lengthy to display here, but you can view the well-commented code in the example workbook.

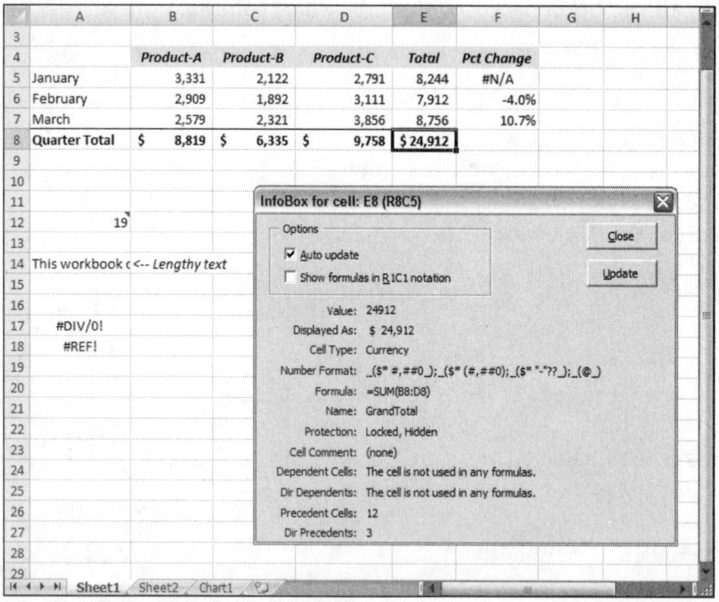

Figure 15-2: This modeless UserForm displays various information about the active cell.

CD-ROM

This example, named `modeless userform2.xlsm`, is available on the companion CD-ROM.

Following are some key points about this more sophisticated version:

- The UserForm has a check box (Auto Update). When this check box is selected, the UserForm is updated automatically. When Auto Update is not turned on, the user can use the Update button to refresh the information.

- The workbook uses a class module to monitor two events for all open workbooks: the `SheetSelectionChange` event and the `SheetActivate` event. As a result, the code to display the information about the current cell is executed automatically whenever these events occur in any workbook (assuming that the Auto Update option is in effect). Some actions (such as changing a cell's number format) do not trigger either of these events. Therefore, the UserForm also contains an Update button.

 CROSS-REFERENCE

Refer to Chapter 29 for more information about class modules.

- The counts displayed for the cell precedents and dependents fields include cells in the active sheet only. This is a limitation of the `Precedents` and `Dependents` properties.

- Because the length of the information will vary, VBA code is used to size and vertically space the labels — and also change the height of the UserForm if necessary.

Displaying a Progress Indicator

One of the most common requests among Excel developers involves progress indicators. A *progress indicator* is a graphical thermometer-type display that shows the progress of a task, such as a lengthy macro.

Displaying a progress indicator is relatively easy. In this section, I describe how to create three types of progress indicators for:

- A macro that's not initiated by a UserForm (a standalone progress indicator).

- A macro that is initiated by a UserForm. In this case, the UserForm uses a `MultiPage` control that displays the progress indicator while the macro is running.

- A macro that is initiated by a UserForm. In this case, the UserForm increases in height while the macro is running, and the progress indicator appears at the bottom of the dialog box.

Displaying Progress in the Status Bar

A simple way to display the progress of a macro is to use Excel's status bar. The advantage is that it's very easy to program. However, the disadvantage is that most users aren't accustomed to watching the status bar and prefer a more visual display.

To write text to the status bar, use a statement such as

```
Application.StatusBar = "Please wait..."
```

You can, of course, update the status bar while your macro progresses. For example, if you have a variable named Pct that represents the percent completed, you can write code that periodically executes a statement such as this:

```
Application.StatusBar = "Processing... " & Pct & "% Completed"
```

When your macro finishes, you must reset the status bar to its normal state with the following statement:

```
Application.StatusBar = False
```

If you don't reset the status bar, the final message will continue to display.

Using a progress indicator requires that you are (somehow) able to gauge how far along your macro might be in completing its given task. How you do this will vary, depending on the macro. For example, if your macro writes data to cells and you know the number of cells that will be written to, it's a simple matter to write code that calculates the percent completed. Even if you can't accurately gauge the progress of a macro, it's a good idea to give the user some indication that the macro is still running and Excel hasn't crashed.

CAUTION

A progress indicator will slow down your macro a bit because of the extra overhead of having to update it. If speed is absolutely critical, you might prefer to forgo using a progress indicator.

Creating a standalone progress indicator

This section describes how to set up a standalone progress indicator — that is, one that is not initiated by displaying a UserForm — to display the progress of a macro. The macro simply clears the worksheet and writes 20,000 random numbers to a range of cells:

```
Sub GenerateRandomNumbers()
'    Inserts random numbers on the active worksheet
     Const RowMax As Integer = 500
```

```
    Const ColMax As Integer = 40
    Dim r As Integer, c As Integer
    If TypeName(ActiveSheet) <> "Worksheet" Then Exit Sub
    Cells.Clear
    For r = 1 To RowMax
        For c = 1 To ColMax
            Cells(r, c) = Int(Rnd * 1000)
        Next c
    Next r
End Sub
```

After you make a few modifications to this macro (described below), the UserForm, shown in Figure 15-3, displays the progress.

	A	B	C	D	E	F	G	H	I	J
1	779	955	381	685	710	755	451	312	570	210
2	472	171	352	413	105	340	885	939	398	97
3	800	870	702	518	819	610	344	257	857	984
4	394	664	96	508	832	121	657	280	403	997
5	23	742	465						136	342
6	97	374	502	Progress					294	803
7	169	404	171	Entering random numbers...					756	242
8	431	758	198	58%					542	98
9	213	938	576						313	890
10	491	523	63						871	714
11	377	674	683	391	749	167	630	528	657	744
12	626	627	226	61	350	42	476	76	253	732
13	133	197	746	312	656	438	837	847	884	510
14	433	276	66	183	57	694	196	887	911	485
15	204	336	270	915	329	976	555	693	341	145
16	761	927	211	451	141	779	929	719	318	555
17	562	175	7	939	552	426	851	868	628	857
18	706	287	541	228	511	567	868	998	196	773
19	431	46	962	371	360	682	42	421	591	102
20	617	314	185	126	329	577	453	400	518	222

Sheet1

Figure 15-3: A UserForm displays the progress of a macro.

CD-ROM

This example, named `progress indicator1.xlsm`, is available on the companion CD-ROM.

BUILDING THE STANDALONE PROGRESS INDICATOR USERFORM

Follow these steps to create the UserForm that will be used to display the progress of your task:

1. Insert a new UserForm and change its `Caption` property setting to `Progress`.

2. Add a `Frame` control and name it `FrameProgress`.

3. Add a `Label` control inside the Frame and name it `LabelProgress`. Remove the label's caption and make its background color (`BackColor` property) something that will stand out. The label's size and placement don't matter for now.

4. Add another label above the frame to describe what's going on (optional). In this example, the label reads, *Entering random numbers...*

5. Adjust the UserForm and controls so that they look something like Figure 15-4.

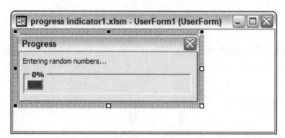

Figure 15-4: This UserForm will serve as a progress indicator.

You can, of course, apply any other type of formatting to the controls. For example, I changed the `SpecialEffect` property for the `Frame` control to make it "sunken."

CREATING THE EVENT HANDLER PROCEDURES
FOR THE STANDALONE PROGRESS INDICATOR

The trick here involves running a procedure automatically when the UserForm is displayed. One option is to use the `Initialize` event. However, this event occurs *before* the UserForm is actually displayed, so it's not appropriate. The `Activate` event, on the other hand, is triggered when the UserForm is displayed, so it's perfect for this application.

Insert the following procedure in the code window for the UserForm. This procedure simply calls a procedure named `GenerateRandomNumbers` when the UserForm is displayed. This procedure, which is stored in a VBA module, is the actual macro that runs while the progress indicator is displayed.

```
Private Sub UserForm_Activate()
    Call GenerateRandomNumbers
End Sub
```

The modified version of the `GenerateRandomNumber` procedure (which was presented earlier) follows. Notice that additional code keeps track of the progress and stores it in a variable named `PctDone`.

```
Sub GenerateRandomNumbers()
'    Inserts random numbers on the active worksheet
    Dim Counter As Integer
    Const RowMax As Integer = 500
    Const ColMax As Integer = 40
    Dim r As Integer, c As Integer
    Dim PctDone As Single

    If TypeName(ActiveSheet) <> "Worksheet" Then Exit Sub
    Cells.Clear
    Counter = 1
    For r = 1 To RowMax
        For c = 1 To ColMax
            Cells(r, c) = Int(Rnd * 1000)
            Counter = Counter + 1
        Next c
        PctDone = Counter / (RowMax * ColMax)
        Call UpdateProgress(PctDone)
    Next r
    Unload UserForm1
End Sub
```

The `GenerateRandomNumbers` procedure contains two loops. Within the inner loop is a call to the `UpdateProgress` procedure, which takes one argument (the `PctDone` variable, which represents the progress of the macro). `PctDone` will contain a value between 0 and 100.

```
Sub UpdateProgress(Pct)
    With UserForm1
        .FrameProgress.Caption = Format(Pct, "0%")
        .LabelProgress.Width = Pct * (.FrameProgress.Width - 10)
        .Repaint
    End With
End Sub
```

CREATING THE START-UP PROCEDURE FOR A STANDALONE PROGRESS INDICATOR

All that's missing is a procedure to display the UserForm. Enter the following procedure in a VBA module:

```
Sub ShowUserForm()
    With UserForm1
        .LabelProgress.Width = 0
        .Show
    End With
End Sub
```

Part IV

TIP

An additional accoutrement is to make the progress bar color match the workbook's current theme. To do so, just add this statement to the ShowUserForm procedure:

```
.LabelProgress.BackColor = ActiveWorkbook.Theme. _
    ThemeColorScheme.Colors(msoThemeAccent1)
```

HOW THE STANDALONE PROGRESS INDICATOR WORKS

When you execute the ShowUserForm procedure, the Label object's width is set to 0. Then the Show method of the UserForm1 object displays the UserForm (which is the progress indicator). When the UserForm is displayed, its Activate event is triggered, which executes the GenerateRandomNumbers procedure. The GenerateRandomNumbers procedure contains code that calls the UpdateProgress procedure every time the r loop counter variable changes. Notice that the UpdateProgress procedure uses the Repaint method of the UserForm object. Without this statement, the changes to the label would not be updated. Before the GenerateRandomNumbers procedure ends, the last statement unloads the UserForm.

To customize this technique, you need to figure out how to determine the percentage completed and assign it to the PctDone variable. This will vary, depending on your application. If your code runs in a loop (as in this example), determining the percentage completed is easy. If your code is not in a loop, you might need to estimate the progress completed at various points in your code.

Showing a progress indicator by using a MultiPage control

In the preceding example, the macro was not initiated by a UserForm. In many cases, your lengthy macro is kicked off when the user clicks the OK button on a UserForm. The technique that I describe in this section is a better solution and assumes the following:

- Your project is completed and debugged.

- Your project uses a UserForm (without a MultiPage control) to initiate a lengthy macro.

- You have a way to gauge the progress of your macro.

CD-ROM

The companion CD-ROM contains an example that demonstrates this technique. The file is named progress indicator2.xlsm.

Like the previous example, this one enters random numbers into a worksheet. The difference here is that the application contains a UserForm that allows the user to specify the number of rows and columns for the random numbers (see Figure 15-5).

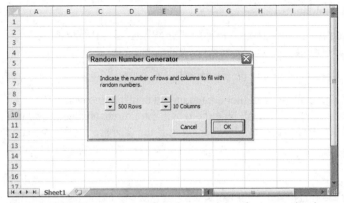

Figure 15-5: The user specifies the number of rows and columns for the random numbers.

MODIFYING YOUR USERFORM FOR A PROGRESS INDICATOR WITH A MULTIPAGE CONTROL

This step assumes that you have a UserForm all set up. You'll add a `MultiPage` control. The first page of the `MultiPage` control will contain all your original UserForm controls. The second page will contain the controls that display the progress indicator. When the macro begins executing, VBA code will change the `Value` property of the `MultiPage` control. This will effectively hide the original controls and display the progress indicator.

The first step is to add a `MultiPage` control to your UserForm. Then move all the existing controls on the UserForm and paste them to `Page1` of the `MultiPage` control.

Next, activate `Page2` of the `MultiPage` control and set it up as shown in Figure 15-6. This is essentially the same combination of controls used in the example in the previous section.

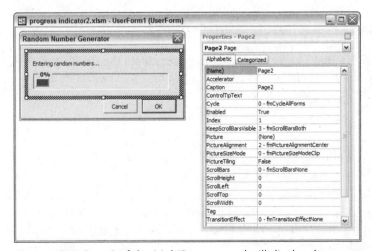

Figure 15-6: Page2 of the MultiPage control will display the progress indicator.

Part IV

1. Add a `Frame` control and name it `FrameProgress`.

2. Add a `Label` control inside the Frame and name it `LabelProgress`. Remove the label's caption and make its background color red.

3. Add another label to describe what's going on (optional).

4. Next, activate the `MultiPage` control itself (not a page on the control) and set its `Style` property to `2 - fmTabStyleNone`. (This will hide the tabs.) You'll probably need to adjust the size of the `MultiPage` control to account for the fact that the tabs are not displayed.

TIP

The easiest way to select the `MultiPage` control when the tabs are hidden is to use the drop-down list in the Properties window.

INSERTING THE UPDATEPROGRESS PROCEDURE FOR A PROGRESS INDICATOR WITH A MULTIPAGE CONTROL

Insert the following procedure in the code module for the UserForm:

```
Sub UpdateProgress(Pct)
    With UserForm1
        .FrameProgress.Caption = Format(Pct, "0%")
        .LabelProgress.Width = Pct * (.FrameProgress.Width - 10)
        .Repaint
    End With
End Sub
```

The `UpdateProgress` procedure is called from the macro that's executed when the user clicks the OK button, and it performs the updating of the progress indicator.

MODIFYING YOUR PROCEDURE FOR A PROGRESS INDICATOR WITH A MULTIPAGE CONTROL

You need to modify the procedure that is executed when the user clicks the OK Button — the `Click` event handler procedure for the button named `OKButton_Click`. First, insert the following statement at the top of your procedure:

```
MultiPage1.Value = 1
```

This statement activates `Page2` of the `MultiPage` control (the page that displays the progress indicator).

In the next step, you're pretty much on your own. You need to write code to calculate the percent completed and assign this value to a variable named `PctDone`. Most likely, this calculation will be performed inside of a loop. Then insert the following statement, which will update the progress indicator:

```
Call UpdateProgress(PctDone)
```

HOW A PROGRESS INDICATOR WITH A MULTIPAGE CONTROL WORKS

This technique is very straightforward and, as you've seen, it involves only one UserForm. The code switches pages of the MultiPage control and converts your normal dialog box into a progress indicator. Because the MultiPage tabs are hidden, it doesn't even resemble a MultiPage control.

Showing a progress indicator without using a MultiPage control

The example in this section is similar to the example in the preceding section. However, this technique is simpler because it doesn't use a MultiPage control. Rather, the progress indicator is stored at the bottom of the UserForm — but the UserForm's height is reduced so that the progress indicator controls are not visible. When it's time to display the progress indicator, the UserForm's height is increased, which makes the progress indicator visible.

CD-ROM

The companion CD-ROM contains an example that demonstrates this technique. The file is named progress indicator3.xlsm.

Figure 15-7 shows the UserForm in the VBE. The Height property of the UserForm is 172. However, before the UserForm is displayed, VBA code changes the Height to 124 (which means the progress indicator controls are not visible to the user). When the user clicks OK, VBA code changes the Height property to 172 with the following statement:

```
Me.Height = 172
```

Figure 15-8 shows the UserForm with the progress indicator section unhidden.

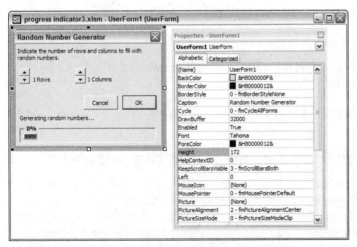

Figure 15-7: The progress indicator will be hidden by reducing the height of the UserForm.

Part IV

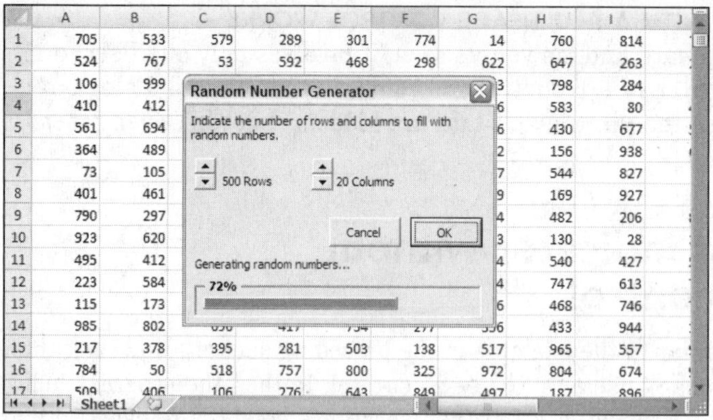

Figure 15-8: The progress indicator in action.

Creating Wizards

Many applications incorporate wizards to guide users through an operation. Excel's Text Import Wizard is a good example. A *wizard* is essentially a series of dialog boxes that solicit information from the user. Usually, the user's choices in earlier dialog boxes influence the contents of later dialog boxes. In most wizards, the user is free to go forward or backward through the dialog box sequence or to click the Finish button to accept all defaults.

You can create wizards by using VBA and a series of UserForms. However, I've found that the most efficient way to create a wizard is to use a single UserForm and a MultiPage control with the tabs hidden.

Figure 15-9 shows an example of a simple four-step wizard, which consists of a single UserForm that contains a MultiPage control. Each step of the wizard displays a different page in the MultiPage control.

CD-ROM

The wizard example in this section is available on the companion CD-ROM. The file is named wizard demo.xlsm.

The sections that follow describe how I created the sample wizard.

Setting up the MultiPage control for the wizard

Start with a new UserForm and add a MultiPage control. By default, this control contains two pages. Right-click the MultiPage tab and insert enough new pages to handle your wizard (one page for each wizard step). The example on the CD-ROM is a four-step wizard, so the MultiPage control has four pages. The names of the MultiPage tabs are irrelevant because they will not be seen. The MultiPage control's Style property will eventually be set to 2 – fmTabStyleNone.

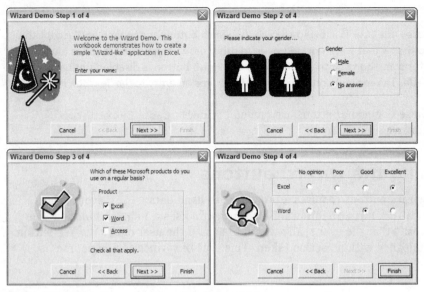

Figure 15-9: This four-step wizard uses a `MultiPage` control.

TIP

While working on the UserForm, you'll want to keep the `MultiPage` tabs visible to make it easier to access various pages.

Next, add the desired controls to each page of the `MultiPage` control. This will, of course, vary depending on your application. You might need to resize the `MultiPage` control while you work in order to have room for the controls.

Adding the buttons to the wizard UserForm

Now add the buttons that control the progress of the wizard. These buttons are placed outside the `MultiPage` control because they are used while any of the pages are displayed. Most wizards have four buttons:

- *Cancel:* Cancels the wizard and performs no action.
- *Back:* Returns to the previous step. During Step 1 of the wizard, this button should be disabled.
- *Next:* Advances to the next step. During the last wizard step, this button should be disabled.
- *Finish:* Finishes the wizard.

NOTE

In some cases, the user is allowed to click the Finish button at any time and accept the defaults for items that were skipped over. In other cases, the wizard requires a user response for some items. If this is the case, the Finish button is disabled until all required input is made. The example on the CD-ROM requires an entry in the TextBox in Step 1.

In the example, these CommandButtons are named `CancelButton`, `BackButton`, `NextButton`, and `FinishButton`.

Programming the wizard buttons

Each of the four wizard buttons requires a procedure to handle its `Click` event. The event handler for `CancelButton` follows. This procedure uses a `MsgBox` function (see Figure 15-10) to verify that the user really wants to exit. If the user clicks the Yes button, the UserForm is unloaded with no action taken. This type of verification, of course, is optional.

```
Private Sub CancelButton_Click()
    Dim Msg As String
    Dim Ans As Integer
    Msg = "Cancel the wizard?"
    Ans = MsgBox(Msg, vbQuestion + vbYesNo, APPNAME)
    If Ans = vbYes Then Unload Me
End Sub
```

Figure 15-10: Clicking the Cancel button displays a confirmation message box.

The event handler procedures for the Back and Next buttons follow:

```
Private Sub BackButton_Click()
    MultiPage1.Value = MultiPage1.Value - 1
    UpdateControls
End Sub

Private Sub NextButton_Click()
    MultiPage1.Value = MultiPage1.Value + 1
    UpdateControls
End Sub
```

These two procedures are very simple. They change the Value property of the MultiPage control and then call another procedure named UpdateControls (which follows).

The UpdateControls procedure is responsible for enabling and disabling the BackButton and NextButton controls.

```
Sub UpdateControls()
    Select Case MultiPage1.Value
        Case 0
            BackButton.Enabled = False
            NextButton.Enabled = True
        Case MultiPage1.Pages.Count - 1
            BackButton.Enabled = True
            NextButton.Enabled = False
        Case Else
            BackButton.Enabled = True
            NextButton.Enabled = True
    End Select

'   Update the caption
    Me.Caption = APPNAME & " Step " _
      & MultiPage1.Value + 1 & " of " _
      & MultiPage1.Pages.Count

'   The Name field is required
    If tbName.Text = "" Then
        FinishButton.Enabled = False
    Else
        FinishButton.Enabled = True
    End If
End Sub
```

The procedure changes the UserForm's caption to display the current step and the total number of steps. APPNAME is a public constant, defined in Module1. The procedure then examines the name field on the first page (a TextBox named tbName). This is a required field, so the user can't click the Finish button if it's empty. If the TextBox is empty, the FinishButton is disabled; otherwise, it's enabled.

Programming dependencies in a wizard

In most wizards, a user's response on a particular step can affect what's displayed in a subsequent step. In this example, the user indicates which products he or she uses in Step 3 and then rates those products in Step 4. The OptionButtons for a product's rating are visible only if the user has indicated a particular product.

Part IV

Programmatically, this is accomplished by monitoring the MultiPage's Change event. Whenever the value of the MultiPage is changed (by clicking the Back or Next button), the MultiPage1_Change procedure is executed. If the MultiPage control is on the last tab (Step 4), the procedure examines the values of the CheckBox controls in Step 3 and makes the appropriate adjustments in Step 4.

In this example, the code uses two arrays of controls — one for the product CheckBox controls (Step 3) and one for the Frame controls (Step 4). The code uses a For-Next loop to hide the Frames for the products that are not used and then adjusts their vertical positioning. If none of the check boxes in Step 3 is checked, everything in Step 4 is hidden except a TextBox that displays Click Finish to exit (if a name is entered in Step 1) or A name is required in Step 1 (if a name is not entered in Step 1). The MultiPage1_Change procedure follows:

```
Private Sub MultiPage1_Change()
'    Set up the Ratings page?
     If MultiPage1.Value = 3 Then
'        Create an array of CheckBox controls
         Dim ProdCB(1 To 3) As MSForms.CheckBox
         Set ProdCB(1) = cbExcel
         Set ProdCB(2) = cbWord
         Set ProdCB(3) = cbAccess

'        Create an array of Frame controls
         Dim ProdFrame(1 To 3) As MSForms.Frame
         Set ProdFrame(1) = FrameExcel
         Set ProdFrame(2) = FrameWord
         Set ProdFrame(3) = FrameAccess

         TopPos = 22
         FSpace = 8
         AtLeastOne = False

'        Loop through all products
         For i = 1 To 3
             If ProdCB(i) Then
                 ProdFrame(i).Visible = True
                 ProdFrame(i).Top = TopPos
                 TopPos = TopPos + ProdFrame(i).Height + FSpace
                 AtLeastOne = True
             Else
                 ProdFrame(i).Visible = False
             End If
         Next i

'        Uses no products?
```

```
        If AtLeastOne Then
            lblHeadings.Visible = True
            Image4.Visible = True
            lblFinishMsg.Visible = False
        Else
            lblHeadings.Visible = False
            Image4.Visible = False
            lblFinishMsg.Visible = True
            If tbName = "" Then
                lblFinishMsg.Caption = _
                  "A name is required in Step 1."
            Else
                lblFinishMsg.Caption = _
                  "Click Finish to exit."
            End If
        End If
    End If
End Sub
```

Performing the task with the wizard

When the user clicks the Finish button, the wizard performs its task: transferring the information from the UserForm to the next empty row in the worksheet. This procedure, named FinishButton_Click , is very straightforward. It starts by determining the next empty worksheet row and assigns this value to a variable (r). The remainder of the procedure simply translates the values of the controls and enters data into the worksheet.

```
Private Sub FinishButton_Click()
    r = Application.WorksheetFunction. _
      CountA(Range("A:A")) + 1

'   Insert the name
    Cells(r, 1) = tbName.Text

'   Insert the gender
    Select Case True
        Case obMale: Cells(r, 2) = "Male"
        Case obFemale: Cells(r, 2) = "Female"
        Case obNoAnswer: Cells(r, 2) = "Unknown"
    End Select

'   Insert usage
    Cells(r, 3) = cbExcel
    Cells(r, 4) = cbWord
```

```
        Cells(r, 5) = cbAccess

'       Insert ratings
        If obExcel1 Then Cells(r, 6) = ""
        If obExcel2 Then Cells(r, 6) = 0
        If obExcel3 Then Cells(r, 6) = 1
        If obExcel4 Then Cells(r, 6) = 2
        If obWord1 Then Cells(r, 7) = ""
        If obWord2 Then Cells(r, 7) = 0
        If obWord3 Then Cells(r, 7) = 1
        If obWord4 Then Cells(r, 7) = 2
        If obAccess1 Then Cells(r, 8) = ""
        If obAccess2 Then Cells(r, 8) = 0
        If obAccess3 Then Cells(r, 8) = 1
        If obAccess4 Then Cells(r, 8) = 2


'       Unload the form
        Unload Me
End Sub
```

After you test your wizard, and everything is working properly, you can set the `MultiPage` control's `Style` property to `2 - fmTabStyleNone` to hide the tabs.

Emulating the MsgBox Function

VBA's `MsgBox` function is a bit unusual because, unlike most functions, it displays a dialog box. But, similar to other functions, it also returns a value: an integer that represents which button the user clicked.

This section describes a custom function that I created that emulates VBA's `MsgBox` function. On first thought, creating such a function might seem rather easy. Think again! The `MsgBox` function is extraordinarily versatile because of the arguments that it accepts. Consequently, creating a function to emulate `MsgBox` is no small feat.

 NOTE

The point of this exercise is not to create an alternative messaging function. Rather, it's to demonstrate how to develop a relatively complex function that also incorporates a UserForm. However, some people might like the idea of being able to customize their messages. If so, you'll find that this function is very easy to customize. For example, you can change the font, colors, button text, and so on.

I named my pseudo-MsgBox function MyMsgBox. The emulation is close, but not perfect. The MyMsgBox function has the following limitations:

- It does not support the Helpfile argument (which adds a Help button that, when clicked, opens a Help file).

- It does not support the Context argument (which specifies the context ID for the Help file).

- It does not support the *system modal* option, which puts everything in Windows on hold until you respond to the dialog box.

- It does not play a sound when it is called.

The syntax for MyMsgBox is

MyMsgBox(*prompt*[, *buttons*] [, *title*])

This syntax is exactly the same as the MsgBox syntax except that it doesn't use the last two optional arguments (Helpfile and Context). MyMsgBox also uses the same predefined constants as MsgBox: vbOKOnly, vbQuestion, vbDefaultButton1, and so on.

NOTE

If you're not familiar with the VBA MsgBox function, consult the Help system to become familiar with its arguments.

MsgBox emulation: MyMsgBox code

The MyMsgBox function uses a UserForm named MyMsgBoxForm. The function itself, which follows, is very short. The bulk of the work is done in the UserForm_Initialize procedure.

CD-ROM

The complete code for the MyMsgBox function is too lengthy to list here, but it's available in a workbook named msgbox emulation.xlsm, available on the companion CD-ROM. The workbook is set up so you can easily try various options.

```
Public Prompt1 As String
Public Buttons1 As Integer
Public Title1 As String
Public UserClick As Integer

Function MyMsgBox(ByVal Prompt As String, _
    Optional ByVal Buttons As Integer, _
```

Part IV

```
     Optional ByVal Title As String) As Integer
        Prompt1 = Prompt
        Buttons1 = Buttons
        Title1 = Title
        MyMsgBoxForm.Show
        MyMsgBox = UserClick
End Function
```

Figure 15-11 shows `MyMsgBox` in use. It looks very similar to the VBA message box, but I used a different font for the message text (Calibri 12-point bold).

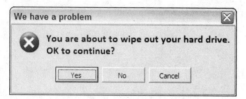

Figure 15-11: The result of the MsgBox emulation function.

Here's the code that I used to execute the function:

```
Prompt = "You are about to wipe out your entire hard drive."
Prompt = Prompt & vbCrLf & vbCrLf & "OK to continue?"
Buttons = vbQuestion + vbYesNo
Title = "We have a problem"
Ans = MyMsgBox(Prompt, Buttons, Title)
```

NOTE

This example, of course, does not really wipe out your entire hard drive.

How the MyMsgBox function works

Notice the use of four `Public` variables. The first three (`Prompt1`, `Buttons1`, and `Title1`) represent the arguments that are passed to the function. The other variable (`UserClick`) represents the values returned by the function. The `UserForm_Initialize` procedure needs a way to get this information and send it back to the function, and using `Public` variables is the only way to accomplish that.

The UserForm (shown in Figure 15-12) contains four `Image` controls (one for each of the four possible icons), three `CommandButton` controls, and a `TextBox` control.

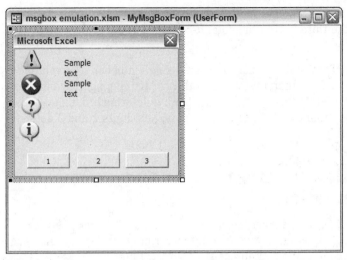

Figure 15-12: The UserForm for the MyMsgBox function.

The code in the `UserForm_Initialize` procedure examines the arguments and does the following:

- Determines which, if any, image to display (and hides the others)
- Determines which button(s) to display (and hides the others)
- Determines which button is the default button
- Centers the buttons in the dialog box
- Determines the captions for the CommandButtons
- Determines the position of the text within the dialog box
- Determines how wide to make the dialog box (by using an API function call to get the video resolution)
- Determines how tall to make the dialog box
- Displays the UserForm

Three additional event handler procedures are included (one for each CommandButton). These routines determine which button was clicked and return a value for the function by setting a value for the `UserClick` variable.

Interpreting the second argument (`buttons`) is a bit challenging. This argument can consist of a number of constants added together. For example, the second argument can be something like this:

```
VbYesNoCancel + VbQuestion + VbDefaultButton3
```

This argument creates a three-button MsgBox (with Yes, No, and Cancel buttons), displays the Question icon, and makes the third button the default button. The actual argument is 547 (3 + 32 + 512).

The challenge was pulling three pieces of information from a single number. The solution involves converting the argument to a binary number and then examining specific bits. For example, 547 in binary is 1000100011. Binary digits 4 through 6 determine the image displayed; digits 8 through 10 determine which buttons to display; and digits 1 and 2 determine which button is the default button.

Using the MyMsgBox function in the MsgBox emulation

To use this function in your own project, export the MyMsgBoxMod module and the MyMsgBoxForm UserForm. Then import these two files into your project. You can then use the MyMsgBox function in your code just as you'd use the MsgBox function.

A UserForm with Movable Controls

I'm not sure of the practical significance of this technique, but the example in this section will help you understand mouse-related events. The UserForm shown in Figure 15-13 contains three Image controls. The user can use the mouse to drag these images around in the dialog box.

Figure 15-13: The three Image controls can be dragged and rearranged by using the mouse.

CD-ROM

This example is available on the companion CD-ROM. The file is named move controls.xlsm.

Each of the `Image` controls has two associated event procedures: `MouseDown` and `MouseMove`. The event procedures for the `Image1` control are shown here (the others are identical except for the control names).

```
Private Sub Image1_MouseDown(ByVal Button As Integer, _
    ByVal Shift As Integer, ByVal X As Single, ByVal Y As Single)
'   Starting position when button is pressed
    OldX = X
    OldY = Y
    Image1.ZOrder 0
End Sub

Private Sub Image1_MouseMove(ByVal Button As Integer, _
    ByVal Shift As Integer, ByVal X As Single, ByVal Y As Single)
'   Move the image
    If Button = 1 Then
        Image1.Left = Image1.Left + (X - OldX)
        Image1.Top = Image1.Top + (Y - OldY)
    End If
End Sub
```

When the mouse button is pressed, the `MouseDown` event occurs, and the X and Y positions of the mouse pointer are stored. Two public variables are used to keep track of the original position of the controls: `OldX` and `OldY`. This procedure also changes the `ZOrder` property, which puts the image "on top" of the others.

When the mouse is being moved, the `MouseMove` event occurs repeatedly. The event procedure checks the mouse button. If the `Button` argument is 1, it means that the left mouse button is depressed. If so, then the `Image` control is shifted relative to its old position.

Also, notice that the mouse pointer changes when it's over an image. That's because the `MousePointer` property is set to `15 - fmMousePointerSizeAll`. This mouse pointer style is commonly used to indicate that something can be moved.

A UserForm with No Title Bar

Excel provides no direct way to display a UserForm without its title bar. But this feat is possible with the help of a few API functions. Figure 15-14 shows a UserForm with no title bar.

Another example of a UserForm without a title bar is in Figure 15-15. This dialog box contains an `Image` control and a `CommandButton` control.

Part IV

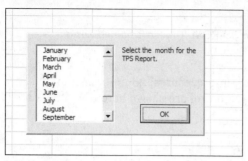

Figure 15-14: This UserForm lacks a title bar.

Figure 15-15: Another UserForm without a title bar.

 CD-ROM

Both of these examples are in a workbook named no title bar.xlsm, which is available on the companion CD-ROM. The CD also contains another version of the splash screen example presented in Chapter 14. This version, named splash screen2.xlsm, displays the UserForm without a title bar.

Displaying a UserForm without a title bar requires four windows API functions: GetWindowLong, SetWindowLong, DrawMenuBar, and FindWindowA (see the example file on the CD for the function declaration) The UserForm_Initialize procedure calls these functions:

```
Private Sub UserForm_Initialize()
    Dim lngWindow As Long, lFrmHdl As Long
    lFrmHdl = FindWindowA(vbNullString, Me.Caption)
    lngWindow = GetWindowLong(lFrmHdl, GWL_STYLE)
```

```
    lngWindow = lngWindow And (Not WS_CAPTION)
    Call SetWindowLong(lFrmHdl, GWL_STYLE, lngWindow)
    Call DrawMenuBar(lFrmHdl)
End Sub
```

One problem is that, without a title bar, the user has no way to reposition the dialog box. The solution is to use the MouseDown and MouseMove events, as described in the preceding section.

NOTE

Because the FindWindowA function uses the UserForm's caption, this technique will not work if the Caption property is set to an empty string.

Simulating a Toolbar with a UserForm

Creating a custom toolbar in versions prior to Excel 2007 was relatively easy. With Excel 2007, it's impossible. More accurately, it's still possible to create a custom toolbar with VBA, but Excel ignores many of your VBA instructions. In Excel 2007, all custom toolbars are displayed in the Add-Ins ⇨ Custom Toolbars Ribbon group. These toolbars cannot be moved, floated, resized, or docked.

This section describes how to create a toolbar alternative: A modeless UserForm that simulates a floating toolbar. Figure 15-16 shows a UserForm that may substitute for a toolbar.

	A	B	C	D	E	F	G	H	I
1	56	92	58	78	82	97	35	15	
2	70	17	10	93	61	82	58	53	
3	29	52	43	11	27	6	67	51	
4	53	66	3	77	7	37	10	85	
5	33	66						20	
6	19	46						49	
7	70	8						44	
8	83	66	5	59	69	62	94	72	
9	59	92	17	18	66	50	74	51	
10	49	90	32	56	5	86	73	40	
11	90	8	28	14	66	56	60	63	
12	27	85	65	92	90	98	100	86	
13	34	36	50	42	38	39	83	85	
14	70	48	48	38	81	22	49	3	

Sheet1 / Sheet2

Figure 15-16: A UserForm set up to function as a toolbar.

CD-ROM

This example, named simulated toolbar.xlm, is available on the companion CD-ROM.

Part IV

The UserForm contains eight `Image` controls, and each executes a macro. Figure 15-17 shows the UserForm in the VBE. Notice that:

- The controls are not aligned.

- The UserForm is not the final size.

- The title bar is the standard size.

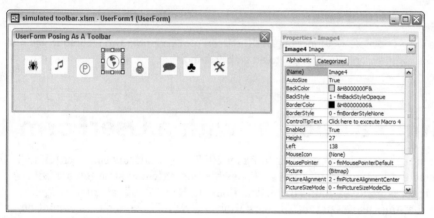

Figure 15-17: The UserForm that simulates a toolbar.

The VBA code takes care of the cosmetic details. It aligns the controls and adjusts the size of the UserForm so there's no wasted space. In addition, the code uses Windows API functions to make the UserForm's title bar smaller — just like a real toolbar. To make the UserForm look even more like a toolbar, I also set the `ControlTipText` property of each `Image` control — which displays a very toolbar-like tooltip when the mouse is hovered over the control.

If you open the file on the CD-ROM, you'll also notice that the images change slightly when the mouse is hovered over them. That's because each Image control has an associated `MouseMove` event handler that changes the `SpecialEffect` property. Here's the `MouseMove` event handler procedure for Image1 (the others are identical):

```
Private Sub Image1_MouseMove(ByVal Button As Integer, _
    ByVal Shift As Integer, ByVal X As Single, ByVal Y As Single)
    Call NoRaise
    Image1.SpecialEffect = fmSpecialEffectRaised
End Sub
```

This procedure calls the `NoRaise` procedure, which turns off the *raised* special effect for each control.

```
Private Sub NoRaise()
'   Remove the raised effect from all controls
    Dim ctl As Control
    For Each ctl In Controls
        ctl.SpecialEffect = fmSpecialEffectFlat
    Next ctl
End Sub
```

The net effect is that the user gets some visual feedback when the mouse moves over a control — just like a real toolbar. The toolbar simulation only goes so far, however. It's not possible to resize the UserForm (for example, make the images display vertically rather than horizontally). And, of course, it's not possible to dock the pseudo-toolbar to one of the Excel window borders.

TIP

The images displayed on the controls are characters from the Wingding font. I used Excel's Insert ⇨ Text ⇨ Symbol command to enter the character into a cell. Then I copied it to the Clipboard and pasted it into the `Picture` property in the Properties box. This is a quick and easy way to add images to UserForm controls.

A Resizable UserForm

Excel uses several resizable dialog boxes. For example, the Name Manager dialog box can be resized by clicking and dragging the bottom-right corner.

If you would like to create a resizable UserForm, you'll quickly discover that there's no direct way to do it. One solution is to resort to Windows API calls. That method works, but it's complicated to set up. In this section, I present a much simpler technique for creating a user-resizable UserForm.

NOTE

Credit for this technique goes to Andy Pope, an Excel expert and Microsoft MVP who lives in the UK. Andy is one of the most creative Excel developers I've ever met. For a real treat (and lots of interesting downloads), visit his Web site at `http://andypope.info`.

Figure 15-18 shows the UserForm that's described in this section. It contains a `ListBox` control that displays data from a worksheet. Notice the scrollbars on the `ListBox`. That means there's a lot more information that doesn't fit. Also, notice the bottom-right corner of the dialog box. It displays a (perhaps) familiar sizing control.

Part IV

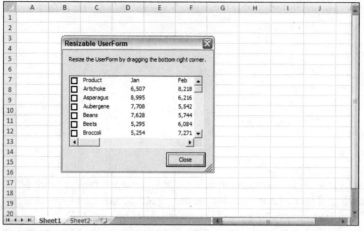

Figure 15-18: This is a resizable UserForm.

Figure 15-19 shows the same UserForm after being resized by the user. Notice that the size of the ListBox is also increased, and the Close button remains in the same relative position. You can stretch this UserForm to the limits of your monitor. A UserForm can have a maximum width and height of 12,287.25 units. The minimum height is 24.75 units (equal to the height of the title bar), and the minimum width is 105 units.

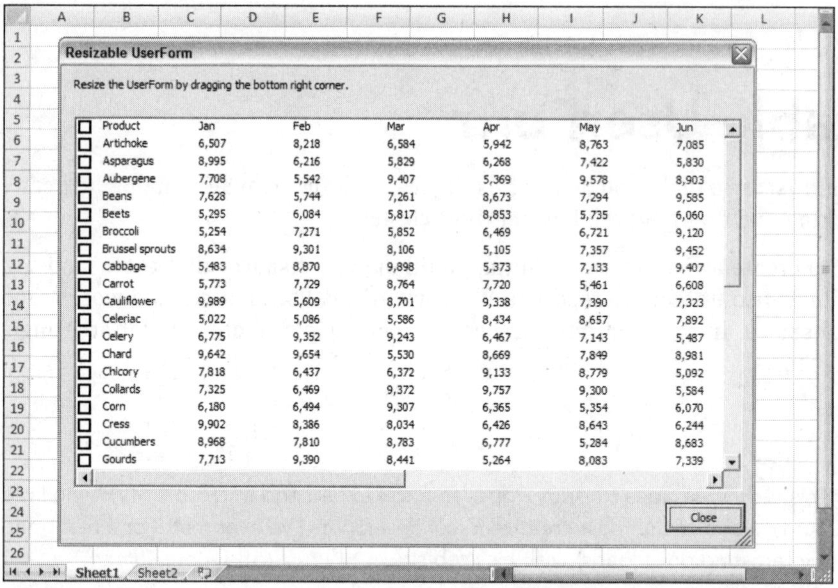

Figure 15-19: The UserForm after being increased in size.

CD-ROM

This example is available on the companion CD-ROM. The filename is `resizable user-form.xlsm`.

The trick here involves a `Label` control, which is added to the UserForm at runtime. The sizing control at the bottom-right corner is actually a `Label` control that displays a single character: The letter *o* (character 111) from the Marlett font, character set 2. This control (named `objResizer`) is added to the UserForm in the `UserForm_Initialize` procedure:

```
Private Sub UserForm_Initialize()
'    Add a resizing control to bottom right corner of UserForm
     Set objResizer = Me.Controls.Add("Forms.label.1", MResizer, True)
     With objResizer
         .Caption = Chr(111)
         .Font.Name = "Marlett"
         .Font.Charset = 2
         .Font.Size = 14
         .BackStyle = fmBackStyleTransparent
         .AutoSize = True
         .ForeColor = RGB(100, 100, 100)
         .MousePointer = fmMousePointerSizeNWSE
         .ZOrder
         .Top = Me.InsideHeight - .Height
         .Left = Me.InsideWidth - .Width
     End With
End Sub
```

NOTE

Although the `Label` control is added at runtime, the event-handler code for the object is contained in the module. Including code for an object that doesn't exist does not present a problem.

This technique relies on these facts:

- The user can move a control on a UserForm (see "A UserForm with Movable Controls," earlier in this chapter).

- Events exist that can identify mouse movements and pointer coordinates. Specifically, these events are `MouseDown` and `MouseMove`.

- VBA code can change the size of a UserForm at runtime, but a user cannot.

Part IV

Do a bit of creative thinking about these facts, and you see that it's possible to translate the user's movement of a Label control into information that can be used to resize a UserForm.

When the user clicks the objResizer Label object, the objResizer_MouseDown event-handler procedure is executed:

```
Private Sub objResizer_MouseDown(ByVal Button As Integer, _
    ByVal Shift As Integer, ByVal X As Single, ByVal Y As Single)
    If Button = 1 Then
        LeftResizePos = X
        TopResizePos = Y
    End If
End Sub
```

This procedure executes only if the left mouse button is pressed (that is, the Button argument is 1) and the cursor is on the objResizer label. The X and Y mouse coordinates at the time of the button click are stored in module-level variables: LeftResizePos and TopResizePos.

Subsequent mouse movements fire the MouseMove event, and the objResizer_ MouseMove event handler kicks into action. Here's an initial take on this procedure:

```
Private Sub objResizer_MouseMove(ByVal Button As Integer, _
    ByVal Shift As Integer, ByVal X As Single, ByVal Y As Single)
    If Button = 1 Then
        With objResizer
            .Move .Left + X - LeftResizePos, .Top + Y - TopResizePos
            Me.Width = Me.Width + X - LeftResizePos
            Me.Height = Me.Height + Y - TopResizePos
            .Left = Me.InsideWidth - .Width
            .Top = Me.InsideHeight - .Height
        End With
    End If
End Sub
```

If you study the code, you'll see that the UserForm's Width and Height properties are adjusted, based on the movement of the objResizer Label control. Figure 15-20 shows how the UserForm looks after the user moves the Label control down and to the right.

The problem, of course, is that the other controls in the UserForm don't respond to the UserForm's new size. The ListBox should be expanded, and the CommandButton should be relocated so it remains in the lower-left corner.

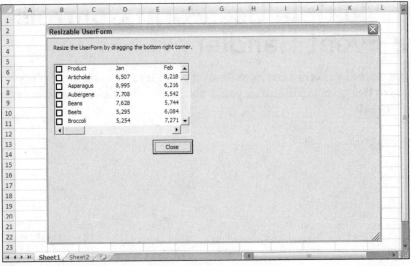

Figure 15-20: VBA code converts Label control movements into new Width and Height properties for the UserForm.

More VBA code is needed to adjust the controls in the UserForm when the UserForm size is changed. The location for this new code is in the `objResizer_MouseMove` event handler procedure. The statements that follow do the job:

```
'   Adjust the ListBox
    On Error Resume Next
    With ListBox1
        .Width = Me.Width - 22
        .Height = Me.Height - 100
    End With
    On Error GoTo 0

'   Adjust the Close Button
    With CloseButton
        .Left = Me.Width - 70
        .Top = Me.Height - 54
    End With
```

These two controls are adjusted relative to the UserForm's size (that is, Me). After adding this new code, the dialog box works like a charm. The user can make it as large as needed, and the controls adjust.

It should be clear that the most challenging part of creating a resizable dialog box is figuring out how to adjust the controls. When you have more than two or three controls, things can get very complicated.

Part IV

Handling Multiple UserForm Controls with One Event Handler

Every CommandButton on a UserForm must have its own procedure to handle its events. For example, if you have two CommandButtons, you'll need two event handler procedures for the controls' click events:

```
Private Sub CommandButton1_Click()
' Code goes here
End Sub

Private Sub CommandButton2_Click()
' Code goes here
End Sub
```

In other words, you cannot assign a macro to execute when *any* CommandButton is clicked. Each Click event handler is hard-wired to its CommandButton. You can, however, have each event handler call another all-inclusive macro in the event handler procedures, but you'll need to pass an argument to indicate which button was clicked. In the following examples, clicking either CommandButton1 or CommandButton2 executes the ButtonClick procedure, and the single argument tells the ButtonClick procedure which button was clicked:

```
Private Sub CommandButton1_Click()
    Call ButtonClick(1)
End Sub

Private Sub CommandButton2_Click()
    Call ButtonClick(2)
End Sub
```

If your UserForm has many CommandButtons, setting up all these event handlers can get tedious. You might prefer to have a single procedure that can determine which button was clicked and take the appropriate action.

This section describes a way around this limitation by using a class module to define a new class.

CD-ROM

This example, named `multiple buttons.xlsm`, is available on the companion CD-ROM.

The following steps describe how to re-create the example UserForm shown in Figure 15-21.

Class Module Demo

1	5	9	13	Clicking any of these Command Buttons (except OK) executes the ButtonGroup_Click subroutine, which is defined in the BtnClass Class Module.
2	6	10	14	
3	7	11	15	Normally, you would need a separate CommandButton_Click subroutine for each CommandButton.
4	8	12	16	OK

Figure 15-21: Many CommandButtons with a single event-handler procedure.

1. Create your UserForm as usual and add several CommandButtons. (The example on the CD contains 16 CommandButton controls.) This example assumes that the form is named UserForm1.

2. Insert a class module into your project (choose Insert ➪ Class Module), give it the name BtnClass, and enter the following code. You will need to customize the ButtonGroup_Click procedure.

```vba
Public WithEvents ButtonGroup As MsForms.CommandButton

Private Sub ButtonGroup_Click()
    Msg = "You clicked " & ButtonGroup.Name & vbCrLf & vbCrLf
    Msg = Msg & "Caption: " & ButtonGroup.Caption & vbCrLf
    Msg = Msg & "Left Position: " & ButtonGroup.Left & vbCrLf
    Msg = Msg & "Top Position: " & ButtonGroup.Top
    MsgBox Msg, vbInformation, ButtonGroup.Name
End Sub
```

TIP

You can adapt this technique to work with other types of controls. You need to change the type name in the Public WithEvents declaration. For example, if you have OptionButtons instead of CommandButtons, use a declaration statement like this:

```vba
Public WithEvents ButtonGroup As MsForms.OptionButton
```

3. Insert a normal VBA module and enter the following code. This routine simply displays the UserForm:

```vba
Sub ShowDialog()
    UserForm1.Show
End Sub
```

4. In the code module for the UserForm, enter the `UserForm_Initialize` code that follows. This procedure is kicked off by the UserForm's `Initialize` event. Notice that the code excludes a button named `OKButton` from the button group. Therefore, clicking the OK button does not execute the `ButtonGroup_Click` procedure.

```
Dim Buttons() As New BtnClass

Private Sub UserForm_Initialize()
    Dim ButtonCount As Integer
    Dim ctl As Control

'   Create the Button objects
    ButtonCount = 0
    For Each ctl In UserForm1.Controls
        If TypeName(ctl) = "CommandButton" Then
            'Skip the OKButton
            If ctl.Name <> "OKButton" Then
                ButtonCount = ButtonCount + 1
                ReDim Preserve Buttons(1 To ButtonCount)
                Set Buttons(ButtonCount).ButtonGroup = ctl
            End If
        End If
    Next ctl
End Sub
```

After performing these steps, you can execute the `ShowDialog` procedure to display the UserForm. Clicking any of the CommandButtons (except the OK button) executes the `ButtonGroup_Click` procedure. Figure 15-22 shows an example of the message displayed when a button is clicked.

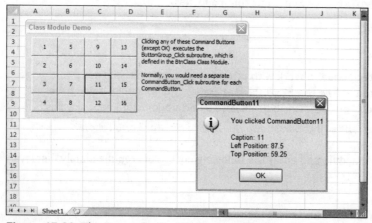

Figure 15-22: The ButtonGroup_Click procedure describes the button that was clicked.

Selecting a Color in a UserForm

The example in this section is a function that displays a dialog box (similar in concept to the MyMsgBox function, presented earlier). The function, named GetAColor, returns a color value:

```
Public ColorValue As Variant

Function GetAColor() As Variant
    UserForm1.Show
    GetAColor = ColorValue
End Function
```

You can use the GetAColor function with a statement like the following:

```
UserColor = GetAColor()
```

Executing this statement displays the UserForm. The user selects a color and clicks OK. The function then assigns the user's selected color value to the UserColor variable.

The UserForm, shown in Figure 15-23, contains three ScrollBar controls — one for each of the color components (red, green, and blue). The value range for each scrollbar is from 0 to 255.

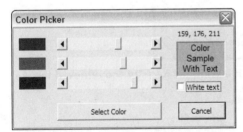

Figure 15-23: This dialog box lets the user select a color by specifying the red, green, and blue components.

 CD-ROM

This example, named getacolor function.xlsm, is available on the companion CD-ROM.

The GetAColor UserForm has another twist: It remembers the last color that was selected. When the function ends, the three Scrollbar values are stored in the Windows Registry, using this code (APPNAME is a string defined in Module1):

```
SaveSetting APPNAME, "Colors", "RedValue", ScrollBarRed.Value
SaveSetting APPNAME, "Colors", "BlueValue", ScrollBarBlue.Value
SaveSetting APPNAME, "Colors", "GreenValue", ScrollBarGreen.Value
```

The `UserForm_Initialize` procedure retrieves these values and assigns them to the scrollbars:

```
ScrollBarRed.Value = GetSetting(APPNAME, "Colors", "RedValue", 128)
ScrollBarGreen.Value = GetSetting(APPNAME, "Colors", "GreenValue", 128)
ScrollBarBlue.Value = GetSetting(APPNAME, "Colors", "BlueValue", 128)
```

The last argument for the `GetSetting` function is the default value, which is used if the Registry key is not found. In this case, each color defaults to 128, which produces middle gray.

The `SaveSetting` and `GetSetting` functions always use this Registry key:

```
HKEY_CURRENT_USER\Software\VB and VBA Program Settings\
```

Figure 15-24 shows the Registry data, displayed with the Windows Regedit.exe program.

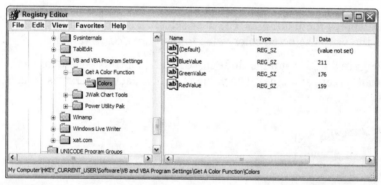

Figure 15-24: The user's ScrollBar values are stored in the Windows Registry and retrieved the next time the GetAColor function is used.

 CROSS-REFERENCE

To learn more about how Excel uses colors, refer to Chapter 30.

Displaying a Chart in a UserForm

Oddly, Excel provides no direct way to display a chart in a UserForm. You can, of course, copy the chart and paste it to the `Picture` property of an `Image` control, but this creates a static image of the chart, so it won't display any changes that are made to the chart.

This section describes a technique to display a chart in a UserForm. Figure 15-25 shows a UserForm with a chart displayed in an `Image` object. The chart actually resides on a worksheet, and the UserForm always displays the current chart. This technique works by copying the chart to a temporary graphics file and then using the `LoadPicture` function to specify that file for the Image control's `Picture` property.

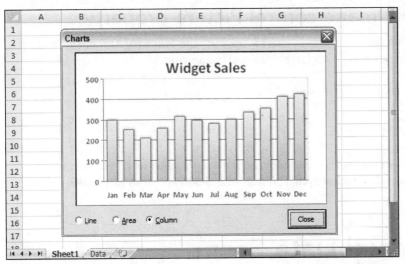

Figure 15-25: With a bit of trickery, a UserForm can display "live" charts.

CD-ROM

This workbook is available on the companion CD-ROM. The filename is `chart in userform.xlsm`.

General steps to display a chart in a userform

To display a chart in a UserForm, follow these general steps:

1. Create your chart or charts as usual.

2. Insert a UserForm and then add an `Image` control.

3. Write VBA code to save the chart as a GIF file and then set the `Image` control's `Picture` property to the GIF file. You need to use VBA's `LoadPicture` function to do this.

4. Add other bells and whistles as desired. For example, the UserForm in the demo file contains controls that let you change the chart type. Alternatively, you could write code to display multiple charts.

Saving a chart as a GIF file

The following code demonstrates how to create a GIF file (named `temp.gif`) from a chart (in this case, the first chart object on the sheet named `Data`):

```
Set CurrentChart = Sheets("Data").ChartObjects(1).Chart
Fname = ThisWorkbook.Path & "\temp.gif"
CurrentChart.Export FileName:=Fname, FilterName:="GIF"
```

Changing the Image control Picture property

If the `Image` control on the UserForm is named `Image1`, the following statement loads the image (represented by the `Fname` variable) into the `Image` control:

```
Image1.Picture = LoadPicture(Fname)
```

NOTE

This technique works fine, but you might notice a slight delay when the chart is saved and then retrieved. On a fast system, however, this delay is barely noticeable.

An Enhanced Data Form

Next is one of the more complex UserForms that you'll encounter. I designed it as a replacement for Excel's built-in Data Form, which is shown in Figure 15-26.

Figure 15-26: Excel's Data Form.

NOTE

Displaying Excel's Data Form is not easy in Excel 2007. You need to use the Excel Options dialog box, click the Customization tab, and add the Form command from the Commands Not in the Ribbon group. Then, the Form command will appear on your Quick Access Toolbar.

Like Excel's Data Form, my Enhanced Data Form works with a list in a worksheet. But as you can see in Figure 15-27, it has a dramatically different appearance and offers several advantages.

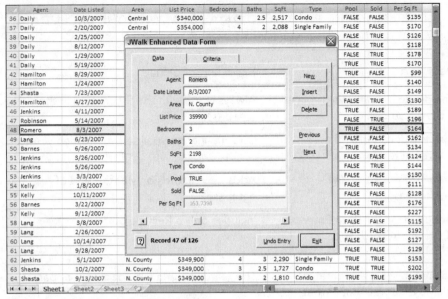

Figure 15-27: My Enhanced Data Form.

About the Enhanced Data Form

The Enhanced Data Form features the enhancements listed in Table 15-1.

TABLE 15-1 COMPARING THE ENHANCED DATA FORM WITH THE EXCEL DATA FORM

Enhanced Data Form	Excel Data Form
Handles any number of records and fields.	Limited to 32 fields.
Dialog box can be displayed in any size that you like.	Dialog box adjusts its size based on the number of fields. In fact, it can take up the entire screen!
Fields can consist of either `InputBox` or `ComboBox` controls.	Uses only InputBoxes.
Record displayed in the dialog box is always visible onscreen and is highlighted so you know exactly where you are.	Doesn't scroll the screen for you and doesn't highlight the current record.

continued

**TABLE 15-1 COMPARING THE ENHANCED DATA FORM WITH THE EXCEL DATA
FORM** *(continued)*

Enhanced Data Form	Excel Data Form
At start-up, the dialog box always displays the record at the active cell.	Always starts with the first record in the database.
When you close the dialog box, the current record is selected for you.	Doesn't change your selection when you exit.
Lets you insert a new record at any position in the database.	Adds new records only at the end of the database.
Includes an Undo button for Data Entry, Insert Record, Delete Record, and New Record.	Includes only a Restore button.
Search criteria are stored in a separate panel, so you always know exactly what you're searching for.	The search criteria are not always apparent.
Supports approximate matches while searching (*, ?, and #).	Excel's Data Form does not support wildcard characters.
The complete VBA source code is available, so you can customize it to your needs.	Data Form is not written in VBA and cannot be customized.

 CD-ROM

The Enhanced Data Form is a commercial product (sort of). The Excel 2003 version of the add-in is available on the companion CD-ROM, and it can be used and distributed freely.

To download a copy of the Excel 2007 version, visit my Web site: `http://j-walk.com/ss`. If you would like to customize the code or UserForm, access to the complete VBA source is available for a modest fee.

Installing the Enhanced Data Form add-in

To try out the Enhanced Data Form, install the add-in:

1. Copy the `dataform2.xla` file from the CD-ROM to a directory on your hard drive.
2. In Excel, choose Office ⇨ Excel Options.

3. In the Excel Options dialog box, click the Add-Ins tab.

4. Select Excel Add-Ins from the Manage drop-down list and click Go to display the Add-Ins dialog box.

5. In the Add-Ins dialog box, click Browse and locate the `dataform2.xla` in the directory from Step 1.

After performing these steps, you can access the Enhanced Data Form by using the Add-Ins ⇨ Menu Commands ⇨ JWalk Enhanced Data Form command. You can use the Enhanced Data Form to work with any worksheet list or table.

 NOTE

Version 3 of this product will be incorporated into the Ribbon and will also feature a resizable UserForm and a few other new features. The updated version was not ready in time to be included on the CD-ROM.

A Puzzle on a UserForm

The final example in this chapter is a familiar sliding puzzle, displayed on a UserForm (see Figure 15-28). This puzzle was invented by Noyes Chapman in the late 1800s.

Figure 15-28: A sliding tile puzzle in a UserForm.

The goal is to arrange the shuffled tiles (`CommandButton` controls) in numerical order. Click a button next to the empty space, and the button moves to the empty space. The `ComboBox` control lets the user choose from three configurations: 3x3, 4x4, and 5x5. The New button shuffles the tiles, and a `Label` control keeps track of the number of moves.

This application uses a class module to handle all the button events (see "Handling Multiple UserForm Controls with One Event Handler," earlier in this chapter).

The VBA code is rather lengthy, so it's not listed here. Here are a few points to keep in mind when examining the code:

- The `CommandButton` controls are added to the UserForm via code. The number and size of the buttons are determined by the `ComboBox` value.

- The tiles are shuffled by simulating a few thousand random clicks on the buttons. Another option is to simply assign random numbers, but that would result in some unsolvable games.

- The blank space is actually a `CommandButton` with its `Visible` property set to `False`.

- The class module contains one event procedure (`MouseUp`), which is executed whenever the user clicks a tile.

- When the user clicks a `CommandButton` tile, its `Caption` is swapped with the hidden button. No buttons are actually moved.

 CD-ROM

This workbook, named `sliding tile puzzle.xlsm`, is available on the companion CD-ROM.

Part  V

Advanced Programming Techniques

Chapter 16

Developing Excel Utilities with VBA

In This Chapter

A *utility*, in general, is something that enhances software, adding useful features or making existing features more accessible. This chapter is about Excel utilities:

- Exploring Excel utilities and utilities in general

- Why use VBA to develop utilities

- What you need to know to develop good utilities

- Step-by-step details for developing a useful Excel utility to manipulate text in cells

- Where to go for more Excel utilities

As you'll see, creating utilities for Excel is an excellent way to make a great product even better.

About Excel Utilities

A utility isn't an end product, such as a quarterly report. Rather, it's a tool that helps you produce an end product. An Excel utility is (almost always) an add-in that enhances Excel with new features or capabilities.

Excel is a great product, but many users soon develop a wish-list of features that they would like to see added to the software. For example, some users prefer to turn off the dotted-line page break display, and they want a feature that toggles this attribute so that they don't have to scroll through the Excel Options dialog box looking for the command. Users who work with dates might want a pop-up calendar feature to facilitate entering dates into cells. And some users desire an easier way to export a range of data to a separate file. These are all examples of features that aren't currently available in Excel. You can, however, add these features by creating a utility.

Utilities don't need to be complicated. Some of the most useful ones are actually very simple. For example, the following VBA procedure is a utility that toggles the page break display in the active window:

```
Sub TogglePageBreaks()
  With ActiveSheet
    .DisplayPageBreaks = Not .DisplayPageBreaks
  End With
End Sub
```

You can store this macro in your Personal Macro Workbook so that it's always available. Or you may prefer to package your favorite utilities in an add-in. For quicker access, you can assign your utility macros to a shortcut key, a right-click shortcut menu, or even modify the Ribbon.

Using VBA to Develop Utilities

Excel 5, released in 1992, was the first version of Excel to include VBA. When I received the beta version of Excel 5, I was very impressed by VBA's potential. VBA was light years ahead of Excel's powerful (but cryptic) XLM macro language, and I decided that I wanted to explore this new language and see what it was capable of.

In an effort to learn VBA, I wrote a collection of Excel utilities by using only VBA. I figured that I would learn the language more quickly if I gave myself a tangible goal. The result was a product that I call the *Power Utility Pak for Excel,* which is available to you at a discount as a benefit of buying this book (use the coupon in the back of the book to order your copy).

I learned several things from my initial efforts on this project:

- VBA can be difficult to grasp at first, but it becomes much easier with practice.

- Experimentation is the key to mastering VBA. Every project that I undertake usually involves dozens of small coding experiments that eventually lead to a finished product.

- VBA enables you to extend Excel in a way that is consistent with Excel's look and feel, including custom worksheet functions and dialog boxes. And, if you're willing to step outside of VBA, you can write XML code to customize the Ribbon.

- Excel can do almost anything. When you reach a dead end, chances are that another path leads to a solution. It helps if you're creative and know where to look for help.

Few other software packages include such an extensive set of tools that enable the end user to extend the software.

What Makes a Good Utility?

An Excel utility, of course, should ultimately make your job easier or more efficient. But if you're developing utilities for other users, what makes an Excel utility valuable? I've put together a list of elements that are common to good utilities:

- *It adds something to Excel.* This could be a new feature, a way to combine existing features, or just a way to make an existing feature easier to use.

- *It's general in nature.* Ideally, a utility should be useful under a wide variety of conditions. Of course, it's more difficult to write a general-purpose utility than it is to write one that works in a highly defined environment.

- *It's flexible.* The best utilities provide many options to handle various situations.

- *It looks, works, and feels like an Excel command.* Although adding your own special touch to utilities is tempting, other users will find them easier to use if they look and act like familiar Excel commands and dialog boxes.

- *It provides help for the user when needed.* In other words, the utility requires documentation that's thorough and accessible.

- *It traps errors.* An end user should never see a VBA error message. Any error messages that appear should be ones that you write.

- *Users can undo its effects.* Users who don't like the result caused by your utility should be able to reverse their path.

Text Tools: The Anatomy of a Utility

In this section, I describe an Excel utility that I developed (and that is part of my Power Utility Pak add-in). The Text Tools utility enables the user to manipulate text in a selected range of cells. Specifically, this utility enables the user to do the following:

- Change the case of the text (uppercase, lowercase, proper case, sentence case, or toggle case).

- Add characters to the text (at the beginning, to the end, or at a specific character position).

- Remove characters from the text (from the beginning, from the end, or from a specific position within the string).

Part V

- Remove spaces from the text (either all spaces or excess spaces).

- Delete characters from text (non-printing characters, alphabetic characters, non-numeric characters, non-alphabetic characters, or numeric characters).

Figure 16-1 shows the Text Tools Utility dialog box.

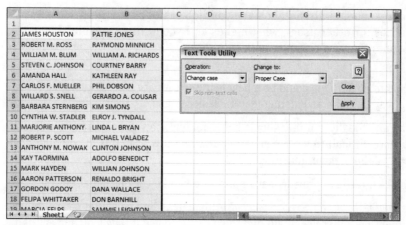

Figure 16-1: Use the Text Tools utility to change the case of selected text.

CD-ROM

The Text Tools utility is available on the CD-ROM that accompanies this book. This is a standalone version of the tool that is included with the Power Utility Pak. The file, named `text tools.xlam`, is a standard Excel add-in. When installed, it adds a new command to the Ribbon: Home ➪ Utilities ➪ Text Tools. The VBA project is not protected with a password, so you can examine the code to see how it works.

Background for Text Tools

Excel has many worksheet functions that can manipulate text strings in useful ways. For example, you can uppercase the text in a cell (UPPER), add characters to text (CONCATENATE), remove spaces (TRIM), and so on. But to perform any of these operations, you need to write formulas, copy them, convert the formulas to values, and then paste the values over the original text. In other words, Excel doesn't make it particularly easy to modify text. Wouldn't it be nice if Excel had some text manipulation tools that didn't require formulas?

By the way, many good utility ideas come from statements that begin: "Wouldn't it be nice if . . .?"

Project goals for Text Tools

The first step in designing a utility is to envision exactly how you want the utility to work. Here's my original plan, stated in the form of ten goals:

- Its main features will be those listed at the beginning of this section.

- It will enable the user to specify that the preceding types of changes work with nontext cells as well as with text cells.

- It will have the same look and feel of other Excel commands. In other words, it will have a dialog box that looks like Excel's dialog boxes.

- It will be in the form of an add-in and will also be accessible from the Ribbon.

- It will operate with the current selection of cells (including multiple selections), and it will enable the user to modify the range selection while the dialog box is displayed.

- It will remember the last operation used and display those settings the next time the dialog box is invoked.

- It will have no effect on cells that contain formulas.

- It will be fast and efficient. For example, if the user selects an entire column, the utility should ignore the empty cells in the column.

- It will enable the user to undo the changes.

- Comprehensive help will be available.

The Text Tools workbook

The Text Tools utility is an XLAM add-in file. During development, I worked with the file as a macro-enabled XLSM workbook. When I was satisfied that all was working properly, I saved the workbook as an add-in.

The Text Tools workbook consists of the following components:

- *One worksheet:* Every workbook must have at least one worksheet. I take advantage of this fact and use this worksheet to handle the undo procedure (see "Implementing Undo," later in this chapter).

- *One VBA module:* This module contains public variable and constant declarations, the code to display the UserForm, and the code to handle the undo procedure.

- *One UserForm:* This contains the dialog box. The code that does the actual text manipulation work is stored in the code module for the UserForm.

Installing an Add-In

To install an add-in, including the `text tools.xlam` add-in, follow these steps:

1. Select Office ➪ Excel Options.

2. In the Excel Options dialog box, click the Add-Ins tab.

3. In the drop-down list labeled Manage, select Excel Add-Ins and then click Go to display the Add-Ins dialog box.

4. If the add-in that you want to install is listed in the Add-Ins Available list, place a check mark next to the item. If the add-in is not listed, click Browse to locate the XLAM or XLA add-in file.

5. Click OK, and the add-in will be installed. It will remain installed until you deselect it from the list.

NOTE

The file also contains some manual modifications that I made in order to get the command to display on the Ribbon. See "Adding the RibbonX code," later in this chapter. Unfortunately, it's not possible to modify Excel's Ribbon using only VBA.

How the Text Tools utility works

The Text Tools add-in contains some RibbonX code that creates a new item in the Ribbon: Home ➪ Utilities ➪ Text Tools. Selecting this item executes the `StartTextTools` procedure, which calls the `ShowTextToolsDialog` procedure.

CROSS-REFERENCE

To find out why this utility requests both the `StartTextTools` procedure and the `ShowTextToolsDialog` procedure, see "Adding the RibbonX code," later in this chapter.

The user can specify various text modifications and click the Apply button to perform them. The changes are visible in the worksheet, and the dialog box remains displayed. Each operation can be undone, or the user can perform additional text modifications. Clicking the Help button displays a help window, and clicking the Close button dismisses the dialog box. Note that this is a *modeless* dialog box. In other words, you can keep working in Excel while the dialog box is displayed. In that sense, it's similar to a toolbar.

The UserForm for the Text Tools utility

When I create a utility, I usually begin by designing the user interface. In this case, it's the dialog box that's displayed to the user. Creating the dialog box forces me to think through the project one more time.

Figure 16-2 shows the UserForm for the Text Tools utility.

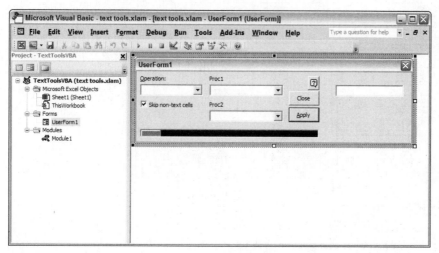

Figure 16-2: The UserForm for the Text Tools utility.

Notice that the controls on this UserForm are laid out differently from how they actually appear to the user. That's because some options use different controls, and the positioning of the controls is handled dynamically in the code. The controls are listed and described next.

- *The Operation ComboBox:* This always appears on the left, and it is used to select the operation to be performed.

- *Proc1 ComboBox:* Most of the text manipulation options use this ComboBox to further specify the operation.

- *Proc2 ComboBox:* Two of the text manipulation options use this ComboBox to specify the operation even further. Specifically, this additional ComboBox is used by Add Text and Remove by Position.

- *Check box:* The Skip Non-Text Cells check box is an option relevant to some of the operations.

- *Help button:* Clicking this CommandButton displays help.

- *Close button:* Clicking this CommandButton unloads the UserForm.

- *Apply button:* Clicking this CommandButton applies the selected text manipulation option.

- *Progress bar:* This consists of a `Label` control inside a `Frame` control.

- *Text box:* This text box is used for the Add Text option.

Figure 16-3 shows how the UserForm looks for each of the five operations. Notice that the configuration of the controls varies, depending on which option is selected.

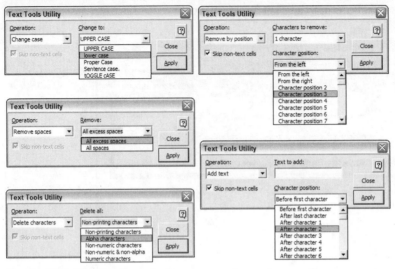

Figure 16-3: The UserForm layout changes for each operation.

NOTE

You'll notice that this utility violates one of the design rules that I outline earlier in this chapter (see "What Makes a Good Utility?"). Unlike most of Excel's built-in dialog boxes, the Text Tools utility dialog box does not have an OK or a Cancel button, and clicking the Apply button does not dismiss the dialog box. The original version of Text Tools had an OK button and was designed so that clicking OK performed the task and closed the dialog box. User feedback, however, convinced me to change the design. Many people, it turns out, like to perform several different manipulations at one time. Therefore, I changed the utility to accommodate user preferences.

The Module1 VBA module

The `Module1` VBA module contains the declarations, a simple procedure that kicks off the utility, and a procedure that handles the undo operation.

DECLARATIONS IN THE MODULE1 VBA MODULE
Following are the declarations at the top of the `Module1` module:

```
Public Const APPNAME As String = "Text Tools Utility"
Public Const PROGRESSTHRESHOLD = 2000
Public UserChoices(1 To 8) As Variant 'stores user's last choices
Public UndoRange As Range ' For undoing
Public UserSelection As Range 'For undoing
```

I declare a `Public` constant containing a string that stores the name of the application. This string is used in the UserForm caption and in various message boxes.

The PROGRESSTHRESHOLD constant specifies the number of cells that will display the progress indicator. When this constant is 2,000, the progress indicator will be shown only if the utility is working on 2,000 or more cells.

The UserChoices array holds the value of each control. This information is stored in the Windows Registry when the user closes the dialog box and is retrieved when the utility is executed again. This is a convenience feature I added because I found that many users tend to perform the same operation every time they use the utility.

Two other Range object variables are used to store information used for undoing.

THE SHOWTEXTTOOLSDIALOG PROCEDURE IN THE MODULE1 VBA MODULE

The ShowTextToolsDialog procedure follows:

```
Sub ShowTextToolsDialog()
    Dim InvalidContext As Boolean
    If Val(Application.Version) < 12 Then
        MsgBox "This utility requires Excel 2007 or later.", vbCritical
        Exit Sub
    End If
    If ActiveSheet Is Nothing Then InvalidContext = True
    If TypeName(ActiveSheet) <> "Worksheet" Then InvalidContext = True
    If InvalidContext Then
        MsgBox "Select some cells in a range.", vbCritical, APPNAME
    Else
        UserForm1.Show vbModeless
    End If
End Sub
```

As you can see, it's rather simple. The procedure starts by checking the version of Excel. If the version is prior to Excel 2007, the user is informed that the utility requires Excel 2007 or later.

NOTE

It's certainly possible to design this utility so it also works with previous versions. For simplicity, I made this an Excel 2007–only application.

If the user is running the appropriate version, the ShowTextToolsDialog procedure checks to make sure that a sheet is active, and then it makes sure that the sheet is a worksheet. If either of these is not true, the InvalidContext variable is set to True. The If-Then-Else construct checks this variable and displays either a message (see Figure 16-4) or the UserForm. Notice that the Show method uses the vbModeless argument, which makes it a *modeless* UserForm (that is, the user can keep working in Excel while it is displayed).

Notice that the code does not ensure that a range is selected. This additional error handling is included in the code that's executed when the Apply button is clicked.

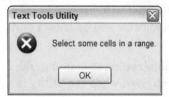

Figure 16-4: This message is displayed if no workbook is active or if the active sheet is not a worksheet.

TIP

While I was developing this utility, I assigned a keyboard shortcut (Ctrl+Shift+T) to the `ShowTextToolsDialog` procedure for testing purposes. That's because I saved the Ribbon modification task for last, and I needed a way to test the utility. After I added the Ribbon button, I removed the keyboard shortcut.

To assign a keyboard shortcut to a macro, press Alt+F8 to display the Macro dialog box. Type **ShowTextToolsDialog** in the Macro Name box and then click Options. Use the Macro Options dialog box to assign the shortcut key combination.

THE UNDOTEXTTOOLS PROCEDURE IN THE MODULE1 VBA MODULE

The `UndoTextTools` procedure is executed when the user clicks the Undo button (or presses Ctrl+Z). This technique is explained later in this chapter (see "Implementing Undo").

The UserForm1 code module

All the real work is done by VBA code contained in the code module for `UserForm1`. Here, I briefly describe each of the procedures in this module. The code is too lengthy to list here, but you can view it by opening the `text tools.xlam` file on the companion CD-ROM.

THE USERFORM_INITIALIZE PROCEDURE IN THE USERFORM1 CODE MODULE

This procedure is executed before the UserForm is displayed. It sizes the UserForm and retrieves (from the Windows Registry) the previously selected values for the controls. It also adds the list items to the ComboBox (named `ComboBoxOperation`) that determines which operation will be performed. These items are:

- Change case
- Add text
- Remove by position
- Remove spaces
- Delete characters

THE COMBOBOXOPERATION_CHANGE PROCEDURE IN THE USERFORM1 CODE MODULE

This procedure is executed whenever the user selects an item in the ComboBoxOperation. It does the work of displaying or hiding the other controls. For example, if the user selects the Change Case option, the code unhides the second ComboBox control (named ComboProc1) and fills it with the following choices:

- UPPER CASE
- lower case
- Proper Case
- Sentence case
- tOGGLE cASE

THE APPLYBUTTON_CLICK PROCEDURE IN THE USERFORM1 CODE MODULE

This procedure is executed when the Apply button is clicked. It does some error checking to ensure that a range is selected and then calls the CreateWorkRange function to make sure empty cells are not included in the cells to be processed. See the upcoming section, "Making the Text Tools utility efficient."

The ApplyButton_Click procedure also calls the SaveForUndo procedure, which saves the current data in case the user needs to undo the operation. See "Implementing Undo," later in this chapter.

The procedure then uses a Select Case construct to call the appropriate procedure to perform the operation. It calls one of the following Sub procedures:

- ChangeCase
- AddText
- RemoveText
- RemoveSpaces
- RemoveCharacters

Some of these procedures make calls to function procedures. For example, the ChangeCase procedure might call the ToggleCase or SentenceCase procedures.

THE CLOSEBUTTON_CLICK PROCEDURE IN THE USERFORM1 CODE MODULE

This procedure is executed when the Close button is clicked. It saves the current control settings to the Windows Registry and then unloads the UserForm.

THE HELPBUTTON_CLICK PROCEDURE IN THE USERFORM1 CODE MODULE

This procedure is executed when the Help button is clicked. It simply displays the Help file (which is a standard compiled HTML help file).

Making the Text Tools utility efficient

The procedures in the Text Tools utility work by looping through a range of cells. It makes no sense to loop through cells that will not be changed — for example, empty cells and cells that contain a formula.

The ApplyButton_Click procedure calls a Function procedure named CreateWorkRange. This function creates and returns a Range object that consists of all non-empty and nonformula cells in the user's selected range. For example, assume that column A contains text in the range A1:A12. If the user selects the entire column, the CreateWorkRange function would convert that complete column range into a subset that consists of only the non-empty cells (that is, the range A:A would be converted to A1:A12). This makes the code much more efficient because empty cells and formulas need not be included in the loop.

The CreateWorkRange function accepts two arguments:

- Rng: A Range object that represents the range selected by the user.

- TextOnly: A Boolean value. If True, the function returns only text cells. Otherwise, it returns all non-empty cells.

```
Private Function CreateWorkRange(Rng, TextOnly)
'   Creates and returns a Range object
    Set CreateWorkRange = Nothing
'   Single cell, has a formula
    If Rng.Count = 1 And Rng.HasFormula Then
        Set CreateWorkRange = Nothing
        Exit Function
    End If
'   Single cell, or single merged cell
    If Rng.Count = 1 Or Rng.MergeCells = True Then
        If TextOnly Then
            If Not IsNumeric(Rng(1).Value) Then
                Set CreateWorkRange = Rng
                Exit Function
            Else
                Set CreateWorkRange = Nothing
                Exit Function
            End If
        Else
            If Not IsEmpty(Rng(1)) Then
                Set CreateWorkRange = Rng
```

```
            Exit Function
        End If
    End If
End If
On Error Resume Next
Set Rng = Intersect(Rng, Rng.Parent.UsedRange)
If TextOnly = True Then
    Set CreateWorkRange = Rng.SpecialCells(xlConstants, xlTextValues)
    If Err <> 0 Then
        Set CreateWorkRange = Nothing
        On Error GoTo 0
        Exit Function
    End If
Else
    Set CreateWorkRange = Rng.SpecialCells _
        (xlConstants, xlTextValues + xlNumbers)
    If Err <> 0 Then
        Set CreateWorkRange = Nothing
        On Error GoTo 0
        Exit Function
    End If
End If
End Function
```

NOTE

The `CreateWorkRange` function makes heavy use of the `SpecialCells` property. To learn more about the `SpecialCells` property, try recording a macro while making various selections in Excel's Go To Special dialog box. You can display this dialog box by pressing F5 and then clicking the Special button in the Go To dialog box.

It's important to understand how the Go To Special dialog box works. Normally, it operates on the current range selection. For example, if an entire column is selected, the result is a subset of that column. But if a single cell is selected, it operates on the entire worksheet. Because of this, the `CreateWorkRange` function checks the number of cells in the range passed to it.

Saving the Text Tools utility settings

The Text Tools utility has a very useful feature: It remembers the last settings that you used. This is handy because many people tend to use the same option each time they invoke it.

The most recently used settings are stored in the Windows Registry. When the user clicks the Close button, the code uses VBA's `SaveSetting` function to save the value of each control. When the Text Tools utility is started, it uses the `GetSetting` function to retrieve those values and set the controls accordingly.

Part V

In the Windows Registry, the settings are stored at the following location:

```
HKEY_CURRENT_USER\Software\VB and VBA Program Settings\
Text Tools Utility\Settings
```

Figure 16-5 shows these settings in the Windows Registry Editor program (regedit.exe).

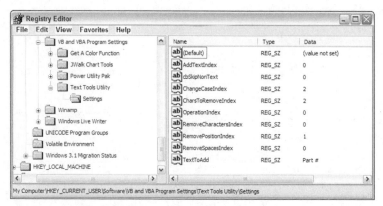

Figure 16-5: Use the Windows Registry Editor program to view the settings stored in the Registry.

If you examine the code for the Text Tools utility, you'll find that I used an eight-element array (named UserChoices) to store the settings. I could have used separate variables for each setting, but using an array made the coding a bit easier.

The following VBA reads the settings from the Registry and stores them in the UserChoices array:

```
'   Get previous settings
    UserChoices(1) = GetSetting(APPNAME, "Settings", "OperationIndex", 0)
    UserChoices(2) = GetSetting(APPNAME, "Settings", "ChangeCaseIndex", 0)
    UserChoices(3) = GetSetting(APPNAME, "Settings", "TextToAdd", "")
    UserChoices(4) = GetSetting(APPNAME, "Settings", "AddTextIndex", 0)
    UserChoices(5) = GetSetting(APPNAME, "Settings", "CharsToRemoveIndex", 0)
    UserChoices(6) = GetSetting(APPNAME, "Settings", "RemovePositionIndex", 0)
    UserChoices(7) = GetSetting(APPNAME, "Settings", "RemoveSpacesIndex", 0)
    UserChoices(8) = GetSetting(APPNAME, "Settings", "RemoveCharactersIndex", 0)
    cbSkipNonText.Value = GetSetting(APPNAME, "cbSkipNonText", 0)
```

The code that follows is executed when the dialog box is closed. These statements retrieve the values from the UserChoices array and write them to the Registry.

```
'   Store settings
    SaveSetting APPNAME, "Settings", "OperationIndex", UserChoices(1)
    SaveSetting APPNAME, "Settings", "ChangeCaseIndex", UserChoices(2)
    SaveSetting APPNAME, "Settings", "TextToAdd", UserChoices(3)
```

```
SaveSetting APPNAME, "Settings", "AddTextIndex", UserChoices(4)

SaveSetting APPNAME, "Settings", "CharsToRemoveIndex", UserChoices(5)

SaveSetting APPNAME, "Settings", "RemovePositionIndex", UserChoices(6)

SaveSetting APPNAME, "Settings", "RemoveSpacesIndex", UserChoices(7)

SaveSetting APPNAME, "Settings", "RemoveCharactersIndex", UserChoices(8)

SaveSetting APPNAME, "Settings", "cbSkipNonText", cbSkipNonText.Value * -1
```

Implementing Undo

Unfortunately, Excel does not provide a direct way to undo an operation performed using VBA. Undoing a VBA macro is possible, but it takes quite a bit of work. And, unlike Excel's Undo feature, the undo technique used in the Text Tools utility is a single level. In other words, the user can undo only the most recent operation. Refer to the sidebar, "Undoing a VBA Procedure," for additional information about using Undo with your applications.

The Text Tools utility implements undo by saving the original data in a worksheet. If the user undoes the operation, that data is then copied back to the user's workbook.

In the Text Tools utility, recall that the `Module1` VBA module declared two public variables for handling undo:

```
Public UndoRange As Range
Public UserSelection As Range
```

Before modifying any data, the `ApplyButton_Click` procedure calls the `SaveForUndo` procedure. The procedure starts with three statements:

```
Set UserSelection = Selection
Set UndoRange = WorkRange
ThisWorkbook.Sheets(1).UsedRange.Clear
```

The `UserSelection` object variable saves the user's current selection so it can be re-selected after the undo operation. `WorkRange` is a `Range` object that's returned by the `CreateWorkRange` function. The range consists of the non-empty and nonformula cells in the user's selection. The preceding third statement erases any existing saved data from the worksheet.

Next, the following loop is executed:

```
For Each RngArea In WorkRange.Areas
    ThisWorkbook.Sheets(1).Range _
        (RngArea.Address).Formula = RngArea.Formula
Next RngArea
```

This code loops through each area of the `WorkRange` and stores the data in the worksheet. (If the `WorkRange` consists of a contiguous range of cells, it will contain only one area.)

After the specified operation is performed, the code then uses the OnUndo method to specify the procedure to execute if the user chooses Undo. For example, after performing a case change operation, this statement is executed:

```
Application.OnUndo "Undo Change Case", "UndoTextTools"
```

Excel's Undo drop-down will then contain a menu item: Undo Change Case (see Figure 16-6). If the user selects the command, the UndoTextTools procedure, shown next, will be executed.

```
Private Sub UndoTextTools()
'    Undoes the last operation
    Dim a As Range
    On Error GoTo ErrHandler
    Application.ScreenUpdating = False
    With UserSelection
        .Parent.Parent.Activate
        .Parent.Activate
        .Select
    End With
    For Each a In UndoRange.Areas
        a.Formula = ThisWorkbook.Sheets(1).Range(a.Address).Formula
    Next a
    Application.ScreenUpdating = True
    On Error GoTo 0
    Exit Sub
ErrHandler:
    Application.ScreenUpdating = True
    MsgBox "Can't undo", vbInformation, APPNAME
    On Error GoTo 0
End Sub
```

Figure 16-6: The Text Tools utility includes a single level of undo.

Undoing a VBA Procedure

Computer users have become accustomed to being able to undo an operation. Almost every operation that you perform in Excel can be undone. Even better, Excel 2007 increased the number of undo levels from 16 to 100.

If you program in VBA, you may have wondered whether it's possible to undo the effects of a procedure. Although the answer is *yes*, the qualified answer is *it's not always easy.*

Making the effects of your VBA procedures undoable isn't automatic. Your procedure needs to store the previous state so that it can be restored if the user chooses the Undo command (which is located in the Quick Access Toolbar). How you do this can vary depending on what the procedure does. You can save the old information in a worksheet or in an array. In extreme cases, you might need to save an entire worksheet. If your procedure modifies a range, for example, you need to save only the contents of that range.

Also, keep in mind that executing a VBA Sub procedure wipes out Excel's undo stack. In other words, after you run a macro, it's impossible to undo previous operations.

The Application object contains an OnUndo method, which lets the programmer specify text to appear on the Undo drop-down and a procedure to execute if the user chooses the Undo command. For example, the following statement causes the Undo drop-down to display Undo my cool macro. If the user chooses Undo ▷ Undo My Cool Macro, the UndoMyMacro procedure is executed:

```
Application.OnUndo "Undo my cool macro", "UndoMyMacro"
```

The `UndoTextTools` procedure first ensures that the correct workbook and worksheet are activated and then selects the original range selected by the user. Then it loops through each area of the stored data (which is available because of the `UndoRange` public variable) and puts the data back to its original location (overwriting the changes, of course).

 CD-ROM

The companion CD-ROM contains a simpler example that demonstrates how to enable the Undo command after a VBA procedure is executed. This example, named simple undo demo.xlsm, stores the data in an array rather than a worksheet. The array is made up of a custom data type that includes the value and address of each cell.

Displaying the Help file

I created a simple compiled HTML Help file named `texttools.chm` for this utility. Clicking the `HelpButton` on the UserForm executes this procedure:

```
Private Sub HelpButton_Click()
    Application.Help (ThisWorkbook.Path & "\" & "texttools.chm")
End Sub
```

Figure 16-7 shows one of the help screens.

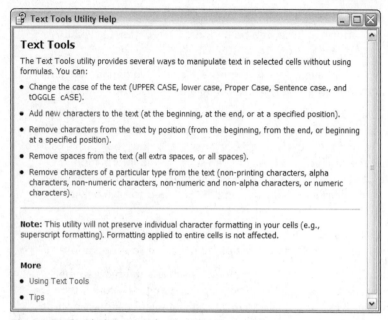

Figure 16-7: A help screen for the Text Tools utility.

CD-ROM

The companion CD-ROM includes all of the source files that were used to create the Help file. These files are in a directory named \helpsource. If you're not familiar with HTML Help files, refer to Chapter 24 for additional information.

Adding the RibbonX code

The final task in creating this utility is to provide a way to execute it. Before Excel 2007, it was relatively easy to insert a new menu command or toolbar button. But, with the new Ribbon user interface, this once-simple job is significantly more challenging.

To add a custom Ribbon interface to an Excel file (which is actually a package of files), you must modify the file in two ways:

- Create a new folder within the package and add a new part — an XML file that describes the Ribbon modification.

- Define a relationship to the new part.

CROSS-REFERENCE

Chapter 22 contains additional information about working with the Ribbon.

Figure 16-8 shows the Ribbon with a new group (called Utilities) added to the end of the Home tab. This group contains a single control that, when clicked, executes this procedure:

```
Sub StartTextTools(control As IRibbonControl)
    Call ShowTextToolsDialog
End Sub
```

Figure 16-8: The Ribbon contains a new group in the Home tab.

Following is a step-by-step list of instructions that will add that single control to the Ribbon. These instructions assume that the workbook is an XLAM add-in file.

1. Close the `text tools.xlam` add-in file.

2. Make a copy of the add-in file and name it `copy of text tools.xlam.zip`.

   Excel 2007 files are actually ZIP compressed files, but without the `.zip` extension. If you add a `.zip` extension, you can work with the individual files within the ZIP file.

3. Use a zip utility to extract the files into a new directory named `copy of text tools`.

   You can use the zip tools built into Windows. Right-click the ZIP file and choose Extract All to launch the Windows Extraction Wizard. Figure 16-9 shows the files in the directory.

Figure 16-9: The files in text tools.xlam.

4. Add a new folder named `customUI` to the `copy of text tools` directory.

5. In the `customUI` folder, create a text file named `customUI.xml` with the following contents (the spacing isn't important). This is the XML part.

```
<customUI xmlns="http://schemas.microsoft.com/office/2006/01/customui">
  <ribbon>
    <tabs>
      <tab idMso="TabHome">
        <group id="Utilities1" label="Utilities">
          <button id="TextToolsButton" label="Text Tools"
onAction="StartTextTools" imageMso="ControlsGallery" size="large"
supertip="Displays a modeless dialog box that contains tools for
working with text in cells. Add-in distributed with 'Excel 2007 Power
Programming With VBA,' by John Walkenbach."/>
        </group>
      </tab>
    </tabs>
  </ribbon>
</customUI>
```

6. Use a text editor (such as Windows Notepad) to edit the `.rels` file in the `_rels` directory. This step defines the relationship of the XML part that was added. Insert the following line into the `.rels` file and save the file:

```
<Relationship Id="12345"
Type="http://schemas.microsoft.com/office/2006/relationships/ui/
extensibility" Target="customUI/customUI.xml"/>
```

Note: The value for `Relationship Id` can be any value or string that's not already in use.

7. Zip all of the files in the `copy of text tools` directory and remove the `.zip` extension. The ZIP file should be named `copy of text tools.xlam`.

8. Open the `copy of text tools.xlam` file with Excel. If all went well, the Home tab of Excel's Ribbon will display a new group.

9. Add this new procedure to `Module1` of `copy of text tools.xlam`.

```
Sub StartTextTools(control As IRibbonControl)
    Call ShowTextToolsDialog
End Sub
```

10. When you're satisfied that all is working, close the file and rename it to `text tools.xlam`.

NOTE

When a workbook has a customized Ribbon, the Ribbon customizations appear only when that workbook is active. But, fortunately, there is an exception to this rule. When the Ribbon customization is contained in an XLAM add-in file (as in this example), the Ribbon modifications appear as long as the add-in file is opened, regardless of which workbook is active.

The preceding steps describe the manual method for adding a `customUI.xml` folder and modifying the `_rels\.rel` file. I will confess that I didn't actually go through these absurdly tedious steps. Rather, I used a utility called Office 2007 Custom UI Editor, written by Doug Mahugh (see Figure 16-10). This utility still requires that you write the XML code manually, but it eliminates the need for all of the zipping and unzipping. Refer to Chapter 22 for more information.

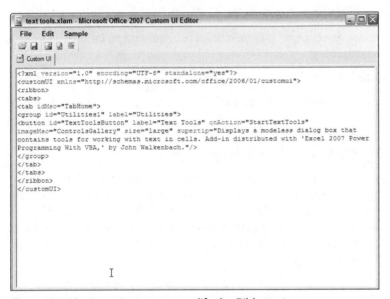

Figure 16-10: An easier way to modify the Ribbon.

Post-mortem of the project

The previous sections describe each component of the Text Tools utility. At this point, it's useful to revisit the original project goals to see whether they were met. The original goals, along with my comments, are as follows:

- *Its main features will be those listed at the beginning of this section.* Accomplished.

- *It will enable the user to request the preceding types of changes on nontext cells as well as text cells.* Accomplished.

- *It will have the same look and feel of other Excel commands. In other words, it will have a dialog box that looks like Excel's dialog boxes.* As I noted earlier, the Text Tools utility deviates from Excel's normal look and feel by using an Apply button rather than an OK button. And, unlike most of Excel's dialog boxes, Text Tools uses a modeless, stay-on-top dialog box. In light of the enhanced usability, I think these deviations are quite reasonable.

- *It will be in the form of an add-in and will be accessible from the Ribbon.* Accomplished.

- *It will operate with the current selection of cells (including multiple selections), and it will enable the user to modify the range selection while the dialog box is displayed.* Accomplished. And because the dialog box need not be dismissed, it didn't require the use of a `RefEdit` control.

- *It will remember the last operation used and display those settings the next time the dialog box is invoked.* Accomplished (thanks to the Windows Registry).

- *It will have no effect on cells that contain formulas.* Accomplished.

- *It will be fast and efficient. For example, if the user selects an entire range, the utility should ignore empty cells.* Accomplished.

- *It will enable the user to undo the changes.* Accomplished.

- *Comprehensive help will be available.* Accomplished.

Understand the Text Tools utility

If you don't fully understand how this utility works, I urge you to load the add-in and use the Debugger to step through the code. Try it out with different types of selections, including an entire worksheet. You will see that regardless of the size of the original selection, only the appropriate cells are processed, and empty cells are completely ignored. If a worksheet has only one cell with text in it, the utility operates just as quickly whether you select that cell or the entire worksheet.

If you convert the add-in to a standard workbook, you'll be able to see how the original data is stored in the worksheet for undo. To convert the add-in to a workbook, double-click the `ThisWorkbook` code module. Press F4 to display the Properties box and then change the `IsAddin` property to `False`.

More about Excel Utilities

You can use the coupon in the back of this book to order a discounted copy of my Power Utility Pak (PUP). This product includes several dozen useful utilities (plus many custom worksheet functions). The complete VBA source code also is available for a small fee.

The Excel 2007 version of PUP was not ready in time to be included on the companion CD-ROM, but you can download a trial version from my Web site: `http://j-walk.com/ss`.

In addition to the Power Utility Pak, many other utilities are available, and most of them can be downloaded from the Internet.

Chapter **17**

Working with Pivot Tables

In This Chapter

Excel's pivot table feature is, arguably, its most innovative and powerful feature. Pivot tables first appeared in Excel 5, and the feature remains unique to Excel. (No other spreadsheet program has anything that comes close to it.) This chapter is not an introduction to pivot tables. I assume that you're familiar with this feature and its terminology and that you know how to create and modify pivot tables manually. In this chapter, I cover the following topics:

◆ What you need to know to create pivot tables with VBA

◆ Examples of VBA procedures that create pivot tables

◆ An example of how to use VBA to create a worksheet table from a summary table

As you probably know, creating a pivot table from a database or list enables you to summarize data in ways that otherwise would not be possible — and it's amazingly fast. You also can write VBA code to generate and modify pivot tables.

An Introductory Pivot Table Example

This section gets the ball rolling with a simple example of using VBA to create a pivot table.

Figure 17-1 shows a very simple worksheet range. It contains four fields: SalesRep, Region, Month, and Sales. Each record describes the sales for a particular sales representative in a particular month.

	A	B	C	D	E
1	SalesRep	Region	Month	Sales	
2	Amy	North	Jan	33,488	
3	Amy	North	Feb	47,008	
4	Amy	North	Mar	32,128	
5	Bob	North	Jan	34,736	
6	Bob	North	Feb	92,872	
7	Bob	North	Mar	76,128	
8	Chuck	South	Jan	41,536	
9	Chuck	South	Feb	23,192	
10	Chuck	South	Mar	21,736	
11	Doug	South	Jan	44,834	
12	Doug	South	Feb	32,002	
13	Doug	South	Mar	23,932	
14					
15					

Sheet1

Figure 17-1: This simple table is a good candidate for a pivot table.

 CD-ROM

This workbook, named `simple pivot table.xlsm`, is available on the companion CD-ROM.

Creating a pivot table

Figure 17-2 shows a pivot table created from the data. This pivot table summarizes the sales performance by sales representative and month. This pivot table is set up with the following fields:

- *Region:* A report filter field in the pivot table.
- *SalesRep:* A row field in the pivot table.
- *Month:* A column field in the pivot table.
- *Sales:* A values field in the pivot table that uses the SUM function.

I turned on the macro recorder before I created this pivot table. I specified a new worksheet for the pivot table location. The code that was generated follows:

```
Sub RecordedMacro()
    Sheets.Add
    ActiveWorkbook.PivotCaches.Create _
        (SourceType:=xlDatabase, _
```

```
            SourceData:="Sheet1!R1C1:R13C4") _
            .CreatePivotTable _
            TableDestination:="Sheet2!R3C1", _
            TableName:="PivotTable1", _
            DefaultVersion:=xlPivotTableVersion12
        Sheets("Sheet2").Select
        With ActiveSheet.PivotTables _
          ("PivotTable1").PivotFields("Region")
            .Orientation = xlPageField
            .Position = 1
        End With
        With ActiveSheet.PivotTables("PivotTable1") _
            .PivotFields("Month")
            .Orientation = xlColumnField
            .Position = 1
        End With
        With ActiveSheet.PivotTables("PivotTable1") _
            .PivotFields("SalesRep")
            .Orientation = xlRowField
            .Position = 1
        End With
        ActiveSheet.PivotTables("PivotTable1").AddDataField _
            ActiveSheet.PivotTables( _
            "PivotTable1").PivotFields("Sales"), _
            "Sum of Sales", xlSum
        ActiveSheet.PivotTables("PivotTable1"). _
            DisplayFieldCaptions = False
    End Sub
```

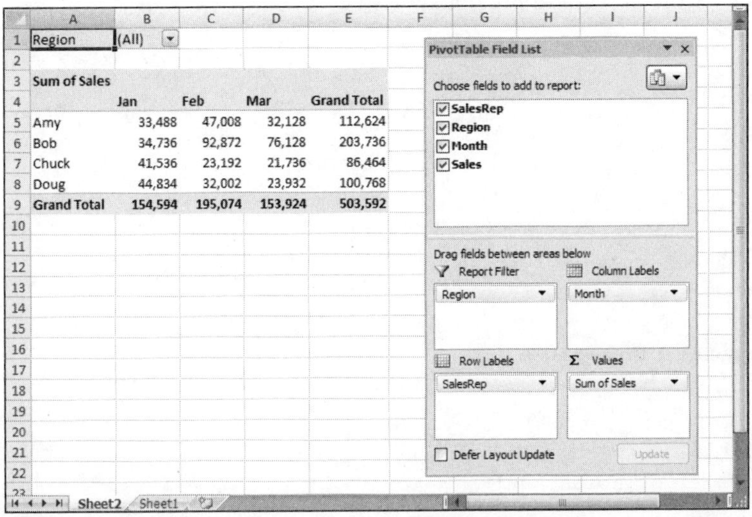

Figure 17-2: A pivot table created from the data in Figure 17-1.

If you execute this macro, it will probably produce an error. Examine the code, and you'll see that the macro recorder "hard-coded" the worksheet name (Sheet2) for the pivot table. If that sheet already exists (or if the new sheet that's added has a different name), the macro ends with an error.

Examining the recorded code for the pivot table

VBA code that works with pivot tables can be confusing. To make any sense of the recorded macro, you need to know about a few relevant objects, all of which are explained in the Help system.

- PivotCaches: A collection of PivotCache objects in a Workbook object (the data used by a pivot table is stored in a pivot cache).

- PivotTables: A collection of PivotTable objects in a Worksheet object.

- PivotFields: A collection of fields in a PivotTable object.

- PivotItems: A collection of individual data items within a field category.

- CreatePivotTable: A method that creates a pivot table by using the data in a pivot cache.

- AddDataField: A method that adds a field to the Value area.

Cleaning up the recorded pivot table code

As with most recorded macros, the preceding example is not as efficient as it could be. And, as I noted, it's very likely to generate an error. The code can be simplified to make it more understandable and also to prevent the error. The hand-crafted code that follows generates the same pivot table as the procedure previously listed.

```
Sub CreatePivotTable()
    Dim PTCache As PivotCache
    Dim PT As PivotTable

'   Create the cache
    Set PTCache = ActiveWorkbook.PivotCaches.Create( _
        SourceType:=xlDatabase, _
        SourceData:=Range("A1").CurrentRegion)

'   Add a new sheet for the pivot table
    Worksheets.Add

'   Create the pivot table
    Set PT = ActiveSheet.PivotTables.Add( _
        PivotCache:=PTCache, _
```

```
        TableDestination:=Range("A3"))

'   Add the fields
    With PT
        .PivotFields("Region").Orientation = xlPageField
        .PivotFields("Month").Orientation = xlColumnField
        .PivotFields("SalesRep").Orientation = xlRowField
        .PivotFields("Sales").Orientation = xlDataField
        'no field captions
        .DisplayFieldCaptions = False
    End With
End Sub
```

The CreatePivotTable procedure is simplified (and might be easier to understand) because it declares two object variables: PTCache and PT. A new PivotCache object is created by using the Create method. A worksheet is added, and it becomes the active sheet (the destination for the pivot table). Then a new PivotTable object is created by using the Add method of the PivotTables collection. The last section of the code adds the fields to the pivot table and specifies their location within it.

What's New in Excel 2007 Pivot Tables?

Excel 2007 pivot tables are easier to use than the old pivot tables. But that's not all that's changed. Here's a list of other new pivot table features:

- *Increased limits:* More rows and columns, more fields (16,000, up from 255), more unique pivot table items (1 million, up from 32,000), and no more truncated labels.

- *Label filtering:* For example, you can display only product names that contain the word *widget*.

- *Value filtering:* For example, you can display only products that have sales in excess of $5,000.

- *Conditional formatting support:* You can incorporate the new conditional formatting features in your pivot table (for example, display data bars).

- *Pivot chart format persistence:* Pivot charts maintain their formatting after the pivot table is refreshed.

- *Styles:* The new pivot table style gallery makes it easy to change the look of your pivot table with a single mouse click.

Also, it's important to understand that Excel 2007 pivot tables are not backward compatible. If you plan to share a workbook that uses an Excel 2007 pivot table with someone who uses an earlier version, you'll need to use "compatibility mode" and save your workbook in the Excel 97–2003 XLS file format.

Part V

The original macro hard-coded both the data range used to create the `PivotCache` object (`'Sheet1!R1C1:R13C4'`) and the pivot table location (`Sheet2`). In the `CreatePivotTable` procedure, the pivot table is based on the current region surrounding cell A1. This ensures that the macro will continue to work properly if more data is added.

Adding the worksheet before the pivot table is created eliminates the need to hard-code the sheet reference. Yet another difference is that the hand-written macro does not specify a pivot table name. Because the `PT` object variable is created, it's never necessary to refer to the pivot table by name.

NOTE

The code also could be more general through the use of indices rather than literal strings for the `PivotFields` collections. This way, if the user changes the column headings, the code will still work. For example, more general code would use `PivotFields(1)` rather than `PivotFields('Region')`.

As always, the best way to master this topic is to record your actions within a macro to find out its relevant objects, methods, and properties. Then study the Help topics to understand how everything fits together. In almost every case, you'll need to modify the recorded macros. Or, after you understand how to work with pivot tables, you can write code from scratch and avoid the macro recorder.

Creating a More Complex Pivot Table

In this section, I present VBA code to create a relatively complex pivot table.

Data for a more complex pivot table

Figure 17-3 shows part of a large worksheet table. This table contains 15,840 rows containing hierarchical budget data for a corporation. There are five divisions, and each division contains 11 departments. Each department has four budget categories, and each budget category contains several budget items. Budgeted and actual amounts are included for each of the 12 months. The goal is to summarize this information with a pivot table.

CD-ROM

This workbook is available on the companion CD-ROM. The file is named `budget pivot table.xlsm`.

Figure 17-4 shows a pivot table created from the data. Notice that the pivot table contains a calculated field named `Variance`. This field is the difference between the `Budget` amount and the `Actual` amount.

	A	B	C	D	E	F	G
1	Division	Department	Category	Item	Month	Budget	Actual
2	N. America	Data Processing	Compensation	Salaries	Jan	2583	3165
3	N. America	Data Processing	Compensation	Benefits	Jan	4496	2980
4	N. America	Data Processing	Compensation	Bonuses	Jan	3768	3029
5	N. America	Data Processing	Compensation	Commissions	Jan	3133	2815
6	N. America	Data Processing	Compensation	Payroll Taxes	Jan	3559	3770
7	N. America	Data Processing	Compensation	Training	Jan	3099	3559
8	N. America	Data Processing	Compensation	Conferences	Jan	2931	3199
9	N. America	Data Processing	Compensation	Entertainment	Jan	2632	2633
10	N. America	Data Processing	Facility	Rent	Jan	2833	2508
11	N. America	Data Processing	Facility	Lease	Jan	3450	2631
12	N. America	Data Processing	Facility	Utilities	Jan	4111	3098
13	N. America	Data Processing	Facility	Maintenance	Jan	3070	2870
14	N. America	Data Processing	Facility	Telephone	Jan	3827	4329
15	N. America	Data Processing	Facility	Other	Jan	3843	3322
16	N. America	Data Processing	Supplies & Services	General Office	Jan	2642	3218
17	N. America	Data Processing	Supplies & Services	Computer Supplies	Jan	3052	4098
18	N. America	Data Processing	Supplies & Services	Books & Subs	Jan	4346	3361
19	N. America	Data Processing	Supplies & Services	Outside Services	Jan	2869	3717
20	N. America	Data Processing	Supplies & Services	Other	Jan	3328	3116
21	N. America	Data Processing	Equipment	Computer Hardware	Jan	3088	2728
22	N. America	Data Processing	Equipment	Software	Jan	4226	2675
23	N. America	Data Processing	Equipment	Photocopiers	Jan	3780	3514
24	N. America	Data Processing	Equipment	Telecommunications	Jan	3893	3664
25	N. America	Data Processing	Equipment	Other	Jan	2851	4380
26	N. America	Human Resources	Compensation	Salaries	Jan	3604	3501
27	N. America	Human Resources	Compensation	Benefits	Jan	2859	4493
28	N. America	Human Resources	Compensation	Bonuses	Jan	3020	2676

Sheet1

Figure 17-3: The data in this workbook will be summarized in a pivot table.

	A	B	C	D	E	F	G	H	I	J	K	L	M	N
1	Division	(All)												
2	Category	(All)												
3														
4		Jan	Feb	Mar	Apr	May	Jun	Jul	Aug	Sep	Oct	Nov	Dec	Grand Total
5	Accounting													
6	Budget	422,455	433,317	420,522	417,964	411,820	414,012	427,431	418,530	412,134	421,678	426,602	418,445	5,044,910
7	Actual	422,662	413,163	416,522	420,672	431,303	429,993	425,879	415,253	417,401	417,806	425,271	420,026	5,055,951
8	Variance	-0,207	20,154	4,000	-2,708	-19,483	-15,981	1,552	3,277	-5,267	3,872	1,331	-1,581	-11,041
9	Advertising													
10	Budget	424,590	419,331	417,949	420,324	427,150	424,169	421,183	420,245	429,454	412,078	411,896	423,101	5,051,470
11	Actual	416,008	420,828	425,437	417,310	419,996	428,330	428,958	420,856	416,067	419,232	411,739	424,492	5,049,253
12	Variance	8,582	-1,497	-7,488	3,014	7,154	-4,161	-7,775	-0,611	13,387	-7,154	0,157	-1,391	2,217
13	Data Processing													
14	Budget	422,197	422,057	419,659	417,260	422,848	421,038	421,676	418,093	419,999	418,752	421,106	428,679	5,053,364
15	Actual	414,743	438,990	430,545	424,214	411,775	421,909	420,210	414,966	419,913	430,262	417,478	408,644	5,053,649
16	Variance	7,454	-16,933	-10,886	-6,954	11,073	-0,871	1,466	3,127	0,086	-11,510	3,628	20,035	-0,285
17	Human Resources													
18	Budget	422,053	425,313	418,634	423,038	423,514	419,602	415,197	419,701	422,762	413,741	410,972	422,746	5,037,273
19	Actual	424,934	429,275	407,053	429,187	410,258	421,870	428,551	422,469	422,252	421,838	415,125	417,222	5,050,034
20	Variance	-2,881	-3,962	11,581	-6,149	13,256	-2,268	-13,354	-2,768	0,510	-8,097	-4,153	5,524	-12,761
21	Operations													
22	Budget	413,530	427,975	419,527	422,299	415,298	414,805	413,149	425,287	412,284	414,242	427,521	420,190	5,026,107
23	Actual	415,819	406,592	426,827	418,223	431,307	413,201	416,350	411,339	422,584	416,132	424,041	426,461	5,028,876
24	Variance	-2,289	21,383	-7,300	4,076	-16,009	1,604	-3,201	13,948	-10,300	-1,890	3,480	-6,271	-2,769
25	Public Relations													
26	Budget	424,896	414,507	415,179	417,100	426,223	408,425	422,138	416,146	429,216	410,282	414,608	421,044	5,019,764
27	Actual	413,526	414,084	415,476	414,040	396,652	416,201	423,826	427,949	423,197	408,537	425,103	412,853	4,991,444
28	Variance	11,370	0,423	-0,297	3,060	29,571	-7,776	-1,688	-11,803	6,019	1,745	-10,495	8,191	28,320
29	R&D													
30	Budget	417,771	429,880	424,066	421,539	417,440	421,174	417,151	413,086	417,919	417,782	419,949	419,881	5,037,638
31	Actual	432,019	426,644	419,595	427,567	412,038	425,932	426,686	424,366	411,557	421,449	423,256	428,113	5,079,222
32	Variance	-14,248	3,236	4,471	-6,028	5,402	-4,758	-9,535	-11,280	6,362	-3,667	-3,307	-8,232	-41,584

PivotSheet Sheet1

PivotTable Field List
Choose fields to add to report:
☑ Division
☑ Department
☑ Category
☐ Item
☑ Month
☑ Budget
☑ Actual
☑ Variance
Drag fields between areas below:
Report Filter: Division, Category
Column Labels: Month
Row Labels: Department, Σ Values
Σ Values: Budget, Actual, Variance
☐ Defer Layout Update
Update

Figure 17-4: A pivot table created from the budget data.

Part V

The code that created the pivot table

Here's the VBA code that created the pivot table:

```vba
Sub CreatePivotTable()
    Dim PTcache As PivotCache
    Dim PT As PivotTable

    Application.ScreenUpdating = False
'   Delete PivotSheet if it exists
    On Error Resume Next
    Application.DisplayAlerts = False
    Sheets("PivotSheet").Delete
    On Error GoTo 0

'   Create a Pivot Cache
    Set PTcache = ActiveWorkbook.PivotCaches.Create( _
        SourceType:=xlDatabase, _
        SourceData:=Range("A1").CurrentRegion.Address)

'   Add new worksheet
    Worksheets.Add
    ActiveSheet.Name = "PivotSheet"
    ActiveWindow.DisplayGridlines = False

'   Create the Pivot Table from the Cache
    Set PT = ActiveSheet.PivotTables.Add( _
        PivotCache:=PTcache, _
        TableDestination:=Range("A1"), _
        TableName:="BudgetPivot")

    With PT
'       Add fields
        .PivotFields("Category").Orientation = xlPageField
        .PivotFields("Division").Orientation = xlPageField
        .PivotFields("Department").Orientation = xlRowField
        .PivotFields("Month").Orientation = xlColumnField
        .PivotFields("Budget").Orientation = xlDataField
        .PivotFields("Actual").Orientation = xlDataField
        .DataPivotField.Orientation = xlRowField

'       Add a calculated field to compute variance
        .CalculatedFields.Add "Variance", "=Budget-Actual"
```

```
        .PivotFields("Variance").Orientation = xlDataField

'       Specify a number format
        .DataBodyRange.NumberFormat = "0,000"

'       Apply a style
        .TableStyle2 = "PivotStyleMedium2"

'       Hide Field Headers
        .DisplayFieldCaptions = False

'       Change the captions
        .PivotFields("Sum of Budget").Caption = " Budget"
        .PivotFields("Sum of Actual").Caption = " Actual"
        .PivotFields("Sum of Variance").Caption = " Variance"
    End With
End Sub
```

How the more complex pivot table works

The `CreatePivotTable` procedure starts by deleting the `PivotSheet` worksheet if it already exists. It then creates a `PivotCache` object, inserts a new worksheet named `PivotSheet`, and creates the pivot table from the `PivotCache`. The code then adds the following fields to the pivot table:

- *Category:* A report filter (page) field.
- *Division:* A report filter (page) field.
- *Department:* A row field.
- *Month:* A column field.
- *Budget:* A data field.
- *Actual:* A data field.

Notice that the `Orientation` property of the `DataPivotField` is set to `xlRowField` in the following statement:

```
.DataPivotField.Orientation = xlRowField
```

This statement determines the overall orientation of the pivot table, and it represents the Sum Value field in the Pivot Table Field list (see Figure 17-5). Try moving that field to the Column Labels section to see how it affects the pivot table layout.

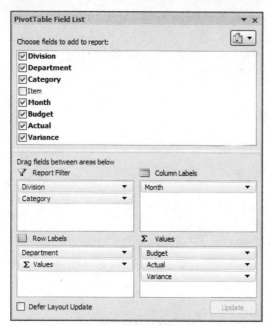

Figure 17-5: The Pivot Table Field List.

Next, the procedure uses the `Add` method of the `CalculatedFields` collection to create the calculated field `Variance`, which subtracts the `Actual` amount from the `Budget` amount. This calculated field is assigned as a data field.

NOTE

To add a calculated field to a pivot table manually, use the PivotTable ⇨ Options ⇨ Tools ⇨ Formulas ⇨ Calculated Field command, which displays the Insert Calculated Field dialog box.

Finally, the code makes a few cosmetic adjustments:

- Applies a number format to the `DataBodyRange` (which represents the entire pivot table data).

- Applies a style.

- Hides the captions (equivalent to the PivotTable Tools ⇨ Options ⇨ Show/Hide ⇨ Field Headers control).

- Changes the captions displayed in the pivot table. For example, `Sum of Budget` is replaced by `Budget`. Note that the string `Budget` is preceded by a space. Excel doesn't allow you to change a caption that corresponds to a field name, so adding a space gets around this restriction.

NOTE

While creating this procedure, I used the macro recorder extensively to learn about the various properties. That, combined with the information in the Help system (and a fair amount of trial and error), provided all the information I needed.

Creating Multiple Pivot Tables

The final example creates a series of pivot tables that summarize data collected in a customer survey. That data is stored in a worksheet database (see Figure 17-6) and consists of 150 rows. Each row contains the respondent's sex plus a numerical rating using a 1–5 scale for each of the 14 survey items.

	A	B	C	D	E	F	G	H	I	J	K	L	M	
1	Name	Sex	Store locations are convenient	Store hours are convenient	Stores are well-maintained	You are easy to reach by phone	I like your web site	Employees are friendly	Employees are helpful	Employee are knowledge able	Pricing is competitive	You have a good selection of products	I like your TV ads	Yo qu prc
2	Subject1	Male	1	4	4	4	1	1	2	1	1	2	5	
3	Subject2	Female	2	5	1	1	4	2	4	3	3	2	2	
4	Subject3	Male	1	1	4	2	3	3	2	1	2	3	2	
5	Subject4	Male	2	1	3	5	1	2	3	4	2	1	3	
6	Subject5	Female	2	2	5	5	4	2	1	5	5	2	3	
7	Subject6	Female	2	4	3	3	1	1	4	4	4	2	2	
8	Subject7	Female	2	4	5	4	5	3	2	5	4	4	1	
9	Subject8	Male	3	2	1	2	3	4	3	1	2	4	3	
10	Subject9	Female	3	4	4	4	5	1	4	1	4	1	2	
11	Subject10	Male	2	1	5	5	5	1	4	1	2	2	5	
12	Subject11	Male	4	3	3	2	1	2	4	2	1	4	2	
13	Subject12	Female	2	1	4	5	5	5	3	1	4	1	2	
14	Subject13	Female	4	3	4	3	2	5	3	3	2	2	5	
15	Subject14	Female	2	3	4	2	1	1	4	2	1	3	3	
16	Subject15	Female	1	3	5	1	2	2	4	1	3	4	2	
17	Subject16	Male	1	4	1	3	4	3	4	4	5	3	4	
18	Subject17	Female	3	4	3	5	5	4	4	3	2	4	2	
19	Subject18	Male	1	5	5	3	5	3	4	2	3	2	3	
20	Subject19	Female	1	3	5	4	5	5	5	1	1	5	3	

K ◀ ▶ ▶I   Summary   **SurveyData**

Figure 17-6: Creating a series of pivot tables will summarize this survey data.

CD-ROM

This workbook, named `survey data pivot tables.xlsm`, is available on the companion CD-ROM.

Figure 17-7 shows a few of the 28 pivot tables produced by the macro. Each survey item is summarized in two pivot tables (one showing percentages, and one showing the actual frequencies).

Part V

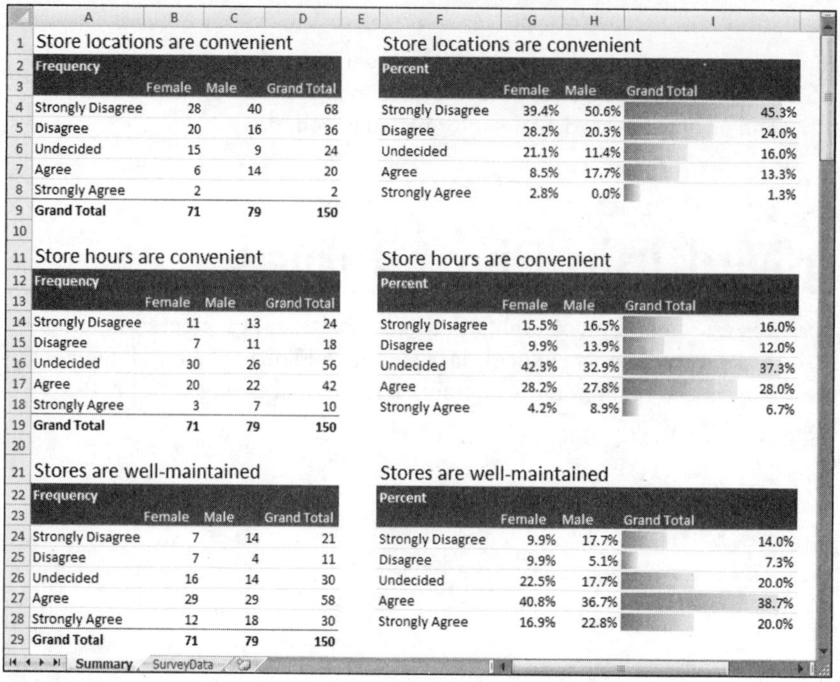

	A	B	C	D	E	F	G	H	I
1	Store locations are convenient					Store locations are convenient			
2	Frequency					Percent			
3		Female	Male	Grand Total			Female	Male	Grand Total
4	Strongly Disagree	28	40	68		Strongly Disagree	39.4%	50.6%	45.3%
5	Disagree	20	16	36		Disagree	28.2%	20.3%	24.0%
6	Undecided	15	9	24		Undecided	21.1%	11.4%	16.0%
7	Agree	6	14	20		Agree	8.5%	17.7%	13.3%
8	Strongly Agree	2		2		Strongly Agree	2.8%	0.0%	1.3%
9	Grand Total	71	79	150					
10									
11	Store hours are convenient					Store hours are convenient			
12	Frequency					Percent			
13		Female	Male	Grand Total			Female	Male	Grand Total
14	Strongly Disagree	11	13	24		Strongly Disagree	15.5%	16.5%	16.0%
15	Disagree	7	11	18		Disagree	9.9%	13.9%	12.0%
16	Undecided	30	26	56		Undecided	42.3%	32.9%	37.3%
17	Agree	20	22	42		Agree	28.2%	27.8%	28.0%
18	Strongly Agree	3	7	10		Strongly Agree	4.2%	8.9%	6.7%
19	Grand Total	71	79	150					
20									
21	Stores are well-maintained					Stores are well-maintained			
22	Frequency					Percent			
23		Female	Male	Grand Total			Female	Male	Grand Total
24	Strongly Disagree	7	14	21		Strongly Disagree	9.9%	17.7%	14.0%
25	Disagree	7	4	11		Disagree	9.9%	5.1%	7.3%
26	Undecided	16	14	30		Undecided	22.5%	17.7%	20.0%
27	Agree	29	29	58		Agree	40.8%	36.7%	38.7%
28	Strongly Agree	12	18	30		Strongly Agree	16.9%	22.8%	20.0%
29	Grand Total	71	79	150					

Summary / SurveyData

Figure 17-7: Six of the 28 pivot tables created by a VBA procedure.

The VBA code that created the pivot tables follows:

```
Sub MakePivotTables()
'    This procedure creates 28 pivot tables
    Dim PTCache As PivotCache
    Dim PT As PivotTable
    Dim SummarySheet As Worksheet
    Dim ItemName As String
    Dim Row As Long, Col As Long, i As Long

    Application.ScreenUpdating = False

'    Delete Summary sheet if it exists
    On Error Resume Next
    Application.DisplayAlerts = False
    Sheets("Summary").Delete
    On Error GoTo 0

'    Add Summary sheet
    Set SummarySheet = Worksheets.Add
    ActiveSheet.Name = "Summary"

'    Create Pivot Cache
```

```vba
Set PTCache = ActiveWorkbook.PivotCaches.Create( _
  SourceType:=xlDatabase, _
  SourceData:=Sheets("SurveyData").Range("A1"). _
    CurrentRegion)

Row = 1
For i = 1 To 14
  For Col = 1 To 6 Step 5 '2 columns
    ItemName = Sheets("SurveyData").Cells(1, i + 2)
    With Cells(Row, Col)
        .Value = ItemName
        .Font.Size = 16
    End With

'   Create pivot table
    Set PT = ActiveSheet.PivotTables.Add( _
      PivotCache:=PTCache, _
      TableDestination:=SummarySheet.Cells(Row + 1, Col))

'   Add the fields
    If Col = 1 Then 'Frequency tables
        With PT.PivotFields(ItemName)
          .Orientation = xlDataField
          .Name = "Frequency"
          .Function = xlCount
        End With
    Else ' Percent tables
    With PT.PivotFields(ItemName)
        .Orientation = xlDataField
        .Name = "Percent"
        .Function = xlCount
        .Calculation = xlPercentOfColumn
        .NumberFormat = "0.0%"
    End With
    End If

    PT.PivotFields(ItemName).Orientation = xlRowField
    PT.PivotFields("Sex").Orientation = xlColumnField
    PT.TableStyle2 = "PivotStyleMedium2"
    PT.DisplayFieldCaptions = False
    If Col = 6 Then
'       add data bars to the last column
        PT.ColumnGrand = False
        PT.DataBodyRange.Columns(3).FormatConditions. _
        AddDatabar
    End If
  Next Col
```

Part V

```
        Row = Row + 10
    Next i

'    Replace numbers with descriptive text
     With Range("A:A,F:F")
        .Replace "1", "Strongly Disagree"
        .Replace "2", "Disagree"
        .Replace "3", "Undecided"
        .Replace "4", "Agree"
        .Replace "5", "Strongly Agree"
     End With
End Sub
End Sub
```

Notice that all of these pivot tables were created from a single `PivotCache` object.

The pivot tables are created within a nested loop. The `Col` loop counter goes from 1 to 6 by using the `Step` parameter. The instructions vary a bit for the second column of pivot tables. Specifically, the pivot tables in the second column, do the following:

- Display the count as a percent of the column.
- Do not show grand totals for the rows.
- Are assigned a number format.
- Display format conditioning data bars.

The `Row` variable keeps track of the starting row of each pivot table. The final step is to replace the numeric categories in columns A and F with text. For example, 1 is replaced with *Strongly Agree*.

Creating a Reverse Pivot Table

A pivot table is a summary of data in a table. But what if you have a summary table, and you'd like to create a table from it? Figure 17-8 shows an example. Range B2:F14 contains a summary table — similar to a very simple pivot table. Columns I:K contain a 48-row table created from the summary table. In the table, each row contains one data point, and the first two columns describe that data point.

Excel doesn't provide a way to transform a summary table into a table, so it's a good job for a VBA macro. After I created this macro, I spent a bit more time and added a UserForm, shown in Figure 17-9. The UserForm gets the input and output ranges and also has an option to convert the output range to a table.

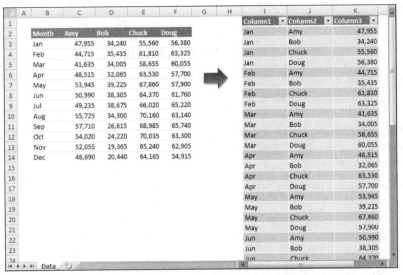

Figure 17-8: The summary table on the left will be converted to the table on the right.

CD-ROM

This workbook, named `reverse pivot table.xlsm`, is available on the companion CD-ROM.

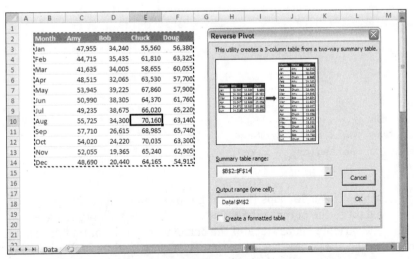

Figure 17-9: This dialog box asks the user for the ranges.

When the user clicks the OK button in the UserForm, VBA code validates the ranges and then calls the `ReversePivot` procedure with this statement:

```
Call ReversePivot(SummaryTable, OutputRange, cbCreateTable)
```

Part V

It passes three arguments:

- `SummaryTable`: A `Range` object that represents the summary table.
- `OutputRange`: A `Range` object that represents the upper-left cell of the output range.
- `cbCreateTable`: The `Checkbox` object on the UserForm.

This procedure will work for any size summary table. The number of data rows in the output table will be equal to the $(r-1) * (c-1)$, where r and c represent the number of rows and columns in the Summary Table.

The code for the `ReversePivot` procedure follows:

```
Sub ReversePivot(SummaryTable As Range, _
   OutputRange As Range, CreateTable As Boolean)
     Dim r As Long, c As Long
     Dim OutRow As Long, OutCol As Long

'    Convert the range
     OutRow = 2
     Application.ScreenUpdating = False
     OutputRange.Range("A1:C3") = Array("Column1", "Column2", "Column3")
     For r = 2 To SummaryTable.Rows.Count
         For c = 2 To SummaryTable.Columns.Count
             OutputRange.Cells(OutRow, 1) = SummaryTable.Cells(r, 1)
             OutputRange.Cells(OutRow, 2) = SummaryTable.Cells(1, c)
             OutputRange.Cells(OutRow, 3) = SummaryTable.Cells(r, c)
             OutRow = OutRow + 1
         Next c
     Next r

'    Make it a table?
     If CreateTable Then _
       ActiveSheet.ListObjects.Add xlSrcRange, _
         OutputRange.CurrentRegion, , xlYes
End Sub
```

The procedure is fairly simple. The code loops through the rows and columns in the input range and then writes the data to the output range. The output range will always have three columns. The `OutRow` variable keeps track of the current row in the output range. Finally, if the user checked the check box, the output range is converted to a table by using the `Add` method of the `ListObjects` collection.

Chapter 18

Working with Charts

In This Chapter

Excel's charting feature lets you create a wide variety of charts using data that's stored in a worksheet. In this chapter, I discuss the following:

◆ Essential background information on Excel charts

◆ The difference between embedded charts and chart sheets

◆ Understanding the `Chart` object model

◆ Using methods other than the macro recorder to help you learn about `Chart` objects

◆ Examples of common charting tasks that use VBA

◆ Examples of more complex charting macros

◆ Some interesting (and useful) chart-making tricks

Excel supports a wide variety of chart types, and you have a great deal of control over nearly every aspect of each chart. In Excel 2007, charts look better than ever.

About Charts

An Excel chart is simply packed with objects, each of which has its own properties and methods. Because of this, manipulating charts with Visual Basic for Applications (VBA) can be a bit of a challenge — and, unfortunately, the macro recorder isn't much help in Excel 2007. In this chapter, I discuss the key concepts that you need to understand in order to write VBA code that generates or manipulates charts. The secret, as you'll see, is a good understanding of the object hierarchy for charts. But first, a bit of background about Excel charts.

Chart locations

In Excel, a chart can be located in either of two places within a workbook:

- *As an embedded object on a worksheet:* A worksheet can contain any number of embedded charts.

- *In a separate chart sheet:* A chart sheet normally holds a single chart.

Most charts are created manually by using the commands in the Insert ➪ Charts group. But you can also create charts by using VBA. And, of course, you can use VBA to modify existing charts.

TIP

The fastest way to create a chart is to select your data and then press Alt+F1. Excel creates an embedded chart and uses the default chart type. To create a new default chart on a chart sheet, select the data and press F11.

A key concept when working with charts is the *active chart* — that is, the chart that's currently selected. When the user clicks an embedded chart or activates a chart sheet, a Chart object is activated. In VBA, the ActiveChart property returns the activated Chart object (if any). You can write code to work with this Chart object, much like you can write code to work with the Workbook object returned by the ActiveWorkbook property.

Here's an example: If a chart is activated, the following statement will display the Name property for the Chart object:

```
MsgBox ActiveChart.Name
```

If a chart is not activated, the preceding statement generates an error.

NOTE

As you see later in this chapter, it's not necessary to activate a chart in order to manipulate it with VBA.

The macro recorder and charts

If you've read other chapters in the book, you know that I often recommend using the macro recorder to learn about objects, properties, and methods. Unfortunately, Microsoft took a major step backward in Excel 2007 when it comes to recording chart actions. Although it's possible to record a macro while you create and customize a chart, there's a pretty good chance that the recorded macro will not produce the same result when you execute it.

Following is a macro that I recorded while I created a column chart, deleted the legend, and then added a shadow effect to the column series.

```
Sub RecordedMacro()
    ActiveSheet.Shapes.AddChart.Select
    ActiveChart.SetSourceData Source:=Range("Sheet1!$A$2:$B$4")
    ActiveChart.ChartType = xlColumnClustered
    ActiveChart.Legend.Select
    Selection.Delete
    ActiveSheet.ChartObjects("Chart 1").Activate
    ActiveChart.SeriesCollection(1).Select
End Sub
```

The chart is shown in Figure 18-1.

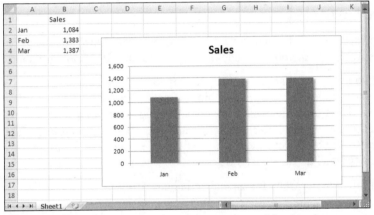

Figure 18-1: The macro recorder was turned on while this chart was created and customized.

Notice the following points:

- Even though I selected the range before I turned on the macro recorder, the source data range is hard-coded in the macro. In other words, the recorded macro does not use the Selection object, which is typical of other recorded macros. In other words, it's not possible to record a macro that creates a chart from the selected range.

- The macro also hard-codes the chart's name. When this macro is played back, it's very unlikely that the newly-created chart will be named Chart 1, so the macro will either select the wrong chart or end with an error if a chart with that name does not exist.

- Although selecting the data series was recorded, the formatting command was not. So, if you would like to find out which objects and properties are used to format a data series, the macro recorder is of no help at all.

Compatibility Note

The VBA code in this chapter uses many new chart-related properties and methods that were introduced in Excel 2007. As a result, most of the code presented here will not work with previous versions of Excel.

Bottom line? In Excel 2007, Microsoft downgraded macro recording for charts to the point where it's virtually useless. I don't know why this happened, but it's likely that they just didn't have the time, and meeting the product ship date was deemed a higher priority.

Despite the flaws, recording a chart-related macro can still be of *some* assistance. For example, you can use a recorded macro to figure out how to insert a chart, change the chart type, add a series, and so on. But when it comes to learning about formatting, you're on your own. More than ever, you'll need to rely on the object browser and the Auto List Members feature.

The Chart object model

When you first start exploring the object model for a `Chart` object, you'll probably be very confused — which is not surprising; the object model *is* very confusing. It's also very deep.

For example, assume that you want to change the title displayed in an embedded chart. The top-level object, of course, is the `Application` object (Excel). The `Application` object contains a `Workbook` object, and the `Workbook` object contains a `Worksheet` object. The `Worksheet` object contains a `ChartObject` object, which contains a `Chart` object. The `Chart` object has a `ChartTitle` object, and the `ChartTitle` object has a `Text` property that stores the text that's displayed as the chart's title.

Here's another way to look at this hierarchy for an embedded chart:

```
Application
    Workbook
        Worksheet
            ChartObject
                Chart
                    ChartTitle
```

Your VBA code must, of course, follow this object model precisely. For example, to set a chart's title to YTD Sales, you can write a VBA instruction like this:

```
WorkSheets("Sheet1").ChartObjects(1).Chart.ChartTitle. _
    .Text = "YTD Sales"
```

This statement assumes the active workbook as the `Workbook` object. The statement works with the first item in the `ChartObjects` collection on the worksheet named

Sheet1. The Chart property returns the actual Chart object, and the ChartTitle property returns the ChartTitle object. Finally, you get to the Text property.

For a chart sheet, the object hierarchy is a bit different because it doesn't involve the Worksheet object or the ChartObject object. For example, here's the hierarchy for the ChartTitle object for a chart in a chart sheet:

```
Application
    Workbook
        Chart
            ChartTitle
```

In terms of VBA, you could use this statement to set the chart title in a chart sheet to YTD Sales:

```
Sheets("Chart1").ChartTitle.Text = "YTD Sales"
```

A chart sheet is essentially a Chart object, and it has no containing ChartObject object. Put another way, the parent object for an embedded chart is a ChartObject object, and the parent object for a chart on a separate chart sheet is a Workbook object.

Both of the following statements will display a message box with the word Chart in it:

```
MsgBox TypeName(Sheets("Sheet1").ChartObjects(1).Chart)
Msgbox TypeName(Sheets("Chart1"))
```

 NOTE

When you create a new embedded chart, you're adding to the ChartObjects collection and the Shapes collection contained in a particular worksheet. (There is no Charts collection for a worksheet.) When you create a new chart sheet, you're adding to the Charts collection and the Sheets collection for a particular workbook.

Common VBA Charting Techniques

In this section, I describe how to use VBA to perform some common tasks that involve charts.

Creating an embedded chart

In Excel 2007, a ChartObject is a special type of Shape object. Therefore, it's a member of the Shapes collection. To create a new chart, use the AddChart method of the Shapes collection. The following statement creates an empty embedded chart:

```
ActiveSheet.Shapes.AddChart
```

The `AddChart` method can use five arguments (all are optional):

- *Type:* The type of chart. If omitted, the default chart type is used. Constants for all of the chart types are provided (for example, `xlArea`, `xlColumnClustered`, and so on).

- *Left:* The left position of the chart, in points. If omitted, Excel centers the chart horizontally.

- *Top:* The top position of the chart, in points. If omitted, Excel centers the chart vertically.

- *Width:* The width of the chart, in points. If omitted, Excel uses 354.

- *Height:* The height of the chart, in points. If omitted, Excel uses 210.

In many cases, you may find it efficient to create an object variable when the chart is created. The following procedure creates a line chart that can be referenced in code by using the `MyChart` object variable:

```
Sub CreateChart()
    Dim MyChart As Chart
    Set MyChart = ActiveSheet.Shapes.AddChart(xlLineMarkers).Chart
End Sub
```

Creating a Chart the Old Way

Using the `AddChart` method of the `Shapes` collection (as described in "Creating an embedded chart") is the "new" way of creating charts, introduced in Excel 2007. For compatibility purposes, you can still use the `Add` method of the `ChartObjects` collection. This method, unlike the `AddChart` method of the `Shapes` objects, does not allow you to specify the chart type as an argument, so you need to use the `ChartType` property if you want to use anything except the default chart type. In addition, the `Left`, `Top`, `Width`, and `Height` arguments are required.

The procedure that follows uses the `Add` method of the `ChartObjects` collection to create an embedded chart.

```
Sub CreateChart2()
    Dim MyChart As Chart
    Dim DataRange As Range
    Set DataRange = ActiveSheet.Range("A1:C7")
    Set MyChart = ActiveSheet.ChartObjects.Add(10, 10, 354, 210).Chart
    MyChart.SetSourceData Source:=DataRange
    MyChart.ChartType = xlColumnClustered
End Sub
```

A chart without data is not very useful, so you'll want to use the `SetSourceData` method to add data to a newly-created chart. The procedure that follows demonstrates the `SetSourceData` method. This procedure creates the chart shown in Figure 18-2.

```
Sub CreateChart()
    Dim MyChart As Chart
    Dim DataRange As Range
    Set DataRange = ActiveSheet.Range("A1:C7")
    Set MyChart = ActiveSheet.Shapes.AddChart.Chart
    MyChart.SetSourceData Source:=DataRange
End Sub
```

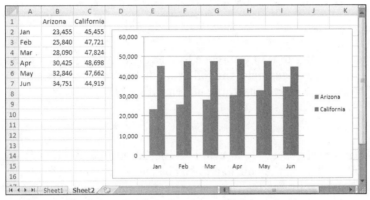

Figure 18-2: A few lines of VBA code created this chart.

Creating a chart on a chart sheet

The preceding section describes the basic procedures for creating an embedded chart. To create a chart on a chart sheet, use the `Add` method of the `Charts` collection. The `Add` method of the `Charts` collection uses several optional arguments, but these arguments specify the position of the chart sheet — not chart-related information.

The example that follows creates a chart on a chart sheet and specifies the data range and chart type:

```
Sub CreateChartSheet()
    Dim MyChart As Chart
    Dim DataRange As Range
    Set DataRange = ActiveSheet.Range("A1:C7")
    Set MyChart = Charts.Add
    MyChart.SetSourceData Source:=DataRange
    ActiveChart.ChartType = xlColumnClustered
End Sub
```

Using VBA to activate a chart

When a user clicks any area of an embedded chart, the chart is activated. Your VBA code can activate an embedded chart with the `Activate` method. Here's a VBA statement that's the equivalent of Ctrl+clicking an embedded chart:

```
ActiveSheet.ChartObjects("Chart 1").Activate
```

If the chart is on a chart sheet, use a statement like this:

```
Sheets("Chart1").Activate
```

Alternatively, you can activate a chart by selecting its containing Shape:

```
ActiveSheet.Shapes("Chart 1").Select
```

When a chart is activated, you can refer to it in your code by using the `ActiveChart` property (which returns a `Chart` object). For example, the following instruction displays the name of the active chart. If there is no active chart, the statement generates an error:

```
MsgBox ActiveChart.Name
```

To modify a chart with VBA, it's not necessary to activate it. The two procedures that follow have exactly the same effect. That is, they change the embedded chart named `Chart 1` to an area chart. The first procedure activates the chart before performing the manipulations; the second one doesn't:

```
Sub ModifyChart1()
    ActiveSheet.ChartObjects("Chart 1").Activate
    ActiveChart.ChartType = xlArea
End Sub

Sub ModifyChart2()
    ActiveSheet.ChartObjects("Chart 1").Chart.ChartType = xlArea
End Sub
```

Moving a chart

A chart embedded on a worksheet can be converted to a chart sheet. To do so manually, just activate the embedded chart and choose Chart Tools ➪ Design ➪ Location ➪ Move Chart. In the Move Chart dialog box, select the New Sheet option and specify a name.

You can also convert an embedded chart to a chart sheet by using VBA. Here's an example that converts the first `ChartObject` on a worksheet named `Sheet1` to a chart sheet named `MyChart`:

```
Sub MoveChart1()
    Sheets("Sheet1").ChartObjects(1).Chart. _
        Location xlLocationAsNewSheet, "MyChart"
End Sub
```

The following example does just the opposite of the preceding procedure: It converts the chart on a chart sheet named `MyChart` to an embedded chart on the worksheet named `Sheet1`.

```
Sub MoveChart2()
    Charts("MyChart") _
        .Location xlLocationAsObject, "Sheet1"
End Sub
```

What's Your Name?

Every `ChartObject` object has a name, and every Chart contained in a `ChartObject` has a name. That certainly seems straightforward enough, but it can be confusing. Create a new chart on `Sheet1` and activate it. Then activate the VBA Immediate window and type a few commands:

```
? ActiveSheet.Shapes(1).Name
Chart 1
? ActiveSheet.ChartObjects(1).Name
Chart 1
? ActiveChart.Name
Sheet1 Chart 1
? Activesheet.ChartObjects(1).Chart.Name
Sheet1 Chart 1
```

If you change the name of the worksheet, the name of the Chart also changes. However, you can't change the name of a Chart that's contained in a `ChartObject`. If you try to do so using VBA, you get an inexplicable "out of memory" error.

What about changing the name of a `ChartObject`? The logical place to do that is in the Name box (to the left of the Formula bar). Although you can rename a shape by using the Name box, you can't rename a chart (even though a chart is actually a shape). To rename an embedded chart, use the Chart Name control in the Chart Tools ➪ Layout ➪ Properties group. This control displays the name of the active chart (which is actually the name of the `ChartObject`), and you can use this control to change the name of the `ChartObject`. Oddly, Excel allows you to use the name of an existing `ChartObject`. In other words, you could have a dozen embedded charts on a worksheet, and every one of them can be named `Chart 1`.

Bottom line? Be aware of this quirk. If you find that your VBA charting macro isn't working, make sure that you don't have two identically named charts.

NOTE

Using the `Location` method also activates the relocated chart.

Using VBA to deactivate a chart

You can use the `Activate` method to activate a chart, but how do you deactivate (that is, unselect) a chart? According to the Help System, you can use the `Deselect` method to deactivate a chart:

```
ActiveChart.Deselect
```

However, this statement simply doesn't work — at least in the initial release of Excel 2007.

As far as I can tell, the only way to deactivate a chart by using VBA is to select something other than the chart. For an embedded chart, you can use the `RangeSelection` property of the `ActiveWindow` object to deactivate the chart and select the range that was selected before the chart was activated:

```
ActiveWindow.RangeSelection.Select
```

Determining whether a chart is activated

A common type of macro performs some manipulations on the active chart (the chart selected by a user). For example, a macro might change the chart's type, apply a style, or export the chart to a graphics file.

The question is, how can your VBA code determine whether the user has actually selected a chart? By selecting a chart, I mean either activating a chart sheet or activating an embedded chart by clicking it. Your first inclination might be to check the `TypeName` property of the `Selection`, as in this expression:

```
TypeName(Selection) = "Chart"
```

In fact, this expression never evaluates to `True`. When a chart is activated, the actual selection will be an object within the `Chart` object. For example, the selection might be a `Series` object, a `ChartTitle` object, a `Legend` object, a `PlotArea` object, and so on.

The solution is to determine whether `ActiveChart` is `Nothing`. If so, then a chart is not active. The following code checks to ensure that a chart is active. If not, the user sees a message and the procedure ends:

```
If ActiveChart Is Nothing Then
    MsgBox "Select a chart."
    Exit Sub
Else
    'other code goes here
End If
```

You may find it convenient to use a VBA function procedure to determine whether a chart is activated. The `ChartIsSelected` function, which follows, returns `True` if a chart sheet is active or if an embedded chart is activated, but returns `False` if a chart is not activated:

```
Private Function ChartIsSelected() As Boolean
    ChartIsSelected = Not ActiveChart Is Nothing
End Function
```

Deleting from the ChartObjects or Charts collection

To delete a chart on a worksheet, you must know the name or index of the `ChartObject`. This statement deletes the `ChartObject` named `Chart 1` on the active worksheet:

```
ActiveSheet.ChartObjects("Chart 1").Delete
```

To delete all `ChartObject` objects on a worksheet, use the `Delete` method of the `ChartObjects` collection:

```
ActiveSheet.ChartObjects.Delete
```

You can also delete embedded charts by accessing the `Shapes` collection. The following statement deletes `Chart 1` on the active worksheet:

```
ActiveSheet.Shapes("Chart 1").Delete
```

And this statement deletes all embedded charts (and all other shapes):

```
ActiveSheet.Shapes.Delete
```

To delete a single chart sheet, you must know the chart sheet's name or index. The following statement deletes the chart sheet named `Chart1`:

```
Charts("Chart1").Delete
```

To delete all chart sheets in the active workbook, use the following statement:

```
ActiveWorkbook.Charts.Delete
```

Deleting sheets causes Excel to display a warning like the one shown in Figure 18-3. The user must reply to this prompt in order for the macro to continue. If you are deleting a sheet with a macro, you probably won't want this warning prompt to appear. To eliminate the prompt, use the following series of statements:

```
Application.DisplayAlerts = False
ActiveWorkbook.Charts.Delete
Application.DisplayAlerts = True
```

Figure 18-3: Attempting to delete one or more chart sheets results in this message.

Looping through all charts

In some cases, you may need to perform an operation on all charts. The following example applies changes to every embedded chart on the active worksheet. The procedure uses a loop to cycle through each object in the ChartObjects collection and then accesses the Chart object in each and changes several properties.

```
Sub FormatAllCharts()
    Dim ChtObj As ChartObject
    For Each ChtObj In ActiveSheet.ChartObjects
      With ChtObj.Chart
        .ChartType = xlLineMarkers
        .ApplyLayout 3
        .ChartStyle = 12
        .ClearToMatchStyle
        .SetElement msoElementChartTitleAboveChart
        .SetElement msoElementLegendNone
        .SetElement msoElementPrimaryValueAxisTitleNone
        .SetElement msoElementPrimaryCategoryAxisTitleNone
        .Axes(xlValue).MinimumScale = 0
        .Axes(xlValue).MaximumScale = 1000
      End With
    Next ChtObj
End Sub
```

 CD-ROM

This example is available on the companion CD-ROM. The filename is format all charts.xlsm.

Figure 18-4 shows four charts that use a variety of different formatting; Figure 18-5 shows the same charts after running the FormatAllCharts macro.

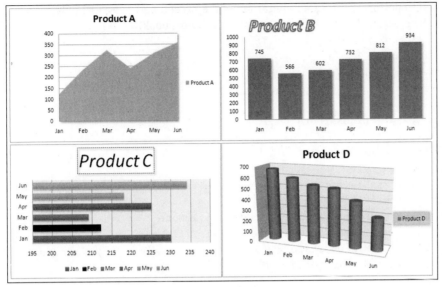

Figure 18-4: These charts use different formatting.

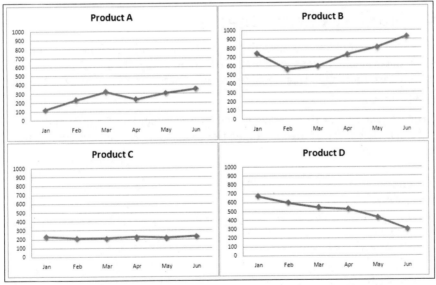

Figure 18-5: A simple macro applied consistent formatting to the four charts.

The following macro performs the same operation as the preceding `FormatAllCharts` procedure but works on all the chart sheets in the active workbook:

```
Sub FormatAllCharts2()
    Dim cht as Chart
    For Each cht In ActiveWorkbook.Charts
      With cht
        .ChartType = xlLineMarkers
        .ApplyLayout 3
        .ChartStyle = 12
        .ClearToMatchStyle
        .SetElement msoElementChartTitleAboveChart
        .SetElement msoElementLegendNone
        .SetElement msoElementPrimaryValueAxisTitleNone
        .SetElement msoElementPrimaryCategoryAxisTitleNone
        .Axes(xlValue).MinimumScale = 0
        .Axes(xlValue).MaximumScale = 1000
      End With
    Next cht
End Sub
```

Sizing and aligning ChartObjects

A `ChartObject` object has standard positional (`Top` and `Left`) and sizing (`Width` and `Height`) properties that you can access with your VBA code. Oddly, the Excel 2007 Ribbon has controls (in the Chart Tools ⇨ Format ⇨ Size group) to set the `Height` and `Width`, but not the `Top` and `Left`.

The following example resizes all `ChartObject` objects on a sheet so that they match the dimensions of the active chart. It also arranges the `ChartObject` objects into a user-specified number of columns.

```
Sub SizeAndAlignCharts()
    Dim W As Long, H As Long
    Dim TopPosition As Long, LeftPosition As Long
    Dim ChtObj As ChartObject
    Dim i As Long, NumCols As Long

    If ActiveChart Is Nothing Then
        MsgBox "Select a chart to be used as the base for the sizing"
        Exit Sub
    End If

    'Get columns
    On Error Resume Next
```

```
    NumCols = InputBox("How many columns of charts?")
    If Err.Number <> 0 Then Exit Sub
    If NumCols < 1 Then Exit Sub
    On Error GoTo 0

    'Get size of active chart
    W = ActiveChart.Parent.Width
    H = ActiveChart.Parent.Height

    'Change starting positions, if necessary
    TopPosition = 100
    LeftPosition = 20
    For i = 1 To ActiveSheet.ChartObjects.Count
        With ActiveSheet.ChartObjects(i)
            .Width = W
            .Height = H
            .Left = LeftPosition + ((i - 1) Mod NumCols) * W
            .Top = TopPosition + Int((i - 1) / NumCols) * H
        End With
    Next i
End Sub
```

If no chart is active, the user is prompted to activate a chart that will be used as the basis for sizing the other charts. I use an `InputBox` function to get the number of columns. The values for the `Left` and `Top` properties are calculated within the loop.

 CD-ROM

This workbook, named `size and align charts.xlsm`, is available on the companion CD-ROM.

Exporting a chart

In some cases, you may need an Excel chart in the form of a graphics file. For example, you may want to post the chart on a Web site. One option is to use a screen capture program and copy the pixels directly from the screen. Another choice is to write a simple VBA macro.

The procedure that follows uses the `Export` method of the `Chart` object to save the active chart as a GIF file.

```
Sub SaveChartAsGIF ()
    Dim Fname as String
    If ActiveChart Is Nothing Then Exit Sub
    Fname = ThisWorkbook.Path & "\" & ActiveChart.Name & ".gif"
    ActiveChart.Export FileName:=Fname, FilterName:="GIF"
End Sub
```

Other choices for the `FilterName` argument are `"JPEG"` and `"PNG"`. Usually, GIF and PNG files look better. Keep in mind that the `Export` method will fail if the user doesn't have the specified graphics export filter installed. These filters are installed in the Office (or Excel) setup program.

Exporting all graphics

One way to export all graphic images from a workbook is to save the file in HTML format. Doing so creates a directory that contains GIF and PNG images of the charts, shapes, clipart, and even copied range images (created with Home ⇨ Clipboard ⇨ Paste ⇨ As Picture ⇨ Paste As Picture).

Here's a VBA procedure that automates the process. It works with the active workbook:

```
Sub SaveAllGraphics()
    Dim FileName As String
    Dim TempName As String
    Dim DirName As String
    Dim gFile As String

    FileName = ActiveWorkbook.FullName
    TempName = ActiveWorkbook.Path & "\" & _
        ActiveWorkbook.Name & "graphics.htm"
    DirName = Left(TempName, Len(TempName) - 4) & "_files"

'   Save active workbookbook as HTML, then reopen original
    ActiveWorkbook.Save
    ActiveWorkbook.SaveAs FileName:=TempName, FileFormat:=xlHtml
    Application.DisplayAlerts = False
    ActiveWorkbook.Close
    Workbooks.Open FileName

'   Delete the HTML file
    Kill TempName

'   Delete all but *.PNG files in the HTML folder
    gFile = Dir(DirName & "\*.*")
    Do While gFile <> ""
        If Right(gFile, 3) <> "png" Then Kill DirName & "\" & gFile
        gFile = Dir
    Loop

'   Show the exported graphics
    Shell "explorer.exe " & DirName, vbNormalFocus
End Sub
```

The procedure starts by saving the active workbook. Then it saves the workbook as an HTML file, closes the file, and re-opens the original workbook. Next, it deletes the HTML file because we're just interested in the folder that it creates (that's where the images are). The code then loops through the folder and deletes everything except the PNG files. Finally, it uses the `Shell` function to display the folder.

CD-ROM

This example is available on the companion CD-ROM. The filename is `export all graphics.xlsm`.

Using VBA to Apply Chart Formatting

A common type of chart macro applies formatting to one or more charts. For example, you may create a macro that applies consistent formatting to all charts on a worksheet. If you experiment with the macro recorder, you'll find that commands in the following Ribbon groups are recorded:

- Chart Tools ⇨ Design ⇨ Chart Layouts
- Chart Tools ⇨ Design ⇨ Chart Styles
- Chart Tools ⇨ Layout ⇨ Labels
- Chart Tools ⇨ Layout ⇨ Axes
- Chart Tools ⇨ Layout ⇨ Background

Unfortunately, formatting any individual chart element (for example, changing the color of a chart series) is *not* recorded by the macro recorder. Therefore, you'll need to figure out the objects and properties on your own.

Formatting a chart

I used output from the macro recorder as the basis for the `FormatChart` procedure shown here, which converts the active chart to a clustered column chart (using Chart Tools ⇨ Design ⇨ Type ⇨ Change Chart Type), applies a particular layout (using Chart Tools ⇨ Design ⇨ Chart Layouts), applies a chart style (using Chart Tools ⇨ Design ⇨ Chart Styles), and removes the gridlines (using Chart Tools ⇨ Layout ⇨ Axes ⇨ Gridlines):

```
Sub FormatChart()
    If ActiveChart Is Nothing Then Exit Sub
    With ActiveChart
        .ChartType = xlColumnClustered
        .ApplyLayout 10
```

```
        .ChartStyle = 30
        .SetElement msoElementPrimaryValueGridLinesNone
        .ClearToMatchStyle
    End With
End Sub
```

Figure 18-6 shows a chart before and after executing the `FormatChart` macro.

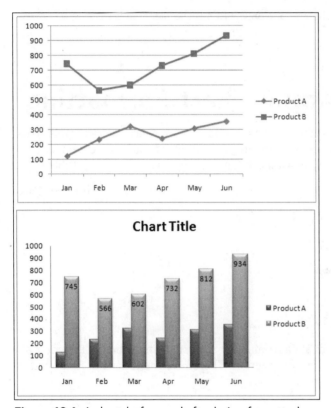

Figure 18-6: A chart, before and after being formatted.

NOTE

Keep in mind that, after executing this macro, the actual appearance of the chart depends on the document theme that's in effect.

CD-ROM

A workbook with this example is available on the companion CD-ROM as a file named `format a chart.xlsm`.

In the `FormatChart` procedure:

- The `ChartType` property is straightforward enough, and VBA provides constants for the various chart types.

- The `ApplyLayout` method uses a number to represent the layout, and the numbers vary with the chart type. These numbers appear as ToolTips when you hover the mouse over an icon in the Chart Tools ⇨ Design ⇨ Chart Layouts gallery. The `ApplyLayout` method can also specify a chart type as its second argument. Therefore, I could have eliminated the statement that changes the `ChartType` property and used this statement:

  ```
  .ApplyLayout 10, xlColumnClustered
  ```

- The `ChartStyle` property also uses a nondescriptive number (from 1 to 48) for its argument. These numbers appear as ToolTips when you hover the mouse over an icon in the Chart Tools ⇨ Design ⇨ Chart Styles gallery.

- The `SetElement` method controls the visibility of just about every aspect of the chart. It accepts more than 120 descriptive constants. For example, the constant `msoElementChartTitleNone` hides the chart's title.

- The `ClearToMatchStyle` method clears all user-applied formatting in the chart. This method is usually used in conjunction with the `ChartStyle` property to ensure that the applied style does not contain any formatting that's not part of the style.

More chart formatting examples

As I noted earlier, the macro recorder in Excel 2007 ignores many formatting commands when working with a chart. This deficiency is especially irksome if you're trying to figure out how to apply some of the new formatting options such as shadows, beveling, and gradient fills.

In this section, I provide some examples of chart formatting. I certainly don't cover all of the options, but it should be sufficient to help you get started so you can explore these features on your own. These examples assume an object variable named `MyChart`, created as follows:

```
Dim MyChart As Chart
Set MyChart = ActiveSheet.ChartObjects(1).Chart
```

If you apply these examples to your own charts, you need to make the necessary modifications so `MyChart` points to the correct `Chart` object.

TIP

To delete all user-applied (or VBA-applied) formatting from a chart, use the `ClearToMatchStyle` method of the `Chart` object. For example:

```
MyChart.ClearToMatchStyle
```

ADDING A SHADOW

One of the most interesting formatting effects in Excel 2007 is shadows. A shadow can give a chart a three-dimensional look and make it appear as if it's floating above your worksheet.

The following statement adds a default shadow to the chart area of the chart:

```
MyChart.ChartArea.Format.Shadow.Visible = msoTrue
```

In this statement, the `Format` property returns a `ChartFormat` object, and the `Shadow` property returns a `ShadowFormat` object. Therefore, this statement sets the `Visible` property of the `ShadowFormat` object, which is contained in the `ChartFormat` object, which is contained in the `ChartArea` object, which is contained in the `Chart` object.

Not surprisingly, the `ShadowFormat` object has some properties that determine the appearance of the shadow. Here's an example of setting five properties of the `ShadowFormat` object, contained in a `ChartArea` object, and Figure 18-7 shows the effect:

```
With MyChart.ChartArea.Format.Shadow
    .Visible = msoTrue
    .Blur = 10
    .Transparency = 0.4
    .OffsetX = 6
    .OffsetY = 6
End With
```

Figure 18-7: Applying a shadow to a chart.

The example that follows adds a subtle shadow to the plot area of the chart:

```
With MyChart.PlotArea.Format.Shadow
    .Visible = msoTrue
    .Blur = 3
    .Transparency = 0.6
```

```
      .OffsetX = 1
      .OffsetY = 1
End With
```

If an object has no fill, applying a shadow to the object has no visible effect. For example, a chart's title usually has a transparent background (no fill color). To apply a shadow to an object that has no fill, you must first add a fill color. This example applies a white fill to the chart's title and then adds a shadow:

```
MyChart.ChartTitle.Format.Fill.BackColor.RGB = RGB(255, 255, 255)
With MyChart.ChartTitle.Format.Shadow
      .Visible = msoTrue
      .Blur = 3
      .Transparency = 0.3
      .OffsetX = 2
      .OffsetY = 2
End With
```

Adding A Bevel

Adding a bevel to a chart can provide an interesting 3-D effect. Figure 18-8 shows a chart with a beveled chart area. To add the bevel, I used the ThreeD property to access the ThreeDFormat object. The code that added the bevel effect is:

```
With MyChart.ChartArea.Format.ThreeD
      .Visible = msoTrue
      .BevelTopType = msoBevelDivot
      .BevelTopDepth = 12
      .BevelTopInset = 32
End With
```

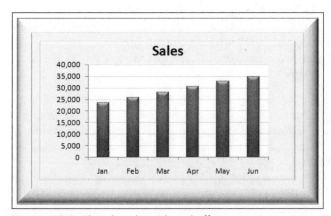

Figure 18-8: This chart has a bevel effect.

Part V

CROSS-REFERENCE

Chapter 30 contains some additional charting examples that deal with color.

Changing the Data Used in a Chart

The examples so far in this chapter have used the `SourceData` property to specify the complete data range for a chart. In many cases, you'll want to adjust the data used by a particular chart series. To do so, access the `Values` property of the `Series` object. The `Series` object also has an `XValues` property that stores the category axis values.

Understanding a Chart's SERIES Formula

The data used in each series in a chart is determined by its SERIES formula. When you select a data series in a chart, the SERIES formula appears in the formula bar. This is not a real formula: In other words, you can't use it in a cell, and you can't use worksheet functions within the SERIES formula. You can, however, edit the arguments in the SERIES formula.

A SERIES formula has the following syntax:

```
=SERIES(series_name, category_labels, values, order, sizes)
```

The arguments that you can use in the SERIES formula are

- `series_name`: (Optional) A reference to the cell that contains the series name used in the legend. If the chart has only one series, the name argument is used as the title. This argument can also consist of text in quotation marks. If omitted, Excel creates a default series name (for example, `Series 1`).

- `category_labels`: (Optional) A reference to the range that contains the labels for the category axis. If omitted, Excel uses consecutive integers beginning with 1. For XY charts, this argument specifies the X values. A noncontiguous range reference is also valid. The ranges' addresses are separated by a comma and enclosed in parentheses. The argument could also consist of an array of comma-separated values (or text in quotation marks) enclosed in curly brackets.

- `values`: (Required) A reference to the range that contains the values for the series. For XY charts, this argument specifies the Y values. A noncontiguous range reference is also valid. The ranges' addresses are separated by a comma and enclosed in parentheses. The argument could also consist of an array of comma-separated values enclosed in curly brackets.

- `order`: (Required) An integer that specifies the plotting order of the series. This argument is relevant only if the chart has more than one series. For example, in a stacked column chart, this parameter determines the stacking order. Using a reference to a cell is not allowed.

- `sizes`: (Only for bubble charts) A reference to the range that contains the values for the size of the bubbles in a bubble chart. A noncontiguous range reference is also valid. The ranges' addresses are separated by a comma and enclosed in parentheses. The argument could also consist of an array of values enclosed in curly brackets.

Range references in a SERIES formula are always absolute, and they always include the sheet name. For example:

```
=SERIES(Sheet1!$B$1,,Sheet1!$B$2:$B$7,1)
```

A range reference can consist of a noncontiguous range. If so, each range is separated by a comma, and the argument is enclosed in parentheses. In the following SERIES formula, the values range consists of B2:B3 and B5:B7:

```
=SERIES(,,(Sheet1!$B$2:$B$3,Sheet1!$B$5:$B$7),1)
```

You can substitute range names for the range references. If you do so (and the name is a workbook-level name), Excel changes the reference in the SERIES formula to include the workbook. For example:

```
=SERIES(Sheet1!$B$1,,budget.xlsx!CurrentData,1)
```

NOTE

The `Values` property corresponds to the third argument of the SERIES formula, and the `XValues` property corresponds to the second argument of the SERIES formula. See the sidebar, "Understanding a Chart's SERIES Formula."

Changing chart data based on the active cell

Figure 18-9 shows a chart that's based on the data in the row of the active cell. When the user moves the cell pointer, the chart is updated automatically.

This example uses an event handler for the `Sheet1` object. The `SelectionChange` event occurs whenever the user changes the selection by moving the cell pointer. The event handler procedure for this event (which is located in the code module for the `Sheet1` object) is as follows:

```
Private Sub Worksheet_SelectionChange(ByVal Target _
  As Excel.Range)
    If CheckBox1 Then Call UpdateChart
End Sub
```

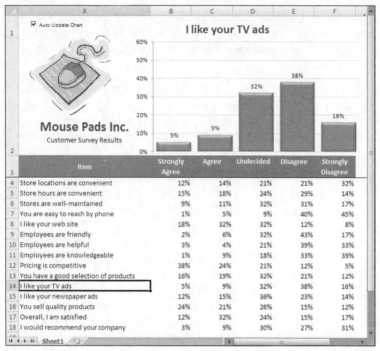

Figure 18-9: This chart always displays the data from the row of the active cell.

In other words, every time the user moves the cell cursor, the `Worksheet_SelectionChange` procedure is executed. If the Auto Update Chart check box (an ActiveX control on the sheet) is checked, this procedure calls the `UpdateChart` procedure, which follows:

```
Sub UpdateChart()
    Dim ChtObj As ChartObject
    Dim UserRow As Long
    Set ChtObj = ActiveSheet.ChartObjects(1)
    UserRow = ActiveCell.Row
    If UserRow < 4 Or IsEmpty(Cells(UserRow, 1)) Then
        ChtObj.Visible = False
    Else
        ChtObj.Chart.SeriesCollection(1).Values = _
            Range(Cells(UserRow, 2), Cells(UserRow, 6))
        ChtObj.Chart.ChartTitle.Text = Cells(UserRow, 1).Text
        ChtObj.Visible = True
    End If
End Sub
```

The `UserRow` variable contains the row number of the active cell. The `If` statement checks that the active cell is in a row that contains data. (The data starts in row 4.) If the cell cursor is in a row that doesn't have data, the `ChartObject` object is hidden, and the underlying text is visible ("Cannot display chart"). Otherwise, the code sets the `Values` property for the `Series` object to the range in columns 2–6 of the active row. It also sets the `ChartTitle` object to correspond to the text in column A.

CD-ROM

This example, named `chart active cell.xlsm`, is available on the companion CD-ROM.

Using VBA to determine the ranges used in a chart

The previous example demonstrated how to use the `Values` property of a `Series` object to specify the data used by a chart series. This section discusses using VBA macros to identify the ranges used by a series in a chart. For example, you might want to increase the size of each series by adding a new cell to the range.

Following is a description of three properties that are relevant to this task:

- `Formula` property: Returns or sets the SERIES formula for the `Series`. When you select a series in a chart, its SERIES formula is displayed in the formula bar. The `Formula` property returns this formula as a string.

- `Values` property: Returns or sets a collection of all the values in the series. This can be a range on a worksheet or an array of constant values, but not a combination of both.

- `XValues` property: Returns or sets an array of X values for a chart series. The `XValues` property can be set to a range on a worksheet or to an array of values, but it can't be a combination of both. The `XValues` property can also be empty.

If you create a VBA macro that needs to determine the data range used by a particular chart series, you might think that the `Values` property of the `Series` object is just the ticket. Similarly, the `XValues` property seems to be the way to get the range that contains the X values (or category labels). In theory, that certainly *seems* correct. But, in practice, it doesn't work.

When you set the `Values` property for a `Series` object, you can specify a `Range` object or an array. But when you read this property, an array is always returned. Unfortunately, the object model provides no way to get a `Range` object used by a `Series` object.

One possible solution is to write code to parse the SERIES formula and extract the range addresses. This sounds simple, but it's actually a difficult task because a SERIES formula can be very complex. Following are a few examples of valid SERIES formulas.

```
=SERIES(Sheet1!$B$1,Sheet1!$A$2:$A$4,Sheet1!$B$2:$B$4,1)
=SERIES(,,Sheet1!$B$2:$B$4,1)
=SERIES(,Sheet1!$A$2:$A$4,Sheet1!$B$2:$B$4,1)
=SERIES("Sales Summary",,Sheet1!$B$2:$B$4,1)
=SERIES(,{"Jan","Feb","Mar"},Sheet1!$B$2:$B$4,1)
=SERIES(,(Sheet1!$A$2,Sheet1!$A$4),(Sheet1!$B$2,Sheet1!$B$4),1)
=SERIES(Sheet1!$B$1,Sheet1!$A$2:$A$4,Sheet1!$B$2:$B$4,1,Sheet1!$C$2:$C$4)
```

As you can see, a SERIES formula can have missing arguments, use arrays, and even use noncontiguous range addresses. And, to confuse the issue even more, a bubble chart has an additional argument (for example, the last SERIES formula in the preceding list). Attempting to parse the arguments is certainly not a trivial programming task.

I spent a lot of time working on this problem, and I eventually arrived at a solution. The trick involves evaluating the SERIES formula by using a dummy function. This function accepts the same arguments as a SERIES formula and returns a 2 x 5 element array that contains all the information in the SERIES formula.

I simplified the solution by creating four custom VBA functions, each of which accepts one argument (a reference to a Series object) and returns a two-element array. These functions are the following:

- SERIESNAME_FROM_SERIES: The first array element contains a string that describes the data type of the first SERIES argument (Range, Empty, or String). The second array element contains a range address, an empty string, or a string.

- XVALUES_FROM_SERIES: The first array element contains a string that describes the data type of the second SERIES argument (Range, Array, Empty, or String). The second array element contains a range address, an array, an empty string, or a string.

- VALUES_FROM_SERIES: The first array element contains a string that describes the data type of the third SERIES argument (Range or Array). The second array element contains a range address or an array.

- BUBBLESIZE_FROM_SERIES: The first array element contains a string that describes the data type of the fifth SERIES argument (Range, Array, or Empty). The second array element contains a range address, an array, or an empty string. This function is relevant only for bubble charts.

Note that I did not create a function to get the fourth SERIES argument (plot order). This argument can be obtained directly by using the PlotOrder property of the Series object.

 CD-ROM

The VBA code for these functions is too lengthy to be listed here, but the code is available on the companion CD-ROM in a file named get series ranges.xlsm. These functions are documented in such a way that they can be easily adapted to other situations.

The following example demonstrates the VALUES_FROM_SERIES function. It displays the address of the values range for the first series in the active chart.

```
Sub ShowValueRange()
    Dim Ser As Series
    Dim x As Variant
    Set Ser = ActiveChart.SeriesCollection(1)
    x = VALUES_FROM_SERIES(Ser)
    If x(1) = "Range" Then
```

```
      MsgBox Range(x(2)).Address
   End If
End Sub
```

The variable x is defined as a variant and will hold the two-element array that's returned by the VALUES_FROM_SERIES function. The first element of the x array contains a string that describes the data type. If the string is Range, the message box displays the address of the range contained in the second element of the x array.

Figure 18-10 shows another example. The chart has three data series. Buttons on the sheet execute macros that expand and contract each of the data ranges.

Figure 18-10: This workbook demonstrates how to expand and contract the chart series by using VBA macros.

The ContractAllSeries procedure is listed below. This procedure loops through the SeriesCollection collection and uses the XVALUE_FROM_SERIES and the VALUES_FROM_SERIES functions to retrieve the current ranges. It then uses the Resize method to decrease the size of the ranges.

```
Sub ContractAllSeries()
   Dim s As Series
   Dim Result As Variant
   Dim DRange As Range
   For Each s In ActiveSheet.ChartObjects(1).Chart.SeriesCollection
      Result = XVALUES_FROM_SERIES(s)
      If Result(1) = "Range" Then
         Set DRange = Range(Result(2))
         If DRange.Rows.Count > 1 Then
            Set DRange = DRange.Resize(DRange.Rows.Count - 1)
            s.XValues = DRange
         End If
      End If
```

```
        Result = VALUES_FROM_SERIES(s)
        If Result(1) = "Range" Then
            Set DRange = Range(Result(2))
            If DRange.Rows.Count > 1 Then
                Set DRange = DRange.Resize(DRange.Rows.Count - 1)
                s.Values = DRange
            End If
        End If
    Next s
End Sub
```

The ExpandAllSeries procedure is very similar. When executed, it expands each range by one cell.

Using VBA to Display Arbitrary Data Labels on a Chart

One of the most frequent complaints about Excel's charting is its inflexible data labeling feature. For example, consider the XY chart in Figure 18-11. It would be useful to display the associated name for each data point. However, you can search all day, and you'll never find the Excel command that lets you do this automatically. Such a command doesn't exist. Data labels are limited to the data values only — unless you want to edit each data label manually and replace it with text (or a formula) of your choice.

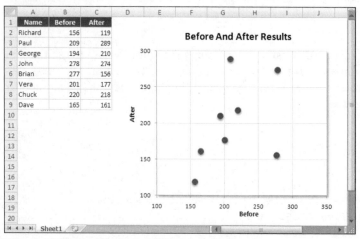

Figure 18-11: An XY chart with no data labels.

The DataLabelsFromRange procedure works with the first chart on the active sheet. It prompts the user for a range and then loops through the Points collection and changes the Text property to the values found in the range.

```
Sub DataLabelsFromRange()
    Dim DLRange As Range
    Dim Cht As Chart
    Dim i As Integer, Pts As Integer

'   Specify chart
    Set Cht = ActiveSheet.ChartObjects(1).Chart

'   Prompt for a range
    On Error Resume Next
    Set DLRange = Application.InputBox _
      (prompt:="Range for data labels?", Type:=8)
    If DLRange Is Nothing Then Exit Sub
    On Error GoTo 0

'   Add data labels
    Cht.SeriesCollection(1).ApplyDataLabels _
      Type:=xlDataLabelsShowValue, _
      AutoText:=True, _
      LegendKey:=False

'   Loop through the Points, and set the data labels
    Pts = Cht.SeriesCollection(1).Points.Count
    For i = 1 To Pts
        Cht.SeriesCollection(1). _
            Points(i).DataLabel.Text = DLRange(i)
    Next i
End Sub
```

CD-ROM

This example, named data labels.xlsm, is available on the companion CD-ROM.

Figure 18-12 shows the chart after running the DataLabelsFromRange procedure and specifying A2:A9 as the data range.

A data label in a chart can also consist of a link to a cell. To modify the DataLabelsFromRange procedure so it creates cell links, just change the statement within the For-Next loop to:

```
Cht.SeriesCollection(1).Points(i).DataLabel.Text = _
    "=" & "'" & DLRange.Parent.Name & "'!" & _
    DLRange(i).Address(ReferenceStyle:=xlR1C1)
```

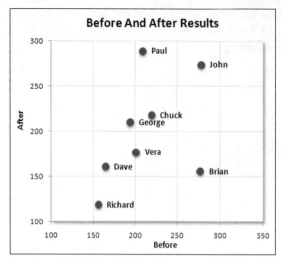

Figure 18-12: This XY chart has data labels, thanks to a VBA procedure.

NOTE

The preceding procedure is rather crude and does very little error checking. In addition, it only works with the first `Series` object. The Power Utility Pak add-in (which you can obtain by using the coupon in the back of the book) includes a much more sophisticated chart data–labeling utility.

Displaying a Chart in a UserForm

In Chapter 15, I describe a way to display a chart in a UserForm. The technique saves the chart as a GIF file and then loads the GIF file into an `Image` control on the UserForm.

The example in this section uses that same technique but adds a new twist: The chart is created on the fly and uses the data in the row of the active cell. Figure 18-13 shows an example.

The UserForm for this example is very simple. It contains an `Image` control and a CommandButton (Close). The worksheet that contains the data has a button that executes the following procedure:

```
Sub ShowChart()
    Dim UserRow As Long
    UserRow = ActiveCell.Row
    If UserRow < 2 Or IsEmpty(Cells(UserRow, 1)) Then
        MsgBox "Move the cell pointer to a row that contains data."
        Exit Sub
```

```
        End If
        CreateChart (UserRow)
        UserForm1.Show
End Sub
```

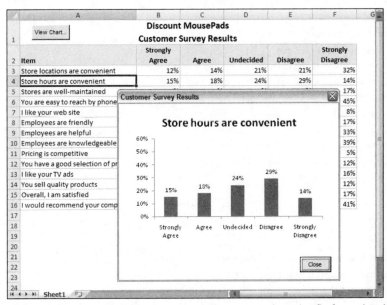

Figure 18-13: The chart in this UserForm is created on the fly from the data in the active row.

Because the chart is based on the data in the row of the active cell, the procedure warns the user if the cell pointer is in an invalid row. If the active cell is appropriate, ShowChart calls the CreateChart procedure to create the chart and then displays the UserForm.

The CreateChart procedure accepts one argument, which represents the row of the active cell. This procedure originated from a macro recording that I cleaned up to make more general.

```
Sub CreateChart(r)
    Dim TempChart As Chart
    Dim CatTitles As Range
    Dim SrcRange As Range, SourceData As Range
    Dim FName As String

    Set CatTitles = ActiveSheet.Range("A2:F2")
    Set SrcRange = ActiveSheet.Range(Cells(r, 1), Cells(r, 6))
    Set SourceData = Union(CatTitles, SrcRange)

'   Add a chart
    Application.ScreenUpdating = False
    Set TempChart = ActiveSheet.Shapes.AddChart.Chart
```

```
    TempChart.SetSourceData Source:=SourceData

'   Fix it up
    With TempChart
        .ChartType = xlColumnClustered
        .SetSourceData Source:=SourceData, PlotBy:=xlRows
        .HasLegend = False
        .PlotArea.Interior.ColorIndex = xlNone
        .Axes(xlValue).MajorGridlines.Delete
        .ApplyDataLabels Type:=xlDataLabelsShowValue, LegendKey:=False
        .Axes(xlValue).MaximumScale = 0.6
        .ChartArea.Format.Line.Visible = False
    End With

'   Adjust the ChartObject's size size
    With ActiveSheet.ChartObjects(1)
        .Width = 300
        .Height = 200
    End With

'   Save chart as GIF
    FName = ThisWorkbook.Path & Application.PathSeparator & "temp.gif"
    TempChart.Export Filename:=FName, filterName:="GIF"
    ActiveSheet.ChartObjects(1).Delete
    Application.ScreenUpdating = True
End Sub
```

When the `CreateChart` procedure ends, the worksheet contains a `ChartObject` with a chart of the data in the row of the active cell. However, the `ChartObject` is not visible because `ScreenUpdating` is turned off. The chart is exported and deleted, and `ScreenUpdating` is turned back on.

The final instruction of the `ShowChart` procedure loads the UserForm. Following is the `UserForm_Initialize` procedure. This procedure simply loads the GIF file into the `Image` control.

```
Private Sub UserForm_Initialize()
    Dim FName As String
    FName = ThisWorkbook.Path & Application.PathSeparator & "temp.gif"
    UserForm1.Image1.Picture = LoadPicture(FName)
End Sub
```

CD-ROM

This workbook, named `chart in userform.xlsm`, is available on the companion CD-ROM.

Understanding Chart Events

Excel supports several events associated with charts. For example, when a chart is activated, it generates an `Activate` event. The `Calculate` event occurs after the chart receives new or changed data. You can, of course, write VBA code that gets executed when a particular event occurs.

CROSS-REFERENCE

Refer to Chapter 19 for additional information about events.

Table 18-1 lists all the chart events.

TABLE 18-1   EVENTS RECOGNIZED BY THE CHART OBJECT

Event	Action That Triggers the Event
Activate	A chart sheet or embedded chart is activated.
BeforeDoubleClick	An embedded chart is double-clicked. This event occurs before the default double-click action.
BeforeRightClick	An embedded chart is right-clicked. The event occurs before the default right-click action.
Calculate	New or changed data is plotted on a chart.
Deactivate	A chart is deactivated.
DragOver	A range of cells is dragged over a chart.
DragPlot	A range of cells is dragged and dropped onto a chart.
MouseDown	A mouse button is pressed while the pointer is over a chart.
MouseMove	The position of the mouse pointer changes over a chart.
MouseUp	A mouse button is released while the pointer is over a chart.
Resize	A chart is resized.
Select	A chart element is selected.
SeriesChange	The value of a chart data point is changed.

Part V

An example of using Chart events

To program an event handler for an event taking place on a chart sheet, your VBA code must reside in the code module for the `Chart` object. To activate this code module, double-click the Chart item in the Project window. Then, in the code module, select Chart from the Object drop-down list on the left and select the event from the Procedure drop-down list on the right (see Figure 18-14).

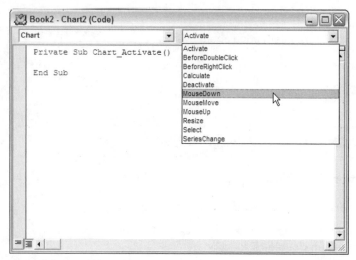

Figure 18-14: Selecting an event in the code module for a Chart object.

 NOTE

Because an embedded chart doesn't have its own code module, the procedure that I describe in this section works only for chart sheets. You can also handle events for embedded charts, but you must do some initial setup work that involves creating a class module. This procedure is described later in "Enabling events for an embedded chart."

The example that follows simply displays a message when the user activates a chart sheet, deactivates a chart sheet, or selects any element on the chart. I created a workbook with a chart sheet; then I wrote three event handler procedures named as follows:

- `Chart_Activate`: Executed when the chart sheet is activated.

- `Chart_Deactivate`: Executed when the chart sheet is deactivated.

- `Chart_Select`: Executed when an element on the chart sheet is selected.

 CD-ROM

This workbook, named `events - chart sheet.xlsm`, is available on the companion CD-ROM.

The `Chart_Activate` procedure follows:

```
Private Sub Chart_Activate()
    Dim msg As String
    msg = "Hello " & Application.UserName & vbCrLf & vbCrLf
    msg = msg & "You are now viewing the six-month sales "
    msg = msg & "summary for Products 1-3." & vbCrLf & vbCrLf
    msg = msg & _
      "Click an item in the chart to find out what it is."
    MsgBox msg, vbInformation, ActiveWorkbook.Name
End Sub
```

This procedure simply displays a message whenever the chart is activated. See Figure 18-15.

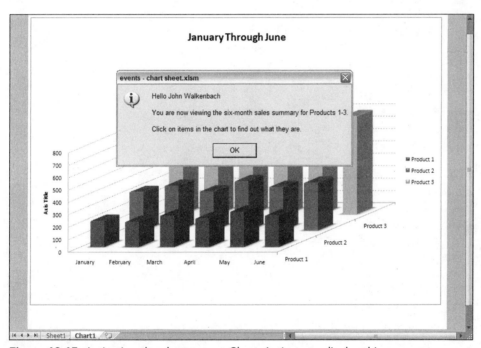

Figure 18-15: Activating the chart causes Chart_Activate to display this message.

The `Chart_Deactivate` procedure that follows also displays a message, but only when the chart sheet is deactivated:

```
Private Sub Chart_Deactivate()
    Dim msg As String
    msg = "Thanks for viewing the chart."
    MsgBox msg, , ActiveWorkbook.Name
End Sub
```

Part V

The `Chart_Select` procedure that follows is executed whenever an item on the chart is selected:

```
Private Sub Chart_Select(ByVal ElementID As Long, _
  ByVal Arg1 As Long, ByVal Arg2 As Long)
    Dim Id As String
    Select Case ElementID
        Case xlAxis: Id = "Axis"
        Case xlAxisTitle: Id = "AxisTitle"
        Case xlChartArea: Id = "ChartArea"
        Case xlChartTitle: Id = "ChartTitle"
        Case xlCorners: Id = "Corners"
        Case xlDataLabel: Id = "DataLabel"
        Case xlDataTable: Id = "DataTable"
        Case xlDownBars: Id = "DownBars"
        Case xlDropLines: Id = "DropLines"
        Case xlErrorBars: Id = "ErrorBars"
        Case xlFloor: Id = "Floor"
        Case xlHiLoLines: Id = "HiLoLines"
        Case xlLegend: Id = "Legend"
        Case xlLegendEntry: Id = "LegendEntry"
        Case xlLegendKey: Id = "LegendKey"
        Case xlMajorGridlines: Id = "MajorGridlines"
        Case xlMinorGridlines: Id = "MinorGridlines"
        Case xlNothing: Id = "Nothing"
        Case xlPlotArea: Id = "PlotArea"
        Case xlRadarAxisLabels: Id = "RadarAxisLabels"
        Case xlSeries: Id = "Series"
        Case xlSeriesLines: Id = "SeriesLines"
        Case xlShape: Id = "Shape"
        Case xlTrendline: Id = "Trendline"
        Case xlUpBars: Id = "UpBars"
        Case xlWalls: Id = "Walls"
        Case xlXErrorBars: Id = "XErrorBars"
        Case xlYErrorBars: Id = "YErrorBars"
        Case Else:: Id = "Some unknown thing"
    End Select
    MsgBox "Selection type: " & Id
End Sub
```

This procedure displays a message box that contains a description of the selected item. When the `Select` event occurs, the `ElementID` argument contains an integer that corresponds to what was selected. The `Arg1` and `Arg2` arguments provide additional information about the selected item (see the Help system for details). The `Select Case` structure converts the built-in constants to descriptive strings.

NOTE

This is not a comprehensive listing of all items that could appear in a `Chart` object. That's why I include the `Case Else` statement.

Enabling events for an embedded chart

As I note in the preceding section, `Chart` events are automatically enabled for chart sheets but not for charts embedded in a worksheet. To use events with an embedded chart, you need to perform the following steps.

CREATE A CLASS MODULE

In the Visual Basic Editor (VBE) window, select your project in the Project window and choose Insert ➪ Class Module. This will add a new (empty) class module to your project. Then use the Properties window to give the class module a more descriptive name (such as `clsChart`). Renaming the class module isn't necessary, but it's a good practice.

DECLARE A PUBLIC CHART OBJECT

The next step is to declare a `Public` variable that will represent the chart. The variable should be of type `Chart`, and it must be declared in the class module by using the `WithEvents` keyword. If you omit the `WithEvents` keyword, the object will not respond to events. Following is an example of such a declaration:

```
Public WithEvents clsChart As Chart
```

CONNECT THE DECLARED OBJECT WITH YOUR CHART

Before your event handler procedures will run, you must connect the declared object in the class module with your embedded chart. You do this by declaring an object of type `clsChart` (or whatever your class module is named). This should be a module-level object variable, declared in a regular VBA module (not in the class module). Here's an example:

```
Dim MyChart As New clsChart
```

Then you must write code to associate the `clsChart` object with a particular chart. The statement below accomplishes this.

```
Set MyChart.clsChart = ActiveSheet.ChartObjects(1).Chart
```

After the preceding statement is executed, the `clsChart` object in the class module points to the first embedded chart on the active sheet. Consequently, the event handler procedures in the class module will execute when the events occur.

Part V

WRITE EVENT HANDLER PROCEDURES FOR THE CHART CLASS

In this section, I describe how to write event handler procedures in the class module. Recall that the class module must contain a declaration such as the following:

```
Public WithEvents clsChart As Chart
```

After this new object has been declared with the `WithEvents` keyword, it appears in the Object drop-down list box in the class module. When you select the new object in the Object box, the valid events for that object are listed in the Procedure drop-down box on the right.

The following example is a simple event handler procedure that is executed when the embedded chart is activated. This procedure simply pops up a message box that displays the name of the `Chart` object's parent (which is a `ChartObject` object).

```
Private Sub clsChart_Activate()
    MsgBox clsChart.Parent.Name & " was activated!"
End Sub
```

CD-ROM

The companion CD-ROM contains a workbook that demonstrates the concepts that I describe in this section. The file is `events - embedded chart.xlsm`.

Example: Using Chart events with an embedded chart

The example in this section provides a practical demonstration of the information presented in the previous section. The example shown in Figure 18-16 consists of an embedded chart that functions as a clickable image map. When chart events are enabled, clicking one of the chart columns activates a worksheet that shows detailed data for the region.

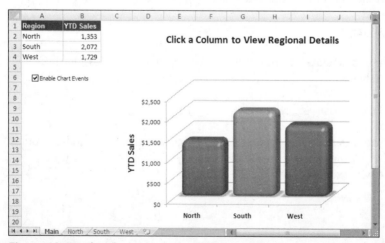

Figure 18-16: This chart serves as a clickable image map.

The workbook is set up with four worksheets. The sheet named Main contains the embedded chart. The other sheets are named North, South, and West. Formulas in B1:B4 sum the data in the respective sheets, and this summary data is plotted in the chart. Clicking a column in the chart triggers an event, and the event handler procedure activates the appropriate sheet so that the user can view the details for the desired region.

The workbook contains both a class module named EmbChartClass and a normal VBA module named Module1. For demonstration purposes, the Main worksheet also contains a check box control (for the Forms group). Clicking the check box executes the CheckBox1_Click procedure, which turns event monitoring on and off:

In addition, each of the other worksheets contains a button that executes the ReturntoMain macro that reactivates the Main sheet.

The complete listing of Module1 follows:

```
Dim SummaryChart As New EmbChartClass

Sub CheckBox1_Click()
    If Worksheets("Main").CheckBoxes("Check Box 1") = xlOn Then
        'Enable chart events
        Range("A1").Select
        Set SummaryChart.myChartClass = _
          Worksheets(1).ChartObjects(1).Chart
    Else
        'Disable chart events
        Set SummaryChart.myChartClass = Nothing
        Range("A1").Select
    End If
End Sub

Sub ReturnToMain()
'   Called by worksheet button
    Sheets("Main").Activate
End Sub
```

The first instruction declares a new object variable SummaryChart to be of type EmbChartClass — which, as you recall, is the name of the class module. When the user clicks the Enable Chart Events button, the embedded chart is assigned to the SummaryChart object, which, in effect, enables the events for the chart. The contents of the class module for EmbChartClass follow:

```
Public WithEvents myChartClass As Chart

Private Sub myChartClass_MouseDown(ByVal Button As Long, _
  ByVal Shift As Long, ByVal X As Long, ByVal Y As Long)

    Dim IDnum As Long
```

```
        Dim a As Long, b As Long

'       The next statement returns values for
'       IDnum, a, and b
        myChartClass.GetChartElement X, Y, IDnum, a, b

'       Was a series clicked?
        If IDnum = xlSeries Then
            Select Case b
                Case 1
                    Sheets("North").Activate
                Case 2
                    Sheets("South").Activate
                Case 3
                    Sheets("West").Activate
            End Select
        End If
        Range("A1").Select
End Sub
```

Clicking the chart generates a `MouseDown` event, which executes the `myChartClass_MouseDown` procedure. This procedure uses the `GetChartElement` method to determine what element of the chart was clicked. The `GetChartElement` method returns information about the chart element at specified X and Y coordinates (information that is available via the arguments for the `myChartClass_MouseDown` procedure).

 CD-ROM

This workbook, named `chart image map.xlsm`, is available on the companion CD-ROM.

VBA Charting Tricks

This section contains a few charting tricks that I've discovered over the years. Some of these techniques might be useful in your applications, and others are simply for fun. At the very least, studying them could give you some new insights into the object model for charts.

Printing embedded charts on a full page

When an embedded chart is selected, you can print the chart by choosing Office ➪ Print. The embedded chart will be printed on a full page by itself (just as if it were on a chart sheet), yet it will remain an embedded chart.

The following macro prints all embedded charts on the active sheet, and each chart is printed on a full page:

```
Sub PrintEmbeddedCharts()
    Dim ChtObj As ChartObject
    For Each ChtObj In ActiveSheet.ChartObjects
        ChtObj.Chart.Print
    Next ChtObj
End Sub
```

Displaying a slide show

The procedure listed below serves as a quick-and-dirty slide show. It displays each embedded chart on the active worksheet in Excel's Print Preview mode. Press Esc or Enter to view the next chart.

```
Sub ChartSlideShow()
    Dim ChtObj As ChartObject
    Application.DisplayFullScreen = True
    For Each ChtObj In ActiveSheet.ChartObjects
        Application.ScreenUpdating = False
        ChtObj.Chart.PrintPreview
    Next ChtObj
    Application.DisplayFullScreen = False
End Sub
```

The version below is similar, but it displays all chart sheets in the active workbook.

```
Sub ChartSlideShow2()
    Dim Cht As Chart
    Application.DisplayFullScreen = True
    For Each Cht In ActiveWorkbook.Charts
        Application.ScreenUpdating = False
        Cht.PrintPreview
    Next Cht
    Application.DisplayFullScreen = False
End Sub
```

 CD-ROM

The companion CD-ROM contains a workbook that demonstrates a chart slide show. The file is named slide show.xlsm.

Hiding series by hiding columns

By default, Excel charts don't display data contained in hidden rows or columns. The workbook shown in Figure 18-17 demonstrates an easy way to allow the user to hide and unhide particular chart series. The chart has seven data series, and it's a confusing mess. A few simple macros allow the user to use the ActiveX CheckBox to indicate which series they'd like to view. Figure 18-18 shows the chart with only three series displayed.

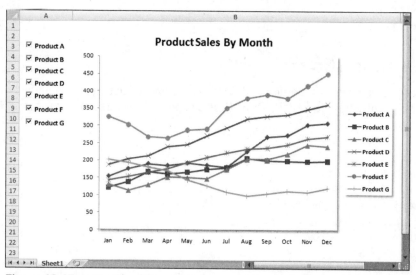

Figure 18-17: Using CheckBox controls to specify which data series to display.

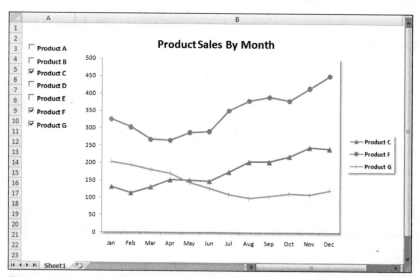

Figure 18-18: A confusing line chart is less confusing when some of the data columns are hidden.

Each series is in a named range: `Product_A`, `Product_B`, and so on. Each check box has its own `Click` event procedure. For example, the procedure that's executed when the user clicks the Product A check box is:

```
Private Sub CheckBox1_Click()
    ActiveSheet.Range("Product_A").EntireColumn.Hidden = _
      Not ActiveSheet.OLEObjects(1).Object.Value
End Sub
```

CD-ROM

This workbook, named `hide and unhide series.xlsm`, is available on the companion CD-ROM.

Creating unlinked charts

Normally, an Excel chart uses data stored in a range. Change the data in the range, and the chart is updated automatically. In some cases, you might want to unlink the chart from its data ranges and produce a *dead chart* (a chart that never changes). For example, if you plot data generated by various what-if scenarios, you might want to save a chart that represents some baseline so that you can compare it with other scenarios.

The three ways to create such a chart are:

- *Copy the chart as a picture.* Activate the chart and choose Home ➪ Clipboard ➪ Paste ➪ As Picture ➪ Copy Picture (accept the defaults in the Copy Picture dialog box). Then click a cell and choose Home ➪ Clipboard ➪ Paste. The result will be a picture of the copied chart.

- *Convert the range references to arrays.* Click a chart series and then click the formula bar. Press F9 to convert the ranges to an array. Repeat this for each series in the chart.

- *Use VBA to assign an array rather than a range to the* `XValues` *or* `Values` *properties of the* `Series` *object.*

The procedure below creates a chart (see Figure 18-19) by using arrays. The data is not stored in the worksheet. As you can see, the SERIES formula contains arrays and not range references.

```
Sub CreateUnlinkedChart()
    Dim MyChart As Chart
    Set MyChart = ActiveSheet.Shapes.AddChart.Chart
    With MyChart
        .SeriesCollection.NewSeries
        .SeriesCollection(1).Name = "Sales"
```

```
        .SeriesCollection(1).XValues = Array("Jan", "Feb", "Mar")
        .SeriesCollection(1).Values = Array(125, 165, 189)
        .ChartType = xlColumnClustered
        .SetElement msoElementLegendNone
    End With
End Sub
```

Because Excel imposes a limit to the length of a chart's SERIES formula, this technique works only for relatively small data sets.

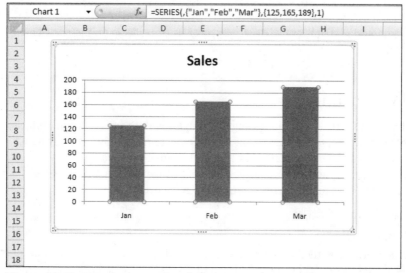

Figure 18-19: This chart uses data from arrays (not stored in a worksheet).

The procedure below creates a picture of the active chart (the original chart is not deleted). It works only with embedded charts.

```
Sub ConvertChartToPicture()
    Dim Cht As Chart
    If ActiveChart Is Nothing Then Exit Sub
    If TypeName(ActiveSheet) = "Chart" Then Exit Sub
    Set Cht = ActiveChart
    Cht.CopyPicture Appearance:=xlPrinter, _
        Size:=xlScreen, Format:=xlPicture
    ActiveWindow.RangeSelection.Select
    ActiveSheet.Paste
End Sub
```

When a chart is converted to a picture, you can create some interesting displays by using the Picture Tools ➪ Format ➪ Picture Styles commands (see Figure 18-20 for an example).

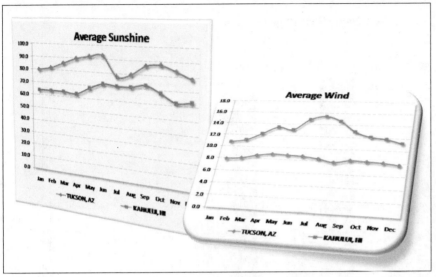

Figure 18-20: After converting a chart to a picture, you can manipulate it by using a variety of commands.

CD-ROM

The two examples in this section are available on the companion CD-ROM. The filename is `unlinked charts.xlsm`.

Displaying text with the MouseOver event

A common charting question deals with modifying chart tips. A *chart tip* is the small message that appears next to the mouse pointer when you move the mouse over an activated chart. The chart tip displays the chart element name and (for series) the value of the data point. The `Chart` object model does not expose these chart tips, so there is no way to modify them.

TIP

To turn chart tips on or off, choose Office ➪ Excel Options to display the Excel Options dialog box. Click the Advanced tab and locate the Display section. The options are labeled Show Chart Element Names on Hover and Show Data Point Values on Hover.

This section describes an alternative to chart tips. Figure 18-21 shows a column chart that uses the `MouseOver` event. When the mouse pointer is positioned over a column, the text box (a `Shape` object) in the upper-left displays information about the data point. The information is stored in a range and can consist of anything you like.

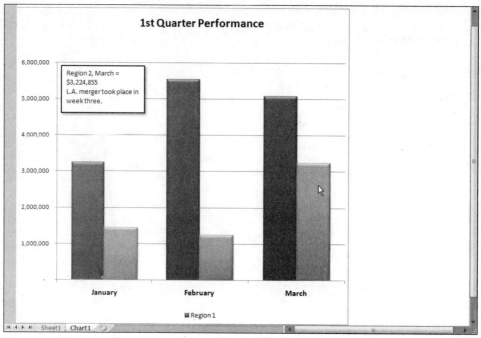

Figure 18-21: A text box displays information about the data point under the mouse pointer.

The event procedure that follows is located in the code module for the Chart sheet that contains the chart.

```
Private Sub Chart_MouseMove(ByVal Button As Long, ByVal Shift As Long, _
  ByVal X As Long, ByVal Y As Long)
    Dim ElementId As Long
    Dim arg1 As Long, arg2 As Long
    Dim NewText As String
    On Error Resume Next

    ActiveChart.GetChartElement X, Y, ElementId, arg1, arg2
    If ElementId = xlSeries Then
        NewText = Sheets("Sheet1").Range("Comments").Offset(arg2, arg1)
    Else
        NewText = ""
    End If
    ActiveChart.Shapes(1).TextFrame.Characters.Text = NewText
End Sub
```

This procedure monitors all mouse movements on the Chart sheet. The mouse coordinates are contained in the X and Y variables, which are passed to the procedure. The Button and Shift arguments are not used in this procedure.

As in the previous example, the key component in this procedure is the `GetChartElement` method. If `ElementId` is `xlSeries`, the mouse pointer is over a series. The `NewText` variable then is assigned the text in a particular cell. This text contains descriptive information about the data point (see Figure 18-22). If the mouse pointer is not over a series, the text box is empty. Otherwise, it displays the contents of `NewText`.

The example workbook also contains a `Workbook_Open` procedure that turns off the normal ChartTip display, and a `Workbook_BeforeClose` procedure that turns the settings back on. The `Workbook_Open` procedure is:

```
Private Sub Workbook_Open()
    Application.ShowChartTipNames = False
    Application.ShowChartTipValues = False
End Sub
```

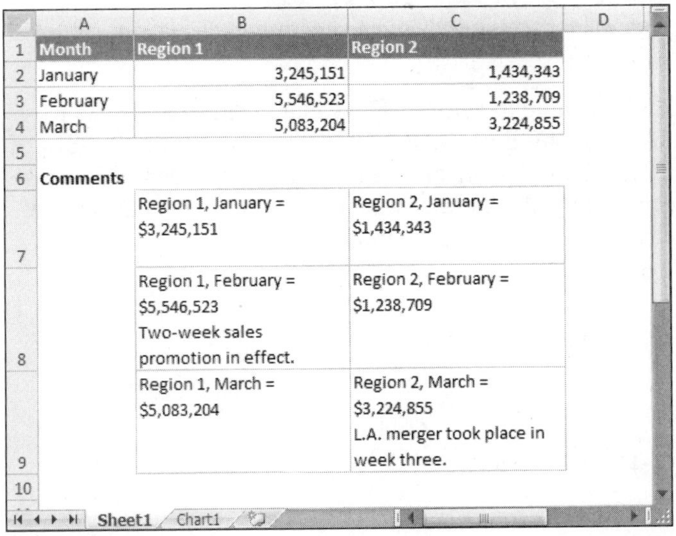

	A	B	C	D
1	Month	Region 1	Region 2	
2	January	3,245,151	1,434,343	
3	February	5,546,523	1,238,709	
4	March	5,083,204	3,224,855	
5				
6	Comments			
7		Region 1, January = $3,245,151	Region 2, January = $1,434,343	
8		Region 1, February = $5,546,523 Two-week sales promotion in effect.	Region 2, February = $1,238,709	
9		Region 1, March = $5,083,204	Region 2, March = $3,224,855 L.A. merger took place in week three.	
10				

Sheet1 / Chart1

Figure 18-22: Range B7:C9 contains data point information that's displayed in the text box on the chart.

CD-ROM

The companion CD-ROM contains this example set up for an embedded chart (`mouseover event - embedded.xlsm`) **and for a chart sheet** (`mouseover event - chart sheet.xlsm`).

Animating Charts

Most people don't realize it, but Excel is capable of performing simple animations. For example, you can animate shapes and charts. Consider the XY chart shown in Figure 18-23.

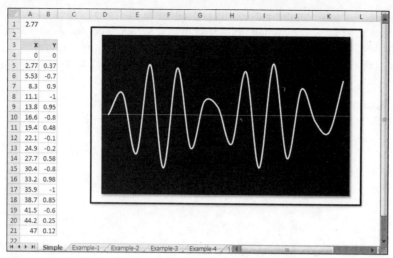

Figure 18-23: A simple VBA procedure will turn this graph into an interesting animation.

The X values (column A) depend on the value in cell A1. The value in each row is the previous row's value plus the value in A1. Column B contains formulas that calculate the SIN of the corresponding value in column A. The following simple procedure produces an interesting animation. It uses a loop to continually change the value in cell A1, which causes the values in the X and Y ranges to change. The effect is an animated chart.

```
Sub AnimateChart()
    Dim i As Long
    Range("A1") = 0
    For i = 1 To 150
        DoEvents
        Range("A1") = Range("A1") + 0.035
        DoEvents
    Next i
    Range("A1") = 0
End Sub
```

The key to chart animation is to use one or more DoEvents statements. This statement passes control to the operating system, which (apparently) causes the chart to be updated when control is passed back to Excel. Without the DoEvents statements the chart's changes would not be displayed inside of the loop.

 CD-ROM

The companion CD-ROM contains a workbook that includes this animated chart, plus several other animation examples. The filename is animated charts.xlsm.

Scrolling a chart

Figure 18-24 shows a chart with 5,218 data points in each series. The workbook contains six names:

- `StartDay`: A name for cell F1.

- `NumDays`: A name for cell F2.

- `Increment`: A name for cell F3 (used for automatic scrolling).

- `Date`: A named formula:

  `=OFFSET(Sheet1!$A$1,StartDay,0,NumDays,1)`

- `ProdA`: A named formula:

  `=OFFSET(Sheet1!$B$1,StartDay,0,NumDays,1)`

- `ProdB`: A named formula:

  `=OFFSET(Sheet1!$C$1,StartDay,0,NumDays,1)`

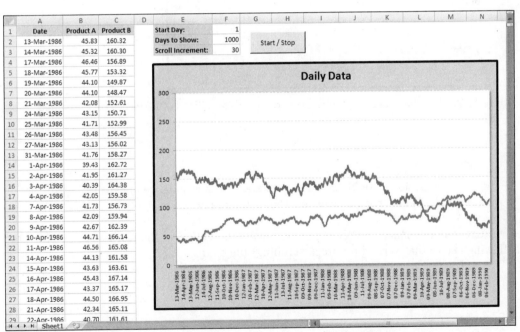

Figure 18-24: The values in column F determine which data to display in the chart.

Each of the SERIES formulas in the chart uses names for the category values and the data. The SERIES formula for the Product A series is as follows (I deleted the sheet name and workbook name for clarity):

```
=SERIES($B$1,Date,ProdA,1)
```

The SERIES formula for the Product B series is:

```
=SERIES($C$1,Date,ProdB,2)
```

Using these names enables the user to specify a value for StartDay and NumDays, and the chart will display a subset of the data. Figure 18-25 shows the chart when StartRow is 700 and NumDays is 365. In other words, the chart display begins with the 700th row, and shows 365 days of data.

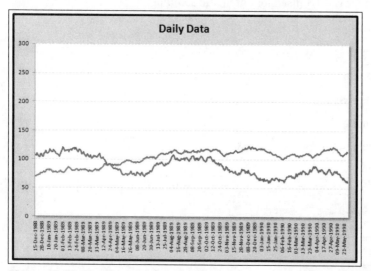

Figure 18-25: The chart displays a subset of the data, determined by the values of two named cells.

 CD-ROM

The companion CD-ROM contains a workbook that includes this animated chart, plus several other animation examples. The filename is scrolling chart.xlsm.

A relatively simple macro makes the chart scroll. The button in the worksheet executes the following macro that scrolls (or stops scrolling) the chart:

```
Public AnimationInProgress As Boolean

Sub AnimateChart()
    Dim StartVal As Long, r As Long
    If AnimationInProgress Then
        AnimationInProgress = False
        End
    End If
    AnimationInProgress = True
```

```
      StartVal = Range("StartDay")
      For r = StartVal To 5219 - Range("NumDays") _
         Step Range("Increment")
           Range("StartDay") = r
           DoEvents
      Next r
      AnimationInProgress = False
End Sub
```

The `AnimateChart` procedure uses a public variable (`AnimationInProgress`) to keep track of the animation status. The animation results from a loop that changes the value in the `StartDay` cell. Because the two chart series use this value, the chart is continually updated with a new starting value. The Scroll Increment setting determines how quickly the chart scrolls.

To stop the animation, I use an `End` statement rather than an `Exit Sub` statement. For some reason, `Exit Sub` doesn't work reliably and may even crash Excel.

Creating a hypocycloid chart

Even if you hated your high school trigonometry class, you'll probably like the example in this section — which relies heavily on trigonometric functions. The workbook shown in Figure 18-26 contains an XY chart that displays a nearly infinite number of dazzling hypocycloid curves. A *hypocycloid* curve is the path formed by a point on a circle that rolls inside of another circle. This, as you might recall from your childhood, is the same technique used in Hasbro's popular Spirograph toy.

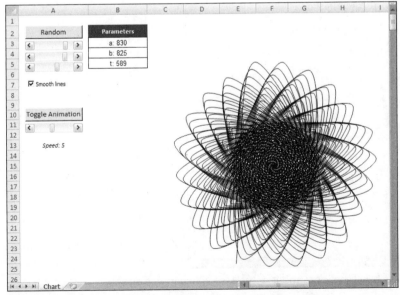

Figure 18-26: This workbook generates hypocycloid curves.

CD-ROM

This workbook is available on the companion CD-ROM. The filename is `hypocycloid - animate.xlsm`.

The chart is an XY chart, with everything hidden except the data series. The X and Y data are generated by using formulas stored in columns A and B. The scroll bar controls at the top let you adjust the three parameters that determine the look of the chart. In addition, clicking the Random button generates random values for the three parameters.

The chart itself is interesting enough, but it gets *really* interesting when it's animated. The animation occurs by changing the starting value for the series within a loop.

Creating a "clock" chart

Figure 18-27 shows an XY chart formatted to look like a clock. It not only looks like a clock, but it also functions as a clock. I can't think of a single reason why anyone would need to display a clock like this on a worksheet, but creating the workbook was challenging, and you might find it instructive.

CD-ROM

This workbook, named `vba clock chart.xlsm`, is available on the companion CD-ROM.

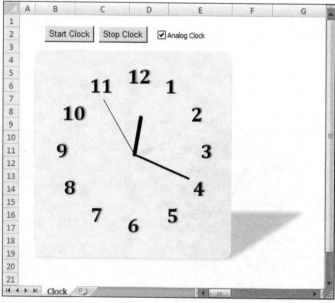

Figure 18-27: This clock is fully functional and is actually an XY chart in disguise.

Besides the clock chart, the workbook contains a text box that displays the time as a normal string, as shown in Figure 18-28. Normally this is hidden, but it can be displayed by deselecting the Analog Clock check box.

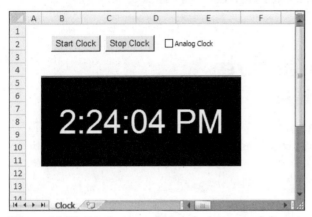

Figure 18-28: Displaying a digital clock in a worksheet is much easier but not as much fun to create.

As you explore this workbook from the CD-ROM, here are a few things to keep in mind:

- The ChartObject is named ClockChart, and it covers up a range named DigitalClock, which is used to display the time digitally.

- The two buttons on the worksheet are from the Forms toolbar, and each has a macro assigned (StartClock and StopClock).

- The CheckBox control (named cbClockType) on the worksheet is from the Forms toolbar — not from the Control Toolbox toolbar. Clicking the object executes a procedure named cbClockType_Click, which simply toggles the Visible property of the ChartObject. When it's invisible, the digital clock is revealed.

- The chart is an XY chart with four Series objects. These series represent the hour hand, the minute hand, the second hand, and the 12 numbers.

- The UpdateClock procedure is executed when the Start Clock button is clicked. It also uses the OnTime method of the Application object to set up a new OnTime event that will occur in one second. In other words, the UpdateClock procedure is called every second.

- Unlike most charts, this one does not use any worksheet ranges for its data. Rather, the values are calculated in VBA and transferred directly to the Values and XValues properties of the chart's Series object.

CAUTION

Although this clock is an interesting demo, it isn't feasible to display a continually updating clock in a worksheet. The VBA macro must be running at all times in the background, and this may interfere with other macros and reduce the overall performance.

Creating an Interactive Chart without VBA

The final example, shown in Figure 18-29, is a useful application that allows the user to choose two U.S. cities (from a list of 284 cities) and view a chart that compares the cities by month in any of the following categories: average precipitation, average temperature, percent sunshine, and average wind speed.

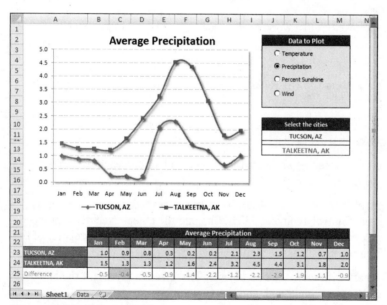

Figure 18-29: This application uses a variety of techniques to plot monthly climate data for two selected U.S. cities.

The most interesting aspect of this application is that it uses no VBA macros. The interactivity is a result of using Excel's built-in features. The cities are chosen from a drop-down list, using Excel's Data Validation feature, and the data option is selected using four Option Button controls, which are linked to a cell. The pieces are all connected using a few formulas.

This example demonstrates that it is indeed possible to create a user-friendly, interactive application without the assistance of macros.

CD-ROM

This workbook, named `climate data.xlsx`, is available on the companion CD-ROM.

The following sections describe the steps I took to set up this application.

Getting the data to create an interactive chart

I did a Web search and spent about five minutes locating the data I needed at the National Climatic Data Center. I copied the data from my browser window, pasted it to an Excel worksheet, and did a bit of clean-up work. The result was four 13-column tables of data, which I named `PrecipitationData`, `TemperatureData`, `SunshineData`, and `WindData`. To keep the interface as clean as possible, I put the data on a separate sheet (named Data).

Creating the Option Button controls for an interactive chart

I needed a way to allow the user to select the data to plot and decided to use `OptionButton` controls from the Forms toolbar. Because option buttons work as a group, the four `OptionButton` controls are all linked to the same cell: cell O3. Cell O3, therefore, contains a value from 1 to 4, depending on which option button is selected.

I needed a way to obtain the name of the data table based on the numeric value in cell O3. The solution was to write a formula (in cell O4) that uses Excel's CHOOSE function:

```
=CHOOSE(O3,"TemperatureData","PrecipitationData","SunshineData","WindData")
```

Therefore, cell O4 displays the name of one of the four named data tables. I then did some cell formatting behind the `OptionButton` controls to make them more visible.

Creating the city lists for the interactive chart

The next step is setting up the application: creating drop-down lists to enable the user to choose the cities to be compared in the chart. Excel's Data Validation feature makes creating a drop-down list in a cell very easy. First, I did some cell merging to create a wider field. I merged cells J11:M11 for the first city list and gave them the name `City1`. I merged cells J13:M13 for the second city list and gave them the name `City2`.

To make working with the list of cities easier, I created a named range, `CityList`, which refers to the first column in the `PrecipitationData` table.

Following are the steps that I used to create the drop-down lists:

1. Select J11:M11. (Remember, these are merged cells.)
2. Choose Data ⇨ Data Validation to display Excel's Data Validation dialog box.
3. Select the Settings tab in the Data Validation dialog box.

4. In the Allow field, choose List.

5. In the Source field, enter **=CityList**.

6. Click OK.

7. Copy J11:M11 to J13:M13. This duplicates the Data Validation settings for the second city.

Figure 18-30 shows the result.

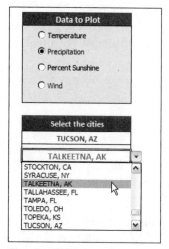

Figure 18-30: Use the Data Validation drop-down list to select a city.

Creating the interactive chart data range

The key to this application is that the chart uses data in a specific range. The data in this range is retrieved from the appropriate data table by using formulas that utilize the VLOOKUP function. (See Figure 18-31.)

	A	B	C	D	E	F	G	H	I	J	K	L	M
20													
21							Average Precipitation						
22		Jan	Feb	Mar	Apr	May	Jun	Jul	Aug	Sep	Oct	Nov	Dec
23	TUCSON, AZ	1.0	0.9	0.8	0.3	0.2	0.2	2.1	2.3	1.5	1.2	0.7	1.0
24	TOLEDO, OH	1.9	1.9	2.6	3.2	3.1	3.8	2.8	3.2	2.8	2.4	2.8	2.6
25	Difference	-0.9	-1.0	-1.8	-3.0	-2.9	-3.6	-0.7	-0.9	-1.4	-1.1	-2.1	-1.6
26													
27													
28													

Sheet1 / Data

Figure 18-31: The chart uses the data retrieved by formulas in A23:M24.

The formula in cell A23, which looks up data based on the contents of City1, is:

```
=VLOOKUP(City1,INDIRECT(DataTable),COLUMN(),FALSE)
```

The formula in cell A24 is the same except that it looks up data based on the contents of City2:

```
=VLOOKUP(City2,INDIRECT(DataTable),COLUMN(),FALSE)
```

After entering these formulas, I simply copied them across to the next 12 columns.

 NOTE

You may be wondering about the use of the COLUMN function for the third argument of the VLOOKUP function. This function returns the column number of the cell that contains the formula. This is a convenient way to avoid hard-coding the column to be retrieved and allows the same formula to be used in each column.

Below the two city rows is another row of formulas that calculate the difference between the two cities for each month. I used Conditional Formatting to apply a different color background for the largest difference and the smallest difference.

The label above the month names is generated by a formula that refers to the DataTable cell and constructs a descriptive title: The formula is:

```
="Average " & LEFT(DataTable,LEN(DataTable)-4)
```

Creating the interactive chart

After completing the previous tasks, the final step — creating the actual chart — is a breeze. The line chart has two data series and uses the data in A22:M24. The chart title is linked to cell A21. The data in A22:M24 changes, of course, whenever an OptionButton control is selected or a new city is selected from either of the Data Validation lists.

Part V

Chapter 19

Chapter **19**

Understanding Excel's Events

In This Chapter
This chapter explains the concept of Excel events, and I include many examples that you can adapt to your own needs. As you will see, understanding events can give your Excel applications a powerful edge. Here, you will find:

◆ An overview of the types of events that Excel can monitor

◆ Essential background information for working with events

◆ Examples of `Workbook` events, `Worksheet` events, `Chart` events, and `UserForm` events

◆ Using `Application` events to monitor all open workbooks

◆ Examples of processing time-based events and keystroke events

In several earlier chapters in this book, I present examples of VBA *event handler procedures,* which are specially named procedures that are executed when a specific event occurs. A simple example is the `CommandButton1_Click` procedure that is executed when the user clicks an object named `CommandButton1` stored on a UserForm or on a worksheet.

629

Excel is capable of monitoring a wide variety of events and executing your VBA code when a particular event occurs. Following are just a few examples of the types of events that Excel recognizes:

- A workbook is opened or closed.

- A window is activated.

- A worksheet is activated or deactivated.

- Data is entered into a cell or the cell is edited.

- A workbook is about to be saved.

- A workbook is about to be printed.

- A worksheet is calculated.

- An object is clicked.

- The data in a chart is updated.

- A particular key or key combination is pressed.

- A particular time of day occurs.

Event Types That Excel Can Monitor

Excel is programmed to monitor many different events that occur. These events can be classified as the following:

- *Workbook events:* Events that occur for a particular workbook. Examples of such events include `Open` (the workbook is opened or created), `BeforeSave` (the workbook is about to be saved), and `NewSheet` (a new sheet is added).

- *Worksheet events:* Events that occur for a particular worksheet. Examples include `Change` (a cell on the sheet is changed), `SelectionChange` (the user moves the cell indicator), and `Calculate` (the worksheet is recalculated).

- *Chart events:* Events that occur for a particular chart. These events include `Select` (an object in the chart is selected) and `SeriesChange` (a value of a data point in a series is changed). To monitor events for an embedded chart, you use a class module, as I demonstrate in Chapter 18.

- *Application events:* Events that occur for the application (Excel). Examples include `NewWorkbook` (a new workbook is created), `WorkbookBeforeClose` (any workbook is about to be closed), and `SheetChange` (a cell in any open workbook is altered). To monitor `Application`-level events, you need to use a class module.

- *UserForm events:* Events that occur for a particular UserForm or an object contained on the UserForm. For example, a UserForm has an `Initialize` event (occurs before the UserForm is displayed), and a CommandButton on a UserForm has a `Click` event (occurs when the button is clicked).

- *Events not associated with objects:* The final category consists of two useful `Application`-level events that I call `On` events: `OnTime` and `OnKey`. These work in a different manner than other events.

This chapter is organized according to the preceding list. Within each section, I provide examples to demonstrate some of the events.

What You Should Know about Events

This section provides some essential information relevant to working with events and writing event handler procedures.

Understanding event sequences

As you can see, some actions trigger multiple events. For example, when you insert a new worksheet into a workbook, this action triggers three `Application`-level events:

- `WorkbookNewSheet`: Occurs when a new worksheet is added.

- `SheetDeactivate`: Occurs when the active worksheet is deactivated

- `SheetActivate`: Occurs when the newly added worksheet is activated.

 NOTE

Event sequencing is a bit more complicated than you might think. The events listed above are `Application`-level events. When adding a new worksheet, additional events occur at the `Workbook` level and at the `Worksheet` level.

At this point, just keep in mind that events fire in a particular sequence, and knowing what the sequence is can be critical when writing event handler procedures. Later in this chapter, I describe how to determine the order of the events that occur for a particular action (see "Monitoring Application-level events").

Where to put event handler procedures

VBA newcomers often wonder why their event handler procedures aren't being executed when the corresponding event occurs. The answer is almost always because these procedures are located in the wrong place.

In the Visual Basic Editor (VBE) window, each project is listed in the Projects window. The project components are arranged in a collapsible list, as shown in Figure 19-1.

Figure 19-1: The components for each VBA project are listed in the Project window.

Each of the following components has its own code module:

- `Sheet` objects (for example, Sheet1, Sheet2, and so on).

- `Chart` objects (that is, chart sheets).

- `ThisWorkbook` object.

- General VBA modules: You never put event handler procedures in a general (that is, non-object) module.

- Class modules.

Even though the event handler procedure must be located in the correct module, the procedure can call other standard procedures stored in other modules. For example, the following event handler procedure, located in the module for the `ThisWorkbook` object, calls a procedure named `WorkbookSetup`, which could be stored in a regular VBA module:

```
Private Sub Workbook_Open()
    Call WorkbookSetup
End Sub
```

Disabling events

By default, all events are enabled. To disable all events, execute the following VBA instruction:

```
Application.EnableEvents = False
```

Events in Older Versions of Excel

Versions of Excel prior to Office 97 also supported events, but the programming techniques required to take advantage of those were quite different from what I describe in this chapter.

For example, if you had a procedure named `Auto_Open` stored in a regular VBA module, this procedure would be executed when the workbook was opened. Beginning with Excel 97, the `Auto_Open` procedure was supplemented by the `Workbook_Open` event handler procedure, which was stored in the code module for the `ThisWorkbook` object and was executed prior to `Auto_Open`.

Before Excel 97, it was often necessary to explicitly set up events. For example, if you needed to execute a procedure whenever data was entered into a cell, you would need to execute a statement such as the following:

```
Sheets("Sheet1").OnEntry = "ValidateEntry"
```

This statement instructs Excel to execute the procedure named `ValidateEntry` whenever data is entered into a cell. With Excel 97 and later, you simply create a procedure named `Worksheet_Change` and store it in the code module for the `Sheet1` object.

For compatibility reasons, Excel 97 and later versions still support the older event mechanism (although they are no longer documented in the Help system). I mention old events just in case you ever encounter an old workbook that seems to have some odd statements.

To enable events, use this one:

```
Application.EnableEvents = True
```

 NOTE

Disabling events does *not* apply to events triggered by UserForm controls — for example, the `Click` event generated by clicking a `CommandButton` control on a UserForm.

Why would you need to disable events? One common reason is to prevent an infinite loop of cascading events.

For example, suppose that cell A1 of your worksheet must always contain a value less than or equal to 12. You can write some code that is executed whenever data is entered into a cell to validate the cell's contents. In this case, you are monitoring the Change event for a Worksheet with a procedure named `Worksheet_Change`. Your procedure checks the user's entry, and, if the entry isn't less than or equal to 12, it displays a message and then clears that entry. The problem is that clearing the entry with your VBA code generates a new Change event, so your event handler procedure is executed again. This is not what you want to happen, so you need to disable events before you clear the cell, and then enable events again so that you can monitor the user's next entry.

Another way to prevent an infinite loop of cascading events is to declare a `Static` Boolean variable at the beginning of your event-handler procedure, such as this:

```
Static AbortProc As Boolean
```

Whenever the procedure needs to make its own changes, set the `AbortProc` variable to `True` (otherwise, make sure that it's set to `False`). Insert the following code at the top of the procedure:

```
If AbortProc Then
    AbortProc = False
    Exit Sub
End if
```

The event procedure is re-entered, but the `True` state of `AbortProc` causes the procedure to end. In addition, `AbortProc` is reset to `False`.

CROSS-REFERENCE

For a practical example of validating data, see "Monitoring a range to validate data entry," later in this chapter.

CAUTION

Disabling events in Excel applies to all workbooks. For example, if you disable events in your procedure and then open another workbook that has, say, a `Workbook_Open` procedure, that procedure will not execute.

Entering event handler code

Every event handler procedure has a predetermined name. Following are some examples of event handler procedure names:

- `Worksheet_SelectionChange`
- `Workbook_Open`
- `Chart_Activate`
- `Class_Initialize`

You can declare the procedure by typing it manually, but a much better approach is to let the VBE do it for you.

Figure 19-2 shows the code module for the `ThisWorkbook` object. To insert a procedure declaration, select `Workbook` from the objects list on the left. Then select the event from the procedures list on the right. When you do so, you get a procedure "shell" that contains the procedure declaration line and an `End Sub` statement.

Figure 19-2: The best way to create an event procedure is to let the VBE do it for you.

For example, if you select `Workbook` from the objects list and `Open` from the procedures list, the VBE inserts the following (empty) procedure:

```
Private Sub Workbook_Open()

End Sub
```

Your VBA code, of course, goes between these two statements.

Event handler procedures that use arguments

Some event handler procedures use an argument list. For example, you might need to create an event handler procedure to monitor the `SheetActivate` event for a workbook. If you use the technique described in the previous section, the VBE creates the following procedure:

```
Private Sub Workbook_SheetActivate(ByVal Sh As Object)

End Sub
```

This procedure uses one argument (`Sh`), which represents the sheet that was activated. In this case, `Sh` is declared as an `Object` data type rather than a `Worksheet` data type because the activated sheet can also be a chart sheet.

Your code can use the data passed as an argument. The following procedure is executed whenever a sheet is activated. It displays the type and name of the activated sheet by using VBA's `TypeName` function and accessing the `Name` property of the object passed in the argument:

```
Private Sub Workbook_SheetActivate(ByVal Sh As Object)
    MsgBox TypeName(Sh) & vbCrLf & Sh.Name
End Sub
```

Figure 19-3 shows the message that appears when Sheet3 is activated.

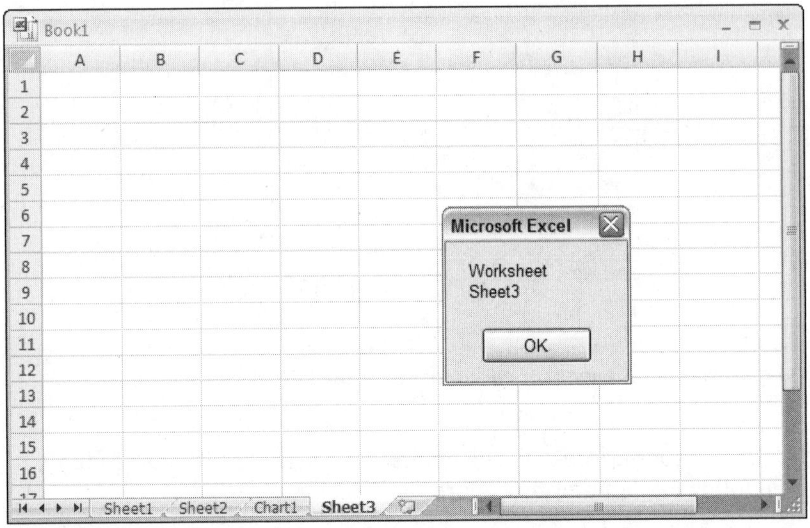

Figure 19-3: This message box was triggered by a SheetActivate event.

Several event handler procedures use a Boolean argument named Cancel. For example, the declaration for a workbook's BeforePrint event is as follows:

```
Private Sub Workbook_BeforePrint(Cancel As Boolean)
```

The value of Cancel passed to the procedure is False. However, your code can set Cancel to True, which will cancel the printing. The following example demonstrates this:

```
Private Sub Workbook_BeforePrint(Cancel As Boolean)
    Dim Msg As String
    Dim Ans As Integer
    Msg = "Have you loaded the 5164 label stock?"
    Ans = MsgBox(Msg, vbYesNo, "About to print...")
    If Ans = vbNo Then Cancel = True
End Sub
```

The Workbook_BeforePrint procedure is executed before the workbook is printed. This routine displays the message box shown in Figure 19-4. If the user clicks the No button, Cancel is set to True and nothing is printed.

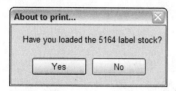

Figure 19-4: You can cancel the print operation by changing the Cancel argument.

TIP

The `BeforePrint` event also occurs when the user previews a worksheet.

Unfortunately, Excel does not provide a sheet-level `BeforePrint` event. Therefore, your code cannot determine which sheet is about to be printed. Often, you can assume that the `ActiveSheet` is the sheet that will be printed. However, there is no way to detect if the user requests that the entire workbook be printed.

Workbook-Level Events

`Workbook`-level events occur within a particular workbook. Table 19-1 lists the workbook events, along with a brief description of each. `Workbook` event handler procedures are stored in the code module for the `ThisWorkbook` object.

TABLE 19-1 WORKBOOK EVENTS

Event	Action That Triggers the Event
Activate	A workbook is activated.
AddinInstall	A workbook is installed as an add-in.
AddinUninstall	A workbook is uninstalled as an add-in.
AfterXMLExport	An XML file has been exported.
AfterXMLImport	An XML file has been imported, or an XML data connection has been refreshed.
BeforeClose	A workbook is about to be closed.
BeforePrint	A workbook (or anything in it) is about to be printed or previewed.
BeforeSave	A workbook is about to be saved.

continued

Part V

TABLE 19-1   WORKBOOK EVENTS (*continued*)

Event	Action That Triggers the Event
BeforeXMLExport	An XML file is about to be exported.
BeforeXMLImport	An XML file is about to be imported, or an XML data connection is about to be refreshed.
Deactivate	A workbook is deactivated.
NewSheet	A new sheet is created in a workbook.
Open	A workbook is opened.
PivotTableCloseConnection	An external data source connection for a pivot table is closed.
PivotTableOpenConnection	An external data source connection for a pivot table is opened.
RowsetComplete*	The user drills through the recordset or invokes the rowset action on an OLAP PivotTable.
SheetActivate	Any sheet is activated.
SheetBeforeDoubleClick	Any worksheet is double-clicked. This event occurs before the default double-click action.
SheetBeforeRightClick	Any worksheet is right-clicked. This event occurs before the default right-click action.
SheetCalculate	Any worksheet is calculated (or recalculated).
SheetChange	Any worksheet is changed by the user or by an external link.
SheetDeactivate	Any sheet is deactivated.
SheetFollowHyperlink	A hyperlink on a sheet is clicked.
SheetPivotTableUpdate	A pivot table is updated with new data.
SheetSelectionChange	The selection on any worksheet is changed.
Sync	A workbook that is part of a Document Workspace is synchronized with the copy on the server.
WindowActivate	Any workbook window is activated.
WindowDeactivate	Any workbook window is deactivated.
WindowResize	Any workbook window is resized.

*A new event, introduced in Excel 2007

CROSS-REFERENCE

If you need to monitor events for any workbook, you need to work with `Application-level events` (see "Application Events," later in this chapter). The remainder of this section presents examples of using `Workbook`-level events. All the example procedures that follow must be located in the code module for the `ThisWorkbook` object. If you put them into any other type of code module, they won't work.

The Open event

One of the most common events that is monitored is the `Open` event for a workbook. This event is triggered when the workbook (or add-in) is opened and executes the procedure named `Workbook_Open`. A `Workbook_Open` procedure is often used for tasks such as these:

- Displaying welcome messages.
- Opening other workbooks.
- Setting up shortcut menus.
- Activating a particular sheet or cell.
- Ensuring that certain conditions are met. For example, a workbook may require that a particular add-in is installed.
- Setting up certain automatic features. For example, you can define key combinations (see "The OnKey event" later in this chapter).
- Setting a worksheet's `ScrollArea` property (which isn't stored with the workbook).
- Setting `UserInterfaceOnly` protection for worksheets so that your code can operate on protected sheets. This setting is an argument for the `Protect` method and is not stored with the workbook.

NOTE

If the user holds down the Shift key when opening a workbook, the workbook's `Workbook_Open` procedure will not execute. And, of course, the procedure will not execute if the workbook is opened with macros disabled.

Following is a simple example of a `Workbook_Open` procedure. It uses VBA's `Weekday` function to determine the day of the week. If it's Friday, a message box appears, reminding the user to perform a weekly file backup. If it's not Friday, nothing happens.

```
Private Sub Workbook_Open()
  If Weekday(Now) = vbFriday Then
      Msg = "Today is Friday. Make sure that you "
      Msg = Msg & "do your weekly backup!"
      MsgBox Msg, vbInformation
  End If
End Sub
```

Part V

The Activate event

The following procedure is executed whenever the workbook is activated. This procedure simply maximizes the active window.

```
Private Sub Workbook_Activate()
    ActiveWindow.WindowState = xlMaximized
End Sub
```

The SheetActivate event

The following procedure is executed whenever the user activates any sheet in the workbook. If the sheet is a worksheet, the code simply selects cell A1. If the sheet is not a worksheet, nothing happens. This procedure uses VBA's TypeName function to ensure that the activated sheet is a worksheet (as opposed to a chart sheet).

```
Private Sub Workbook_SheetActivate(ByVal Sh As Object)
    If TypeName(Sh) = "Worksheet" Then _
        Range("A1").Select
End Sub
```

An alternative method to avoid the error that occurs when you try to select a cell on a chart sheet is to simply ignore the error.

```
Private Sub Workbook_SheetActivate(ByVal Sh As Object)
    On Error Resume Next
    Range("A1").Select
End Sub
```

The NewSheet event

The following procedure is executed whenever a new sheet is added to the workbook. The sheet is passed to the procedure as an argument. Because a new sheet can be a worksheet or a chart sheet, this procedure determines the sheet type. If it's a worksheet, the code inserts a date and time stamp in cell A1 on the new sheet.

```
Private Sub Workbook_NewSheet(ByVal Sh As Object)
    If TypeName(Sh) = "Worksheet" Then _
        Sh.Range("A1") = "Sheet added " & Now()
End Sub
```

The BeforeSave event

The BeforeSave event occurs before the workbook is actually saved. As you know, choosing the Office ➪ Save command sometimes brings up the Save As dialog box. This happens if the workbook has never been saved or if it was opened in read-only mode.

When the `Workbook_BeforeSave` procedure is executed, it receives an argument (`SaveAsUI`) that indicates whether the Save As dialog box will be displayed. The following example demonstrates this:

```
Private Sub Workbook_BeforeSave _
   (ByVal SaveAsUI As Boolean, Cancel As Boolean)
    If SaveAsUI Then
        MsgBox "Make sure you save this file on drive J."
    End If
End Sub
```

When the user attempts to save the workbook, the `Workbook_BeforeSave` procedure is executed. If the save operation will bring up Excel's Save As dialog box, the `SaveAsUI` variable is `True`. The procedure above checks this variable and displays a message only if the Save As dialog box will be displayed. If the procedure sets the `Cancel` argument to `True`, the file will not be saved (or the Save As dialog box will not be shown).

The Deactivate event

The following example demonstrates the `Deactivate` event. This procedure is executed whenever the workbook is deactivated and essentially never lets the user deactivate the workbook. When the `Deactivate` event occurs, the code reactivates the workbook and displays a message.

```
Private Sub Workbook_Deactivate()
    Me.Activate
    MsgBox "Sorry, you may not leave this workbook"
End Sub
```

NOTE

I do not recommend using procedures, such as this one, that attempt to "take over" Excel. It can be very frustrating and confusing for the user. Rather, I would recommend training the user how to use your application correctly.

This simple example illustrates the importance of understanding event sequences. If you try out this procedure, you'll see that it works well if the user attempts to activate another workbook. However, it's important to understand that the workbook `Deactivate` event is also triggered by the following actions:

- Closing the workbook
- Opening a new workbook
- Minimizing the workbook

Part V

In other words, this procedure might not perform as it was originally intended. It does prevent the user from activating a different workbook directly, but he or she can still close the workbook, open a new one, or minimize the workbook. The message box will still appear, but the actions will occur anyway.

The BeforePrint event

The `BeforePrint` event occurs when the user requests a print or a print preview but before the printing or previewing actually occurs. The event uses a `Cancel` argument, so your code can cancel the printing or previewing by setting the `Cancel` variable to `True`. Unfortunately, there is no way to determine whether the `BeforePrint` event was triggered by a print request or a preview request.

UPDATING A HEADER OR FOOTER

Excel's page header and footer options are very flexible, but it's still not possible to print the contents of a specific cell in the header or footer from within Excel. The `Workbook_BeforePrint` event provides a way to display the current contents of a cell in the header or footer when the workbook is printed. The following code updates each sheet's left footer whenever the workbook is printed or previewed. Specifically, it inserts the contents of cell A1 on Sheet1:

```
Private Sub Workbook_BeforePrint(Cancel As Boolean)
    Dim sht As Object
    For Each sht In ThisWorkbook.Sheets
        sht.PageSetup.LeftFooter = _
            Worksheets("Sheet1").Range("A1")
    Next sht
End Sub
```

This procedure loops through each sheet in the workbook and sets the `LeftFooter` property of the `PageSetup` object to the value in cell A1 on Sheet1.

TIP

When testing `BeforePrint` event handlers, you can save time (and paper) by previewing rather than actually printing.

HIDING COLUMNS BEFORE PRINTING

The example that follows uses a `Workbook_BeforePrint` procedure to hide columns B:D in Sheet1 before printing or previewing.

```
Private Sub Workbook_BeforePrint(Cancel As Boolean)
    'Hide columns B:D on Sheet1 before printing
    Worksheets("Sheet1").Range("B:D").EntireColumn.Hidden = True
End Sub
```

Ideally, you would want to unhide the columns after printing has occurred. It would be nice if Excel provided an `AfterPrint` event, but that event doesn't exist. However, there is a way to unhide the columns automatically. The modified procedure that follows schedules an `OnTime` event, which calls a procedure named `UnhideColumns` five seconds after printing or previewing.

```
Private Sub Workbook_BeforePrint(Cancel As Boolean)
    'Hide columns B:D on Sheet1 before printing
    Worksheets("Sheet1").Range("B:D").EntireColumn.Hidden = True
    Application.OnTime Now()+ TimeValue("0:00:05"), "UnhideColumns"
End Sub
```

The `UnhideColumns` procedure goes in a standard VBA module.

```
Sub UnhideColumns()
    Worksheets("Sheet1").Range("B:D").EntireColumn.Hidden = False
End Sub
```

CD-ROM

This example, named `hide columns before printing.xlsm`, is available on the companion CD-ROM.

CROSS-REFERENCE

For more information about `OnTime` events, see "The OnTime event," later in this chapter.

The BeforeClose event

The `BeforeClose` event occurs before a workbook is closed. This event is often used in conjunction with a `Workbook_Open` event handler. For example, you might use the `Workbook_Open` procedure to add shortcut menu items for your workbook and then use the `Workbook_BeforeClose` procedure to delete the shortcut menu items when the workbook is closed. That way, the custom menu is available only when the workbook is open.

Unfortunately, the `Workbook_BeforeClose` event is not implemented very well. For example, if you attempt to close a workbook that hasn't been saved, Excel displays a prompt asking whether you want to save the workbook before closing, as shown in Figure 19-5. The problem is, the `Workbook_BeforeClose` event has already occurred by the time the user sees this message. If the user cancels, your event handler procedure has already executed.

Figure 19-5: When this message appears, Workbook_BeforeClose has already done its thing.

Consider this scenario: You need to display custom shortcut menus when a particular work-book is open. Therefore, your workbook uses a `Workbook_Open` procedure to create the menu items when the workbook is opened, and it uses a `Workbook_BeforeClose` proce-dure to remove the menu items when the workbook is closed. These two event handler pro-cedures follow. Both of these call other procedures, which are not shown here.

```
Private Sub Workbook_Open()
    Call CreateShortcutMenuItems
End Sub

Private Sub Workbook_BeforeClose(Cancel As Boolean)
    Call DeleteShortcutMenuItems
End Sub
```

As I note earlier, Excel's Do you want to save . . . prompt displays *after* the
`Workbook_BeforeClose` event handler runs. So, if the user clicks `Cancel`, the workbook
remains open, but the custom menu items have already been deleted.

One solution to this problem is to bypass Excel's prompt and write your own code in the
`Workbook_BeforeClose` procedure to ask the user to save the workbook. The following
code demonstrates:

```
Private Sub Workbook_BeforeClose(Cancel As Boolean)
    Dim Msg As String
    If Me.Saved = False Then
        Msg = "Do you want to save the changes you made to "
        Msg = Msg & Me.Name & "?"
        Ans = MsgBox(Msg, vbQuestion + vbYesNoCancel)
        Select Case Ans
            Case vbYes
                Me.Save
            Case vbCancel
                Cancel = True
                Exit Sub
        End Select
    End If
    Call DeleteShortcutMenuItems
    Me.Saved = True
End Sub
```

This procedure checks the `Saved` property of the `Workbook` object to determine whether the workbook has been saved. If so, no problem — the `DeleteShortcutMenuItems` procedure is executed, and the workbook is closed. But, if the workbook has not been saved, the procedure displays a message box that duplicates the one that Excel would normally show. The effect of clicking each of the three buttons is:

- *Yes:* The workbook is saved, the menu is deleted, and the workbook is closed.

- *No:* The code sets the `Saved` property of the `Workbook` object to `True` (but doesn't actually save the file), deletes the menu, and the file is closed.

- *Cancel:* The `BeforeClose` event is canceled, and the procedure ends without deleting the shortcut menu items.

 CD-ROM

A workbook with this example is available on the companion CD-ROM. The file is named `workbook_beforeclose workaround.xlsm`.

Worksheet Events

The events for a `Worksheet` object are some of the most useful. Monitoring these events can make your applications perform feats that would otherwise be impossible.

Table 19-2 lists the worksheet events, with a brief description of each.

TABLE 19-2   WORKSHEET EVENTS

Event	Action That Triggers the Event
Activate	The worksheet is activated.
BeforeDoubleClick	The worksheet is double-clicked.
BeforeRightClick	The worksheet is right-clicked.
Calculate	The worksheet is calculated (or recalculated).
Change	Cells on the worksheet are changed by the user or by an external link.
Deactivate	The worksheet is deactivated.
FollowHyperlink	A hyperlink on the sheet is clicked.
PivotTableUpdate	A pivot table on the sheet is updated.
SelectionChange	The selection on the worksheet is changed.

Part V

Remember that the code for a worksheet event must be stored in the code module for the specific worksheet.

TIP

To quickly activate the code module for a worksheet, right-click the sheet tab and then choose View Code.

The Change event

The Change event is triggered when any cell in a worksheet is changed by the user or by a VBA procedure. The Change event is not triggered when a calculation generates a different value for a formula or when an object is added to the sheet.

When the Worksheet_Change procedure is executed, it receives a Range object as its Target argument. This Range object represents the changed cell or range that triggered the event. The following procedure is executed whenever the worksheet is changed. It displays a message box that shows the address of the Target range:

```
Private Sub Worksheet_Change(ByVal Target As Excel.Range)
    MsgBox "Range " & Target.Address & " was changed."
End Sub
```

To get a better feel for the types of actions that generate a Change event for a worksheet, enter the preceding procedure in the code module for a Worksheet object. After entering this procedure, activate Excel and make some changes to the worksheet by using various techniques. Every time the Change event occurs, you'll see a message box that displays the address of the range that was changed.

When I ran this procedure, I discovered some interesting quirks. Some actions that should trigger the event don't, and other actions that should not trigger the event do!

- Changing the formatting of a cell does not trigger the Change event (as expected). But copying formats using the Paste Special dialog box *does* trigger the Change event. Choosing the Home ➪ Editing ➪ Clear ➪ Clear Formats command also triggers the event.

- Adding, editing, or deleting a cell comment does not trigger the Change event.

- Pressing Delete generates an event even if the cell is empty to start with.

- Cells that are changed by using Excel commands may or may not trigger the Change event. For example, sorting a range does not trigger the event. But using the spell checker does.

- If your VBA procedure changes a cell, it *does* trigger the Change event.

As you can see from the preceding list, it's not a good idea to rely on the Change event to detect cell changes for critical applications.

Monitoring a specific range for changes

The Change event occurs when any cell on the worksheet is changed. But, in most cases, all you care about are changes made to a specific cell or range. When the Worksheet_Change event handler procedure is called, it receives a Range object as its argument. This Range object represents the cell or cells that were changed.

Assume that your worksheet has a range named InputRange, and you would like to monitor changes made only within this range. There is no Change event for a Range object, but you can perform a quick check within the Worksheet_Change procedure:

```
Private Sub Worksheet_Change(ByVal Target As Excel.Range)
    Dim MRange As Range
    Set MRange = Range("InputRange")
    If Not Intersect(Target, MRange) Is Nothing Then _
        MsgBox "A changed cell is in the input range."
End Sub
```

This example uses a Range object variable named MRange, which represents the worksheet range that you are interested in monitoring for changes. The procedure uses VBA's Intersect function to determine whether the Target range (passed to the procedure in its argument) intersects with MRange. The Intersect function returns an object that consists of all the cells that are contained in both of its arguments. If the Intersect function returns Nothing, the ranges have no cells in common. The Not operator is used so the expression returns True if the ranges *do* have at least one cell in common. Therefore, if the changed range has any cells in common with the range named InputRange, a message box is displayed. Otherwise, the procedure ends, and nothing happens.

MONITORING A RANGE TO MAKE FORMULAS BOLD

The following example monitors a worksheet and also makes formula entries bold and non-formula entries not bold.

```
Private Sub Worksheet_Change(ByVal Target As Excel.Range)
    Dim cell As Range
    For Each cell In Target
        cell.Font.Bold = cell.HasFormula
    Next cell
End Sub
```

Because the object passed to the Worksheet_Change procedure can consist of a multicell range, the procedure loops through each cell in the Target range. If the cell has a formula, it is made bold. Otherwise, the Bold property is set to False.

The procedure works, but it has a problem. What if the user deletes a row or column? In such a case, the Target range consists of a huge number of cells. The For Each loop would take a very long time to examine them all — and it wouldn't find any formulas.

The modified procedure listed next solves this problem by changing the Target range to be the intersection of the Target range and the worksheet's used range. The check to ensure that Target is Not Nothing handles the case in which an empty row or column outside of the used range is deleted.

```
Private Sub Worksheet_Change(ByVal Target As Excel.Range)
    Dim cell As Range
    Set Target = Intersect(Target, Target.Parent.UsedRange)
    If Not Target Is Nothing Then
        For Each cell In Target
            cell.Font.Bold = cell.HasFormula
        Next cell
    End If
End Sub
```

CD-ROM

This example, named make formulas bold.xlsm, is available on the companion CD-ROM.

CAUTION

A potentially serious side-effect of using a Worksheet_Change procedures is that it effectively turns off Excel's Undo feature. Excel's Undo stack is destroyed whenever a macro is executed. Using a Worksheet_Change event procedure executes a macro every time the worksheet is changed.

MONITORING A RANGE TO VALIDATE DATA ENTRY

Excel's data validation feature is a useful tool, but it suffers from a potentially serious problem. When you paste data to a cell that uses data validation, the pasted value not only fails to get validated, but it also deletes the validation rules associated with the cell! This fact makes the data validation feature practically worthless for critical applications. In this section, I demonstrate how you can use the Change event for a worksheet to create your own data validation procedure.

CD-ROM

The companion CD-ROM contains two versions of this example. One (named validate entry1.xlsm) uses the EnableEvents property to prevent cascading Change events; the other (named validate entry2.xlsm) uses a Static variable. See "Disabling events," earlier in this chapter.

The Worksheet_Change procedure that follows is executed when a user changes a cell. The validation is restricted to the range named InputRange. Values entered into this range must be integers between 1 and 12.

```
Private Sub Worksheet_Change(ByVal Target As Range)
    Dim VRange As Range, cell As Range
    Dim Msg As String
    Dim ValidateCode As Variant
    Set VRange = Range("InputRange")
    If Intersect(VRange, Target) Is Nothing Then Exit Sub
    For Each cell In Intersect(VRange, Target)
        ValidateCode = EntryIsValid(cell)
        If TypeName(ValidateCode) = "String" Then
            Msg = "Cell " & cell.Address(False, False) & ":"
            Msg = Msg & vbCrLf & vbCrLf & ValidateCode
            MsgBox Msg, vbCritical, "Invalid Entry"
            Application.EnableEvents = False
            cell.ClearContents
            cell.Activate
            Application.EnableEvents = True
        End If
    Next cell
End Sub
```

The `Worksheet_Change` procedure creates a `Range` object (named `VRange`) that represents the worksheet range that is validated. Then it loops through each cell in the `Target`
argument, which represents the cell or cells that were changed. The code determines
whether each cell is contained in the range to be validated. If so, it passes the cell as an
argument to a custom function (`EntryIsValid`), which returns `True` if the cell is a valid
entry.

If the entry is not valid, the `EntryIsValid` function returns a string that describes the
problem, and the user is informed via a message box (see Figure 19-6). When the message
box is dismissed, the invalid entry is cleared from the cell, and the cell is activated. Notice
that events are disabled before the cell is cleared. If events were not disabled, clearing the
cell would produce a `Change` event that causes an endless loop.

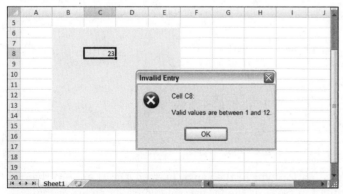

Figure 19-6: This message box describes the problem when the user makes an invalid entry.

The `EntryIsValid` function procedure is shown here:

```
Private Function EntryIsValid(cell) As Variant
'   Returns True if cell is an integer between 1 and 12
'   Otherwise it returns a string that describes the problem

'   Numeric?
    If Not WorksheetFunction.IsNumber (cell) Then
        EntryIsValid = "Non-numeric entry."
        Exit Function
    End If
'   Integer?
    If CInt(cell) <> cell Then
        EntryIsValid = "Integer required."
        Exit Function
    End If
'   Between 1 and 12?
    If cell < 1 Or cell > 12 Then
        EntryIsValid = "Valid values are between 1 and 12."
        Exit Function
    End If
'   It passed all the tests
    EntryIsValid = True
End Function
```

The preceding technique works, but it can be rather tedious to set up. Wouldn't it be nice if you could take advantage of Excel's data validation feature, yet ensure that the data validation rules don't get deleted if the user pastes data into the validation range? The next example solves the problem.

```
Private Sub Worksheet_Change(ByVal Target As Range)
    Dim VT As Long
    'Do all cells in the validation range
    'still have validation?
    On Error Resume Next
    VT = Range("InputRange").Validation.Type
    If Err.Number <> 0 Then
        Application.Undo
        MsgBox "Your last operation was canceled." & _
        "It would have deleted data validation rules.", vbCritical
    End If
End Sub
```

This event procedure checks the validation type of the range (named `InputRange`) that is *supposed* to contains the data validation rules. If the `VT` variable contains an error, that means that one or more cells in the `InputRange` no longer contain data validation. In other words, the worksheet change probably resulted from data being copied into the range that contains data validation. If that's the case, the code executes the Undo method of the Application object and reverses the user's action. Then it displays the message box shown in Figure 19-7.

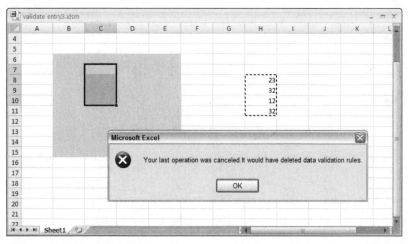

Figure 19-7: The Worksheet_Change procedure ensures that data validation does not get deleted.

 NOTE
A nice side-benefit to using this procedure is that the Undo stack is not destroyed.

 CD-ROM
This example, named `validate entry3.xlsm`, is available on the companion CD-ROM.

The SelectionChange event

The following procedure demonstrates the SelectionChange event. It's executed whenever the user makes a new selection on the worksheet.

```
Private Sub Worksheet_SelectionChange(ByVal Target _
  As Excel.Range)
    Cells.Interior.ColorIndex = xlNone
    With ActiveCell
        .EntireRow.Interior.Color = RGB(219, 229, 241)
        .EntireColumn.Interior.Color = RGB(219, 229, 241)
    End With
End Sub
```

This procedure shades the row and column of the active cell, which makes it very easy to identify the active cell. The first statement removes the background color for all cells in the worksheet. Next, the entire row and column of the active cell is shaded light blue. Figure 19-8 shows the shading in effect.

	A	B	C	D	E	F	G	H	I	J	K
1		Project-1	Project-2	Project-3	Project-4	Project-5	Project-6	Project-7	Project-8	Project-9	Project-10
2	Jan-2007	2158	1527	3870	4863	3927	3993	2175	2143	3965	288
3	Feb-2007	4254	28	4345	2108	412	2857	3098	87	2181	446
4	Mar-2007	3631	1240	4208	452	3443	2965	91	2935	170	304
5	Apr-2007	724	4939	1619	1721	3631	3487	3581	3082	3729	23
6	May-2007	3060	1034	1646	345	978	526	4422	1390	3566	306
7	Jun-2007	394	1241	2965	1411	3545	4499	2477	735	2533	495
8	Jul-2007	2080	3978	3304	1460	4533	3335	2675	1687	2475	396
9	Aug-2007	411	753	732	1207	1902	4009	1793	2262	916	288
10	Sep-2007	2711	95	2267	2634	1944	3920	2020	402	3183	358
11	Oct-2007	2996	4934	3932	2938	4730	1139	3776	3366	2239	15
12	Nov-2007	2837	1116	3879	1740	1466	3628	212	780	4518	476
13	Dec-2007	300	2917	321	1219	841	3554	1924	1786	3967	24
14	Jan-2008	1604	768	2617	3414	4732	863	2993	4184	3432	197
15	Feb-2008	1662	1380	4590	531	4143	1758	2990	2938	4400	75
16	Mar-2008	1001	3454	4611	4852	456	46	4475	1340	859	13
17	Apr-2008	4407	46	4185	4868	2313	2750	4948	4525	3896	4
18	May-2008	3948	1292	1462	1977	2418	1816	4810	2803	4973	9
19	Jun-2008	160	2908	3834	2396	4120	2231	3689	486	4751	31
20	Jul-2008	1131	118	3193	40	1965	424	4802	3379	3645	325
21	Aug-2008	2480	2564	373	3893	4932	4362	4472	3707	2411	32
22	Sep-2008	4949	2649	2335	9	2309	3454	657	3519	658	36
23	Oct-2008	3268	2652	2164	1898	1598	1237	1524	4752	1237	476

Figure 19-8: Moving the cell cursor causes the active cell's row and column to be shaded.

You won't want to use the procedure if your worksheet contains any background shading because it will be wiped out. The exceptions are tables with a style applied and background colors resulting from conditional formatting. In both of these instances, the background color *is* maintained. Keep in mind, however, that executing the `Worksheet_SelectionChange` macro destroys the Undo stack, so using this technique essentially disables Excel's Undo feature.

CD-ROM

This example, named `shade active row and column.xlsm`, is available on the companion CD-ROM.

The BeforeDoubleClick event

You can set up a VBA procedure to be executed when the user double-clicks a cell. In the following example (which is stored in the Code window for a `Sheet` object), double-clicking a cell makes the cell bold (if it's not bold) or not bold (if it is bold):

```
Private Sub Worksheet_BeforeDoubleClick _
   (ByVal Target As Excel.Range, Cancel As Boolean)
    Target.Font.Bold = Not Target.Font.Bold
    Cancel = True
End Sub
```

If `Cancel` is set to `True`, the default double-click action doesn't occur. In other words, double-clicking the cell won't put Excel into cell edit mode.

The BeforeRightClick event

When the user right-clicks in a worksheet, Excel displays a shortcut menu. If, for some reason, you'd like to prevent the shortcut menu from appearing in a particular sheet, you can trap the `RightClick` event. The following procedure sets the `Cancel` argument to `True`, which cancels the `RightClick` event and thereby cancels the shortcut menu. Instead, a message box is displayed.

```
Private Sub Worksheet_BeforeRightClick _
   (ByVal Target As Excel.Range, Cancel As Boolean)
    Cancel = True
    MsgBox "The shortcut menu is not available."
End Sub
```

Keep in mind that the user can still access the shortcut menu by using Shift+F10. However, only a tiny percentage of Excel users are aware of that keystroke combination.

 CROSS-REFERENCE
To find out how to intercept the Shift+F10 key combination, see "The OnKey event," later in this chapter. Chapter 24 describes other methods for disabling shortcut menus.

Following is another example that uses the `BeforeRightClick` event. This procedure checks to see whether the cell that was right-clicked contains a numeric value. If so, the code displays the Format Number dialog box and sets the `Cancel` argument to `True` (avoiding the normal shortcut menu display). If the cell does not contain a numeric value, nothing special happens — the shortcut menu is displayed as usual.

```
Private Sub Worksheet_BeforeRightClick _
   (ByVal Target As Excel.Range, Cancel As Boolean)
    If IsNumeric(Target) And Not IsEmpty(Target) Then
        Application.Dialogs(xlDialogFormatNumber).Show
        Cancel = True
    End If
End Sub
```

Notice that the code makes an additional check to see if the cell is not empty. This is because VBA considers empty cells to be numeric.

NOTE

An alternative statement that displays the Format Number dialog box is:

```
Application.CommandBars.ExecuteMso ("NumberFormatsDialog")
```

This statement works only in Excel 2007.

Chart Events

This section describes some of the events associated with charts. By default, events are enabled only for charts that reside on a chart sheet. To work with events for an embedded chart, you need to create a class module.

 CROSS-REFERENCE

Refer to Chapter 18 for examples that deal with Chart events. Chapter 18 also describes how to create a class module to enable events for embedded charts.

Table 19-3 contains a list of the chart events as well as a brief description of each.

TABLE 19-3   EVENTS RECOGNIZED BY A CHART SHEET

Event	Action That Triggers the Event
Activate	The chart sheet or embedded chart is activated.
BeforeDoubleClick	The chart sheet or an embedded chart is double-clicked. This event occurs before the default double-click action.
BeforeRightClick	The chart sheet or an embedded chart is right-clicked. The event occurs before the default right-click action.
Calculate	New or changed data is plotted on a chart.
Deactivate	The chart is deactivated.
MouseDown	A mouse button is pressed while the pointer is over a chart.
MouseMove	The position of the mouse pointer changes over a chart.
MouseUp	A mouse button is released while the pointer is over a chart.
Resize	The chart is resized.
Select	A chart element is selected.
SeriesChange	The value of a chart data point is changed.

Using the Object Browser to Locate Events

The Object Browser is a useful tool that can help you learn about objects and their properties and methods. It can also help you find out which objects support a particular event. For example, say you'd like to find out which objects support the MouseMove event. Activate the VBE and press F2 to display the Object Browser window. Make sure that <All Libraries> is selected; then type **MouseMove** and click the binoculars icon (see the accompanying figure).

The Object Browser displays a list of matching items. Events are indicated with a small yellow lightning bolt. From this list, you can see which objects support the MouseMove event. Most of the objects located are controls in the MSForms library, home of the UserForm control. But you can also see that Excel's Chart object supports the MouseMove event.

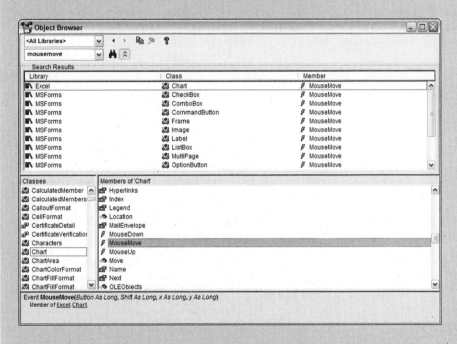

Notice how the list is divided into three columns: Library, Class, and Member. The match for the item that you're searching for might appear in any of these columns. This brings up a crucial point: The name of an event or term belonging to one library or class could be the same as that for another belonging to a different library or class — although they probably don't share the same functionality. So be sure to click each item in the Object Browser list and check the status bar at the bottom of the list for the syntax. You might find, for instance, that one class or library treats an event differently.

Application Events

In earlier sections, I discuss `Workbook` events and `Worksheet` events. Those events are monitored for a particular workbook. If you want to monitor events for all open workbooks or all worksheets, you use `Application`-level events.

 NOTE
Creating event handler procedures to handle `Application` events always requires a class module and some setup work.

Table 19-4 lists the `Application` events with a brief description of each.

TABLE 19-4   EVENTS RECOGNIZED BY THE APPLICATION OBJECT

Event	Action That Triggers the Event
AfterCalculate*	A calculation has been completed and no outstanding queries exist.
NewWorkbook	A new workbook is created.
SheetActivate	Any sheet is activated.
SheetBeforeDoubleClick	Any worksheet is double-clicked. This event occurs before the default double-click action.
SheetBeforeRightClick	Any worksheet is right-clicked. This event occurs before the default right-click action.
SheetCalculate	Any worksheet is calculated (or recalculated).
SheetChange	Cells in any worksheet are changed by the user or by an external link.
SheetDeactivate	Any sheet is deactivated.
SheetFollowHyperlink	A hyperlink is clicked.
SheetPivotTableUpdate	Any pivot table is updated.
SheetSelectionChange	The selection changes on any worksheet except a chart sheet.
WindowActivate	Any workbook window is activated.
WindowDeactivate	Any workbook window is deactivated.
WindowResize	Any workbook window is resized.
WorkbookActivate	Any workbook is activated.
WorkbookAddinInstall	A workbook is installed as an add-in.

Event	Action That Triggers the Event
WorkbookAddinUninstall	Any add-in workbook is uninstalled.
WorkbookAfterXMLExport	An XML file has been exported.
WorkbookAfterXMLImport	An XML file has been imported, or an XML data connection has been refreshed.
WorkbookBeforeClose	Any open workbook is closed.
WorkbookBeforePrint	Any open workbook is printed.
WorkbookBeforeSave	Any open workbook is saved.
WorkbookBeforeXMLExport	An XML file is about to be exported, or an XML data connection is about to be refreshed.
WorkbookBeforeXMLImport	An XML file is about to be imported.
WorkbookDeactivate	Any open workbook is deactivated.
WorkbookNewSheet	A new sheet is created in any open workbook.
WorkbookOpen	A workbook is opened.
WorkbookPivotTableCloseConnection	An external data source connection for any pivot table is closed.
WorkbookPivotTableOpenConnection	An external data source connection for any pivot table is opened.
WorkbookRowSetComplete*	The user drills through the recordset or invokes the rowset action on an OLAP PivotTable.
WorkbookSync	A workbook that is part of a Document Workspace is synchronized with the copy on the server.

This event was introduced in Excel 2007.

Part V

Enabling Application-level events

To use Application-level events, you need to do the following:

1. Create a new class module.

2. Set a name for this class module in the Properties window under *Name*.

   By default, VBA gives each new class module a default name like Class1, Class2, and so on. You might want to give your class module a more meaningful name, such as clsApp.

3. In the class module, declare a public `Application` object by using the `WithEvents` keyword. For example:

```
Public WithEvents XL As Application
```

4. Create a variable that you will use to refer to the declared `Application` object in the class module. This should be a module-level object variable declared in a regular VBA module (not in the class module). For example:

```
Dim X As New clsApp
```

5. Connect the declared object with the `Application` object. This is often done in a `Workbook_Open` procedure. For example:

```
Set X.XL = Application
```

6. Write event handler procedures for the `XL` object in the class module.

 CROSS-REFERENCE

This procedure is virtually identical to that required to use events with an embedded chart. See Chapter 18.

Determining when a workbook is opened

The example in this section keeps track of every workbook that is opened by storing information in a comma-separated variable (CSV) text file. This file can be imported into Excel.

I start by inserting a new class module and naming it `clsApp`. The code in the class module is:

```
Public WithEvents AppEvents As Application

Private Sub AppEvents_WorkbookOpen _
  (ByVal Wb As Excel.Workbook)
    Call UpdateLogFile(Wb)
End Sub
```

This code declares `AppEvents` as an `Application` object with events. The `AppEvents_WorkbookOpen` procedure will be called whenever a workbook is opened. This event handler procedure calls `UpdateLogFile` and passes the `Wb` variable, which represents the workbook that was opened. I then added a VBA module and inserted the following code:

```
Dim AppObject As New clsApp

Sub Init()
'   Called by Workbook_Open
    Set AppObject.AppEvents = Application
```

```
End Sub

Sub UpdateLogFile(Wb)
    Dim txt As String
    Dim Fname As String
    txt = Wb.FullName
    txt = txt & "," & Date & "," & Time
    txt = txt & "," & Application.UserName
    Fname = Application.DefaultFilePath & "\logfile.csv"
    Open Fname For Append As #1
    Write #1, txt
    Close #1
    MsgBox txt
End Sub
```

Notice at the top that the `AppObject` variable is declared as type `clsApp` (the name of the class module). The call to `Init` is in the `Workbook_Open` procedure, which is in the code module for `ThisWorkbook`. This procedure is as follows:

```
Private Sub Workbook_Open()
    Call Init
End Sub
```

The `UpdateLogFile` procedure opens a text file — or creates it if it doesn't exist. It then writes key information about the workbook that was opened: the filename and full path, the date, the time, and the username.

The `Workbook_Open` procedure calls the `Init` procedure. Therefore, when the workbook opens, the `Init` procedure creates the object variable.

 CD-ROM

This example, named `log workbook open.xlsm`, is available on the companion CD-ROM.

Monitoring Application-level events

To get a feel for the event-generation process, you might find it helpful to see a list of events that get generated as you go about your work.

I created an application that displays (in a UserForm) each `Application`-level event as it occurs (see Figure 19-9). You might find this helpful in learning about the types and sequence of events that occur.

 CD-ROM

This example is available on the companion CD-ROM. The file is named `application event tracker.xlsm`.

Part V

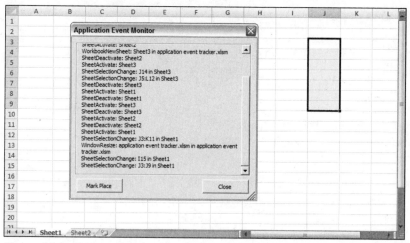

Figure 19-9: This workbook uses a class module to monitor all Application-level events.

The workbook contains a class module with 21 procedures defined, one for each Application-level event. Here's an example of one of them:

```
Private Sub XL_NewWorkbook(ByVal Wb As Excel.Workbook)
    LogEvent "NewWorkbook: " & Wb.Name
End Sub
```

Each of these procedures calls the LogEvent procedure and passes an argument that consists of the event name and the object. The LogEvent procedure follows:

```
Sub LogEvent(txt)
    EventNum = EventNum + 1
    With UserForm1
        With .lblEvents
            .AutoSize = False
            .Caption = .Caption & vbCrLf & txt
            .Width = UserForm1.FrameEvents.Width - 20
            .AutoSize = True
        End With
        .FrameEvents.ScrollHeight = .lblEvents.Height + 20
        .FrameEvents.ScrollTop = EventNum * 20
    End With
End Sub
```

The LogEvent procedure updates the UserForm by modifying the Caption property of the Label control named lblEvents. The procedure also adjusts the ScrollHeight and ScrollTop properties of the Frame named FrameEvents, which contains the Label. Adjusting these properties causes the most recently added text to be visible while older text scrolls out of view. You can also adjust the vertical size of this UserForm. It uses the technique described in Chapter 15.

UserForm Events

A UserForm supports quite a few events, and each control placed on a UserForm has its own set of events. Table 19-5 lists the UserForm events that you can use.

TABLE 19-5   EVENTS RECOGNIZED BY A USERFORM

Event	Action That Triggers the Event
Activate	The UserForm is activated.
AddControl	A control is added at runtime.
BeforeDragOver	A drag-and-drop operation is in progress while the pointer is over the form.
BeforeDropOrPaste	The user is about to drop or paste data: that is, when the user has released the mouse button.
Click	A mouse is clicked while the pointer is over the form.
DblClick	A mouse is double-clicked while the pointer is over the form.
Deactivate	The UserForm is deactivated.
Error	A control detects an error and cannot return the error information to a calling program.
Initialize	The UserForm is about to be shown.
KeyDown	A key is pressed.
KeyPress	The user presses any ANSI key.
KeyUp	A key is released.
Layout	A UserForm changes size.
MouseDown	A mouse button is pressed.
MouseMove	The mouse is moved.
MouseUp	A mouse button is released.
QueryClose	Occurs before a UserForm closes.
RemoveControl	A control is removed from the UserForm at runtime.
Resize	The UserForm is resized.
Scroll	The UserForm is scrolled.
Terminate	The UserForm is terminated.
Zoom	The UserForm is zoomed.

Part V

CROSS-REFERENCE

Many of the examples in Chapters 13 through 15 demonstrate event handling for UserForms and UserForm controls.

Events Not Associated with an Object

The events that I discuss earlier in this chapter are all associated with an object (Application, Workbook, Sheet, and so on). In this section, I discuss two additional rogue events: OnTime and OnKey. These events are not associated with an object. Rather, they are accessed by using methods of the Application object.

NOTE

Unlike the other events discussed in this chapter, you program these On events in a general VBA module.

The OnTime event

The OnTime event occurs at a specified time of day. The following example demonstrates how to program Excel so that it beeps and then displays a message at 3 p.m.:

```
Sub SetAlarm()
    Application.OnTime TimeValue("15:00:00"), "DisplayAlarm"
End Sub

Sub DisplayAlarm()
    Beep
    MsgBox "Wake up. It's time for your afternoon break!"
End Sub
```

In this example, the SetAlarm procedure uses the OnTime method of the Application object to set up the OnTime event. This method takes two arguments: the time (3 p.m., in the example) and the procedure to execute when the time occurs (DisplayAlarm in the example). After SetAlarm is executed, the DisplayAlarm procedure will be called at 3 p.m., bringing up the message in Figure 19-10.

Figure 19-10: This message box was programmed to display at a particular time of day.

If you want to schedule an event relative to the current time — for example, 20 minutes from now — you can write an instruction like this:

```
Application.OnTime Now + TimeValue("00:20:00"), "DisplayAlarm"
```

You can also use the OnTime method to schedule a procedure on a particular day. The following statement runs the DisplayAlarm procedure at 12:01 a.m. on April 1, 2008:

```
Application.OnTime DateSerial(2008, 4, 1) + _
    TimeValue("00:00:01"), "DisplayAlarm"
```

NOTE

The OnTime method has two additional arguments. If you plan to use this method, you should refer to the online help for complete details.

The two procedures that follow demonstrate how to program a repeated event. In this case, cell A1 is updated with the current time every five seconds. Executing the UpdateClock procedures writes the time to cell A1 and also programs another event five seconds later. This event re-runs the UpdateClock procedure. To stop the events, execute the StopClock procedure (which cancels the event). Note that NextTick is a module-level variable that stores the time for the next event.

CD-ROM

This example, named ontime event demo.xlsm, is available on the companion CD-ROM.

```
Dim NextTick As Date

Sub UpdateClock()
'   Updates cell A1 with the current time
    ThisWorkbook.Sheets(1).Range("A1") = Time
'   Set up the next event five seconds from now
    NextTick = Now + TimeValue("00:00:05")
    Application.OnTime NextTick, "UpdateClock"
End Sub

Sub StopClock()
'   Cancels the OnTime event (stops the clock)
    On Error Resume Next
    Application.OnTime NextTick, "UpdateClock", , False
End Sub
```

CAUTION

The OnTime event persists even after the workbook is closed. In other words, if you close the workbook without running the StopClock procedure, the workbook will reopen itself in five seconds (assuming that Excel is still running). To prevent this, use a Workbook_BeforeClose event procedure that contains the following statement:

```
Call StopClock
```

CROSS-REFERENCE

To see an example of a repeating OnTime event, see the analog clock example in Chapter 18.

The OnKey event

While you're working, Excel constantly monitors what you type. Because of this, you can set up a keystroke or a key combination that, when pressed, executes a particular procedure. The only time these keystrokes won't be recognized is when you're entering a formula or working with a dialog box.

CAUTION

It's important to understand that creating a procedure to respond to an OnKey event is not limited to a single workbook. The re-mapped keystroke is valid in all open workbooks, not just the one in which you created the event procedure.

Also, if you set up an OnKey event, make sure that you provide a way to cancel the event. A common way to do this is to use the Workbook_BeforeClose event procedure.

AN ONKEY EVENT EXAMPLE

The following example uses the OnKey method to set up an OnKey event. This event reassigns the PgDn and PgUp keys. After the Setup_OnKey procedure is executed, pressing PgDn executes the PgDn_Sub procedure, and pressing PgUp executes the PgUp_Sub procedure. The net effect is that pressing PgDn moves the cursor down one row, and pressing PgUp moves the cursor up one row.

```
Sub Setup_OnKey()
    Application.OnKey "{PgDn}", "PgDn_Sub"
    Application.OnKey "{PgUp}", "PgUp_Sub"
End Sub

Sub PgDn_Sub()
    On Error Resume Next
    ActiveCell.Offset(1, 0).Activate
```

```
End Sub

Sub PgUp_Sub()
    On Error Resume Next
    ActiveCell.Offset(-1, 0).Activate
End Sub
```

 CD-ROM

This example, named `onkey event demo.xlsm`, is available on the companion CD-ROM.

In the preceding examples, I use `On Error Resume Next` to ignore any errors that are generated. For example, if the active cell is in the first row, trying to move up one row causes an error. Also, if the active sheet is a chart sheet, an error will occur because there is no such thing as an active cell in a chart sheet.

By executing the following procedure, you cancel the `OnKey` events and return these keys to their normal functionality:

```
Sub Cancel_OnKey()
    Application.OnKey "{PgDn}"
    Application.OnKey "{PgUp}"
End Sub
```

Contrary to what you might expect, using an empty string as the second argument for the `OnKey` method does *not* cancel the `OnKey` event. Rather, it causes Excel to simply ignore the keystroke and do nothing at all. For example, the following instruction tells Excel to ignore Alt+F4 (the percent sign represents the Alt key):

```
Application.OnKey "%{F4}", ""
```

 CROSS-REFERENCE

Although you can use the `OnKey` method to assign a shortcut key for executing a macro, it's better to use the Macro Options dialog box for this task. For more details, see Chapter 9.

KEY CODES

In the previous section, notice that the PgDn keystroke appears in braces. Table 19-6 shows the key codes that you can use in your `OnKey` procedures.

Part V

TABLE 19-6   KEY CODES FOR THE ONKEY EVENT

Key	Code
Backspace	{BACKSPACE} or {BS}
Break	{BREAK}
Caps Lock	{CAPSLOCK}
Delete or Del	{DELETE} or {DEL}
Down Arrow	{DOWN}
End	{END}
Enter	~ (tilde)
Enter (on the numeric keypad)	{ENTER}
Escape	{ESCAPE} or {ESC}
Home	{HOME}
Ins	{INSERT}
Left Arrow	{LEFT}
NumLock	{NUMLOCK}
Page Down	{PGDN}
Page Up	{PGUP}
Right Arrow	{RIGHT}
Scroll Lock	{SCROLLLOCK}
Tab	{TAB}
Up Arrow	{UP}
F1 through F15	{F1} through {F15}

You can also specify keys combined with Shift, Ctrl, and Alt. To specify a key combined with another key or keys, use the following symbols:

- *Shift:* Plus sign (+)
- *Ctrl:* Caret (^)
- *Alt:* Percent sign (%)

For example, to assign a procedure to the Ctrl+Shift+A key, use this code:

```
Application.OnKey "^+A", "SubName"
```

To assign a procedure to Alt+F11 (which is normally used to switch to the VB Editor window), use this code:

```
Application.OnKey "^{F11}", "SubName"
```

DISABLING SHORTCUT MENUS

Earlier in this chapter, I discuss a `Worksheet_BeforeRightClick` procedure that disables the right-click shortcut menu. The following procedure is placed in the `ThisWorkbook` code module:

```
Private Sub Worksheet_BeforeRightClick _
    (ByVal Target As Excel.Range, Cancel As Boolean)
    Cancel = True
    MsgBox "The shortcut menu is not available."
End Sub
```

I also noted that the user could still display the shortcut menu by pressing Shift+F10. To intercept the Shift+F10 key combination, add these procedures to a standard VBA module:

```
Sub SetupNoShiftF10()
    Application.OnKey "+{F10}", "NoShiftF10"
End Sub

Sub TurnOffNoShiftF10()
    Application.OnKey "+{F10}"
End Sub

Sub NoShiftF10()
    MsgBox "Nice try, but that doesn't work either."
End Sub
```

After the `SetupNoShiftF10` procedure is executed, pressing Shift+F10 displays the message box shown in Figure 19-11. Remember that the `Worksheet_BeforeRightClick` procedure is valid only in its own workbook. The Shift+F10 key event, on the other hand, applies to all open workbooks.

NOTE

Some keyboards have a dedicated key that displays a shortcut menu. On my keyboard, that key is on the right side of the keyboard between the Windows key and the Ctrl key. I was surprised to discover that intercepting the Shit+F10 key combination also disables the dedicated shortcut menu key.

Part V

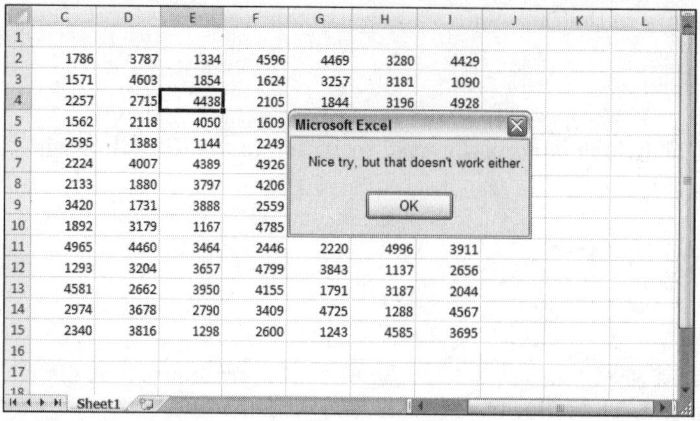

	C	D	E	F	G	H	I	J	K	L
1										
2	1786	3787	1334	4596	4469	3280	4429			
3	1571	4603	1854	1624	3257	3181	1090			
4	2257	2715	4438	2105	1844	3196	4928			
5	1562	2118	4050	1609						
6	2595	1388	1144	2249						
7	2224	4007	4389	4926						
8	2133	1880	3797	4206						
9	3420	1731	3888	2559						
10	1892	3179	1167	4785						
11	4965	4460	3464	2446	2220	4996	3911			
12	1293	3204	3657	4799	3843	1137	2656			
13	4581	2662	3950	4155	1791	3187	2044			
14	2974	3678	2790	3409	4725	1288	4567			
15	2340	3816	1298	2600	1243	4585	3695			
16										
17										

Microsoft Excel

Nice try, but that doesn't work either.

OK

Sheet1

Figure 19-11: Pressing Shift+F10 displays this message.

CD-ROM

The companion CD-ROM contains a workbook that includes all of these procedures. The file, named no shortcut menus.xlsm, includes workbook event handler procedures: Workbook_Open executes the SetupNoShiftF10 procedure, and Workbook_ BeforeClose calls the TurnOffNoShiftF10 procedure.

Chapter 20

Chapter 20

Interacting with Other Applications

In This Chapter

In this chapter, I describe some of the ways in which your Excel applications can interact with other applications. Of course, I also provide several examples.

- ◆ Starting or activating another application from Excel

- ◆ Displaying Windows Control Panel dialog boxes

- ◆ Using Automation to control another application

- ◆ A simple example of using ADO to retrieve data

- ◆ Using `SendKeys` as a last resort

In the early days of personal computing, interapplication communication was rare. In the pre-multitasking era, users had no choice but to use one program at a time. Interapplication communication was usually limited to importing files; even copying information and pasting it into another application — something that virtually every user now takes for granted — was impossible.

Nowadays, most software is designed to support at least some type of communication with other applications. At the very least, most Windows programs support the Clipboard for copy-and-paste operations between applications. Many Windows products also support Automation.

Starting an Application from Excel

Starting up another application from Excel is often useful. For example, you might want to execute another Microsoft Office application or even a DOS batch file from Excel. Or, as an application developer, you might want to make it easy for a user to access the Windows Control Panel.

Using the VBA Shell function

The VBA `Shell` function makes launching other programs relatively easy. The `StartCalc` procedure that follows launches the Windows Calculator application.

```
Sub StartCalc()
    Dim Program As String
    Dim TaskID As Double
    On Error Resume Next
    Program = "calc.exe"
    TaskID = Shell(Program, 1)
    If Err <> 0 Then
        MsgBox "Cannot start " & Program, vbCritical, "Error"
    End If
End Sub
```

You'll probably recognize the application that this procedure launches in Figure 20-1.

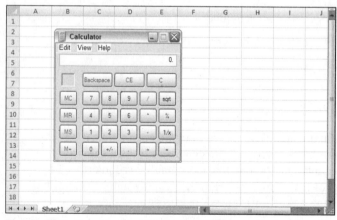

Figure 20-1: Running the Windows Calculator program from Excel.

The `Shell` function returns a task identification number for the application. You can use this number later to activate the task. The second argument for the `Shell` function determines how the application is displayed. (1 is the code for a normal-size window, with the focus.) Refer to the Help system for other values for this argument.

Displaying a Folder Window

The Shell function is also handy if you need to display a particular directory using Windows Explorer. For example, the statement that follows displays the folder of the active workbook (but only if the workbook has been saved):

```
If ActiveWorkbook.Path <> "" Then _
    Shell "explorer.exe " & ActiveWorkbook.Path, vbNormalFocus
```

If the Shell function is not successful, it generates an error. Therefore, this procedure uses an On Error statement to display a message if the executable file cannot be found or if some other error occurs.

It's important to understand that your VBA code does not pause while the application that was started with the Shell function is running. In other words, the Shell function runs the application *asynchronously*. If the procedure has more instructions after the Shell function is executed, they are executed concurrently with the newly loaded program. If any instruction requires user intervention (for example, displaying a message box), Excel's title bar flashes while the other application is active.

In some cases, you might want to launch an application with the Shell function, but you need your VBA code to pause until the application is closed. For example, the launched application might generate a file that is used later in your code. Although you can't pause the execution of your code, you *can* create a loop that does nothing except monitor the application's status. The example that follows displays a message box when the application launched by the Shell function has ended:

```
Declare Function OpenProcess Lib "kernel32" _
    (ByVal dwDesiredAccess As Long, _
    ByVal bInheritHandle As Long, _
    ByVal dwProcessId As Long) As Long

Declare Function GetExitCodeProcess Lib "kernel32" _
    (ByVal hProcess As Long, _
    lpExitCode As Long) As Long

Sub StartCalc2()
    Dim TaskID As Long
    Dim hProc As Long
    Dim lExitCode As Long
    Dim ACCESS_TYPE As Integer, STILL_ACTIVE As Integer
    Dim Program As String

    ACCESS_TYPE = &H400
    STILL_ACTIVE = &H103

    Program = "Calc.exe"
```

```
    On Error Resume Next

'   Shell the task
    TaskID = Shell(Program, 1)

'   Get the process handle
    hProc = OpenProcess(ACCESS_TYPE, False, TaskID)

    If Err <> 0 Then
        MsgBox "Cannot start " & Program, vbCritical, "Error"
        Exit Sub
    End If

    Do  'Loop continuously
'       Check on the process
        GetExitCodeProcess hProc, lExitCode
'       Allow event processing
        DoEvents
    Loop While lExitCode = STILL_ACTIVE

'   Task is finished, so show message
    MsgBox Program & " was closed"
End Sub
```

While the launched program is running, this procedure continually calls the GetExitCodeProcess function from within a Do-Loop structure, testing for its returned value (lExitCode). When the program is finished, lExitCode returns a different value, the loop ends, and the VBA code resumes executing.

CD-ROM

Both of the preceding examples are available on the companion CD-ROM. The filename is start calculator.xlsm.

Using the Windows ShellExecute API function

ShellExecute is a Windows Application Programming Interface (API) function that is useful for starting other applications. Importantly, this function can start an application only if an associated filename is known (assuming that the file type is registered with Windows). For example, you can use ShellExecute to open a Web document by starting the default Web browser. Or you can use an e-mail address to start the default e-mail client.

The API declaration follows (this code goes at the top of a VBA module):

```
Private Declare Function ShellExecute Lib "shell32.dll" _
   Alias "ShellExecuteA" (ByVal hWnd As Long, _
   ByVal lpOperation As String, ByVal lpFile As String, _
```

```
ByVal lpParameters As String, ByVal lpDirectory As String, _
ByVal nShowCmd As Long) As Long
```

The following procedure demonstrates how to call the `ShellExecute` function. In this example, it opens a graphics file by using the graphics program that's set up to handle GIF files. If the result returned by the function is less than 32, then an error occurred.

```
Sub ShowGraphic()
    Dim FileName As String
    Dim Result As Long
    FileName = ThisWorkbook.Path & "\flower.jpg"
    Result = ShellExecute(0&, vbNullString, FileName, _
        vbNullString, vbNullString, vbNormalFocus)
    If Result < 32 Then MsgBox "Error"
End Sub
```

The next procedure opens a text file, using the default text file program:

```
Sub OpenTextFile()
    Dim FileName As String
    Dim Result As Long
    FileName = ThisWorkbook.Path & "\textfile.txt"
    Result = ShellExecute(0&, vbNullString, FileName, _
        vbNullString, vbNullString, vbNormalFocus)
    If Result < 32 Then MsgBox "Error"
End Sub
```

The following example is similar, but it opens a Web URL by using the default browser.

```
Sub OpenURL()
    Dim URL As String
    Dim Result As Long
    URL = "http://office.microsoft.com"
    Result = ShellExecute(0&, vbNullString, URL, _
        vbNullString, vbNullString, vbNormalFocus)
    If Result < 32 Then MsgBox "Error"
End Sub
```

This technique can also be used with an e-mail address. The example below opens the default e-mail client and then addresses an e-mail to the recipient.

```
Sub StartEmail()
    Dim Addr As String
    Dim Result As Long
    Addr = "mailto:bgates@microsoft.com"
    Result = ShellExecute(0&, vbNullString, Addr, _
        vbNullString, vbNullString, vbNormalFocus)
    If Result < 32 Then MsgBox "Error"
End Sub
```

Part V

CD

These examples are available on the companion CD-ROM in a file named
`shellexecute examples.xlsm`.

Activating an Application with Excel

In the previous section, I discuss various ways to start an application. You might find that if an application is already running, using the `Shell` function could start another instance of it. In most cases, however, you want to *activate* the instance that's running — not start another instance of it.

Using AppActivate

The following `StartCalculator` procedure uses the `AppActivate` statement to activate an application if it's already running (in this case, the Windows Calculator). The argument for `AppActivate` is the caption of the application's title bar. If the `AppActivate` statement generates an error, it indicates that the Calculator is not running. Therefore, the routine starts the application.

```
Sub StartCalculator()
    Dim AppFile As String
    Dim CalcTaskID As Double

    AppFile = "Calc.exe"
    On Error Resume Next
    AppActivate "Calculator"
    If Err <> 0 Then
        Err = 0
        CalcTaskID = Shell(AppFile, 1)
        If Err <> 0 Then MsgBox "Can't start Calculator"
    End If
End Sub
```

CD-ROM

This example is available on the companion CD-ROM. The filename is `start calculator.xlsm`.

Activating a Microsoft Office application

If the application that you want to start is one of several Microsoft applications, you can use the `ActivateMicrosoftApp` method of the `Application` object. For example, the following procedure starts Word:

```
Sub StartWord()
    Application.ActivateMicrosoftApp xlMicrosoftWord
End Sub
```

If Word is already running when the preceding procedure is executed, it is activated. The other constants available for this method are:

- `xlMicrosoftPowerPoint`
- `xlMicrosoftMail` (activates Outlook)
- `xlMicrosoftAccess`
- `xlMicrosoftFoxPro`
- `xlMicrosoftProject`
- `xlMicrosoftSchedulePlus`

Running Control Panel Dialog Boxes

Windows provides quite a few system dialog boxes and wizards, most of which are accessible from the Windows Control Panel. You might need to display one or more of these from your Excel application. For example, you might want to display the Windows Date and Time Properties dialog box, shown in Figure 20-2.

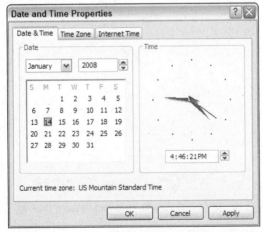

Figure 20-2: Use VBA to display a Control Panel dialog box.

The key to running other system dialog boxes is to execute the `rundll32.exe` application by using the VBA `Shell` function.

The following procedure displays the Date and Time dialog box:

```
Sub ShowDateTimeDlg()
  Dim Arg As String
  Dim TaskID As Double
  Arg = "rundll32.exe shell32.dll,Control_RunDLL timedate.cpl"
  On Error Resume Next
  TaskID = Shell(Arg)
  If Err <> 0 Then
      MsgBox ("Cannot start the application.")
  End If
End Sub
```

Following is the general format for the `rundll32.exe` application:

```
rundll32.exe shell32.dll,Control_RunDLL filename.cpl, n,t
```

- `filename.cpl`: The name of one of the Control Panel *.CPL files.
- n: The zero-based number of the applet within the *.CPL file.
- t: The number of the tab (for multi-tabbed applets).

 CD-ROM

A workbook that displays12 additional Control Panel applets, depicted in Figure 20-3, is available on the companion CD-ROM. The filename is `control panel dialogs.xlsm`.

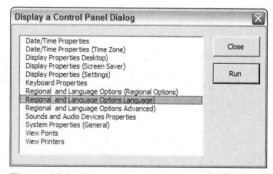

Figure 20-3: The workbook that displays this dialog box demonstrates how to run system dialog boxes from Excel.

Using Automation in Excel

You can write an Excel macro to control other applications, such as Microsoft Word. More accurately, the Excel macro will control Word's automation server. In such circumstances,

Excel is the *client application,* and Word is the *server application.* Or you can write a Visual Basic application to control Excel. The process of one application's controlling another is sometimes known as *Object Linking and Embedding (OLE),* or simply *automation.*

The concept behind automation is quite appealing. A developer who needs to generate a chart, for example, can just reach into another application's grab bag of objects, fetch a `Chart` object, and then manipulate its properties and use its methods. Automation, in a sense, blurs the boundaries between applications. An end user might be working with an Access object and not even realize it.

NOTE
Some applications, such as Excel, can function as either a client application or a server application. Other applications can function only as client applications or only as server applications.

In this section, I demonstrate how to use VBA to access and manipulate the objects exposed by other applications. The examples use Microsoft Word, but the concepts apply to any application that exposes its objects for automation — which accounts for an increasing number of applications.

Working with foreign objects using automation

As you might know, you can use Excel's Insert ⇨ Text ⇨ Object command to embed an object, such as a Word document, in a worksheet. In addition, you can create an object and manipulate it with VBA. (This action is the heart of Automation.) When you do so, you usually have full access to the object. For developers, this technique is generally more beneficial than embedding the object in a worksheet. When an object is embedded, the user must know how to use the automation object's application. But, when you use VBA to work with the object, you can program the object so that the user can manipulate it by an action as simple as a button click.

Early versus late binding

Before you can work with an external object, you must create an instance of the object. This can be done in either of two ways: early binding or late binding. *Binding* refers to matching the function calls written by the programmer to the actual code that implements the function.

EARLY BINDING
To use early binding, create a reference to the object library by choosing the Tools ⇨ References command in the Visual Basic Editor (VBE), which brings up the dialog box shown in Figure 20-4. Then put a check mark next to the object library you need to reference.

Part V

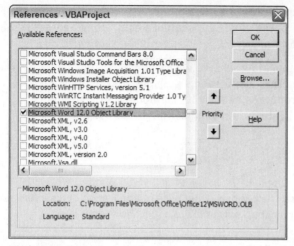

Figure 20-4: Adding a reference to an object library file.

After the reference to the object library is established, you can use the Object Browser, shown in Figure 20-5, to view the object names, methods, and properties. To access the Object Browser, press F2 in the VBE.

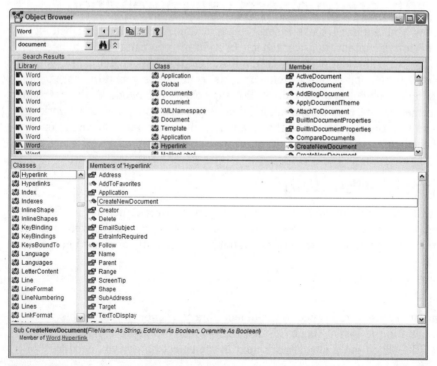

Figure 20-5: Use the Object Browser to learn about the objects in a referenced library.

When you use early binding, you must establish a reference to a version-specific object library. For example, you can specify Microsoft Word 10.0 Object Library (for Word 2002), or Microsoft Word 11.0 Object Library (for Word 2003), or Microsoft Word 12.0 Object Library (for Word 2007). Then you use a statement like the following to create the object:

```
Dim WordApp As New Word.Application
```

Using early binding to create the object by setting a reference to the object library usually is more efficient and also often yields better performance. Early binding is an option, however, only if the object that you are controlling has a separate type library or object library file. You also need to ensure that the user of the application actually has a copy of the specific library installed.

Another advantage of early binding is that you can use constants that are defined in the object library. For example, Word (like Excel) contains many predefined constants that you can use in your VBA code. If you use early binding, you can use the constants in your code. If you use late binding, you'll need to use the actual value rather than the constant.

Still another benefit of using early binding is that you can take advantage of the VBE Object Browser and Auto List Members option to make it easier to access properties and methods; this feature doesn't work when you use late binding because the type of the object is known only at runtime.

LATE BINDING

At runtime, you use either the `CreateObject` function to create the object or the `GetObject` function to obtain a saved instance of the object. Such an object is declared as a generic `Object` type, and its object reference is resolved at runtime.

GetObject versus CreateObject

VBA's `GetObject` and `CreateObject` functions both return a reference to an object, but they work in different ways.

The `CreateObject` function creates an interface to a new instance of an application. Use this function when the application is not running. If an instance of the application is already running, a new instance is started. For example, the following statement starts Excel, and the object returned in XLApp is a reference to the `Excel.Application` object that it created.

```
Set XLApp = CreateObject("Excel.Application")
```

The `GetObject` function is either used with an application that's already running or to start an application with a file already loaded. The following statement, for example, starts Excel with the file `Myfile.xls` already loaded. The object returned in XLBook is a reference to the `Workbook` object (the `Myfile.xlsx` file):

```
Set XLBook = GetObject("C:\Myfile.xlsx")
```

You can use late binding even when you don't know which version of the application is installed on the user's system. For example, the following code, which works with Word 97 and later, creates a `Word` object:

```
Dim WordApp As Object
Set WordApp = CreateObject("Word.Application")
```

If multiple versions of Word are installed, you can create an object for a specific version. The following statement, for example, uses Word 2003:

```
Set WordApp = CreateObject("Word.Application.11")
```

The Registry key for Word's Automation object and the reference to the `Application` object in VBA just happen to be the same: `Word.Application`. They do not, however, refer to the same thing. When you declare an object `As Word.Application` or `As New Word.Application`, the term refers to the `Application` object in the `Word` library. But when you invoke the function `CreateObject("Word.Application")`, the term refers to the moniker by which the latest version of Word is known in the Windows System Registry. This isn't the case for all automation objects, although it is true for the main Office 2007 components. If the user replaces Word 2003 with Word 2007, `CreateObject("Word.Application")` will continue to work properly, referring to the new application. If Word 2007 is removed, however, `CreateObject("Word.Application.12")`, which uses the alternate version-specific name for Word 2007, will fail to work.

The `CreateObject` function used on an automation object such as `Word.Application` or `Excel.Application` always creates a new *instance* of that automation object. That is, it starts up a new and separate copy of the automation part of the program. Even if an instance of the automation object is already running, a new instance is started, and then an object of the specified type is created.

To use the current instance or to start the application and have it load a file, use the `GetObject` function.

NOTE

If you need to automate an Office application, it is recommended that you use early binding and reference the earliest version of the product that you expect could be installed on your client's system. For example, if you need to be able to automate Word 2000, Word 2002, Word 2003, and Word 2007, you should use the type library for Word 2000 to maintain compatibility with all four versions. This, of course, will mean that you can't use features found only in the later version of Word.

A simple example of late binding

The following example demonstrates how to create a `Word` object by using late binding. This procedure creates the object, displays the version number, closes the Word application, and then destroys the object (thus freeing the memory that it used):

```
Sub GetWordVersion()
    Dim WordApp As Object
    Set WordApp = CreateObject("Word.Application")
    MsgBox WordApp.Version
    WordApp.Quit
    Set WordApp = Nothing
End Sub
```

 NOTE

The `Word` object that's created in this procedure is invisible. If you'd like to see the object's window while it's being manipulated, set its `Visible` property to `True`, as follows:

```
WordApp.Visible = True
```

This example can also be programmed using early binding. Before doing so, choose Tools ➪ References to set a reference to the Word object library. Then you can use the following code:

```
Sub GetWordVersion()
    Dim WordApp As New Word.Application
    MsgBox WordApp.Version
    WordApp.Quit
    Set WordApp = Nothing
End Sub
```

Controlling Word from Excel

The example in this section demonstrates Automation by using Word. The `MakeMemos` procedure creates three customized memos in Word and then saves each document to a file. The information used to create the memos is stored in a worksheet, as shown in Figure 20-6.

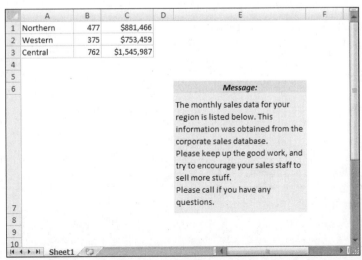

Figure 20-6: Word automatically generates three memos based on this Excel data.

The MakeMemos procedure starts by creating an object called WordApp. The routine cycles through the three rows of data in Sheet1 and uses Word's properties and methods to create each memo and save it to disk. A range named Message (in cell E6) contains the text used in the memo. All the action occurs behind the scenes: That is, Word is not visible.

```
Sub MakeMemos()
'    Creates memos in word using Automation
     Dim WordApp As Object
     Dim Data As Range, message As String
     Dim Records As Integer, i As Integer
     Dim Region As String, SalesAmt As String, SalesNum As String
     Dim SaveAsName As String

'    Start Word and create an object (late binding)
     Set WordApp = CreateObject("Word.Application")

'    Information from worksheet
     Set Data = Sheets("Sheet1").Range("A1")
     Message = Sheets("Sheet1").Range("Message")

'    Cycle through all records in Sheet1
     Records = Application.CountA(Sheets("Sheet1").Range("A:A"))
     For i = 1 To Records
'        Update status bar progress message
         Application.StatusBar = "Processing Record " & i

'        Assign current data to variables
         Region = Data.Cells(i, 1).Value
         SalesNum = Data.Cells(i, 2).Value
         SalesAmt = Format(Data.Cells(i, 3).Value, "#,000")

'        Determine the filename
         SaveAsName = Application.DefaultFilePath & _
             "\" & Region & ".docx"

'        Send commands to Word
         With WordApp
             .Documents.Add
             With .Selection
                 .Font.Size = 14
                 .Font.Bold = True
                 .ParagraphFormat.Alignment = 1
                 .TypeText Text:="M E M O R A N D U M"
                 .TypeParagraph
                 .TypeParagraph
                 .Font.Size = 12
                 .ParagraphFormat.Alignment = 0
                 .Font.Bold = False
```

```
            .TypeText Text:="Date:" & vbTab & _
                Format(Date, "mmmm d, yyyy")
            .TypeParagraph
            .TypeText Text:="To:" & vbTab & Region & _
             " Manager"
            .TypeParagraph
            .TypeText Text:="From:" & vbTab & _
                Application.UserName
            .TypeParagraph
            .TypeParagraph
            .TypeText Message
            .TypeParagraph
            .TypeParagraph
            .TypeText Text:="Units Sold:" & vbTab & _
             SalesNum
            .TypeParagraph
            .TypeText Text:="Amount:" & vbTab & _
                Format(SalesAmt, "$#,##0")
        End With
            .ActiveDocument.SaveAs FileName:=SaveAsName
    End With
 Next i


'    Kill the object
     WordApp.Quit
     Set WordApp = Nothing


'    Reset status bar
     Application.StatusBar = ""
     MsgBox Records & " memos were created and saved in " & _
        Application.DefaultFilePath
End Sub
```

Figure 20-7 shows one of the documents created by the MakeMemos procedure.

 **CD-ROM**

This workbook, named make memos.xlsm, is available on the companion CD-ROM.

Creating this macro involved several steps. I started by recording a macro in Word. I recorded my actions while creating a new document, adding and formatting some text, and saving the file. That Word macro provided the information that I needed about the appropriate properties and methods. I then copied the macro to an Excel module. Notice that I used With-End With. I added a dot before each instruction between With and End With. For example, the original Word macro contained (among others) the following instruction:

```
Documents.Add
```

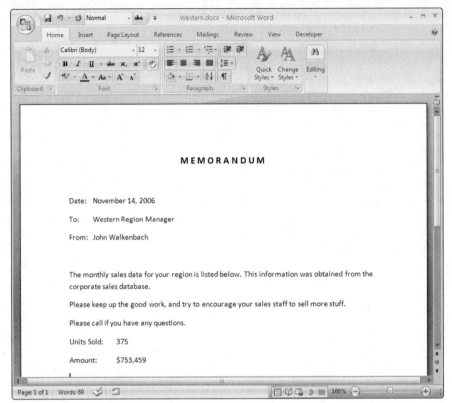

Figure 20-7: An Excel procedure created this Word document.

I modified the macro as follows:

```
With WordApp
    .Documents.Add
'   more instructions here
End With
```

The macro that I recorded in Word used a few of Word's built-in constants. Because this example uses late binding, I had to substitute actual values for those constants. I was able to learn the values by using the Immediate window in Word's VBE.

Controlling Excel from another application

You can, of course, also control Excel from another application (such as another programming language or a Word VBA procedure). For example, you might want to perform some calculations in Excel and return the result to a Word document.

You can create any of the following Excel objects with the adjacent functions:

- `Application` object: `CreateObject("Excel.Application")`
- `Workbook` object: `CreateObject("Excel.Sheet")`
- `Chart` object: `CreateObject("Excel.Chart")`

The code that follows is a procedure that is located in a VBA module in a Word 2007 document. This procedure creates an Excel `Worksheet` object (whose moniker is `"Excel.Sheet"`) from an existing workbook and pastes it into the Word file.

```
Sub MakeLoanTable()
    Dim XLSheet As Object
    Dim LoanAmt
    Dim Wbook As String

'   Prompt for values
    LoanAmt = InputBox("Loan Amount?")
    If LoanAmt = "" Then Exit Sub

'   Clear the document
    ThisDocument.Content.Delete

'   Create Sheet object
    Wbook = ThisDocument.Path & "\mortgagecalcs.xlsx"
    Set XLSheet = GetObject(Wbook, "Excel.Sheet").ActiveSheet

'   Put values in sheet
    XLSheet.Range("LoanAmount") = LoanAmt
    XLSheet.Calculate

'   Insert page heading
    Selection.Style = "Title"
    Selection.TypeText "Loan Amount: " & _
        Format(LoanAmt, "$#,##0")
    Selection.TypeParagraph
    Selection.TypeParagraph

'   Copy data from sheet & paste to document
    XLSheet.Range("DataTable").Copy
    Selection.Paste

    Selection.TypeParagraph
    Selection.TypeParagraph

'   Copy chart and paste to document
    XLSheet.ChartObjects(1).Copy
```

```
    Selection.PasteSpecial _
        Link:=False, _
        DataType:=wdPasteMetafilePicture, _
        Placement:=wdInLine


'   Kill the object
    Set XLSheet = Nothing
End Sub
```

CD

This example is available on the companion CD-ROM. The Word document is named `automate excel.docm`, and the Excel workbook is named `mortgagecalcs.xlsx`. When you open the Word file, execute the MakeLoanTable macro by choosing Insert ➪ Mortgage ➪ Get Mortgage Amount.

The Excel worksheet used by this Word procedure is shown in Figure 20-8. The `MakeLoanTable` procedure prompts the user for a loan amount and inserts the value into cell C7 (named `LoanAmount`).

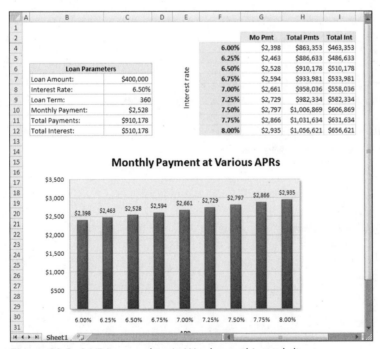

Figure 20-8: A VBA procedure in Word uses this worksheet.

Recalculating the worksheet updates a data table in range F2:I12 (named `DataTable`), and also updates the chart. The `DataTable` range and the chart are then copied from the Excel object and pasted into the Word document. The result is shown in Figure 20-9.

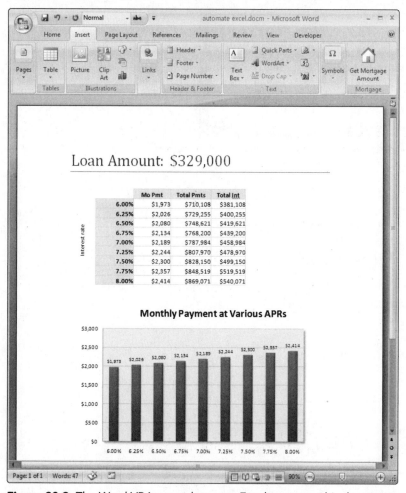

Figure 20-9: The Word VBA procedure uses Excel to create this document.

Sending Personalized E-Mail via Outlook

The example in this section demonstrates automation with Microsoft Outlook.

Figure 20-10 shows a worksheet that contains data used in the e-mail messages: name, e-mail address, and bonus amount. The SendMail procedure loops through the rows in the worksheet, retrieves the data, and creates an individualized message (stored in the Msg variable).

	A	B	C	D
1	**Name**	**Email**	**Bonus**	
2	John Jones	jjones@zx-prrtgfw.com	$2,000	
3	Bob Smith	bsmith@zx-prrtgfw.com	$3,500	
4	Fred Simpson	fsimpson@zx-prrtgfw.com	$1,250	
5				
6				
7				
8				

Sheet1

Figure 20-10: This information is used in the Outlook e-mail messages.

```
Sub SendEmail()
  'Uses early binding
  'Requires a reference to the Outlook Object Library
  Dim OutlookApp As Outlook.Application
  Dim MItem As Outlook.MailItem
  Dim cell As Range
  Dim Subj As String
  Dim EmailAddr As String
  Dim Recipient As String
  Dim Bonus As String
  Dim Msg As String

  'Create Outlook object
  Set OutlookApp = New Outlook.Application

  'Loop through the rows
  For Each cell In Columns("B").Cells.SpecialCells(xlCellTypeConstants)
    If cell.Value Like "*@*" Then
      'Get the data
      Subj = "Your Annual Bonus"
      Recipient = cell.Offset(0, -1).Value
      EmailAddr = cell.Value
      Bonus = Format(cell.Offset(0, 1).Value, "$0,000.")

     'Compose message
      Msg = "Dear " & Recipient & vbCrLf & vbCrLf
      Msg = Msg & "I am pleased to inform you that your annual bonus is "
      Msg = Msg & Bonus & vbCrLf & vbCrLf
      Msg = Msg & "William Rose" & vbCrLf
      Msg = Msg & "President"

      'Create Mail Item and send it
      Set MItem = OutlookApp.CreateItem(olMailItem)
      With MItem
        .To = EmailAddr
```

```
        .Subject = Subj
        .Body = Msg
        .Send
      End With
    End If
  Next
End Sub
```

Figure 20-11 shows one of the e-mail messages displayed in Outlook.

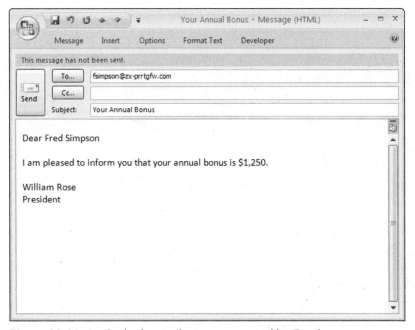

Figure 20-11: An Outlook e-mail message created by Excel.

This example uses early binding, so it requires a reference to the Outlook Object Library. Notice that two objects are involved: an `Outlook` object and a `MailItem` object. The `Outlook` object is created with this statement:

```
Set OutlookApp = New Outlook.Application
```

The `MailItem` object is created with this statement:

```
Set MItem = OutlookApp.CreateItem(olMailItem)
```

The code sets the `To`, `Subject`, and `Body` properties and then uses the `Send` method to send each message.

TIP

To save the messages in your Draft folder (rather than send them), use the `Save` method instead of the `Send` method. This change is particularly useful while you're testing and debugging the code.

Unless you've changed your security settings, you'll probably see the dialog box shown in Figure 20-12 for each message that's sent. To eliminate this dialog box, activate Outlook and choose Tools ⇨ Trust Center. In the Trust Center dialog box, click the Programmatic Access tab and choose the option labeled Never Warn Me about Suspicious Activity (Not Recommended). But do this at your own risk.

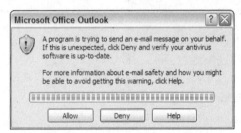

Figure 20-12: Using Excel to send e-mail via Outlook normally causes a warning message from Outlook.

CD-ROM

This example, named `personalized email - outlook.xlsm`, is available on the companion CD-ROM. You must have Microsoft Outlook installed. The CD also contains a slightly modified version that uses late binding: `personalized email - outlook (late binding).xlsm`.

NOTE

Subsequent sections in this chapter describe other ways of sending e-mail through Excel. See "Sending E-Mail Attachments from Excel" and "Using SendKeys."

Sending E-Mail Attachments from Excel

As you probably know, Excel has the ability to send a workbook via e-mail as an attachment. And, of course, you can use VBA to automate these types of tasks. The procedure below uses the `SendMail` method to send the active workbook (as an attachment) to `joeblow@zx-prrtgfw.com`. The e-mail message has the subject `My Workbook`.

```
Sub SendWorkbook()
    ActiveWorkbook.SendMail "joeblow@zx-prrtgfw.com", "My Workbook"
End Sub
```

 NOTE

The SendMail method uses the default e-mail client.

If you would like to e-mail only a single sheet from a workbook, you need to copy the sheet to a new (temporary) workbook, send that workbook as an attachment, and then close the temporary file. Here's an example that sends `Sheet1` from the active workbook.

```
Sub Sendasheet()
    ActiveWorkbook.Worksheets("sheet1").Copy
    ActiveWorkbook.SendMail "joeblow@zx-prrtgfw.com", "My Sheet"
    ActiveWorkbook.Close False
End Sub
```

In the preceding example, the file will have the default workbook name (for example, `Book2 .xlsx`). If you would like to give the single-sheet workbook attachment a more meaningful name, you need to save the temporary workbook and then delete it after it's sent. The following procedure saves `Sheet1` to a file named `my file.xlsx`. After sending this temporary workbook as an e-mail attachment, the code uses VBA's `Kill` statement to delete the file.

```
Sub SendOneSheet()
    Dim Filename As String
    Filename = "my file.xlsx"
    ActiveWorkbook.Worksheets("sheet1").Copy
    ActiveWorkbook.SaveAs Filename
    ActiveWorkbook.SendMail "joeblow@zx-prrtgfw.com", "My Sheet"
    ActiveWorkbook.Close False
    Kill Filename
End Sub
```

Excel 2007 includes a new command to send a workbook as a PDF file (the command is Office ⇨ Send ⇨ Email as PDF Attachment).

 NOTE

Because of some legal issues with Adobe Systems Incorporated, the ability to save a workbook as a PDF file is not built into Office 2007. This feature is available only if you've downloaded and installed the PDF add-in from Microsoft's Web site.

Unfortunately, Excel does not provide a way to automate saving a workbook as a PDF file and sending it as an attachment. You can, however, automate part of the process. The `SendSheetAsPDF` procedure below saves the active sheet as a PDF file and then displays the compose message window from your default e-mail client (with the PDF file attached) so you can fill in the recipient's name and click Send:

```
Sub SendSheetAsPDF()
    CommandBars.ExecuteMso ("FileEmailAsPdfEmailAttachment")
End Sub
```

When Excel is lacking powers, it's time to call on Outlook. The procedure that follows saves the active workbook as a PDF file and automates Outlook to create an e-mail message with the PDF file as an attachment.

```
Sub SendAsPDF()
'   Uses early binding
'   Requires a reference to the Outlook Object Library
    Dim OutlookApp As Outlook.Application
    Dim MItem As Object
    Dim Recipient As String, Subj As String
    Dim Msg As String, Fname As String

'   Message details
    Recipient = "myboss@xrediyh.com"
    Subj = "Sales figures"
    Msg = "Hey boss, here's the PDF file you wanted."
    Msg = Msg & vbNewLine & vbNewLine & "-Frank"
    Fname = Application.DefaultFilePath & "\" & _
      ActiveWorkbook.Name & ".pdf"

'   Create the attachment
    ActiveSheet.ExportAsFixedFormat _
        Type:=xlTypePDF, _
        Filename:=Fname

'   Create Outlook object
    Set OutlookApp = New Outlook.Application

'   Create Mail Item and send it
    Set MItem = OutlookApp.CreateItem(olMailItem)
    With MItem
      .To = Recipient
      .Subject = Subj
      .Body = Msg
      .Attachments.Add Fname
      .Save 'to Drafts folder
      '.Send
    End With
```

```
    Set OutlookApp = Nothing

'   Delete the file
    Kill Fname
End Sub
```

 CD

This example, named `send pdf via outlook.xlsm`, is available on the companion CD-ROM.

Using SendKeys

Not all applications support Automation. In some cases, you can still control some aspects of the application even if it doesn't support Automation. You can use Excel's `SendKeys` method to send keystrokes to an application, simulating actions that a live human might perform.

Although using the `SendKeys` method might seem like a good solution, you'll find that it can be very tricky. A potential problem is that it relies on a specific user interface. If a later version of the program that you're sending keystrokes has a different user interface, your application might no longer work. Consequently, you should use `SendKeys` only as a last resort.

Following is a very simple example. This procedure runs the Windows Calculator program and displays its Scientific mode: That is, it executes the View ➪ Scientific command.

```
Sub TestKeys()

    Shell "calc.Exe", vbNormalFocus
    Application.SendKeys "%vs"
End Sub
```

In this example, the code sends out Alt+V (the percent sign represents the Alt key) followed by S.

`SendKeys` is documented in the Help system, which describes how to send nonstandard keystrokes, such as Alt and Ctrl key combinations.

The code that follows is a more elaborate procedure that uses `SendKeys`. This routine is similar to the Outlook example that I present earlier in this chapter (see "Sending Personalized E-Mail via Outlook"). The difference is that it creates e-mail messages for Outlook Express — Microsoft's e-mail client that doesn't support automation.

```
Sub SendEmailViaOutlookExpress()
  Dim cell As Range
  Dim Subj As String
  Dim EmailAddr As String
  Dim Recipient As String
  Dim Bonus As String
```

```
Dim Msg As String
Dim HLink As String
For Each cell In Columns("B").Cells.SpecialCells(xlCellTypeConstants)
  If cell.Value Like "*@*" Then
    'Get the data
    Subj = "Your Annual Bonus"
    Recipient = cell.Offset(0, -1).Value
    EmailAddr = cell.Value
    Bonus = Format(cell.Offset(0, 1).Value, "$0,000.")

    'Compose message
    Msg = "Dear " & Recipient & "%0A"
    Msg = Msg & "%0A" & "I am pleased to inform "
    Msg = Msg & "you that your annual bonus is "
    Msg = Msg & Bonus & "%0A"
    Msg = Msg & "%0A" & "William Rose"
    Msg = Msg & "%0A" & "President"

    'Build hyperlink
    HLink = "mailto:" & EmailAddr & "?"
    HLink = HLink & "subject=" & Subj & "&"
    HLink = HLink & "body=" & Msg

    'Send it
    ActiveWorkbook.FollowHyperlink HLink
    Application.Wait (Now + TimeValue("0:00:02"))
    SendKeys "%s", True
  End If
Next
End Sub
```

 CD

This example, named `personalized email - OE sendkeys.xlsm`, is available on the companion CD-ROM. The procedure works correctly only if Outlook Express is your default e-mail client. If you use a different e-mail client, you may be able to modify the procedure so that it sends keystrokes appropriate for your software.

Figure 20-13 shows a worksheet that contains data used in the e-mail messages: name, e-mail address, and bonus amount.

The `SendEmail` procedure assumes that Outlook Express is the default e-mail client. It loops through the rows in the worksheet and creates a message (stored in the `Msg` variable). It uses the `FollowHyperlink` method to launch Outlook Express's New Message window. For the first record, the hyperlink is as follows:

```
mailto:jjones@prrtgfw.com?subject=Your Annual Bonus
&body=Dear John Jones%0A%0AI am pleased to inform you
that your annual bonus is $2,000.%0A%0AWilliam Rose%0APresident
```

	A	B	C	D
1	Name	Email	Bonus	
2	John Jones	jjones@zx-prrtgfw.com	$2,000	
3	Bob Smith	bsmith@zx-prrtgfw.com	$3,500	
4	Fred Simpson	fsimpson@zx-prrtgfw.com	$1,250	
5				
6				
7				

Sheet1

Figure 20-13: This information is used in the Outlook Express e-mail messages.

NOTE

The %0A character sequence represents a line break.

The procedure pauses for two seconds and then uses SendKeys to issue the Alt+S command, which puts the message in the Outlook Express Outbox. This pause is required to ensure that the e-mail message is onscreen when the keystrokes are sent. You might need to adjust the delay, depending on your system. You might find that a one-second delay is sufficient, but others might need to increase it to three or more seconds.

Although this technique works fine, note the character limit on the length of the hyperlink (around 730 characters). Therefore, this is suitable only for short messages.

Figure 20-14 shows one of the messages in Outlook Express.

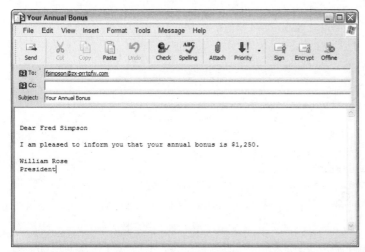

Figure 20-14: This Outlook Express message uses data stored in a worksheet.

Part V

Working with ADO

ADO (ActiveX Data Objects) is an object model that enables you to access data stored in a variety of database formats. Importantly, this methodology allows you to use a single object model for all your databases. This is currently the preferred data access methodology and should not be confused with DAO (Data Access Objects).

This section presents a simple example that uses ADO to retrieve data from an Access database.

> **NOTE**
>
> ADO programming is a very complex topic. If you need to access external data in your Excel application, you'll probably want to invest in one or more books that cover this topic in detail.

The `ADO_Demo` example retrieves data from an Access 2007 database named `budget data.accdb`. This database contains one table (named Budget). This example retrieves the data in which the `Item` field contains the text *Lease*, the `Division` field contains the text *N. America,* and the `Year` field contains *2006.* The qualifying data is stored in a `Recordset` object, and the data is then transferred to a worksheet (see Figure 20-15).

```
Sub ADO_Demo()
'   This demo requires a reference to
'   the Microsoft ActiveX Data Objects 2.x Library

    Dim DBFullName As String
    Dim Cnct As String, Src As String
    Dim Connection As ADODB.Connection
    Dim Recordset As ADODB.Recordset
    Dim Col As Integer

    Cells.Clear

'   Database information
    DBFullName = ThisWorkbook.Path & "\budget data.accdb"

'   Open the connection
    Set Connection = New ADODB.Connection
    Cnct = "Provider=Microsoft.ACE.OLEDB.12.0;"
    Cnct = Cnct & "Data Source=" & DBFullName & ";"
    Connection.Open ConnectionString:=Cnct

'   Create RecordSet
    Set Recordset = New ADODB.Recordset
    With Recordset
```

```
'       Filter
        Src = "SELECT * FROM Budget WHERE Item = 'Lease' "
        Src = Src & "and Division = 'N. America' "
        Src = Src & "and Year = '2006'"
        .Open Source:=Src, ActiveConnection:=Connection

'       Write the field names
        For Col = 0 To Recordset.Fields.Count - 1
            Range("A1").Offset(0, Col).Value = _
                Recordset.Fields(Col).Name
        Next

'       Write the recordset
        Range("A1").Offset(1, 0).CopyFromRecordset Recordset
    End With
    Set Recordset = Nothing
    Connection.Close
    Set Connection = Nothing
End Sub
```

	A	B	C	D	E	F	G	H	I	J	K	L
1	ID	SORT	DIVISION	DEPARTMEN	CATEGORY	ITEM	YEAR	MONTH	BUDGET	ACTUAL	VARIANCE	
2	15850	15850	N. Amer	Data Process	Facility	Lease	2006	Jan	4084	2662	-1422	
3	15874	15874	N. Amer	Human Resc	Facility	Lease	2006	Jan	3760	3749	-11	
4	15898	15898	N. Amer	Accounting	Facility	Lease	2006	Jan	4155	3489	-666	
5	15922	15922	N. Amer	Training	Facility	Lease	2006	Jan	3120	4142	1022	
6	15946	15946	N. Amer	Security	Facility	Lease	2006	Jan	3953	4461	508	
7	15970	15970	N. Amer	R&D	Facility	Lease	2006	Jan	3256	3188	-68	
8	15994	15994	N. Amer	Operations	Facility	Lease	2006	Jan	3927	3334	-593	
9	16018	16018	N. Amer	Shipping	Facility	Lease	2006	Jan	4106	3333	-773	
10	16042	16042	N. Amer	Sales	Facility	Lease	2006	Jan	2983	2920	-63	
11	16066	16066	N. Amer	Advertising	Facility	Lease	2006	Jan	3607	3308	-299	
12	16090	16090	N. Amer	Public Relati	Facility	Lease	2006	Jan	4344	3910	-434	
13	17170	17170	N. Amer	Data Process	Facility	Lease	2006	Feb	4113	4551	438	
14	17194	17194	N. Amer	Human Resc	Facility	Lease	2006	Feb	4314	3655	-659	
15	17218	17218	N. Amer	Accounting	Facility	Lease	2006	Feb	2885	4324	1439	
16	17242	17242	N. Amer	Training	Facility	Lease	2006	Feb	3999	4507	508	
17	17266	17266	N. Amer	Security	Facility	Lease	2006	Feb	3908	3796	-112	
18	17290	17290	N. Amer	R&D	Facility	Lease	2006	Feb	3896	3920	24	
19	17314	17314	N. Amer	Operations	Facility	Lease	2006	Feb	4742	3126	-1616	
20	17338	17338	N. Amer	Shipping	Facility	Lease	2006	Feb	2878	3874	996	
21	17362	17362	N. Amer	Sales	Facility	Lease	2006	Feb	3764	3887	123	
22	17386	17386	N. Amer	Advertising	Facility	Lease	2006	Feb	3106	3766	660	
23	17410	17410	N. Amer	Public Relati	Facility	Lease	2006	Feb	3438	3673	235	
24	18490	18490	N. Amer	Data Process	Facility	Lease	2006	Mar	4775	3065	-1710	
25	18514	18514	N. Amer	Human Resc	Facility	Lease	2006	Mar	3131	3198	67	
26	18538	18538	N. Amer	Accounting	Facility	Lease	2006	Mar	3687	4762	1075	
27	18562	18562	N. Amer	Training	Facility	Lease	2006	Mar	2615	3486	871	

Sheet1 / Description

Figure 20-15: This data was retrieved from an Access database.

CD-ROM

This example (named simple ado example.xlsm), along with the Access database file (named budget data.accdb), is available on the companion CD-ROM.

Chapter 21

Creating and Using Add-Ins

In This Chapter

In this chapter, I explain the benefits of using add-ins, and I show you how to create your own add-ins by using only the tools built into Excel.

- ◆ An overview of add-ins and why this concept is important for developers

- ◆ Details about Excel's Add-In Manager

- ◆ How to create an add-in, including a hands-on example

- ◆ How XLSA add-in files differ from XLSM files

- ◆ Examples of VBA code that manipulates add-ins

- ◆ How to detect whether an add-in is installed properly

One of Excel's most useful features for developers is the ability to create add-ins. Creating add-ins adds a professional touch to your work and, as you'll see, add-ins offer several key advantages over standard workbook files.

What Is an Add-In?

Generally speaking, a *spreadsheet add-in* is something added to a spreadsheet to give it additional functionality. For example, Excel ships with several add-ins. One of the most popular is the *Analysis ToolPak*, which adds statistical and analysis capabilities that are not built into Excel.

699

Some add-ins also provide new worksheet functions that can be used in formulas. With a well-designed add-in, the new features blend in well with the original interface, so they appear to be part of the program.

Comparing an add-in with a standard workbook

Any knowledgeable Excel user can create an add-in from an Excel workbook file; no additional software or programming tools are required. Any workbook file can be converted to an add-in, but not every workbook is appropriate for an add-in. An Excel add-in is basically a normal XLSM workbook with the following differences:

- The `IsAddin` property of the `ThisWorkbook` object is `True`. By default, this property is `False`.

- The workbook window is hidden in such a way that it can't be unhidden by choosing the View ➪ Window ➪ Unhide command. This means that you can't display worksheets or chart sheets contained in an add-in unless you write code to copy the sheet to a standard workbook.

- An add-in is not a member of the `Workbooks` collection. Rather, it's a member of the `AddIns` collection. However, you *can* access an add-in via the `Workbooks` collection (see "XLAM file VBA collection membership," later in this chapter).

- Add-ins can be installed and uninstalled by using the Add-Ins dialog box. To display this dialog box, choose Office ➪ Excel Options ➪ Add-Ins. Then, in the Excel Options dialog box, choose Excel Add-Ins from the Manage drop-down list and click Go. After it's installed, an add-in remains installed across Excel sessions.

- The Macro dialog box (invoked by choosing Developer ➪ Code ➪ Macros or View ➪ Macros ➪ Macros) does not display the names of the macros contained in an add-in.

- A custom worksheet function stored within an add-in can be used in formulas without having to precede its name with the source workbook's filename.

 NOTE

In the past, Excel allowed you to use any extension for an add-in. In Excel 2007, you can still use any extension for an add-in, but if it's not XLA or XLAM, you see the warning shown in Figure 21-1. This prompt occurs even if it's an installed add-in that opens automatically when Excel starts.

Figure 21-1: Excel warns you if an add-in uses a non-standard file extension.

Why create add-ins?

You might decide to convert your Excel application into an add-in for any of the following reasons:

- *To restrict access to your code and worksheets:* When you distribute an application as an add-in and you protect its VBA project with a password, users can't view or modify the sheets or the VBA code in the workbook. Therefore, if you use proprietary techniques in your application, you can prevent anyone from copying the code — or at least make it more difficult to do so.

- *To avoid confusion:* If a user loads your application as an add-in, the file is not visible and is, therefore, less likely to confuse novice users or get in the way. Unlike a hidden workbook, an add-in can't be unhidden.

- *To simplify access to worksheet functions:* Custom worksheet functions stored within an add-in don't require the workbook name qualifier. For example, if you store a custom function named MOVAVG in a workbook named `Newfuncs.xlsm`, you must use a syntax like the following to use this function in a formula that's in a different workbook:

```
=Newfuncs.xlsm!MOVAVG(A1:A50)
```

  But if this function is stored in an add-in file that's open, you can use a much simpler syntax because you don't need to include the file reference:

```
=MOVAVG(A1:A50)
```

- *To provide easier access for users:* After you identify the location of your add-in, it appears in the Add-Ins dialog box with a friendly name and a description of what it does.

- *To gain better control over loading:* Add-ins can be opened automatically when Excel starts, regardless of the directory in which they are stored.

- *To avoid displaying prompts when unloading:* When an add-in is closed, the user never sees the `Do you want to save change?` prompt.

About COM Add-Ins

Excel also supports COM (Component Object Model) add-ins. These files have a `.dll` or `.exe` file extension. A COM add-in can be written so it works with all Office applications that support add-ins. An additional advantage is that the code is compiled, thereby offering better security. Unlike XLAM add-ins, a COM add-in cannot contain Excel sheets or charts. COM add-ins are developed with Visual Basic 5 (or later) or Visual Basic .NET. Discussion of creating COM add-in procedures is well beyond the scope of this book.

Part V

NOTE

The ability to use add-ins is determined by the user's security settings in the Trust Center dialog box. To display this dialog box, choose Developer ⇨ Macro Security. Or, if the Developer tab is not displayed, choose Office ⇨ Excel Options ⇨ Trust Center and then click the Trust Center Settings button.

Understanding Excel's Add-In Manager

The most efficient way to load and unload add-ins is with Excel's Add-Ins dialog box, which you access by choosing Office ⇨ Excel Options ⇨ Add-Ins. Then, in the Excel Options dialog box, choose Excel Add-Ins from the Manage drop-down box and click Go.

TIP

The Alt+TI shortcut key sequence used in earlier versions of Excel is a quicker way to display the Add-Ins dialog box. Also, consider adding the Add-Ins button to your Quick Access Toolbar (QAT). Right-click the QAT and choose Customize. In the Excel Options dialog box, choose Commands Not in the Ribbon, select Add-ins, and click Add.

Figure 21-2 shows the Add-Ins dialog box. The list contains the names of all add-ins that Excel knows about, and check marks identify add-ins that are open. You can open and close add-ins from this dialog box by clearing or marking the check boxes.

Figure 21-2: The Add-Ins dialog box.

CAUTION

You can also open most add-in files by choosing the Office ⇨ Open command. Because an add-in is never the active workbook, however, you can't close an add-in by choosing Office ⇨ Close. You can remove the add-in only by exiting and restarting Excel or by executing VBA code to close the add-in. For example:

```
Workbooks("myaddin.xlam").Close
```

Opening an add-in with the Office ⇨ Open command opens the file, but the add-in is not officially installed.

When you open an add-in, you might notice something different about Excel. In almost every case, the user interface changes in some way: Excel displays either a new command in the Ribbon or new menu items on a shortcut menu. For example, when the Analysis ToolPak add-in is installed, it gives you a new command: Data ⇨ Analysis ⇨ Data Analysis. When you install Excel's Euro Currency Tools add-in, you get a new group in the Formulas tab: Solutions.

If the add-in contains only custom worksheet functions, the new functions appear in the Insert Function dialog box.

Creating an Add-in

As I note earlier, you can convert any workbook to an add-in, but not all workbooks are appropriate candidates for add-ins. First, an add-in must contain macros (otherwise, it's useless).

Generally, a workbook that benefits most from being converted to an add-in is one that contains general-purpose macro procedures. A workbook that consists only of worksheets would be inaccessible as an add-in because worksheets within add-ins are hidden from the user. You can, however, write code that copies all or part of a sheet from your add-in to a visible workbook.

Creating an add-in from a workbook is simple. The following steps describe how to create an add-in from a normal workbook file:

1. Develop your application and make sure that everything works properly.

   Don't forget to include a way to execute the macro or macros in the add-in. You might want to add a new command to the Ribbon or a new menu item to a shortcut menu. See Chapters 22 and 23 for more information about modifying Excel's user interface.

2. Activate the Visual Basic Editor (VBE) and select the workbook in the Project window. Choose Tools ⇨ *xxx* Properties (where *xxx* represents the name of the project) and then click the Protection tab. Select the Lock Project for Viewing check box and then enter a password (twice). Click OK.

Part V

A Few Words about Passwords

Microsoft has never promoted Excel as a product that creates applications in which the source code is secure. The password feature provided in Excel is sufficient to prevent casual users from accessing parts of your application that you'd like to keep hidden. Excel 2002 and later versions include stronger security than previous versions, but your passwords can be cracked. If you must be absolutely sure that no one ever sees your code or formulas, Excel is not your best choice as a development platform.

This step is necessary only if you want to prevent others from viewing or modifying your macros or UserForms.

3. Reactivate Excel and choose Office ➪ Prepare ➪ Properties to display the Document Properties panel. Enter a brief descriptive title in the Title field and a longer description in the Comments field.

This step is not required, but it makes the add-in easier to use by displaying descriptive text in the Add-Ins dialog box.

4. Choose Office ➪ Save As to display the Save As dialog box.

5. In the Save As dialog box, select Excel Add-In (*.xlam) from the Save as Type drop-down list.

6. Click Save. A copy of the workbook is saved (with an .xlam extension), and the original workbook remains open.

7. Close the original workbook and then install the add-in version.

8. Test the add-in to make sure it works correctly. If not, make changes to your code. And don't forget to save your changes.

 CAUTION

A workbook being converted to an add-in must have at least one worksheet. For example, if your workbook contains only chart sheets or Excel 5/95 dialog sheets, the Excel Add-In (*.xlam) option does not appear in the Save As dialog box. Also, this option appears only when a worksheet is active when you choose the Office ➪ Save As command.

An Add-In Example

In this section, I discuss the steps involved in creating a useful add-in. The example uses the Text Tools utility that I describe in Chapter 16.

CD-ROM

The XLSM version of the Text Tools utility (named `text tools.xlsm`) is available on the companion CD-ROM. You can use this file to create the described add-in.

Setting up the workbook for the example add-in

In this example, you'll be working with a workbook that has already been developed and debugged. The workbook consists of the following items:

- *A worksheet named* `Sheet1`*:* This sheet is used to hold pre-processed data, which can be restored if the user chooses to undo the operation.

- *A UserForm named* `UserForm1`*:* This dialog box serves as the primary user interface. The code module for this UserForm contains several event handler procedures.

- *A UserForm named UserForm2:* This dialog box is displayed when the workbook is opened. It briefly describes how to access the Text Tools utility. It also contains a Don't Show This Message Again check box.

- *A VBA module named* `Module1`*:* This module contains several procedures, including a procedure that displays the `UserForm1` UserForm.

- `ThisWorkbook` *code module:* This module contains two event handler procedures (`Workbook_Open` and `Workbook_BeforeClose`) that contain code to create and delete shortcut menu items.

- *XML code to customize the Ribbon:* This customization was done outside of Excel. See Chapter 22 for more information about customizing the Ribbon by using RibbonX.

CROSS-REFERENCE

See Chapter 16 for details about how the Text Tools utility works. The version presented here is a modified version of the application presented in Chapter 16.

Adding descriptive information for the example add-in

To enter a title and description for your add-in, choose Office ➪ Prepare ➪ Properties, which displays the Document Properties panel below the Ribbon (see Figure 21-3).

Document Properties ▼		Location: C:\text tools.xlsm		∗ Required field ✕
Author:	Title:	Subject:	Keywords:	
John Walkenbach	Text Tools			
Category:	Status:			
Comments:				
Adds text manipulation features to Excel.				

Figure 21-3: Use the Document Properties panel to enter descriptive information about your add-in.

Part V

Enter a title for the add-in in the Title field. This text appears in list in the Add-Ins dialog box. In the Comments field, enter a description of the add-in. This information appears at the bottom of the Add-Ins dialog box when the add-in is selected.

Adding a title and description for the add-in is optional, but highly recommended.

Creating an add-in

To create an add-in, do the following:

1. Activate the VBE and select the future add-in workbook in the Project window.

2. Choose Debug ⇨ Compile. This step forces a compilation of the VBA code and also identifies any syntax errors so that you can correct them. When you save a workbook as an add-in, Excel creates the add-in even if it contains syntax errors.

About Excel's Add-In Manager

You install and uninstall add-ins by using Excel's Add-Ins dialog box. To display this dialog box, choose Office ⇨ Excel Options ⇨ Add-Ins. Then, in the Excel Options dialog box, choose Excel Add-Ins from the Manage drop-down list and click Go. This dialog box lists the names of all the available add-ins. Those that are checked are open.

In VBA terms, the Add-In dialog box lists the Title property of each AddIn object in the AddIns collection. Each add-in that appears with a check mark has its Installed property set to True.

You can install an add-in by marking its check box, and you can clear an installed add-in by removing the check mark from its box. To add an add-in to the list, use the Browse button to locate its file. By default, the Add-In dialog box lists files of the following types:

- XLAM: An Excel 2007 add-in created from an XLSM file

- XLA: A pre–Excel 2007 add-in created from an XLS file

- XLL: A standalone compiled DLL file

If you click the Automation button (available only in Excel 2002 and later), you can browse for COM add-ins. Note that the Automation Servers dialog box will probably list many files, and the file list is not limited to COM add-ins that work with Excel.

You can enroll an add-in file into the AddIns collection with the Add method of VBA's AddIns collection, but you can't remove one by using VBA. You can also open an add-in from within VBA code by setting the AddIn object's Installed property to True. Setting it to False closes the add-in.

The Add-In Manager stores the installed status of the add-ins in the Windows Registry when you exit Excel. Therefore, all add-ins that are installed when you close Excel are automatically opened the next time you start Excel.

3. Choose Tools ⇨ *xxx* Properties (where *xxx* represents the name of the project) to display the Project Properties dialog box. Click the General tab and enter a new name for the project. By default, all VB projects are named *VBProject*. In this example, the project name is changed to *TextToolsVBA*. This step is optional but recommended.

4. Save the workbook one last time using its *.XLSM name. Strictly speaking this step is not really necessary, but it gives you an XLSM backup (with no password) of your XLAM add-in file.

5. With the Project Properties dialog box still displayed, click the Protection tab. Select the Lock Project for Viewing check box and enter a password (twice). The code will remain viewable, and the password protection will take effect the next time the file is opened. Click OK.

   If you don't need to protect the project, you can skip this step.

6. In Excel, choose Office ⇨ Save As. Excel displays its Save As dialog box.

7. In the Save as Type drop-down list, select Excel Add-In (*.xlam).

8. Click Save. A new add-in file is created, and the original XLSM version remains open.

Add-ins can be located in any directory. By default, Excel proposes the following directory:

```
C:\Documents and Settings\<username>\Application Data\Microsoft\AddIns
```

Installing an add-in

To avoid confusion, close the XLSM workbook before installing the add-in created from that workbook.

To install an add-in, do the following:

1. Choose Office ⇨ Excel Options ⇨ Add-Ins. Then, in the Excel Options dialog box, choose Excel Add-Ins from the Manage drop-down list and click Go (or, press Alt+TI). Excel displays the Add-Ins dialog box.

2. Click the Browse button and locate and double-click the add-in that you just created.

   After you find your new add-in, the Add-Ins dialog box displays the add-in in its list. As shown in Figure 21-4, the Add-Ins dialog box also displays the descriptive information that you provided in the Properties dialog box.

3. Click OK to close the dialog box and open the add-in.

When the Text Tools add-in is opened, the Add-Ins tab displays a new group: Text Tools. This group has two controls. In addition, the Text Tools utility adds a new menu item to the shortcut menu that appears when you right-click a range, row, or column.

Part V

Figure 21-4: The Add-Ins dialog box with the new add-in selected.

Testing the add-in

After installing the add-in, it's a good idea to perform some additional testing. For this example, open a new workbook to try out the various features in the Text Tools utility. Do everything you can think of to try to make it fail. Better yet, seek the assistance of someone unfamiliar with the application to give it a crash test.

If you discover any errors, you can correct the code in the add-in (the original file is not required). After making changes, save the file by choosing File ⇨ Save in the VBE.

Distributing an add-in

You can distribute this add-in to other Excel users simply by giving them a copy of the XLAM file (they don't need the XLSM version) along with instructions on how to install it. If you locked the file with a password, your macro code cannot be viewed or modified by others unless they know the password.

Modifying an add-in

If you need to modify an add-in, first open it and then unlock the VB project if you applied a password. To unlock it, activate the VBE and then double-click its project's name in the Project window. You'll be prompted for the password. Make your changes and then save the file from the VBE (choose File ⇨ Save).

If you create an add-in that stores its information in a worksheet, you must set its IsAddIn property to False before you can view that workbook in Excel. You do this in the Properties window shown in Figure 21-5 when the ThisWorkbook object is selected. After you make your changes, set the IsAddIn property back to True before you save the file. If you leave the IsAddIn property set to False, Excel will not let you save the file with the XLAM extension.

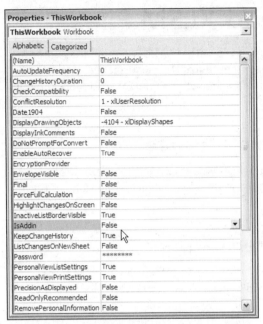

Figure 21-5: Making an add-in not an add-in.

Creating an Add-In: A Checklist

Before you release your add-in to the world, take a few minutes to run through this checklist:

- Did you test your add-in with all supported platforms and Excel versions?

- Did you give your VB project a new name? By default, every project is named `VBProject`. It's a good idea to give your project a more meaningful name.

- Does your add-in make any assumptions about the user's directory structure or directory names?

- When you use the Add-Ins dialog box to load your add-in, is its name and description correct and appropriate?

- If your add-in uses VBA functions that aren't designed to be used in a worksheet, have you declared the functions as `Private`? If not, these functions will appear in the Paste Function dialog box.

- Did you remember to remove all `Debug.Print` statements from your code?

- Did you force a recompile of your add-in to ensure that it contains no syntax errors?

- Did you account for any international issues?

- Is your add-in file optimized for speed? See "Optimizing the Performance of Add-Ins" later in this chapter.

Part V

Comparing XLAM and XLSM Files

This section begins by comparing an XLAM add-in file with its XLSM source file. Later in this chapter, I discuss methods that you can use to optimize the performance of your add-in. I describe a technique that might reduce its file size, which makes it load more quickly and use less disk space and memory.

XLSM and XLAM file size and structure

An add-in based on an XLSM source file is exactly the same size as the original. The VBA code in XLAM files is not optimized in any way, so faster performance is not among the benefits of using an add-in.

XLAM file VBA collection membership

An add-in is a member of the `AddIns` collection but is not an official member of the `Workbooks` collection. You can refer to an add-in by using the `Workbooks` method of the `Application` object and supplying the add-in's filename as its index. The following instruction creates an object variable that represents an add-in named `myaddin.xlam`:

```
Dim TestAddin As Workbook
Set TestAddin = Workbooks("myaddin.xlam")
```

Add-ins cannot be referenced by an index number in the `Workbooks` collection. If you use the following code to loop through the `Workbooks` collection, the `myaddin.xlam` workbook is not displayed:

```
Dim w as Workbook
For Each w in Application.Workbooks
    MsgBox w.Name
Next w
```

The following `For-Next` loop, on the other hand, displays `myaddin.xlam` — assuming that Excel "knows" about it — in the Add-Ins dialog box:

```
Dim a as Addin
For Each a in Application.AddIns
    MsgBox a.Name
Next a
```

Visibility of XLSM and XLAM files

Ordinary workbooks are displayed in one or more windows. For example, the following statement displays the number of windows for the active workbook:

```
MsgBox ActiveWorkbook.Windows.Count
```

You can manipulate the visibility of each window for a workbook by choosing the View ⇨ Window ⇨ Hide command or by changing the `Visible` property using VBA. The following code hides all windows for the active workbook:

```
Dim Win As Window
For Each Win In ActiveWorkbook.Windows
    Win.Visible = False
Next Win
```

Add-in files are never visible, and they don't officially have windows, even though they have unseen worksheets. Consequently, add-ins don't appear in the windows list when you choose the View ⇨ Window ⇨ Switch Windows command. If `myaddin.xlam` is open, the following statement returns 0:

```
MsgBox Workbooks("myaddin.xlam").Windows.Count
```

Worksheets and chart sheets in XLSM and XLAM files

Add-in files, like normal workbook files, can have any number of worksheets or chart sheets. But, as I note earlier in this chapter, an XLSM file must have at least one worksheet in order for it to be converted to an add-in.

When an add-in is open, your VBA code can access its sheets as if it were an ordinary workbook. Because add-in files aren't part of the `Workbooks` collection, however, you must always reference an add-in by its name and not by an index number. The following example displays the value in cell A1 of the first worksheet in `myaddin.xla`, which is assumed to be open:

```
MsgBox Workbooks("myaddin.xlam").Worksheets(1).Range("A1").Value
```

If your add-in contains a worksheet that you would like the user to see, you can either copy it to an open workbook or create a new workbook from the sheet.

The following code, for example, copies the first worksheet from an add-in and places it in the active workbook (as the last sheet):

```
Sub CopySheetFromAddin()
    Dim AddinSheet As Worksheet
    Dim NumSheets As Long
    Set AddinSheet = Workbooks("myaddin.xlam").Sheets(1)
    NumSheets = ActiveWorkbook.Sheets.Count
    AddinSheet.Copy After:=ActiveWorkbook.Sheets(NumSheets)
End Sub
```

Part V

Creating a new workbook from a sheet within an add-in is even simpler:

```
Sub CreateNewWorkbook()
    Workbooks("myaddin.xlam").Sheets(1).Copy
End Sub
```

NOTE

The preceding examples assume that the code is in a file other than the add-in file. VBA code within an add-in should always use `ThisWorkbook` to qualify references to sheets or ranges within the add-in. For example, the following statement is assumed to be in a VBA module in an add-in file. This statement displays the value in cell A1 on Sheet 1:

```
MsgBox ThisWorkbook.Sheets("Sheet1").Range("A1").Value
```

Accessing VBA procedures in an add-in

Accessing the VBA procedures in an add-in is a bit different from accessing procedures in a normal XLSM workbook. First of all, when you choose the View ➪ Macros ➪ Macros command, the Macro dialog box does not display the names of macros that are in open add-ins. It's almost as if Excel is trying to prevent you from accessing them.

TIP

If you know the name of the procedure in the add-in, you can enter it directly into the Macro dialog box and click Run to execute it. The `Sub` procedure must be in a general VBA module and not in a code module for an object.

Because procedures contained in an add-in aren't listed in the Macro dialog box, you must provide other means to access them. Your choices include direct methods (such as shortcut keys, Ribbon commands, and shortcut menu items) as well as indirect methods (such as event handlers). One such candidate, for example, may be the `OnTime` method, which executes a procedure at a specific time of day.

You can use the `Run` method of the `Application` object to execute a procedure in an add-in. For example,

```
Application.Run "myaddin.xlam!DisplayNames"
```

Another option is to use the Tools ➪ References command in the VBE to enable a reference to the add-in. Then you can refer directly to one of its procedures in your VBA code without the filename qualifier. In fact, you don't need to use the `Run` method; you can call the procedure directly as long as it's not declared as `Private`. The following statement executes a procedure named `DisplayNames` in an add-in that has been added as a reference:

```
Call DisplayNames
```

Sleuthing a Protected Add-In

The Macro dialog box does not display the names of procedures contained in add-ins. But what if you'd like to run such a procedure, but the add-in is protected so that you can't view the code to determine the name of the procedure? Use the Object Browser!

To illustrate, install the Lookup Wizard add-in. This add-in is distributed with Excel and is protected, so you can't view the code.

1. Activate the VBE and then select the `Lookup.xla` project in the Project window.

2. Press F2 to activate the Object Browser.

3. In the Libraries drop-down list, select Lookup. This displays all the classes in the `Lookup.xla` add-in, as depicted in the following figure.

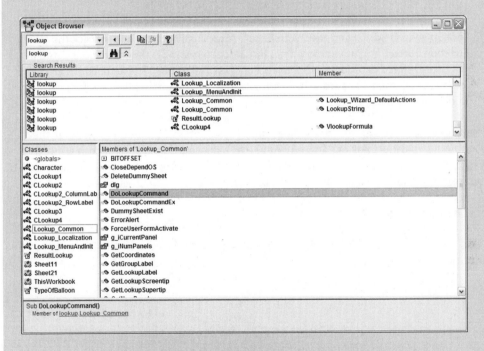

4. Select various items in the Classes list to see what class they are and the members that they contain.

In the example above, the `Lookup_Common` class is a module, and its members consist of a number of variables, constants, procedures, and functions. One of these procedures, `DoLookupCommand`, sounds like it might be the main procedure that starts the wizard. To test this theory, activate Excel and then choose View ➪ Macros ➪ Macros. Type **DoLookupCommand** in the Macro Name box and then click Run. Sure enough! You'll see the first dialog box of the Lookup Wizard.

Armed with this information, you can write VBA code to start the Lookup Wizard — assuming, of course, that you can think of a reason to do so.

NOTE

Even when a reference to the add-in has been established, its macro names do not appear in the Macro dialog box.

Function procedures defined in an add-in work just like those defined in an XLSM workbook. They're easy to access because Excel displays their names in the Insert Function dialog box under the User Defined category (by default). The only exception is if the Function procedure was declared with the Private keyword; then the function does not appear there. That's why it's a good idea to declare custom functions as Private if they will be used only by other VBA procedures and are not designed to be used in worksheet formulas.

NOTE

An example of an add-in that does *not* declare its functions as Private is Microsoft's Lookup Wizard add-in (included with Excel). After installing this add-in, click the Insert Function button. You'll find more than three-dozen non-worksheet functions listed in the User Defined category of the Insert Function dialog box. These functions are not intended to be used in a worksheet formula, but it appears that the programmer forgot to declare them as Private.

As I discuss earlier, you can use worksheet functions contained in add-ins without the workbook name qualifier. For example, if you have a custom function named MOVAVG stored in the file newfuncs.xlsm, you would use the following instruction to address the function from a worksheet that's in a different workbook:

```
=newfuncs.xlsm!MOVAVG(A1:A50)
```

But if this function is stored in an add-in file that's open, you can omit the file reference and write the following instead:

```
=MOVAVG(A1:A50)
```

Manipulating Add-Ins with VBA

In this section, I present information that will help you write VBA procedures that manipulate add-ins.

Understanding the AddIns collection

The AddIns collection consists of all add-ins that Excel knows about. These add-ins can either be installed or not. The Add-Ins dialog box lists all members of the AddIns collection. Those entries accompanied by a check mark are installed.

ADDING AN ITEM TO THE ADDINS COLLECTION

The add-in files that make up the `AddIns` collection can be stored anywhere. Excel maintains a partial list of these files and their locations in the Windows Registry. For Excel 2007, this list is stored at

```
HKEY_CURRENT_USER\Software\Microsoft\Office\12.0\Excel\Add-in Manager
```

You can use the Windows Registry Editor (`regedit.exe`) to view this Registry key. Note that the standard add-ins that are shipped with Excel do not appear in this Registry key. In addition, add-in files stored in the following directory also appear in the list but are not listed in the Registry:

```
C:\Documents and Settings\<username>\Application Data\Microsoft\AddIns
```

You can add a new `AddIn` object to the `AddIns` collection either manually or programmatically by using VBA. To add a new add-in to the collection manually, display the Add-Ins dialog box, click the Browse button, and locate the add-in.

To enroll a new member of the `AddIns` collection with VBA, use the collection's `Add` method. Here's an example:

```
Application.AddIns.Add "c:\files\newaddin.xlam"
```

After the preceding instruction is executed, the `AddIns` collection has a new member, and the Add-Ins dialog box shows a new item in its list. If the add-in already exists in the collection, nothing happens, and an error is not generated.

If the add-in that you're enrolling is on removable media (for example, a CD-ROM), you can also copy the file to Excel's library directory with the `Add` method. The following example copies `myaddin.xlam` from drive E and adds it to the `AddIns` collection. The second argument (`True`, in this case) specifies whether the add-in should be copied. If the add-in resides on a hard drive, the second argument can be ignored.

```
Application.AddIns.Add "e:\myaddin.xla", True
```

 NOTE

Enrolling a new workbook in the `AddIns` collection does not install it. To install the add-in, set its `Installed` property to `True`.

 CAUTION

The Windows Registry does not actually get updated until Excel closes normally. Therefore, if Excel ends abnormally (that is, if it crashes), the add-in's name will not get added to the Registry, and the add-in will not be part of the `AddIns` collection when Excel restarts.

Part V

REMOVING AN ITEM FROM THE ADDINS COLLECTION

Oddly, there is no direct way to remove an add-in from the `AddIns` collection. The `AddIns` collection does not have a `Delete` or `Remove` method. One way to remove an add-in from the Add-Ins dialog box is to edit the Windows Registry database (using `regedit.exe`). After you do this, the add-in will not appear in the Add-Ins dialog box the next time that you start Excel. Note that this method is not guaranteed to work with all add-in files.

Another way to remove an add-in from the `AddIns` collection is to delete, move, or rename its XLAM (or XLA) file. You'll get a warning like the one in Figure 21-6 the next time you try to install or uninstall the add-in, along with an opportunity to remove it from the `AddIns` collection.

Figure 21-6: One very direct way to remove a member of the AddIns collection.

AddIn object properties

An `AddIn` object is a single member of the `AddIns` collection. For example, to display the filename of the first member of the `AddIns` collection, use the following:

```
Msgbox AddIns(1).Name
```

An `AddIn` object has 14 properties, which you can read about in the Help system. Five of these properties are hidden properties. Some of the terminology is a bit confusing, so I discuss a few of the more important properties in the sections that follow.

THE NAME PROPERTY OF AN ADDIN OBJECT

This property holds the filename of the add-in. `Name` is a read-only property, so you can't change the name of the file by changing the `Name` property.

THE PATH PROPERTY OF AN ADDIN OBJECT

This property holds the drive and path where the add-in file is stored. It does not include a final backslash or the filename.

THE FULLNAME PROPERTY OF AN ADDIN OBJECT

This property holds the add-in's drive, path, and filename. This property is a bit redundant because this information is also available from the `Name` and `Path` properties. The following instructions produce exactly the same message:

```
MsgBox AddIns(1).Path & "\" & AddIns(1).Name
MsgBox AddIns(1).FullName
```

THE TITLE PROPERTY OF AN ADDIN OBJECT

This hidden property holds a descriptive name for the add-in. The Title property is what appears in the Add-Ins dialog box. This property is read-only, and the only way to add or change the Title property of an add-in is to use the Document Properties panel (choose Office ⇨ Prepare ⇨ Properties command). You must use this menu command with the XLSM version of the file before converting it to an add-in.

Typically, a member of a collection is addressed by way of its Name property setting. The AddIns collection is different; it uses the Title property instead. The following example displays the filename for the Analysis ToolPak add-in (that is, analys32.xll), whose Title property is "Analysis ToolPak".

```
Sub ShowName()
    MsgBox AddIns("Analysis Toolpak").Name
End Sub
```

You can, of course, also reference a particular add-in with its index number if you happen to know it. But in the vast majority of cases, you will want to refer to an add-in by using its Name property.

THE COMMENTS PROPERTY OF AN ADDIN OBJECT

This hidden property stores text that is displayed in the Add-Ins dialog box when a particular add-in is selected. Comments is a read-only property. The only way to change it is to use the Properties dialog box before you convert the workbook to an add-in. Comments can be as long as 255 characters, but the Add-Ins dialog box can display only about 100 characters.

If your code attempts to read the Comments property of an add-in that has no Comments, you get an error.

THE INSTALLED PROPERTY OF AN ADDIN OBJECT

The Installed property is True if the add-in is currently installed — that is, if it is checked in the Add-Ins dialog box. Setting the Installed property to True opens the add-in. Setting it to False unloads it. Here's an example of how to install (that is, open) the Analysis ToolPak add-in with VBA:

```
Sub InstallATP()
    AddIns("Analysis ToolPak").Installed = True
End Sub
```

After this procedure is executed, the Add-Ins dialog box displays a check mark next to Analysis ToolPak. If the add-in is already installed, setting its Installed property to True has no effect. To remove this add-in (uninstall it), simply set the Installed property to False.

Part V

CAUTION

If an add-in was opened with the Office ⇨ Open command, it is not considered to be officially installed. Consequently, its `Installed` property is `False`.

The `ListAllAddIns` procedure that follows creates a table that lists all members of the `AddIns` collection and displays the following properties: `Name`, `Title`, `Installed`, `Comments`, and `Path`.

```vba
Sub ListAllAddins()
    Dim ai As AddIn
    Dim Row As Long
    Dim Table1 As ListObject
    Cells.Clear
    Range("A1:E1") = Array("Name", "Title", "Installed", _
        "Comments", "Path")
    Row = 2
    On Error Resume Next
    For Each ai In AddIns
        Cells(Row, 1) = ai.Name
        Cells(Row, 2) = ai.Title
        Cells(Row, 3) = ai.Installed
        Cells(Row, 4) = ai.Comments
        Cells(Row, 5) = ai.Path
        Row = Row + 1
    Next ai
    On Error GoTo 0
    Range("A1").Select
    ActiveSheet.ListObjects.Add
    ActiveSheet.ListObjects(1).TableStyle = _
        "TableStyleMedium2"
End Sub
```

Figure 21-7 shows the result of executing this procedure.

CD

This procedure is available on the companion CD-ROM. The filename is `list add-in information.xlsm`.

NOTE

You can determine whether a particular workbook is an add-in by accessing its `IsAddIn` property. This is not a read-only property, so you can also convert a workbook to an add-in by setting the `IsAddIn` property to `True`.

And, conversely, you can convert an add-in to a workbook by setting the `IsAddIn` property to `False`. After doing so, the add-in's worksheets will be visible in Excel — even if the add-in's VBA project is protected.

	A	B	C	D	E
1	Name	Title	Installed	Comments	Path
2	ANALYS32.XLL	Analysis ToolPak	TRUE		C:\Program Files\Microsoft Office\Offi
3	ATPVBAEN.XLAM	Analysis ToolPak - VBA	FALSE		C:\Program Files\Microsoft Office\Offi
4	Budget Tools.addin	Budget Tools	FALSE		C:\Documents and Settings\jw\My Doc
5	change case.xlam	Change Case	FALSE	Changes the case of text in selected	C:\Documents and Settings\jw\Applica
6	SUMIF.XLAM	Conditional Sum Wizard	FALSE		C:\Program Files\Microsoft Office\Offi
7	EUROTOOL.XLAM	Euro Currency Tools	FALSE		C:\Program Files\Microsoft Office\Offi
8	hello world.xlam	Hello World	FALSE		C:\Documents and Settings\jw\Applica
9	HTML.XLAM	Internet Assistant VBA	FALSE		C:\Program Files\Microsoft Office\Offi
10	is addin installed.xlam	Is Add-In Installed	FALSE	Demonstrates how to determine if a	C:\Documents and Settings\jw\My Doc
11	LOOKUP.XLAM	Lookup Wizard	FALSE		C:\Program Files\Microsoft Office\Offi
12	page break display.xlsm	Page Break Display	FALSE		C:\Documents and Settings\jw\Applica
13	page break display add-in.xlam	Page Break Toggle	FALSE	RibbonX Demo adds a new control tc	C:\Documents and Settings\jw\Applica
14	pup6.xla	Power Utility Pak v6	TRUE	Add-In Tools For Excel - Licensed≡≡¢	C:\Program Files\pup6
15	WaterfallChart.xla	PTS Waterfall Chart Utility	FALSE	Create Waterfall Charts from simple	C:\Program Files\PTS Charts
16	SOLVER.XLAM	Solver Add-in	FALSE		C:\Program Files\Microsoft Office\Offi
17	text tools.xlam	Text Tools	TRUE	Adds text manipulation features to E	C:\Documents and Settings\jw\My Doc
18					

Figure 21-7: A table that lists all members of the AddIns collection.

Accessing an add-in as a workbook

As I mention earlier, there are two ways to open an add-in file: by using the Add-Ins dialog box and by choosing the Office ⇨ Open command. The former method is the preferred method for the following reason: When you open an add-in with the Office ⇨ Open command, its `Installed` property is *not* set to `True`. Therefore, you cannot close the file by using the Add-Ins dialog box. In fact, the only way to close such an add-in is with a VBA statement such as the following:

```
Workbooks("myaddin.xlam").Close
```

 CAUTION

Using the `Close` method on an installed add-in removes the add-in from memory, but it does not set its `Installed` property to `False`. Therefore, the Add-Ins dialog box still lists the add-in as installed, which can be very confusing. The proper way to remove an installed add-in is to set its `Installed` property to `False`.

As you might have surmised, Excel's add-in capability is a bit quirky, and this component has not been improved in many years. Therefore, as a developer, you need to pay particular attention to issues involving installing and uninstalling add-ins.

AddIn object events

An `AddIn` object has two events: `AddInInstall` (raised when the add-in is installed) and `AddInUninstall` (raised when it is uninstalled). You can write event handler procedures for these events in the `ThisWorkbook` code module for the add-in.

The following example is displayed as a message when the add-in is installed:

```
Private Sub Workbook_AddInInstall()
    MsgBox ThisWorkbook.Name & _
        " add-in has been installed."
End Sub
```

CAUTION

Don't confuse the AddInInstall event with the Open event. The AddInInstall event occurs only when the add-in is first installed — not every time it is opened. If you need to execute code every time the add-in is opened, use a Workbook_Open procedure.

CROSS-REFERENCE

For additional information about events, see Chapter 19.

Optimizing the Performance of Add-Ins

If you ask a dozen Excel programmers to automate a particular task, chances are that you'll get a dozen different approaches. Most likely, not all these approaches will perform equally well.

Following are a few tips that you can use to ensure that your code runs as quickly as possible. These tips apply to all VBA code, not just the code in add-ins.

- *Set the* Application.ScreenUpdating *property to* False *when writing data to a worksheet or performing any other actions that cause changes to the display.*

- *Declare the data type for all variables used and avoid variants whenever possible.* Use an Option Explicit statement at the top of each module to force yourself to declare all variables.

- *Create object variables to avoid lengthy object references.* For example, if you're working with a Series object for a chart, create an object variable by using code like this:

  ```
  Dim S1 As Series
  Set S1 = ActiveWorkbook.Sheets(1).ChartObjects(1). _
      Chart.SeriesCollection(1)
  ```

- *Whenever possible, declare object variables as a specific object type* — not As Object.

- *Use the* With-End With *construct,* when appropriate, to set multiple properties or call multiple methods for a single object.

- *Remove all extraneous code.* This is especially important if you've used the macro recorder to create procedures.

- If possible, *manipulate data with VBA arrays rather than worksheet ranges.* Reading and writing to a worksheet takes much longer than manipulating data in memory. This is not a firm rule, however. For best results, test both options.

- *Avoid linking UserForm controls to worksheet cells.* Doing so may trigger a recalculation whenever the user changes the UserForm control.

- *Compile your code before creating the add-in.* This could increase the file size, but it eliminates the need for Excel to compile the code before executing the procedures.

Special Problems with Add-Ins

Add-ins are great, but you should realize by now that there's no free lunch. Add-ins present their share of problems — or should I say *challenges?* In this section, I discuss some issues that you need to know about if you'll be developing add-ins for widespread user distribution.

Ensuring that an add-in is installed

In some cases, you might need to ensure that your add-in is installed properly: that is, opened using the Add-Ins dialog box and not the Office ⇨ Open command. This section describes a technique that determines how an add-in was opened and gives the user an opportunity to install the add-in if it is not properly installed.

If the add-in isn't properly installed, the code displays a message (see Figure 21-8). Clicking Yes installs the add-in. Clicking No leaves the file open but doesn't install it. Clicking Cancel closes the file.

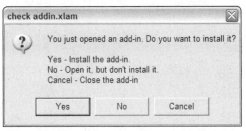

Figure 21-8: When attempting to open the add-in incorrectly, the user sees this message.

The code that follows is the code module for the add-in's `ThisWorkbook` object. This technique relies on the fact that the `AddInInstall` event occurs before the `Open` event for the workbook.

```vba
Dim InstalledProperly As Boolean

Private Sub Workbook_AddinInstall()
    InstalledProperly = True
End Sub

Private Sub Workbook_Open()
    Dim ai As AddIn, NewAi As AddIn
    Dim M As String
    Dim Ans As Integer
    'Was just installed using the Add-Ins dialog box?
    If InstalledProperly Then Exit Sub

    'Is it in the AddIns collection?
    For Each ai In AddIns
        If ai.Name = ThisWorkbook.Name Then
            If ai.Installed Then
                MsgBox "This add-in is properly installed.", _
                    vbInformation, ThisWorkbook.Name
                Exit Sub
            End If
        End If
    Next ai

    'It's not in AddIns collection, prompt user.
    M = "You just opened an add-in. Do you want to install it?"
    M = M & vbNewLine
    M = M & vbNewLine & "Yes - Install the add-in. "
    M = M & vbNewLine & "No - Open it, but don't install it."
    M = M & vbNewLine & "Cancel - Close the add-in"
    Ans = MsgBox(M, vbQuestion + vbYesNoCancel, _
        ThisWorkbook.Name)
    Select Case Ans
        Case vbYes
            ' Add it to the AddIns collection and install it.
            Set NewAi = _
                Application.AddIns.Add(ThisWorkbook.FullName)
            NewAi.Installed = True
        Case vbNo
            'no action, leave it open
        Case vbCancel
            ThisWorkbook.Close
    End Select
End Sub
```

The procedure covers the following possibilities:

- The add-in was opened automatically because it's an installed add-in, listed (and checked) in the Add-Ins dialog box. The user does not see a message.

- The user uses the Add-ins dialog box to install the add-in. The user does not see a message.

- The add-in was opened manually (by using Office ⇨ Open), and it's not a member of the AddIns collection. The user sees the message and must take one of the three actions.

- The add-in was opened manually, and it's a member of the AddIns collection — but it is not installed (not checked). The user sees the message and must take one of the three actions.

By the way, this code can also be used as a way to simplify the installation of an add-in that you give to someone. Just tell them to double-click the add-in's filename (which opens it in Excel) and respond Yes to the prompt. Better yet, modify the code so the add-in is installed without a prompt.

 CD-ROM

This add-in, named check addin.xlam, is available on the companion CD-ROM. Try opening it using both methods (the Add-Ins dialog box and by choosing Office ⇨ Open).

Referencing other files from an add-in

If your add-in uses other files, you need to be especially careful when distributing the application. You can't assume anything about the storage structure of the system that users will run the application on. The easiest approach is to insist that all files for the application be copied to a single directory. Then you can use the Path property of your application's workbook to build path references to all other files.

For example, if your application uses a custom help file, be sure that the help file is copied to the same directory as the application itself. Then you can use a procedure like the following to make sure that the help file can be located:

```
Sub GetHelp()
    Application.Help ThisWorkbook.Path & "\userhelp.chm "
End Sub
```

If your application uses Application Programming Interface (API) calls to standard Windows DLLs, you can assume that these can be found by Windows. But if you use custom DLLs, the best practice is to make sure that they're installed in the Windows\System directory (which might or might not be named Windows\System). You'll need to use the GetSystemDirectory Windows API function to determine the exact path of the System directory.

Detecting the proper Excel version for your add-in

As you may know, those who use an earlier version of Excel can open Excel 2007 files if they've installed Microsoft's Compatibility Pak. If your add-in uses any features unique to Excel 2007, you'll want to warn users who attempt to open the add-in with an earlier version. The following code does the trick:

```
Sub CheckVersion()
    If Val(Application.Version) < 12 Then
        MsgBox "This works only with Excel 2007 or later"
        ThisWorkbook.Close
    End If
End Sub
```

The `Version` property of the `Application` object returns a string. For example, this might return `12.0a`. This procedure uses VBA's `Val` function, which ignores everything after the first alphabetic character.

 CROSS-REFERENCE

See Chapter 26 for additional information about compatibility.

Part VI

Developing Applications

Chapter 22

Working with the Ribbon

In This Chapter

Perhaps the most significant change in Office 2007 is the new Ribbon-based user interface. This chapter provides an overview of the Ribbon and describes how it relates to VBA.

◆ The new Excel 2007 Ribbon UI, from a user's perspective

◆ How you can use VBA to work with the Ribbon

◆ An introduction to customizing the Ribbon with RibbonX code

◆ Examples of workbooks that modify the Ribbon

◆ Boiler-plate code for creating an old-style toolbar

The Ribbon is a brand new concept in user interface design. You use XML to modify the Ribbon, but there are a few Ribbon-related operations that you can perform with VBA.

Ribbon Basics

The first thing you notice about Excel 2007 is its new look. The time-honored menu-and-toolbar user interface has been scrapped and replaced with a new *tab-and-Ribbon* interface. Although the new interface kind of resembles the old-fashioned menus-and-toolbars interface, you'll find that it's radically different.

Long-time Excel users have probably noticed that the menu system has become increasingly complicated with each new version. In addition, the number of toolbars has become almost overwhelming. After all, every new feature must be accessible. In the past, this access meant adding more items to the menus and building new toolbars. The Microsoft designers set out to solve this overcrowding problem, and the new Ribbon interface is their solution.

Time will tell how users will accept the new Ribbon interface. As I write this book, the reaction can best be described as *mixed*. As with anything new, some people love it, and others hate it.

I think many experienced Excel users will suffer from a mild case of bewilderment when they realize that all their familiar command sequences no longer work. Beginning users, on the other hand, will be able to get up to speed much more quickly because they won't be overwhelmed with irrelevant menus and toolbars.

Because the Ribbon UI is new, I provide some additional user-oriented information in the sections that follow.

Ribbon tabs

The commands available in the Ribbon vary, depending on which tab is selected. The Ribbon is arranged into groups of related commands. Here's a quick overview of Excel's tabs:

- *Home:* You'll probably spend most of your time in the Home tab. This tab contains the basic Clipboard commands, formatting commands, style commands, commands to insert and delete rows and columns, plus an assortment of worksheet-editing commands.

- *Insert:* Select this tab when you need to insert something in a worksheet — a table, a diagram, a chart, a symbol, and so on.

- *Page Layout:* This tab contains commands that affect the overall appearance of your worksheet, including settings that deal with printing.

- *Formulas:* Use this tab to insert a formula, name a range, access the formula-auditing tools, or control how Excel performs calculations.

- *Data:* Excel's data-related commands are on this tab.

- *Review:* This tab contains tools to check spelling, translate words, add comments, and protect sheets.

- *View:* The View tab contains commands that control various aspects of how a sheet is viewed. Some commands on this tab are also available on the status bar.

- *Developer:* This tab isn't visible by default. It contains commands that are useful for programmers. To display the Developer tab, choose Office ➪ Excel Options and then select Popular. Place a check mark next to Show Developer Tab in the Ribbon.

- *Add-Ins:* This tab is visible only if you've loaded a workbook or add-in that customizes the menu or toolbars (by using the `CommandBars` object). Because menus and toolbars are no longer available in Excel 2007, these customizations appear in the Add-Ins tab.

The CommandBar Object in Excel 2007

Excel 97 introduced a completely new way of handling toolbars and menus. These UI elements are `CommandBar` objects. What's commonly called a toolbar is actually one of three types of command bars:

- *Toolbar:* This is a bar with one or more clickable controls.
- *Menu bar:* The two built-in menu bars are Worksheet menu bar and Chart menu bar.
- *Shortcut menu:* This is the menu that pops up when you right-click an object.

For compatibility purposes, Excel 2007 still supports the `CommandBar` object — but its functionality has been significantly deprecated. It's no longer possible for an end user to create a custom toolbar. However, a VBA programmer can still create and work with `CommandBar` objects (see "Creating an Old-Style Toolbar," later in this chapter). The problem, however, is that many of the `CommandBar` properties and methods are simply ignored in Excel 2007. For example, every toolbar or customized menu appears in the Add-Ins tab of the Ribbon. Properties that control a toolbar's dimensions and position no longer work. In addition, floating toolbars are no longer possible.

The accompanying figures show a customized menu and toolbar in Excel 2003, and the same menu and toolbar in Excel 2007. Although these UI elements are still functional in Excel 2007, it's clearly not what the developer (me!) had in mind. Needless to say, many VBA developers will want to redo the UI for their applications.

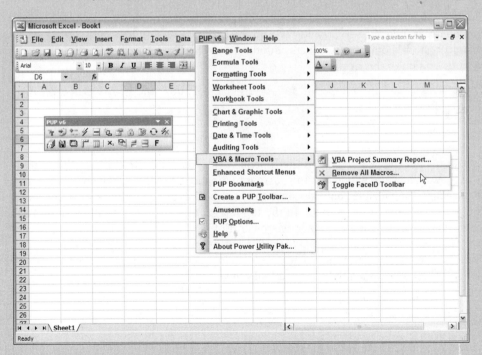

continued

Part VI

continued

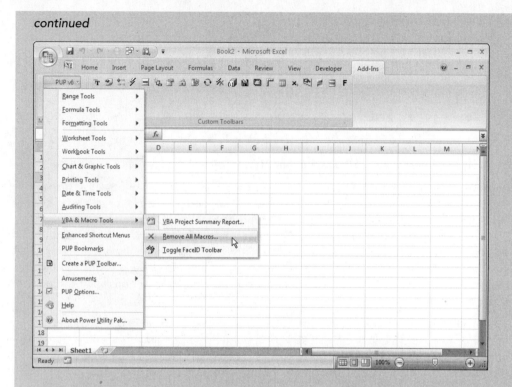

In this chapter, I present a simple example of creating a custom toolbar by using the CommandBar object (see "Creating an Old-Style Toolbar"). For complete details on creating custom menus and toolbars with the CommandBar object, consult the previous edition of this book.

Customizing shortcut menus is still supported in Excel 2007, and I cover that topic in Chapter 23.

The appearance of the commands on the Ribbon varies, depending on the width of the Excel window. When the window is too narrow to display everything, the commands adapt and may seem to be missing, but the commands are still available. Figure 22-1 shows three views of the Home tab of the Ribbon. In the top image, all controls are fully visible. In the middle image, Excel's window is made narrower. Notice that some of the descriptive text is gone, and some of the icons are smaller. The bottom image shows the extreme case in which the window is very narrow. Some groups display a single icon. However, if you click the icon, all the group commands are available to you.

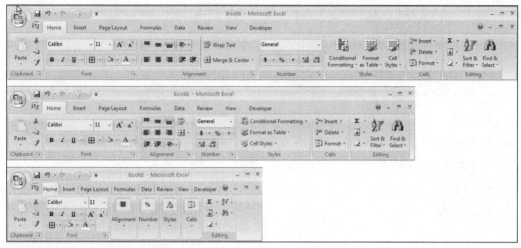

Figure 22-1: The Home tab of the Ribbon, with varying widths of the Excel window.

TIP

If you would like to hide the Ribbon to increase your worksheet view, just double-click any of the tabs. The Ribbon goes away (but the tabs remain), and you're able to see about five additional rows of your worksheet. When you need to use the Ribbon again, just click a tab, and it comes back temporarily. To permanently restore the Ribbon, double-click a tab. You can also press Ctrl+F1 to toggle the Ribbon display on and off.

VBA and the Ribbon

Now, the big question: What can a VBA programmer do with the Ribbon? The simple answer is this: not much.

Following is a list of what you can do with the Ribbon using VBA:

- Determine whether a particular control is enabled.
- Determine whether a particular control is visible.
- Determine whether a particular control is pressed (for toggle buttons and check boxes).
- Get a control's label, screen tip, or supertip (a more detailed description of the control).
- Display the image associated with a control.
- Execute a particular control.

Following is a list of things that you might like to do with the Ribbon but that are not possible:

- Determine which tab is currently selected.
- Activate a particular tab.
- Add a new tab.
- Add a new group to a tab.
- Add a new control.
- Remove a control.
- Disable a control.
- Hide a control.

Accessing a Ribbon control

All told, Excel has more than 1,700 Ribbon controls. Every Ribbon control has a name, and you use that name when you work with the control using VBA.

For example, the statement that follows displays a message box that shows the Enabled status of the ViewCustomViews control. (This control is located in the View ⇨ Workbook Views group.)

```
MsgBox Application.CommandBars.GetEnabledMso("ViewCustomViews")
```

Determining the name of a particular control is a manual task. First, display the Customize tab of the Office ⇨ Excel Options dialog box. Locate the control in the list box on the left, and then hover the mouse pointer over the item. The control's name appears in a pop-up screen tip (see Figure 22-2)

Unfortunately, it's not possible to write VBA code to loop through all the controls on the Ribbon and display a list of their names.

CD-ROM

The companion CD-ROM contains a workbook with the names of all Excel controls. The workbook also displays additional information about each control, including the control type, the tab name, and the group name. Figure 22-3 shows a portion of this file, which is named ribbon control names.xlsx.

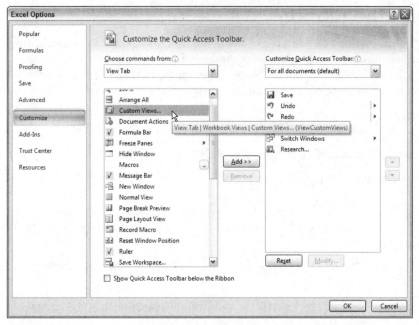

Figure 22-2: Using the Customize tab of the Excel Options dialog box to determine the name of a control.

	Control Name	Control Type	Tab Set Name	Tab Name	Group Name	Paren
3	FileNewDefault	button	None (Quick Access Toolbar)	Quick Access Toolbar		
4	FileOpen	button	None (Quick Access Toolbar)	Quick Access Toolbar		
5	FileSave	button	None (Quick Access Toolbar)	Quick Access Toolbar		
6	FileSendAsAttachment	button	None (Quick Access Toolbar)	Quick Access Toolbar		
7	FilePrintQuick	button	None (Quick Access Toolbar)	Quick Access Toolbar		
8	FilePrintPreview	button	None (Quick Access Toolbar)	Quick Access Toolbar		
9	Spelling	button	None (Quick Access Toolbar)	Quick Access Toolbar		
10	Undo	gallery	None (Quick Access Toolbar)	Quick Access Toolbar		
11	Redo	gallery	None (Quick Access Toolbar)	Quick Access Toolbar		
12	SortAscendingExcel	button	None (Quick Access Toolbar)	Quick Access Toolbar		
13	SortDescendingExcel	button	None (Quick Access Toolbar)	Quick Access Toolbar		
14	FileNew	button	None (Office Menu)	Office Menu		
15	FileOpen	button	None (Office Menu)	Office Menu		
16	UpgradeWorkbook	button	None (Office Menu)	Office Menu		
17	FileSave	button	None (Office Menu)	Office Menu		
18	FileSaveAsMenu	splitButton	None (Office Menu)	Office Menu		
19	FileSaveAs	button	None (Office Menu)	Office Menu	FileSaveAsMenu	
20	FileSaveAsExcelXlsx	button	None (Office Menu)	Office Menu	FileSaveAsMenu	
21	FileSaveAsExcelXlsxMacro	button	None (Office Menu)	Office Menu	FileSaveAsMenu	
22	FileSaveAsExcelXlsb	button	None (Office Menu)	Office Menu	FileSaveAsMenu	
23	FileSaveAsExcel97_2003	button	None (Office Menu)	Office Menu	FileSaveAsMenu	
24	AdvertisePublishAs	button	None (Office Menu)	Office Menu	FileSaveAsMenu	
25	FileSaveAsPdfOrXps	button	None (Office Menu)	Office Menu	FileSaveAsMenu	
26	FileSaveAsOtherFormats	button	None (Office Menu)	Office Menu	FileSaveAsMenu	
27	FilePrintMenu	splitButton	None (Office Menu)	Office Menu		
28	FilePrint	button	None (Office Menu)	Office Menu	FilePrintMenu	
29	FilePrint	button	None (Office Menu)	Office Menu	FilePrintMenu	
30	FilePrintQuick	button	None (Office Menu)	Office Menu	FilePrintMenu	

Figure 22-3: A workbook that displays information about each Ribbon control.

Working with the Ribbon

In the previous section I provided an example of using the GetEnabledMso method of the CommandBars object. Following is a list of all the methods that are relevant to working with the Ribbon via the CommandBars object. All of these methods take one argument: idMso, which represents the name of the command.

- ExecuteMso: Executes a control
- GetEnabledMso: Returns True if the specified control is enabled
- GetImageMso: Returns the image for a control
- GetLabelMso: Returns the label for a control
- GetPressedMso: Returns True if the specified control is pressed (applies to check box and toggle button controls)
- GetScreentipMso: Returns the screen tip for a control (the text that appears in the control)
- GetSupertipMso: Returns the supertip for a control (the description of the control that appears when you hove the mouse pointer over the control)

Some of these methods are fairly worthless. Why would a VBA programmer need to determine the screen tip for a control? I can't think of a reason.

The VBA statement that follows toggles the Selection pane (a new feature that facilitates selecting objects on a worksheet):

```
Application.CommandBars.ExecuteMso("SelectionPane")
```

The following statement displays the Paste Special dialog box:

```
Application.CommandBars.ExecuteMso("PasteSpecialDialog")
```

Here's a command that tells you whether the formula bar is visible (it corresponds to the state of the Formula Bar control in the View ➪ Show/Hide group):

```
MsgBox Application.CommandBars.GetPressedMso("ViewFormulaBar")
```

Note, however, that your code cannot change the visibility of the formula bar by accessing the Ribbon control. Rather, use the DisplayFormulaBar property of the Application object:

```
Application.DisplayFormulaBar = True
```

The statement that follows displays True if the Merge & Center control is enabled. (This control is disabled if the sheet is protected or if the active cell is within a table.)

```
MsgBox Application.CommandBars.GetEnabledMso("MergeCenter")
```

The following VBA code adds an ActiveX Image control to the active worksheet and uses the `GetImageMso` method to display the image from the Find & Select control in the Home ⇨ Editing group:

```
Sub ImageOnSheet()
    Dim MyImage As OLEObject
    Set MyImage = ActiveSheet.OLEObjects.Add _
      (ClassType:="Forms.Image.1", _
      Left:=50, _
      Top:=50)
    With MyImage.Object
        .AutoSize = True
        .BorderStyle = 0
        .Picture = Application.CommandBars. _
          GetImageMso("FindDialog", 32, 32)
    End With
End Sub
```

Activating a tab

Microsoft provides no direct way to activate a Ribbon tab from VBA. But if you really need to do so, using `SendKeys` is your only option. The `SendKeys` method simulates keystrokes. The keystrokes required to activate the Home tab are Alt, followed by H. These keystrokes display the keytips in the Ribbon. To hide the keytips, press F6. Using this information, the following statement sends the keystrokes required to activate the Home tab:

```
Application.SendKeys "%h{F6}"
```

The `SendKeys` arguments for the other tabs are:

- Insert: `"%n{F6}"`
- Page Layout: `"%p{F6}"`
- Formulas: `"%m{F6}"`
- Data: `"%a{F6}"`
- Review: `"%r{F6}"`
- View: `"%w{F6}"`
- Developer: `"%l{F6}"`
- Add-Ins: `"%x{F6}"`

Part VI

About the Quick Access Toolbar

In previous versions of Excel, it was relatively easy for end users to change the user interface. They could create custom toolbars that contained frequently used commands, and they could even remove menu items that they never used. Users could display any number of toolbars and move them wherever they liked. Those days are over.

The Quick Access Toolbar (QAT) is the only user-customizable UI element in Excel 2007. It's very easy for a user to add a command to the QAT, so the command is available no matter which Ribbon tab is active. The QAT can't be moved, but Microsoft does allow users to determine whether the QAT is displayed: above or below the Ribbon.

The QAT is not part of the object model, so there is nothing you can do with it using VBA.

The QAT information is stored in an XML file named `Excel.qat`. The file is located here:

```
C:\Documents and Settings\<username>\Local Settings\
Application Data\Microsoft\Office
```

You can view this file with a text editor or an XML viewer. If you make a copy of the file and rename it with an `XML` extension, you can even open it with Excel (when prompted for how to open the file, specify as an XML table). However, you cannot modify the `Excel.qat` file using Excel.

Customizing the Ribbon

You can't perform any Ribbon modifications using VBA. Rather, you must write RibbonX code and insert the code into the workbook file — which is done outside of Excel. You can, however, create VBA callback procedures. A *callback procedure* is a VBA macro that is executed when a custom Ribbon control is activated.

RibbonX code is XML markup that describes the controls, where in the Ribbon they are displayed, what they look like, and what happens when they are activated. This book does not cover RibbonX — it's complex enough to be the subject of an entire book. I do, however, provide a few simple examples so you can understand what's involved in modifying the Excel 2007 UI and decide if it's something you'd like to learn.

A simple RibbonX example

This section contains a step-by-step walkthrough that will give you a feel for what it takes to modify Excel's Ribbon. This example creates a new Ribbon group (named Custom) on the Data tab. It also creates two buttons in the new Ribbon group, labeled Hello World and Goodbye World. Clicking either of these buttons executes a VBA macro.

See Your Errors

Before you do any work with Ribbon customization, you should enable the display of RibbonX errors. Access the Office ⇨ Excel Options dialog box and click the Advanced tab. Scroll down to the General section and place a check mark next to Show Add-in User Interface Errors.

When this setting is enabled, RibbonX errors (if any) are displayed when the workbook opens — which is very helpful for debugging.

Follow these steps to create a workbook that contains RibbonX code that modifies the Ribbon:

1. Create a new Excel workbook, insert a VBA module, and enter two callback procedures. These are the procedures that are executed when the buttons are clicked:

```
Sub HelloWorld(control As IRibbonControl)
    MsgBox "Hello World!"
End Sub

Sub GoodbyeWorld(control As IRibbonControl)
    ThisWorkbook.Close
End Sub
```

2. Save the workbook and name it `ribbon modification.xlsm`.

3. Close the workbook.

4. Activate the folder that contains the `ribbon modification.xlsm` file and create a folder named customUI.

5. Inside that folder, use a text editor (such as Windows Notepad) to create a text file named `customUI.xml` with the following RibbonX XML code:

```
<customUI xmlns="http://schemas.microsoft.com/office/2006/01/customui">
<ribbon>
<tabs>
<tab idMso="TabData">
  <group  id="Group1" label="Custom">
    <button id="Button1"
        label="Hello World"
        size="normal"
        onAction="HelloWorld"
        imageMso="HappyFace" />
    <button id="Button2"
        label="Goodbye World"
        size="normal"
        onAction="GoodbyeWorld"
```

```
        imageMso="DeclineInvitation" />
      </group>
   </tab>
   </tabs>
   </ribbon>
   </customUI>
```

6. Using Windows Explorer, add a `.zip` extension to the `ribbon modification.xlsm` file in Windows Explorer. The filename should now be `ribbon modification.xlsm.zip`.

7. Drag the customUI folder you created in Step 4 into the `ribbon modification.xlsm.zip` file. Windows treats ZIP files as if they were folders, so drag-and-drop operations are allowed.

8. Double-click the `ribbon modification.xlsm.zip` file to open it. Figure 22-4 shows the contents of the ZIP file. As you see, the file contains several folders.

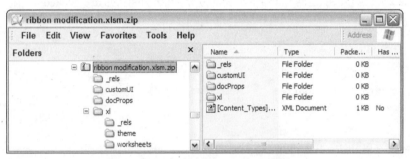

Figure 22-4: An Excel workbook, displayed as a ZIP file.

9. Double-click the _rels folder within the ZIP file. This folder contains one file, named `.rels`.

10. Drag the `.rels` file to a location outside the ZIP file (to your Desktop, for example).

11. Open the `.rels` file (which is an XML file) with a text editor, such as Notepad.

12. Add the following line to the `.rels` file, before the `</Relationships>` tag:

```
<Relationship
Type="http://schemas.microsoft.com/office/2006/relationships/ui/
extensibility" Target="/customUI/customUI.xml" Id="12345" />
```

13. Save the `.rels` file and drag it back into the ZIP file, overwriting the original version.

14. Remove the `.zip` extension so that the file is back to its original name: `ribbon modification.xlsm`.

Open the workbook in Excel. If all went well, you should see a new group with two buttons in the Data tab (see Figure 22-5).

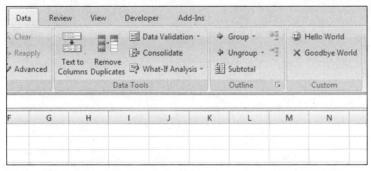

Figure 22-5: RibbonX code created a new group with two buttons.

CD-ROM

This workbook, named `ribbon modification.xlsm`, is available on the companion CD-ROM.

It's important to understand that the Ribbon modification is document-specific. In other words, the new Ribbon group is displayed only when the workbook that contains the RibbonX code is the active workbook. This is a major departure from how UI modifications worked in previous versions of Excel.

TIP

To display Ribbon customizations when any workbook is active, convert the workbook to an add-in file, or add the RibbonX code to your Personal Macro Workbook.

If you've concluded that modifying Excel's Ribbon is not worth the effort, don't despair. Tools will be available that make the process much less tedious than I've described. As I write this book, only one such tool is available: Office 2007 Custom UI Editor, written by Trang Luu (see Figure 22-6). This program still requires that you create the RibbonX code manually, but it will validate the code for you. It also eliminates all the tedious manual file manipulations. And finally, it can generate the VBA callback procedure declarations, which you can copy and paste to your VBA module.

More about the simple RibbonX example

This section provides some additional details about the `ribbon modification.xlsm` workbook I discuss in the previous section.

VBA CALLBACK PROCEDURES

Recall that the workbook contains two VBA procedures, `HelloWorld` and `GoodbyeWorld`. These procedure names correspond to the `onAction` parameters in the RibbonX code. The `onAction` parameter is one way to link the RibbonX code to your VBA code.

Figure 22-6: The Office 2007 Custom UI Editor.

Both the VBA procedures contain an argument named `control`, which is an
`IRibbonControl` object. This object has three properties, which you can access in your
VBA code:

- `Context`: A handle to the active window containing the Ribbon that triggered the callback. For example, use the following expression to get the name of the workbook that
  contains the RibbonX code:

  `control.Context.Caption`

- `Id`: Contains the name of the control, specified as its `Id` parameter.

- `Tag`: Contains any arbitrary text that's associated with the control.

The VBA callback procedures can be as complex as necessary.

THE .RELS FILE

Inserting the file that contains the RibbonX code has no effect unless you specify a relationship between the document file and the customization file. These relationships, written
in XML, are stored in the `.rels` file, which is in the _rels folder. Here's the relationship
for the example presented in the previous section:

```
<Relationship Type="http://schemas.microsoft.com/office/2006/
   relationships/ui/extensibility" Target="/customUI/customUI.xml"
   Id="12345" />
```

The `Target` parameter points to the `customUI.xml` file that contains the RibbonX code.
The `Id` parameter contains an arbitrary text string. The string can contain anything, as
long as it's unique to the file (that is, as long as no other `<Relationship>` tag uses the
same `Id`).

THE RIBBONX CODE

And now, the tricky part. Writing the XML code that defines your UI modification is no easy task. As I've noted, this is not the book that will teach you how to write RibbonX code. You'll find a few simple examples here, but you'll need to consult other sources for the fine points.

Using imageMso Images

Microsoft Office 2007 provides more than 2,500 named images that are associated with various commands. You can specify any of these images for your custom Ribbon controls — if you know the image's name.

The accompanying figure shows a workbook that contains the names of all the imageMso images. Scroll through the image names, and you see 50 images at a time (in small or large size), beginning with the image name in the active cell. This workbook, named mso image browser.xlsm, is available on the companion CD-ROM.

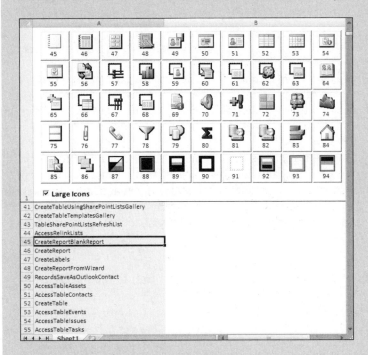

You can also use these images in an Image control placed on a UserForm. The statement below assigns the imageMso image named ReviewAcceptChanges to the Picture property of a UserForm Image control named Image1. The size of the image is specified as 32 x 32 pixels.

```
Image1.Picture = Application.CommandBars. _
  GetImageMso("ReviewAcceptChange", 32, 32)
```

Part VI

When you're starting out, it's best to start with examples that work (search the Web) and then make small modifications, testing frequently along the way. It can be very frustrating to spend an hour working on code that appears to be perfect in every way — and then realize that XML is case-sensitive. *ID* is not the same as *Id*.

NOTE

You may be curious about the `imageMso` parameter, which determines which icon is displayed next to the control. Microsoft Office includes more than 2,500 icons that you can use with Ribbon controls. Each is accessed by its name. For more information, see the sidebar "Using imageMso Images."

Another RibbonX example

This section contains another example of using RibbonX to modify the UI. This workbook creates a new group on the Page Layout tab and adds a check box control that toggles the display of page breaks.

NOTE

Although Excel has more than 1,700 commands, it does not have a command that toggles the page break display. After printing or previewing a worksheet, the only way to hide the page break display is to use the Excel Options dialog box. Therefore, this example also has some practical value.

This example is a bit tricky because it requires that the new Ribbon control be in synch with the active sheet. For example, if you activate a worksheet that doesn't display page breaks, the check box control should be in its unchecked state. If you activate a worksheet that displays page breaks, the control should be checked. Furthermore, page breaks aren't relevant for a chart sheet, so the control should be disabled if you activate a chart sheet.

THE RIBBONX CODE

The RibbonX code that adds a new group (with a `CheckBox` control) to the Page Layout tab follows:

```
<customUI
   xmlns="http://schemas.microsoft.com/office/2006/01/customui"
   onLoad="Initialize">
<ribbon>
<tabs>
<tab idMso="TabPageLayoutExcel">
   <group id="Group1" label="Custom">
     <checkBox id="Checkbox1"
         label="Page Breaks"
```

```
        onAction="TogglePageBreakDisplay"
        getPressed="GetPressed"
        getEnabled="GetEnabled"/>
    </group>
</tab>
</tabs>
</ribbon>
</customUI>
```

This RibbonX code references four VBA callback procedures (each of which is described later):

- `Initialize`: Executed when the workbook is opened.

- `TogglePageBreakDisplay`: Executed when the user clicks the check box control.

- `GetPressed`: Executed when the control is invalidated (the user activates a different sheet).

- `GetEnabled`: Executed when the control is invalidated (the user activates a different sheet).

Figure 22-7 shows the new control.

Figure 22-7: This check box control is always in synch with the page break display of the active sheet.

THE VBA CODE

The `CustomUI` tag includes an `onLoad` parameter, which specifies the `Initialize` VBA callback procedure, as follows:

```
Public MyRibbon As IRibbonUI

Sub Initialize(Ribbon As IRibbonUI)
'    Executed when the workbook loads
    Set MyRibbon = Ribbon
End Sub
```

The Initialize procedure creates an IRibbonUI object named MyRibbon. Notice that MyRibbon is a Public variable, so it's accessible from other procedures in the module.

I created a simple event-procedure that is executed whenever a worksheet is activated. This procedure, which is located in the ThisWorkbook code module, calls the CheckPageBreakDisplay procedure:

```
Private Sub Workbook_SheetActivate(ByVal Sh As Object)
    Call CheckPageBreakDisplay
End Sub
```

The CheckPageBreakDisplay procedure *invalidates* the check box control. In other words, it destroys any data associated with that control.

```
Sub CheckPageBreakDisplay()
'   Executed when a sheet is activated
    MyRibbon.InvalidateControl ("Checkbox1")
End Sub
```

When a control is invalidated, the GetPressed and GetEnabled procedures are called.

```
Sub GetPressed(control As IRibbonControl, ByRef returnedVal)
'   Executed when the control is invalidated
    On Error Resume Next
    returnedVal = ActiveSheet.DisplayPageBreaks
End Sub
```

```
Sub GetEnabled(control As IRibbonControl, ByRef returnedVal)
'   Executed when the control is invalidated
    returnedVal = TypeName(ActiveSheet) = "Worksheet"
End Sub
```

Notice that the returnedVal argument is passed ByRef. This means that your code is able to change the value. And that's exactly what happens. In the GetPressed procedure, the returnedVal variable is set to the status of the DisplayPageBreaks property of the active sheet. The result is that the control's Pressed parameter is True if page breaks are displayed (and the control is checked). Otherwise, the control is not checked.

In the GetEnabled procedure, the returnedVal variable is set to True if the active sheet is a worksheet (as opposed to a chart sheet). Therefore, the control is enabled only when the active sheet is a worksheet.

The only other VBA procedure is the onAction procedure, TogglePageBreakDisplay, which is executed when the user checks or unchecks the check box:

```
Sub TogglePageBreakDisplay(control As IRibbonControl, pressed As Boolean)
'   Executed when check box is clicked
    On Error Resume Next
    ActiveSheet.DisplayPageBreaks = pressed
End Sub
```

This `pressed` argument is `True` if the user checks the check box and `False` if he unchecks the check box. The code sets the `DisplayPageBreaks` property accordingly.

CD-ROM

This workbook, named `page break display.xlsm`, is available on the companion CD-ROM. The CD also contains an add-in version of this workbook (named `page break display add-in.xlam`), which makes the new UI command available for all workbooks. The add-in version uses a class module to monitor sheet activation events for all workbooks. Refer to Chapter 19 for more information about events, and Chapter 29 for more information about class modules.

Ribbon controls demo

Figure 22-8 shows a custom Ribbon tab (My Stuff) with four groups of controls. In this section, I briefly describe the RibbonX code and the VBA callback procedures.

Figure 22-8: A new Ribbon tab with four groups of controls.

CD-ROM

This workbook, named `ribbon controls demo.xlsm`, is available on the companion CD-ROM.

CREATING A NEW TAB
The RibbonX code that creates the new tab is

```
<ribbon>
  <tabs>
    <tab id="CustomTab" label="My Stuff">
  </tabs>
</ribbon>
```

Part VI

TIP

If you'd like to create a minimal UI, the `ribbon` tag has a `startFromScratch` attribute. If set to `True`, all the built-in tabs are hidden. In addition, all the Office button menu commands are hidden except for New, Open, Excel Options, and Exit.

```
<ribbon startFromScratch="true" >
```

CREATING A RIBBON GROUP

The code in the `ribbon controls demo.xlsm` example creates four groups on the My Stuff tab. Here's the code that creates the four groups:

```
<group  id="Group1" label="Stuff">
</group>

<group  id="Group2" label="More Stuff">
</group>

<group  id="Group3" label="Built In Stuff">
</group>

<group  id="Group4" label="Galleries">
</group>
```

Theses pairs of `<group>` and `</group>` tags are located within the `<tab>` and `</tab>` tags that create the new tab.

CREATING CONTROLS

Following is the RibbonX code that creates the controls in the first group (Stuff), shown in Figure 22-9. Notice that the controls are defined within the first set of `<group>` `</group>` tags.

```
<group id="Group1" label="Stuff">
    <labelControl id="Label1" getLabel="getLabel1" />
    <labelControl id="Label2" getLabel="getLabel2" />

    <editBox id="EditBox1"
       showLabel="true"
       label="Number:"
       onChange="EditBox1_Change"/>

    <button id="Button1"
       label="Calculator"
       size="large"
       onAction="ShowCalculator"
       imageMso="Calculator" />
</group>
```

Two label controls each have an associated VBA callback procedure (named `getLabel1` and `getLabel2`). These procedures are:

```
Sub getLabel1(control As IRibbonControl, ByRef returnedVal)
    returnedVal = "Hello " & Application.UserName
End Sub

Sub getLabel2(control As IRibbonControl, ByRef returnedVal)
    returnedVal = "Today is " & Date
End Sub
```

Figure 22-9: A Ribbon group with four controls.

When the RibbonX code is loaded, these two procedures are executed, and the captions of the label controls are dynamically updated with the username and the date.

The `editBox` control has an `onChange` callback procedure named `EditBox1_Change`, which displays the square root of the number entered (or an error message if the square root can't be calculated). The `EditBox1_Change` procedure is

```
Sub EditBox1_Change(control As IRibbonControl, text As String)
    Dim squareRoot As Double
    On Error Resume Next
    squareRoot = Sqr(text)
    If Err.Number = 0 Then
        MsgBox "The square root of " & text & " is: " & squareRoot
    Else
        MsgBox "Enter a positive number.", vbCritical
    End If
End Sub
```

The last control in the Stuff group is a simple button. It's `onAction` parameter executes a VBA procedure named `ShowCalculator` — which uses the VBA `Shell` function to display the Windows calculator:

```
Sub ShowCalculator(control As IRibbonControl)
    On Error Resume Next
    Shell "calc.exe", vbNormalFocus
    If Err.Number <> 0 Then MsgBox "Can't start calc.exe"
End Sub
```

Figure 22-10 shows the controls in the second group, labeled More Stuff.

Figure 22-10: Three controls in a custom Ribbon group.

The RibbonX code for the second group is as follows:

```
<group  id="Group2" label="More Stuff">
  <toggleButton id="ToggleButton1"
      size="large"
      imageMso="FileManageMenu"
      label="Toggle Me"
      onAction="ToggleButton1_Click" />

  <separator id="sep1" />

  <checkBox id="Checkbox1"
      label="Checkbox"
      onAction="Checkbox1_Change"/>

  <comboBox id="Combo1"
     label="Month"
     onChange="Combo1_Change">
    <item id="Month1" label="January" />
    <item id="Month2" label="February"/>
    <item id="Month3" label="March"/>
    <item id="Month4" label="April"/>
    <item id="Month5" label="May"/>
    <item id="Month6" label="June"/>
    <item id="Month7" label="July"/>
    <item id="Month8" label="August"/>
    <item id="Month9" label="September"/>
    <item id="Month10" label="October"/>
    <item id="Month11" label="November"/>
    <item id="Month12" label="December"/>
  </comboBox>
</group>
```

The group contains a `toggleButton`, a `separator`, a `checkBox`, and a `comboBox` control. These controls are fairly straightforward. Except for the `separator` control (which inserts a vertical line), each has an associated callback procedure that simply displays the status of the control:

```
Sub ToggleButton1_Click(control As IRibbonControl, ByRef returnedVal)
    MsgBox "Toggle value: " & returnedVal
```

```
End Sub

Sub Checkbox1_Change(control As IRibbonControl, pressed As Boolean)
    MsgBox "Checkbox value: " & pressed
End Sub

Sub Combo1_Change(control As IRibbonControl, text As String)
    MsgBox text
End Sub
```

NOTE

The comboBox control also accepts user-entered text. If you would like to limit the choices to those that you provide, use a dropDown control.

The controls in the third group consist of built-in controls (see Figure 22-11). To include a built-in control in a custom group, you just need to know its name (the idMso parameter).

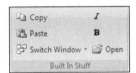

Figure 22-11: This group contains built-in controls.

The RibbonX code is

```
<group id="Group3" label="Built In Stuff">
    <control idMso="Copy" label="Copy" />
    <control idMso="Paste" label="Paste" enabled="true" />
    <control idMso="WindowSwitchWindowsMenuExcel"
        label="Switch Window" />
    <control idMso="Italic" />
    <control idMso="Bold" />
    <control idMso="FileOpen" />
</group>
```

These controls don't have callback procedures because they perform the standard action.

Figure 22-12 shows the final group of controls, which consists of two galleries.

Figure 22-12: This Ribbon group contains two galleries.

The RibbonX code for these two gallery controls is

```
<group id="Group4" label="Galleries">
  <gallery id="Gallery1"
      imageMso="ViewAppointmentInCalendar"
      label="Pick a Month:"
      columns="2" rows="6"
      onAction="MonthSelected" >
    <item id="January" label="January"
      imageMso="QuerySelectQueryType"/>
    <item id="February" label="February"
      imageMso="QuerySelectQueryType"/>
    <item id="March" label="March"
      imageMso="QuerySelectQueryType"/>
    <item id="April" label="April"
      imageMso="QuerySelectQueryType"/>
    <item id="May" label="May"
      imageMso="QuerySelectQueryType"/>
    <item id="June" label="June"
      imageMso="QuerySelectQueryType"/>
    <item id="July" label="July"
      imageMso="QuerySelectQueryType"/>
    <item id="August" label="August"
      imageMso="QuerySelectQueryType"/>
    <item id="September" label="September"
      imageMso="QuerySelectQueryType"/>
    <item id="October" label="October"
      imageMso="QuerySelectQueryType"/>
    <item id="November" label="November"
      imageMso="QuerySelectQueryType"/>
    <item id="December" label="December"
      imageMso="QuerySelectQueryType"/>
    <button id="Today"
       label="Today..."
       imageMso="ViewAppointmentInCalendar"
       onAction="ShowToday"/>
  </gallery>

  <gallery id="Gallery2"
      label="Banjo Players"
      size="large"
      columns="4"
      itemWidth="100" itemHeight="125"
      imageMso=  "Camera"
      onAction="OnAction">
    <item id="bp01" image="bp01" />
    <item id="bp02" image="bp02" />
```

```
        <item id="bp03" image="bp03" />
        <item id="bp04" image="bp04" />
        <item id="bp05" image="bp05" />
        <item id="bp06" image="bp06" />
        <item id="bp07" image="bp07" />
        <item id="bp08" image="bp08" />
        <item id="bp09" image="bp09" />
        <item id="bp10" image="bp10" />
        <item id="bp11" image="bp11" />
        <item id="bp12" image="bp12" />
        <item id="bp13" image="bp13" />
        <item id="bp14" image="bp14" />
        <item id="bp15" image="bp15" />
    </gallery>
</group>
```

Figure 22-13 shows the first gallery, a list of month names in two columns. The `onAction` parameter executes the `MonthSelected` callback procedure, which displays the selected month (which is stored as the `id` parameter):

```
Sub MonthSelected(control As IRibbonControl, _
    id As String, index As Integer)
    MsgBox "You selected " & id
End Sub
```

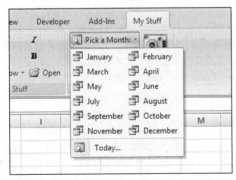

Figure 22-13: A gallery that displays month names, plus a button.

The Pick a Month gallery also contains a button control with its own callback procedure (labeled Today) at the bottom:

```
Sub ShowToday(control As IRibbonControl)
    MsgBox "Today is " & Date
End Sub
```

The second gallery, shown in Figure 22-14, displays 15 photos.

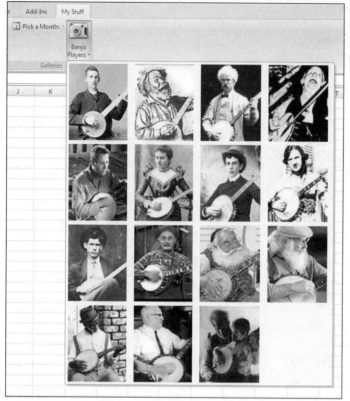

Figure 22-14: A gallery of photos.

These photos are stored in the workbook file, in a folder named images, within the customUI folder. Adding images also requires a _rels folder, with a list of relationships. To see how this works, add a .zip extension to the workbook and then examine its contents.

A DynamicMenu Control Example

One of the most interesting Ribbon controls is the dynamicMenu control. This control lets your VBA code feed XML data into the control — which provides the basis for menus that change based on context.

Setting up a dynamicMenu control is not a simple task, but this control probably offers the most flexibility in terms of using VBA to modify the Ribbon dynamically.

I created a simple dynamicMenu control demo that displays a different menu for each of the three worksheets in a workbook. Figure 22-15 shows the menu that appears when Sheet1 is active. When a sheet is activated, a VBA procedure sends XML code specific for the sheet. For this demo, I stored the XML code directly in the worksheets to make it easier to read. Alternatively, the XML markup can be stored as a string variable in your code.

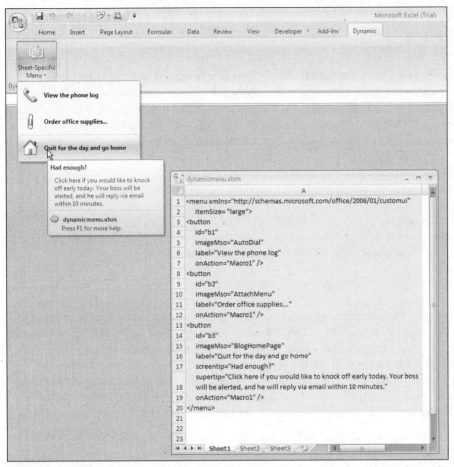

Figure 22-15: The dynamicMenu control lets you create a menu that varies depending on the context.

The RibbonX code that creates the new tab, the new group, and the `dynamicMenu` control follows:

```
<customUI xmlns="http://schemas.microsoft.com/office/2006/01/customui"
onLoad="ribbonLoaded">
  <ribbon>
  <tabs>
    <tab id="CustomTab" label="Dynamic">
        <group id="group1" label="Dynamic Menu Demo">
          <dynamicMenu id="DynamicMenu"
              getContent="dynamicMenuContent"
              imageMso="RegionLayoutMenu"
              size = "large"
              label="Sheet-Specific Menu"/>
        </group>
  </tab>
```

```
    </tabs>
   </ribbon>
</customUI>
```

This example needs a way to invalidate the Ribbon whenever the user activates a new sheet. I use the same method I used for the page break display example earlier in this chapter (see "Another RibbonX example"): I declared a `Public` variable, MyRibbon, of type `IRibbonUI`. I used a `Workbook_SheetActivate` procedure that called the UpdateDynamicRibbon procedure whenever a new sheet is activated:

```
Sub UpdateDynamicRibbon()
'    Invalidate the Ribbon to force a call to dynamicMenuContent
    On Error Resume Next
    MyRibbon.Invalidate
    If Err.Number <> 0 Then
        MsgBox "Lost the Ribbon object. Save and reload."
    End If
End Sub
```

The UpdateDynamicRibbon procedure invalidates the MyRibbon object, which forces a call to the VBA callback procedure named dynamicMenuContent (a procedure referenced by the getContent parameter in the RibbonX code). Notice the error-handling code. Some edits to your VBA code destroy the MyRibbon object, which is created when the workbook is opened. Attempting to invalidate an object that doesn't exist causes an error, and the message box informs the user that the workbook must be saved and reopened. Unfortunately, reopening the workbook is the only way to re-create the MyRibbon object.

The dynamicMenuContent procedure follows. This procedure loops through the cells in column A of the active sheet, reads the XML code, and stores it in a variable named XMLcode. When all the XML has been appended, it's passed to the returnedVal argument. The net effect is that the dynamicMenu control has new code, so it displays a different set of menu options.

```
Sub dynamicMenuContent(control As IRibbonControl, _
    ByRef returnedVal)
    Dim r As Long
    Dim XMLcode As String
'    Read the XML markup from the active sheet
    For r = 1 To Application.CountA(Range("A:A"))
        XMLcode = XMLcode & ActiveSheet.Cells(r, 1) & " "
    Next r
    returnedVal = XMLcode
End Sub
```

 CD-ROM

The workbook that contains this example is available on the companion CD-ROM. The filename is dynamicmenu.xlsm.

More on Ribbon customization

I conclude this section with some additional points to keep in mind as you explore the wonderful world of Excel Ribbon customization:

- When you're working with the Ribbon, make sure that you turn on error message display. Refer to the "See Your Errors" sidebar, earlier in this chapter.

- Remember that RibbonX code is case-sensitive.

- All the named control IDs are in English, and they are the same across all language versions of Excel. Therefore, Ribbon modifications work regardless of what language version of Excel is used.

- Ribbon modifications appear only when the workbook that contains the RibbonX code is active. To make Ribbon modifications appear for all workbooks, the RibbonX code must be in an add-in.

- The built-in controls scale themselves when the Excel window is resized. Custom controls are always the same size; they don't scale.

- Adding or removing controls from a built-in Ribbon group is not possible.

- You can, however, hide tabs. The RibbonX code that follows hides three tabs:

```
<customUI xmlns="http://schemas.microsoft.com/office/2006/01/customui">
<ribbon>
  <tabs>
    <tab idMso="TabPageLayoutExcel" visible="false" />
    <tab idMso="TabData" visible="false" />
    <tab idMso="TabReview" visible="false" />
  </tabs>
</ribbon>
</customUI>
```

- You can also hide groups within a tab. Here's RibbonX code that hides four groups on the Insert tab (leaving only the Charts group):

```
<customUI xmlns="http://schemas.microsoft.com/office/2006/01/customui">
<ribbon>
  <tabs>
    <tab idMso="TabInsert">
     <group idMso="GroupInsertTablesExcel" visible="false" />
     <group idMso="GroupInsertIllustrations" visible="false" />
     <group idMso="GroupInsertLinks" visible="false" />
     <group idMso="GroupInsertText" visible="false" />
    </tab>
  </tabs>
</ribbon>
</customUI>
```

- You can assign your own macro to a built-in control. This is known as *repurposing the control.* The RibbonX code that follows intercepts three built-in commands:

```
<customUI xmlns="http://schemas.microsoft.com/office/2006/01/customui">
<commands>
  <command idMso="FileSave" onAction="mySave"/>
  <command idMso="FilePrint" onAction="myPrint"/>
  <command idMso="FilePrintQuick" onAction="myPrint"/>
</commands>
</customUI>
```

- You can also write RibbonX code to disable one or more built-in controls. The code that follows disables the Insert ClipArt command.

```
<customUI xmlns="http://schemas.microsoft.com/office/2006/01/customui">
<commands>
  <command idMso="ClipArtInsert" enabled="false"/>
</commands>
</customUI>
```

- If you have two or more workbooks (or add-ins) that add controls to the same custom Ribbon group, you must make sure that they both use the same namespace. Do this in the <CustomUI> tag at the top of the RibbonX code.

Creating an Old-Style Toolbar

If you find that customizing the Ribbon is just too much work, you may be content to create a simple custom toolbar using the pre–Excel 2007 CommandBar object. This technique is perfectly suitable for any workbook that only you will be using. It's an easy way to provide quick access to a number of macros.

In this section, I provide boilerplate code that you can adapt as needed. I don't offer much in the way of explanation. For more information about CommandBar objects, search the Web or consult the previous edition of this book. CommandBar objects can be much more powerful than the example presented here.

Limitations of old-style toolbars in Excel 2007

If you decide to create a toolbar for Excel 2007, be aware of the following limitations:

- It cannot be free-floating.
- It will always appear in the Add-Ins ⇨ Custom Toolbars group (along with any other toolbars).
- Some of the CommandBar properties and methods are simply ignored by Excel.

Code to create a toolbar

The code in this section assumes that you have a workbook with two macros (named `Macro1` and `Macro2`). It also assumes that you want the toolbar to be created when the workbook is opened and deleted when the workbook is closed.

NOTE

Unlike Ribbon modifications, custom toolbars are visible regardless of which workbook is active.

In the `ThisWorkbook` code module, enter the following procedures. The first one calls the procedure that creates the toolbar when the workbook is opened. The second calls the procedure to delete the toolbar when the workbook is closed:

```
Private Sub Workbook_Open()
    Call CreateToolbar
End Sub

Private Sub Workbook_BeforeClose(Cancel As Boolean)
    Call DeleteToolbar
End Sub
```

CROSS-REFERENCE

In Chapter 19, I describe a potentially serious problem with the `Workbook_BeforeClose` event. Excel's "Do you want to save . . ." prompt displays after the `Workbook_BeforeClose` event handler runs. So if the user clicks `Cancel`, the workbook remains open, but the custom menu items have already been deleted. In Chapter 19, I also present a way to get around this problem.

The CreateToolbar procedure follows:

```
Const TOOLBARNAME As String = "MyToolbar"

Sub CreateToolbar()
    Dim TBar As CommandBar
    Dim Btn As CommandBarButton

'   Delete existing toolbar (if it exists)
    On Error Resume Next
    CommandBars(TOOLBARNAME).Delete
    On Error GoTo 0

'   Create toolbar
    Set TBar = CommandBars.Add
    With TBar
```

Part VI

```
        .Name = TOOLBARNAME
        .Visible = True
    End With


'   Add a button
    Set Btn = TBar.Controls.Add(Type:=msoControlButton)
    With Btn
        .FaceId = 300
        .OnAction = "Macro1"
        .Caption = "Macro1 Tooltip goes here"
    End With


'   Add another button
    Set Btn = TBar.Controls.Add(Type:=msoControlButton)
    With Btn
        .FaceId = 25
        .OnAction = "Macro2"
        .Caption = "Macro2 Tooltip goes here"
    End With
End Sub
```

CD-ROM

A workbook that contains this code is available on the companion CD-ROM. The filename is `old-style toolbar.xlsm`.

Figure 22-16 shows the two-button toolbar.

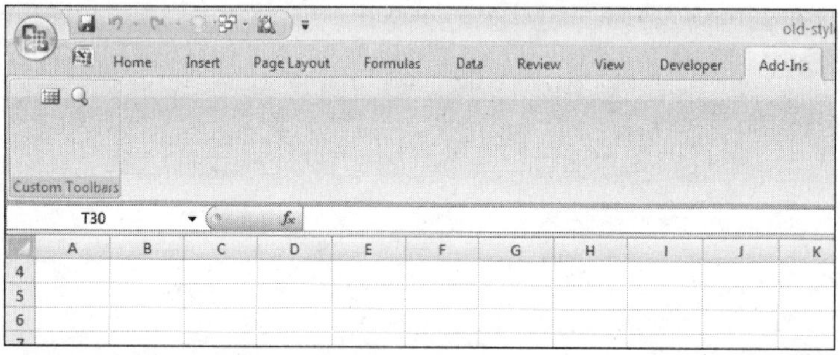

Figure 22-16: An old-style toolbar, located in the Custom Toolbars group of the Add-Ins tab.

I use a module-level constant, TOOLBAR, which stores the toolbar's name. This name is also used in the DeleteToolbar procedure, so using a constant ensures that both procedures work with the same name.

The procedure starts by deleting the existing toolbar that has the same name (if such a toolbar exists). Including this statement is useful during development and also eliminates the error you get if you attempt to create a toolbar using a duplicate name.

The toolbar is created by using the `Add` method of the `CommandBars` object. The two buttons are added by using the `Add` method of the `Controls` object. Each button has three properties:

- `FaceID`: A number that determines the image displayed on the button.
- `OnAction`: The macro that is executed when the button is clicked.
- `Caption`: The screen tip that appears when you hover the mouse pointer over the button.

TIP

Rather than set the `FaceID` property, you can set the `Picture` property using any of the `imageMso` images. For example, the statement below displays a green check mark:

```
.Picture = Application.CommandBars.GetImageMso _
    ("AcceptInvitation", 16, 16)
```

For more information about `imageMso` images, see the sidebar, "Using imageMso Images."

When the workbook is closed, the `Workbook_BeforeClose` event procedure fires, which calls `DeleteToolbar`:

```
Sub DeleteToolbar()
    On Error Resume Next
    CommandBars(TOOLBARNAME).Delete
    On Error GoTo 0
End Sub
```

Chapter 23

Working with Shortcut Menus

In This Chapter

Although the Ribbon has replaced menus and toolbars, Excel 2007 still offers developers the opportunity to customize the shortcut menus. Typically, right-clicking an item displays a context-sensitive shortcut menu containing relevant commands. In this chapter, I cover the following:

- ◆ How to identify shortcut menus

- ◆ How to customize the shortcut menus

- ◆ How to disable shortcut menus

- ◆ How to use events in conjunction with shortcut menus

- ◆ How to create a completely new shortcut menu

The `CommandBar` object takes on a much less significant role in Excel 2007. This chapter covers the `CommandBar` object as it relates to customizing shortcut menus.

CommandBar Overview

A `CommandBar` object is used for three Excel user interface elements:

- Custom toolbars
- Custom menus
- Customs shortcut (right-click) menus

In Excel 2007, the `CommandBar` object is in a rather odd position. If you write VBA code to customize a menu or a toolbar, Excel intercepts that code and ignores many of your commands. As I describe in Chapter 22, menu and toolbar customizations performed with the `CommandBar` object appear in the Add-Ins ⇨ Menu Commands or the Add-Ins ⇨ Custom Toolbars group. So, for all practical purposes, the `CommandBar` object in Excel 2007 is limited to shortcut menu operations.

In this section, I provide some background information about CommandBars.

CommandBar types

Excel supports three types of CommandBars, differentiated by their `Type` property. The `Type` property can be any of these three values:

- `msoBarTypeNormal`: A toolbar (`Type` = 0)
- `msoBarTypeMenuBar`: A menu bar (`Type` = 1)
- `msoBarTypePopUp`: A shortcut menu (`Type` = 2)

Even though toolbars and menu bars aren't used in Excel 2007, these UI elements are still included in the object model for compatibility with older applications. However, attempting to display a CommandBar of Type 0 or 1 has no effect in Excel 2007. In Excel 2003, for example, the following statement displays the Standard toolbar.

```
CommandBars("Standard").Visible = True
```

In Excel 2007, that statement is ignored.

This chapter focuses exclusively on Type 2 CommandBars (shortcut menus).

Listing shortcut menus

Excel 2007 has 65 shortcut menus. How do I know that? I ran the `ShowShortcutMenuNames` procedure that follows, which loops through all CommandBars. If the `Type` property is `msoBarTypePopUp` (a built-in constant that has a value of 2), it displays the CommandBar's index and name in a worksheet.

```
Sub ShowShortcutMenuNames()
    Dim Row As Long
    Dim cbar As CommandBar
    Row = 1
    For Each cbar In CommandBars
        If cbar.Type = msoBarTypePopUp Then
            Cells(Row, 1) = cbar.Index
            Cells(Row, 2) = cbar.Name
            Row = Row + 1
        End If
    Next cbar
End Sub
```

Figure 23-1 shows part of the output from this procedure. The shortcut menu index values range from 21 to 145. Also, notice that not all the names are unique. For example, CommandBar 36 and CommandBar 39 both have a Name of Cell. This is because right-clicking a cell gives a different shortcut menu when the worksheet is in Page Break Preview mode.

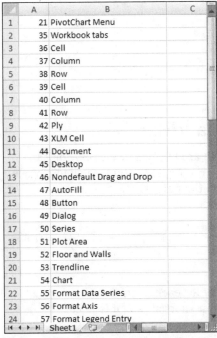

	A	B	C
1	21	PivotChart Menu	
2	35	Workbook tabs	
3	36	Cell	
4	37	Column	
5	38	Row	
6	39	Cell	
7	40	Column	
8	41	Row	
9	42	Ply	
10	43	XLM Cell	
11	44	Document	
12	45	Desktop	
13	46	Nondefault Drag and Drop	
14	47	AutoFill	
15	48	Button	
16	49	Dialog	
17	50	Series	
18	51	Plot Area	
19	52	Floor and Walls	
20	53	Trendline	
21	54	Chart	
22	55	Format Data Series	
23	56	Format Axis	
24	57	Format Legend Entry	

Figure 23-1: A simple macro generates a list of all shortcut menus.

CD

This example is available on the companion CD-ROM. The filename is show shortcut menu names.xlsm

Referring to CommandBars

You can reference a particular `CommandBar` object by its `Index` or by its `Name` property. For example, the expressions that follow both refer to the shortcut menu that displays when you right-click the Excel desktop (the area that's visible when no documents are open):

```
Application.CommandBars (45)
Application.CommandBars("Desktop")
```

The `CommandBars` collection is a member of the `Application` object. When you reference this collection in a regular VBA module or in a module for a sheet, you can omit the reference to the `Application` object. For example, the following statement (contained in a standard VBA module) displays the name of the object in the `CommandBars` collection that has an index of 45:

```
MsgBox CommandBars(45).Name
```

When you reference the `CommandBars` collection from a code module for a `ThisWorkbook` object, you must precede it with a reference to the `Application` object, like this:

```
MsgBox Application.CommandBars(45).Name
```

 NOTE
Unfortunately, the Index numbers have not always remained constant across the different Excel versions.

Referring to controls in a CommandBar

A `CommandBar` object contains `Control` objects, which are buttons or menus. You can refer to a control by its `Index` property or by its `Caption` property. Here's a simple procedure that displays the caption of the first menu item on the Cell shortcut menu:

```
Sub ShowCaption()
    MsgBox Application.CommandBars("Cell"). _
        Controls(1).Caption
End Sub
```

The following procedure displays the `Caption` property for each control in the shortcut menu that appears when you right-click a sheet tab (that shortcut menu is named `Ply`):

```
Sub ShowCaptions()
    Dim txt As String
    Dim ctl As CommandBarControl
    For Each ctl In CommandBars("Ply").Controls
        txt = txt & ctl.Caption & vbNewLine
    Next ctl
    MsgBox txt
End Sub
```

When you execute this procedure, you see the message box shown in Figure 23-2. The ampersand is used to indicate the underlined letter in the text — the keystroke that will execute the menu item.

Microsoft Excel
&Insert...
&Delete
&Rename
&Move or Copy...
&View Code
&Protect Sheet...
Tab Color
&Hide
&Unhide...
&Select All Sheets
&Ungroup Sheets
OK

Figure 23-2: Displaying the Caption property for controls.

In some cases, Control objects on a shortcut menu contain other Control objects. For example, the Filter control on the Cell right-click menu contains other controls. The Filter control is a submenu, and the additional items are submenu items.

Finding a Control

If you are writing code that will be used by a different language version of Excel, avoid using the Caption property to access a particular shortcut menu item. The Caption property is language-specific, so your code will fail if the user has a different language version of Excel.

Instead, use the FindControl method in conjunction with the ID of the control (which is language-independent). For example, assume that you want to disable the Rename menu on the shortcut menu that appears when you right-click a sheet tab. If your workbook will be used only by people who have the English version of Excel, this statement will do the job:

```
CommandBars("Ply").Controls("Rename").Enabled = False
```

To ensure that the command will work with non-English versions, you need to know the ID of the control. The following statement will tell you that the ID is 889:

```
MsgBox CommandBars("Ply").Controls("Rename").ID
```

Then, to disable that control, use this statement:

```
CommandBars.FindControl(ID:=889).Enabled = False
```

The CommandBar names are not internationalized, so a reference to CommandBars("Desktop") will always work.

The statement that follows displays the first submenu item in the Filter submenu:

```
MsgBox CommandBars("Cell").Controls("Filter").Controls(1).Caption
```

Properties of CommandBar controls

`CommandBar` controls have a number of properties that determine how the controls look and work. This list contains some of the more useful properties for `CommandBar` controls:

- `Caption`: The text displayed for the control. If the control shows only an image, the Caption appears when you move the mouse over the control.

- `ID`: A unique numeric identifier for the control.

- `FaceID`: A number that represents a graphic image displayed next to the control's text.

- `Type`: A value that determines whether a control is a button (`msoControlButton`) or a submenu (`msoControlPopup`).

- `Picture`: A graphics image displayed next to the control's text.

- `BeginGroup`: True if a separator bar appears before the control.

- `OnAction`: The name of a VBA macro that executes when the user clicks the control.

- `BuiltIn`: True if the control is an Excel built-in control.

- `Enabled`: True if the control can be clicked.

- `Visible`: True if the control is visible. Many of the shortcut menus contains hidden controls.

- `ToolTipText`: Text that appears when the user moves the mouse pointer over the control. (Not applicable for shortcut menus.)

Displaying all shortcut menu items

The `ShowShortcutMenuItems` procedure that follows creates a table that lists all of the first-level controls on every shortcut menu. For each control, the table includes the shortcut menu's `Index` and `Name`, plus the `ID`, `Caption`, `Type`, `Enabled`, and `Visible` property values.

```
Sub ShowShortcutMenuItems()
  Dim Row As Long
  Dim Cbar As CommandBar
  Dim ctl As CommandBarControl
  Range("A1:G1") = Array("Index", "Name", "ID", "Caption", _
    "Type", "Enabled", "Visible")
  Row = 2
```

```
Application.ScreenUpdating = False
For Each Cbar In Application.CommandBars
    If Cbar.Type = 2 Then
        For Each ctl In Cbar.Controls
            Cells(Row, 1) = Cbar.Index
            Cells(Row, 2) = Cbar.Name
            Cells(Row, 3) = ctl.ID
            Cells(Row, 4) = ctl.Caption
            If ctl.Type = 1 Then
                Cells(Row, 5) = "Button"
            Else
                Cells(Row, 5) = "Submenu"
            End If
            Cells(Row, 6) = ctl.Enabled
            Cells(Row, 7) = ctl.Visible
            Row = Row + 1
        Next ctl
    End If
Next Cbar
End Sub
```

Figure 23-3 shows a portion of the output.

	A	B	C	D	E	F	G
1	Index	Name	ID	Caption	Type	Enabled	Visible
2	21	PivotChart Menu	460	Field Setti&ngs	Button	TRUE	TRUE
3	21	PivotChart Menu	1604	&Options...	Button	FALSE	TRUE
4	21	PivotChart Menu	459	&Refresh Data	Button	TRUE	TRUE
5	21	PivotChart Menu	3956	&Hide PivotChart Field Buttons	Button	FALSE	TRUE
6	21	PivotChart Menu	30254	For&mulas	Submenu	TRUE	TRUE
7	21	PivotChart Menu	5416	Remo&ve Field	Button	FALSE	TRUE
8	35	Workbook tabs	957	Sheet1	Button	TRUE	TRUE
9	35	Workbook tabs	957	&Sheet List	Button	TRUE	FALSE
10	35	Workbook tabs	957	&Sheet List	Button	TRUE	FALSE
11	35	Workbook tabs	957	&Sheet List	Button	TRUE	FALSE
12	35	Workbook tabs	957	&Sheet List	Button	TRUE	FALSE
13	35	Workbook tabs	957	&Sheet List	Button	TRUE	FALSE
14	35	Workbook tabs	957	&Sheet List	Button	TRUE	FALSE
15	35	Workbook tabs	957	&Sheet List	Button	TRUE	FALSE
16	35	Workbook tabs	957	&Sheet List	Button	TRUE	FALSE
17	35	Workbook tabs	957	&Sheet List	Button	TRUE	FALSE
18	35	Workbook tabs	957	&Sheet List	Button	TRUE	FALSE
19	35	Workbook tabs	957	&Sheet List	Button	TRUE	FALSE
20	35	Workbook tabs	957	&Sheet List	Button	TRUE	FALSE
21	35	Workbook tabs	957	&Sheet List	Button	TRUE	FALSE
22	35	Workbook tabs	957	&Sheet List	Button	TRUE	FALSE
23	35	Workbook tabs	957	&Sheet List	Button	TRUE	FALSE
24	36	Cell	21	Cu&t	Button	TRUE	TRUE
25	36	Cell	19	&Copy	Button	TRUE	TRUE
26	36	Cell	22	&Paste	Button	TRUE	TRUE
27	36	Cell	755	Paste &Special...	Button	TRUE	TRUE
28	36	Cell	3181	&Insert...	Button	TRUE	TRUE
29	36	Cell	292	&Delete...	Button	TRUE	TRUE
30	36	Cell	3125	Clear Co&ntents	Button	TRUE	TRUE

Figure 23-3: Listing the items in all shortcut menus.

Part VI

If you run the ShowShortcutMenuItems macro, you see that many of the shortcut menus contain hidden or disabled controls. These hidden or disabled menu items represent items that are not available because of the current context. For example, the Desktop shortcut menu (Index 45) contains the following menu items:

- &New...

- &Open...

- Save &Workspace...

- &Calculate Now

- F&ull Screen

The Full Screen menu item is normally hidden — unless Excel is in full screen mode. In such a case, the menu item is made visible and its caption is changed to &Close Full Screen.

 CD-ROM

This example, named show shortcut menu items.xlsm, is available on the companion CD-ROM.

Using VBA to Customize Shortcut Menus

In this section, I present some practical examples of VBA code that manipulates Excel's shortcut menus. These examples give you an idea of the types of things you can do with shortcut menus, and they can all be modified to suit your needs.

Resetting a shortcut menu

The Reset method restores a shortcut menu to its original, default condition. The following procedure resets the Cell shortcut menu to its normal state:

```
Sub ResetCellMenu()
    CommandBars("Cell").Reset
End Sub
```

As I noted earlier, Excel has two shortcut menus named Cell. The preceding code resets only the first one (index of 36). To reset the second Cell shortcut menu, use its index number (39) instead of its name.

The following procedure resets all built-in toolbars to their original states:

```
Sub ResetAll()
    Dim cbar As CommandBar
    For Each cbar In Application.CommandBars
        If cbar.Type = msoBarTypePopup Then
            cbar.Reset
            cbar.Enabled = True
        End If
    Next cbar
End Sub
```

NOTE

If your application adds items to a shortcut menu, it's better to remove the items individually when your application closes. If you simply reset the shortcut menu, it will delete customizations made by other applications.

Disabling a Shortcut Menu

The `Enabled` property lets you disable an entire shortcut menu. For example, you can set this property so that right-clicking a cell does not display the normal shortcut menu. The following statement disables the Cell shortcut menu:

```
Application.CommandBars("Cell").Enabled = False
```

To re-enable the shortcut menu, simply set its `Enabled` property to `True`.

If you want to disable *all* shortcut menus, use the following procedure:

```
Sub DisableAllShortcutMenus()
    Dim cb As CommandBar
    For Each cb In CommandBars
        If cb.Type = msoBarTypePopup Then _
            cb.Enabled = False
    Next cb
End Sub
```

CAUTION

Disabling shortcut menus "sticks" between sessions. Therefore, you'll probably want to restore the shortcut menus before closing Excel. To restore the shortcut menus, modify the preceding procedure to set the `Enabled` property to `True`.

Disabling shortcut menu items

You might want to disable one or more shortcut menu items on certain shortcut menus while your application is running. When an item is disabled, its text appears in light gray, and clicking it has no effect. The following procedure disables the Hide menu item from the Row and Column shortcut menus:

```
Sub DisableHideMenuItems()
    CommandBars("Column").Controls("Hide").Enabled = False
    CommandBars("Row").Controls("Hide").Enabled = False
End Sub
```

Adding a new item to the Cell shortcut menu

The `AddToShortcut` procedure that follows adds a new menu item to the Cell shortcut menu: Toggle Word Wrap. Recall that Excel has two Cell shortcut menus. This procedure modifies the normal right-click menu, but not the right-click menu that appears in Page Break Preview mode.

```
Sub AddToShortCut()
'   Adds a menu item to the Cell shortcut menu
    Dim Bar As CommandBar
    Dim NewControl As CommandBarButton
    DeleteFromShortcut
    Set Bar = CommandBars("Cell")
    Set NewControl = Bar.Controls.Add _
        (Type:=msoControlButton, _
        temporary:=True)
    With NewControl
        .Caption = "Toggle &Word Wrap"
        .OnAction = "ToggleWordWrap"
        .Picture = Application.CommandBars.GetImageMso _
            ("WrapText", 16, 16)
        .Style = msoButtonIconAndCaption
    End With
End Sub
```

Figure 23-4 shows the new menu item displayed after right-clicking a cell.

The first actual command after the declaration of a couple of variables calls the `DeleteFromShortcut` procedure (listed later in this section). This statement ensures that only one Toggle Word Wrap menu item appears on the shortcut Cell menu. Notice that the underlined hot key for this menu item is W, not T. That's because T is already used by the Cut menu item.

The `Picture` property is set by referencing the image used in the Ribbon for the Wrap Text command. Refer to Chapter 22 for more information about images used in Ribbon commands.

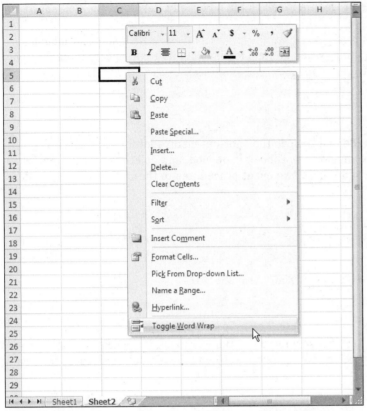

Figure 23-4: The Cell shortcut menu with a custom menu item.

The macro that is executed when the menu item is select is specified by the `OnAction` property. In this case, the macro is named `ToggleWordWrap`:

```
Sub ToggleWordWrap()
    CommandBars.ExecuteMso ("WrapText")
End Sub
```

This procedure simply executes the `WrapText` Ribbon command.

NOTE

When you modify a shortcut menu, that modification remains in effect until you restart Excel. In other words, modified shortcut menus don't reset themselves when you close the workbook that contains the VBA code. Therefore, if you write code to modify a shortcut menu, you almost always write code to reverse the effect of your modification.

Part VI

The `DeleteFromShortcut` procedure removes the new menu item from the Cell shortcut menu.

```
Sub DeleteFromShortcut()
    On Error Resume Next
    CommandBars("Cell").Controls _
      ("Toggle &Word Wrap").Delete
End Sub
```

In most cases, you want to add and remove the shortcut menu additions automatically: Add the shortcut menu item when the workbook is opened, and delete the menu item when the workbook is closed. Just add these two event procedures to the `ThisWorkbook` code module:

```
Private Sub Workbook_Open()
    Call AddToShortCut
End Sub

Private Sub Workbook_BeforeClose(Cancel As Boolean)
    Call DeleteFromShortcut
End Sub
```

The `Workbook_Open` procedure is executed when the workbook is opened, and the `Workbook_BeforeClose` procedure is executed before the workbook is closed. Just what the doctor ordered.

NOTE

Menu items added to a shortcut menu are available in all workbooks, not just the workbook that creates the menu items.

CD

The workbook described in this section is available on the companion CD-ROM. The filename is `add to cell shortcut.xlsm`.

Adding a submenu to a shortcut menu

The example in this section adds a submenu with three options to a shortcut menu. Actually, it adds the submenu to *six* shortcut menus. Figure 23-5 shows the worksheet after right-clicking a row. Each of the submenu items executes a macro that changes the case of text in the selected cells.

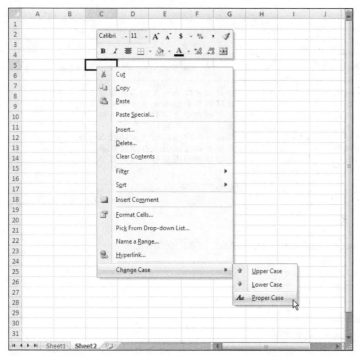

Figure 23-5: This shortcut menu has a submenu with three submenu items.

Finding FaceID Images

The icon that's displayed on a shortcut menu item is determined by one of two property settings:

- `Picture`: This option lets you use an `imageMso` from the Ribbon. For an example, see "Adding a new item to the Cell shortcut menu," earlier in this chapter.

- `FaceID`: This is the easiest option because the `FaceID` property is just a numeric value that represents one of hundreds of images.

But how do you find out which number corresponds to a particular `FaceID` image? Excel doesn't provide a way, so I created an application the lets you enter a beginning and ending `FaceID` number. Click a button, and the images are displayed in the worksheet. Each image has a name that corresponds to its `FaceID` value. See the accompanying figure, which shows `FaceID` values from 1 to 300. This workbook, named `show faceids.xlsm`, is available on the companion CD-ROM.

continued

Part VI

continued

The code that creates the submenu and submenu items is as follows:

```
Sub AddSubmenu()
'    Adds a submenu to the six shortcut menus
    Dim Bar As CommandBar
    Dim NewMenu As CommandBarControl
    Dim NewSubmenu As CommandBarButton
    Dim cbIndex As Long

    DeleteSubmenu
    For cbIndex = 36 To 41
        Set Bar = CommandBars(cbIndex)
'       Add submenu
        Set NewMenu = Bar.Controls.Add _
            (Type:=msoControlPopup, _
             temporary:=True)
        NewMenu.Caption = "Ch&ange Case"
        NewMenu.BeginGroup = True
'       Add first submenu item
        Set NewSubmenu = NewMenu.Controls.Add _
           (Type:=msoControlButton)
        With NewSubmenu
           .FaceId = 38
           .Caption = "&Upper Case"
           .OnAction = "MakeUpperCase"
        End With
'       Add second submenu item
        Set NewSubmenu = NewMenu.Controls.Add _
           (Type:=msoControlButton)
        With NewSubmenu
           .FaceId = 40
           .Caption = "&Lower Case"
```

```
                .OnAction = "MakeLowerCase"
        End With
'       Add third submenu item
        Set NewSubmenu = NewMenu.Controls.Add _
          (Type:=msoControlButton)
        With NewSubmenu
            .FaceId = 476
            .Caption = "&Proper Case"
            .OnAction = "MakeProperCase"
        End With
    Next cbIndex
End Sub
```

The `AddSubmenu` procedure uses a loop to modify the six `CommandBar` objects that have an Index between 36 and 41. These shortcut menus are the ones that appear when you right-click a cell, row, or column (different shortcut menus appear when Excel is in Page Break preview mode).

The submenu is added first, and its `Type` property is `msoControlPopup`. Then the three submenu items are added, and each has a different `OnAction` property.

CD

The workbook described in this section is available on the companion CD-ROM. The file-name is `shortcut with submenu.xlsm`.

Shortcut Menus and Events

The examples in this section demonstrate various shortcut-menu programming techniques used in conjunction with events.

CROSS-REFERENCE

I discuss event programming in depth in Chapter 19.

Adding and deleting menus automatically

If you need to modify a shortcut menu when a workbook is opened, use the `Workbook_Open` event. The following code, stored in the code module for the `ThisWorkbook` object, executes the `ModifyShortcut` procedure (not shown here):

```
Private Sub Workbook_Open()
    Call ModifyShortcut
End Sub
```

To return the shortcut back to its state before the modification, use a procedure such as the following. This procedure is executed before the workbook closes, and it executes the `RestoreShortcut` procedure (not shown here):

```
Private Sub Workbook_BeforeClose(Cancel As Boolean)
    Call RestoreShortcut
End Sub
```

A problem could arise, however, if the workbook is not saved when the user closes it. Excel's "Do you want to save the changes?" prompt occurs *after* the `Workbook_BeforeClose` event handler runs. So if the user clicks Cancel, the workbook remains open, but your custom menu has already been deleted!

One solution to this problem is to bypass Excel's prompt and write your own code in the `Workbook_BeforeClose` procedure to ask the user to save the workbook. The following code demonstrates how:

```
Private Sub Workbook_BeforeClose(Cancel As Boolean)
    If Not Me.Saved Then
        Msg = "Do you want to save the changes you made to "
        Msg = Msg & Me.Name & "?"
        Ans = MsgBox(Msg, vbQuestion + vbYesNoCancel)
        Select Case Ans
            Case vbYes
                Me.Save
            Case vbNo
                Me.Saved = True
            Case vbCancel
                Cancel = True
                Exit Sub
        End Select
    End If
    Call RestoreShortcut
End Sub
```

This procedure determines whether the workbook has been saved. If it has been saved, no problem; the `RestoreShortcut` procedure is executed, and the workbook is closed. But if the workbook has not been saved, the procedure displays a message box that duplicates the one Excel normally shows. If the user clicks Yes, the workbook is saved, the menu is deleted, and the workbook is closed. If the user clicks No, the code sets the `Saved` property of the `Workbook` object to `True` (without actually saving the file) and deletes the menu. If the user clicks Cancel, the `BeforeClose` event is canceled, and the procedure ends without restoring the shortcut menu.

Disabling or hiding shortcut menu items

When a menu item is disabled, its text appears in a faint shade of gray, and clicking it has no effect. When a menu item is hidden, it does not appear on the shortcut menu. You can, of course, write VBA code to enable or disable shortcut menu items. Similarly, you can write code to hide shortcut menu items. The key, of course, is tapping into the correct event.

The following code, for example, disables the Change Case shortcut menu item (which was added to the Cells menu) when Sheet2 is activated. This procedure is located in the code module for Sheet2:

```
Private Sub Worksheet_Activate()
    CommandBars("Cell").Controls("Change Case").Enabled = False
End Sub
```

To enable the menu item when Sheet2 is deactivated, add this procedure. The net effect is that the Change Case menu item is available at all times except when Sheet2 is active.

```
Private Sub Worksheet_Deactivate()
    CommandBars("Cell").Controls("Change Case").Enabled = True
End Sub
```

To hide the menu item rather than disable it, simply access the `Visible` property instead of the `Enabled` property.

Creating a context-sensitive shortcut menu

You can create an entirely new shortcut menu and display it in response to a particular event. The code that follows creates a shortcut menu named `MyShortcut` and adds six menu items to it. These menu items have their `OnAction` property set to execute a simple procedure that displays one of the tabs in the Format Cells dialog box (see Figure 23-6).

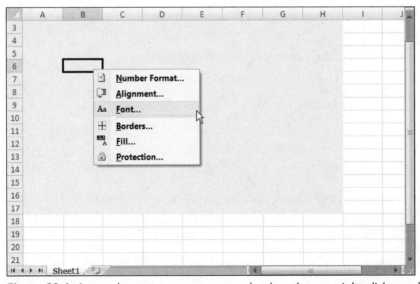

Figure 23-6: A new shortcut menu appears only when the user right-clicks a cell in the shaded area of the worksheet.

```
Sub CreateShortcut()
    Set myBar = CommandBars.Add _
        (Name:="MyShortcut", Position:=msoBarPopup, _
         Temporary:=True)

'   Add a menu item
    Set myItem = myBar.Controls.Add(Type:=msoControlButton)
    With myItem
        .Caption = "&Number Format..."
        .OnAction = "ShowFormatNumber"
        .FaceId = 1554
    End With

'   Add a menu item
    Set myItem = myBar.Controls.Add(Type:=msoControlButton)
    With myItem
        .Caption = "&Alignment..."
        .OnAction = "ShowFormatAlignment"
        .FaceId = 217
    End With

'   Add a menu item
    Set myItem = myBar.Controls.Add(Type:=msoControlButton)
    With myItem
        .Caption = "&Font..."
        .OnAction = "ShowFormatFont"
        .FaceId = 291
    End With

'   Add a menu item
    Set myItem = myBar.Controls.Add(Type:=msoControlButton)
    With myItem
        .Caption = "&Borders..."
        .OnAction = "ShowFormatBorder"
        .FaceId = 149
        .BeginGroup = True
    End With

'   Add a menu item
    Set myItem = myBar.Controls.Add(Type:=msoControlButton)
    With myItem
        .Caption = "&Patterns..."
        .OnAction = "ShowFormatPatterns"
        .FaceId = 1550
    End With

'   Add a menu item
```

```
    Set myItem = myBar.Controls.Add(Type:=msoControlButton)
    With myItem
        .Caption = "Pr&otection..."
        .OnAction = "ShowFormatProtection"
        .FaceId = 2654
    End With
End Sub
```

After the shortcut menu is created, you can display it by using the ShowPopup method. The following procedure, located in the code module for a Worksheet object, is executed when the user right-clicks a cell:

```
Private Sub Worksheet_BeforeRightClick _
  (ByVal Target As Excel.Range, Cancel As Boolean)
    If Union(Target.Range("A1"), Range("data")).Address = _
      Range("data").Address Then
        CommandBars("MyShortcut").ShowPopup
        Cancel = True
    End If
End Sub
```

If the active cell is within a range named data when the user right-clicks, the MyShortcut menu appears. Setting the Cancel argument to True ensures that the normal shortcut menu is not displayed. Note that the mini toolbar is not displayed.

You can also display this shortcut menu without even using the mouse. Create a simple procedure and assign a shortcut key by using the Options button in the Macro dialog box.

```
Sub ShowMyShortcutMenu()
'   Ctrl+Shift+M shortcut key
    CommandBars("MyShortcut").ShowPopup
End Sub
```

 CD-ROM

The companion CD-ROM contains an example (named new shortcut menu.xlsm) that creates a new shortcut menu and displays it in place of the normal Cell shortcut menu.

Chapter 24

Providing Help for Your Applications

In This Chapter

In this chapter, I discuss several methods of providing help for the users of your Excel applications:

◆ Why you should provide user help for your applications

◆ How to provide help by using only the components supplied with Excel

◆ How to display help files created with the HTML Help System

◆ How to associate a help file with your application

◆ Other ways to display HTML Help

Computer users have become rather spoiled over the years. In the early days of personal computers, software companies rarely provided onscreen help. And the "help" provided often proved less than helpful. Now, just about all commercial software provides help. And more often than not, the help serves as the primary documentation. Thick software manuals are an endangered species.

Help for Your Excel Applications

If you develop a nontrivial application in Excel, you might want to consider building in some sort of help for end users. Doing so makes the users feel more comfortable with the application and could eliminate many of those time-wasting phone calls from users with basic questions. Another advantage is that help is always available: That is, the instructions can't be misplaced or buried under a pile of books.

You can provide help for your Excel applications in a number of ways, ranging from simple to complex. The method that you choose depends on your application's scope and complexity and how much effort you're willing to put into this phase of development. Some applications might require only a brief set of instructions on how to start them. Others could benefit from a full-blown, searchable Help system. Most often, applications need something in between.

This chapter classifies user help into two categories:

- *Unofficial Help system:* This method of displaying help uses standard Excel components (such as a UserForm).

- *Official Help system:* This Help system uses a compiled CHM file produced by Microsoft's HTML Help Workshop.

Creating a compiled help file is not a trivial task, but it is worth the effort if your application is complex or if it will be used by a large number of people.

 CD-ROM

All the examples in this chapter are available on the companion CD-ROM. Because most examples consist of multiple files, each example is in a separate directory on the CD.

Online Help?

In the past, I've referred to Excel's onscreen assistance as *online help.* In fact, that's the common name for this type of assistance. But in recent years, the term *online* has come to refer to information available via the Internet. Some people were confused by the expression *online help* because the help information is actually stored on their local drives.

Therefore, I now use the expression *Help system* to refer to assistance provided by an application. But, beginning with Excel 2003, things have come full circle. The Help system for Excel 2003 and later is (optionally) truly online. You can view locally stored help information or (with an Internet connection) search for more up-to-date information at the Microsoft Web site.

About the Examples in This Chapter

Many of the examples in this chapter use a simple workbook application to demonstrate various ways of providing help. The application uses data stored in a worksheet to generate and print form letters.

As you can see in the following figure, cells display the total number of records in the database (C2, calculated by a formula), the current record number (C3), the first record to print (C4), and the last record to print (C5). To display a particular record, the user enters a value into cell C3. To print a series of form letters, the user specifies the first and last record numbers in cells C4 and C5.

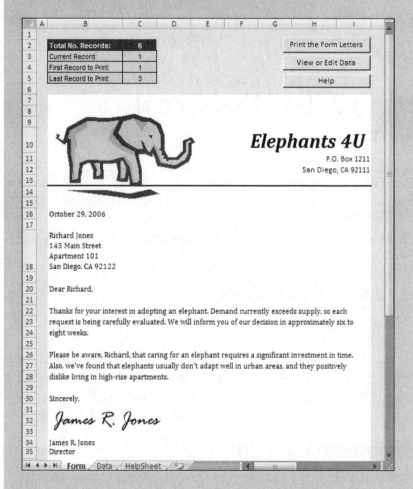

The application is very simple, but it does consist of several discrete components. I use this example to demonstrate various ways of displaying context-sensitive help.

continued

continued

The form letter workbook consists of the following components:

- `Form`: A worksheet that contains the text of the form letter.
- `Data`: A worksheet that contains a seven-field database table.
- `HelpSheet`: A worksheet that's present only in the examples that store help text on a worksheet.
- `PrintMod`: A VBA module that contains macros to print the form letters.
- `HelpMod`: A VBA module that contains macros that control the help display. The content of this module varies depending on the type of help being demonstrated.
- `UserForm1`: A UserForm present only if the help technique involves a UserForm.

Help Systems That Use Excel Components

Perhaps the most straightforward method of providing help to your users is to use the features contained in Excel itself. The primary advantage of this method is that you don't need to learn how to create HTML Help files — which can be a major undertaking and might take longer to develop than your application.

In this section, I provide an overview of some help techniques that use the following built-in Excel components:

- *Cell comments:* This is about as simple as it gets.
- A *text box control:* A simple macro is all it takes to toggle the display of a text box that shows help information.
- A *worksheet:* A simple way to add help is to insert a worksheet, enter your help information, and name its tab *Help.* When the user clicks the tab, the worksheet is activated.
- A *custom UserForm:* A number of techniques involve displaying help text in a UserForm.

Using cell comments for help

Perhaps the simplest way to provide user help is to use cell comments. This technique is most appropriate for describing the type of input that's expected in a cell. When the user moves the mouse pointer over a cell that contains a comment, that comment appears in a small window, like a ToolTip (see Figure 24-1). Another advantage is that this technique does not require any macros.

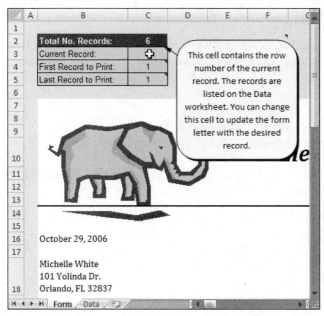

Figure 24-1: Using cell comments to display help.

Automatic display of cell comments is an option. The following VBA instruction, which can be placed in a `Workbook_Open` procedure, ensures that cell comment indicators are displayed for cells that contain comments:

```
Application.DisplayCommentIndicator = xlCommentIndicatorOnly
```

 CD-ROM

A workbook that demonstrates using cell comments is available on the companion CD-ROM. The filename is `cell comments\formletter.xlsm`.

 TIP

Most users don't realize it, but a comment can also display an image. Right-click the comment's border and choose Format Comment from the shortcut menu. In the Format Comment dialog box, select the Colors and Lines tab. Click the Color drop-down list and select Fill Effects. In the Fill Effects dialog box, click the Picture tab and then click the Select Picture button to choose the image file.

Another option is to use Excel's Data ➪ Data Tools ➪ Data Validation command, which displays a dialog box that lets you specify validation criteria for a cell or range. You can just ignore the data validation aspect and use the Input Message tab of the Data Validation dialog box to specify a message that's displayed when the cell is activated. This text is limited to approximately 250 characters.

Part VI

Using a text box for help

Using a text box to display help information is also easy to implement. Simply create a text box by choosing Insert ➪ Text ➪ Text Box, enter the help text, and format it to your liking.

TIP

In lieu of a text box, you can use a different shape and add text to it. Choose Insert ➪ Illustrations ➪ Shapes and choose a shape. Then, just starting typing the text.

Figure 24-2 shows an example of a shape set up to display help information. I added a shadow effect to make the object appear to float above the worksheet.

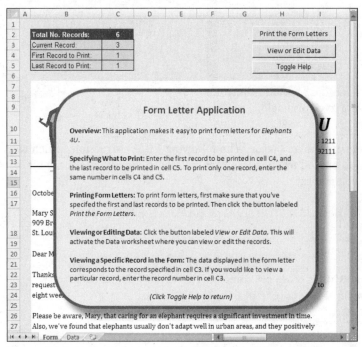

Figure 24-2: Using a shape object with text to display help for the user.

Most of the time, you won't want the text box to be visible. Therefore, you can add a button to your application to execute a macro that toggles the `Visible` property of the text box. An example of such a macro follows. In this case, the TextBox is named `HelpText`.

```
Sub ToggleHelp()
    ActiveSheet.TextBoxes("HelpText").Visible = _
      Not ActiveSheet.TextBoxes("HelpText").Visible
End Sub
```

CD-ROM

A workbook that demonstrates using a text box for help is available on the companion CD-ROM. The filename is `textbox\formletter.xlsm`.

Using a worksheet to display help text

Another easy way to add help to your application is to create a macro that activates a separate worksheet that holds the help information. Just attach the macro to a button control, toolbar button, or menu item, and voilà! . . . quick-and-dirty help.

Figure 24-3 shows a sample help worksheet. I designed the range that contains the help text to simulate a page from a yellow notebook pad — a fancy touch that you might or might not like.

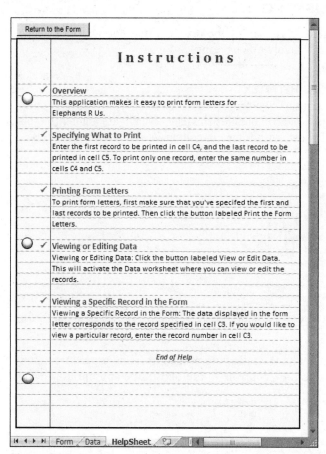

Figure 24-3: Putting user help in a separate worksheet is an easy way to go.

To keep the user from scrolling around the `HelpSheet` worksheet, the macro sets the `ScrollArea` property of the worksheet. Because this property is not stored with the workbook, it's necessary to set it when the worksheet is activated. I also protected the worksheet to prevent the user from changing the text and selecting cells, and I "froze" the first row so that the Return button is always visible, regardless of how far down the sheet the user scrolls.

The main disadvantage of using this technique is that the help text isn't visible along with the main work area. One possible solution is to write a macro that opens a new window to display the sheet.

CD-ROM

The companion CD-ROM contains a workbook named `worksheet\formletter.xlsm` that demonstrates using a worksheet for help.

Displaying help in a UserForm

Another way to provide help to the user is to display the text in a UserForm. In this section, I describe several techniques that involve UserForms.

USING LABEL CONTROLS TO DISPLAY HELP TEXT

Figure 24-4 shows a UserForm that contains two `Label` controls: one for the title and one for the actual help text. A `SpinButton` control enables the user to navigate among the topics. The text itself is stored in a worksheet, with topics in column A and text in column B.

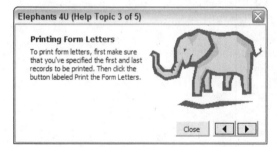

Figure 24-4: Clicking one of the arrows on the SpinButton changes the text displayed in the Labels.

Clicking the `SpinButton` control executes the following procedure. This procedure simply sets the `Caption` property of the two `Label` controls to the text in the appropriate row of the worksheet (named `HelpSheet`).

```
Private Sub SpinButton1_Change()
    HelpTopic = SpinButton1.Value
    LabelTopic.Caption = Sheets("HelpSheet"). _
      Cells(HelpTopic, 1)
    LabelText.Caption = Sheets("HelpSheet").Cells(HelpTopic, 2)
    Me.Caption = APPNAME & " (Help Topic " & HelpTopic & " of " _
      & SpinButton1.Max & ")"
End Sub
```

Using Control Tips in a UserForm

Every UserForm control has a `ControlTipText` property, which can store brief descriptive text. When the user moves the mouse pointer over a control, the Control tip (if any) is displayed in a pop-up window. See the accompanying figure.

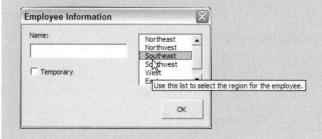

Here, APPNAME is a global constant that contains the application's name.

 CD-ROM

A workbook that demonstrates this technique is available on the companion CD-ROM. The filename is `userform1\formletter.xlsm`.

USING A SCROLLING LABEL TO DISPLAY HELP TEXT

This technique displays help text in a single `Label` control. Because a `Label` control cannot contain a vertical scrollbar, the Label is placed inside a `Frame` control, which *can* contain a scrollbar. Figure 24-5 shows an example of a UserForm set up in this manner. The user can scroll through the text by using the Frame's scrollbar.

Figure 24-5: Inserting a Label control inside a Frame control adds scrolling to the Label.

The text displayed in the Label is read from a worksheet named `HelpSheet` when the UserForm is initialized. Here's the `UserForm_Initialize` procedure for this worksheet.

```
Private Sub UserForm_Initialize()
    Dim LastRow As Long
    Dim r As Long
    Dim txt As String
    Me.Caption = APPNAME & " Help"
    LastRow = Sheets("HelpSheet").Cells(Rows.Count, 1) _
        .End(xlUp).Row
      .End(xlUp).Row
    txt = ""
    For r = 1 To LastRow
        txt = txt & Sheets("HelpSheet").Cells(r, 1) _
          .Text & vbCrLf
    Next r
    With Label1
        .Top = 0
        .Caption = txt
        .Width = 160
        .AutoSize = True
    End With
    With Frame1
        .ScrollHeight = Label1.Height
        .ScrollTop = 0
    End With
End Sub
```

Notice that the code adjusts the Frame's `ScrollHeight` property to ensure that the scrolling covers the complete height of the Label. Again, APPNAME is a global constant that contains the application's name.

Because a Label cannot display formatted text, I used underscore characters in the `HelpSheet` worksheet to delineate the Help topic titles.

 CD-ROM

A workbook that demonstrates this technique is available on the companion CD-ROM as a file named `userform2\formletter.xlsm`.

Using a ComboBox control to select a Help topic

The example in this section improves upon the previous example. Figure 24-6 shows a UserForm that contains a `ComboBox` control and a `Label` control. The user can select a topic from the ComboBox or view the topics sequentially by clicking the Previous or Next buttons.

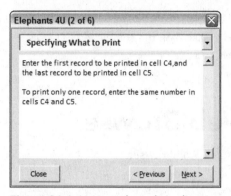

Figure 24-6: Using a drop-down list control to select a help topic.

This example is a bit more complex than the example in the previous section, but it's also much more flexible. It uses the label-within-a-scrolling-frame technique (described previously) to support help text of any length.

The help text is stored in a worksheet named `HelpSheet` in two columns (A and B). The first column contains the topic headings, and the second column contains the text. The ComboBox items are added in the `UserForm_Initialize` procedure. The `CurrentTopic` variable is a module-level variable that stores an integer that represents the Help topic.

```
Private Sub UpdateForm()
    ComboBoxTopics.ListIndex = CurrentTopic - 1
    Me.Caption = HelpFormCaption & _
      " (" & CurrentTopic & " of " & TopicCount & ")"

    With LabelText
        .Caption = HelpSheet.Cells(CurrentTopic, 2)
        .AutoSize = False
        .Width = 212
        .AutoSize = True
    End With
    With Frame1
        .ScrollHeight = LabelText.Height + 5
        .ScrollTop = 1
    End With

    If CurrentTopic = 1 Then
        NextButton.SetFocus
    ElseIf CurrentTopic = TopicCount Then
        PreviousButton.SetFocus
    End If
    PreviousButton.Enabled = CurrentTopic <> 1
    NextButton.Enabled = CurrentTopic <> TopicCount
End Sub
```

> ✍ **CD-ROM**
>
> A workbook that demonstrates this technique is available on the companion CD-ROM. The filename is userform3\formletter.xlsm.

Displaying Help in a Web Browser

This section describes two ways to display user help in a Web browser.

Using HTML files

Yet another way to display help for an Excel application is to create one or more HTML files and provide a hyperlink that displays the file in the default Web browser. The HTML files can be stored locally or on your corporate intranet. You can create the hyperlink to the help file in a cell (macros not required). Figure 24-7 shows an example of help in a browser.

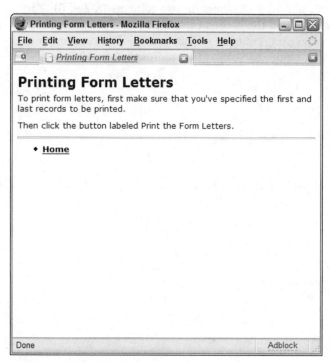

Figure 24-7: Displaying help in a Web browser.

Easy-to-use HTML editors are readily available, and your HTML-based help system can be as simple or as complex as necessary. A disadvantage is that you may need to distribute a large number of HTML files. One solution to this problem is to use an MHTML file, which I describe next.

CD-ROM

A workbook that demonstrates this technique is available on the companion CD-ROM. The filename is `web browser\formletter.xlsm`.

Using an MHTML file

MHTML, which stands for MIME Hypertext Markup Language, is a Web archive format. MHTML files can be displayed by Microsoft Internet Explorer.

The nice thing about using an MHTML file for an Excel Help system is that you can create these files in Excel. Just create your help text using any number of worksheets. Then, choose Office ➪ Save As, click the Save As Type drop-down list, and select Single File Web Page (*.mht; *.mhtml). VBA macros are not saved in this format.

Figure 24-8 shows an MHTML file displayed in Internet Explorer.

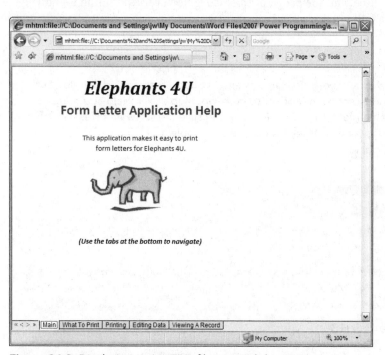

Figure 24-8: Displaying an MHTML file in a Web browser.

In Excel, you can create a hyperlink to display the MHTML file.

CD-ROM

A workbook that demonstrates this technique is available on the companion CD-ROM. The filename is `mhtml file\formletter.xlsm`.

NOTE

If you save a multisheet Excel workbook as an MHTML file, the file will contain Javascript code — which may generate a security warning when the file is opened.

Using the HTML Help System

Currently, the most common Help system used in Windows applications is HTML Help, which uses CHM files. This system replaces the old Windows Help System (WinHelp), which used HLP files (see the sidebar, "Microsoft's Help System Evolution"). Both of these Help systems enable the developer to associate a context ID with a particular help topic. This makes it possible to display a particular help topic in a context-sensitive manner.

In this section, I briefly describe the HTML help-authoring system. Details on creating such Help systems are well beyond the scope of this book. However, you'll find lots of information and examples online.

NOTE

If you plan to develop a large-scale Help system, I strongly recommend that you purchase a help-authoring software product to make your job easier. Help-authoring software makes it much easier to develop Help files because the software takes care of lots of the tedious details for you. Many products are available, including freeware, shareware, and commercial offerings.

Microsoft's Help System Evolution

Over the years, Microsoft has incorporated four different Help systems in its applications and operating systems:

- *WinHelp:* Based on RTF (rich-text formatting) files. This Help system was first used in Windows 3.0, 1990. Multiple RTF files are compiled into a single help file with an .hlp extension. Versions of Microsoft Office prior to Office 2000 use WinHelp.

- *HTML Help:* Based on HTML (HyperText Markup Language) files. This Help system was first used in Internet Explorer 4.0, in 1997. Multiple HTML files are compiled into a single help file with a .chm extension. Office 2000 was the first version of Office to use HTML Help.

- *Microsoft Help 2:* Supports HTML, DHTML, XML, VBScript, and JavaScript. Multiple files are compiled into an .hsx file. This is the Help technology used in Office 2007. This help system is intended for large-scale applications.

- *Assistance Platform Help:* AP Help is the help system used by Windows Vista. This help system may eventually be available for Windows XP.

A compiled HTML Help system transforms a series of HTML files into a compact Help system. Additionally, you can create a combined table of contents and index as well as use keywords for advanced hyperlinking capability. HTML Help can also use additional tools such as graphics files, ActiveX controls, scripting, and DHTML (Dynamic HTML). Figure 24-9 shows an example of a simple HTML Help System.

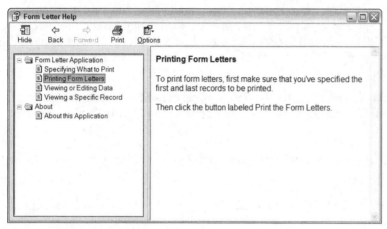

Figure 24-9: An example of HTML Help.

Displaying an Excel Help Topic

In some cases, you may want your VBA code to display a particular topic from Excel's Help system. For example, assume that you'd like to give the user the option to view Excel's Help system information on chart types.

First, you need to determine the Topic ID number of the topic. To do so, locate the topic in the Help system; then right-click and choose Copy Topic ID *xxxx* (where *xxxx* is the ID number for the topic). This shortcut menu command places the Topic ID on the Clipboard so you can paste it into your code. Next, just paste the copied number as the argument for the `ShowHelp` method:

```
Application.Assistance.ShowHelp "HA01233737"
```

Unfortunately, this statement works only if the user's Help system is set up to display local contents only (that is, the Help system is in Offline mode). If the Help system is in Online mode, the preceding statement displays the Help contents. I'm not aware of any way to check if the Help system is currently in Online or Offline mode.

Another option is to use the SearchHelp method, which *does* work when the Help system is in Online mode. Just supply a search term, and the user will see a list of matching Help topics. Here's an example:

```
Application.Assistance.SearchHelp "format chart elements"
```

CD-ROM

A workbook that demonstrates this technique is available on the companion CD-ROM. The filename is `html help\formletter.xlsm`.

HTML Help is displayed by the HTML Help Viewer, which uses the layout engine of Internet Explorer. The information is displayed in a window, and the table of contents, index, and search tools are displayed in a separate pane. In addition, the help text can contain standard hyperlinks that display another topic or even a document on the Internet. It's also important that HTML Help can access files stored on a Web site. This is ideal for directing users to a source of up-to-date information that might not have been available when the Help system was created.

You need a special compiler to create an HTML Help System. The HTML Help Workshop, along with lots of additional information, is available free from the Microsoft Web site at this address:

```
http://msdn.microsoft.com/library/default.asp?url=/library/en-us/htmlhelp/
html/vsconhh1start.asp
```

Figure 24-10 shows the HTML Help Workshop with the project file that created the help system shown in Figure 24-9.

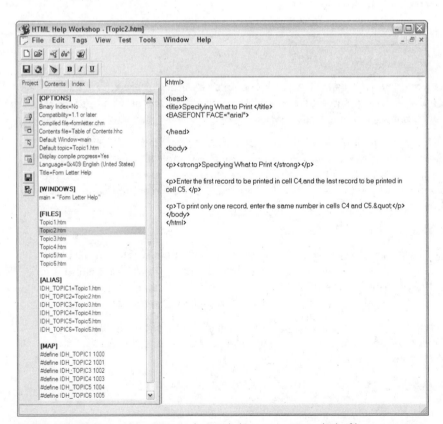

Figure 24-10: Using the HTML Help Workshop to create a help file.

Using the Help method to display HTML Help

Use the `Help` method of the `Application` object to display a Help file — either a WinHelp HLP file or an HTML Help CHM file. This method works even if the Help file doesn't have any context IDs defined.

The syntax for the `Help` method is as follows:

```
Application.Help(helpFile, helpContextID)
```

Both arguments are optional. If the name of the Help file is omitted, Excel's Help file is displayed. If the context ID argument is omitted, the specified Help file is displayed with the default topic.

The following example displays the default topic of `myapp.chm`, which is assumed to be in the same directory as the workbook that it's called from. Note that the second argument is omitted.

```
Sub ShowHelpContents()
    Application.Help ThisWorkbook.Path & "\myapp.chm"
End Sub
```

The following instruction displays the Help topic with a context ID of `1002` from an HTML Help file named `myapp.chm`:

```
Application.Help ThisWorkbook.Path & "\myapp.chm", 1002
```

Using an API function to display HTML help

The `Application.Help` method sometimes doesn't work reliably, so many Excel developers prefer to use an API function to display HTML Help. The API declaration is as follows:

```
Private Declare Function HtmlHelp Lib "HHCtrl.ocx" Alias "HtmlHelpA" _
  (ByVal hwndCaller As Long, ByVal pszFile As String, _
  ByVal uCommand As Long, ByVal dwData As Long) As Long
```

Here's a procedure that calls the `HtmlHelp` function and displays topic 1000. The function returns a value of 0 if the file is not found.

```
Sub ShowHelp()
    Dim Result As Long
    Dim Topic As Long
    Topic = 1000
    Result = HtmlHelp(0, ThisWorkbook.Path & "\formletter.chm", &HF, Topic)
    If Result = 0 Then MsgBox "Cannot display Help", vbCritical, APPNAME
End Sub
```

Associating a Help File with Your Application

You can associate a particular HTML Help file with your Excel application in one of two ways: by using the Project Properties dialog box or by writing VBA code.

In the Visual Basic Editor (VBE), choose Tools ⇨ *xxx* Properties (where *xxx* corresponds to your project's name). In the Project Properties dialog box, click the General tab and specify a compiled HTML Help file for the project. This file should have a .chm extension.

The statement that follows demonstrates how to associate a Help file with your application by using a VBA statement. The following instruction sets up an association to myfuncs.chm, which is assumed to be in the same directory as the workbook:

```
ThisWorkbook.VBProject.HelpFile = ThisWorkbook.Path & "\myfuncs.chm"
```

When a Help file is associated with your application, you can call up a particular Help topic in the following situations:

- When the user presses F1 while a custom worksheet function is selected in the Insert Function dialog box.

- When the user presses F1 while a UserForm is displayed. The Help topic associated with the control that has the focus is displayed.

Associating a help topic with a VBA function

If you create custom worksheet functions with VBA, you might want to associate a Help file and context ID with each function. After these items are assigned to a function, the Help topic can be displayed from the Insert Function dialog box by pressing F1.

To specify a context ID for a custom worksheet function, follow these steps:

1. Create the function as usual.

2. Make sure that your project has an associated Help file (refer to the preceding section).

3. In the VBE, press F2 to activate the Object Browser.

4. Select your project from the Project/Library drop-down list.

5. In the Classes window, select the module that contains your function.

6. In the Members Of window, select the function.

7. Right-click the function and then select Properties from the shortcut menu. This displays the Member Options dialog box, shown in Figure 24-11.

8. Enter the context ID of the Help topic for the function. You can also enter a description of the function.

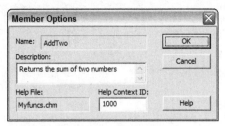

Figure 24-11: Specify a context ID for a custom function in the Member Options dialog box.

 NOTE

The Member Options dialog box does not let you specify the Help file. It always uses the Help file associated with the project.

You might prefer to write VBA code that sets up the context ID and Help file for your custom functions. You can do this by using the `MacroOptions` method.

The following procedure uses the `MacroOptions` method to specify a description, Help file, and context ID for two custom functions (`AddTwo` and `Squared`). You need to execute this macro only one time.

```
Sub SetOptions()
'   Set options for the AddTwo function
    Application.MacroOptions Macro:="AddTwo", _
        Description:="Returns the sum of two numbers", _
        HelpFile:=ThisWorkbook.Path & "\myfuncs.chm", _
        HelpContextID:=1000

'   Set options for the Squared function
    Application.MacroOptions Macro:="Squared", _
        Description:="Returns the square of an argument", _
        HelpFile:=ThisWorkbook.Path & "\myfuncs.chm", _
        HelpContextID:=2000
End Sub
```

After executing these procedures, the user can get help directly from the Insert Function dialog box by pressing F1 or by clicking the Help on This Function hyperlink.

 CD-ROM

A workbook that demonstrates this technique is available on the companion CD-ROM. The filename is `function help\myfuncs.xlsm`.

Chapter 25

Developing User-Oriented Applications

In This Chapter
In this chapter, I attempt to pull together some of the information presented in the previous chapters.

- ◆ A description of a user-oriented application

- ◆ A close look at the Loan Amortization Wizard, which generates a worksheet with an amortization schedule for a fixed-rate loan

- ◆ A demonstration of application development concepts and techniques by the Loan Amortization Wizard

- ◆ An application development checklist

This discussion centers around a user-oriented application called the Loan Amortization Wizard. Useful in its own right, this workbook demonstrates quite a few important application development techniques.

What Is a User-Oriented Application?

I reserve the term *user-oriented application* for an Excel application that can be used by someone with minimal training. These applications produce useful results even for users who know virtually nothing about Excel.

The Loan Amortization Wizard discussed in this chapter qualifies as a user-oriented application because it's designed in such a way that the end user doesn't need to know the intimate details of Excel to use it. Replying to a few simple prompts produces a useful and flexible worksheet complete with formulas.

The Loan Amortization Wizard

The Loan Amortization Wizard generates a worksheet that contains an amortization schedule for a fixed-rate loan. An amortization schedule projects month-by-month details for a loan. The details include the monthly payment amount, the amount of the payment that goes toward interest, the amount that goes toward reducing the principal, and the new loan balance.

An alternative to creating an amortization schedule using a wizard is to create a template file. As you'll see, this wizard approach offers several advantages.

Figure 25-1 shows an amortization schedule generated by the Loan Amortization Wizard.

Pmt No.	Year	Month	Payment	Interest	Principal	Balance
1	2007	6	$2,262.03	$1,983.33	$278.70	$339,721.30
2	2007	7	$2,262.03	$1,981.71	$280.32	$339,440.98
3	2007	8	$2,262.03	$1,980.07	$281.96	$339,159.03
4	2007	9	$2,262.03	$1,978.43	$283.60	$338,875.43
5	2007	10	$2,262.03	$1,976.77	$285.26	$338,590.17
6	2007	11	$2,262.03	$1,975.11	$286.92	$338,303.25
7	2007	12	$2,262.03	$1,973.44	$288.59	$338,014.66
8	2008	1	$2,262.03	$1,971.75	$290.28	$337,724.38
9	2008	2	$2,262.03	$1,970.06	$291.97	$337,432.41
10	2008	3	$2,262.03	$1,968.36	$293.67	$337,138.74
11	2008	4	$2,262.03	$1,966.64	$295.39	$336,843.36
12	2008	5	$2,262.03	$1,964.92	$297.11	$336,546.25
13	2008	6	$2,262.03	$1,963.19	$298.84	$336,247.40
14	2008	7	$2,262.03	$1,961.44	$300.59	$335,946.82
15	2008	8	$2,262.03	$1,959.69	$302.34	$335,644.48
16	2008	9	$2,262.03	$1,957.93	$304.10	$335,340.38
17	2008	10	$2,262.03	$1,956.15	$305.88	$335,034.50
18	2008	11	$2,262.03	$1,954.37	$307.66	$334,726.84

Figure 25-1: This amortization schedule shows details for a 30-year mortgage.

CD-ROM

The Loan Amortization Wizard is available on the CD-ROM that accompanies this book. It's an unprotected add-in named `loan amortization wizard.xlam`.

Using the Loan Amortization Wizard

The Loan Amortization Wizard consists of a five-step dialog box sequence that collects information from the user. Typical of a wizard, this enables the user to go forward and backward through the steps. Clicking the Finish button creates the new worksheet. If all the steps haven't been completed when the user clicks Finish, default values are used. Clicking the Cancel button closes the UserForm, and no action is taken.

This application uses a single UserForm with a `MultiPage` control to display the five steps, shown in Figures 25-2 through 25-6.

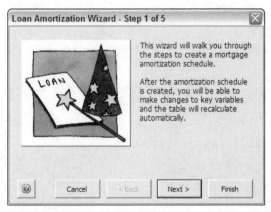

Figure 25-2: Step 1 of the Loan Amortization Wizard.

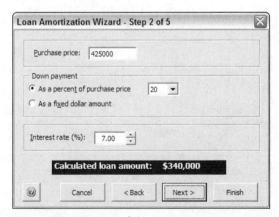

Figure 25-3: Step 2 of the Loan Amortization Wizard.

Part VI

Figure 25-4: Step 3 of the Loan Amortization Wizard.

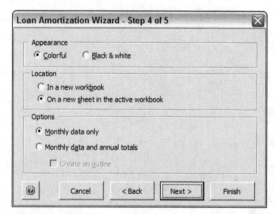

Figure 25-5: Step 4 of the Loan Amortization Wizard.

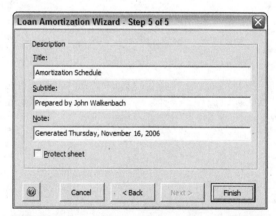

Figure 25-6: Step 5 of the Loan Amortization Wizard.

The Loan Amortization Wizard workbook structure

The Loan Amortization Wizard consists of the following components:

- `FormMain`: A UserForm that serves as the primary user interface.

- `FormHelp`: A UserForm that displays online help.

- `FormMessage`: A UserForm that displays a message when the add-in is opened. The user can disable this display.

- `HelpSheet`: A worksheet that contains the text used in the online help.

- `ModMain`: A VBA module that contains a procedure that displays the main UserForm.

- `ThisWorkbook`: The code module for this object contains the `Workbook_Open` event handler procedure.

In addition, the workbook file contains some simple RibbonX XML code that creates the Loan Amortization Wizard button in the Ribbon.

How the Loan Amortization Wizard works

The Loan Amortization Wizard is an add-in, so you should install it by using the Add-Ins dialog box. To display this dialog box, choose Office ➪ Excel Options ➪ Add-Ins. Then, in the Excel Options dialog box, choose Excel Add-Ins from the Manage drop-down list and click Go. Use the Browse button to locate the add-in file. After it's installed, an add-in remains installed across Excel sessions. The add-in works perfectly well, however, if it's opened with the Office ➪ Open command.

Creating the Loan Amortization Wizard

The Loan Amortization Wizard application started out as a simple concept and evolved into a relatively complex project. My primary goal was to demonstrate as many development concepts as possible and still have a useful end product. I would like to say that I clearly envisioned the end result before I began developing the application, but I'd be lying.

My basic idea was much less ambitious. I simply wanted to create an application that gathered user input and created a worksheet. But, after I got started, I began thinking of ways to enhance my simple program. I eventually stumbled down several blind alleys. Some folks would consider my wanderings time-wasting, but those false starts became a vital part of the development process.

I completed the entire project in one (long) day, and I spent a few more hours fine-tuning and testing it. I added a few more accouterments for the version included in this edition of the book.

MODIFYING THE USER INTERFACE

Every add-in needs a way to be accessed. I added some simple RibbonX code to the file that adds a button to a new group in the Insert tab (see Figure 25-7). Clicking this button executes the StartAmortizationWizard procedure, which simply displays the FormMain UserForm.

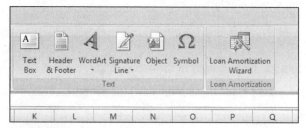

Figure 25-7: A new group on the Insert tab contains one control.

The RibbonX code that creates the Ribbon control is:

```
<customUI xmlns="http://schemas.microsoft.com/office/2006/01/customui">
  <ribbon>
    <tabs>
      <tab idMso="TabInsert">
        <group id="gpUtils" label="Loan Amortization">
          <button id="b1"
            size="large"
            imageMso="CreateQueryFromWizard"
            label="Loan Amortization Wizard"
            supertip="Click here to create an amortization schedule."
            onAction="StartAmortizationWizard"/>
        </group>
      </tab>
    </tabs>
  </ribbon>
</customUI>
```

CROSS-REFERENCE

Refer to Chapter 22 for information about modifying the Ribbon.

DISPLAYING AN INITIAL MESSAGE

I've installed many Excel add-ins over the years, and I've found that many of them don't provide a clue as to how to access the add-in. So, in order to make this application as user-friendly as possible, I added a UserForm that is displayed when the workbook is opened. This form simply tells the user how to start the wizard. Figure 25-8 shows the UserForm.

Figure 25-8: This form is displayed when the Loan Amortization Wizard is opened.

Importantly, this UserForm includes an option to turn off the message in the future.

Following is the `Workbook_Open` procedure that displays the dialog box:

```
Private Sub Workbook_Open()
    If GetSetting(APPNAME, "Defaults", "ShowMessage", "Yes") = "Yes" Then
        FormMessage.Show
    End If
End Sub
```

The user's choice regarding the future display of the UserForm is stored in the Windows Registry. The Registry key is specified by the application's name (a global constant, APP-NAME). The default value is "Yes," so the UserForm will display at least one time.

Following is the code that is executed when the user clicks the OK button:

```
Private Sub OKButton_Click()
    If cbMessage Then
        SaveSetting APPNAME, "Defaults", "ShowMessage", "No"
    Else
        SaveSetting APPNAME, "Defaults", "ShowMessage", "Yes"
    End If
    Unload Me
End Sub
```

If the user checks the check box control, then the registry setting is set to "No," and the UserForm will not be displayed again.

INITIALIZING FORMMAIN FOR THE WIZARD

The `UserForm_Initialize` procedure for `FormMain` does quite a bit of work:

- It sets the `MultiPage` control's `Style` property to `fmTabStyleNone`. The tabs are present in the Visual Basic Editor to make the UserForm easier to edit.

- It sets the `MultiPage` control's `Value` property to `0`. This ensures that it displays the first page, regardless of its value when the workbook was last saved.

- It adds items to three `ComboBox` controls used on the form.

- It calls the GetDefaults procedure, which retrieves the most recently used setting from the Windows Registry (see the upcoming section "Saving and retrieving default settings").

- It checks whether a workbook is active. If no workbook is active, the code disables the OptionButton that enables the user to create the new worksheet in the active workbook.

- If a workbook is active, an additional check determines whether the workbook's structure is protected. If so, the procedure disables the OptionButton that enables the user to create the worksheet in the active workbook.

PROCESSING EVENTS WHILE THE USERFORM IS DISPLAYED

The code module for the FormMain UserForm contains several event handler procedures that respond to the Click and Change events for the controls on the UserForm.

CROSS-REFERENCE

Clicking the Back and Next buttons determines which page of the MultiPage control is displayed. The MultiPage1_Change procedure adjusts the UserForm's caption and enables and disables the Back and Next buttons as appropriate. See Chapter 15 for more information about programming a wizard.

DISPLAYING HELP IN THE WIZARD

You have several options when it comes to displaying online help. I chose a simple technique that employs the UserForm shown in Figure 25-9 to display text stored in a worksheet. You'll notice that this help is context-sensitive. When the user clicks the Help button, the Help topic displayed is relevant to the current page of the MultiPage control.

Figure 25-9: User help is presented in a UserForm that copies text stored in a worksheet.

CROSS-REFERENCE

For more information about the technique of transferring worksheet text to a UserForm, consult Chapter 24.

CREATING THE NEW WORKSHEET

When the user clicks the Finish button, the action begins. The `Click` event handler procedure for this button performs the following actions:

- It calls a function named `DataIsValid`, which checks the user's input to ensure that it's valid. If all the entries are valid, the function returns `True`, and the procedure continues. If an invalid entry is encountered, `DataIsValid` sets the focus to the control that needs to be corrected and returns a descriptive error message (see Figure 25-10).

Figure 25-10: If an invalid entry is made, the focus is set back to the control that contains the error.

- If the user's responses are valid, the procedure creates a new worksheet either in the active workbook or in a new workbook, per the user's request.

- The loan *parameters* (purchase price, down payment information, loan amount, term, and interest rate) are written to the worksheet. This requires the use of some `If` statements because the down payment can be expressed as a percentage of the purchase price or as a fixed amount.

- The column headers are written to the worksheet.

- The first row of formulas is written below the column headers. The first row is different from the remaining rows because its formulas refer to data in the loan parameters section. The other formulas all refer to the previous row. Notice that I use named ranges in the formulas. These are sheet-level names, so the user can store more than one amortization schedule in the same workbook.

- For unnamed references, I use row number and column number notation, which is much easier than trying to determine actual cell addresses.

- The second row of formulas is written to the worksheet and then copied down one row for each month.

- If the user requested annual totals as opposed to simply monthly data, the procedure uses the Subtotal method to create subtotals. This, by the way, is an example of how using a native feature in Excel can save *lots* of coding.

- Because subtotaling the Balance column isn't appropriate, the procedure replaces formulas in the balance column with a formula that returns the year-end balance.

- When Excel adds subtotals, it also creates an outline. If the user didn't request an outline, the procedure uses the ClearOutline method to remove it. If an outline was requested, the procedure hides the outline symbols.

- Next, the procedure applies formatting to the cells: number formatting, plus an AutoFormat if the user requested color output.

- The amortization schedule is then converted to a table, and a style is applied based on the user's choice of black-and-white or color.

- The procedure then adjusts the column widths, freezes the titles just below the header row, and protects the formulas and a few other key cells that shouldn't be changed.

- If the Protect Sheet option is specified in Step 5, the sheet is protected (but not with a password).

- Finally, the SaveDefaults procedure writes the current values of the UserForm's controls to the Windows Registry. These values will be the new default settings the next time the user creates an amortization schedule. (See the following section.)

SAVING AND RETRIEVING DEFAULT SETTINGS

If you run this application, you'll notice that the FormMain UserForm always displays the setting that you most recently used. In other words, it remembers your last choices and uses them as the new default values. This step makes it very easy to generate multiple *what-if* amortization schedules that vary in only a single parameter. This is accomplished by storing the values in the Windows Registry and then retrieving them when the UserForm is initialized. When the application is used for the first time, the Registry doesn't have any values, so it uses the default values stored in the UserForm controls.

The following GetDefaults procedure loops through each control on the UserForm. If the control is a TextBox, ComboBox, OptionButton, CheckBox, or SpinButton, it calls VBA's GetSetting function and reads the value to the Registry. Note that the third argument for GetSetting is the value to use if the setting is not found. In this case, it uses the value of the control specified at design time. APPNAME is a global constant that contains the name of the application.

```
Sub GetDefaults()
'    Reads default settings from the registry
    Dim ctl As Control
    Dim CtrlType As String
```

```
For Each ctl In Me.Controls
    CtrlType = TypeName(ctl)
    If CtrlType = "TextBox" Or _
        CtrlType = "ComboBox" Or _
        CtrlType = "OptionButton" Or _
        CtrlType = "CheckBox" Or _
        CtrlType = "SpinButton" Then
        ctl.Value = GetSetting _
            (APPNAME, "Defaults", ctl.Name, ctl.Value)
    End If
    Next ctl
End Sub
```

Figure 25-11 shows how these values appear in the Registry, from the perspective of the Windows Registry Editor program.

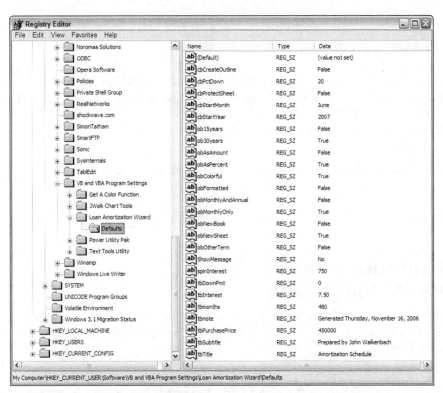

Figure 25-11: The Windows Registry stores the default values for the wizard.

The following `SaveDefaults` procedure is similar. It uses VBA's `SaveSetting` statement to write the current values to the Registry:

```
Sub SaveDefaults()
'   Writes current settings to the registry
    Dim ctl As Control
    Dim CtrlType As String

    For Each ctl In Me.Controls
        CtrlType = TypeName(ctl)
        If CtrlType = "TextBox" Or _
            CtrlType = "ComboBox" Or _
            CtrlType = "OptionButton" Or _
            CtrlType = "CheckBox" Or _
            CtrlType = "SpinButton" Then
            SaveSetting APPNAME, "Defaults", ctl.Name, CStr(ctl.Value)
        End If
    Next ctl
End Sub
```

Notice that the code uses the `CStr` function to convert each setting to a string. This is to avoid problems for those who use non-English regional settings. Without the string conversion, `True` and `False` are translated to the user's language before they are stored in the Registry. But they are *not* translated back to English when the setting is retrieved — which causes an error.

The `SaveSetting` statement and the `GetSetting` function always use the following Registry key:

```
HKEY_CURRENT_USER\Software\VB and VBA Program Settings\
```

Potential enhancements for the Loan Amortization Wizard

It's been said that you never finish writing an application — you just stop working on it. Without even thinking too much about it, I can come up with several enhancements for the Loan Amortization Wizard:

- An option to display cumulative totals for interest and principal

- An option to work with adjustable-rate loans and make projections based on certain interest rate scenarios

- More formatting options (for example, no decimal places, no dollar signs, and so on)

- Options to enable the user to specify page headers or footers

Application Development Concepts

It's often difficult to follow the logic in an application developed by someone other than yourself. To help you understand my work, I included lots of comments in the code and described the general program flow in the preceding sections. But, if you really want to understand this application, I suggest that you use the Debugger to step through the code.

At the very least, the Loan Amortization Wizard demonstrates some useful techniques and concepts that are important for Excel developers:

- Modifying the Ribbon.

- Using a wizard-like UserForm to gather information.

- Setting the `Enabled` property of a control dynamically.

- Linking a `TextBox` and a `SpinButton` control.

- Displaying online help to a user.

- Naming cells with VBA.

- Writing and copying formulas with VBA.

- Reading from and writing to the Windows Registry.

Application Development Checklist

When developing user-oriented applications, you need to keep in mind many things. Let the following checklist serve as a reminder:

- *Do the dialog boxes all work from the keyboard?* Don't forget to add hot keys and check the tab order carefully.

- *Did you make any assumptions about directories?* If your application reads or writes files, you can't assume that a particular directory exists or that it's the current directory.

- *Did you make provisions for canceling all dialog boxes?* You can't assume that the user will end a dialog box by clicking the OK button.

- *Did you assume that no other worksheets are open?* If your application is the only workbook open during testing, you could overlook something that happens when other workbooks are open.

- *Did you assume that a workbook is visible?* It's possible, of course, to use Excel with no workbooks visible.

continued

continued

- *Did you attempt to optimize the speed of your application?* For example, you often can speed up your application by declaring variable types and defining object variables.

- *Are your procedures adequately documented?* Will you understand your code if you revisit it in six months?

- *Did you include appropriate end-user documentation?* Doing so often eliminates (or at least reduces) the number of follow-up questions.

- *Did you allow time to revise your application?* Chances are the application won't be perfect the first time out. Build in some time to fix it.

Developing user-oriented applications in Excel is not easy. You must be keenly aware of how people will use (and abuse) the application in real life. Although I tried to make this application completely bulletproof, I did not do extensive real-world testing, so I wouldn't be surprised if it fails under some conditions.

Part VII

Other Topics

Chapter 26

Compatibility Issues

In This Chapter

If your application also needs to run on earlier versions of Excel, Excel for Macintosh, or international versions of Excel, you must be aware of some potential issues. These issues are the topic of this chapter:

◆ How to increase the probability that your Excel 2007 applications will also work with previous versions of Excel

◆ Issues to be aware of if you're developing Excel applications for international use

If the applications that you've developed with Excel 2007 will be used only by others who also use the same version of Excel, you can skip this chapter.

What Is Compatibility?

Compatibility is an oft-used term among computer people. In general, it refers to how well software performs under various conditions. These conditions might be defined in terms of hardware, software, or a combination of the two. For example, software that is written specifically for a 32-bit operating system such as Windows XP will not run under the older 16-bit versions of Windows 3.*x*. In other words, 32-bit applications are not compatible with Windows 3.*x*. And, as I'm sure you realize, software written for Windows will not run directly on other operating systems, such as Macintosh or Linux.

In this chapter, I discuss a more specific compatibility issue involving how your Excel 2007 applications will work with earlier versions of Excel for Windows and Excel for Macintosh. The fact that two versions of Excel might use the same file format isn't always enough to ensure complete compatibility between the contents of their files. For example, Excel 97, Excel 2000, Excel 2002, Excel 2003, and Excel 2002 for Macintosh all use the same file format, but compatibility issues are rampant. Just because a particular version of Excel can open a worksheet file or an add-in doesn't guarantee that that version of Excel can carry out the VBA macro instructions contained in it.

The past few releases of Excel have been relatively minor upgrades. Consequently, compatibility problems were minimal. The introduction of Excel 2007, however, greatly increases the number and types of potential compatibility problems. Besides using a new file format, Excel 2007 includes many new features that aren't available in earlier versions.

Excel is a moving target, and there is really no way that you can guarantee complete compatibility. Unfortunately, cross-version compatibility doesn't happen automatically. In most cases, you need to do quite a bit of additional work to achieve compatibility.

Types of Compatibility Problems

You need to be aware of several categories of potential compatibility problems. These are listed here and discussed further in this chapter:

- *File format issues:* Workbooks can be saved in several different Excel file formats. Earlier versions of Excel might not be able to open workbooks that were saved in a later version's file format. For more information about sharing Excel 2007 files, see the sidebar, "The Office 2007 Compatibility Pack."

- *New feature issues:* It should be obvious that a feature introduced in a particular version of Excel cannot be used in previous versions of Excel.

- *Microsoft issues:* For whatever reason, Microsoft itself is responsible for some types of compatibility issues. For example, as I note in Chapter 23, index numbers for shortcut menus have not remained consistent across Excel versions.

- *Windows versus Macintosh issues:* If your application must work on both platforms, plan to spend lots of time ironing out various compatibility problems.

- *International issues:* If your application will be used by those who speak another language, you must address a number of additional issues.

After reading this chapter, it should be clear that there is only one way to ensure compatibility: You must test your application on every target platform and with every target version of Excel. Often, this is simply not feasible. However, there are measures that you, as a developer, can take to help ensure that your application works with different versions of Excel.

The Office 2007 Compatibility Pack

If you plan to share your Excel 2007 application with others who haven't upgraded to Excel 2007, you have two choices:

- Always save your files in the older XLS file format.

- Make sure the recipients of your files have installed the Microsoft Office Compatibility Pack.

The Microsoft Office Compatibility Pack is a free download available at www.microsoft.com. When installed, Office XP and Office 2003 users can open, edit, and save documents, workbooks, and presentations in the new file formats for Word 2007, Excel 2007, and PowerPoint 2007.

Keep in mind that this compatibility pack does not endow earlier versions of Excel with any of the new features in Excel 2007. It simply allows those users to open and save files in the new file format.

NOTE

If you're reading this chapter in search of a complete list of specific compatibility issues among the various versions of Excel, you will be disappointed. As far as I know, no such list exists, and it would be virtually impossible to compile one. These types of issues are far too numerous and complex.

TIP

A good source for information about potential compatibility problems is Microsoft's online Knowledge Base. The URL is:

> http://search.support.microsoft.com

This will often help you identify bugs that appear in a particular version of Excel.

Avoid Using New Features

If your application must work with both Excel 2007 and earlier versions, you need to avoid any features that were added after the earliest Excel version that you will support. Another alternative is to incorporate the new features selectively. In other words, your code can determine which version of Excel is being used and then take advantage of the new features or not.

VBA programmers must be careful not to use any objects, properties, or methods that aren't available in earlier versions. In general, the safest approach is to develop your application for the lowest common denominator. For compatibility with Excel 2000 and later, you should use Excel 2000 for development; then test thoroughly by using the other versions.

Determining Excel's Version Number

The `Version` property of the `Application` object returns the version of Excel. The returned value is a string, so you might need to convert it to a value. VBA's `Val` function is perfect for this. The following function, for example, returns `True` if the user is running Excel 2007 or later. (**Note:** Excel 2007 is version 12.)

```
Function XL12OrLater()
    XL12OrLater = Val(Application.Version) >= 12
End Function
```

A very useful feature in Excel 2007 is the Compatibility Checker, shown in Figure 26-1. Display this dialog box by choosing Office ⇨ Prepare ⇨ Run Compatibility Checker. The Compatibility Checker identifies any compatibility issues that might cause a problem if the file is opened using an earlier version of Excel.

Unfortunately, the Compatibility Checker doesn't even look at the VBA code — which is a prime candidate for compatibility problems.

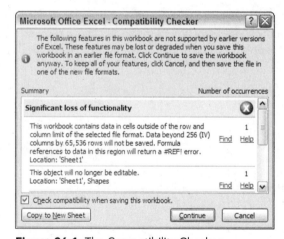

Figure 26-1: The Compatibility Checker.

But Will It Work on a Mac?

One of the most prevalent problems that I hear about is Macintosh compatibility. Excel for Macintosh represents a very small proportion of the total Excel market, and many developers choose simply to ignore it. The good news is that the old Excel XLS file format is compatible across both platforms. The bad news is that the features supported are not identical, and VBA macro compatibility is far from perfect.

NOTE

As I write this, Microsoft has not released a compatibility pack for the Macintosh version of Excel — although, apparently, one is in the works. In addition, Microsoft has announced that future versions of Excel for Macintosh will no longer support VBA.

You can write VBA code to determine which platform your application is running. The following function accesses the OperatingSystem property of the Application object and returns True if the operating system is any version of Windows (that is, if the returned string contains the text "Win"):

```
Function WindowsOS() As Boolean
    If Application.OperatingSystem like "*Win*" Then
        WindowsOS = True
    Else
        WindowsOS = False
    End If
End Function
```

Many subtle (and not so subtle) differences exist between the Windows versions and the Mac versions of Excel. Many of those differences are cosmetic (for example, different default fonts), but others are much more serious. For example, Excel for Macintosh doesn't include ActiveX controls. Also, it uses the 1904 date system as the default, so workbooks that use dates could be off by four years. Excel for Windows, by default, uses the 1900 date system. On the Macintosh, a date serial number of 1 refers to January 1, 1904; in Excel for Windows, that same serial number represents January 1, 1900.

Another limitation concerns Windows API functions: They won't work with Excel for Macintosh. If your application depends on such functions, you need to develop a workaround.

If your code deals with paths and filenames, you need to construct your path with the appropriate path separator (a colon for the Macintosh, a backslash for Windows). A better approach is to avoid hard-coding the path separator character and use VBA to determine it. The following statement assigns the path separator character to a variable named PathSep:

```
PathSep = Application.PathSeparator
```

After this statement is executed, your code can use the PathSep variable in place of a hard-coded colon or backslash.

Rather than try to make a single file compatible with both platforms, most developers choose to develop on one platform (typically Excel for Windows) and then modify the application so that it works on the Mac platform. In other words, you'll probably need to maintain two separate versions of your application.

There is only one way to make sure that your application is compatible with the Macintosh version of Excel: You must test it thoroughly on a Macintosh — and be prepared to develop some workarounds for routines that don't work correctly.

Part VII

Creating an International Application

The final compatibility concern deals with language issues and international settings. Excel is available in many different language versions. The following statement displays the country code for the version of Excel:

```
MsgBox Application.International(xlCountryCode)
```

The United States/English version of Excel has a country code of 1. Other country codes are listed in Table 26-1.

TABLE 26-1 EXCEL COUNTRY CODES

Country	Country Code
English	1
Russian	7
Greek	30
Dutch	31
French	33
Spanish	34
Hungarian	36
Italian	39
Czech	42
Danish	45
Swedish	46
Norwegian	47
Polish	48
German	49
Portuguese (Brazil)	55
Thai	66
Japanese	81
Korean	82
Vietnamese	84
Simplified Chinese	86

Country	Country Code
Turkish	90
Indian	91
Urdu	92
Portuguese	351
Finnish	358
Traditional Chinese	886
Arabic	966
Hebrew	972
Farsi	982

If your application will be used by those who speak another language, you need to ensure that the proper language is used in your dialog boxes. Also, you need to identify the user's decimal and thousands separator characters. In the United States, these are almost always a period and a comma, respectively. However, users in other countries might have their systems set up to use other characters. Yet another issue is date and time formats: The United States is one of the few countries that use the (illogical) month/day/year format.

If you're developing an application that will be used only by people with your company, you probably won't need to be concerned with international compatibility. But, if your company has offices throughout the world, or if you plan to distribute your application outside your country, you need to address a number of issues to ensure that your application will work properly. I discuss these issues in the following sections.

Multilanguage applications

An obvious consideration involves the language that is used in your application. For example, if you use one or more dialog boxes, you probably want the text to appear in the language of the user. Fortunately, this is not too difficult (assuming, of course, that you can translate your text or know someone who can).

 CD-ROM

The companion CD-ROM contains an example that demonstrates how to allow the user to choose from three languages in a dialog box: English, Spanish, or German. The filename is `multilingual wizard.xlsm`.

The first step of the multilingual wizard (found on the CD) contains three OptionButtons that enable the user to select a language. The text for the three languages is stored in a worksheet.

Figure 26-2 shows the UserForm displaying text in all three languages.

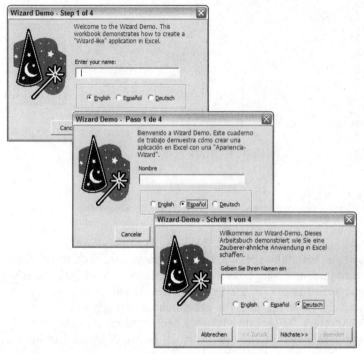

Figure 26-2: The Wizard Demo in English, Spanish, and German.

VBA language considerations

In general, you need not be concerned with the language in which you write your VBA code. Excel uses two object libraries: the Excel object library and the VBA object library. When you install Excel, it registers the English language version of these object libraries as the default libraries. (This is true regardless of the language version of Excel.)

Using local properties

If your code will display worksheet information, such as a formula or a range address, you probably want to use the local language. For example, the following statement displays the formula in cell A1:

```
MsgBox Range("A1").Formula
```

For international applications, a better approach is to use the FormulaLocal property rather than the Formula property:

```
MsgBox Range("A1").FormulaLocal
```

Several other properties also have local versions. These are shown in Table 26-2 (refer to the Help system for specific details).

TABLE 26-2   PROPERTIES THAT HAVE LOCAL VERSIONS

Property	Local Version	Return Contents
Address	AddressLocal	An address
Category	CategoryLocal	A function category
Formula	FormulaLocal	A formula
FormulaR1C1	FormulaR1C1Local	A formula, using R1C1 notation
Name	NameLocal	A name
NumberFormat	NumberFormatLocal	A number format
RefersTo	RefersToLocal	A reference
RefersToR1C1	RefersToR1C1Local	A reference, using R1C1 notation

Identifying system settings

Generally, you cannot assume that the end user's system is set up like the system on which you develop your application. For international applications, you need to be aware of the following settings:

- *Decimal separator:* The character used to separate the decimal portion of a value.

- *Thousands separator:* The character used to delineate every three digits in a value.

- *List separator:* The character used to separate items in a list.

You can determine the current separator settings by accessing the `International` property of the `Application` object. For example, the following statement displays the decimal separator, which won't always be a period:

```
MsgBox Application.International(xlDecimalSeparator)
```

The 45 international settings that you can access with the `International` property are listed in Table 26-3.

TABLE 26-3   CONSTANTS FOR THE INTERNATIONAL PROPERTY

Constant	What It Returns
xlCountryCode	Country version of Microsoft Excel.
xlCountrySetting	Current country setting in the Windows Control Panel.
xlDecimalSeparator	Decimal separator.
xlThousandsSeparator	Thousands separator.
xlListSeparator	List separator.
xlUpperCaseRowLetter	Uppercase row letter (for R1C1-style references).
xlUpperCaseColumnLetter	Uppercase column letter.
xlLowerCaseRowLetter	Lowercase row letter.
xlLowerCaseColumnLetter	Lowercase column letter.
xlLeftBracket	Character used instead of the left bracket ([) in R1C1-style relative references.
xlRightBracket	Character used instead of the right bracket (]) in R1C1-style references.
xlLeftBrace	Character used instead of the left brace ({) in array literals.
xlRightBrace	Character used instead of the right brace (}) in array literals.
xlColumnSeparator	Character used to separate columns in array literals.
xlRowSeparator	Character used to separate rows in array literals.
xlAlternateArraySeparator	Alternate array item separator to be used if the current array separator is the same as the decimal separator.
xlDateSeparator	Date separator (/).
xlTimeSeparator	Time separator (:).
xlYearCode	Year symbol in number formats (y).
xlMonthCode	Month symbol (m).
xlDayCode	Day symbol (d).
xlHourCode	Hour symbol (h).
xlMinuteCode	Minute symbol (m).
xlSecondCode	Second symbol (s).
xlCurrencyCode	Currency symbol.

Constant	What It Returns
xlGeneralFormatName	Name of the General number format.
xlCurrencyDigits	Number of decimal digits to be used in currency formats.
xlCurrencyNegative	A value that represents the currency format for negative currency values.
xlNoncurrencyDigits	Number of decimal digits to be used in noncurrency formats.
xlMonthNameChars	Always returns three characters for backward-compatibility; abbreviated month names are read from Microsoft Windows and can be any length.
xlWeekdayNameChars	Always returns three characters for backward-compatibility; abbreviated weekday names are read from Microsoft Windows and can be any length.
xlDateOrder	An integer that represents the order of date elements.
xl24HourClock	True if the system is using 24-hour time; False if the system is using 12-hour time.
xlNonEnglishFunctions	True if the system is not displaying functions in English.
xlMetric	True if the system is using the metric system; False if the system is using the English measurement system.
xlCurrencySpaceBefore	True if a space is added before the currency symbol.
xlCurrencyBefore	True if the currency symbol precedes the currency values; False if it follows them.
xlCurrencyMinusSign	True if the system is using a minus sign for negative numbers; False if the system is using parentheses.
xlCurrencyTrailingZeros	True if trailing zeros are displayed for zero currency values.
xlCurrencyLeadingZeros	True if leading zeros are displayed for zero currency values.
xlMonthLeadingZero	True if a leading zero is displayed in months (when months are displayed as numbers).
xlDayLeadingZero	True if a leading zero is displayed in days.
xl4DigitYears	True if the system is using four-digit years; False if the system is using two-digit years.

continued

TABLE 26-3   CONSTANTS FOR THE INTERNATIONAL PROPERTY *(continued)*

Constant	What It Returns
xlMDY	True if the date order is month-day-year for dates displayed in the long form; False if the date order is day/month/year.
xlTimeLeadingZero	True if a leading zero is displayed in times.

Date and time settings

If your application writes formatted dates and will be used in other countries, you might want to make sure that the date is in a format familiar to the user. The best approach is to specify a date by using VBA's DateSerial function and let Excel take care of the formatting details (it will use the user's short date format).

The following procedure uses the DateSerial function to assign a date to the StartDate variable. This date is then written to cell A1 with the local short date format.

```
Sub WriteDate()
    Dim StartDate As Date
    StartDate = DateSerial(2007, 4, 15)
    Range("A1") = StartDate
End Sub
```

If you need to do any other formatting for the date, you can write code to do so after the date has been entered into the cell. Excel provides several named date and time formats, plus quite a few named number formats. These are all described in the online help (search for *named date/time formats* or *named numeric formats*).

Chapter 27

Manipulating Files with VBA

In This Chapter

In this chapter, I describe how to use Visual Basic for Applications (VBA) to perform common (and not so common) file operations and work directly with text files.

- ◆ A basic overview of VBA text file manipulation features
- ◆ Performing common file operations
- ◆ Various ways to open a text file
- ◆ Displaying extended file information, such as details for media files
- ◆ Examples of reading and writing a text file with VBA
- ◆ Sample code for exporting a range to HTML and XML format
- ◆ Zipping and unzipping files

Many applications that you develop for Excel require working with external files. For example, you might need to get a listing of files in a directory, delete files, rename files, and so on. Excel, of course, can import and export several types of text files. In many cases, however, Excel's built-in text file handling isn't sufficient. For example, you might want to export a range of cells to a simple HyperText Markup Language (HTML) file.

Performing Common File Operations

Excel provides two ways to perform common file operations:

- *Use traditional VBA statements and functions.* This method works for all versions of Excel.
- *Use the FileSystemObject object, which uses the Microsoft Scripting Library.* This method works for Excel 2000 and later.

 NEW

Previous versions of Excel also supported the use of the `FileSearch` object. That feature has been removed from Excel 2007. If you execute an old macro that uses the `FileSearch` object, the macro will fail.

In the sections that follow, I discuss these two methods and present examples.

Using VBA file-related commands

The VBA commands that you can use to work with files are summarized in Table 27-1. Most of these commands are straightforward, and all are described in the Help system.

TABLE 27-1   VBA FILE-RELATED COMMANDS

Command	What It Does
ChDir	Changes the current directory.
ChDrive	Changes the current drive.
Dir	Returns a filename or directory that matches a specified pattern or file attribute.
FileCopy	Copies a file.
FileDateTime	Returns the date and time when a file was last modified.
FileLen	Returns the size of a file, in bytes.
GetAttr	Returns a value that represents an attribute of a file.
Kill	Deletes a file.
MkDir	Creates a new directory.
Name	Renames a file or directory.
RmDir	Removes an empty directory.
SetAttr	Changes an attribute for a file.

The remainder of this section consists of examples that demonstrate some of the file manipulation commands.

A VBA FUNCTION TO DETERMINE WHETHER A FILE EXISTS

The following function returns `True` if a particular file exists and `False` if it does not exist. If the `Dir` function returns an empty string, the file could not be found, so the function returns `False`.

```
Function FileExists(fname) As Boolean
    FileExists = Dir(fname) <> ""
End Function
```

The argument for the `FileExists` function consists of a full path and filename. The function can be either used in a worksheet or called from a VBA procedure.

A VBA FUNCTION TO DETERMINE WHETHER A PATH EXISTS

The following function returns `True` if a specified path exists and `False` otherwise:

```
Function PathExists(pname) As Boolean
'   Returns TRUE if the path exists
    On Error Resume Next
    PathExists = (GetAttr(pname) And vbDirectory) = vbDirectory
End Function
```

CD-ROM

The `FileExists` and `PathExists` functions are available on the CD-ROM. The filename is `file functions.xlsm`.

A VBA PROCEDURE TO DISPLAY A LIST OF FILES IN A DIRECTORY

The following procedure displays (in the active worksheet) a list of files contained in a particular directory, along with the file size and date:

```
Sub ListFiles()
    Dim Directory As String
    Dim r As Long
    Dim f As String
    Directory = "f:\excelfiles\budgeting\"
    r = 1
'   Insert headers
    Cells(r, 1) = "FileName"
    Cells(r, 2) = "Size"
    Cells(r, 3) = "Date/Time"
    Range("A1:C1").Font.Bold = True
'   Get first file
```

```
    f = Dir(Directory, vbReadOnly + vbHidden + vbSystem)
    Do While f <> ""
        r = r + 1
        Cells(r, 1) = f
        Cells(r, 2) = FileLen(Directory & f)
        Cells(r, 3) = FileDateTime(Directory & f)
    '   Get next file
        f = Dir()
    Loop
End Sub
```

Figure 27-1 shows an example of the output of the `ListFiles` subroutine.

	A	B	C	D	E
1	Files in C:\Program Files\Mozilla Firefox\	Size	Date/Time		
2	.autoreg	0	8/13/2006 13:04		
3	AccessibleMarshal.dll	8322	8/13/2006 13:04		
4	active-update.xml	57	8/13/2006 13:04		
5	browserconfig.properties	230	8/13/2006 13:04		
6	components.ini	24	9/25/2005 15:11		
7	defaults.ini	24	9/25/2005 15:11		
8	firefox.exe	7183469	8/13/2006 13:04		
9	install.log	27042	5/19/2006 7:41		
10	install_status.log	1921	12/1/2005 10:12		
11	install_wizard.log	2983	12/1/2005 10:12		
12	js3250.dll	416359	8/13/2006 13:04		
13	LICENSE	30869	8/13/2006 13:04		
14	nspr4.dll	155758	8/13/2006 13:04		
15	nss3.dll	364646	8/13/2006 13:04		
16	nssckbi.dll	237677	8/13/2006 13:04		
17	plc4.dll	28787	8/13/2006 13:04		
18	plds4.dll	24686	8/13/2006 13:04		
19	readme.txt	177	8/13/2006 13:04		
20	removed-files	1644	8/13/2006 13:04		

Figure 27-1: Output from the ListFiles procedure.

Notice that the procedure uses the `Dir` function twice. The first time (used with an argument), it retrieves the first filename found. Subsequent calls (without an argument) retrieve additional filenames. When no more files are found, the `Dir` function returns an empty string.

 CD-ROM

The companion CD-ROM contains a version of this procedure that uses the `GetDirectory` function (described in Chapter 12), which allows you to select a directory from a dialog box. The filename is `create file list.xlsm`.

The `Dir` function also accepts wildcard file specifications in its first argument. To get a list of Excel files, for example, you could use a statement such as this:

```
f = Dir(Directory & "*.xl??", vbReadOnly + vbHidden + vbSystem)
```

This statement retrieves the name of the first `*.xl??` file in the specified directory. The wildcard specification returns a four-character extension that begins with XL. For example, the extension could be XLSX, XLTX, or XLAM. The second argument for the `Dir` function lets you specify the attributes of the files (in terms of built-in constants). In this example, the `Dir` function retrieves filenames that have no attributes, read-only files, hidden files, and system files.

Table 27-2 lists the built-in constants for the `Dir` function.

TABLE 27-2   FILE ATTRIBUTE CONSTANTS FOR THE DIR FUNCTION

Constant	Value	Description
`vbNormal`	0	Files with no attributes. This is the default setting and is always in effect.
`vbReadOnly`	1	Read-only files.
`vbHidden`	2	Hidden files.
`vbSystem`	4	System files.
`vbVolume`	8	Volume label. If any other attribute is specified, this attribute is ignored.
`vbDirectory`	16	Directories. This attribute does not work. Calling the `Dir` function with the `vbDirectory` attribute does not continually return subdirectories.

CAUTION

If you use the `Dir` function to loop through files and call another procedure to process the files, make sure the other procedure does not use the `Dir` function. Only one "set" of `Dir` calls can be active at any time.

A RECURSIVE VBA PROCEDURE TO DISPLAY A LIST OF FILES IN NESTED DIRECTORIES

The example in this section creates a list of files in a specified directory, including all of its subdirectories. This procedure is unusual because it calls itself — a concept known as *recursion*.

```vba
Public Sub RecursiveDir(ByVal CurrDir As String, Optional ByVal Level As Long)
    Dim Dirs() As String
    Dim NumDirs As Long
    Dim FileName As String
    Dim PathAndName As String
    Dim i As Long

'   Make sure path ends in backslash
    If Right(CurrDir, 1) <> "\" Then CurrDir = CurrDir & "\"

'   Put column headings on active sheet
    Cells(1, 1) = "Path"
    Cells(1, 2) = "Filename"
    Cells(1, 3) = "Size"
    Cells(1, 4) = "Date/Time"
    Range("A1:D1").Font.Bold = True

'   Get files
    FileName = Dir(CurrDir & "*.*", vbDirectory)
    Do While Len(FileName) <> 0
      If Left(FileName, 1) <> "." Then 'Current dir
        PathAndName = CurrDir & FileName
        If (GetAttr(PathAndName) And vbDirectory) = vbDirectory Then
          'store found directories
           ReDim Preserve Dirs(0 To NumDirs) As String
           Dirs(NumDirs) = PathAndName
           NumDirs = NumDirs + 1
        Else
          'Write the path and file to the sheet
          Cells(WorksheetFunction.CountA(Range("A:A")) + 1, 1) = _
             CurrDir
          Cells(WorksheetFunction.CountA(Range("B:B")) + 1, 2) = _
             FileName
          Cells(WorksheetFunction.CountA(Range("C:C")) + 1, 3) = _
             FileLen(PathAndName)
          Cells(WorksheetFunction.CountA(Range("D:D")) + 1, 4) = _
             FileDateTime(PathAndName)
        End If
      End If
        FileName = Dir()
    Loop
    ' Process the found directories, recursively
    For i = 0 To NumDirs - 1
        RecursiveDir Dirs(i), Level + 2
    Next i
End Sub
```

The procedure takes one argument, `CurrDir`, which is the directory being examined. Information for each file is displayed in the active worksheet. As the procedure loops through the files, it stores the subdirectory names in an array named `Dirs`. When no more files are found, the procedure calls itself using an entry in the `Dirs` array for its argument. When all of the directories in the `Dirs` array have been processed, the procedure ends.

Because the `RecursiveDir` procedure uses an argument, it must be executed from another procedure by using a statement like this:

```
Call RecursiveDir("c:\directory\")
```

CD-ROM

The companion CD-ROM contains a version of this procedure that allows you to select a directory from a dialog box. The filename is `recursive file list.xlsm`.

Using the FileSystemObject object

The `FileSystemObject` object is a member of the Windows Scripting Host and provides access to a computer's file system. This object is often used in script-oriented Web pages (for example, VBScript and JavaScript) and can be used with Excel 2000 and later versions.

CAUTION

The Windows Scripting Host is sometimes used as a way to spread computer viruses. Consequently, the Windows Scripting Host may be disabled on some systems. Therefore, use caution if you are designing an application that will be used on many different systems.

The name `FileSystemObject` is a bit misleading because it actually includes a number of objects, each designed for a specific purpose:

- *Drive:* Represents a drive or a collection of drives.

- *File:* Represents a file or a collection of files.

- *Folder:* Represents a folder or a collection of folders.

- *TextStream:* Represents a stream of text that is read from, written to, or appended to a text file.

The first step in using the `FileSystemObject` object is to create an instance of the object. This can be done in two ways: early binding and late binding.

The late binding method uses two statements, like this:

```
Dim FileSys As Object
Set FileSys = CreateObject("Scripting.FileSystemObject")
```

Note that the `FileSys` object variable is declared as a generic `Object` rather than as an actual object type. The object type is resolved at runtime.

The early binding method of creating the object requires that you set up a reference to the Windows Scripting Host Object Model. You do this by using Tools ➪ References in the VBE (see Figure 27-2). After you've established the reference, create the object by using statements like these:

```
Dim FileSys As FileSystemObject
Set FileSys = CreateObject("Scripting.FileSystemObject")
```

Using the early binding method enables you to take advantage of the VBE's Auto List Members feature to help you identify properties and methods as you type. In addition, you can use the Object Browser (by pressing F2) to learn more about the object model.

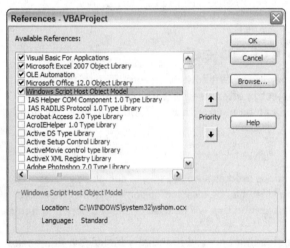

Figure 27-2: Creating a reference to the Windows Script Host Object Model.

The examples that follow demonstrate various tasks using the `FileSystemObject` object.

USING FILESYSTEMOBJECT TO DETERMINE WHETHER A FILE EXISTS

The `Function` procedure that follows accepts one argument (the path and filename) and returns `True` if the file exists:

```
Function FileExists3(fname) As Boolean
    Dim FileSys As Object 'FileSystemObject
    Set FileSys = CreateObject("Scripting.FileSystemObject")
    FileExists3 = FileSys.FileExists(fname)
End Function
```

The function creates a new `FileSystemObject` object named `FileSys` and then accesses the `FileExists` property for that object.

USING FILESYSTEMOBJECT TO DETERMINE WHETHER A PATH EXISTS

The `Function` procedure that follows accepts one argument (the path) and returns `True` if the path exists:

```
Function PathExists2(path) As Boolean
    Dim FileSys As Object 'FileSystemObject
    Dim FolderObj As Object 'Folder
    Set FileSys = CreateObject("Scripting.FileSystemObject")
    On Error Resume Next
    Set FolderObj = FileSys.GetFolder(path)
    PathExists2 = Err = 0
End Function
```

The function attempts to create a reference to a `Folder` object named `FolderObj`. If this operation is successful, the directory exists. If an error occurs, the directory does not exist.

USING FILESYSTEMOBJECT TO LIST INFORMATION ABOUT ALL AVAILABLE DISK DRIVES

The example in this section uses `FileSystemObject` to retrieve and display information about all disk drives. The procedure loops through the `Drives` collection and writes various property values to a worksheet.

Figure 27-3 shows the results run on a system with six drives. The data shown is the drive letter, whether the drive is "ready," the drive type, the volume name, the total size, and the available space.

	A	B	C	D	E	F
1	Drive	Ready	Type	Vol. Name	Size	Available
2	C	TRUE	Fixed		156,230,967,296	77,212,749,824
3	D	FALSE	CD-ROM			
4	E	TRUE	CD-ROM	ExcelPPVBA	127,907,840	0
5	F	TRUE	Fixed	MUSIC DRIVE	300,009,586,688	135,937,425,408
6	G	TRUE	Fixed	MUSICBACKUP	300,009,586,688	111,668,985,856
7						
8						
9						

Sheet1

Figure 27-3: Output from the ShowDriveInfo procedure.

CD-ROM

This workbook, named `show drive info.xlsm`, is available on the companion CD-ROM.

```
Sub ShowDriveInfo()
    Dim FileSys As FileSystemObject
    Dim Drv As Drive
```

```
    Dim Row As Long
    Set FileSys = CreateObject("Scripting.FileSystemObject")
    Cells.ClearContents
    Row = 1
'   Column headers
    Range("A1:F1") = Array("Drive", "Ready", "Type", "Vol. Name", _
        "Size", "Available")
    On Error Resume Next
'   Loop through the drives
    For Each Drv In FileSys.Drives
        Row = Row + 1
        Cells(Row, 1) = Drv.DriveLetter
        Cells(Row, 2) = Drv.IsReady
        Select Case Drv.DriveType
            Case 0: Cells(Row, 3) = "Unknown"
            Case 1: Cells(Row, 3) = "Removable"
            Case 2: Cells(Row, 3) = "Fixed"
            Case 3: Cells(Row, 3) = "Network"
            Case 4: Cells(Row, 3) = "CD-ROM"
            Case 5: Cells(Row, 3) = "RAM Disk"
        End Select
        Cells(Row, 4) = Drv.VolumeName
        Cells(Row, 5) = Drv.TotalSize
        Cells(Row, 6) = Drv.AvailableSpace
    Next Drv
    'Make a table
    ActiveSheet.ListObjects.Add xlSrcRange, _
        Range("A1").CurrentRegion, , xlYes
End Sub
```

CROSS REFERENCE

Chapter 11 describes another method of getting drive information by using Windows API functions.

Displaying Extended File Information

The example in this section displays extended file properties for all files in a specified directory. The information that's available depends on the file type. For example, image files have properties such as Camera Model and Dimensions; audio files have properties such as Artist, Title, Duration, and so on. Following is a complete list of extended properties retrieved by this procedure:

- Name
- Size
- Type
- Date Modified
- Date Created
- Date Accessed
- Attributes
- Status
- Owner
- Author
- Title
- Subject
- Category
- Pages
- Comments
- Copyright

- Artist
- Album Title
- Year
- Track Number
- Genre
- Duration
- Bit Rate
- Protected
- Camera Model
- Date Picture Taken
- Dimensions
- Program Description
- Audio sample size
- Audio sample rate
- Channels

The `FileInfo` procedure, which uses the Windows `Shell.Application` object, follows:

```
Sub FileInfo()
    Dim c As Long, r As Long, i As Long
    Dim FileName As Object 'FolderItem2
    Dim objShell As Object 'IShellDispatch4
    Dim objFolder As Object 'Folder3

'   Create the object
    Set objShell = CreateObject("Shell.Application")

'   Prompt for the folder
    Set objFolder = objShell.Namespace(GetDirectory)

'   Insert headers on active sheet
    Worksheets.Add
    c = 0
    For i = 0 To 34
        If i = 27 Or i = 28 Or i = 29 Or i = 31 Then
            'Nothing. These items are not used
        Else
            c = c + 1
```

```
            Cells(1, c) = objFolder.GetDetailsOf(objFolder.Items, i)
        End If
    Next i

'   Loop through the files
    r = 1
    For Each FileName In objFolder.Items
        c = 0
        r = r + 1
        For i = 0 To 34
            If i = 27 Or i = 28 Or i = 29 Or i = 31 Then
            'Nothing. These items are not used
            Else
                c = c + 1
                Cells(r, c) = objFolder.GetDetailsOf(FileName, i)
            End If
        Next i
    Next FileName
'   Make it a table
    ActiveSheet.ListObjects.Add xlSrcRange, _
      Range("A1").CurrentRegion
End Sub
```

Figure 27-4 shows part of the output of this procedure.

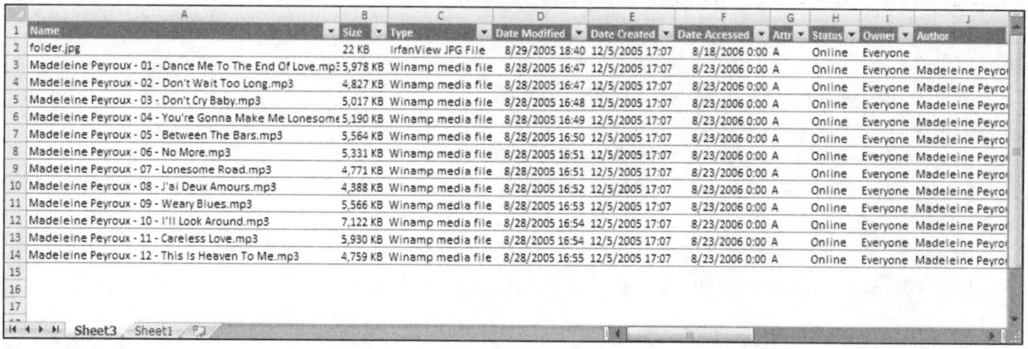

Name	Size	Type	Date Modified	Date Created	Date Accessed	Attr	Status	Owner	Author
folder.jpg	22 KB	IrfanView JPG File	8/29/2005 18:40	12/5/2005 17:07	8/18/2006 0:00	A	Online	Everyone	
Madeleine Peyroux - 01 - Dance Me To The End Of Love.mp3	5,978 KB	Winamp media file	8/28/2005 16:47	12/5/2005 17:07	8/23/2006 0:00	A	Online	Everyone	Madeleine Peyro
Madeleine Peyroux - 02 - Don't Wait Too Long.mp3	4,827 KB	Winamp media file	8/28/2005 16:47	12/5/2005 17:07	8/23/2006 0:00	A	Online	Everyone	Madeleine Peyro
Madeleine Peyroux - 03 - Don't Cry Baby.mp3	5,017 KB	Winamp media file	8/28/2005 16:48	12/5/2005 17:07	8/23/2006 0:00	A	Online	Everyone	Madeleine Peyro
Madeleine Peyroux - 04 - You're Gonna Make Me Lonesome	5,190 KB	Winamp media file	8/28/2005 16:49	12/5/2005 17:07	8/23/2006 0:00	A	Online	Everyone	Madeleine Peyro
Madeleine Peyroux - 05 - Between The Bars.mp3	5,564 KB	Winamp media file	8/28/2005 16:50	12/5/2005 17:07	8/23/2006 0:00	A	Online	Everyone	Madeleine Peyro
Madeleine Peyroux - 06 - No More.mp3	5,331 KB	Winamp media file	8/28/2005 16:51	12/5/2005 17:07	8/23/2006 0:00	A	Online	Everyone	Madeleine Peyro
Madeleine Peyroux - 07 - Lonesome Road.mp3	4,771 KB	Winamp media file	8/28/2005 16:51	12/5/2005 17:07	8/23/2006 0:00	A	Online	Everyone	Madeleine Peyro
Madeleine Peyroux - 08 - J'ai Deux Amours.mp3	4,388 KB	Winamp media file	8/28/2005 16:52	12/5/2005 17:07	8/23/2006 0:00	A	Online	Everyone	Madeleine Peyro
Madeleine Peyroux - 09 - Weary Blues.mp3	5,566 KB	Winamp media file	8/28/2005 16:53	12/5/2005 17:07	8/23/2006 0:00	A	Online	Everyone	Madeleine Peyro
Madeleine Peyroux - 10 - I'll Look Around.mp3	7,122 KB	Winamp media file	8/28/2005 16:54	12/5/2005 17:07	8/23/2006 0:00	A	Online	Everyone	Madeleine Peyro
Madeleine Peyroux - 11 - Careless Love.mp3	5,930 KB	Winamp media file	8/28/2005 16:54	12/5/2005 17:07	8/23/2006 0:00	A	Online	Everyone	Madeleine Peyro
Madeleine Peyroux - 12 - This Is Heaven To Me.mp3	4,759 KB	Winamp media file	8/28/2005 16:55	12/5/2005 17:07	8/23/2006 0:00	A	Online	Everyone	Madeleine Peyro

Figure 27-4: A table of information about the files in a directory.

This example uses late binding to create a `Shell.Application` object, so the objects are declared generically. To use early binding, use the VBE Tools ➪ References command and create a reference to Microsoft Shell Controls and Automation.

CROSS-REFERENCE

This procedure prompts the user for a directory by a function named `GetDirectory`. The `GetDirectory` function uses a Windows API function, which is described in Chapter 12.

CD-ROM

This example, named `file information.xlsm`, is available on the companion CD-ROM.

Working with Text Files

VBA contains a number of statements that allow low-level manipulation of files. These Input/Output (I/O) statements give you much more control over files than Excel's normal text file import and export options.

A file can be accessed in any of three ways:

- *Sequential access:* By far the most common method. This allows reading and writing individual characters or entire lines of data.

- *Random access:* Used only if you're programming a database application — something that's not really appropriate for VBA.

- *Binary access:* Used to read or write to any byte position in a file, such as storing or displaying a bitmap image. This access method is rarely used in VBA.

Because random and binary access files are rarely used with VBA, this chapter focuses on sequential access files, which are accessed sequentially. In other words, your code starts reading from the beginning of the file and reads each line sequentially. For output, your code writes data to the end of the file.

NOTE

The method of reading and writing text files discussed in this book is the traditional data-channel approach. Another option is to use the object approach. The `FileSystemObject` object contains a `TextStream` object that can be used to read and write text files. The `FileSystemObject` object is part of the Windows Scripting Host. As I mention earlier, this scripting service is disabled on some systems because of the possibility of transferring a virus.

Opening a text file

VBA's `Open` statement (not to be confused with the `Open` method of the `Workbooks` object) opens a file for reading or writing. Before you can read from or write to a file, you must open it.

The `Open` statement is quite versatile and has a rather complex syntax:

```
Open pathname For mode [Access access] [lock]  _
  As [#]filenumber [Len=reclength]
```

- `pathname`: (Required) The `pathname` part of the `Open` statement is quite straightforward. It simply contains the name and path (optional) of the file to be opened.
- `mode`: (Required) The file mode must be one of the following:
  - `Append`: A sequential access mode that either allows the file to be read or allows data to be appended to the end of the file.
  - `Input`: A sequential access mode that allows the file to be read but not written to.
  - `Output`: A sequential access mode that allows the file to be read or written to. In this mode, a new file is always created. (An existing file with the same name is deleted.)
  - `Binary`: A random access mode that allows data to be read or written to on a byte-by-byte basis.
  - `Random`: A random access mode that allows data to be read or written in units determined by the `reclength` argument of the `Open` statement.
- `access`: (Optional) The `access` argument determines what can be done with the file. It can be `Read`, `Write`, or `Read Write`.
- `lock`: (Optional) The `lock` argument is useful for multiuser situations. The options are `Shared`, `Lock Read`, `Lock Write`, and `Lock Read Write`.
- `filenumber`: (Required) A file number ranging from `1` to `511`. You can use the `FreeFile` function to get the next available file number. (Read about `FreeFile` in the upcoming section, "Getting a file number.")
- `reclength`: (Optional) The record length (for random access files) or the buffer size (for sequential access files).

Reading a text file

The basic procedure for reading a text file with VBA consists of the following steps:

1. Open the file by using the `Open` statement.
2. Specify the position in the file by using the `Seek` function (optional).

3. Read data from the file (by using the `Input`, `Input #`, or `Line Input #` statements).

4. Close the file by using the `Close` statement.

Writing a text file

The basic procedure for writing a text file is:

1. Open or create the file by using the `Open` statement.

2. Specify the position in the file by using the `Seek` function (optional).

3. Write data to the file by using the `Write #` or `Print #` statements.

4. Close the file by using the `Close` statement.

Getting a file number

Most VBA programmers simply designate a file number in their `Open` statement. For example:

```
Open "myfile.txt" For Input As #1
```

Then you can refer to the file in subsequent statements as `#1`.

If a second file is opened while the first is still open, you would designate the second file as `#2`:

```
Open "another.txt" For Input As #2
```

Another approach is to use VBA's `FreeFile` function to get a file handle. Then you can refer to the file by using a variable. Here's an example:

```
FileHandle = FreeFile
Open "myfile.txt" For Input As FileHandle
```

Determining or setting the file position

For sequential file access, it's rarely necessary to know the current location in the file. If for some reason you need to know this, you can use the `Seek` function.

Statements for reading and writing

VBA provides several statements to read and write data to a file.

Excel's Text File Import and Export Features

Excel supports three types of text files:

- *CSV (Comma-Separated Value) files:* Columns of data are separated by a comma, and each row of data ends in a carriage return. For some non-English versions of Excel, a semicolon rather than a comma is used.

- *PRN:* Columns of data are aligned by character position, and each row of data ends in a carriage return.

- *TXT (Tab-delimited) files:* Columns of data are separated by Tab characters, and each row of data ends in a carriage return.

When you attempt to open a text file with the Office ⇨ Open command, the Text Import Wizard might appear in order to help you delineate the columns. If the text file is tab-delimited or comma-delimited, Excel usually opens the file without displaying the Text Import Wizard. If the data is not interpreted correctly, close the file and try renaming it to use a .TXT extension.

The Text to Columns Wizard (accessed by choosing Data ⇨ Data Tools ⇨ Text to Table) is identical to the Text Import Wizard but works with data stored in a single worksheet column.

Three statements are used for reading data from a sequential access file:

- `Input`: Reads a specified number of characters from a file.

- `Input #`: Reads data as a series of variables, with variables separated by a comma.

- `Line Input #`: Reads a complete line of data (delineated by a carriage return and/or linefeed character).

Two statements are used for writing data to a sequential access file:

- `Write #`: Writes a series of values, with each value separated by a comma and enclosed in quotes. If you end the statement with a semicolon, a carriage return/linefeed sequence is not inserted after each value. Data written with `Write #` is usually read from a file with an `Input #` statement.

- `Print #`: Writes a series of values, with each value separated by a Tab character. If you end the statement with a semicolon, a carriage return/linefeed sequence is not inserted after each value. Data written with `Print #` is usually read from a file with a `Line Input #` or an `Input` statement.

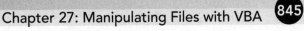

Text File Manipulation Examples

This section contains a number of examples that demonstrate various techniques that manipulate text files.

Importing data in a text file

The following example reads a text file and then places each line of data in a single cell (beginning with the active cell):

```
Sub ImportData()
    Open "c:\data\textfile.txt" For Input As #1
    r = 0
    Do Until EOF(1)
        Line Input #1, data
        ActiveCell.Offset(r, 0) = data
        r = r + 1
    Loop
    Close #1
End Sub
```

In most cases, this procedure won't be very useful because each line of data is simply dumped into a single cell. It would be easier to just open the text file directly by using Office ⇨ Open.

Exporting a range to a text file

The example in this section writes the data in a selected worksheet range to a CSV text file. Excel, of course, can export data to a CSV file, but it exports the entire worksheet. This macro works with a specified range of cells.

```
Sub ExportRange()
    Dim Filename As String
    Dim NumRows As Long, NumCols As Integer
    Dim r As Long, c As Integer
    Dim Data
    Dim ExpRng As Range
    Set ExpRng = Selection
    NumCols = ExpRng.Columns.Count
    NumRows = ExpRng.Rows.Count
    Filename = Application.DefaultFilePath & "\textfile.csv"
    Open Filename For Output As #1
        For r = 1 To NumRows
            For c = 1 To NumCols
                Data = ExpRng.Cells(r, c).Value
                If IsNumeric(Data) Then Data = Val(Data)
```

```
          If IsEmpty(ExpRng.Cells(r, c)) Then Data = ""
          If c <> NumCols Then
             Write #1, Data;
          Else
             Write #1, Data
          End If
        Next c
      Next r
    Close #1
End Sub
```

Notice that the procedure uses two `Write #` statements. The first statement ends with a semicolon, so a carriage return/linefeed sequence is not written. For the last cell in a row, however, the second `Write #` statement does not use a semicolon, which causes the next output to appear on a new line.

I use a variable named `Data` to store the contents of each cell. If the cell is numeric, the variable is converted to a value. This step ensures that numeric data will not be stored with quotation marks. If a cell is empty, its `Value` property returns 0. Therefore, the code also checks for a blank cell (by using the `IsEmpty` function) and substitutes an empty string instead of a zero.

Figure 27-5 shows the contents of the resulting file, viewed in Windows Notepad.

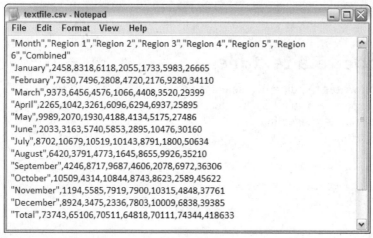

Figure 27-5: This text file was generated by VBA.

CD-ROM

This example and the example in the next section are available on the companion CD-ROM. The filename is `export and import csv.xlsm`.

Importing a text file to a range

The example in this section reads the CSV file created in the previous example and then stores the values beginning at the active cell in the active worksheet. The code reads each character and essentially parses the line of data, ignoring quote characters and looking for commas to delineate the columns.

```
Sub ImportRange()
    Dim ImpRng As Range
    Dim Filename As String
    Dim r As Long, c As Integer
    Dim txt As String, Char As String * 1
    Dim Data
    Dim i As Integer

    Set ImpRng = ActiveCell
    On Error Resume Next
    Filename = Application.DefaultFilePath & "\textfile.csv"
    Open Filename For Input As #1
    If Err <> 0 Then
        MsgBox "Not found: " & Filename, vbCritical, "ERROR"
        Exit Sub
    End If
    r = 0
    c = 0
    txt = ""
    Application.ScreenUpdating = False
    Do Until EOF(1)
        Line Input #1, Data
        For i = 1 To Len(Data)
            Char = Mid(Data, i, 1)
            If Char = "," Then 'comma
                ActiveCell.Offset(r, c) = txt
                c = c + 1
                txt = ""
            ElseIf i = Len(Data) Then 'end of line
                If Char <> Chr(34) Then txt = txt & Char
                ActiveCell.Offset(r, c) = txt
                txt = ""
            ElseIf Char <> Chr(34) Then
                txt = txt & Char
            End If
        Next i
        c = 0
        r = r + 1
    Loop
    Close #1
    Application.ScreenUpdating = True
End Sub
```

NOTE

The preceding procedure has a flaw: It doesn't handle data that contains a comma or a quote character. In addition, an imported date will be surrounded by number signs: for example, #2007-05-12#.

Logging Excel usage

The example in this section writes data to a text file every time Excel is opened and closed. In order for this to work reliably, the procedure must be located in a workbook that's opened every time you start Excel. The Personal Macro Workbook is an excellent choice.

The following procedure, stored in the code module for the `ThisWorkbook` object, is executed when the file is opened:

```
Private Sub Workbook_Open()
    Open Application.Path & "\excelusage.txt" For Append As #1
    Print #1, "Started " & Now
    Close #1
End Sub
```

The procedure appends a new line to a file named `excelusage.txt`. The new line contains the current date and time and might look something like this:

```
Started 11/16/09 9:27:43 PM
```

The following procedure is executed before the workbook is closed. It appends a new line that contains the word *Stopped* along with the current date and time.

```
Private Sub Workbook_BeforeClose(Cancel As Boolean)
    Open Application.Path & "\excelusage.txt" _
      For Append As #1
    Print #1, "Stopped " & Now
    Close #1
End Sub
```

CROSS-REFERENCE

Refer to chapter 19 for more information about event handler procedures such as `Workbook_Open` and `Workbook_BeforeClose`.

Filtering a text file

The example in this section demonstrates how to work with two text files at once. The `FilterFile` procedure that follows reads a text file (`infile.txt`) and copies only the rows that contain a specific text string to a second text file (`output.txt`).

```
Sub FilterFile()
    Open ThisWorkbook.Path & "\infile.txt" For Input As #1
    Open Application.DefaultFilePath & "\output.txt" For Output As #2
    TextToFind = "January"
    Do Until EOF(1)
        Line Input #1, data
        If InStr(1, data, TextToFind) Then
            Print #2, data
        End If
    Loop
    Close #1
End Sub
```

 CD-ROM

This example, named `filter text file.xlsm`, is available on the companion CD-ROM.

Exporting a range to HTML format

The example in this section demonstrates how to export a range of cells to an HTML file. An *HTML file,* as you might know, is simply a text file that contains special formatting tags that describe how the information will be presented in a Web browser.

Why not use Excel's Office ➪ Save As command and choose the Web Page file type? The procedure listed here has a distinct advantage: It does not produce bloated HTML code. For example, I used the `ExportToHTML` procedure to export a range of 70 cells. The file size was 2.6KB. Then I used Excel's Office ➪ Save as Web Page command to export the sheet. The result was 15.8KB — more than six times larger.

But, on the other hand, the `ExportToHTML` procedure does not maintain all the cell formatting. In fact, the only formatting information that it produces is bold, italic, and horizontal alignment. However, the procedure is good enough for many situations, and it serves as the basis for additional enhancements.

```
Sub ExportToHTML()
    Dim Filename As Variant
    Dim TDOpenTag As String, TDCloseTag As String
    Dim CellContents As String
    Dim Rng As Range
    Dim r As Long, c As Integer

'   Use the selected range of cells
    Set Rng = Application.Intersect(ActiveSheet.UsedRange, Selection)
    If Rng Is Nothing Then
        MsgBox "Nothing to export.", vbCritical
```

```
            Exit Sub
        End If


    '   Get a file name
        Filename = Application.GetSaveAsFilename( _
            InitialFileName:="myrange.htm", _
            fileFilter:="HTML Files(*.htm), *.htm")
        If Filename = False Then Exit Sub


    '   Open the text file
        Open Filename For Output As #1


    '   Write the tags
        Print #1, "<HTML>"
        Print #1, "<TABLE BORDER=0 CELLPADDING=3>"


    '   Loop through the cells
        For r = 1 To Rng.Rows.Count
            Print #1, "<TR>"
            For c = 1 To Rng.Columns.Count
                Select Case Rng.Cells(r, c).HorizontalAlignment
                    Case xlHAlignLeft
                        TDOpenTag = "<TD ALIGN=LEFT>"
                    Case xlHAlignCenter
                        TDOpenTag = "<TD ALIGN=CENTER>"
                    Case xlHAlignGeneral
                        If IsNumeric(Rng.Cells(r, c)) Then
                          TDOpenTag = "<TD ALIGN=RIGHT>"
                        Else
                          TDOpenTag = "<TD ALIGN=LEFT>"
                        End If
                    Case xlHAlignRight
                        TDOpenTag = "<TD ALIGN=RIGHT>"
                End Select

                TDCloseTag = "</TD>"
                If Rng.Cells(r, c).Font.Bold Then
                    TDOpenTag = TDOpenTag & "<B>"
                    TDCloseTag = "</B>" & TDCloseTag
                End If
                If Rng.Cells(r, c).Font.Italic Then
                    TDOpenTag = TDOpenTag & "<I>"
                    TDCloseTag = "</I>" & TDCloseTag
                End If
                CellContents = Rng.Cells(r, c).Text
```

```
            Print #1, TDOpenTag & CellContents & TDCloseTag
        Next c
        Print #1, "</TR>"
    Next r
'   Close the table
    Print #1, "</TABLE>"
    Print #1, "</HTML>"

'   Close the file
    Close #1

'   Tell the user
    MsgBox Rng.Count & " cells were exported to " & Filename
End Sub
```

The procedure starts by determining the range to export. This is based on the intersection of the selected range and the used area of the worksheet. This ensures that entire rows or columns are not processed. Next, the user is prompted for a filename, and the text file is opened. The bulk of the work is done within two For-Next loops. The code generates the appropriate HTML tags and writes the information to the text file. The only complicated part is determining the cell's horizontal alignment. (Excel doesn't report this information directly.) Finally, the file is closed, and the user sees a summary message.

Figure 27-6 shows a range in a worksheet, and Figure 27-7 shows how it looks in a Web browser after being converted to HTML.

	A	B	C	D	E	F	G
1							
2			New York	Los Angeles	Chicago	Total	
3		January	$11,249.09	$11,423.69	$4,936.33	$5,438.79	
4		February	$9,265.44	$10,778.64	$10,519.65	$5,044.97	
5		March	$11,606.05	$8,306.11	$11,055.09	$8,388.56	
6		April	$7,956.91	$11,509.05	$6,951.02	$8,965.71	
7		May	$7,850.21	$9,937.65	$9,346.92	$10,907.65	
8		June	$8,399.23	$6,456.32	$8,669.86	$4,898.50	
9		July	$6,298.21	$6,530.04	$8,403.11	$8,848.34	
10		August	$5,013.93	$7,690.16	$9,527.34	$7,327.38	
11		September	$8,986.08	$11,600.23	$5,740.46	$11,394.59	
12		October	$5,574.59	$5,011.99	$9,417.73	$10,519.65	
13		November	$10,320.80	$9,994.88	$7,996.68	$7,659.12	
14		December	$11,436.30	$6,500.94	$10,557.48	$10,421.68	
15		Total	$103,956.84	$105,739.70	$103,121.67	$312,818.21	
16							
17							

Sheet1

Figure 27-6: A worksheet range, ready to be converted to HTML.

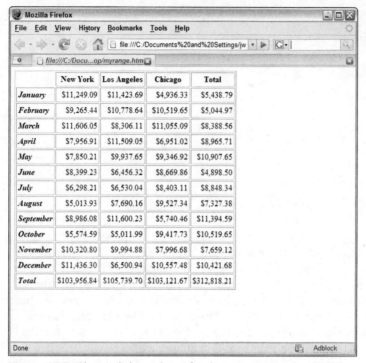

	New York	Los Angeles	Chicago	Total
January	$11,249.09	$11,423.69	$4,936.33	$5,438.79
February	$9,265.44	$10,778.64	$10,519.65	$5,044.97
March	$11,606.05	$8,306.11	$11,055.09	$8,388.56
April	$7,956.91	$11,509.05	$6,951.02	$8,965.71
May	$7,850.21	$9,937.65	$9,346.92	$10,907.65
June	$8,399.23	$6,456.32	$8,669.86	$4,898.50
July	$6,298.21	$6,530.04	$8,403.11	$8,848.34
August	$5,013.93	$7,690.16	$9,527.34	$7,327.38
September	$8,986.08	$11,600.23	$5,740.46	$11,394.59
October	$5,574.59	$5,011.99	$9,417.73	$10,519.65
November	$10,320.80	$9,994.88	$7,996.68	$7,659.12
December	$11,436.30	$6,500.94	$10,557.48	$10,421.68
Total	$103,956.84	$105,739.70	$103,121.67	$312,818.21

Figure 27-7: The worksheet data after being converted to HTML.

CD-ROM

This example, named `export to HTML.xlsm`, is available on the companion CD-ROM.

Exporting a range to an XML file

This example exports an Excel range to a simple XML data file. As you might know, an *XML file* uses tags to wrap each data item. The procedure in this section uses the labels in the first row as the XML tags. Figure 27-8 shows the range in a worksheet table, and Figure 27-9 shows the XML file displayed in a Web browser.

NOTE

Although Excel 2003 introduced improved support for XML files, it can't create an XML file from an arbitrary range of data unless you have a map file (schema) for the data.

	EmployeeID	LastName	FirstName	Title	BirthDate	HireDate	Address	City
2	9001	Davolio	Nancy	Sales Representative	12/8/68	5/1/01	507 - 20th Ave. E. Apt. 2A	Sea
3	9002	Fuller	Andrew	Vice President, Sales	2/19/52	8/14/02	908 W. Capital Way	Tac
4	9003	Leverling	Janet	Sales Representative	8/30/63	4/1/06	722 Moss Bay Blvd.	Kirk
5	9004	Peacock	Margaret	Sales Representative	9/19/58	5/3/99	4110 Old Redmond Rd.	Rec
6	9005	Buchanan	Steven	Sales Manager	3/4/55	10/17/93	14 Garrett Hill	Lon
7	9006	Suyama	Michael	Sales Representative	7/2/63	10/17/97	Coventry House▯Miner Rd.	Lon
8	9007	King	Robert	Sales Representative	5/29/60	1/2/98	Edgeham Hollow Winchester Way	Lon
9	9008	Callahan	Laura	Inside Sales Coordinator	1/9/58	3/5/94	4726 - 11th Ave. N.E.	Sea
10	9009	Dodsworth	Anne	Sales Representative	7/2/69	11/15/03	7 Houndstooth Rd.	Lon
11	9102	Jackson	Raymond	Sales Representative	2/16/52	3/4/00	11 Franklin Way	Por

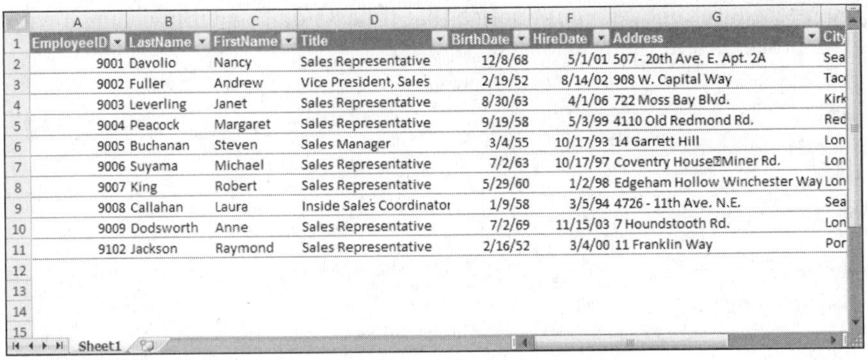

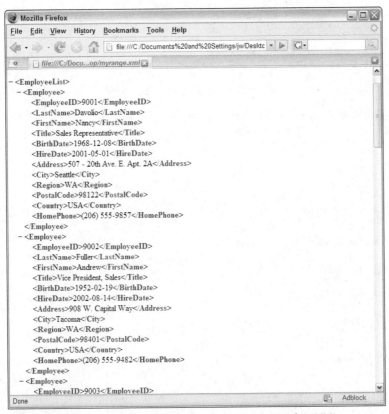

Figure 27-8: The data in this range will be converted to XML.

Figure 27-9: The worksheet data after being converted to XML.

The ExportToXML procedure follows. You'll notice that it has a quite a bit in common with the ExportToHTML procedure in the previous section.

```vba
Sub ExportToXML()
    Dim Filename As Variant
    Dim Rng As Range
    Dim r As Long, c As Long

'   Set the range
    Set Rng = Range("Table1[#All]")

'   Get a file name
    Filename = Application.GetSaveAsFilename( _
        InitialFileName:="myrange.xml", _
        fileFilter:="XML Files(*.xml), *.xml")
    If Filename = False Then Exit Sub

'   Open the text file
    Open Filename For Output As #1

'   Write the <xml> tags
    Print #1, "<?xml version=""1.0"" encoding=""UTF-8"" standalone=""yes""?>"
    Print #1, "<EmployeeList xmlns:xsi=""http://www.w3.org/2001/XMLSchema-instance"">"

'   Loop through the cells
    For r = 2 To Rng.Rows.Count
        Print #1, "<Employee>"
        For c = 1 To Rng.Columns.Count
            Print #1, "<" & Rng.Cells(1, c) & ">";
            If IsDate(Rng.Cells(r, c)) Then
                Print #1, Format(Rng.Cells(r, c), "yyyy-mm-dd");
            Else
                Print #1, Rng.Cells(r, c).Text;
            End If
            Print #1, "</" & Rng.Cells(1, c) & ">"
        Next c
        Print #1, "</Employee>"
    Next r
'   Close the table
    Print #1, "</EmployeeList>"

'   Close the file
    Close #1

'   Tell the user
    MsgBox Rng.Rows.Count - 1 & " records were exported to " & Filename
End Sub
```

CD-ROM

This example, named `export to XML.xlsm`, is available on the companion CD-ROM.

The exported XML file can be opened with Excel. When opening an XML file, you'll see the dialog box shown in Figure 27-10. If you choose the As an XML Table option, the file will be displayed as a table. Keep in mind that any formulas in the original table are not preserved.

Figure 27-10: When opening an XML file, Excel offers three options.

Zipping and Unzipping Files

Perhaps the most commonly used type of file compression is the ZIP format. Even Excel 2007 files are stored in the ZIP format (although they don't use the `.zip` extension). A ZIP file can contain any number of files, and even complete directory structures. The content of the files determines the degree of compression. For example, JPG image files are already compressed, so zipping such a file will have little effect on the file size.

CD-ROM

The examples in this section are available on the companion CD-ROM. The files are named `'zip files.xlsm'` and `'unzip a file.xlsm'`.

Zipping files

The example in this section demonstrates how to create a ZIP file from a group of user-selected files. The `ZipFiles` procedure displays a dialog box so the user can select the files. It then creates a ZIP file named `compressed.zip` in Excel's default directory.

```
Sub ZipFiles()
    Dim ShellApp As Object
    Dim FileNameZip As Variant
    Dim FileNames As Variant
    Dim i As Long, FileCount As Long

'   Get the file names
    FileNames = Application.GetOpenFilename _
        (FileFilter:="All Files (*.*),*.*", _
```

```
            FilterIndex:=1, _
            Title:="Select the files to ZIP", _
            MultiSelect:=True)

'   Exit if dialog box canceled
    If Not IsArray(FileNames) Then Exit Sub

    FileCount = UBound(FileNames)
    FileNameZip = Application.DefaultFilePath & "\compressed.zip"

    'Create empty Zip File with zip header
    Open FileNameZip For Output As #1
    Print #1, Chr$(80) & Chr$(75) & Chr$(5) & Chr$(6) & String(18, 0)
    Close #1

    Set ShellApp = CreateObject("Shell.Application")
    'Copy the files to the compressed folder
    For i = LBound(FileNames) To UBound(FileNames)
        ShellApp.Namespace(FileNameZip).CopyHere FileNames(i)
    Next i

    'Keep script waiting until Compressing is done
    On Error Resume Next
    Do Until ShellApp.Namespace(FileNameZip).items.Count = FileCount
        Application.Wait (Now + TimeValue("0:00:01"))
    Loop

    If MsgBox(FileCount & " files were zipped to:" & _
        vbNewLine & FileNameZip & vbNewLine & vbNewLine & _
        "View the zip file?", vbQuestion + vbYesNo) = vbYes Then _
        Shell "Explorer.exe /e," & FileNameZip, vbNormalFocus
End Sub
```

Figure 27-11 shows the file selection dialog box generated by using the GetOpenFilename method of the Application object (see Chapter 12 for more information). This dialog box allows the user to select multiple files from a single directory.

The ZipFiles procedure creates a file named compressed.zip and writes a string of characters, which identify it as a ZIP file. Next, a Shell.Application object is created, and the code uses its CopyHere method to copy the files into the ZIP archive. The next section of the code is a Do Until loop, which checks the number of files in the ZIP archive every second. This is necessary because copying the files could take some time, and, if the procedure ends before the files are copied, the ZIP file will be incomplete (and probably corrupt).

When the number of files in the ZIP archive matches the number that should be there, the loop ends, and the user is presented with a message like the one shown in Figure 27-12. Clicking the Yes button opens a Windows Explorer window that shows the zipped files (see Figure 27-13).

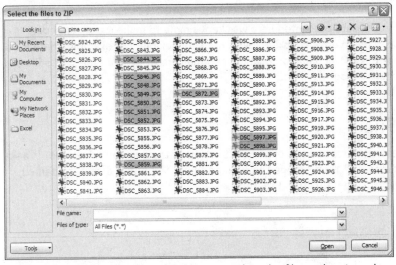

Figure 27-11: This dialog box lets the user select the files to be zipped.

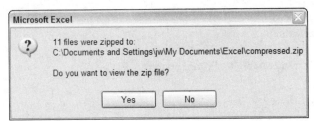

Figure 27-12: The user is informed when the ZIP file is complete.

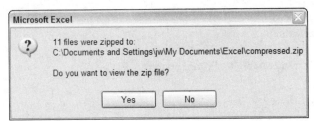

Figure 27-13: This Explorer window shows the ZIP file contents.

CAUTION

The ZipFiles procedure presented here was kept simple to make it easy to understand. The code does no error checking and is not very flexible. For example, there is no option to choose the ZIP filename or location, and the current compressed.zip file is always overwritten without warning.

Unzipping a File

The example in this section performs the opposite function of the previous example. It asks the user for a ZIP filename and then unzips the files and puts them in a directory named Unzipped, located in Excel's default file directory.

```
Sub UnzipAFile()
    Dim ShellApp As Object
    Dim TargetFile
    Dim ZipFolder

'   Target file & temp dir
    TargetFile = Application.GetOpenFilename _
        (FileFilter:="Zip Files (*.zip), *.zip")
    If TargetFile = False Then Exit Sub

    ZipFolder = Application.DefaultFilePath & "\Unzipped\"

'   Create a temp folder
    On Error Resume Next
    RmDir ZipFolder
    MkDir ZipFolder
    On Error GoTo 0

'   Copy the zipped files to the newly created folder
    Set ShellApp = CreateObject("Shell.Application")
    ShellApp.Namespace(ZipFolder).CopyHere _
        ShellApp.Namespace(TargetFile).items

    If MsgBox("The files was unzipped to:" & _
        vbNewLine & ZipFolder & vbNewLine & vbNewLine & _
        "View the folder?", vbQuestion + vbYesNo) = vbYes Then _
        Shell "Explorer.exe /e," & ZipFolder, vbNormalFocus
End Sub
```

The UnzipAFile procedure uses the GetOpenFilename method to get the ZIP file. It then creates the new folder and uses the Shell.Application object to copy the contents of the ZIP file to the new folder. Finally, the user can choose to display the new directory.

Chapter 28

Manipulating Visual Basic Components

In This Chapter

This chapter covers a topic that some readers might find extremely useful: writing Visual Basic for Applications (VBA) code that manipulates components in a VBA project. Read on to discover the following:

◆ An overview of the VBA Integrated Development Environment (IDE) and its object model

◆ How to use VBA to add and remove modules from a project

◆ How to write VBA code that creates more VBA code

◆ How to use VBA to help create UserForms

◆ A useful function that creates a UserForm on the fly

The VBA IDE contains an object model that exposes key elements of your VBA projects, including the Visual Basic Editor (VBE) itself. This object model enables you to write VBA code that adds or removes modules, generates other VBA code, or even creates UserForms on the fly.

Introducing the IDE

The *IDE* is essentially an Object Linking and Embedding (OLE) automation interface for the Visual Basic Editor. After you establish a reference to the object, you have access to all the VBE's objects, properties, and methods, and you can also declare objects from the IDE's member classes.

Use the VBE's Tools ⇨ References command to display the References dialog box, where you can add a reference to the Microsoft Visual Basic for Applications Extensibility Library (see Figure 28-1). This gives you access to an object called VBIDE. Creating a reference to VBIDE enables you to declare object variables contained in the VBIDE and also gives you access to a number of predefined constants that relate to the IDE. Actually, you can access the objects in the IDE *without* creating a reference, but you won't be able to use the constants in your code, nor will you be able to declare specific objects that refer to IDE components.

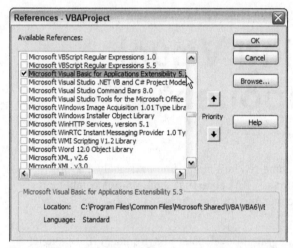

Figure 28-1: Adding a reference to the Microsoft Visual Basic for Applications Extensibility Library.

 CROSS-REFERENCE
Refer to Chapter 20 for background information about OLE automation.

After you understand how the IDE object model works, you can write code to perform a variety of operations, including the following:

- Adding and removing VBA modules
- Inserting VBA code
- Creating UserForms
- Adding controls to a UserForm

An Important Security Note

If you're using Excel to develop applications for others to use, be aware that the procedures in this chapter may not work. Because of the threat of macro viruses, Microsoft (beginning with Excel 2002) made it much more difficult for a VBA macro to modify components in a VBA project. If you attempt to execute any of the procedures in this chapter, you may see an error message.

Whether you see this error message depends on a setting in Excel's Trust Center dialog box. To view or change this setting,

1. Choose Office ⇨ Excel Options.

2. In the Excel options dialog box, click the Trust Center Tab.

3. In the Trust Center Tab, click the Trust Center Settings button.

4. In the Trust Center dialog box, click the Macro Settings tab.

You'll find a check box labeled Trust Access to the VBA Project Object Model.

This setting is turned off by default. Even if the user chooses to trust the macros contained in the workbook, the macros cannot modify the VBA project if this setting is turned off. Note that this setting applies to all workbooks and cannot be changed for only a particular workbook.

You can't directly determine the value of this particular setting by using VBA. The only way to detect this setting is to attempt to access the VBProject object and then check for an error. The following code demonstrates:

```
On Error Resume Next
Set x = ActiveWorkbook.VBProject
If Err <> 0 Then
  MsgBox "Your security settings do not allow this macro to run."
  Exit Sub
End If
```

Not all the examples in this chapter are intended to be used by end users. Many of them are designed to help developers create projects. For these projects, you'll want to enable the Trust Access to Visual Basic Project setting.

The IDE Object Model

Programming the IDE requires an understanding of its object model. The top object in the object hierarchy is the VBE (Visual Basic Environment). As with Excel's object model, the VBE contains other objects. A simplified version of the IDE object hierarchy is as follows:

```
VBE
    VBProject
        VBComponent
            CodeModule
            Designer
            Property
        Reference
    Window
    CommandBar
```

NOTE

This chapter ignores the Extensibility Library's `Windows` collection and `CommandBars` collection, which aren't all that useful for Excel developers. Rather, the chapter focuses on the `VBProject` object, which can be very useful for developers — but make sure that you read the "An Important Security Note" sidebar.

The VBProjects collection

Every open workbook or add-in is represented by a `VBProject` object. To access the `VBProject` object for a workbook, make sure that you've established a reference to the Microsoft Visual Basic for Applications Extensibility Library (see "Introducing the IDE," earlier in this chapter).

The `VBProject` property of the `Workbook` object returns a `VBProject` object. The following instructions, for example, create an object variable that represents the `VBProject` object for the active workbook:

```
Dim VBP As VBProject
Set VBP = ActiveWorkbook.VBProject
```

NOTE

If you get an error message when VBA encounters the `Dim` statement, make sure that you've added a reference to Microsoft Visual Basic for Applications Extensibility Library.

Each `VBProject` object contains a collection of the VBA component objects in the project (UserForms, modules, class modules, and document modules). Not surprisingly, this collection is called `VBComponents`. A `VBProject` object also contains a `References` collection for the project, representing the libraries being referenced currently by the project.

You cannot add a new member to the `VBProjects` collection directly. Rather, you do so indirectly by opening or creating a new workbook in Excel. Doing so automatically adds a new member to the `VBProjects` collection. Similarly, you can't remove a `VBProject` object directly; closing a workbook removes the `VBProject` object from the collection.

THE VBCOMPONENTS COLLECTION

To access a member of the VBComponents collection, use the VBComponents property with an index number or name as its argument. The following instructions demonstrate the two ways to access a VBA component and create an object variable:

```
Set VBC = ThisWorkbook.VBProject.VBComponents(1)
Set VBC = ThisWorkbook.VBProject.VBComponents("Module1")
```

THE REFERENCES COLLECTION

Every VBA project in Excel contains a number of references. You can view, add, or delete the references for a project by choosing the Tools ➪ References command (refer to Figure 28-1 to see the References dialog box). Every project contains some references (such as VBA itself, Excel, OLE Automation, and the Office object library), and you can add more references to a project as needed.

You can also manipulate the references for a project by using VBA. The References collection contains Reference objects, and these objects have properties and methods. The following procedure, for example, displays a message box that lists the Name, Description, and FullPath property for each Reference object in the active workbook's project:

```
Sub ListReferences()
    Dim Ref As Reference
    Msg = ""
    For Each Ref In ActiveWorkbook.VBProject.References
        Msg = Msg & Ref.Name & vbNewLine
        Msg = Msg & Ref.Description & vbNewLine
        Msg = Msg & Ref.FullPath & vbNewLine & vbNewLine
    Next Ref
    MsgBox Msg
End Sub
```

Figure 28-2 shows the result of running this procedure when a workbook that contains six references is active.

NOTE   Because it declares an object variable of type Reference, the ListReferences procedure requires a reference to the VBA Extensibility Library. If you declare Ref as a generic Object, the VBA Extensibility Library reference is not needed.

You can also add a reference programmatically by using either of two methods of the Reference class. The AddFromFile method adds a reference if you know its filename and path. AddFromGuid adds a reference if you know the reference's *globally unique identifier,* or GUID. Refer to the Help system for more information.

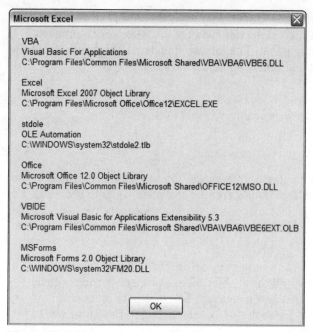

Figure 28-2: This message box displays information about the references for a project.

Displaying All Components in a VBA Project

The ShowComponents procedure, which follows, loops through each VBA component in the active workbook and writes the following information to a worksheet:

- The component's name

- The component's type

- The number of lines of code in the code module for the component

```
Sub ShowComponents()
    Dim VBP As VBIDE.VBProject
    Dim VBC As VBComponent
    Dim row As Long

    Set VBP = ActiveWorkbook.VBProject

'   Write headers
    Cells.ClearContents
```

```
    Range("A1:C1") = Array("Name", "Type", "Code Lines")
    Range("A1:C1").Font.Bold = True
    row = 1

'   Loop through the VB Components
    For Each VBC In VBP.VBComponents
        row = row + 1
'       Name
        Cells(row, 1) = VBC.Name
'       Type
        Select Case VBC.Type
            Case vbext_ct_StdModule
                Cells(row, 2) = "Module"
            Case vbext_ct_ClassModule
                Cells(row, 2) = "Class Module"
            Case vbext_ct_MSForm
                Cells(row, 2) = "UserForm"
            Case vbext_ct_Document
                Cells(row, 2) = "Document Module"
        End Select
'       Lines of code
        Cells(row, 3) = VBC.CodeModule.CountOfLines
    Next VBC
End Sub
```

Notice that I used built-in constants (for example vbext_ct_StdModule) to determine the component type. These constants are not defined unless you've established a reference to the Microsoft Visual Basic for Applications Extensibility Library.

Figure 28-3 shows the result of running the ShowComponents procedure. In this case, the VBA project contained seven components, and only one of them had a nonempty code module.

	A	B	C	D
1	Name	Type	Code Lines	
2	ThisWorkbook	Document Module	0	
3	Sheet1	Document Module	0	
4	Module1	Module	46	
5	Class1	Class Module	0	
6	UserForm1	UserForm	0	
7	Sheet2	Document Module	0	
8	Sheet3	Document Module	0	
9				
10				

Sheet1 / Sheet2 / Sheet3

Figure 28-3: The result of executing the ShowComponents procedure.

CD-ROM

This workbook, named `list VB components.xlsm`, is available on the companion CD-ROM. Notice that it contains a reference to the VBA Extensibility Library.

Listing All VBA Procedures in a Workbook

The `ListProcedures` macro in this section creates a list (in a message box) of all VBA procedures in the active workbook.

```
Sub ListProcedures()
    Dim VBP As VBIDE.VBProject
    Dim VBC As VBComponent
    Dim CM As CodeModule
    Dim StartLine As Long
    Dim Msg As String
    Dim ProcName As String

'   Use the active workbook
    Set VBP = ActiveWorkbook.VBProject

'   Loop through the VB components
    For Each VBC In VBP.VBComponents
        Set CM = VBC.CodeModule
        Msg = Msg & vbNewLine
        StartLine = CM.CountOfDeclarationLines + 1
        Do Until StartLine >= CM.CountOfLines
            Msg = Msg & VBC.Name & ": " & _
                CM.ProcOfLine(StartLine, vbext_pk_Proc) & vbNewLine
            StartLine = StartLine + CM.ProcCountLines _
                (CM.ProcOfLine(StartLine, vbext_pk_Proc), _
                vbext_pk_Proc)
        Loop
    Next VBC
    MsgBox Msg
End Sub
```

Figure 28-4 shows the result for a workbook that has nine procedures.

CD-ROM

This example, named `list all procedures.xlsm`, is available on the companion CD-ROM.

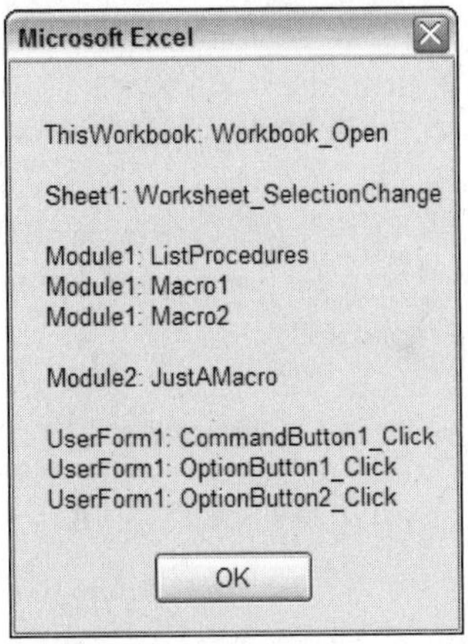

```
Microsoft Excel                    [X]


  ThisWorkbook: Workbook_Open

  Sheet1: Worksheet_SelectionChange

  Module1: ListProcedures
  Module1: Macro1
  Module1: Macro2

  Module2: JustAMacro

  UserForm1: CommandButton1_Click
  UserForm1: OptionButton1_Click
  UserForm1: OptionButton2_Click


            [    OK    ]
```

Figure 28-4: The message box lists all procedures in the active workbook.

Replacing a Module with an Updated Version

The example in this section demonstrates how to replace a VBA module with a different VBA module. Besides demonstrating three VBComponent methods (Export, Remove, and Import), the procedure also has a practical use. For example, you might distribute a workbook to a group of users and then later discover that a macro contains an error or needs to be updated. Because the users could have added data to the workbook, it's not practical to replace the entire workbook. The solution, then, is to distribute another workbook that contains a macro that replaces the VBA module with an updated version stored in a file.

This example consists of two workbooks:

- UserBook.xlsm: Contains a module (Module1) that needs to be replaced.

- UpdateUserBook.xlsm: Contains VBA procedures to replace Module1 in UserBook.xlsm with a later version of Module1 (which is stored in UpdateUserBook.xlsm).

The BeginUpdate procedure follows. This macro is contained in the UpdateUserBook.xlsm workbook, which would be distributed to users of UserBook.xlsm. This procedure ensures that UserBook.xlsm is open. It then informs the user of what is about to happen with the message shown in Figure 28-5.

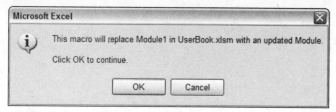

Figure 28-5: This message box informs the user that a module will be replaced.

```vba
Sub BeginUpdate()
    Dim Filename As String
    Dim Msg As String
    Filename = "UserBook.xlsm"

'   Activate workbook
    On Error Resume Next
    Workbooks(Filename).Activate
    If Err <> 0 Then
        MsgBox Filename & " must be open.", vbCritical
        Exit Sub
    End If

    Msg = "This macro will replace Module1 in UserBook.xlsm "
    Msg = Msg & "with an updated Module." & vbCrLf & vbCrLf
    Msg = Msg & "Click OK to continue."
    If MsgBox(Msg, vbInformation + vbOKCancel) = vbOK Then
        Call ReplaceModule
    Else
        MsgBox "Module not replaced,", vbCritical
    End If
End Sub
```

When the user clicks OK to confirm the replacement, the `ReplaceModule` procedure is called. This procedure replaces `Module1` in the `UserBook.xlsm` with the copy of `Module1` in the `UpdateUserBook.xlsm` file:

```vba
Sub ReplaceModule()
    Dim ModuleFile As String
    Dim VBP As VBIDE.VBProject

'   Export Module1 from this workbook
    ModuleFile = Application.DefaultFilePath & "\tempmodxxx.bas"
    ThisWorkbook.VBProject.VBComponents("Module1") _
        .Export ModuleFile

'   Replace Module1 in UserBook
    Set VBP = Workbooks("UserBook.xlsm").VBProject
```

```
On Error GoTo ErrHandle
With VBP.VBComponents
    .Remove VBP.VBComponents("Module1")
    .Import ModuleFile
End With

'   Delete the temporary module file
    Kill ModuleFile
    MsgBox "The module has been replaced.", vbInformation
    Exit Sub

ErrHandle:
'   Did an error occur?
    MsgBox "ERROR. The module may not have been replaced.", _
        vbCritical
End Sub
```

This procedure performs the following actions:

1. It exports `Module1` (the updated module) to a file. The file has an unusual name to reduce the likelihood of overwriting an existing file.

2. It removes `Module1` (the old module) from `UserBook.xlsm`, using the `Remove` method of the `VBComponents` collection.

3. It imports the module (saved in Step 1) to `UserBook.xlsm`.

4. It deletes the file saved in Step 1.

5. It reports the action to the user. General error handling is used to inform the user that an error occurred.

 CD-ROM

This example is available on the companion CD-ROM. It requires two workbooks: `UserBook.xlsm` and `UpdateUserBook.xlsm`.

Using VBA to Write VBA Code

The example in this section demonstrates how you can write VBA code that writes more VBA code. The `AddButtonAndCode` procedure does the following:

1. Inserts a new worksheet.

2. Adds an ActiveX `CommandButton` control to the worksheet.

3. Adjusts the position, size, and caption of the CommandButton.

4. Inserts an event handler procedure for the CommandButton named CommandButton1_ Click in the sheet's code module. This procedure simply activates Sheet1.

The AddButtonAndCode procedure follows.

```
Sub AddButtonAndCode()
    Dim NewSheet As Worksheet
    Dim NewButton As OLEObject

'   Add the sheet
    Set NewSheet = Sheets.Add

'   Add a CommandButton
    Set NewButton = NewSheet.OLEObjects.Add _
      ("Forms.CommandButton.1")
    With NewButton
        .Left = 4
        .Top = 4
        .Width = 100
        .Height = 24
        .Object.Caption = "Return to Sheet1"
    End With

'   Add the event handler code
    Code = "Sub CommandButton1_Click()" & vbCrLf
    Code = Code & "    On Error Resume Next" & vbCrLf
    Code = Code & "    Sheets(""Sheet1"").Activate" & vbCrLf
    Code = Code & "    If Err <> 0 Then" & vbCrLf
    Code = Code & "        MsgBox ""Cannot activate Sheet1.""" _
     & vbCrLf
    Code = Code & "    End If" & vbCrLf
    Code = Code & "End Sub"

    With ActiveWorkbook.VBProject. _
      VBComponents(NewSheet.Name).CodeModule
        NextLine = .CountOfLines + 1
        .InsertLines NextLine, Code
    End With
End Sub
```

Figure 28-6 shows the worksheet and the CommandButton control that were added by the AddButtonAndCode procedure.

Figure 28-6: This sheet, the CommandButton, and its event handler were added by using VBA.

CD-ROM

This example is available on the companion CD-ROM. The filename is `add button and code.xlsm`.

The tricky part of this procedure is inserting the VBA code into the code module for the new worksheet. The code is stored in a variable named `Code`, with each instruction separated by a carriage return and linefeed sequence. The `InsertLines` method adds the code to the code module for the inserted worksheet.

The `NextLine` variable stores the number of existing lines in the module incremented by one. This ensures that the procedure is added to the end of the module. If you simply insert the code beginning at line 1, it causes an error if the user's system is set up to add an `Option Explicit` statement to each module automatically.

Figure 28-7 shows the procedure that is created by the `AddButtonAndCode` procedure in its new home in the code window.

```
add button and code.xlsm - Sheet2 (Code)

CommandButton1                          Click

Sub CommandButton1_Click()
    On Error Resume Next
    Sheets("Sheet1").Activate
    If Err <> 0 Then
        MsgBox "Cannot activate Sheet1."
    End If
End Sub
```

Figure 28-7: VBA generated this event handler procedure.

Adding Controls to a UserForm at Design Time

If you've spent any time developing UserForms, you probably know that it can be quite tedious to add and adjust the controls so that they're aligned and sized consistently. Even if you take full advantage of the VBE formatting commands, it can still take a considerable amount of time to get the controls to look just right.

The UserForm shown in Figure 28-8 contains 100 CommandButtons, all of which are identical in size and positioned precisely on the form. Furthermore, each CommandButton has its own event handler procedure. Adding these buttons manually and creating their event handlers would take some time — lots of time. Adding them automatically at design time by using a VBA procedure takes less than a second.

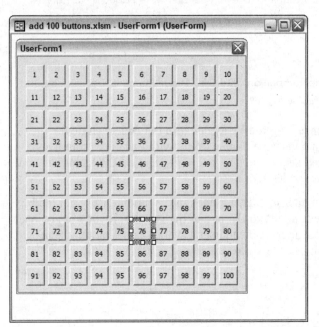

Figure 28-8: A VBA procedure added the CommandButtons on this UserForm.

Design-time versus runtime UserForm manipulations

It's important to understand the distinction between manipulating UserForms or controls at design time and manipulating these objects at runtime. Runtime manipulations are apparent when the UserForm is shown, but the changes made are not permanent. For example, you might write code that changes the Caption property of the UserForm before the form is displayed. The new caption appears when the UserForm is shown, but when you return to the VBE, the UserForm displays its original caption. Runtime manipulation is very common, and Part IV of this book contains many examples of code that perform run-time manipulation of UserForms and controls.

Design-time manipulations, on the other hand, are permanent — just as if you made the changes manually by using the tools in the VBE. Normally, you perform design-time manipulations as a way to automate some of the tedious chores in designing a UserForm. To make design-time manipulations, you access the Designer object for the UserForm.

To demonstrate the difference between design-time and runtime manipulations, I developed two simple procedures that add a CommandButton to a UserForm. One procedure adds the button at runtime; the other adds it at design time.

The following RunTimeButton procedure is very straightforward. When used in a general (non-UserForm) module, it simply adds a CommandButton, changes a few of its properties, and then displays the UserForm. The CommandButton appears on the form when the form is shown, but when you view the form in the VBE, the CommandButton is not there.

```
Sub RunTimeButton()
'   Adds a button at runtime
    Dim Butn As CommandButton
    Set Butn = UserForm1.Controls.Add("Forms.CommandButton.1")
    With Butn
        .Caption = "Added at runtime"
        .Width = 100
        .Top = 10
    End With
    UserForm1.Show
End Sub
```

Following is the DesignTimeButton procedure. What's different here is that this procedure uses the Designer object, which is contained in the VBComponent object. Specifically, it uses the Add method to add the CommandButton control. Because the Designer object was used, the CommandButton is added to the UserForm just as if you did it manually in the VBE.

```
Sub DesignTimeButton()
'   Adds a button at design time
    Dim Butn As CommandButton
    Set Butn = ThisWorkbook.VBProject. _
      VBComponents("UserForm1") _
      .Designer.Controls.Add("Forms.CommandButton.1")
    With Butn
        .Caption = "Added at design time"
        .Width = 120
        .Top = 40
    End With
End Sub
```

Adding 100 CommandButtons at design time

The example in this section demonstrates how to take advantage of the `Designer` object to help you design a UserForm. In this case, the code adds 100 CommandButtons (perfectly spaced and aligned), sets the `Caption` property for each CommandButton, and also creates 100 event handler procedures (one for each CommandButton).

```vba
Sub Add100Buttons()
    Dim UFvbc As VBComponent
    Dim CMod As CodeModule
    Dim ctl As Control
    Dim cb As CommandButton
    Dim n As Long, c As Long, r As Long
    Dim code As String

    Set UFvbc = ThisWorkbook.VBProject.VBComponents("UserForm1")

' Delete all controls, if any
    For Each ctl In UFvbc.Designer.Controls
        UFvbc.Designer.Controls.Remove ctl.Name
    Next ctl

' Delete all VBA code
    UFvbc.CodeModule.DeleteLines 1, UFvbc.CodeModule.CountOfLines

' Add 100 CommandButtons
    n = 1
    For r = 1 To 10
      For c = 1 To 10
        Set cb = UFvbc.Designer. _
          Controls.Add("Forms.CommandButton.1")
        With cb
          .Width = 22
          .Height = 22
          .Left = (c * 26) - 16
          .Top = (r * 26) - 16
          .Caption = n
        End With

'       Add the event handler code
        With UFvbc.CodeModule
          code = ""
          code = code & "Private Sub CommandButton" & n & _
            "_Click" & vbCr
          code = code & "Msgbox ""This is CommandButton" & n & _
            """"" & vbCr
```

```
      code = code & "End Sub"
        .InsertLines .CountOfLines + 1, code
      End With
      n = n + 1
    Next c
  Next r
End Sub
```

CD-ROM

This example is available on the companion CD-ROM. The file is named add 100 buttons.xlsm.

The Add100Buttons procedure requires a UserForm named UserForm1. You'll need to make the UserForm a bit larger than its default size so that the buttons will fit. The procedure starts by deleting all controls on the form by using the Remove method of the Controls collection and then deleting all the code in the code module by using the DeleteLines method of the CodeModule object. Next, the CommandButtons are added, and the event handler procedures are created within two For-Next loops. These event handlers are very simple. Here's an example of such a procedure for CommandButton1:

```
Private Sub CommandButton1_Click()
  MsgBox "This is CommandButton1"
End Sub
```

If you'd like to show the form after adding the controls at design time, you need to add the following instruction right before the End Sub statement:

```
  VBA.UserForms.Add("UserForm1").Show
```

It took me quite a while to figure out how to actually display the UserForm. When VBA generates the 100-button UserForm, it indeed exists in VBA's memory, but it isn't officially part of the project yet. So you need the Add method to formally enroll UserForm1 into the collection of UserForms. The return value of this method is a reference to the form itself, which is why the Show method can be appended to the end of the Add method. So, as a rule, the UserForm must be added to the UserForms collection before it can be used.

Creating UserForms Programmatically

The final topic in this chapter demonstrates how to use VBA code to create UserForms at runtime. I present two examples. One is relatively simple, and the other is quite a bit more complex.

A simple runtime UserForm example

The example in this section isn't all that useful — in fact, it's completely useless. But it does demonstrate some useful concepts. The MakeForm procedure performs several tasks:

1. It creates a temporary UserForm in the active workbook by using the Add method of the VBComponents collection.

2. It adds a CommandButton control to the UserForm by using the Designer object.

3. It adds an event handler procedure to the UserForm's code module (CommandButton1_Click). This procedure, when executed, simply displays a message box and then unloads the form.

4. It displays the UserForm.

5. It deletes the UserForm.

The net result is a UserForm that's created on the fly, put to use, and then deleted. This example and the one in the next section both blur the distinction between modifying forms at design time and modifying forms at runtime. The form is created by using design-time techniques, but it all happens at runtime.

The following shows the MakeForm procedure:

```
Sub MakeForm()
    Dim TempForm As Object
    Dim NewButton As Msforms.CommandButton
    Dim Line As Integer

    Application.VBE.MainWindow.Visible = False

'   Create the UserForm
    Set TempForm = ThisWorkbook.VBProject. _
      VBComponents.Add(3) 'vbext_ct_MSForm
    With TempForm
        .Properties("Caption") = "Temporary Form"
        .Properties("Width") = 200
        .Properties("Height") = 100
    End With

'   Add a CommandButton
    Set NewButton = TempForm.Designer.Controls _
      .Add("Forms.CommandButton.1")
    With NewButton
        .Caption = "Click Me"
        .Left = 60
        .Top = 40
    End With
```

```
'   Add an event-hander sub for the CommandButton
    With TempForm.CodeModule
        Line = .CountOfLines
        .InsertLines Line + 1, "Sub CommandButton1_Click()"
        .InsertLines Line + 2, "   MsgBox ""Hello!"""
        .InsertLines Line + 3, "   Unload Me"
        .InsertLines Line + 4, "End Sub"
    End With

'   Show the form
    VBA.UserForms.Add(TempForm.Name).Show
'
'   Delete the form
    ThisWorkbook.VBProject.VBComponents.Remove TempForm
End Sub
```

CD-ROM

This example, named `create userform on the fly.xlsm`, is available on the companion CD-ROM.

The `MakeForm` procedure creates and shows the simple UserForm shown in Figure 28-9.

Figure 28-9: This UserForm and its underlying code were generated on the fly.

NOTE

The workbook that contains the `MakeForm` procedure does not need a reference to the VBA Extensibility Library because it declares `TempForm` as a generic `Object` (not specifically as a `VBComponent` object). Moreover, it doesn't use any built-in constants.

Notice that one of the first instructions hides the VBE window by setting its `Visible` property to `False`. This eliminates the onscreen flashing that might occur while the form and code are being generated.

A useful (but not so simple) dynamic UserForm example

The example in this section is both instructive and useful. It consists of a function named GetOption that displays a UserForm. Within this UserForm are a number of OptionButtons whose captions are specified as arguments to the function. The function returns a value that corresponds to the OptionButton selected by the user.

CD-ROM

The example in this section is available on the companion CD-ROM. The filename is 'getoption function.xlsm'.

The GetOption function procedure follows.

```
Function GetOption(OpArray, Default, Title)
    Dim TempForm As Object
    Dim NewOptionButton As Msforms.OptionButton
    Dim NewCommandButton1 As Msforms.CommandButton
    Dim NewCommandButton2 As Msforms.CommandButton
    Dim i As Integer, TopPos As Integer
    Dim MaxWidth As Long
    Dim Code As String

'   Hide VBE window to prevent screen flashing
    Application.VBE.MainWindow.Visible = False

'   Create the UserForm
    Set TempForm = _
        ThisWorkbook.VBProject.VBComponents.Add(3)
    TempForm.Properties("Width") = 800

'   Add the OptionButtons
    TopPos = 4
    MaxWidth = 0 'Stores width of widest OptionButton
    For i = LBound(OpArray) To UBound(OpArray)
        Set NewOptionButton = TempForm.Designer.Controls. _
            Add("Forms.OptionButton.1")
        With NewOptionButton
            .Width = 800
            .Caption = OpArray(i)
            .Height = 15
            .Accelerator = Left(.Caption, 1)
            .Left = 8
            .Top = TopPos
            .Tag = i
            .AutoSize = True
```

```
            If Default = i Then .Value = True
            If .Width > MaxWidth Then MaxWidth = .Width
        End With
        TopPos = TopPos + 15
    Next i

'   Add the Cancel button
    Set NewCommandButton1 = TempForm.Designer.Controls. _
        Add("Forms.CommandButton.1")
    With NewCommandButton1
        .Caption = "Cancel"
        .Cancel = True
        .Height = 18
        .Width = 44
        .Left = MaxWidth + 12
        .Top = 6
    End With

'   Add the OK button
    Set NewCommandButton2 = TempForm.Designer.Controls. _
        Add("Forms.CommandButton.1")
    With NewCommandButton2
        .Caption = "OK"
        .Default = True
        .Height = 18
        .Width = 44
        .Left = MaxWidth + 12
        .Top = 28
    End With

'   Add event-hander subs for the CommandButtons
    Code = ""
    Code = Code & "Sub CommandButton1_Click()" & vbCrLf
    Code = Code & "  GETOPTION_RET_VAL=False" & vbCrLf
    Code = Code & "  Unload Me" & vbCrLf
    Code = Code & "End Sub" & vbCrLf
    Code = Code & "Sub CommandButton2_Click()" & vbCrLf
    Code = Code & "  Dim ctl" & vbCrLf
    Code = Code & "  GETOPTION_RET_VAL = False" & vbCrLf
    Code = Code & "  For Each ctl In Me.Controls" & vbCrLf
    Code = Code & "    If TypeName(ctl) = ""OptionButton""" _
        & " Then" & vbCrLf
    Code = Code & "      If ctl Then GETOPTION_RET_VAL = " _
        & "ctl.Tag" & vbCrLf
    Code = Code & "    End If" & vbCrLf
    Code = Code & "  Next ctl" & vbCrLf
    Code = Code & "  Unload Me" & vbCrLf
```

```
    Code = Code & "End Sub"

    With TempForm.CodeModule
        .InsertLines .CountOfLines + 1, Code
    End With

'   Adjust the form
    With TempForm
        .Properties("Caption") = Title
        .Properties("Width") = NewCommandButton1.Left + _
          NewCommandButton1.Width + 10
        If .Properties("Width") < 160 Then
            .Properties("Width") = 160
            NewCommandButton1.Left = 106
            NewCommandButton2.Left = 106
        End If
        .Properties("Height") = TopPos + 24
    End With

'   Show the form
    VBA.UserForms.Add(TempForm.Name).Show

'   Delete the form
    ThisWorkbook.VBProject.VBComponents.Remove VBComponent:=TempForm

'   Pass the selected option back to the calling procedure
    GetOption = GETOPTION_RET_VAL
End Function
```

The GetOption function is remarkably fast, considering all that's going on behind the scenes. On my system, the form appears almost instantaneously. The UserForm is deleted after it has served its purpose.

USING THE GETOPTION FUNCTION

The GetOption function takes three arguments:

- OpArray: A string array that holds the items to be displayed in the form as OptionButtons.

- Default: An integer that specifies the default OptionButton that is selected when the UserForm is displayed. If 0, none of the OptionButtons are selected (the user clicks Cancel).

- Title: The text to display in the title bar of the UserForm.

How GetOption works

The GetOption function performs the following operations:

1. Hides the VBE window to prevent any flashing that could occur when the UserForm is created or the code is added.

2. Creates a UserForm and assigns it to an object variable named TempForm.

3. Adds the OptionButton controls by using the array passed to the function via the OpArray argument. It uses the Tag property of the control to store the index number. The Tag setting of the chosen option is the value that's eventually returned by the function.

4. Adds two CommandButton controls: the OK button and the Cancel button.

5. Creates an event handler procedure for each of the CommandButtons.

6. Does some final cleanup work. It adjusts the position of the CommandButtons as well as the overall size of the UserForm.

7. Displays the UserForm. When the user clicks OK, the CommandButton1_Click procedure is executed. This procedure determines which OptionButton is selected and also assigns a number to the GETOPTION_RET_VAL variable (a Public variable).

8. Deletes the UserForm after it's dismissed.

9. Returns the value of GETOPTION_RET_VAL as the function's result.

NOTE

A significant advantage of creating the UserForm on the fly is that the function is self-contained in a single module and doesn't even require a reference to the VBA Extensibility Library. Therefore, you can simply export this module (which is named modOptionsForm) and then import it into any of your workbooks, thus giving you access to the GetOption function.

The following procedure demonstrates how to use the GetOption function. In this case, the UserForm presents five options (contained in the Ops array).

```
Sub TestGetOption()
    Dim Ops(1 To 5)
    Dim UserOption
    Ops(1) = "North"
    Ops(2) = "South"
    Ops(3) = "West"
    Ops(4) = "East"
    Ops(5) = "All Regions"
    UserOption = GetOption(Ops, 5, "Select a region")
    Debug.Print UserOption
    MsgBox Ops(UserOption)
End Sub
```

The `UserOption` variable contains the index number of the option selected by the user. If the user clicks Cancel (or presses Escape), the `UserOption` variable is set to `False`.

Notice that the `Accelerator` property is set to the first character of each option's caption, so the user can use an Alt+letter combination to make a choice. I made no attempt to avoid duplicate Accelerator keys, so the user may need to press the key combination multiple times to make a selection.

Figure 28-10 shows the UserForm that this function generates.

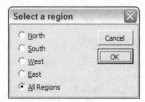

Figure 28-10: The GetOption function generated this UserForm.

 NOTE

The UserForm adjusts its size to accommodate the number of elements in the array passed to it. Theoretically, the `UserOption` function can accept an array of any size. Practically speaking, however, you'll want to limit the number of options to keep the UserForm at a reasonable size. Figure 28-11 shows how the form looks when the options contain more text.

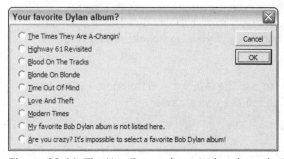

Figure 28-11: The UserForm adjusts its height and width to accommodate the number of options and the length of the text.

GETOPTION EVENT-HANDLER CODE

Following are the event handler procedures for the two CommandButtons. This is the code generated within the `GetOption` function and placed in the code module for the temporary UserForm.

```
Sub CommandButton1_Click()
  GETOPTION_RET_VAL = False
  Unload Me
End Sub

Sub CommandButton2_Click()
  Dim ctl
  GETOPTION_RET_VAL = False
  For Each ctl In Me.Controls
    If TypeName(ctl) = "OptionButton" Then
      If ctl Then GETOPTION_RET_VAL = ctl.Tag
    End If
  Next ctl
  Unload Me
End Sub
```

NOTE

Because the UserForm is deleted after it's used, you can't see what it looks like in the VBE. So, if you'd like to view the UserForm, convert the following instruction to a comment by typing an apostrophe (') in front of it:

```
ThisWorkbook.VBProject.VBComponents.Remove _
  VBComponent:=TempForm
```

Chapter 29

Understanding Class Modules

In This Chapter

This chapter presents an introduction to class modules and includes several examples that might help you better understand this feature and give you ideas for using class modules in your own projects.

♦ An introduction to class modules

♦ Some typical uses for class modules

♦ Examples that demonstrate some key concepts related to class modules

For many VBA programmers, the concept of a class module is a mystery, even though this feature has been available in Visual Basic for several years — it was added to Excel beginning with Excel 97. The examples in this chapter may help to make this powerful feature less mysterious.

What Is a Class Module?

A *class module* is a special type of VBA module that you can insert into a VBA project. Basically, a class module enables the programmer (you) to create a new object class. As you should know by now, programming Excel really boils down to manipulating objects. A class module allows you to create new objects, along with corresponding properties, methods, and events.

CROSS-REFERENCE

Examples in previous chapters in this book use class modules. See Chapters 15, 18, 19, and 22.

At this point, you might be asking, "Do I really need to create new objects?" The answer is no. You don't *need* to, but you might want to after you understand some of the benefits of doing so. In many cases, a class module simply serves as a substitute for functions or procedures, but it could be a more convenient and manageable alternative. In other cases, however, you'll find that a class module is the only way to accomplish a particular task.

Following is a list of some typical uses for class modules:

- *To handle events associated with embedded charts.* (See Chapter 18 for an example.)

- *To monitor application-level events,* such as activating any worksheet. (See Chapters 19 and 22 for examples.)

- *To encapsulate a Windows Application Programming Interface (API) function to make it easier to use in your code.* For example, you can create a class that makes it easy to detect or set the state of the Num Lock or Caps Lock key. Or you can create a class that simplifies access to the Windows Registry.

- *To enable multiple objects in a UserForm to execute a single procedure.* Normally, each object has its own event handler. The example in Chapter 15 demonstrates how to use a class module so that multiple CommandButtons have a single `Click` event handler procedure.

- *To create reusable components that can be imported into other projects.* After you create a general-purpose class module, you can import it into other projects to reduce your development time.

Example: Creating a NumLock Class

In this section, I provide step-by-step instructions for creating a useful, albeit simple, class module. This class module creates a `NumLock` class that has one property (`Value`) and one method (`Toggle`).

Detecting or changing the state of the Num Lock key requires several Windows API functions, and the procedure varies depending on the version of Windows. In other words, it's fairly complicated. The purpose of this class module is to simplify things. All the API declarations and code are contained in a class module (not in your normal VBA modules). The benefits? Your code will be much easier to work with, and you can reuse this class module in your other projects.

After the class is created, your VBA code can determine the current state of the Num Lock key by using an instruction such as the following, which displays the `Value` property:

```
MsgBox NumLock.Value
```

Or your code can change the state of the Num Lock key by changing the `Value` property. The following instruction, for example, turns on the Num Lock key:

```
NumLock.Value = True
```

In addition, your code can toggle the Num Lock key by using the `Toggle` method:

```
NumLock.Toggle
```

It's important to understand that a class module contains the code that *defines* the object, including its properties and methods. You can then create an instance of this object in your VBA general code modules and manipulate its properties and methods.

To better understand the process of creating a class module, you might want to follow the instructions in the sections that follow. Start with an empty workbook.

Inserting a class module

Activate the Visual Basic Editor (VBE) and choose Insert ⇨ Class Module. This adds an empty class module named `Class1`. If the Properties window isn't displayed, press F4 to display it. Then change the name of the class module to `NumLockClass` (see Figure 29-1).

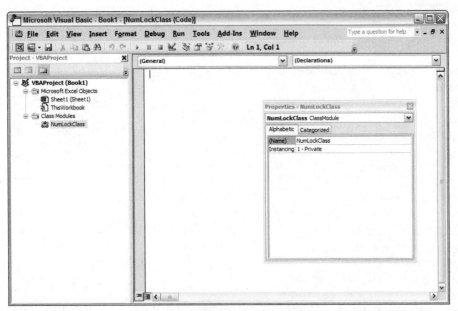

Figure 29-1: An empty class module named NumLockClass.

Adding VBA code to the class module

In this step, you create the code for the Value property. To detect or change the state of the Num Lock key, the class module needs the required Windows API declarations that are used to detect and set the Num Lock key. That code follows:

 NOTE

The VBA code for this example was adapted from an example at the Microsoft Web site.

```
' Type declaration
Private Type OSVERSIONINFO
    dwOSVersionInfoSize As Long
    dwMajorVersion As Long
    dwMinorVersion As Long
    dwBuildNumber As Long
    dwPlatformId As Long
    szCSDVersion As String * 128
End Type


' API declarations
Private Declare Function GetVersionEx Lib "Kernel32" _
    Alias "GetVersionExA" _
    (lpVersionInformation As OSVERSIONINFO) As Long

Private Declare Sub keybd_event Lib "user32" _
    (ByVal bVk As Byte, _
    ByVal bScan As Byte, _
    ByVal dwflags As Long, ByVal dwExtraInfo As Long)

Private Declare Function GetKeyboardState Lib "user32" _
    (pbKeyState As Byte) As Long

Private Declare Function SetKeyboardState Lib "user32" _
    (lppbKeyState As Byte) As Long

'Constant declarations
Const VK_NUMLOCK = &H90
Const VK_SCROLL = &H91
Const VK_CAPITAL = &H14
Const KEYEVENTF_EXTENDEDKEY = &H1
Const KEYEVENTF_KEYUP = &H2
Const VER_PLATFORM_WIN32_NT = 2
Const VER_PLATFORM_WIN32_WINDOWS = 1
```

Next, you need a procedure that retrieves the current state of the Num Lock key. I'll call this the Value property of the object. You can use any name for the property, but

`Value` seems like a good choice. To retrieve the state, insert the following `Property Get` procedure:

```
Property Get Value() As Boolean
'    Get the current state
     Dim keys(0 To 255) As Byte
     GetKeyboardState keys(0)
     Value = keys(VK_NUMLOCK)
End Property
```

CROSS-REFERENCE

The details of `Property` procedures are described later in this chapter. See "Programming properties of objects."

This procedure, which uses the `GetKeyboardState` Windows API function to determine the current state of the Num Lock key, is called whenever VBA code reads the `Value` property of the object. For example, after the object is created, a VBA statement such as this executes the `Property Get` procedure:

```
MsgBox NumLock.Value
```

You now need a procedure that sets the Num Lock key to a particular state: either on or off. You can do this with the following `Property Let` procedure:

```
Property Let Value(boolVal As Boolean)
    Dim o As OSVERSIONINFO
    Dim keys(0 To 255) As Byte
    o.dwOSVersionInfoSize = Len(o)
    GetVersionEx o
    GetKeyboardState keys(0)
'    Is it already in that state?
    If boolVal = True And keys(VK_NUMLOCK) = 1 Then Exit Property
    If boolVal = False And keys(VK_NUMLOCK) = 0 Then Exit Property
'    Toggle it
    If o.dwPlatformId = VER_PLATFORM_WIN32_WINDOWS Then '(Win95)
        'Toggle numlock
       keys(VK_NUMLOCK) = IIf(keys(VK_NUMLOCK) = 0, 1, 0)
       SetKeyboardState keys(0)
    ElseIf o.dwPlatformId = VER_PLATFORM_WIN32_NT Then ' (WinNT)
        'Simulate Key Press
        keybd_event VK_NUMLOCK, &H45, KEYEVENTF_EXTENDEDKEY Or 0, 0
        'Simulate Key Release
        keybd_event VK_NUMLOCK, &H45, KEYEVENTF_EXTENDEDKEY Or _
           KEYEVENTF_KEYUP, 0
    End If
End Property
```

The `Property Let` procedure takes one argument, which is either `True` or `False`. A VBA statement such as the following sets the `Value` property of the `NumLock` object to `True` by executing the `Property Let` procedure:

```
NumLock.Value = True
```

Finally, you need a procedure to toggle the `NumLock` state:

```
Sub Toggle()
'    Toggles the state
     Dim o As OSVERSIONINFO
     o.dwOSVersionInfoSize = Len(o)
     GetVersionEx o
     Dim keys(0 To 255) As Byte
     GetKeyboardState keys(0)
     If o.dwPlatformId = VER_PLATFORM_WIN32_WINDOWS Then '(Win95)
         'Toggle numlock
         keys(VK_NUMLOCK) = IIf(keys(VK_NUMLOCK) = 0, 1, 0)
         SetKeyboardState keys(0)
     ElseIf o.dwPlatformId = VER_PLATFORM_WIN32_NT Then ' (WinNT)
         'Simulate Key Press
         keybd_event VK_NUMLOCK, &H45, KEYEVENTF_EXTENDEDKEY Or 0, 0
         'Simulate Key Release
         keybd_event VK_NUMLOCK, &H45, KEYEVENTF_EXTENDEDKEY Or _
            KEYEVENTF_KEYUP, 0
     End If
End Sub
```

Notice that `Toggle` is a standard `Sub` procedure (not a `Property Let` or `Property Get` procedure). A VBA statement such as the following one toggles the state of the `NumLock` object by executing the `Toggle` procedure.

```
NumLock.Toggle
```

Using the NumLockClass class

Before you can use the `NumLockClass` class module, you must create an instance of the object. The following statement, which resides in a regular VBA module (not the class module), does just that:

```
Dim NumLock As New NumLockClass
```

Notice that the object type is `NumLockClass` (that is, the name of the class module). The object variable itself can have any name, but `NumLock` certainly seems like a logical name for this.

The following procedure sets the `Value` property of the `NumLock` object to `True`, which results in the Num Lock key being turned on:

```
Sub NumLockOn()
    Dim NumLock As New NumLockClass
    NumLock.Value = True
End Sub
```

The next procedure displays a message box that indicates the current state of the Num Lock key (`True` is on; `False` is off):

```
Sub GetNumLockState()
    Dim NumLock As New NumLockClass
    MsgBox NumLock.Value
End Sub
```

The following procedure toggles the Num Lock key:

```
Sub ToggleNumLock()
    Dim NumLock As New NumLockClass
    NumLock.Toggle
End Sub
```

Notice that there's another way to toggle the Num Lock key without using the `Toggle` method:

```
Sub ToggleNumLock2()
    Dim NumLock As New NumLockClass
    NumLock.Value = Not NumLock.Value
End Sub
```

It should be clear that using the `NumLock` class is much simpler than using the API functions. After you create a class module, you can reuse it in any other project simply by importing the class module.

 CD-ROM

The completed class module for this example is available on the companion CD-ROM. The workbook, named `keyboard classes.xlsm`, also contains class modules to detect and set the state of the Caps Lock key and the Scroll Lock key.

More about Class Modules

The example in the preceding section demonstrates how to create a new object class with a single property named `Value` and a single method named `Toggle`. An object class can contain any number of properties, methods, and events.

Naming the object class

The name that you use for the class module in which you define the object class is also the name of the object class. By default, class modules are named `Class1`, `Class2`, and so on. Usually, you'll want to provide a more meaningful name for your object class.

Programming properties of objects

Most objects have at least one property, and you can give them as many as you need. After a property is defined and the object is created, you can use it in your code using the standard "dot" syntax:

```
object.property
```

The VBE Auto List Members option works with objects defined in a class module. This makes it easier to select properties or methods when writing code.

Properties for the object that you define can be read-only, write-only, or read/write. You define a read-only property with a single procedure — using the `Property Get` keyword. Here's an example of a `Property Get` procedure:

```
Property Get FileNameOnly() As String
    FileNameOnly = ""
    For i = Len(FullName) To 1 Step -1
        Char = Mid(FullName, i, 1)
        If Char = "\" Then
            Exit Function
        Else
            FileNameOnly = Char & FileNameOnly
        End If
    Next i
End Property
```

You might have noticed that a `Property Get` procedure works like a `Function` procedure. The code performs calculations and then returns a property value that corresponds to the procedure's name. In this example, the procedure's name is `FileNameOnly`. The property value returned is the filename part of a path string (contained in a `Public` variable named `FullName`). For example, if `FullName` is `c:\data\myfile.txt`, the procedure returns a property value of `myfile.txt`. The `FileNameOnly` procedure is called when VBA code references the object and property.

For read/write properties, you create two procedures: a `Property Get` procedure (which reads a property value) and a `Property Let` procedure (which writes a property value). The value being assigned to the property is treated as the final argument (or the only argument) of a `Property Get` procedure.

Two example procedures follow:

```
Dim XLFile As Boolean

Property Get SaveAsExcelFile() As Boolean
    SaveAsExcelFile = XLFile
End Property

Property Let SaveAsExcelFile(boolVal As Boolean)
    XLFile = boolVal
End Property
```

NOTE

Use `Property Set` in place of `Property Let` when the property is an object data type.

A `Public` variable in a class module can also be used as a property of the object. In the preceding example, the `Property Get` and `Property Let` procedures could be eliminated and replaced with this module-level declaration:

```
Public SaveAsExcelFile As Boolean
```

In the unlikely event that you need to create a write-only property, you create a single `Property Let` procedure with no corresponding `Property Get` procedure.

The preceding examples use a Boolean module-level variable named `XLFile`. The `Property Get` procedure simply returns the value of this variable as the property value. If the object were named `FileSys`, for example, the following statement would display the current value of the `SaveAsExcelFile` property:

```
MsgBox FileSys.SaveAsExcelFile
```

The `Property Let` statement, on the other hand, accepts an argument and uses the argument to change the value of a property. For example, you could write a statement such as the following to set the `SaveAsExcelFile` property to `True`:

```
FileSys.SaveAsExcelFile = True
```

In this case, the value `True` is passed to the `Property Let` statement, thus changing the property's value.

The preceding examples use a module-level variable named `XLFile` that actually stores the property value. You'll need to create a variable that represents the value for each property that you define within your class module.

NOTE

Normal procedure-naming rules apply to property procedures, and you'll find that VBA won't let you use some names if they are reserved words. So, if you get a syntax error when creating a property procedure, try changing the name of the procedure.

Programming methods for objects

A method for an object class is programmed by using a standard Sub or Function procedure placed in the class module. An object might or might not use methods. Your code executes a method by using standard notation:

```
object.method
```

Like any other VBA method, a method that you write for an object class will perform some type of action. The following procedure is an example of a method that saves a workbook in one of two file formats, depending on the value of the XLFile variable. As you can see, there is nothing special about this procedure.

```
Sub SaveFile()
    If XLFile Then
        ActiveWorkbook.SaveAs FileName:=FName, _
            FileFormat:=xlWorkbookNormal
    Else
        ActiveWorkbook.SaveAs FileName:=FName, _
            FileFormat:=xlCSV
    End If
End Sub
```

The CSVFileClass example in the next section should clarify the concepts of properties and methods for object classes defined in a class module.

Class module events

Every class module has two events: Initialize and Terminate. The Initialize event is triggered when a new instance of the object is created; the Terminate event is triggered when the object is destroyed. You might want to use the Initialize event to set default property values.

The frameworks for these event handler procedures are as follows:

```
Private Sub Class_Initialize()
'    Initialization code goes here
End Sub

Private Sub Class_Terminate()
'    Termination code goes here
End Sub
```

An object is *destroyed* (and the memory it uses is freed) when the procedure or module in which it is declared finishes executing. You can destroy an object at any time by setting it to Nothing. The following statement, for example, destroys the object named MyObject:

```
Set MyObject = Nothing
```

Example: A CSV File Class

The example presented in this section defines an object class called CSVFileClass. This class has two properties and two methods:

- *Properties:*
    - ExportRange: (Read/write) A worksheet range to be exported as a CSV file.
    - ImportRange: (Read/write) The range into which a CSV file will be imported.
- *Methods:*
    - Import: Imports the CSV file represented by the CSVFileName argument into the range represented by the ImportRange property.
    - Export: Exports the range represented by the ExportRange property to a CSV file represented by the CSVFileName argument.

 CD-ROM

The example in this section is available on the companion CD-ROM. The filename is 'csv class.xlsm'.

Class module–level variables for the CSVFileClass

A class module must maintain its own private variables that mirror the property settings for the class. The CSVFileClass class module uses two variables to keep track of the two property settings. These variables are declared at the top of the class module:

```
Private RangeToExport As Range
Private ImportToCell As Range
```

RangeToExport is a Range object that represents the range to be exported. ImportToCell is a Range object that represents the upper-left cell of the range into which the file will be imported. These variables are assigned values by the Property Get and Property Let procedures listed in the next section.

Property procedures for the CSVFileClass

The property procedures for the CSVFileClass class module follow. The Property Get procedures return the value of a variable, and the Property Let procedures set the value of a variable.

```
Property Get ExportRange() As Range
    Set ExportRange = RangeToExport
End Property

Property Let ExportRange(rng As Range)
    Set RangeToExport = rng
End Property

Property Get ImportRange() As Range
    Set ImportRange = ImportToCell
End Property

Property Let ImportRange(rng As Range)
    Set ImportToCell = rng
End Property
```

Method procedures for the CSVFileClass

The CSVFileClass class module contains two procedures that represent the two methods. These are listed and discussed in the sections that follow.

THE EXPORT PROCEDURE

The Export procedure is called when the Export method is executed. It takes one argument: the full name of the file receiving the exported range. The procedure provides some basic error handling. For example, it ensures that the ExportRange property has been set by checking the RangeToExport variable. The procedure sets up an error handler to trap other errors.

```
Sub Export(CSVFileName)
'    Exports a range to CSV file
    If RangeToExport Is Nothing Then
        MsgBox "ExportRange not specified"
        Exit Sub
    End If

    On Error GoTo ErrHandle
    Application.ScreenUpdating = False
    Set ExpBook = Workbooks.Add(xlWorksheet)
    RangeToExport.Copy
```

```
        Application.DisplayAlerts = False

        With ExpBook
            .Sheets(1).Paste
            .SaveAs FileName:=CSVFileName, FileFormat:=xlCSV
            .Close SaveChanges:=False
        End With
        Application.CutCopyMode = False
        Application.ScreenUpdating = True
        Application.DisplayAlerts = True
        Exit Sub
ErrHandle:
        ExpBook.Close SaveChanges:=False
        Application.CutCopyMode = False
        Application.ScreenUpdating = True
        Application.DisplayAlerts = True
        MsgBox "Error " & Err & vbCrLf & vbCrLf & Error(Err), _
            vbCritical, "Export Method Error"
End Sub
```

The Export procedure works by copying the range specified by the RangeToExport variable to a new temporary workbook, saving the workbook as a CSV text file, and closing the file. Because screen updating is turned off, the user does not see this happening. If an error occurs — for example, an invalid filename is specified — the procedure jumps to the ErrHandle section and displays a message box that contains the error number and description.

THE IMPORT PROCEDURE

The Import procedure imports a CSV file specified by the CSVFileName argument and copies its contents to a range specified by the ImportToCell variable, which maintains the ImportRange property. The file is then closed. Again, screen updating is turned off, so the user does not see the file being opened. Like the Export procedure, the Import procedure incorporates some basic error handling.

```
Sub Import(CSVFileName)
'   Imports a CSV file to a range
    If ImportToCell Is Nothing Then
        MsgBox "ImportRange not specified"
        Exit Sub
    End If

    If CSVFileName = "" Then
        MsgBox "Import FileName not specified"
        Exit Sub
    End If

    On Error GoTo ErrHandle
```

```
    Application.ScreenUpdating = False
    Application.DisplayAlerts = False
    Workbooks.Open CSVFileName
    Set CSVFile = ActiveWorkbook
    ActiveSheet.UsedRange.Copy Destination:=ImportToCell
    CSVFile.Close SaveChanges:=False
    Application.ScreenUpdating = True
    Application.DisplayAlerts = True
    Exit Sub
ErrHandle:
    CSVFile.Close SaveChanges:=False
    Application.ScreenUpdating = True
    Application.DisplayAlerts = True
    MsgBox "Error " & Err & vbCrLf & vbCrLf & Error(Err), _
        vbCritical, "Import Method Error"
End Sub
```

Using the CSVFileClass object

To create an instance of a CSVFileClass object in your code, start by declaring a variable as type CSVFileClass. Here's an example:

```
Dim CSVFile As New CSVFileClass
```

You might prefer to declare the object variable first and then create the object when needed. This requires a Dim statement and a Set statement:

```
Dim CSVFile As CSVFileClass
' other code may go here
Set CSVFile = New CSVFileClass
```

The advantage of using both a Dim and a Set statement is that the object isn't actually created until the Set statement is executed. You might want to use this technique to save memory by not creating an object if it's not needed. For example, your code might contain logic that determines whether the object is actually created. In addition, using the Set command enables you to create multiple instances of an object.

After creating an instance of the object, you can write other instructions to access the properties and methods defined in the class module.

As you can see in Figure 29-2, the VBE Auto List Members feature works just like any other object. After you type the variable name and a dot, you see a list of properties and methods for the object.

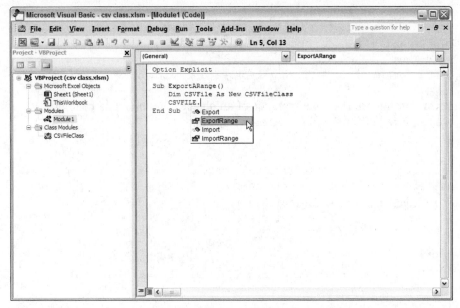

Figure 29-2: The Auto List Members feature displays the available properties and methods.

The following procedure demonstrates how to save the current range selection to a CSV file named `temp.csv`, which is stored in the same directory as the current workbook:

```
Sub ExportARange()
    Dim CSVFile As New CSVFileClass
    With CSVFile
        .ExportRange = ActiveWindow.RangeSelection
        .Export CSVFileName:=ThisWorkbook.Path & "\temp.csv"
    End With
End Sub
```

Using the `With-End With` structure isn't mandatory. For example, the procedure could be written as follows:

```
Sub ExportARange()
    Dim CSVFile As New CSVFileClass
    CSVFile.ExportRange = ActiveWindow.RangeSelection
    CSVFile.Export CSVFileName:=ThisWorkbook.Path & "\temp.csv"
End Sub
```

The following procedure demonstrates how to import a CSV file, beginning at the active cell:

```
Sub ImportAFile()
    Dim CSVFile As New CSVFileClass
    With CSVFile
    On Error Resume Next
```

```
        .ImportRange = ActiveCell
        .Import CSVFileName:=ThisWorkbook.Path & "\temp.csv"
    End With
    If Err <> 0 Then _
      MsgBox "Cannot import " & ThisWorkbook.Path & "\temp.csv"    End Sub
```

Your code can work with more than one instance of an object. The following code, for example, creates an array of three CSVFileClass objects:

```
Sub Export3Files()
    Dim CSVFile(1 To 3) As New CSVFileClass
    CSVFile(1).ExportRange = Range("A1:A20")
    CSVFile(2).ExportRange = Range("B1:B20")
    CSVFile(3).ExportRange = Range("C1:C20")

    For i = 1 To 3
        CSVFile(i).Export CSVFileName:="File" & i & ".csv"
    Next i
End Sub
```

Chapter 30

Working with Colors

In This Chapter

One of the most significant changes in Excel 2007 is the abandonment of the old 56-color workbook palette. This chapter describes how color is used in Excel 2007, including the new *themes*. I include many examples that should help you understand how these changes affect your workbooks. Here you will find

- ◆ Specifying colors in VBA code
- ◆ VBA conversion functions for various color models
- ◆ Converting colors to grayscale
- ◆ Working with Excel 2007 document themes
- ◆ Modifying colors in Shape objects
- ◆ Modifying colors in charts

Dealing with color in Excel 2007 is no trivial matter. I'm the first to admit that it can be complicated. And often, recording a macro while you change the color of a cell or object only adds to the confusion. In this chapter, I attempt to pull it all together.

Back in the pre–Excel 2007 days, a workbook stored a palette of 56-colors. These colors were the only ones available for cell backgrounds, cell text, and charts. Sure, you could modify any or all those colors, but there was no way to exceed the 56-color limit for a workbook.

But things have changed. You now have access to a virtually unlimited number of colors in a workbook — actually, the limit is 16,777,216 colors, but that certainly qualifies as virtually unlimited in my book.

Specifying Colors

In VBA, you can specify a color as a decimal color value, which is a number between 0 and 16,777,215. For example, the VBA statement that follows changes the background color of the active cell to a dark maroon:

```
ActiveCell.Interior.Color = 5911168
```

In addition, VBA has some predefined constants for some common colors. For example, vbRed has a value of 255 (the decimal value for pure red) and vbGreen has a value of 65,280.

No one, of course, can keep track of nearly 17 million colors, and the predefined constants are limited. A better way to change a color is to specify the color in terms of its red, green, and blue components — the RGB color system.

The RGB color system

The RGB color system combines various levels of three colors: red, green, and blue. Each of these colors can range from 0 through 255. Therefore, the total number of possible colors is 256 x 256 x 256 = 16,777,216. When all three color components are 0, the color is pure black. When all three components are 255, the color is pure white. When all three are 128 (the half-way point), the color is middle gray. The remaining 16,777,213 possible combinations of these three values represent other colors.

To specify a color using the RGB system in VBA, use the RGB function. This function accepts three arguments that represent the red, blue, and green components of a color. The function returns a decimal color value.

The statement that follows uses the RGB function to assign a color that's exactly the same as the one assigned in the preceding section (that dark maroon, 5911168):

```
ActiveCell.Interior.Color = RGB(128, 50, 90)
```

Table 30-1 shows the RGB values and the decimal color code of some common colors:

TABLE 30-1   COLOR EXAMPLES

Name	Red Component	Green Component	Blue Component	Color Value
Black	0	0	0	0
White	255	255	255	16777215
Red	255	0	0	255
Green	0	255	0	65280
Blue	0	0	255	16711680
Yellow	255	255	0	65535
Pink	255	0	255	16711935
Turquoise	0	255	255	16776960
Brown	153	51	0	13209
Indigo	51	51	153	10040115
80% Gray	51	51	51	3355443

The HSL color system

If you select the More Colors option when choosing a color in Excel, you see the Colors dialog box. Click the Custom tab, and you can choose from two color models to specify your color: RGB and HSL. Figure 30-1 shows the Colors dialog box with the HSL color model selected.

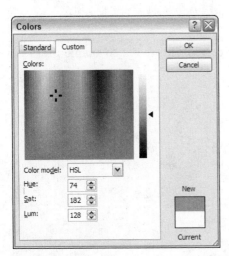

Figure 30-1: Choosing a color using the HSL color system.

In the HSL color system, colors are specified using three parameters: Hue, Saturation, and Luminance. As with RGB colors, each of these parameters can range from 0 to 255. Each RGB color has an equivalent HSL color, and each HSL color has an equivalent decimal color value. In other words, any of the 16,777,216 colors can be specified by using any of the three color systems: RGB, HSL, or decimal.

Although the Colors dialog box lets you specify a color using the HSL color model, this is actually the *only* area in which Excel supports the HSL color model. For example, when you specify a color using VBA, it must be decimal color value. You can, of course, use the RGB function to return a decimal color value. However, VBA does not have a corresponding HSL function.

Converting colors

If you know the three color component values, converting an RGB color to a decimal color is easy. Just use VBA's RGB function. Assume three variables (r, g, and b), each of which represents a color component value between 0 and 255. To calculate the equivalent decimal color value, use a statement like this:

```
DecimalColor = RGB(r, g, b)
```

To perform this conversion in a worksheet formula, create this simple VBA wrapper function:

```
Function RGB2DECIMAL(R, G, B)
'   Converts from RGB to decimal color
    RGB2DECIMAL = RGB(R, G, B)
End Function
```

The following example worksheet formula assumes the three color values are in A1:C1:

```
=RGB2DECIMAL(A1,B1,C1)
```

Converting a decimal color to its red, green, and blue components is not so simple. Here's a function that returns a three-element array:

```
Function DECIMAL2RGB(ColorVal) As Variant
'   Converts a color value to an RGB triplet
'   Returns a 3-element variant array
    DECIMAL2RGB = Array(ColorVal \ 256 ^ 0 And 255, _
      ColorVal \ 256 ^ 1 And 255, ColorVal \ 256 ^ 2 And 255)
End Function
```

To use the DECIMAL2RGB function in a worksheet formula, the formula must be entered as a three-cell array formula. For example, assume that cell A1 contains a decimal color value. To convert that color value to its RGB components, select a three-cell horizontal range and then enter the following formula. Press Ctrl+Shift+Enter to make it an array formula, and don't enter the braces.

```
{=DECIMAL2RGB(A1)}
```

If the three-cell range is vertical, you need to transpose the array, as follows:

```
{=TRANSPOSE(DECIMAL2RGB(A1))}
```

Figure 30-2 shows the DECIMAL2RGB function in use in a worksheet.

	A	B	C	D	E	F
1	**Decimal**			**Decimal-To-RGB**		
2	Color Value		R	G	B	
3	0		0	0	0	
4	167,772		92	143	2	
5	335,544		184	30	5	
6	503,316		20	174	7	
7	671,088		112	61	10	
8	838,860		204	204	12	
9	1,006,632		40	92	15	
10	1,174,404		132	235	17	
11	1,342,176		224	122	20	
12	1,509,948		60	10	23	
13	1,677,720		152	153	25	
14	1,845,492		244	40	28	
15	2,013,264		80	184	30	
16	2,181,036		172	71	33	
17	2,348,808		8	215	35	
18	2,516,580		100	102	38	
19	2,684,352		192	245	40	
20	2,852,124		28	133	43	
21	3,019,896		120	20	46	
22	3,187,668		212	163	48	

Figure 30-2: The DECIMAL2RGB function converts a decimal color value to its red, green, and blue components.

CD-ROM

The companion CD-ROM contains a workbook with the following color conversion functions: DECIMAL2RGB, DECIMAL2HSL, HSL2RGB, RGB2DECIMAL, RGB2HSL, and HSL2DECIMAL. The file is named color conversion functions.xlsm.

More about Decimal Color Values

You may be curious about how the 16,777,216 decimal color values are arranged. Color 0 is black, and color 16,777,216 is white, but what about all those colors in between?

It might help to think of the decimal color values as being generated by nested `For-Next` loops, as shown in the following code:

```
Sub GenerateColorValues()
    Dim Red As Long, Blue As Long, Green As Long
    Dim AllColors(0 To 16777215) As Long
    Dim ColorNum As Long
    ColorNum = 0
    For Blue = 0 To 255
        For Green = 0 To 255
            For Red = 0 To 255
                AllColors(ColorNum) = RGB(Red, Blue, Green)
                ColorNum = ColorNum + 1
            Next Red
        Next Green
    Next Blue

End Sub
```

After this procedure runs, the values in the `AllColors` array correspond exactly to the decimal color values used by Excel.

Understanding Grayscale

When you create worksheets and charts, it's important to remember that not everyone has a color printer. And even if your chart is printed on a color printer, it's possible that it may be photocopied, faxed, or viewed by someone who is color-blind (a condition that affects about 8 percent of the male population).

When content is printed on a non-color device, colors are converted to grayscale. Sometimes you'll be lucky and your colors will display nicely when converted to grayscale. Other times, you won't be so lucky. For example, the columns in a chart may be indistinguishable when the colors are converted.

Every grayscale color has an equal component of red, green, and blue. Pure black is `RGB(0, 0, 0)`. Pure white is `RGB(255, 255, 255)`. Neutral gray is `RGB(128, 128, 128)`. Using this color system produces 256 shades of gray.

To create a 256-color grayscale in a range of cells, execute the procedure that follows. It colors the background of cells in the range A1:A256, starting with black and ending with white. You might want to zoom out on the worksheet to see the entire range.

```
Sub GenerateGrayScale()
    Dim r As Long
    For r = 0 To 255
        Cells(r + 1, 1).Interior.Color = RGB(r, r, r)
    Next r
End Sub
```

Converting colors to gray

One approach to grayscale conversion is to simply average the Red, Green, and Blue components of a color and use that single value for the Red, Green, and Blue components of its grayscale equivalent. That approach, however, does not take into account the fact that different colors are perceived as varying levels of brightness. For example, green is perceived to be brighter than red, and red is perceived to be brighter than blue.

Perceptual experiments have arrived at the following "recipe" to convert an RGB color value to a grayscale value

- 28.7% of the red component
- 58.9% of the green component
- 11.4% of the blue component

For example, consider color value 16751001, a shade of violet that corresponds to RGB(153, 153, 255). Applying the factors listed previously, the RGB values are

- Red: $28.7\% \times 153 = 44$
- Green: $58.9\% \times 153 = 90$
- Blue: $11.4\% \times 255 = 29$

The sum of these values is 163. Therefore, the corresponding grayscale RGB value for color value 16751001 is RGB(163, 163, 163).

Following is a VBA function that accepts a decimal color value as its argument and returns the corresponding grayscale decimal value.

```
Function Grayscale(color)
    Dim r As Long, g As Long, b As Long
    r = (color \ 256 ^ 0 And 255) * 0.287
    g = (color \ 256 ^ 1 And 255) * 0.589
    b = (color \ 256 ^ 2 And 255) * 0.114
    Grayscale = RGB(r + g + b, r + g + b, r + g + b)
End Function
```

Viewing charts as grayscale

One way to approximate how your colors will look when converted to grayscale is to use Excel's Print Preview feature with the printer set to a non-color device (such as a fax).

Here's a technique that lets you see how an embedded chart looks converted to grayscale:

1. Select the chart.

2. Press Ctrl+C to copy the chart to the Clipboard.

3. Click a cell and choose Home ➪ Clipboard ➪ Paste ➪ Paste As Picture.

4. Select the picture and choose Picture Tools ➪ Format ➪ Recolor and then choose the Grayscale color mode from the drop-down gallery.

These steps are automated in the macro that follows. The ShowChartAsGrayScale procedure copies the active chart as a picture and converts the picture to grayscale. After you've determined whether the colors are satisfactory, you can delete the picture.

```
Sub ShowChartAsGrayScale()
'   Copies the active chart as a grayscale picture
'   Embedded charts only
    If ActiveChart Is Nothing Then
        MsgBox "Select a chart."
        Exit Sub
    End If
    ActiveChart.Parent.CopyPicture
    ActiveChart.Parent.TopLeftCell.Select
    ActiveSheet.Pictures.Paste
    ActiveSheet.Pictures(ActiveSheet.Pictures.Count). _
      ShapeRange.PictureFormat.ColorType = msoPictureGrayscale
End Sub
```

 CD-ROM

A workbook with this example is available on the companion CD-ROM. The filename is chart to grayscale picture.xlsm.

Experimenting with Colors

Figure 30-3 shows a workbook that I created that deals with colors. If you're at all confused about how the RGB color model works, spending some time with this color demo workbook will probably make it all very clear.

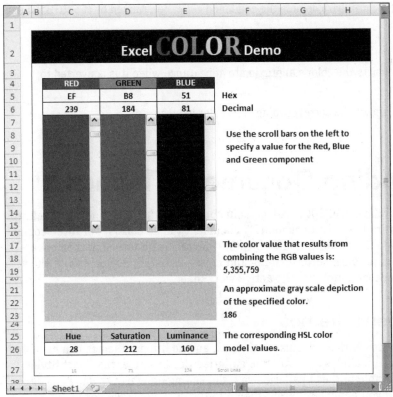

Figure 30-3: This workbook demonstrates how red, green, and blue colors combine.

 CD-ROM

This workbook, named RGB color demo.xlsm, is available on the companion CD-ROM.

This workbook contains three vertical scrollbars, each of which controls the background color of a range. Use these scrollbars to specify the red, green, and blue component for a color to values between 0 and 255. Moving the scrollbars changes several areas of the worksheet:

- The cells above the scrollbars display the color components in hexadecimal (00–FF) and in decimal (0–255).Hexadecimal RGB color values are often used in specifying colors for HTML documents.

- The ranges next to each scrollbar change intensity, corresponding to the scrollbar's position (that is, the value of the color component).

- A range below the scrollbars depicts the combined color, determined by the RGB values you specify.

- A cell displays the decimal color value.

- Another range depicts the color's approximate appearance when it is converted to grayscale.

- A range of cells shows the corresponding HSL color values.

Understanding Document Themes

A significant new feature in Excel 2007 is document themes. With a single mouse click, the user can change the entire look of a document. A document theme consists of three components: colors, fonts, and effects (for graphic objects). The rationale for using themes is that they may help users produce better-looking and more consistent documents. A theme applies to the entire workbook, not just the active worksheet.

About document themes

Microsoft Office 2007 ships with 20 document themes, and additional themes can be added. The user interface Ribbon includes several style galleries (for example, the Chart Styles gallery). The styles available in these galleries vary depending on which theme is assigned to the document. And, if you apply a different theme to the document, the document changes to reflect the new theme's colors, fonts, and effects.

 CD-ROM

If you haven't explored document themes, open the workbook named `document theme demo.xlsx` found on the companion CD-ROM. This workbook contains a range that shows each theme color, two shapes, text (using the headings and body fonts), and a chart. Choose Page Layout ⇨ Themes ⇨ Themes Gallery to see how the worksheet changes with each theme.

Users can also mix and match theme elements. For example, it's possible to use the colors from one theme, the fonts from another theme, and the effects from yet a different theme. In addition, the user can create a new color set or a new font set. These customized themes can be saved and then applied to other workbooks.

NOTE

The concept of document themes is based on the notion that users will apply little, if any, non-theme formatting to the document. If the user applies colors or fonts that aren't part of the current theme, this formatting will not be modified if a new theme is applied to the document. Therefore, it's still very easy to create an ugly document with mismatched colors and too many different fonts.

Understanding document theme colors

When a user applies a color to a cell or object, the color is selected from a control like the one shown in Figure 30-4. The control displays the 60 theme colors (10 columns by 6 rows) plus 10 additional standard colors. Clicking the More Colors option displays the Color dialog box, in which the user can specify any of the 16,777,216 available colors.

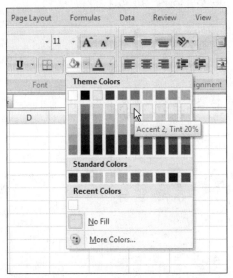

Figure 30-4: A color-selection control.

The 60 theme colors are identified by pop-up ToolTips. For example, the color in the second row of the sixth column is known as "Accent 2, Tint 20%." Table 30-2 shows the names of all 60 theme colors. Examine the table, and you see that there isn't much of a pattern — although the Accent colors are consistent in terms of the tint and shade variations. Also, note that some color variations are known as a *tint* and others are known as a *shade*.

TABLE 30-2 THEME COLOR NAMES

Row/Column	1	2	3	4	5	6	7	8	9	10
1	Text/Background 1	Text/Background 2	Text/Background 3	Text/Background 4	Accent 1	Accent 2	Accent 3	Accent 4	Accent 5	Accent 6
2	Shade 95%	Tint 95%	Shade 90%	Tint 20%	Tint 20%	Tint 20%	Tint 20%	Tint 20%	Tint 20%	Tint 20%
3	Shade 85%	Tint 65%	Shade 75%	Tint 40%	Tint 40%	Tint 40%	Tint 40%	Tint 40%	Tint 40%	Tint 40%
4	Shade 75%	Tint 75%	Shade 50%	Tint 60%	Tint 60%	Tint 60%	Tint 60%	Tint 60%	Tint 60%	Tint 60%
5	Shade 65%	Tint 85%	Shade 25%	Shade 75%	Shade 75%	Shade 75%	Shade 75%	Shade 75%	Shade 75%	Shade 75%
6	Shade 50%	Tint 95%	Shade 10%	Shade 50%	Shade 50%	Shade 50%	Shade 50%	Shade 50%	Shade 50%	Shade 50%

Keep in mind that these color names remain the same, even if a different document theme is applied. The document theme colors actually consist of the 10 colors displayed in the top row (four text/background colors and six accent colors), and each of these 10 colors has five tint/shade variations.

NOTE

If you select Page Layout ⇨ Themes ⇨ Colors ⇨ Create New Theme Colors, you see that a theme has two additional colors: Hyperlink and Followed Hyperlink. These are the colors applied when a hyperlink is created, and they are not shown in the color selector control.

You may find it enlightening to record a macro while you change the fill color and text color of a range. Following is a macro that I recorded when a range was selected. For the fill color, I chose "Accent 2, Shade 75%," and for the text color, I chose "Text/Background 3, Shade 90%."

```
Sub Macro1()
    With Selection.Interior
        .Pattern = xlSolid
        .PatternColorIndex = 56
        .ThemeColor = 6
        .TintAndShade = -0.249977111117893
        .PatternTintAndShade = 0
    End With
    With Selection.Font
        .ThemeColor = 3
        .TintAndShade = -9.99786370433668E-02
    End With
End Sub
```

First of all, you can safely ignore the three pattern-related properties (`Pattern`, `PatternColorIndex`, and `PatternTintAndShade`). These properties refer to the ugly, old-fashioned (but still supported) cell patterns, which you can specify in the Fill tab of the Format Cells dialog box. These properties simply maintain any existing pattern that may exist in the range.

The recorded macro, after I delete the three pattern-related properties, is

```
Sub Macro1()
    With Selection.Interior
        .ThemeColor = 6
        .TintAndShade = -0.249977111117893
    End With
    With Selection.Font
        .ThemeColor = 3
        .TintAndShade = -9.99786370433668E-02
    End With
End Sub
```

Part VII

As you can see, each color is specified in terms of a `ThemeColor` property and a `TintAndShade` property. The `ThemeColor` property is easy enough to decipher. It's simply the column number of the 10-x-6 theme color table. But what about the `TintAndShade` property?

The `TintAndShade` property can have a value between –1 and +1. A value of –1 results in black, and a value of +1 results in white. A `TintAndShade` property value of 0 gives the *pure* color. In other words, as the `TintAndShade` value goes negative, the color gets increasingly darker until it's pure black. As the `TintAndShade` value goes positive, the color gets increasingly lighter until it's pure white.

To arrive at the `TintAndShade` property value that corresponds to a particular theme color variation, look at Table 30-2.

- If the color variation is expressed as a Tint, the `TintAndShade` property value is 1 minus the percent value (a positive value, making the variation lighter than the original color).

- If the color variation is expressed as a Shade, the `TintAndShade` property value is the percent value minus 1 (a negative value, making the variation darker than the original value).

CD-ROM

For a demonstration of how the `TintAndShade` property changes a color, open the `tintandshade demo.xlsm` workbook on the companion CD-ROM (see Figure 30-5). Specify a starting color, and the macro displays that color with 50 levels of the `TintAndShade` property values, ranging from –1 to +1. It also displays the decimal color value and the red, green, and blue components of the color (which are displayed in a chart).

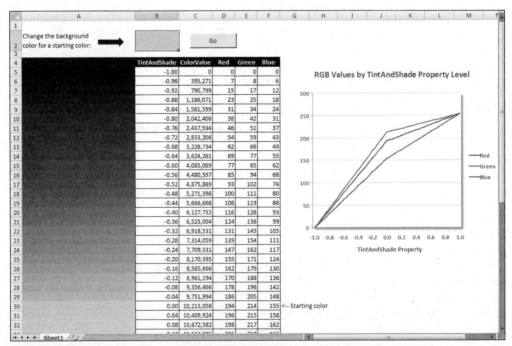

Figure 30-5: This workbook demonstrates how the TintAndShade property affects a color.

Displaying all theme colors

Using the information in Table 30-1, I wrote a macro that displays all 60 theme color variations in a range of cells.

```
Sub ShowThemeColors()
  Dim r As Long, c As Long
  For r = 1 To 6
    For c = 1 To 10
        With Cells(r, c).Interior
        .ThemeColor = c
        Select Case c
            Case 1 'Text/Background 1
            Select Case r
                Case 1: .TintAndShade = 0
                Case 2: .TintAndShade = -0.05
                Case 3: .TintAndShade = -0.15
                Case 4: .TintAndShade = -0.25
                Case 5: .TintAndShade = -0.35
                Case 6: .TintAndShade = -0.5
            End Select
        Case 2 'Text/Background 2
            Select Case r
                Case 1: .TintAndShade = 0
                Case 2: .TintAndShade = 0.5
                Case 3: .TintAndShade = 0.35
                Case 4: .TintAndShade = 0.25
                Case 5: .TintAndShade = 0.15
                Case 6: .TintAndShade = 0.05
            End Select
        Case 3 'Text/Background 3
            Select Case r
                Case 1: .TintAndShade = 0
                Case 2: .TintAndShade = -0.1
                Case 3: .TintAndShade = -0.25
                Case 4: .TintAndShade = -0.5
                Case 5: .TintAndShade = -0.75
                Case 6: .TintAndShade = -0.9
            End Select
        Case Else  'Text/Background 4, and Accent 1-6
            Select Case r
                Case 1: .TintAndShade = 0
                Case 2: .TintAndShade = 0.8
                Case 3: .TintAndShade = 0.6
                Case 4: .TintAndShade = 0.4
                Case 5: .TintAndShade = -0.25
                Case 6: .TintAndShade = -0.5
```

```
          End Select
        End Select
      Cells(r, c) = .TintAndShade
        End With
    Next c
  Next r
End Sub
```

Figure 30-6 shows the result of executing the ShowThemeColors procedure (it looks better in color). If you change to a different document theme, the colors will be updated to reflect those in the new theme.

	A	B	C	D	E	F	G	H	I	J
1	0	0	0	0	0	0	0	0	0	0
2	-0.04999	0.499985	-0.09998	0.799982	0.799982	0.799982	0.799982	0.799982	0.799982	0.799982
3	-0.15	0.349986	-0.24998	0.599994	0.599994	0.599994	0.599994	0.599994	0.599994	0.599994
4	-0.24998	0.249977	-0.49998	0.399976	0.399976	0.399976	0.399976	0.399976	0.399976	0.399976
5	-0.34999	0.149998	-0.74999	-0.24998	-0.24998	-0.24998	-0.24998	-0.24998	-0.24998	-0.24998
6	-0.49998	0.049989	-0.89999	-0.49998	-0.49998	-0.49998	-0.49998	-0.49998	-0.49998	-0.49998
7										

Figure 30-6: A VBA macro generated these theme colors.

CD-ROM

This example, named generate theme colors.xlsm, is available on the companion CD-ROM.

So far in this chapter, I've described how to change the fill color of a range by setting the Color property of the Interior object. As I noted, using the VBA RGB function makes this easier. These two statements demonstrate how to change the fill color of a range (they both have the same result):

```
Range("A1:F24").Interior.Color = 5913728
Range("A1:F24").Interior.Color = RGB(128, 60, 90)
```

What if you'd like your code to change the background color of a range to a specific theme color, such as the color in the third row of the sixth column (the color identified as "Accent 2, Tint 40%")?

Unfortunately, the Excel 2007 designers seemed to have forgotten to include a direct way to specify a theme color using this type of indexing. You might think the ColorIndex property would do the job, but it doesn't. The ColorIndex property refers to colors in the (pre–Excel 2007) 56-color palette.

In actual practice, this omission is not a serious problem. When setting a color, the important property is the `ThemeColor` property, which ranges from 1 to 10. Your code can assign a value to the `TintAndShade` property to vary that color (a negative value for a darker variation, a positive value for a lighter variation). If the user applies a different document theme, the color still changes in a relative manner.

Working with Shape Objects

So far, this chapter has focused exclusively on modifying the color of a range. This section provides examples of changing colors in Shape objects. In Excel, use the Insert ⇨ Illustrations ⇨ Shapes group to add a shape to a worksheet.

Figure 30-7 shows a Shape object inserted on a worksheet. This object's default name is Right Arrow 1. The number in the name varies, depending on how many shapes you have inserted. For example, if you had previously inserted two other shapes (of any style), the name would be Right Arrow 3.

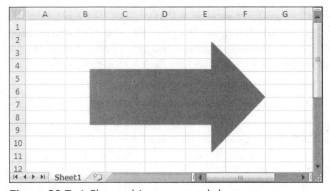

Figure 30-7: A Shape object on a worksheet.

A shape's background color

The background color of a Shape object is determined by the RGB property. So, to get the decimal color value of this shape, use a statement like this:

```
MsgBox ActiveSheet.Shapes("Right Arrow 1").Fill.ForeColor.RGB
```

This statement may be a bit confusing, so I'll break it down. The `Fill` property of the Shape object returns a `FillFormat` object. The `ForeColor` property of the `FillFormat` object returns a `ColorFormat` object. So the RGB property actually applies to the `ColorFormat` object, and this property contains the decimal color value.

NOTE

If you're confused about the use of the `ForeColor` property in this example, you're not alone. Most people, myself included, would expect to use the `BackColor` property of the `FillFormat` object to change the background color of an object. As it turns out, the `BackColor` property is used for the second color if the object is shaded or filled with a pattern. For an unfilled Shape with no pattern, the `ForeColor` property controls the background color.

When working with Shape objects, you almost always want your code to perform multiple actions. Therefore, it's efficient to create an object variable. The code that follows creates an object variable named `Shp`:

```
Dim Shp As Shape
Set Shp = ActiveSheet.Shapes("Right Arrow 1")
MsgBox Shp.Fill.ForeColor.RGB
```

TIP

An additional advantage to creating an object variable is that you can take advantage of the VBE's Auto List Members feature, which displays the possible properties and objects as you type (see Figure 30-8). This is particularly helpful in the case of Shape objects because actions you take with Shapes are not recorded by Excel's macro recorder.

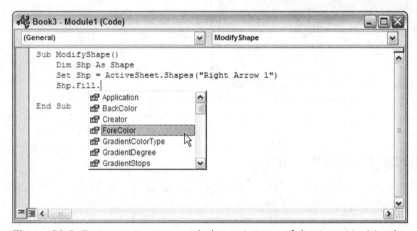

Figure 30-8: Typing a statement with the assistance of the Auto List Members feature.

If you'll be working only with the shape's colors, you can create an object variable for the shape's `ColorFormat` object, like this:

```
Dim ShpCF As ColorFormat
Set ShpCF = ActiveSheet.Shapes("Right Arrow 1").Fill.ForeColor
MsgBox ShpCF.RGB
```

The RGB property of the `ColorFormat` object controls the color of the shape. Following are some additional properties. If you're not familiar with document theme colors, see "Understanding document theme colors," earlier in this chapter.

- `ObjectThemeColor`: A number between 1 and 10 that represents the theme color (that is, a color in the first row of the 10-x-6 theme color grid)

- `SchemeColor`: A number that ranges from 0 to 80 that represents the color as an index in the current color scheme. These are colors from the old 56-color palette, and I don't see any need to ever use the `SchemeColor` property.

- `TintAndShade`: A number between –1 and +1 that represents the tint or shade of the theme color.

- `Type`: A number that represents the `ColorFormat` object type. As far as I can tell, this read-only property is always 1, which represents the RGB color system.

Changing the background color of a shape does not affect the shape's outline color. To modify the color of a shape's outline, access the `ColorFormat` object of the shape's `LineFormat` object. The following statements set a Shape's background color and outline to red:

```
Dim Shp As Shape
Set Shp = ActiveSheet.Shapes("Right Arrow 1")
Shp.Fill.ForeColor.RGB = RGB(255, 0, 0)
Shp.Line.ForeColor.RGB = RGB(255, 0, 0)
```

Here's an alternative way to accomplish the same effect, using object variables:

```
Dim Shp As Shape
Dim FillCF As ColorFormat
Dim LineCF As ColorFormat
Set Shp = ActiveSheet.Shapes("Right Arrow 1")
Set FillCF = Shp.Fill.ForeColor
Set LineCF = Shp.Line.ForeColor
FillCF.RGB = RGB(255, 0, 0)
LineCF.RGB = RGB(255, 0, 0)
```

Using other fill types with a shape

Shapes can also display other types of fills, such as gradients, pictures, and textures. The examples in this section demonstrate how to apply these other types of fills to a Shape object.

CD-ROM

All the examples in this section are available on the companion CD-ROM. The filename is `shape object colors.xlsm`.

The following code creates a rectangle, hides its border, and applies a two-color gradient. One of the colors is set specifically; the other color is one of the document theme colors. Figure 30-9 shows the result of running this macro.

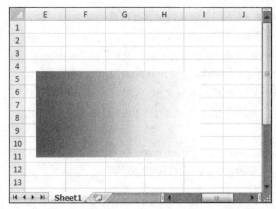

Figure 30-9: A Shape object with a two-color gradient fill.

```
Sub MakeShapeWithGradient()
    Dim Shp As Shape

'    Create the shape
    Set Shp = ActiveSheet.Shapes.AddShape( _
        Type:=msoShapeRectangle, _
        Left:=100, _
        Top:=10, _
        Width:=200, _
        Height:=100)

'    Hide the border
    Shp.Line.Visible = False

'    Add 2-color gradient
    With Shp.Fill
        .TwoColorGradient _
            Style:=msoGradientVertical, Variant:=2
        .ForeColor.RGB = RGB(255, 255, 255) 'white
        .BackColor.ObjectThemeColor = msoThemeColorAccent4
    End With
End Sub
```

The code that follows creates a Shape that uses pattern fill. See Figure 30-10.

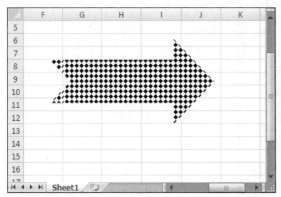

Figure 30-10: This Shape uses a diamond-pattern fill.

```
Sub MakeShapeWithPattern()
    Dim Shp As Shape

'   Create the shape
    Set Shp = ActiveSheet.Shapes.AddShape( _
        Type:=msoShapeNotchedRightArrow, _
        Left:=100, _
        Top:=10, _
        Width:=200, _
        Height:=100)

'   Hide the border
    Shp.Line.Visible = False

'   Add a pattern
    With Shp.Fill
        .Patterned Pattern:=msoPatternSolidDiamond
        .ForeColor.RGB = RGB(0, 0, 0) 'black
        .BackColor.RGB = RGB(255, 255, 255) 'white
    End With
End Sub
```

The next procedure is similar, but it uses a picture for the Shape's background. The graphic file is loaded from the disk. The code also adds a reflection to the Shape. Figure 30-11 shows the result.

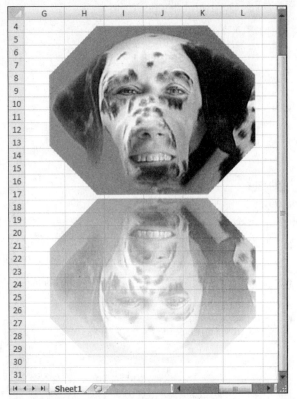

Figure 30-11: A Shape that uses a picture.

```
Sub MakeShapeWithPicture()
    Dim Shp As Shape

'    Create the shape
    Set Shp = ActiveSheet.Shapes.AddShape( _
        Type:=msoShapeOctagon, _
        Left:=100, _
        Top:=10, _
        Width:=250, _
        Height:=196)

'    Hide the border
    Shp.Line.Visible = False

'    Add a picture
    Shp.Fill.UserPicture _
        ThisWorkbook.Path & "\weirddog.jpg"

'    Give it a reflection
    Shp.Reflection.Type = msoReflectionType5
End Sub
```

The next Shape object example creates a shape with a texture and applies some 3-D effects and a shadow. Figure 30-12 shows the result.

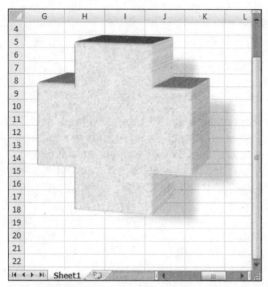

Figure 30-12: A shape with a texture fill and a few other accoutrements.

```
Sub MakeShapeWithTexture()
    Dim Shp As Shape
'   Create the shape
    Set Shp = ActiveSheet.Shapes.AddShape( _
        Type:=msoShapeCross, _
        Left:=100, _
        Top:=10, _
        Width:=200, _
        Height:=200)

'   Hide the border
    Shp.Line.Visible = False

'   Give it a texture
    Shp.Fill.PresetTextured _
        PresetTexture:=msoTextureBlueTissuePaper

'   Some 3D effects
    With Shp.ThreeD
        .Visible = True
        .Depth = 60
        .BevelTopDepth = 10
        .RotationY = 10
    End With
```

```
'    And a shadow
     With Shp.Shadow
          .Visible = True
          .Transparency = 0.8
          .OffsetX = 30
          .OffsetY = 30
          .Blur = 12
     End With
End Sub
```

The final Shape example involves text. The procedure adds a shape, sets the shape's background, adjusts the border, adds text, and then formats the text — very similar to what happens when you insert a WordArt object. That's because there's really nothing special about WordArt. When you use the Insert ⇨ Text ⇨ WordArt command, you're just inserting a shape that has text. Your code can manipulate WordArt just as it can manipulate Shape objects.

```
Sub MakeShapeWithText()
     Dim Shp As Shape
'    Create the shape
     Set Shp = ActiveSheet.Shapes.AddShape( _
          Type:=msoShapeRectangle, _
          Left:=200, _
          Top:=10, _
          Width:=200, _
          Height:=100)

'    Shape's background color
     Shp.Fill.ForeColor.ObjectThemeColor = msoThemeColorLight2
     Shp.Shadow.Visible = True

'    Shape's border
     Shp.Line.ForeColor.ObjectThemeColor = msoThemeColorAccent2
     Shp.Line.Weight = 6

'    Add text
     Shp.TextFrame2.TextRange.Text = "Microsoft Excel"

'    Format the text
     With Shp.TextFrame2.TextRange.Font
          .Size = 38
          .Bold = True
          .Fill.ForeColor.ObjectThemeColor = msoThemeColorAccent2
          .Shadow.Visible = True
     End With
End Sub
```

Figure 30-13 shows the result of executing the MakeShapeWithText procedure.

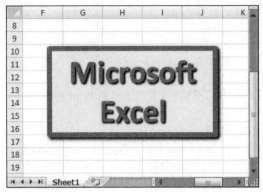

Figure 30-13: A Shape object that contains text.

Learning more about shapes

The information in this section barely scratches the surface when it comes to working with Shape objects. Programming shapes with VBA could easily serve as the subject matter for a complete book.

To learn more about Shape objects, use the Object Browser (press F2, in the VBE), the Help system, the macro recorder (which is of limited value), and the Internet. And don't forget the best learning tool of them all: experimentation.

Modifying Chart Colors

This section describes how to change colors in a chart. The most important point is to identify the specific chart element that you want to modify. In other words, you need to identify the object and then set the appropriate properties.

Figure 30-14 shows a simple column chart named Chart 1. This chart has two data series, a legend, and a chart title.

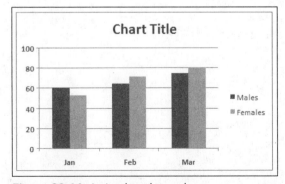

Figure 30-14: A simple column chart.

Following is a VBA statement that changes the color of the first data series to red.

```
ActiveSheet.ChartObjects("Chart 1").Chart. _
    SeriesCollection(1).Format.Fill.ForeColor.RGB = vbRed
```

To the uninitiated, this statement is probably confusing because so many objects are involved. The object hierarchy is as follows:

The active sheet contains a ChartObjects collection. One object in that collection is the ChartObject named Chart 1. The Chart property of the ChartObject object returns a Chart object. The Chart object has a SeriesCollection collection, and one Series object in the collection has an index number of 1. The Format property of the Series object returns a ChartFormat object. The Fill property of the ChartFormat object returns a FillFormat object. The ForeColor property of the FillFormat object returns a ColorFormat object. The RGB property of the ColorFormat object is set to red.

 ## CROSS-REFERENCE
Refer to Chapter 18 for more information about using VBA to work with charts.

Another way of writing the preceding statement, using object variables to identify the individual objects (and, perhaps, clarify the objects' relationships), is

```
Sub ChangeSeries1Color
    Dim MyChartObject As ChartObject
    Dim MyChart As Chart
    Dim MySeries As Series
    Dim MyChartFormat As ChartFormat
    Dim MyFillFormat As FillFormat
    Dim MyColorFormat As ColorFormat

'   Create the objects
    Set MyChartObject = ActiveSheet.ChartObjects("Chart 1")
    Set MyChart = MyChartObject.Chart
    Set MySeries = MyChart.SeriesCollection(1)
    Set MyChartFormat = MySeries.Format
    Set MyFillFormat = MyChartFormat.Fill
    Set MyColorFormat = MyFillFormat.ForeColor

'   Change the color
    MyColorFormat.RGB = vbRed
End Sub
```

The RGB property accepts a decimal color value, which I specified using a built-in VBA constant. Other color-related properties of the ColorFormat object are

- ObjectThemeColor: A number between 0 and 16 that represents the theme color. VBA provides constants for these values. For example, msoThemeColorAccent3 contains the value 7.

- TintAndShade: A number between −1 and +1 that represents the tint or shade of the theme color.

 CD-ROM

The examples in this section are available on the companion CD-ROM. The filename is chart colors.xlsm.

You can also specify color gradients. Here's an example that applies a preset gradient to the second data series in a chart. Notice that the gradient is set using the FillFormat object:

```
Sub AddPresetGradient()
    Dim MyChart As Chart
    Set MyChart = ActiveSheet.ChartObjects("Chart 1").Chart
    With MyChart.SeriesCollection(1).Format.Fill
        .PresetGradient _
            Style:=msoGradientHorizontal, _
            Variant:=1, _
            PresetGradientType:=msoGradientFire
    End With
End Sub
```

Working with other chart elements is similar. The procedure that follows changes the colors of the chart's chart area and plot area, using colors from the current document theme:

```
Sub RecolorChartAndPlotArea()
    Dim MyChart As Chart
    Set MyChart = ActiveSheet.ChartObjects("Chart 1").Chart
    With MyChart
        .ChartArea.Format.Fill.ForeColor.ObjectThemeColor = _
            msoThemeColorAccent6
        .ChartArea.Format.Fill.ForeColor.TintAndShade = 0.9
        .PlotArea.Format.Fill.ForeColor.ObjectThemeColor = _
            msoThemeColorAccent6
        .PlotArea.Format.Fill.ForeColor.TintAndShade = 0.5
    End With
End Sub
```

The final example in this section applies a random color to each chart element. Using this macro virtually guarantees an ugly chart. However, this code demonstrates how to change the color for other chart elements. The UseRandomColors procedure uses a simple function, RandomColor, to determine the color used.

```
Sub UseRandomColors()
    Dim MyChart As Chart
    Set MyChart = ActiveSheet.ChartObjects("Chart 4").Chart
    With MyChart
        .ChartArea.Format.Fill.ForeColor.RGB = RandomColor
        .PlotArea.Format.Fill.ForeColor.RGB = RandomColor
        .SeriesCollection(1).Format.Fill.ForeColor.RGB = RandomColor
        .SeriesCollection(2).Format.Fill.ForeColor.RGB = RandomColor
        .Legend.Font.Color = RandomColor
        .ChartTitle.Font.Color = RandomColor
        .Axes(xlValue).MajorGridlines.Border.Color = RandomColor
        .Axes(xlValue).TickLabels.Font.Color = RandomColor
        .Axes(xlValue).Border.Color = RandomColor
        .Axes(xlCategory).TickLabels.Font.Color = RandomColor
        .Axes(xlCategory).Border.Color = RandomColor
    End With
End Sub


Function RandomColor()
    RandomColor = Application.RandBetween(0, RGB(255, 255, 255))
End Function
```

Chapter 31

Frequently Asked Questions about Excel Programming

In This Chapter

If you like to cruise the Internet, you're undoubtedly familiar with *FAQs* — lists of *frequently asked questions* (and their answers) about a particular topic. FAQs are prevalent in the discussion groups and are posted in an attempt to reduce the number of messages that ask the same questions over and over again. They rarely serve their intended purpose, however, because the same questions keep appearing despite the FAQs.

I've found that people tend to ask the same questions about Excel programming, so I put together a list of FAQs that cover programming topics for Excel.

◆ Excel 2007 quirks that you can and can't work around

◆ Frequently asked questions about Excel programming

◆ Some help getting around in the VBE

Although this FAQ list certainly won't answer all your questions, it covers many common questions and might set you straight about a thing or two.

What If My Question Isn't Answered Here?

If this chapter doesn't provide an answer to your question, start by checking this book's index. This book includes lots of information that doesn't qualify as a frequently asked question. If you still come up empty-handed, check out the resources listed in Appendix A.

I organized this list of questions by assigning each question to one of these categories:

- General Excel questions
- The Visual Basic Editor (VBE)
- Sub procedures
- Function procedures
- Objects, properties, methods, and events
- UserForms
- Add-ins
- Excel user interface modification

In some cases, my classifications are rather arbitrary; a question could justifiably be assigned to other categories. Moreover, questions within each category are listed in no particular order.

By the way, most of the information in this chapter is discussed in greater detail in other chapters in this book.

General Excel Questions

How do I record a macro?

Click the little square icon in the left side of the status bar.

How do I run a macro?

Choose View ➪ Macros ➪ Macros. Or, choose Developer ➪ Code ➪ Macros.

What do I do if I don't have a Developer tab?

Display the Excel Options dialog box (Office ➪ Excel Options), click Popular, and then enable Show Developer Tab in the Ribbon.

I recorded a macro and saved my workbook. When I reopened it, the macros were gone! Where did they go?

By default, Excel proposes that you destroy your macros when you first save a new workbook. When you save the file, read Excel's warning very carefully and don't accept the default Yes button. If your workbook contains macros, you must save it as an XLSM file, not an XLSX file.

Before saving my workbook as an XLSM file, I converted all my VBA statements to comments so I could debug the code later. When I re-opened the workbook, all my VBA code was gone.

Unfortunately, that's how Excel 2007 works. If a module contains no executable procedures, it is deleted. I'd call that a dumb design decision on the part of Microsoft.

How do I hide the Ribbon so it doesn't take up so much space?

Press Ctrl+F1 to toggle the display of the Ribbon. If you'd like to toggle the Ribbon display using VBA, you must resort to using the Sendkeys method:

```
Sub ToggleRibbon()
  Application.SendKeys "^{F1}"
End Sub
```

Where are my old custom toolbars?

Click the Add-Ins tab, and you'll see them in the Custom Toolbars group.

Can I make my old custom toolbars float?

No, you can't. The old custom toolbars are fixed in place in the Add-Ins ➪ Custom Toolbars group.

Where can I find examples of VBA code?

The Internet has thousands of VBA examples. A good starting point is my Web site:

http://j-walk.com/ss

Or, do a search at

www.google.com

How can I hide the status bar in Excel 2007?

You must use VBA to hide the status bar. The following statement will do the job:

```
Application.DisplayStatusBar = False
```

Is there a utility that will convert my Excel application into a standalone EXE file?

No.

Why doesn't Ctrl+A select all the cells in my worksheet?

That's probably because the cell pointer is inside a table. When the active cell is in a table, you must press Ctrl+A three times to select all worksheet cells.

Why is the Custom Views command is grayed out?

That's probably because your workbook contains a table. Convert the table to a range, and then you can use Views ➪ Workbook Views ➪ Custom Views.

How can I add a drop-down list to a cell so the user can choose a value from the list?

This technique does not require any macros. Type the list of valid entries in a single column. You can hide this column from the user if you wish. Select the cell or cells that will display the list of entries, choose Data ➪ Data Tools ➪ Data Validation, and then click the Settings tab in the Data Validation dialog box. From the Allow drop-down list, select List. In the Source box, enter a range address or a reference to the single-column list on your sheet. Make sure the In-Cell Dropdown check box is selected. If the list is short, you can simply type the items, each separated by a comma.

Can I use this drop-down list method if my list is stored on a different worksheet in the workbook?

Yes. You need to create a name for the list (for example, ListEntries). Then, in the Data Validation dialog box, enter **=ListEntries** in the Source box. Make sure that you include the initial equal sign; otherwise, it won't work.

I use Application.Calculation to set the calculation mode to manual. However, this seems to affect all workbooks and not just the active workbook.

The `Calculation` property is a member of the `Application` object. Therefore, the calculation mode affects all workbooks. You cannot set the calculation mode for only one workbook. Excel 2000 and later versions provide a new `Worksheet` object property: `EnableCalculation`. When this property is `False`, the worksheet will not be calculated, even if the user requests a calculation. Setting the property to `True` will cause the sheet to be calculated.

Why doesn't the F4 function key repeat all my operations?

I don't know. Unfortunately, the very useful F4 key is much less useful in Excel 2007. For example, if you click the Insert Worksheet icon and then press F4, Excel does *not* repeat the Insert Worksheet command. However, if you insert the worksheet by using Shift+F11, then F4 *does* repeat the command.

Another example: If you apply a style to a chart (using Chart Tools ⇨ Design ⇨ Chart Styles), you can't use F4 to repeat that command on another chart.

Hopefully, this problem will be fixed in a subsequent update.

What happened to the ability to "speak" the cell contents?

To use those commands, you must customize your Quick Access Toolbar (QAT). Right-click the QAT and choose Customize Quick Access Toolbar. The speech commands are listed in the Commands Not in the Ribbon category (they all begin with the word "Speak").

How can I increase the number of columns in a worksheet?

You can't. This number is fixed and cannot be changed. Excel 2007 worksheets contain 16,384 columns.

How can I increase the number of rows in a worksheet?

See the answer to the previous question. If you need more than 1,048,576 rows, Excel is probably not the solution to your problem.

I opened a workbook, and it has only 65,546 rows. What happened?

When Excel opens a workbook that was saved in a previous version's file format, it does not automatically convert it to an Excel 2007 workbook. You need to do it manually: Save the workbook in an Excel 2007 file format, close it, and then re-open it. You'll then see the additional rows.

How do I get my old workbook to use the new fonts?

Press Ctrl+N to create a blank workbook. Activate your old workbook and choose the Home tab. Click the very bottom of the vertical scrollbar in the Styles gallery and choose Merge Styles. In the Merge Styles dialog box, double-click the new workbook you created with Ctrl+N, and the old styles will be replaced with the new styles. But this works only with cells that have not been formatted with other font attributes. For example, bold cells retain their old fonts.

How do I get a print preview?

Try using the Page Layout view (the icon on the right side of the status bar). Or, add the Print Preview button to your QAT. To add this button to your QAT, click the down arrow control to the right of the QAT and choose Print Preview from the list.

When I switch to a new document template, my worksheet no longer fits on a single page.

That's probably because the new theme uses different fonts. After applying the theme, use the Page Layout ⇨ Themes ⇨ Fonts control to select your original fonts to use with the new theme. Or, modify the font size for the Normal style. If page fitting is critical, you should choose the theme before you do much work on the document.

How do I get rid of the annoying dotted-line page break display in Normal view mode?

Open the Excel Options dialog box, click the Advanced tab, scroll down to the Display Options for This Worksheet section, and remove the check mark from Show Page Breaks.

Can I add that Show Page Breaks option to my QAT?

No. For some reason, this very useful command isn't available as a QAT icon.

I changed the text in a cell to use Angle Clockwise orientation (in the Home ⇨ Alignment group). How do I get the orientation back to normal? There's no Horizontal Alignment option.

To change the cell back to normal, click the option that corresponds to the current orientation (that option is highlighted). Or, choose the Format Cell Alignment option and make the change in the Format Cells dialog box.

I'm trying to apply a table style to a table, but it has no visible effect. What can I do?

That's probably because the table cells were formatted manually. Removing the old cell background colors and applying a style should work.

How do I get Office 2007 to support PDF output?

You need to download a free add-in from Microsoft (try `http://office.microsoft.com`). After you download and install the add-in, click the Office Menu button and then choose Save As ⇨ PDF or XPS. Why isn't it built into Office 2007? Blame the attorneys at Adobe Systems.

Can I change the color of the sheet tabs?

Right-click the sheet tab and select Tab Color. Versions prior to Excel 2002 do not allow you to change the tab color.

Can I change the font of the sheet tabs?

Yes, but you must go outside Excel to do so. If you use Windows XP, access the Windows Control Panel and select Display. In the Display Properties dialog box, click the Appearance tab and then click the Advanced button. In the Advanced Appearance dialog box, access the Item list and select Scrollbar. Enter a different font size or use the spinner to increase or decrease the size. This setting will affect other programs. The procedure varies slightly with other versions of Windows.

Can I change the default font and color of cell comments?

Yes. See the answer to the previous question — but select ToolTip in the Item list. Use the controls to change the settings. Changing the setting will not affect existing comments.

Can I write VBA macros that play sounds?

Yes, you can play WAV and MIDI files, but it requires Windows Application Programming Interface (API) functions (see Chapter 11). If you're using Excel 2002 or later, you can take advantage of the Speech object. The following statement, when executed, greets the user by name:

```
Application.Speech.Speak ("Hello" & Application.UserName)
```

When I open a workbook, Excel asks whether I want to update the links. I've searched all my formulas and cannot find any links in this workbook. Is this a bug?

Probably not. Try using the Office ⇨ Prepare ⇨ Edit Links to Files command. In the Edit Links dialog box, click Break Link. Keep in mind that links can occur in places other than formulas. If you have a chart in your workbook, click each data series in the chart and examine the SERIES formula in the formula bar. If the formula refers to another workbook, you've identified the link. To eliminate it, move the chart's data into the current workbook and re-create your chart.

If your workbook contains any Excel 5/95 dialog sheets, select each object in each dialog box and examine the formula bar. If any object contains a reference to another workbook, edit or delete that reference.

Choose Formulas ⇨ Defined Name ⇨ Name Manager. Scroll down the list in the Name Manager dialog box and examine the Refers To column. Delete names that refer to another workbook or that contain an erroneous reference (such as #REF!). This is the most common cause of "phantom links."

Why does Excel crash every time I start it?

When Excel starts, it opens an *.xlb file, which contains menu and toolbar customizations. If this file is damaged, it might cause Excel to crash when it's started. Also, this file might (for some reason) be very large. In such a case, this could also cause Excel to crash. Typically, your *.xlb file should be 100K or smaller.

If Excel crashes when it is started, try deleting your *.xlb file. To do so, close Excel and search your hard drive for *.xlb. (The filename and location will vary.) Create a backup copy of this file, delete the original file, and then try restarting Excel. Hopefully, Excel will now start up normally and create a new *.xlb file.

Deleting your *.xlb file will also delete any toolbar or menu customizations that appear in the Add-Ins tab.

The Visual Basic Editor

Can I use the VBA macro recorder to record all my macros?

No. Recording is useful for very simple macros only. Macros that use variables, looping, or any other type of program flow changes cannot be recorded. You can, however, often take advantage of the macro recorder to write some parts of your code or to discover the relevant properties or methods.

I turned on the macro recorder when I edited a chart, but many of the commands weren't recorded.

Yes, that's a problem with the initial release of Excel 2007. Perhaps it will be fixed in a later update.

I have some macros that are general in nature. I would like to have these available all the time. What's the best way to do this?

Consider storing those general-purpose macros in your Personal Macro Workbook. This is a (normally) hidden workbook that is loaded automatically by Excel. When you record a macro, you have the option of recording it to your Personal Macro Workbook. The file, Personal.xlsb, is stored in your \XLStart directory.

I can't find my Personal Macro Workbook. Where is it?

The Personal.xlsb file doesn't exist until you record a macro to it.

I locked my VBA project with a password, and I forget what it was. Is there any way to unlock it?

Several third-party password-cracking products exist. Use a Web search engine to search for *Excel password*. The existence of these products should tell you that Excel passwords are not very secure.

How can I write a macro to change the password of my project?

You can't. The protection elements of a VBA project are not exposed in the object model. Most likely, this was done to make it more difficult for password-cracking software.

When I insert a new module, it always starts with an Option Explicit line. What does this mean?

If Option Explicit is included at the top of a module, it means that you must declare every variable before you use it in a procedure (which is a good idea). If you don't want this line to appear in new modules, activate the VBE, choose Tools ⇨ Options, click the Editor tab, and clear the Require Variable Declaration check box. Then you can either declare your variables or let VBA handle the data typing automatically.

Why does my VBA code appear in different colors? Can I change these colors?

VBA uses color to differentiate various types of text: comments, keywords, identifiers, statements with a syntax error, and so on. You can adjust these colors and the font used by choosing the Tools ⇨ Options command (Editor Format tab) in the VBE.

Can I delete a VBA module by using VBA code?

Yes. The following code deletes Module1 from the active workbook:

```
With ActiveWorkbook.VBProject
     .VBComponents.Remove  .VBComponents("Module1")
End With
```

This might not work with Excel 2002 and later. See the next question.

I wrote a macro in Excel 2000 that adds VBA code to the VB project. When I run it in Excel 2007, I get an error message. What's wrong?

Excel 2002 introduced a new setting: Trust Access to Visual Basic Project. By default, this setting is turned off. To change it in Excel 2007, choose Office ⇨ Excel Options ⇨ Trust Center. Click the Trust Center Settings button to display the Trust Center dialog box. Click the Macro Settings tab and place a check mark next to Trust Access to the VBA Project Object Model.

How can I write a macro to change the user's macro security setting? I want to avoid the "this workbook contains macros" message when my application is opened.

The ability to change the security level using VBA would pretty much render the entire macro security system worthless. Think about it.

Part VII

How does the UserInterfaceOnly option work when protecting a worksheet?

When protecting a worksheet using VBA code, you can use a statement such as

```
ActiveSheet.Protect UserInterfaceOnly:=True
```

This causes the sheet to be protected, but your macros can still make changes to the sheet. It's important to understand that this setting is not saved with the workbook. When the workbook is re-opened, you'll need to re-execute the statement in order to reapply the UserInterfaceOnly protection.

How can I tell whether a workbook has a macro virus?

In the VBE, activate the project that corresponds to the workbook. Examine all the code modules (including the ThisWorkbook code module) and look for VBA code that is not familiar to you. Usually, virus code will not be formatted well and will contain many unusual variable names. Another option is to use a commercial virus-scanning program.

I'm having trouble with the concatenation operator (&) in VBA. When I try to concatenate two strings, I get an error message.

VBA is probably interpreting the ampersand as a type-declaration character. Make sure that you insert a space before and after the concatenation operator.

I can't seem to get the VBA line continuation character (underscore) to work.

The line continuation sequence is actually two characters: a space followed by an underscore.

I distributed an Excel application to many users. On some machines, my VBA error-handling procedures don't work. Why not?

The error-handling procedures won't work if the user has the Break on All Errors option set. This option is available in the Options dialog box (General tab) in the VBE. Unfortunately, you can't change this setting with VBA.

Procedures

What's the difference between a VBA procedure and a macro?

Nothing, really. The term *macro* is a carry-over from the old days of spreadsheets. These terms are now used interchangeably.

What's a procedure?

A *procedure* is a grouping of VBA instructions that can be called by name. If these instructions are to give an explicit result (such as a value) back to the instruction that called them, they most likely belong to a `Function` procedure. Otherwise, they probably belong to a `Sub` procedure.

What is a variant data type?

Variables that aren't specifically declared are assigned the `Variant` type by default, and VBA automatically converts the data to the proper type when it's used. This is particularly useful for retrieving values from a worksheet cell when you don't know in advance what the cell contains. Generally, it's a good idea to specifically declare your variables with the `Dim`, `Public`, or `Private` statement because using variants is a bit slower and is not the most efficient use of memory.

What's the difference between a variant array and an array of variants?

A *variant* is a unit of memory with a special data type that can contain any kind of data: a single value or an array of values (that is, a *variant array*). The following code creates a variant that contains a three-element array:

```
Dim X As Variant
X = Array(30, 40, 50)
```

A normal array can contain items of a specified data type, including nontyped variants. The following statement creates an array that consists of three variants:

```
Dim X (0 To 2) As Variant
```

Although a variant containing an array is conceptually different from an array whose elements are of type `Variant`, the array elements are accessed in the same way.

What's a type-definition character?

VBA lets you append a character to a variable's name to indicate the data type. For example, you can declare the `MyVar` variable as an integer by tacking % onto the name, as follows:

```
Dim MyVar%
```

VBA supports these type-declaration characters:

- Integer: %
- Long: &
- Single: !
- Double: #
- Currency: @
- String: $

Type-definition characters are included primarily for compatibility. Declaring variables by using words is the standard approach.

I would like to create a procedure that automatically changes the formatting of a cell based on the data that I enter. For example, if I enter a value greater than 0, the cell's background color should be red. Is this possible?

It's certainly possible, and you don't need any programming. Use Excel's Conditional Formatting feature, accessed with the Home ⇨ Styles ⇨ Conditional Formatting command.

The Conditional Formatting feature is useful, but I'd like to perform other types of operations when data is entered into a cell.

In that case, you can take advantage of the `Change` event for a worksheet object. Whenever a cell is changed, the `Change` event is triggered. If the code module for the `Sheet` object contains a procedure named `Worksheet_Change`, this procedure will be executed automatically.

What other types of events can be monitored?

Lots! Search the Help system for *events* to get a complete listing.

I tried entering an event procedure (Sub Workbook_Open), but the procedure isn't executed when the workbook is opened. What's wrong?

You probably put the procedure in the wrong place. Workbook event procedures must be in the code module for the ThisWorkbook object. Worksheet event procedures must be in the code module for the appropriate Sheet object, as shown in the VBE Project window.

I can write an event procedure for a particular workbook, but can I write an event procedure that will work for any workbook that's open?

Yes, but you need to use a class module. Details are in Chapter 19.

I'm very familiar with creating formulas in Excel. Does VBA use the same mathematical and logical operators?

Yes. And it includes some additional operators that aren't valid in worksheet formulas. These additional VBA operators are listed in the following table:

Operator	Function
\	Division with an integer result
Eqv	Returns True if both expressions are true or both are false
Imp	A bitwise logical implication on two expressions (rarely used)
Is	Compares two object variables
Like	Compares two strings by using wildcard characters
Xor	Returns True if only one expression is true

How can I execute a procedure that's in a different workbook?

Use the Run method of the Application object. The following instruction executes a procedure named Macro1 located in the Personal.xlsb workbook:

```
Run "Personal.xlsb!Macro1"
```

Another option is to add a reference to the workbook. Do this by choosing the Tools ➪ References command in the VBE. After you've added a reference, you can then run the procedures in the referenced workbook without including the name of the workbook.

I've used VBA to create several custom functions. I like to use these functions in my worksheet formulas, but I find it inconvenient to precede the function name with the workbook name. Is there any way around this?

Yes. Convert the workbook that holds the function definitions to an XLAM add-in. When the add-in is open, you can use the functions in any other worksheet without referencing the function's filename.

In addition, if you set up a reference to the workbook that contains the custom functions, you can use the function without preceding it with the workbook name. To create a reference, choose the Tools ➪ References command in the VBE.

I would like a particular workbook to be loaded every time I start Excel. I would also like a macro in this workbook to execute automatically. Am I asking too much?

Not at all. To open the workbook automatically, just store it in your \XLStart directory. To have the macro execute automatically, create a Workbook_Open macro in the code module for the workbook's ThisWorkbook object.

I have a workbook that uses a Workbook_Open procedure. Is there a way to prevent this from executing when I open the workbook?

Yes. Hold down Shift when you issue the Office ➪ Open command. To prevent a Workbook_ BeforeClose procedure from executing, press Shift when you close the workbook. Using the Shift key will not prevent these procedures from executing when you're opening an add-in.

Can a VBA procedure access a cell's value in a workbook that is not open?

VBA can't do it, but Excel's old XLM language can. Fortunately, you can execute XLM from VBA. Here's a simple example that retrieves the value from cell A1 on Sheet1 in a workbook named myfile.xlsx in the c:\files directory:

```
MsgBox ExecuteExcel4Macro("'c:\files\[myfile.xlsx]Sheet1'!R1C1")
```

Note that the cell address must be in R1C1 notation.

How can I prevent the "save file" prompt from being displayed when I close a workbook from VBA?

You can use this statement:

```
ActiveWorkbook.Close SaveChanges:=False
```

Or, you can set the workbook's `Saved` property to `True` by using a statement like this:

```
ActiveWorkbook.Saved = True
```

This statement, when executed, does not actually save the file, so any unsaved changes will be lost when the workbook is closed.

A more general solution to avoid Excel prompts is to insert the following instruction:

```
Application.DisplayAlerts = False
```

Normally, you'll want to set the `DisplayAlerts` property back to `True` after the file is closed.

How can I set things up so that my macro runs once every hour?

You need to use the `OnTime` method of the `Application` object. This enables you to specify a procedure to execute at a particular time of day. When the procedure ends, use the `OnTime` method again to schedule another event in one hour.

How do I prevent a macro from showing in the macro list?

Declare the procedure by using the `Private` keyword:

```
Private Sub MyMacro()
```

Or you can add a dummy optional argument, declared as a specific data type:

```
Sub MyMacro (Optional FakeArg as Long)
```

Can I save a chart as a GIF file?

Yes. The following code saves the first embedded chart on `Sheet1` as a GIF file named `Mychart.gif`:

```
Set CurrentChart = Sheets("Sheet1").ChartObjects(1).Chart
Fname = ThisWorkbook.Path & "\Mychart.gif"
CurrentChart.Export Filename:=Fname, FilterName:="GIF"
```

Are variables in a VBA procedure available to other VBA procedures? What if the procedure is in a different module? Or in a different workbook?

You're talking about a variable's *scope*. There are three levels of scope: local, module, and public. Local variables have the narrowest scope and are declared within a procedure. A local variable is visible only to the procedure in which it was declared. Module-level variables are declared at the top of a module, prior to the first procedure. Module-level variables are visible to all procedures in the module. Public variables have the broadest scope, and they are declared by using the Public keyword.

Functions

I created a VBA function for use in worksheet formulas. However, it always returns #NAME?. What went wrong?

You probably put the function in the code module for a Sheet (for example, Sheet1) or in the ThisWorkbook module. Custom worksheet functions must reside in standard VBA modules.

I wrote a VBA function that works perfectly when I call it from another procedure, but it doesn't work when I use it in a worksheet formula. What's wrong?

VBA functions called from a worksheet formula have some limitations. In general, they must be strictly *passive*. That is, they can't change the active cell, apply formatting, open workbooks, or change the active sheet. If the function attempts to do any of these things, the formula will return an error.

Functions can only perform calculations and return a value. An exception to this rule is the VBA MsgBox function. A custom function can display a message box whenever it is recalculated. This is very handy for debugging a custom function.

When I access a custom worksheet function with the Insert Function dialog box, it reads "No help available." How can I get the Insert Function dialog box to display a description of my function?

To add a description for your custom function, activate the workbook that contains the Function procedure. Then choose View ➪ Macros ➪ Macros to display the Macro dialog box. Your function won't be listed, so you must type it into the Macro Name box. After typing the function's name, click Options to display the Macro Options dialog box. Enter the descriptive text in the Description box.

Can I also display help for the arguments for my custom function in the Insert Function dialog box?

Unfortunately, no.

My custom worksheet function appears in the User Defined category in the Insert Function dialog box. How can I make my function appear in a different function category?

You need to use VBA to do this. The following instruction assigns the function named MyFunc to Category 1 (Financial):

```
Application.MacroOptions Macro:="MyFunc", Category:=1
```

The following table lists the valid function category numbers:

Number	Category
0	No category (appears only in All)
1	Financial
2	Date & Time
3	Math & Trig
4	Statistical
5	Lookup & Reference
6	Database

continued

Number	Category
7	Text
8	Logical
9	Information
10	Commands (normally hidden)
11	Customizing (normally hidden)
12	Macro Control (normally hidden)
13	DDE/External (normally hidden)
14	User Defined (default)
15	Engineering

How can I create a new function category?

You can create a new function category by using an XLM macro. However, this method is not reliable and is not recommended.

I have a custom function that will be used in a worksheet formula. If the user enters arguments that are not appropriate, how can I make the function return a true error value (#VALUE!)?

If your function is named `MyFunction`, you can use the following instruction to return an error value to the cell that contains the function:

```
MyFunction = CVErr(xlErrValue)
```

In this example, `xlErrValue` is a predefined constant. Constants for the other error values are listed in the Help system.

How can I force a recalculation of formulas that use my custom worksheet function?

Press Ctrl+Alt+F9.

Can I use Excel's built-in worksheet functions in my VBA code?

In most cases, yes. Excel's worksheet functions are accessed via the WorksheetFunction method of the Application object. For example, you could access the SUM worksheet function with a statement such as the following:

```
Ans = Application.WorksheetFunction.Sum(Range("A1:A3"))
```

This example assigns the sum of the values in A1:A3 (on the active sheet) to the Ans variable.

Generally, if VBA includes an equivalent function, you cannot use Excel's worksheet version. For example, because VBA has a function to compute square roots (Sqr), you can't use the SQRT worksheet function in your VBA code.

Is there any way to force a line break in the text of a message box?

Use a carriage return or a linefeed character to force a new line. The following statement displays the message box text on two lines. vbNewLine is a built-in constant that represents a carriage return.

```
MsgBox "Hello" & vbNewLine & Application.UserName
```

Objects, Properties, Methods, and Events

Is there a listing of the Excel objects I can use?

Yes. The Help system has that information.

I'm overwhelmed with all the properties and methods available. How can I find out which methods and properties are available for a particular object?

There are several ways. You can use the Object Browser available in the VBE. Press F2 to access the Object Browser and then choose Excel from the Libraries/Workbooks drop-down list. The Classes list (on the left) shows all the Excel objects. When you select an object, its corresponding properties and methods appear in the Member Of list on the right.

You can also get a list of properties and methods as you type. For example, enter the following:

```
Range("A1").
```

When you type the dot, you'll see a list of all properties and methods for a `Range` object. If the list doesn't appear, choose Tools ⇨ Options (in the VBE), click the Editor tab, and place a check mark next to Auto List Members. Unfortunately, Auto List Members doesn't work for all objects. For example, you won't see a list of properties and methods when you type this statement:

```
ActiveSheet.Shapes(1).
```

And, of course, the Help system for VBA is very extensive; it lists the properties and methods available for most objects of importance. The easiest way to access these lists is to type the object name into the Immediate window at the bottom of the VBE and move the cursor anywhere within the object name. Then press F1, and you'll get the help topic appropriate for the object.

What's the story with collections? Is a collection an object? What are collections?

A *collection,* which is an object that contains a group of related objects, is designated by a plural noun. For example, the `Worksheets` collection is an object that contains all the `Worksheet` objects in a workbook. You can think of this as an array: `Worksheets(1)` refers to the first `Worksheet` object in the `Workbook`. Rather than use index numbers, you can also use the actual worksheet name, such as `Worksheets("Sheet1")`. The concept of a collection makes it easy to work with all related objects at once and to loop through all objects in a collection by using the `For Each-Next` construct.

When I refer to a worksheet in my VBA code, I get a "subscript out of range" error. I'm not using any subscripts. What gives?

This error occurs when you attempt to access an element in a collection that doesn't exist. For example, the following instruction generates the error if the active workbook does not contain a worksheet named `MySheet`:

```
Set X = ActiveWorkbook.Worksheets("MySheet")
```

How can I prevent the user from scrolling around the worksheet?

You can either hide the unused rows and columns or use a VBA instruction to set the scroll area for the worksheet. The following instruction, for example, sets the scroll area on Sheet1 so that the user cannot activate any cells outside of B2:D50:

```
Worksheets("Sheet1").ScrollArea = "B2:D50"
```

To set scrolling back to normal, use a statement like this:

```
Worksheets("Sheet1").ScrollArea = ""
```

Keep in mind that the ScrollArea setting is not saved with the workbook. Therefore, you need to execute the ScrollArea assignment instruction whenever the workbook is opened. This instruction can go in the Workbook_Open event handler procedure.

What's the difference between using Select and Application.Goto?

The Select method of the Range object selects a range on the *active* worksheet only. Use Application.Goto to select a range on any worksheet in a workbook. Application.Goto might or might not make another sheet the active sheet. The Goto method also lets you scroll the sheet so that the range is in the upper-left corner.

What's the difference between activating a range and selecting a range?

In some cases, the Activate method and the Select method have exactly the same effect. But in other cases, they produce quite different results. Assume that range A1:C3 is selected. The following statement activates cell C3. The original range remains selected, but C3 becomes the active cell — that is, the cell that contains the cell pointer.

```
Range("C3").Activate
```

Again, assuming that range A1:C3 is selected, the following statement selects a single cell, which also becomes the active cell.

```
Range("C3").Select
```

Is there a quick way to delete all values from a worksheet yet keep the formulas intact?

Yes. The following code works on the active sheet and deletes all nonformula cells. (The cell formatting is not affected.)

```
On Error Resume Next
Cells.SpecialCells(xlCellTypeConstants, 23).ClearContents
```

The second argument, 23, is the sum of the values of the following built-in constants: `xlErrors` (16), `xlLogical` (4), `xlNumbers` (1), and `xlTextValues` (2).

Using `On Error Resume Next` prevents the error message that occurs if no cells qualify.

I know how to write a VBA instruction to select a range by using a cell address, but how can I write one to select a range if I know only its row and column number?

Use the `Cells` method. The following instruction, for example, selects the cell in the 5th row and the 12th column (that is, cell L5):

```
Cells(5, 12).Select
```

When I try to record the Office ⇨ Exit Excel command, Excel closes down before I can see what code it generates. Is there a VBA command to quit Excel?

Use the following instruction to end Excel:

```
Application.Quit
```

How can I turn off screen updating while a macro is running?

The following instruction turns off screen updating and speeds up macros that modify the display:

```
Application.ScreenUpdating = False
```

When your procedure ends, the `ScreenUpdating` property is set back to `True`. However, you can resume screen updating at any time by executing this statement:

```
Application.ScreenUpdating = False
```

What's the easiest way to create a range name in VBA?

If you turn on the macro recorder while you name a range, you get code something like this:

```
Range("D14:G20").Select
ActiveWorkbook.Names.Add Name:="InputArea", _
    RefersToR1C1:="=Sheet1!R14C4:R20C7"
```

A much simpler method is to use a statement like this:

```
Sheets("Sheet1").Range("D14:G20").Name = "InputArea"
```

How can I determine whether a particular cell or range has a name?

You need to check the Name property of the Name object contained in the Range object. The following function accepts a range as an argument and returns the name of the range (if it has one). If the range has no name, the function returns False.

```
Function RangeName(rng) As Variant
    On Error Resume Next
    RangeName = rng.Name.Name
    If Err <> 0 Then RangeName = False
End Function
```

Can I disable the Setup and Margins buttons that are displayed in Excel's Print Preview window?

Yes, use a statement like this:

```
ActiveSheet.PrintPreview EnableChanges:=False
```

I have a lengthy macro, and it would be nice to display its progress in the status bar. Can I display messages in the status bar while a macro is running?

Yes. Assign the text to the StatusBar property of the Application object. Here's an example:

```
Application.StatusBar = "Now processing File " & FileNum
```

Before your routine finishes, return the status bar back to normal with the following instruction:

```
Application.StatusBar = False
```

I recorded a VBA macro that copies a range and pastes it to another area. The macro uses the Select method. Is there a more efficient way to copy and paste?

Yes. Although the macro recorder generally selects cells before doing anything with them, selecting is not necessary and can actually slow down your macro. Recording a very simple copy-and-paste operation generates four lines of VBA code, two of which use the Select method. Here's an example:

```
Range("A1").Select
Selection.Copy
Range("B1").Select
ActiveSheet.Paste
```

These four lines can be replaced with a single instruction, such as the following:

```
Range("A1").Copy Range("B1")
```

Notice that this instruction does not use the Select method.

I have not been able to find a method to sort a VBA array. Does this mean that I have to copy the values to a worksheet and then use the Range.Sort method?

There is no built-in way to sort an array in VBA. Copying the array to a worksheet is one method, but you'll probably be better off if you write your own sorting procedure. Many sorting algorithms are available, and some are quite easy to code in VBA. This book contains VBA code for several sorting techniques.

My macro works with the selected cells, but it fails if something else (like a chart) is selected. How can I make sure that a range is selected?

You can use VBA's TypeName function to check the Selection object. Here's an example:

```
If TypeName(Selection) <> "Range" Then
    MsgBox "Select a range!"
    Exit Sub
End If
```

Another approach is to use the RangeSelection property, which returns a Range object that represents the selected cells on the worksheet in the specified window, even if a graphic object is active or selected. This property applies to a `Window` object — not a `Workbook` object. The following instruction, for example, displays the address of the selected range:

```
MsgBox ActiveWindow.RangeSelection.Address
```

How can I determine if a chart is activated?

Use a statement like this:

```
If ActiveChart Is Nothing Then MsgBox "Select a chart"
```

The message box will be displayed only if a chart is not activated. (This includes embedded charts and charts on a chart sheet.)

My VBA macro needs to count the number of rows selected by the user. Using Selection.Rows.Count doesn't work when nonadjacent rows are selected. Is this a bug?

Actually, this is the way it's supposed to work. The `Count` method returns the number of elements in only the *first* area of the selection (a noncontiguous selection has multiple areas). To get an accurate row count, your VBA code must first determine the number of areas in the selection and then count the number of rows in each area. Use `Selection.Areas.Count` to count the number of areas. Here's an example that stores the total number of selected rows in the `NumRows` variable:

```
NumRows = 0
For Each area In Selection.Areas
    NumRows = NumRows + area.Rows.Count
Next area
```

By the way, this process is also relevant to counting columns and cells.

I use Excel to create invoices. Can I generate a unique invoice number?

One way to do this is to use the Windows Registry. The following code demonstrates:

```
Counter = GetSetting("XYZ Corp", "InvoiceNum", "Count", 0)
Counter = Counter + 1
SaveSetting "XYZ Corp", "InvoiceNum", "Count", Counter
```

When these statements are executed, the current value is retrieved from the Registry, incremented by one, and assigned to the Counter variable. Then this updated value is stored back to the Registry. You can use the value of Counter as your unique invoice number.

You can adapt this technique for other purposes. For example, you can keep track of the number of times a workbook has been opened by including similar code in a Workbook_Open procedure.

Is there a workbook property that forces an Excel workbook to always remain visible so it won't be hidden by another application's window?

No.

Is there a VBA instruction to select the last entry in a column or row? Normally, I can use Ctrl+Shift+↓ or Ctrl+Shift+→ to do this, but how can I do it with a macro?

The VBA equivalent for Ctrl+Shift+↓ is the following:

```
Selection.End(xlDown).Select
```

The constants used for the other directions are xlToLeft, xlToRight, and xlUp.

How can I determine the last non-empty cell in a particular column?

The following instruction displays the address of the last non-empty cell in column A:

```
MsgBox ActiveSheet.Cells(Rows.Count, 1).End(xlUp).Address
```

But that instruction won't work if the last cell in the column is not empty. To handle that unlikely occurrence, use this code:

```
With ActiveSheet.Cells(Rows.Count, 1)
    If IsEmpty(.Value) Then
        MsgBox .End(xlUp).Address
    Else
        MsgBox .Address
    End If
End With
```

VBA references can become very lengthy, especially when I need to fully qualify an object by referencing its sheet and workbook. Can I reduce the length of these references?

Yes. Use the Set statement to create an object variable. Here's an example:

```
Dim MyRange as Range
Set MyRange = ThisWorkbook.Worksheets("Sheet1").Range("A1")
```

After the Set statement is executed, you can refer to this single-cell Range object simply as MyRange. For example, you can assign a value to the cell with the following:

```
MyRange.Value = 10
```

Besides making it easier to refer to objects, using object variables can also help your code execute more quickly.

Can I declare an array if I don't know how many elements it will have?

Yes. You can declare a dynamic array with the Dim statement by using empty parentheses; then allocate storage for that array later with the ReDim statement when you know how many elements the array should have. Use ReDim Preserve if you don't want to lose the current array contents when reallocating it.

Can I let the user undo my macro?

In most cases, yes — but undoing a macro is not something that can be done automatically. To enable the user to undo the effects of your macro, your VBA code module must keep track of what was changed by the macro and then be capable of restoring the original state if the user chooses Undo.

To enable the Undo command, use the OnUndo method as the last action in your macro. This method enables you to specify text that will appear on the Undo menu item and also to specify a procedure to run if the user chooses Undo. Here's an example:

```
Application.OnUndo "The Last Macro", "MyUndoMacro"
```

Can I pause a macro so the user can enter data into a certain cell?

You can use Excel's InputBox statement to get a value from a user and place it in a particular cell. The first instruction that follows, for example, displays an input box. When the user enters a value, that value is placed in cell A1.

```
UserVal = Application.InputBox(prompt:="Value?", Type:=1)
If TypeName(UserVal)<>"Boolean" Then Range("A1") = UserVal
```

VBA has an InputBox function, but there's also an InputBox method for the Application object. Are these the same?

No. Excel's InputBox method is more versatile because it allows validation of the user's entry. The preceding example uses 1 (which represents a numeric value) for the `Type` argument of the InputBox method. This ensures that the user enters a value into the input box.

I'm trying to write a VBA instruction that creates a formula. To do so, I need to insert a quote character (") within quoted text. How can I do that?

Assume that you want to enter the following formula into cell B1 with VBA:

```
=IF(A1="Yes",TRUE,FALSE)
```

The following instruction generates a syntax error because of the embedded quote characters:

```
Range("B1").Formula = "=IF(A1="Yes",TRUE,FALSE)"    'erroneous
```

The solution is to use two double quotes side by side. When two quotes are embedded within another set of quotes, Excel interprets the double quote characters as a single quote. The following instruction produces the desired result:

```
Range("B1").Formula = "=IF(A1=""Yes"",TRUE,FALSE)"
```

Another approach is to use VBA's Chr function with an argument of 34, which returns a quotation mark. The following example demonstrates:

```
Range("B1").Formula = _
   "=IF(A1=" & Chr(34) & "Yes" & Chr(34) & ",TRUE,FALSE)"
```

Yet another technique is to compose your formula using apostrophes in place of the quote marks. Then use VBA's Replace function to replace the apostrophes with quote characters:

```
TheFormula = "=IF(A1='Yes',TRUE,FALSE)"
Range("B1").Formula = Replace(TheFormula, "'", Chr(34))
```

I created an array, but the first element in that array is being treated as the second element. What's wrong?

Unless you tell it otherwise, VBA uses 0 as the first index number for an array. If you want all your arrays to always start with 1, insert the following statement at the top of your VBA module:

```
Option Base 1
```

Or you can specify the upper and lower bounds of an array when you declare it. Here's an example:

```
Dim Months(1 To 12) As String
```

I would like my VBA code to run as quickly as possible. Any suggestions?

Here are a few general tips:

- Make sure that you declare all your variables. Use `Option Explicit` at the top of your modules to force yourself to do this.

- If you reference an Excel object more than once, create an object variable for it.

- Use the `With-End With` construct whenever possible.

- If your macro writes information to a worksheet, turn off screen updating by using `Application.ScreenUpdating = False`.

- If your application enters data into cells that are referenced by one or more formulas, set the calculation mode to manual to avoid unnecessary calculations.

UserForms

My macro needs to get just a few pieces of information from the user, and a UserForm seems like overkill. Are there any alternatives?

Yes, check out VBA's `MsgBox` function and its `InputBox` function. Alternatively, you might want to use Excel's InputBox method.

I have 12 CommandButtons on a UserForm. How can I assign a single macro to be executed when any of the buttons is clicked?

There is no easy way to do this because each CommandButton has its own Click event procedure. One solution is to call another procedure from each of the CommandButton_Click procedures. Another solution is to use a class module to create a new class. This technique is described in Chapter 15.

How can I display a chart in a UserForm?

There is no direct way to do this. One solution is to write a macro that saves the chart to a GIF file and then loads the GIF file into an Image control on the UserForm.

How can I remove the "X" from the title bar of my UserForm? I don't want the user to click that button to close the form.

Removing the Close button on a UserForm's title bar requires some complex API functions. A simpler approach is to intercept all attempts to close the UserForm by using a UserForm_QueryClose event procedure in the code module for the UserForm. The following example does not allow the user to close the form by clicking the Close button:

```
Private Sub UserForm_QueryClose _
   (Cancel As Integer, CloseMode As Integer)
    If CloseMode = vbFormControlMenu Then
        MsgBox "You can't close the form like that."
        Cancel = True
    End If
End Sub
```

I created a UserForm with controls that are linked to cells on the worksheet with the ControlSource property. Is this the best way to do this?

In some cases, using links to worksheet cells can slow your application because the worksheet is recalculated every time a control changes the cell. In addition, if your UserForm has a Cancel button, the cells might have already been changed when the user clicks Cancel.

Can I create a control array for a UserForm? It's possible with Visual Basic, but I can't figure out how to do it with Excel VBA.

You can't create a control array, but you can create an array of `Control` objects. The following code creates an array consisting of all `CommandButton` controls:

```
Private Sub UserForm_Initialize()
    Dim Buttons() As CommandButton
    Cnt = 0
    For Each Ctl In UserForm1.Controls
        If TypeName(Ctl) = "CommandButton" Then
            Cnt = Cnt + 1
            ReDim Preserve Buttons(1 To Cnt)
            Set Buttons(Cnt) = Ctl
        End If
    Next Ctl
End Sub
```

Is there any difference between hiding a UserForm and unloading a UserForm?

Yes, the `Hide` method keeps the UserForm in memory but makes it invisible. The `Unload` statement unloads the UserForm, beginning the "termination" process (invoking the `Terminate` event for the UserForm) and removing the UserForm from memory.

How can I make my UserForm stay open while I do other things?

By default, each UserForm is *modal*, which means that it must be dismissed before you can do anything else. However, you can make a UserForm modeless by using `vbModeless` as the argument for the `Show` method. Here's an example:

```
UserForm1.Show vbModeless
```

Excel 97 gives me a compile error when I write UserForm1.Show vbModeless. How can I make the form modeless in Excel 2000 and later while allowing it to remain modal in Excel 97?

Test for the version of Excel that the user is running and then execute a separate procedure if the version is Excel 2000 or later. The following code demonstrates how:

```
Sub ShowUserForm()
    If Val(Application.Version) >= 9 Then
      ShowModelessForm
    Else
      UserForm1.Show
    End If
End Sub

Sub ShowModelessForm()
    Dim frm As Object
    Set frm = UserForm1
    frm.Show 0   ' vbModeless
End Sub
```

Because the ShowModelessForm procedure is not executed in Excel 97, it will not cause a compile error.

I need to display a progress indicator like those you see when you're installing software while a lengthy process is being executed. How can I do this?

You can do this with a UserForm. Chapter 15 describes several different techniques, including one in which the code gradually stretches a shape inside a frame while the lengthy macro is running.

How can I use Excel's shapes on my UserForm?

You can't use the shapes directly with a UserForm, but you can do so indirectly. Start by adding a shape to a worksheet. Then select the shape and choose Home ⇨ Clipboard ⇨ Copy. Activate your UserForm and insert an Image object. Press F4 to display the Properties window. Select the Picture property and press Ctrl+V to paste the Clipboard contents to the Image control. You might also need to set the AutoSize property to True.

How can I generate a list of files and directories into my UserForm so the user can select a file from the list?

There's no need to do that. Use VBA's GetOpenFilename method. This method displays an Open dialog box in which the user can select a drive, directory, and file.

I need to concatenate strings and display them in a ListBox control. But when I do so, they aren't aligned properly. How can I get them to display equal spacing between strings?

You can use a monospaced font such as Courier New for the ListBox. A better approach, however, is to set up your ListBox to use two columns. (See Chapter 14 for details.)

Is there an easy way to fill a ListBox or ComboBox control with items?

Yes, you can use an array. The statement that follows adds three items to ListBox1.

```
ListBox1.List = Array("Jan", "Feb", "Mar")
```

Can I display a built-in Excel dialog box from VBA?

Many of Excel's dialog boxes can be displayed by using the Application.Dialogs method. For example, the following instruction displays the dialog box that enables you to format numbers in cells:

```
Application.Dialogs(xlDialogFormatNumber).Show
```

Use the Object Browser to display a list of the constants for the built-in dialog boxes. Press F2 from the VBE, select the Excel library, and search for *xlDialog*. You'll probably need to use some trial and error to locate the constant that corresponds to the dialog box that you want to display.

In Excel 2007, you can execute Ribbon commands (including those that display a dialog box) by using the ExecuteMso method along with the control name. The statement that follows, for example, displays the dialog box that enables you to format numbers in a cell:

```
Application.CommandBars.ExecuteMso("NumberFormatsDialog")
```

See Chapter 22 for more information.

I tried the technique described in the preceding question and received an error message. Why is that?

The Dialogs method (and the ExecuteMso method) will fail if the context isn't appropriate. For example, if you attempt to display the Chart Type dialog box (xlDialogChartType) when a chart is not activated, you'll get an error message.

Every time I create a UserForm, I go through the steps of adding an OK button and a Cancel button. Is there a way to get these controls to appear automatically?

Yes. Set up a UserForm with the controls that you use most often. Then choose File ⇨ Export File to save the UserForm. When you want to add a new form to another project, choose File ⇨ Import File.

Can I create a UserForm without a title bar?

Yes, but it requires some complex API functions.

When I click a button on my UserForm, nothing happens. What am I doing wrong?

Controls added to a UserForm do nothing unless you write event handler procedures for them. These procedures must be located in the code module for the UserForm, and they must have the correct name.

Can I create a UserForm whose size is always the same, regardless of the video display resolution?

You can, but it's probably not worth the effort. You can write code to determine the video resolution and then use the Zoom property of a UserForm to change its size. The normal way to deal with this matter is simply to design your UserForm for the lowest resolution that will be used — probably a 1024 × 768 display.

Can I create a UserForm box that lets the user select a range in a worksheet by pointing?

Yes. Use the RefEdit control for this. See Chapter 14 for an example.

Can I change the startup position of a UserForm?

Yes, you can set the UserForm's Left and Top properties. But for these to be effective, you need to set the UserForm's StartUpPosition property to 0.

Can I make a UserForm that's resizable by the user?

Yes. See Chapter 15 for an example.

Add-ins

Where can I get Excel add-ins?

You can get Excel add-ins from a number of places:

- Excel includes several add-ins that you can use whenever you need them. Use the Add-Ins dialog box to install them.

- You can download more add-ins from the Microsoft Office Update Web site.

- Third-party developers distribute and sell add-ins for special purposes.

- Many developers create free add-ins and distribute them via their Internet sites.

- You can create your own add-ins.

How do I install an add-in?

The most common way to install an add-in is by using the Add-Ins dialog box. Choose Office ⇨ Excel Options. In the Excel Options dialog box, select the Add-Ins tab. Then, select Excel Add-ins from the Manage drop-down control and click Go. A quicker method to display the dialog box is to press Alt+TI.

You can also install an add-in by using the Office ⇨ Open command, but using the Add-Ins dialog box is the preferred method. An add-in opened with Office ⇨ Open cannot be closed without using VBA.

When I install my add-in from Excel's Add-Ins dialog box, it shows up without a name or description. How can I give my add-in a description?

Before creating the add-in, use the Office ⇨ Prepare ⇨ Properties command to display the Properties panel. In the Title field, enter the text that you want to appear in the Add-Ins dialog box. In the Comments field, enter the description for the add-in. Then create the add-in as usual.

I have several add-ins that I no longer use, but I can't figure out how to remove them from the Add-Ins Available list in the Add-Ins dialog box. What's the story?

Oddly, there is no way to remove unwanted add-ins from the list directly from Excel. One way to remove an add-in from the list is to move or delete the add-in file. Then, when you attempt to open the add-in from the Add-Ins dialog box, Excel will ask whether you want to remove the add-in from the list. Answer yes.

How do I create an add-in?

Activate any worksheet and then choose Office ⇨ Save As. Then select Excel Add-in (*.xlam) from the Save as Type drop-down list. The add-in is created, and the original workbook remains open.

I try to create an add-in, but the Save as Type drop-down box doesn't provide Add-in as an option.

The most likely reason is that the active sheet is not a worksheet.

Should I convert all my essential workbooks to add-ins?

No! Although you *can* create an add-in from any workbook, not all workbooks are suitable. When a workbook is converted to an add-in, it is essentially invisible. For most workbooks, being invisible isn't a good thing.

Do I need to keep two copies of my workbook: the XLSM version and the XLAM version?

No, you can edit an add-in and even convert an add-in back to a normal workbook.

How do I modify an add-in after it has been created?

If you need to modify only the VBA code, no special action is required; you can access the code from the VBE and then save your changes in the VBE. If you need to modify information on a worksheet, activate the VBE (press Alt+F11) and then set the `IsAddIn` property of the `ThisWorkbook` object to `False`. Make your changes to the worksheet, set the `IsAddIn` property to `True`, and resave the file.

What's the difference between an XLSM file and an XLAM file created from an XLSM file? Is the XLAM version compiled? Does it run faster?

There isn't a great deal of difference between the files, and you generally won't notice any speed differences. VBA code is always compiled before it is executed. This is true whether it's in an XLSM file or an XLAM file. However, XLAM files still contain the actual VBA code — not some special compiled code. Another difference is that the workbook is never visible in an XLAM file.

How do I protect the code in my add-in from being viewed by others?

Activate the VBE and choose Tools ⇨ *xxxx* Properties (where *xxxx* is the name of your project). Click the Protection tab, select Lock Project for Viewing, and enter a password. Then save the file.

Are my add-ins safe? In other words, if I distribute an XLAM file, can I be assured that no one else will be able to view my code?

Protect your add-in by locking it with a password. This prevents most users from being able to access your code. Recent versions of Excel have improved the security features, but the password still might be broken by using any of a number of utilities. Bottom line? Don't think of an XLAM as being a secure file.

User Interface

How do I use VBA to add a simple button to the Ribbon?

You can't. You must write special XML code (known as RibbonX code) and insert the XML document into a workbook file by using third-party tools. Or, if you're a glutton for punishment (and know what you're doing), you can do it by unzipping the document and making the edits manually.

What are my options for modifying the user interface to make it easy for a user to run my macros?

In Excel 2007, you have these choices:

- Modify the Ribbon (not an easy task).
- Add your macro to the Quick Access Toolbar (a manual task that's not possible to perform using VBA).
- Assign a shortcut key to the macro.
- Add a new menu item to a shortcut menu.
- Create an old-style toolbar or menu, which will display in the Add-Ins tab.

How do I add a macro to the Quick Access Toolbar?

Right-click the QAT and choose Customize Quick Access Toolbar from the shortcut menu. In the Customize tab of the Excel Options dialog box, choose Macros from the drop-down list on the left. Select your macro and click Add. To change the icon or text displayed, click the Modify button.

I added my macro to the QAT, but clicking the icon generates an error.

In order to execute a macro from the QAT, the workbook that contains the macro must be the active workbook. This is not the case, however, if the macro is in an add-in or stored in your Personal Macro Workbook.

How do I use VBA to activate a particular tab on the Ribbon?

SendKeys is your only choice. Press the Alt key to find out the keystroke(s) required. For example, to switch to the Page Layout tab, use this:

```
Application.SendKeys "%p{F6}"
```

How can I disable all the right-click shortcut menus?

The following procedure will do the job:

```
Sub DisableAllShortcutMenus()
    Dim cb As CommandBar
    For Each cb In CommandBars
        If cb.Type = msoBarTypePopup Then _
            cb.Enabled = False
    Next cb
End Sub
```

Part

Appendixes

Appendix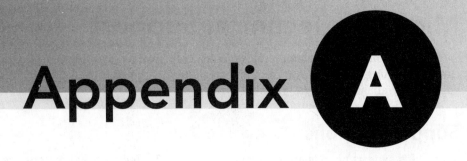

Excel Resources Online

If I've done my job, the information provided in this book will be very useful to you. The book, however, can't cover every conceivable topic about Excel. Therefore, I've compiled a list of additional resources that you may find helpful.

I classify these resources into four categories: Excel's Help System, Microsoft technical support, Internet newsgroups, and Internet Web sites.

The Excel Help System

Many users forget about an excellent source of information: the Excel Help system. This Help information is available by clicking the question mark icon in the upper-right corner of Excel's window or just by pressing F1. Either of these methods displays Excel Help in a new window. You can then type your search query and click Search.

If you're working in the Visual Basic Editor, you can get help by using either of these methods:

- Type a search query in the box to the right of the menu bar and press Enter.
- Move the blinking cursor within any keyword, object, property, or method, and press F1.

The Excel Help system isn't perfect — it often provides only superficial help and ignores some topics altogether. But if you're stuck, a quick search of the Help system may be worth a try.

Microsoft Technical Support

Technical support is the common term for assistance provided by a software vendor. In this case, I'm talking about assistance that comes directly from Microsoft. Microsoft's technical support is available in several different forms.

Support options

Microsoft's support options are constantly changing. To find out what options are available (both free and fee-based), go to

http://support.microsoft.com

Microsoft Knowledge Base

Perhaps your best bet for solving a problem may be the Microsoft Knowledge Base, which is the primary Microsoft product information source. It's an extensive, searchable database that consists of tens of thousands of detailed articles containing technical information, bug lists, fix lists, and more.

You have free and unlimited access to the Knowledge Base via the Internet. To access the Knowledge Base, go to the following URL, enter some search terms, and click Search:

http://support.microsoft.com/search

Microsoft Excel home page

The official home page of Excel is at

www.microsoft.com/office/excel

This site contains a variety of material, such as tips, templates, answers to questions, training materials, and links to companion products.

Microsoft Office home page

For information about Office 2007 (including Excel), try this site:

http://office.microsoft.com

You'll find product updates, add-ins, examples, and lots of other useful information.

NOTE

As you know, the Internet is a dynamic entity that changes rapidly. Web sites are often reorganized, so a particular URL listed in this Appendix may not be available when you try to access it.

Internet Newsgroups

Usenet is an Internet service that provides access to several thousand special interest groups and enables you to communicate with people who share common interests. A newsgroup works like a public bulletin board. You can post a message or questions, and (usually) others reply to your message.

Thousands of newsgroups cover virtually every topic you can think of (and many that you haven't thought of). Typically, questions posed on a newsgroup are answered within 24 hours — assuming, of course, that you ask the questions in a manner that makes others want to reply.

Accessing newsgroups by using a newsreader

You can use newsreader software to access the Usenet newsgroups. Many such programs are available, but you probably already have one installed: Microsoft Outlook Express, which is installed with Internet Explorer.

Microsoft maintains an extensive list of newsgroups, including quite a few devoted to Excel. If your Internet service provider doesn't carry the Microsoft newsgroups, you can access them directly from Microsoft's news server. (In fact, that's the preferred method.) You need to configure your newsreader software (not your Web browser) to access Microsoft's news server at this address:

```
msnews.microsoft.com
```

Accessing newsgroups by using a Web browser

As an alternative to using newsreader software, you can read and post to the Microsoft newsgroups directly from your Web browser. This option is often significantly slower than using standard newsgroup software and is best suited for situations in which newsgroup access is prohibited by network policies.

- Access thousands of newsgroups at Google Groups:

  ```
  http://groups.google.com
  ```

- Access the Microsoft newsgroups (including Excel newsgroups) from this URL:

  ```
  www.microsoft.com/communities/newsgroups/default.mspx
  ```

Table A-1 lists the most popular English-language Excel newsgroups found on Microsoft's news server (and also available at Google Groups).

Part VIII

TABLE A-1   THE MICROSOFT.COM EXCEL-RELATED NEWSGROUPS

Newsgroup	Topic
microsoft.public.excel	General Excel topics
microsoft.public.excel.charting	Building charts with Excel
microsoft.public.excel.interopoledde	OLE, DDE, and other cross-application issues
microsoft.public.excel.macintosh	Excel issues on the Macintosh operating system
microsoft.public.excel.misc	General topics that don't fit one of the other categories
microsoft.public.excel.newusers	Help for newcomers to Excel
microsoft.public.excel.printing	Printing with Excel
microsoft.public.excel.programming	Programming Excel with VBA macros
microsoft.public.excel.templates	Spreadsheet Solutions templates and other XLT files
microsoft.public.excel.worksheet.functions	Worksheet functions

Searching newsgroups

The fastest way to find a quick answer to a question is to search past newsgroup postings. Often, searching past newsgroup postings is an excellent alternative to posting a question to the newsgroup because you can get the answer immediately. Unless your question is very obscure, there's an excellent chance that your question has already been asked and answered. The best source for searching newsgroup postings is Google Groups:

```
http://groups.google.com
```

How does searching work? Suppose that you have a problem identifying unique values in a range of cells. You can perform a search using the following keywords: **Excel**, **Range**, and **Unique**. The Google search engine probably will find dozens of newsgroup postings that deal with these topics.

If the number of results is too large, refine your search by adding search terms. Sifting through the messages may take a while, but you have an excellent chance of finding an answer to your question. In fact, I estimate that at least 90 percent of the questions posted in the Excel newsgroups can be answered by searching Google.

Tips for Posting to a Newsgroup

If you're new to online newsgroups, here are some pointers:

1. Conduct a search first to make sure that your question has not already been answered.

2. Make the subject line descriptive. Postings with a subject line like "Help me!" and "Another Question" are less likely to be answered than postings with a more specific subject, such as "Sizing a Chart's Plot Area."

3. Specify the Excel version that you use. In many cases, the answer to your question depends on your version of Excel.

4. For best results, ask only one question per message.

5. Make your question as specific as possible.

6. Keep your question brief and to the point but provide enough information so that someone can answer it adequately.

7. Indicate what you've done to try to answer your own question.

8. Post in the appropriate newsgroup, and don't cross-post to other groups unless the question applies to multiple groups.

9. Don't type in all uppercase or all lowercase; check your grammar and spelling.

10. Don't include a file attachment.

11. Avoid posting in HTML format. Plain text is the preferred format.

12. If you request an e-mail reply in addition to a newsgroup reply, don't use an anti-spam e-mail address that requires the responder to modify your address. Why cause extra work for someone doing you a favor?

Internet Web Sites

The World Wide Web has dozens of excellent sites devoted to Excel. I list a few of my favorites here.

The Spreadsheet Page

```
http://www.j-walk.com/ss
```

This is my own Web site, which contains files to download, developer tips, instructions for accessing Excel Easter eggs, spreadsheet jokes, an extensive list of links to other Excel sites, and information about my books.

Daily Dose of Excel

http://DailyDoseOfExcel.com

This is a frequently updated Web log created by Dick Kusleika, with about a dozen contributors (including me). It covers a variety of topics, and readers can leave comments.

Jon Peltier's Excel Page

http://peltiertech.com/Excel

Those who frequent the microsoft.public.excel.charting newsgroup are familiar with Jon Peltier. Jon has an uncanny ability to solve practically any chart-related problem. His Web site contains many Excel tips and an extensive collection of charting examples.

Pearson Software Consulting

www.cpearson.com/excel.htm

This site, maintained by Chip Pearson, contains dozens of useful examples of VBA and clever formula techniques.

Stephen Bullen's Excel Page

www.bmsltd.co.uk/excel

Stephen's Web site contains some fascinating examples of Excel code, including a section titled "They Said It Couldn't Be Done."

David McRitchie's Excel Pages

www.mvps.org/dmcritchie/excel/excel.htm

David's site is jam-packed with useful Excel information and is updated frequently.

Mr. Excel

www.MrExcel.com

Mr. Excel, also known as Bill Jelen, maintains an extensive site devoted to Excel. The site also features a message board.

Appendix B

VBA Statements and Functions Reference

This Appendix contains a complete listing of all Visual Basic for Applications (VBA) statements and built-in functions. For details, consult Excel's online help.

 NOTE
There are no new VBA statements in Excel 2007.

TABLE B-1 SUMMARY OF VBA STATEMENTS

Statement	Action
AppActivate	Activates an application window
Beep	Sounds a tone via the computer's speaker
Call	Transfers control to another procedure
ChDir	Changes the current directory
ChDrive	Changes the current drive
Close	Closes a text file
Const	Declares a constant value
Date	Sets the current system date

continued

TABLE B-1 SUMMARY OF VBA STATEMENTS *(continued)*

Statement	Action
Declare	Declares a reference to an external procedure in a Dynamic Link Library (DLL)
DefBool	Sets the default data type to `Boolean` for variables that begin with specified letters
DefByte	Sets the default data type to `Byte` for variables that begin with specified letters
DefCur	Sets the default data type to `Currency` for variables that begin with specified letters
DefDate	Sets the default data type to `Date` for variables that begin with specified letters
DefDec	Sets the default data type to `Decimal` for variables that begin with specified letters
DefDbl	Sets the default data type to `Double` for variables that begin with specified letters
DefInt	Sets the default data type to `Integer` for variables that begin with specified letters
DefLng	Sets the default data type to `Long` for variables that begin with specified letters
DefObj	Sets the default data type to `Object` for variables that begin with specified letters
DefSng	Sets the default data type to `Single` for variables that begin with specified letters
DefStr	Sets the default data type to `String` for variables that begin with specified letters
DefVar	Sets the default data type to `Variant` for variables that begin with specified letters
DeleteSetting	Deletes a section or key setting from an application's entry in the Windows Registry
Dim	Declares variables and (optionally) their data types
Do-Loop	Loops through a set of instructions
End	Used by itself, exits the program; also used to end a block of statements that begin with `If`, `With`, `Sub`, `Function`, `Property`, `Type`, or `Select`

Statement	Action
Enum	Declares a type for enumeration
Erase	Re-initializes an array
Error	Simulates a specific error condition
Event	Declares a user-defined event
Exit Do	Exits a block of Do-Loop code
Exit For	Exits a block of Nor-Next code
Exit Function	Exits a Function procedure
Exit Property	Exits a property procedure
Exit Sub	Exits a subroutine procedure
FileCopy	Copies a file
For Each-Next	Loops through a set of instructions for each member of a series
For-Next	Loops through a set of instructions a specific number of times
Function	Declares the name and arguments for a Function procedure
Get	Reads data from a text file
GoSub...Return	Branches to and returns from a procedure
GoTo	Branches to a specified statement within a procedure
If-Then-Else	Processes statements conditionally
Implements	Specifies an interface or class that will be implemented in a class module
Input #	Reads data from a sequential text file
Kill	Deletes a file from a disk
Let	Assigns the value of an expression to a variable or property
Line Input #	Reads a line of data from a sequential text file
Load	Loads an object but doesn't show it
Lock...Unlock	Controls access to a text file
Lset	Left-aligns a string within a string variable
Mid	Replaces characters in a string with other characters
MkDir	Creates a new directory

continued

Part VIII

TABLE B-1   SUMMARY OF VBA STATEMENTS *(continued)*

Statement	Action
`Name`	Renames a file or directory
`On Error`	Gives specific instructions for what to do in the case of an error
`On...GoSub`	Branches on a condition
`On...GoTo`	Branches on a condition
`Open`	Opens a text file
`Option Base`	Changes the default lower limit for arrays
`Option Compare`	Declares the default comparison mode when comparing strings
`Option Explicit`	Forces declaration of all variables in a module
`Option Private`	Indicates that an entire module is `Private`
`Print #`	Writes data to a sequential file
`Private`	Declares a local array or variable
`Property Get`	Declares the name and arguments of a `Property Get` procedure
`Property Let`	Declares the name and arguments of a `Property Let` procedure
`Property Set`	Declares the name and arguments of a `Property Set` procedure
`Public`	Declares a public array or variable
`Put`	Writes a variable to a text file
`RaiseEvent`	Fires a user-defined event
`Randomize`	Initializes the random number generator
`ReDim`	Changes the dimensions of an array
`Rem`	Specifies a line of comments (same as an apostrophe ['])
`Reset`	Closes all open text files
`Resume`	Resumes execution when an error-handling routine finishes
`RmDir`	Removes an empty directory
`RSet`	Right-aligns a string within a string variable
`SaveSetting`	Saves or creates an application entry in the Windows Registry
`Seek`	Sets the position for the next access in a text file
`Select Case`	Processes statements conditionally

Statement	Action
SendKeys	Sends keystrokes to the active window
Set	Assigns an object reference to a variable or property
SetAttr	Changes attribute information for a file
Static	Declares variables at the procedure level so that the variables retain their values as long as the code is running
Stop	Pauses the program
Sub	Declares the name and arguments of a Sub procedure
Time	Sets the system time
Type	Defines a custom data type
Unload	Removes an object from memory
While...Wend	Loops through a set of instructions as long as a certain condition remains true
Width #	Sets the output line width of a text file
With	Sets a series of properties for an object
Write #	Writes data to a sequential text file

Invoking Excel Functions in VBA Instructions

If a VBA function that's equivalent to one you use in Excel is not available, you can use Excel's worksheet functions directly in your VBA code. Just precede the function with a reference to the WorksheetFunction object. For example, VBA does not have a function to convert radians to degrees. Because Excel has a worksheet function for this procedure, you can use a VBA instruction such as the following:

```
Deg = Application.WorksheetFunction.Degrees(3.14)
```

The WorksheetFunction object was introduced in Excel 97. For compatibility with earlier versions of Excel, you can omit the reference to the WorksheetFunction object and write an instruction such as the following:

```
Deg = Application.Degrees(3.14)
```

NOTE

There are no new VBA functions in Excel 2007.

TABLE B-2 SUMMARY OF VBA FUNCTIONS

Function	Action
Abs	Returns the absolute value of a number
Array	Returns a variant containing an array
Asc	Converts the first character of a string to its ASCII value
Atn	Returns the arctangent of a number
CallByName	Executes a method, or sets or returns a property of an object
CBool	Converts an expression to a Boolean data type
CByte	Converts an expression to a Byte data type
CCur	Converts an expression to a Currency data type
CDate	Converts an expression to a Date data type
CDbl	Converts an expression to a Double data type
CDec	Converts an expression to a Decimal data type
Choose	Selects and returns a value from a list of arguments
Chr	Converts a character code to a string
CInt	Converts an expression to an Integer data type
CLng	Converts an expression to a Long data type
Cos	Returns the cosine of a number
CreateObject	Creates an Object Linking and Embedding (OLE) Automation object
CSng	Converts an expression to a Single data type
CStr	Converts an expression to a String data type
CurDir	Returns the current path
CVar	Converts an expression to a variant data type
CVDate	Converts an expression to a Date data type (for compatibility, not recommended)
CVErr	Returns a user-defined error value that corresponds to an error number

Function	Action
Date	Returns the current system date
DateAdd	Adds a time interval to a date
DateDiff	Returns the time interval between two dates
DatePart	Returns a specified part of a date
DateSerial	Converts a date to a serial number
DateValue	Converts a string to a date
Day	Returns the day of the month of a date
DDB	Returns the depreciation of an asset
Dir	Returns the name of a file or directory that matches a pattern
DoEvents	Yields execution so the operating system can process other events
Environ	Returns an operating environment string
EOF	Returns True if the end of a text file has been reached
Error	Returns the error message that corresponds to an error number
Exp	Returns the base of natural logarithms (e) raised to a power
FileAttr	Returns the file mode for a text file
FileDateTime	Returns the date and time when a file was last modified
FileLen	Returns the number of bytes in a file
Filter	Returns a subset of a string array, filtered
Fix	Returns the integer portion of a number
Format	Displays an expression in a particular format
FormatCurrency	Returns an expression formatted with the system currency symbol
FormatDateTime	Returns an expression formatted as a date or time
FormatNumber	Returns an expression formatted as a number
FormatPercent	Returns an expression formatted as a percentage
FreeFile	Returns the next available file number when working with text files
FV	Returns the future value of an annuity
GetAllSettings	Returns a list of settings and values from the Windows Registry

continued

TABLE B-2   SUMMARY OF VBA FUNCTIONS *(continued)*

Function	Action
GetAttr	Returns a code representing a file attribute
GetObject	Retrieves an OLE Automation object from a file
GetSetting	Returns a specific setting from the application's entry in the Windows Registry
Hex	Converts from decimal to hexadecimal
Hour	Returns the hour of a time
IIf	Evaluates an expression and returns one of two parts
Input	Returns characters from a sequential text file
InputBox	Displays a box to prompt a user for input
InStr	Returns the position of a string within another string
InStrRev	Returns the position of a string within another string from the end of the string
Int	Returns the integer portion of a number
IPmt	Returns the interest payment for a given period of an annuity
IRR	Returns the internal rate of return for a series of cash flows
IsArray	Returns True if a variable is an array
IsDate	Returns True if a variable is a date
IsEmpty	Returns True if a variable has not been initialized
IsError	Returns True if an expression is an error value
IsMissing	Returns True if an optional argument was not passed to a procedure
IsNull	Returns True if an expression contains a Null value
IsNumeric	Returns True if an expression can be evaluated as a number
IsObject	Returns True if an expression references an OLE Automation object
Join	Combines strings contained in an array
LBound	Returns the smallest subscript for a dimension of an array
LCase	Returns a string converted to lowercase
Left	Returns a specified number of characters from the left of a string
Len	Returns the number of characters in a string

Function	Action
Loc	Returns the current read or write position of a text file
LOF	Returns the number of bytes in an open text file
Log	Returns the natural logarithm of a number
LTrim	Returns a copy of a string with no leading spaces
Mid	Returns a specified number of characters from a string
Minute	Returns the minute of a time
MIRR	Returns the modified internal rate of return for a series of periodic cash flows
Month	Returns the month of a date as a number
MonthName	Returns the month of a date as a string
MsgBox	Displays a modal message box
Now	Returns the current system date and time
NPer	Returns the number of periods for an annuity
NPV	Returns the net present value of an investment
Oct	Converts from decimal to octal
Partition	Returns a string representing a range in which a value falls
Pmt	Returns a payment amount for an annuity
Ppmt	Returns the principal payment amount for an annuity
PV	Returns the present value of an annuity
QBColor	Returns a red/green/blue (RGB) color code
Rate	Returns the interest rate per period for an annuity
Replace	Returns a string in which a substring is replaced with another string
RGB	Returns a number representing an RGB color value
Right	Returns a specified number of characters from the right of a string
Rnd	Returns a random number between 0 and 1
Round	Returns a rounded number
RTrim	Returns a copy of a string with no trailing spaces
Second	Returns the seconds portion of a specified time

continued

TABLE B-2 SUMMARY OF VBA FUNCTIONS *(continued)*

Function	Action
Seek	Returns the current position in a text file
Sgn	Returns an integer that indicates the sign of a number
Shell	Runs an executable program
Sin	Returns the sine of a number
SLN	Returns the straight-line depreciation for an asset for a period
Space	Returns a string with a specified number of spaces
Spc	Positions output when printing to a file
Split	Returns a one-dimensional array containing a number of substrings
Sqr	Returns the square root of a number
Str	Returns a string representation of a number
StrComp	Returns a value indicating the result of a string comparison
StrConv	Returns a converted string
String	Returns a repeating character or string
StrReverse	Returns a string, reversed
Switch	Evaluates a list of Boolean expressions and returns a value associated with the first True expression
SYD	Returns the sum-of-years' digits depreciation of an asset for a period
Tab	Positions output when printing to a file
Tan	Returns the tangent of a number
Time	Returns the current system time
Timer	Returns the number of seconds since midnight
TimeSerial	Returns the time for a specified hour, minute, and second
TimeValue	Converts a string to a time serial number
Trim	Returns a string without leading spaces and/or trailing spaces
TypeName	Returns a string that describes the data type of a variable
UBound	Returns the largest available subscript for a dimension of an array

Function	Action
UCase	Converts a string to uppercase
Val	Returns the number formed from any initial numeric characters of a string
VarType	Returns a value indicating the subtype of a variable
Weekday	Returns a number indicating a day of the week
WeekdayName	Returns a string indicating a day of the week
Year	Returns the year of a date

Part VIII

Appendix C

VBA Error Codes

This Appendix contains a complete listing of the error codes for all trappable errors in Visual Basic for Applications (VBA). This information is useful for error trapping. For complete details, consult Excel's help system.

Error Code	Message
3	Return without `GoSub`.
5	Invalid procedure call or argument.
6	Overflow (for example, value too large for an integer).
7	Out of memory. This error rarely refers to the amount of physical memory installed on your system. Rather, it usually refers to a fixed-size area of memory used by Excel or Windows (for example, the area used for graphics or custom formats).
9	Subscript out of range. You will also get this error message if a named item is not found in a collection of objects. For example, if your code refers to `Sheets("Sheet2")`, and `Sheet2` does not exist.
10	This array is fixed or temporarily locked.
11	Division by zero.
13	Type mismatch.
14	Out of string space.

continued

Error Code	Message
16	Expression too complex.
17	Can't perform requested operation.
18	User interrupt occurred. This error occurs if the user interrupts a macro by pressing the Cancel key.
20	Resume without error. This error probably indicates that you forgot the `Exit Sub` statement before your error handler code.
28	Out of stack space.
35	`Sub` or `Function` not defined.
47	Too many Dynamic Link Library (DLL) application clients.
48	Error in loading DLL.
49	Bad DLL calling convention.
51	Internal error.
52	Bad filename or number.
53	File not found.
54	Bad file mode.
55	File already open.
57	Device Input/Output (I/O) error.
58	File already exists.
59	Bad record length.
61	Disk full.
62	Input past end of file.
63	Bad record number.
67	Too many files.
68	Device unavailable.
70	Permission denied.
71	Disk not ready.
74	Can't rename with different drive.
75	Path/File access error.
76	Path not found.

Error Code	Message
91	Object variable or `With` block variable not set. This error occurs if you don't use `Set` at the beginning of a statement that creates an object variable. Or, it occurs if you refer to a worksheet object (such as `ActiveCell`) when a chart sheet is active.
92	`For` loop not initialized.
93	Invalid pattern string.
94	Invalid use of `Null`.
96	Unable to sink events of object because the object is already firing events to the maximum number of event receivers that it supports.
97	Cannot call friend function on object that is not an instance of defining class.
98	A property or method call cannot include a reference to a private object, either as an argument or as a return value.
321	Invalid file format.
322	Can't create necessary temporary file.
325	Invalid format in resource file.
380	Invalid property value.
381	Invalid property array index.
382	`Set` not supported at runtime.
383	`Set` not supported (read-only property).
385	Need property array index.
387	`Set` not permitted.
393	`Get` not supported at runtime.
394	`Get` not supported (write-only property).
422	Property not found.
423	Property or method not found.
424	Object required. This error occurs if text preceding a dot is not recognized as an object.
429	ActiveX component can't create object (might be a registration problem with a library that you've referenced).
430	Class doesn't support Automation or doesn't support expected interface.
432	Filename or class name not found during Automation operation.
438	Object doesn't support this property or method.

continued

Error Code	Message
440	Automation error.
442	Connection to type library or object library for remote process has been lost. Press OK for dialog box to remove reference.
443	Automation object does not have a default value.
445	Object doesn't support this action.
446	Object doesn't support named arguments.
447	Object doesn't support current locale setting.
448	Named argument not found.
449	Argument not optional.
450	Wrong number of arguments or invalid property assignment.
451	`Property Let` procedure not defined, and `Property Get` procedure did not return an object.
452	Invalid ordinal.
453	Specified DLL function not found.
454	Code resource not found.
455	Code resource lock error.
457	Key is already associated with an element of this collection.
458	Variable uses an Automation type not supported in Visual Basic.
459	Object or class does not support the set of events.
460	Invalid Clipboard format.
461	Method or data member not found.
462	Remote server machine doesn't exist or is unavailable.
463	Class not registered on local machine.
481	Invalid picture.
482	Printer error.
735	Can't save file to TEMP.
744	Search text not found.
746	Replacements too long.
1004	Application-defined or object-defined error. This is a very common catch-all error message. This error occurs when an error doesn't correspond to an error defined by VBA. In other words, the error is defined by Excel (or some other object) and is propagated back to VBA.

Appendix D

What's on the CD-ROM

This appendix describes the contents of the CD-ROM that accompanies this book. For any last-minute changes, please refer to the ReadMe file located at the root of the CD.

This appendix provides information on the following topics:

- System requirements
- Using the CD
- Files and software on the CD
- Troubleshooting

System Requirements

Make sure that your computer meets the minimum system requirements listed in this section. If your computer doesn't match up to most of these requirements, you may have a problem using the contents of the CD.

- A Windows PC with Microsoft Excel 2007.
- A CD-ROM drive.

Using the CD

To install the items from the CD to your hard drive, follow these steps:

1. Insert the CD into your computer's CD-ROM drive.

   Note: The interface won't launch if you have autorun disabled. In that case, choose Start ⇨ Run. In the dialog box that appears, type **D:\start.exe**. (Replace *D* with the proper letter if your CD drive uses a different letter. If you don't know the letter, see how your CD drive is listed under My Computer.) Click OK.

2. The CD-ROM interface appears. The interface provides a simple point-and-click way to explore the contents of the CD.

Files and Software on the CD

The following sections provide more details about the software and other materials available on the CD.

eBook version of *Excel 2007 Power Programming with VBA*

The complete text of the book you hold in your hands is provided on the CD in Adobe's Portable Document Format (PDF). You can read and quickly search the content of this PDF file by using Adobe's Acrobat Reader, also included on the CD.

Sample files for *Excel 2007 Power Programming with VBA*

The files discussed in the book are organized by chapter. With a few exceptions, the files are all Excel 2007 files that have one of the following extensions:

- `.xlsx`: An Excel workbook file.
- `.xlsm`: An Excel workbook file that contains VBA macros.
- `.xlam`: An Excel add-in file that contains VBA macros.

When you open an XLSM file, Excel may display a security warning that tells you that macros have been disabled. To enable macros, click the Options button in the security warning panel and then select Enable This Content.

Because the files on this CD are from a trusted source, you may want to copy the files to your hard drive and then designate the folder as a trusted location. To do so, follow these steps:

1. Open an Explorer window and double-click the CD-ROM drive that contains the companion CD-ROM.

2. Right-click the folder that corresponds to the root folder for the samples files and select Copy from the shortcut menu.

3. Activate the folder on your hard drive where you'd like to copy the files. Right-click the directory and choose Paste from the shortcut menu.

   The CD-ROM files will be copied to a subfolder in the folder you specified in Step 3.

To designate this new folder as a trusted location:

1. Start Excel and choose Office ➪ Excel Options to display the Excel Options dialog box.

2. In the Excel Options dialog box, click the Trust Center tab.

3. Click the Trust Center Settings button.

4. In the Trust Center dialog box, click the Trusted Locations tab.

5. Click the Add New Location button to display the Microsoft Office Trusted Location dialog box.

6. In the Microsoft Office Trusted Location dialog box, click the Browse button and locate the folder that contains the files copied from the CD-ROM.

7. Make sure you select the option labeled Subfolders of This Location Are Also Trusted.

After performing these steps, when you open XLSM files from this location, the macros are enabled and you don't see the security warning.

Following is a list of the sample files, along with a brief description.

 NOTE

Some chapters don't use any sample files.

CHAPTER 3

- `array formula examples.xlsx`: A workbook that contains various examples of array formulas.

- `counting and summing examples.xlsx`: A workbook that contains examples of counting and summing formulas.

- `extended date functions help.docx`: A Word document that describes the extended date functions.

- `extended date functions.xlsm`: A workbook that contains VBA functions that enable formulas to work with dates prior to 1900.

- `megaformula.xlsm`: A workbook that demonstrates intermediate formulas, a megaformula, and a VBA function.

- `named formulas.xlsx`: A workbook that contains several examples of named formulas.

CHAPTER 4

- `sample.xlsm`: A sample file used to demonstrate the file structure of an Excel workbook.

CHAPTER 6

- `worksheet controls.xlsx`: A workbook that demonstrates the use of ActiveX controls on a worksheet (with no macros).

CHAPTER 7

- `comment object.xlsm`: A workbook that demonstrates some ways to manipulate Comment objects using VBA.

CHAPTER 8

- `timing test.xlsm`: A workbook that demonstrates the speed advantage of declaring variables as a specific data type.

CHAPTER 9

- `sheet sorter.xlsm`: A macro that sorts worksheets in a workbook.

CHAPTER 10

- `array argument.xlsm`: A workbook that contains an example of a function that uses an array argument.

- `commission functions.xlsm`: A workbook that contains an example of a function that uses an argument.

- `draw.xlsm`: A workbook that contains a function that selects a cell randomly.

- `key press.xlsm`: A workbook that uses an API function to determine if the Ctrl, Shift, or Alt key is pressed.

- `month names.xlsm`: A workbook that demonstrates returning an array from a function.

- `mysum function.xlsm`: A workbook that contains a function that simulates Excel's SUM function.

- `no argument.xlsm`: A workbook that contains functions that don't use an argument.

- `remove vowels.xlsm`: A workbook that contains a function that removes the vowels from its argument.

- `upper case.xlsm`: A workbook that contains a function that converts text to uppercase.

- `win32api.txt`: A text file that contains Windows API declarations and constants.

- `windows directory.xlsm`: A workbook that uses an API function to determine the Windows directory.

CHAPTER 11

- `about range selection.xlsm`: A workbook that contains a macro that describes the current range selection.

- `batch processing.xlsm`: A workbook that contains a macro that performs batch process on three files.

- `celltype function.xlsm`: A workbook that contains a function that describes the data type of its single-cell argument.

- `copy multiple selection.xlsm`: A workbook that contains a macro that copies a noncontiguous range selection.

- `date and time.xlsm`: A workbook that contains a macro that displays the current date and time.

- `delete empty rows.xlsm`: A workbook that contains a macro that deletes all empty rows in a workbook.

- `drive information.xlsm`: A workbook that contains a macro that lists information about all disk drives.

- `duplicate rows.xlsm`: A workbook that contains a macro that duplicates rows, based on the contents of a cell.

- `efficient looping.xlsm`: A workbook that demonstrates an efficient way to loop through a range.

- `file association.xlsm`: A workbook that contains an API function that returns the application associated with a particular file.

- `hide rows and columns.xlsm`: A workbook that contains a macro that hides all rows and columns that are outside of the current range selection.

- `inputbox demo.xlsm`: A workbook that contains a macro that demonstrates how to prompt for a value.

- `inrange function.xlsm`: A workbook that contains a function that determines whether a range is contained in another range.

- `list fonts.xlsm`: A workbook that contains a macro that lists all installed fonts.

- `loop vs array fill range.xlsm`: A workbook that contains macros that demonstrate ways to fill a range of cells.

- `myworkbook.xlsx`: A workbook used by the value from a closed `workbook.xlsm` example.

- `next empty cell.xlsm`: A workbook that contains a macro that determines the next empty cell in a column.

- `page count.xlsm`: A workbook that contains a macro that counts the number of printed pages in a workbook.

- `printer info.xlsm`: A workbook that contains an API function that returns information about the active printer.

- `prompt for a range.xlsm`: A workbook that contains a macro that demonstrates how to prompt for a user-selected range.

- `range selections.xlsm`: A workbook that contains macros that perform various types of range selections.

- `select by value.xlsm`: A workbook that contains a macro that demonstrates how to select cells based on their values.

- `sorting demo.xlsm`: A workbook that contains macros that demonstrate four ways to sort an array.

- `sound.wav`: A sound file used by the `sound.xlsm` workbook.

- `sound.xlsm`: A workbook that contains examples of generating sound in Excel.

- `synchronize sheets.xlsm`: A workbook that contains a macro that synchronizes worksheets.

- `text01.txt, text02.txt, text03.txt`: Text files used in the `batch processing.xlsm` example.

- `value from a closed workbook.xlsm`: A workbook that contains a function that retrieves a value from a closed workbook.

- `variant transfer.xlsm`: A workbook that contains a macro that transfers a range to a variant array.

- `video mode.xlsm`: A workbook that contains an API function that determines the current video mode.

- `windows registry.xlsm`: A workbook that contains macros that read from and write to the Windows Registry.

- `worksheet functions.xlsm`: A workbook that contains some useful worksheet functions created using VBA.

CHAPTER 12

- `data form example.xlsm`: A workbook that contains a macro that displays Excel's built-in data form.
- `get directory.xlsm`: A workbook that contains macros that demonstrate two ways to prompt a user for a directory.
- `inputbox method.xlsm`: A workbook that contains macros that demonstrate the use of Excel's InputBox method.
- `ribbon control names.xlsx`: A workbook that lists all of the Excel 2007 Ribbon control names.
- `VBA inputbox.xlsm`: A workbook that contains macros that demonstrate the use of the VBA `InputBox` function.

CHAPTER 13

- `activex worksheet controls.xlsx`: A workbook that demonstrates the use of ActiveX controls on a worksheet (with no macros).
- `all userform controls.xlsm`: A workbook that contains a UserForm that uses all available controls.
- `get name and sex.xlsm`: A workbook that contains a simple UserForm example.
- `newcontrols.pag`: A file that contains customized controls that can be imported into your UserForm Toolbox as a new page.
- `spinbutton and textbox.xlsm`: A workbook that demonstrates the use of a paired `SpinButton` and `TextBox` control in a UserForm.
- `spinbutton events.xlsm`: A workbook that demonstrates SpinButton events.
- `userform events.xlsm`: A workbook that demonstrates UserForm events.

CHAPTER 14

- `change userform size.xlsm`: A workbook that demonstrates how to use VBA to change the size of a UserForm.
- `date and time picker.xlsm`: A workbook that demonstrates the use of the Date and Time Picker control.
- `fill listbox.xlsm`: A workbook that demonstrates how to fill a `ListBox` control in a UserForm.

Part VIII

- `listbox activate sheet.xlsm`: A workbook that demonstrates how to allow a user to select a sheet by using a `ListBox` control.

- `listbox item transfer.xlsm`: A workbook that demonstrates how to transfer items between two `ListBox` controls.

- `listbox move items.xlsm`: A workbook that demonstrates how to allow the user to change the order of items in a `ListBox` control.

- `listbox multicolumn1.xlsm`: A workbook that demonstrates a range-based multicolumn `ListBox` control.

- `listbox multicolumn2.xlsm`: A workbook that demonstrates an array-based multicolumn `ListBox` control.

- `listbox multiple lists.xlsm`: A workbook that demonstrates how to display multiple lists in a single `ListBox` control.

- `listbox select rows.xlsm`: A workbook that demonstrates how to allow a user to select worksheet rows by using a `ListBox` control.

- `listbox selected items.xlsm`: A workbook that demonstrates how to identify the selected item(s) in a `ListBox`.

- `listbox unique items1.xlsm`: A workbook that demonstrates how to fill a `ListBox` control with unduplicated items.

- `listbox unique items2.xlsm`: A variation of the `listbox unique items1.xlsm` example that also sorts the items.

- `multipage control demo.xlsm`: A workbook that demonstrates the `MultiPage` control in a UserForm.

- `queryclose demo.xlsm`: A workbook that demonstrates how to prevent a user from closing a UserForm by clicking its Close button in the title bar.

- `random number generator.xlsm`: A workbook that demonstrates how to program simple animation in a UserForm.

- `range selection demo.xlsm`: A workbook that demonstrates the `RefEdit` control in a UserForm.

- `splash screen.xlsm`: A workbook that demonstrates how to use a UserForm as a splash screen that displays when a workbook is opened.

- `userform menus.xlsm`: A workbook that demonstrates how use a UserForm to display a menu of macros.

- `zoom and scroll sheet.xlsm`: A workbook that demonstrates how to zoom and scroll a worksheet while a UserForm is displayed.

- `zoom userform.xlsm`: A workbook that demonstrates how to allow the user to change the size of a UserForm.

CHAPTER 15

- `chart in userform.xlsm`: A workbook that demonstrates how to display a chart in a UserForm.

- `getacolor function.xlsm`: A workbook that contains a function that allows the user to select a color by using controls on a UserForm.

- `modeless userform1.xlsm`: A workbook that demonstrates how to display a modeless UserForm to display information about the active cell.

- `modeless userform2.xlsm`: A more sophisticated version of `modeless userform1.xlsm`.

- `move controls.xlsm`: A workbook that demonstrates how to allow the user to move controls on a UserForm.

- `msgbox emulation.xlsm`: A workbook that contains macros that simulate the VBA `MsgBox` function.

- `multiple buttons.xlsm`: A workbook that demonstrates how to use a class module to allow a single procedure to handle events for multiple controls on a UserForm.

- `no title bar.xlsm`: A workbook that uses API functions to display a UserForm without a title bar.

- `progress indicator1.xlsm`: A workbook that displays a progress indicator in a UserForm.

- `progress indicator2.xlsm`: A workbook that uses a `MultiPage` control to display a progress indicator in a UserForm.

- `progress indicator3.xlsm`: A workbook that displays a progress indicator in a UserForm by changing the size of the UserForm.

- `resizable userform.xlsm`: A workbook that demonstrates a UserForm that's resizable by the user.

- `simulated toolbar.xlsm`: A workbook that uses a UserForm to simulate a toolbar.

- `sliding tile puzzle.xlsm`: A workbook that contains a UserForm with a sliding tile puzzle.

- `splash screen2.xlsm`: The `splash screen.xlsm` example from Chapter 14, with a UserForm that doesn't have a title bar.

- `wizard demo.xlsm`: A workbook that uses a `MultiPage` control to display a simple wizard UserForm.

- `\dataform`: This directory contains the Enhanced Data Form add-in created by the author.

CHAPTER 16

- `simple undo demo.xlsm`: A workbook that demonstrates a method to undo the effects of a VBA macro.

- `text tools.xlam`: An add-in that adds text manipulation features to Excel.

- `texttools.chm`: The help file for `text tools.xlam`.

- `\helpsource`: The source files used to create the `texttools.chm` help file.

CHAPTER 17

- `budget pivot table.xlsm`: A workbook that contains data suitable for a pivot table.

- `reverse pivot table.xlsm`: A workbook that contains a macro that converts a summary table into a 3-column data table.

- `simple pivot table.xlsm`: A workbook that contains data suitable for a pivot table.

- `survey data pivot tables.xlsm`: A workbook that contains a macro to generate 28 pivot tables from a range of data.

CHAPTER 18

- `animated charts.xlsm`: A workbook that demonstrates how to use VBA to animate charts.

- `chart active cell.xlsm`: A workbook that contains a macro that displays a chart that uses data based on the active cell position.

- `chart image map.xlsm`: A workbook that uses chart events to create a simple clickable image map.

- `chart in userform.xlsm`: A workbook that displays a chart in a UserForm, using the data based on the active cell position.

- `climate data.xlsx`: An interactive chart application that uses no macros.

- `data labels.xlsm`: A workbook that contains a macro that applies chart data labels that are stored in a range.

- `events - chart sheet.xlsm`: A workbook that demonstrates events for a chart on a chart sheet.

- `events - embedded chart.xlsm`: A workbook that demonstrates events for an embedded chart.

- `export all graphics.xlsm`: A workbook that contains a macro that exports all graphic objects in a workbook.

- `format a chart.xlsm`: A workbook that contains a macro that applies formatting to a chart.

- `format all charts.xlsm`: A workbook that contains a macro that changes the formatting of all charts on a worksheet.

- `get series ranges.xlsm`: A workbook that contains functions that identify the ranges used in a chart.

- `hide and unhide series.xlsm`: A workbook that contains check boxes that allow a user to indicate which chart series to display.

- `hypocycloid - animated.xlsm`: A workbook that includes macros to display an animated hypocycloid chart.

- `mouseover event - chart sheet.xlsm`: A workbook that demonstrates the `MouseOver` event for a chart sheet.

- `mouseover event - embedded.xlsm`: A workbook that demonstrates the `MouseOver` event for an embedded chart.

- `scrolling chart.xlsm`: A workbook that demonstrates how to create an animated scrolling chart.

- `size and align charts.xlsm`: A workbook that contains a macro that sizes and aligns all charts on a worksheet.

- `slide show.xlsm`: A workbook that contains a macro that displays a full-screen slide show of all charts in a workbook.

- `unlinked chart.xlsm`: A workbook that contains macros that demonstrate two ways to unlink a chart from its source data.

- `vba clock chart.xlsm`: A workbook that displays a chart that resembles an analog clock.

CHAPTER 19

- `application event tracker.xlsm`: A workbook that demonstrates how to monitor application-level events.

- `hide columns before printing.xlsm`: A workbook that uses an event to hide columns before printing and unhide the columns after printing.

- `log workbook open.xlsm`: A workbook that demonstrates how to keep track of every workbook that is opened by using a class module.

- `make formulas bold.xlsm`: A workbook that demonstrates the `Worksheet Change` event.

- `no shortcut menus.xlsm`: A workbook that uses the `Workbook_Open` event to disable shortcut keys and the `Workbook_BeforeClose` event to re-enable shortcut keys.

- `onkey event demo.xlsm`: A workbook that demonstrates the `OnKey` event.

- `ontime event demo.xlsm`: A workbook that demonstrates the `OnTime` event.

- `shade active row and column.xlsm`: A workbook that uses the `Worksheet SelectionChange` event to apply shading to the row and column of the active cell.

- `validate entry1.xlsm`: A workbook that demonstrates how to validate data entered into a cell by using VBA (uses the `EnableEvents` property).

- `validate entry2.xlsm`: A workbook that demonstrates how to validate data entered into a cell by using VBA (uses a static variable).

- `validate entry3.xlsm`: A workbook that demonstrates how to validate data by using Excel's data validation feature — and ensuring that the data validation conditions do not get erased..

- `workbook_beforeclose workaround.xlsm`: A workbook that demonstrates how to overcome a problem with the `Workbook BeforeClose` event.

CHAPTER 20

- `automate excel.docm`: A Word document that contains macros that automate Excel.

- `budget data.accdb`: An Access file used by the `simple ado example.xlsm` example.

- `control panel dialogs.xlsm`: A workbook that contains macros that display Windows Control Panel dialog boxes.

- `flower.jpg`: A graphics file used by the `shellexecute examples.xlsm` example.

- `make memos.xlsm`: A workbook that automates Word and creates a customized memo.

- `mortgagecalcs.xlsx`: A workbook that's used by the `automate excel.docm` example.

- `personalized email - OE sendkeys.xlsm`: A workbook that contains a macro to send personalized e-mail via Outlook Express.

- `personalized email - outlook.xlsm`: A workbook that contains a macro to send personalized e-mail via Outlook (using early binding).

- `personalized email - outlook (late binding).xlsm`: A workbook that contains a macro to send personalized e-mail via Outlook (using late binding).

- `send pdf via outlook.xlsm`: A workbook that contains a macro that sends e-mail with a PDF file attachment using Outlook.

- `shellexecute examples.xlsm`: A workbook that contains macros that demonstrate the `ShellExecute` API function.

- `simple ado example.xlsm`: A workbook that contains a macro that demonstrates ADO (ActiveX Data Objects).

- `start calculator.xlsm`: A workbook that contains a macro that launches the Calculator application.

- `textfile.txt`: A text file used by the `shellexecute examples.xlsm` example.

CHAPTER 21

- `check addin.xlam`: A workbook that contains code to ensure that an add-in is installed properly.

- `list add-in information.xlsm`: A workbook that contains a macro that lists information about all add-ins.

- `text tools.xlsm`: The Text Tools Utility workbook, which can be converted to an add-in.

- `texttools.chm`: The help file for the `text tools.xlsm` workbook.

- `\text tools helpsource`: A directory that contains the source files that were used to create the `texttools.chm` help file.

CHAPTER 22

- `dynamicmenu.xlsm`: A workbook that demonstrates the `dynamicMenu` control.

- `mso image browser.xlsm`: A workbook that contains a macro that displays the images associated with Ribbon commands.

- `old-style toolbar.xlsm`: A workbook that demonstrates how to create a toolbar, used in previous versions of Excel.

- `page break display add-in.xlam`: An add-in that adds a useful control to Excel's Ribbon.

- `page break display.xlsm`: The workbook file used to create the `page break display add-in.xlam` add-in.

- `ribbon control names.xlsx`: A workbook that contains the names of all Excel Ribbon controls.

- `ribbon controls demo.xlsm`: A workbook that demonstrates several types of Ribbon controls.

- `ribbon modification.xlsm`: A workbook that contains a simple example that modifies Excel's Ribbon.

CHAPTER 23

- `add to cell shortcut.xlsm`: A workbook that contains a macro that adds a new menu item to a shortcut menu.

- `new shortcut menu.xlsm`: A workbook that contains a macro that creates a new shortcut menu.

- `shortcut with submenu.xlsm`: A workbook that contains a macro that adds new menu and submenu items to a shortcut menu.

- `show faceids.xlsm`: A workbook that contains a macro that displays `FaceId` images.

- `show shortcut menu items.xlsm`: A workbook that contains a macro that lists all menu items on all shortcut menus.

- `show shortcut menu names.xlsm`: A workbook that contains a macro that lists the names of all shortcut menus.

CHAPTER 24

- `\cell comments`: A directory that contains a workbook that demonstrates using cell comments to display help information.

- `\function help`: A workbook that demonstrates how to display help for custom VBA worksheet functions.

- `\html help`: A directory that contains files that demonstrate using compiled HTML help.

- `\mhtml file`: A directory that contains files that demonstrate using an MHTML file to display help information in Internet Explorer.

- `\textbox`: A directory that contains a workbook that demonstrates using a text box to display help information.

- `\userform1`: A directory that contains a workbook that demonstrates using a UserForm with a `SpinButton` control to display help information.

- `\userform2`: A directory that contains a workbook that demonstrates using a UserForm with a scrolling `Label` control to display help information.

- `\userform3`: A directory that contains a workbook that demonstrates using a UserForm with a `ComboBox` control to display help information.

- `\web browser`: A directory that contains files that demonstrate using a UserForm to display help information.

- `\worksheet`: A directory that contains a file that demonstrates using a worksheet to display help information.

CHAPTER 25

- `loan amortization wizard.xlam`: An add-in used for the loan amortization wizard example.

CHAPTER 26

- `multilingual wizard.xlsm`: A workbook used for the multilingual wizard example.

CHAPTER 27

- `create file list.xlsm`: A workbook that contains a macro that creates a list of files contained in a directory.

- `export and import csv.xlsm`: A workbook that contains macros that export and import a CSV file.

- `export to HTML.xlsm`: A workbook that contains a macro that exports worksheet data to an HTML file.

- `export to XML.xlsm`: A workbook that contains a macro that exports worksheet data to an XML file.

- `file functions.xlsm`: A workbook that contains the `FileExists` and `PathExists` functions.

- `file information.xlsm`: A workbook that contains a macro that creates a list of files and extended file information.

- `filter text file.xlsm`: A workbook that contains a macro that imports only selected information from a text file.

- `infile.txt`: A text file used by the `filter text file.xlsm` example.

- `recursive file list.xlsm`: A workbook that contains a macro that creates a list of files contained in a directory, including all subdirectories.

- `show drive info.xlsm`: A workbook that contains a macro that displays information about all disk drives.

- `unzip a file.xlsm`: A workbook that contains a macro that unzips a file.

- `zip files.xlsm`: A workbook that contains a macro that zips files.

CHAPTER 28

- `add 100 buttons.xlsm`: A workbook that contains a macro that adds 100 `CommandButton` controls and code to a UserForm at design time.

- `add button and code.xlsm`: A workbook that contains a macro that adds a button to a worksheet, and VBA code that is executed when the button is clicked.

- `create userform on the fly.xlsm`: A workbook that contains a macro that creates a UserForm.

- `getoption function.xlsm`: A workbook that contains a function that creates a UserForm (with `OptionButton` controls) on the fly and returns a value that corresponds to the user's choice.

- `list all procedures.xlsm`: A workbook that contains a macro that lists all VBA procedures in a workbook.

- `list VB components.xlsm`: A workbook that contains a macro that lists all VB components in a workbook.

- `UpdateUserBook.xlsm`: A workbook that contains a macro that replaces a VBA module with a new module.

- `UserBook.xlsm`: A workbook that's used by the `UpdateUserBook.xlsm` example.

Chapter 29

- `csv class.xlsm`: A workbook that makes it easy to import and export a CSV file.

- `keyboard class.xlsm`: A workbook that contains a class module that defines a `NumLock`, a `CapsLock`, and a `ScrollLock` class.

Chapter 30

- `chart colors.xlsm`: A workbook that contains macros that work with chart colors.

- `chart to grayscale picture.xlsm`: A workbook that contains a macro that creates a grayscale image from a chart.

- `color conversion functions.xlsm`: A workbook that contains functions that convert between various color systems.

- `document theme gallery.xlsx`: A workbook that contains various elements that demonstrate the effects of applying a different theme.

- `generate theme colors.xlsm`: A workbook that contains a macro that demonstrates theme colors.

- `rgb color demo.xlsm`: A workbook that contains an interactive demonstration of the RGB color system.

- `shape object colors.xlsx`: A workbook that contains macros that work with shapes.

- `tintandshade demo.xlsm`: A workbook that demonstrates how the `TintAndShade` property works.

- `weirddog.jpg`: A graphics file that's used by the `shape object colors.xlsm` example.

Troubleshooting

If you have difficulty installing or using any of the materials on the companion CD, try the following solutions:

- *Turn off any antivirus software that you may have running.* Installers sometimes mimic virus activity and can make your computer incorrectly believe that it is being infected by a virus. (Be sure to turn the antivirus software back on later.)

- *Close all running programs.* The more programs you're running, the less memory is available to other programs. Installers also typically update files and programs; if you keep other programs running, installation may not work properly.

- *Reference the ReadMe file.* Refer to the `ReadMe` file located at the root of the CD-ROM for the latest product information (if any) at the time of publication.

If you still have trouble with the CD-ROM, please call the Wiley Product Technical Support phone number at (800) 762-2974. Outside the United States, call 1(317) 572-3994. You can also contact Wiley Product Technical Support at `http://support.wiley.com`. John Wiley & Sons will provide technical support only for installation and other general quality control items. For technical support on the applications themselves, consult the program's vendor or author.

To place additional orders or to request information about other Wiley products, please call (877) 762-2974.

Index

Symbols

error, 60

A

Abs function, 982
absolute cell references, 49
  macro recorder, 159–162
absolute value of number, 982
Activate event, 603, 640, 654
Activate method, 319, 578
ActivateMicrosoftApp method, 674–675
activating
  application windows, 977
  charts, 578
  ranges, selecting and, 950
  sheets, ListBoxes and, 476–479
active chart, 572
active objects, 137
active sheet, 16
active workbook, 16
ActiveCell property, 178
ActiveChart property, 178, 572
ActiveSheet property, 178
ActiveWindow property, 178
ActiveWorkbook property, 178
ActiveX component can't create object
    error, 991
ActiveX controls
  drawing layer, 118
  Form controls comparison, 120
  UserForms, 118
  worksheets, 118–120
AddButtonAndCode procedure, 870

Add100Buttons procedure, 874–875
AddChart method, 575–576
AddComment method, 177
AddControl event, 661
AddDataField method, 558
Add-In Manager, 702–703, 706
AddIn object
  Comments property, 717
  events, 719–720
  FullName property, 716
  Installed property, 717
  Name property, 716
  Path property, 716
  Title property, 717
AddInInstall event, 719–720
add-ins
  accessing as workbook, 719
  checklist for creating, 709
  creating, 703–704, 706–707
  custom functions and, 310
  description, 699–700
  descriptive information, 705–706
  distributing, 708
  Excel version, detecting, 724
  files, 90–91
  installation, 538, 707–708
  installation, ensuring, 721–723
  introduction, 43
  ListAllAddIns procedure, 718
  modifying, 708
  optimization, 720–721
  password-protected, 124
  procedures, accessing, 712–714
  protected, 713

continued

continued

continued

continued

continued

continued

continued

J

continued

continued

BUSINESS, CAREERS & PERSONAL FINANCE

0-7645-9847-3

0-7645-2431-3

Also available:
- Business Plans Kit For Dummies
  0-7645-9794-9
- Economics For Dummies
  0-7645-5726-2
- Grant Writing For Dummies
  0-7645-8416-2
- Home Buying For Dummies
  0-7645-5331-3
- Managing For Dummies
  0-7645-1771-6
- Marketing For Dummies
  0-7645-5600-2

- Personal Finance For Dummies
  0-7645-2590-5*
- Resumes For Dummies
  0-7645-5471-9
- Selling For Dummies
  0-7645-5363-1
- Six Sigma For Dummies
  0-7645-6798-5
- Small Business Kit For Dummies
  0-7645-5984-2
- Starting an eBay Business For Dummies
  0-7645-6924-4
- Your Dream Career For Dummies
  0-7645-9795-7

HOME & BUSINESS COMPUTER BASICS

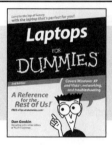

0-470-05432-8

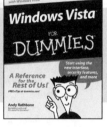

0-471-75421-8

Also available:
- Cleaning Windows Vista For Dummies
  0-471-78293-9
- Excel 2007 For Dummies
  0-470-03737-7
- Mac OS X Tiger For Dummies
  0-7645-7675-5
- MacBook For Dummies
  0-470-04859-X
- Macs For Dummies
  0-470-04849-2
- Office 2007 For Dummies
  0-470-00923-3

- Outlook 2007 For Dummies
  0-470-03830-6
- PCs For Dummies
  0-7645-8958-X
- Salesforce.com For Dummies
  0-470-04893-X
- Upgrading & Fixing Laptops For Dummies
  0-7645-8959-8
- Word 2007 For Dummies
  0-470-03658-3
- Quicken 2007 For Dummies
  0-470-04600-7

FOOD, HOME, GARDEN, HOBBIES, MUSIC & PETS

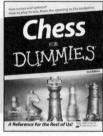

0-7645-8404-9

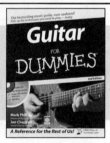

0-7645-9904-6

Also available:
- Candy Making For Dummies
  0-7645-9734-5
- Card Games For Dummies
  0-7645-9910-0
- Crocheting For Dummies
  0-7645-4151-X
- Dog Training For Dummies
  0-7645-8418-9
- Healthy Carb Cookbook For Dummies
  0-7645-8476-6
- Home Maintenance For Dummies
  0-7645-5215-5

- Horses For Dummies
  0-7645-9797-3
- Jewelry Making & Beading For Dummies
  0-7645-2571-9
- Orchids For Dummies
  0-7645-6759-4
- Puppies For Dummies
  0-7645-5255-4
- Rock Guitar For Dummies
  0-7645-5356-9
- Sewing For Dummies
  0-7645-6847-7
- Singing For Dummies
  0-7645-2475-5

INTERNET & DIGITAL MEDIA

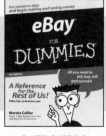

0-470-04529-9

0-470-04894-8

Also available:
- Blogging For Dummies
  0-471-77084-1
- Digital Photography For Dummies
  0-7645-9802-3
- Digital Photography All-in-One Desk Reference For Dummies
  0-470-03743-1
- Digital SLR Cameras and Photography For Dummies
  0-7645-9803-1
- eBay Business All-in-One Desk Reference For Dummies
  0-7645-8438-3
- HDTV For Dummies
  0-470-09673-X

- Home Entertainment PCs For Dummies
  0-470-05523-5
- MySpace For Dummies
  0-470-09529-6
- Search Engine Optimization For Dummies
  0-471-97998-8
- Skype For Dummies
  0-470-04891-3
- The Internet For Dummies
  0-7645-8996-2
- Wiring Your Digital Home For Dummies
  0-471-91830-X

* Separate Canadian edition also available
† Separate U.K. edition also available

Available wherever books are sold. For more information or to order direct: U.S. customers visit www.dummies.com or call 1-877-762-2974.
U.K. customers visit www.wileyeurope.com or call 0800 243407. Canadian customers visit www.wiley.ca or call 1-800-567-4797.

SPORTS, FITNESS, PARENTING, RELIGION & SPIRITUALITY

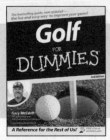

0-471-76871-5

0-7645-7841-3

Also available:

- Catholicism For Dummies
0-7645-5391-7
- Exercise Balls For Dummies
0-7645-5623-1
- Fitness For Dummies
0-7645-7851-0
- Football For Dummies
0-7645-3936-1
- Judaism For Dummies
0-7645-5299-6
- Potty Training For Dummies
0-7645-5417-4
- Buddhism For Dummies
0-7645-5359-3

- Pregnancy For Dummies
0-7645-4483-7 †
- Ten Minute Tone-Ups For Dummies
0-7645-7207-5
- NASCAR For Dummies
0-7645-7681-X
- Religion For Dummies
0-7645-5264-3
- Soccer For Dummies
0-7645-5229-5
- Women in the Bible For Dummies
0-7645-8475-8

TRAVEL

0-7645-7749-2

0-7645-6945-7

Also available:

- Alaska For Dummies
0-7645-7746-8
- Cruise Vacations For Dummies
0-7645-6941-4
- England For Dummies
0-7645-4276-1
- Europe For Dummies
0-7645-7529-5
- Germany For Dummies
0-7645-7823-5
- Hawaii For Dummies
0-7645-7402-7

- Italy For Dummies
0-7645-7386-1
- Las Vegas For Dummies
0-7645-7382-9
- London For Dummies
0-7645-4277-X
- Paris For Dummies
0-7645-7630-5
- RV Vacations For Dummies
0-7645-4442-X
- Walt Disney World & Orlando
For Dummies
0-7645-9660-8

GRAPHICS, DESIGN & WEB DEVELOPMENT

0-7645-8815-X

0-7645-9571-7

Also available:

- 3D Game Animation For Dummies
0-7645-8789-7
- AutoCAD 2006 For Dummies
0-7645-8925-3
- Building a Web Site For Dummies
0-7645-7144-3
- Creating Web Pages For Dummies
0-470-08030-2
- Creating Web Pages All-in-One Desk
Reference For Dummies
0-7645-4345-8
- Dreamweaver 8 For Dummies
0-7645-9649-7

- InDesign CS2 For Dummies
0-7645-9572-5
- Macromedia Flash 8 For Dummies
0-7645-9691-8
- Photoshop CS2 and Digital
Photography For Dummies
0-7645-9580-6
- Photoshop Elements 4 For Dummies
0-471-77483-9
- Syndicating Web Sites with RSS Feeds
For Dummies
0-7645-8848-6
- Yahoo! SiteBuilder For Dummies
0-7645-9800-7

NETWORKING, SECURITY, PROGRAMMING & DATABASES

0-7645-7728-X

0-471-74940-0

Also available:

- Access 2007 For Dummies
0-470-04612-0
- ASP.NET 2 For Dummies
0-7645-7907-X
- C# 2005 For Dummies
0-7645-9704-3
- Hacking For Dummies
0-470-05235-X
- Hacking Wireless Networks
For Dummies
0-7645-9730-2
- Java For Dummies
0-470-08716-1

- Microsoft SQL Server 2005 For Dummies
0-7645-7755-7
- Networking All-in-One Desk Reference
For Dummies
0-7645-9939-9
- Preventing Identity Theft For Dummies
0-7645-7336-5
- Telecom For Dummies
0-471-77085-X
- Visual Studio 2005 All-in-One Desk
Reference For Dummies
0-7645-9775-2
- XML For Dummies
0-7645-8845-1

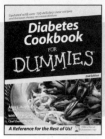